# Guidelines for determining your purpose

**1. What are the requirements of my writing project?**
❏ If I am writing to fulfill an assignment, do I understand that assignment? ❏ If writing on my own, do I have definite expectations of what I will accomplish? ❏ Does the assignment require graphics? ❏ What is my purpose in adding graphics?

**2. As I proceed, what do I need to know?**
❏ Do I understand my subject, or do I need more information? ❏ Who are the possible audiences who might read my writing? ❏ Have I researched ways to make my text visually effective?

**3. What hypothesis can I use as my working purpose?**
❏ How many different hypotheses can I formulate about my subject? ❏ Which of them seems to direct and control my information in the most eff[...]nable me to cr[...]

**4. Has my [...]**
❏ How [...] more about my subject [...]ave I discovered, by working with a hypothesis, what I want to do in my writing? ❏ Have I found ways to use graphics to demonstrate my purpose?

**5. What is my thesis?**
❏ How can I state my main idea about my subject in a thesis sentence? ❏ Does my thesis limit the scope of my writing to what I can demonstrate in the available space? ❏ Does it focus my writing on one specific assertion? ❏ Does it make an exact statement about what my writing intends to do? ❏ How might a design element call attention to my thesis?

# Guidelines for revising your style

**1. What is my general impression of my writing?**
❏ Is my writing clear, unambiguous, and likely to engage my readers? ❏ Does the *how* of my writing—its attitude, organization, and language—convey the *what* of my ideas? ❏ Is there an effective balance between words and graphics?

**2. What tone have I established in my writing?**
❏ Is my tone informative, affective, or a blend of both? ❏ How much distance have I maintained between myself and my readers? ❏ Is my tone appropriate for my subject and audience? ❏ Is it maintained consistently? ❏ How do my illustrations enrich the tone or the look of my writing?

**3. What is my style of writing?**
❏ Have I written in a moderate style, with appropriate colloquialism or formality? ❏ Does my purpose require me to be overtly colloquial or formal? ❏ Is there a consistent, logical, and appropriate look to my design?

**4. Are my sentences well constructed and easy on the ear?**
❏ Have I written sentences varying in length and style so that they hold my readers' interest? ❏ Have I avoided the choppiness that comes from too many basic or loosely coordinated sentences? ❏ Have I avoided the density that comes from too many complicated sentences with multiple subordinate clauses? ❏ How effectively have I used graphics to break up the density of my text?

**5. Have I used words effectively?**
❏ Do the connotations and denotations of my words support my purpose? ❏ Have I avoided unnecessary formalities and slang? Is my language specific and vivid? ❏ Do I have any mixed metaphors? ❏ Have I used imagery successfully to heighten effects? ❏ Have I selected appropriate pictures to illustrate my words?

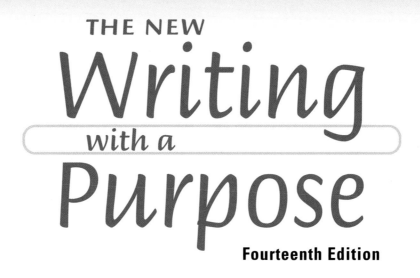

# THE NEW
# Writing
## with a
# Purpose

**Fourteenth Edition**

## Joseph F. Trimmer

*Ball State University*

**HOUGHTON MIFFLIN COMPANY**
**Boston    New York**

DEDICATION

**In memory of Dean Johnson**
**Editor, mentor, friend**

*Senior sponsoring editor:* Suzanne Phelps Weir
*Senior development editor:* Sarah Helyar Smith
*Senior project editor:* Rosemary Winfield
*Senior production/design coordinator:* Jill Haber
*Manufacturing manager:* Florence Cadran
*Marketing manager:* Cindy Graff Cohen

*Cover illustration* © Paul Wearing

Acknowledgments continue on page A-1, which constitutes an extension of the copyright page.

Printed in the U.S.A.

Library of Congress Catalog Card Number: 2002109686

ISBN: 0-618-31847-X

1 2 3 4 5 6 7 8 9 - DOC - 06 05 04 03

# Brief Contents

THE NEW
## Writing with a Purpose

# Contents

# Tone and Style  289

# PART III
# Writing Research  333

# Planning the Research Paper  318

# Writing the Research Paper  350

# PART IV
# Readings with a Purpose   395

# Writing Strategies   396

# PART V
## Handbook of Grammar and Usage   473

*Writing with a Purpose* has always been distinguished by its emphasis on the role of purpose in the writing process, by its comprehensive coverage of the materials and problems basic to the introductory writing course, and by its effective use of examples and exercises to illustrate how writers make decisions that produce successful writing. The Fourteenth Edition retains the book's traditional strengths but now also addresses the demands of writing in a visual culture. The result is a blend of familiar and new material invigorated by fresh approaches, enlivened by student writing composed in different contexts, and presented in a four-color design that demonstrates how visual texts need to be created with a purpose.

## New Features

**Designing**    At the heart of *The New Writing with a Purpose* is Chapter 5, Designing. Presented as the fourth stage in the writing process, Chapter 5 explains how students can use basic elements and principles to create effective visual texts. The electronic revolution has given students the power to write *and* design their texts. But students need to know how to assess and create designs that reinforce their text's purpose. Chapter 5 illustrates the designing strategies students need to clarify their subject, acknowledge their audience, and advance their purpose.

**Text Design**    Chapter 5 gives students a language to analyze design in every aspect of their lives. Most immediately, however, it encourages them to analyze the features in the four-color design of *The New Writing with a Purpose*. Everything on every page becomes a subject for analysis. Students can discuss whether the layout, typeface, illustrations, and graphics are rendered in an effective and purposeful design.

**Image Gallery**    Positioned near the end of each chapter, the Image Gallery presents the subject and strategies discussed in each chapter in evocative images. Some galleries contrast single dramatic images; others create clusters of related images. Each Image Gallery asks students to analyze its subject, audience, and purpose.

**Web Site Design**    The major writing document in each chapter—some written by students, others written by professionals—serves as an exercise for composition students to practice their designing skills. Two possible Web sites are presented at the end of each chapter. These images include annotations and instructional material to help students evaluate the effectiveness of textual and graphic presentations on the Web, to critique sites as research tools, and to understand the role of purpose in designing and assessing Web sites.

**Argument**   The student writing featured in Chapter 7, Argument, focuses on the complex relationship between the media and the military. This topic creates an opportunity to present stronger advice on critical analysis and thinking. It also provides guidance on how to use textual and visual formats to create effective arguments in various contexts and media.

**Research**   The speed of the electronic revolution requires that each new edition of *Writing with a Purpose* must revise its presentation of the research process both as a fundamental planning strategy and as a special academic writing assignment—the research paper. This edition features special icons and boxed material about research in every chapter. Chapter 12, Planning the Research Paper, and Chapter 13, Writing the Research Paper, present new information on selecting, evaluating, and documenting sources, with a special emphasis on online sources.

**Readings**   Over thirty percent of the essays by professional and student writers are new to this edition. In particular, new case studies of student writing-in-progress are featured in Chapter 5, Designing; Chapter 7, Argument; Chapter 12, Planning the Research Paper; and Chapter 13, Writing the Research Paper. Part IV, Readings with a Purpose, contains provocative and engaging new readings that focus on contemporary issues and ideas.

## Organization of the Text

**Part I: The Writing Process**   Part I, Chapters 1–5, covers all aspects of composing from planning through designing. Chapter 1, which provides an overview of this process, details the variety of approaches that writers take and discusses the three activities that are common to every writing situation: selecting your subject, analyzing your audience, and especially determining your purpose, which is defined in detail and carefully reinforced throughout the text as the principle touchstone by which writers measure their progress through the writing process.

The remainder of Part I, enriched by new examples and exercises, focuses on the four stages of the writing process: planning, drafting, revising, and designing. Chapter 2 offers multiple planning strategies to demonstrate how students can discover and evaluate thinking in writing. Chapter 3 presents methods to arrange and assess the material discovered in planning to guide the creation of a discovery draft and then a more cohesive, precise second draft. Chapter 4 defines the revising process, demonstrates methods for revising an essay, and provides an extended case study of revising from discovery to final draft. Chapter 5 explains the basic elements and principles necessary to arrange words and images in an effective design.

All the chapters in Part I are unified by recurring student writing-in-progress that illustrates a range of projects from expressive writing about personal experience to investigative writing about academic subjects.

**Part II: Writing Structures**  Part II, Chapters 6–11, places the discrete skills of effective writing—methods of development, argument, paragraphs, sentences, diction, tone and style—within the composing process. This is done partly through the use of quotations from personal interviews with professional writers who explain their own method for using certain structures and partly through the work of student writers who try to employ those structures in their own writing process. In particular, Chapter 6, Common Methods of Development, and Chapter 7, Argument, illustrate how a student writer works with patterns of exposition and the structures of argument to plan, draft, revise, and design a compelling piece of writing.

The writing examples and exercises in each chapter have been selected to cluster around a different disciplinary theme to provide readers with the opportunity to discover provocative comparisons. Chapter 6 has a thematic emphasis on animal rights and environmental awareness, Chapter 7 on the military and the media, Chapter 8 on families and ethnic groups, Chapter 9 on art and medicine, Chapter 10 on biology and the physical sciences, and Chapter 11 on travel and transportation.

**Part III: Writing Research**  Part III, Chapters 12–13, focuses on an academic assignment central to most composition courses—the research paper—providing extensive analysis and illustrations of the many steps embedded in planning and writing the research paper. Chapter 12, Planning the Research Paper, explains how to select a subject for research and how to use print and electronic search strategies to select, assess, and analyze sources. Chapter 13, Writing the Research Paper, presents the methods by which information composed by other researchers can be incorporated into and help advance the student's own research paper. Special attention is given to the purpose and procedure of quoting, documenting, and listing sources. The whole range of planning and writing activities required to produce a successful paper is illustrated by one student's progress through the process. Erin McMullen's paper, "The Possibilities and Limitations of Online Learning," is fully annotated so that readers can assess the decisions she made during the writing process and the methods she used to embody those decisions in an appropriate format.

**Part IV: Readings with a Purpose**     Part IV is an anthology of student and professional essays arranged in the same pattern of rhetorical strategies featured in Chapters 6 and 7 and corresponding to the sequence of writing assignments that conclude every chapter in the text.

Strategy One: Narration and Description
Strategy Two: Process Analysis
Strategy Three: Comparison and Contrast
Strategy Four: Division and Classification
Strategy Five: Definition
Strategy Six: Causal Analysis
Strategy Seven: Argument

Each section opens with general observations about choosing your subject, audience, and purpose and ends with specific advice about using the strategy effectively. Each student essay is annotated, each professional essay is followed by questions, and each section ends with A Sampler of Other Essays, which directs readers to other essays in the text that have used the same strategy.

**Part V: Handbook of Grammar and Usage**     The grammar and usage handbook, identified by the colored bar at the top of its pages, is a concise guide for you to refer to when editing your papers. It provides a brief overview of the history of English and then progresses from the broader elements of sentence logic and structure to the finer points of word choice, punctuation, and mechanics. A handy glossary of usage helps you understand the meaning and use of common words.

## Supplements for the Student

*The New Writing with a Purpose, Fourteenth Edition,* website for students
*The New Writing with a Purpose* website at <**http://college.hmco.com/english**> provides support directly related to the book. The fully integrated website contains

▶ A downloadable checklist for your writing project, encompassing selecting your subject, analyzing your audience, determining your purpose, and revising your style and including questions to help you make sure any visual elements support and further the purpose of your work;

- Real-world Web links to the thematic contents and activities throughout the book;

- Activities to enhance and expand the Image Gallery in each chapter to provide practice in seeing with a purpose;

- Activities based on the Web design feature in each chapter to apply composition skills to visual elements;

- Expanded activities from the textbook to reinforce writing and editing skills;

- An online version of the Handbook of Grammar and Usage for easy reference; and

- Additional student models.

**Student Resource Center**   The Student Resource Center—at the Houghton Mifflin website for students, <**http://college.hmco.com/ english**>—provides additional support for coursework:

- The **Internet Research Guide** contains Learning Modules on the purpose of research; email, listservs, newsgroups, and chat rooms; surfing and browsing, evaluating information on the Web; building an argument with Web research; and plagiarism and documentation.

- The **eLibrary** is full of self-quizzes that give students the opportunity to increase their grammar and writing skills in 30 areas. As they sharpen their skills and strengthen their knowledge with over 700 exercises, they'll work at their own pace wherever they want—at home, in the computer lab, or in the classroom.

- **SMARTHINKING**™ provides online tutoring in English (as well as in seven other disciplines). Students have three different kinds of support: Live Help provides access to 20 hours a week of real-time, one-on-one instruction from Sunday to Thursday, 9 a.m. to 1 a.m. Eastern time. Questions Anytime allows students to submit questions 24 hours a day, 7 days a week, for response by an e-structor within 24 hours. And Independent Study Resources connects students around-the-clock to additional educational services, ranging from interactive web sites to frequently asked questions.

## Supplements for the Instructor

*Teaching with a Purpose*   This Instructor's Resource Manual, prepared by Sarah Bricker, offers advice for each chapter on how to use the text in the writing center and in a conventional or collaborative classroom setting. It also provides chapter synopses, suggested answers for exercises, commentary on readings, additional writing and designing assignments, sample syllabi, special sections on how teachers and students can use the writing center to expand classroom instruction, and a bibliography of useful sources.

*Teaching Writing with Computers: An Introduction*   by Pamela Takayoshi and Brian Huot, addresses writing technologies for composition pedagogies, learning to teach with technology, teaching beyond physical boundaries, teaching and learning new media, and assigning and assessing student writing.

*The Writing Teacher's Companion: Planning, Teaching, and Evaluating in the Composition Classroom*   by Rai Peterson, helps instructors with organizing the course, assessment, classroom management, and selecting textbooks.

**Instructor's Resource Center** at the Houghton Mifflin website, <**http://college.hmco.com/english**>, provides numerous and varied sources of assistance:

▶ The **Instructor's Resource Manual online** is a downloadable version of the print Instructor's Resource Manual, enhanced with an overview of website offerings, instructions on how to use the site most effectively, and Web links for instructors.

▶ **SMARTHINKING™** provides personalized, text-specific tutoring to students when they need it—online during their typical study hours—leaving instructors more time for other demands on campus. The three levels of unparalleled service and innovative use of Web-based educational technology provide increased support for instructors and help improve student performance.

▶ The **Guide to the Current Conflict,** a cross-curricular resource center, enables instructors to help students learn more about Afghanistan's cultural and political history, the world of Islam, the Al Qaeda network, and more. The wealth of resources provided here can be used as discussion starters, for homework assignments, or for further research. Some topics also include model lesson plans and tips for teaching.

▶ **After the Test**   Taking a final exam signifies the end of class work for students, but for instructors the work is just beginning when exams are turned in. See the tips on grading tests and dealing with students after they've received their grades.

▶ **Adjuncts.com** is dedicated to helping adjunct faculty make the most of their teaching careers.

# Acknowledgments

It is a pleasure to acknowledge those who have shaped *The New Writing with a Purpose*. For teaching me about the intricacies of design, my special thanks go to Jamie Miles, media director, Virginia Ball Center for Creative Inquiry, Ball State University. For guiding me through the latest developments on the information highway, thanks also go to Lisa J. Barnett, Instructional Services, Bracken Library, Ball State University. For his substantial work on the Handbook of Grammar and Usage, my continuing thanks go to Robert Perrin, Indiana State University.

For their helpful comments on the *New Writing with a Purpose,* I would like to thank the following people: Mary Adams, Peru State College; Jim Addison, Western Carolina University; Mary Ann Bretzlauf, The College of Lake County; Sandy Cavanah, Hopkinsville Community College; Rachelle L. Darabi, Indiana University–Purdue University, Fort Wayne; Paul R. Lehman, University of Central Oklahoma; Mitchell R. Lewis, Elmira College; Kate Mohler, Mesa Community College; David Ragsdale, Kingwood College; Nancy Ruff, Southern Illinois University, Edwardsville; and James R. Sodon, St. Louis Community College at Florissant Valley.

For their willingness to talk with me at length about the craft they practice with such precision and intelligence, I would like to thank Bill Barich, Annie Dillard, Patricia Hampl, John McPhee, Anna Quindlen, Richard Selzer, and Calvin Trillin.

For their eagerness to participate in a variety of writing and designing experiments, I would like to thank the students in my composition classes. In particular, I am indebted to the inventive, humorous, and informative observations of the students whose writing and designing give this edition its unique voice and look: Wallace Armstrong, Brett Booher, Larry Bush, Andrew Gaub, Jane Graham, Ellen Haack, Jim Jones, Sue Kirby, Joni Leisure, Erin McMullen, Kris Modlin, Sarah S. Penning, Christine Ragsdale, Susan Reidenback, Jon Seidel, Yili Shi, Rod Sturma, Jill Taraskiewicz., and Lisa Widenhofer.

For her thorough analysis and thoughtful suggestions about the writing and designing of this book, I am deeply indebted to Lynn Walterick. For her diligence in guiding this book through the various stages of its publication, I would like to thank Sarah Helyar Smith. And for her faith in the abiding power of this book to teach college students to write with a purpose, I would like to thank Suzanne Phelps Weir.

Joseph F. Trimmer

THE NEW
Writing with a Purpose

# PART 1

# The Writing Process

Toward Purposeful Writing **1**

Planning **2**

Drafting **3**

Revising **4**

Designing **5**

# 1

# Toward Purposeful Writing

Some people find writing easy. They sit down and write, work until they are finished, and turn out a first draft that is so good that it is their final draft. Everyone has heard stories about students who dash off perfect term papers the night before the assignment is due. And many people know the story of how Jack Kerouac wrote his novel *On the Road*—composing it in fourteen days and typing it on a roll of Teletype paper to avoid changing pages. But such ease of composition is rare. Kerouac himself had been writing and rewriting his book for years before hammering out its final version. Most people—whether they are students writing papers, teachers researching articles, journalists assembling news stories, business people composing memos, or novelists hammering out lengthy works of fiction— find writing hard work.

But writing is also *opportunity*. It allows you to express something about yourself, to explore and explain ideas, and to assess the claims of other people. By formulating and organizing ideas, and finding the right words to present them, you gain power. At times the task may seem overwhelming, but the rewards make the hard work worthwhile. As you come to see writing positively, as an opportunity for communication, you will develop the confidence you need to overcome its occasional frustrations.

You can gain this confidence by writing and learning from your own work and that of others. Experienced writers are one source of lessons that you may find helpful. Consider what Ernest Hemingway says about his early writing experiences in Paris in the 1920s.

> It was wonderful to walk down the long flights of stairs knowing that I'd had good luck working. I always worked until I had

something done and I always stopped when I knew what was going to happen next. That way I could be sure of going on the next day. But sometimes when I was starting a new story and I could not get it going, I would sit in front of the fire and squeeze the peel of the little oranges into the edge of the flame and watch the sputter of blue that they made. I would stand and look out over the roofs of Paris and think, "Do not worry. You have always written before and you will write now. All you have to do is write one true sentence. Write the truest sentence that you know." So finally I would write one true sentence, and then go on from there. It was easy then because there was always one true sentence that I knew or had seen or had heard someone say. If I started to write elaborately, or like someone introducing or presenting something, I found that I could cut that scrollwork or ornament out and throw it away and start with the first true simple declarative sentence I had written. Up in that room I decided that I would write one story about each thing that I knew about. I was trying to do this all the time I was writing, and it was good and severe discipline.

(Ernest Hemingway, *A Moveable Feast*)

Hemingway's account contains some helpful pointers for all writers.

1. *Develop writing habits that work for you and trust in them.* Because they have written successfully before, experienced writers believe they will write successfully again. They put this belief at risk each time they write, for each new piece of writing will inevitably contain new challenges. At times their confidence may fluctuate, but they do not lose faith. They believe the habits that have worked before— composing in a special environment, maintaining a disciplined schedule, and using familiar tools—will work again.

2. *Understand the stages of the writing process.* Identifying the predictable stages of the writing process builds confidence. Experienced writers recognize the obstacles they encounter in each stage, the strategies that help them overcome those obstacles, and the signs that prompt them to repeat one or all of the stages. As they move forward from stage to stage, or backward to repeat a stage, they are confident that they are making progress because they are identifying and solving problems.

3. *Rely on three basic elements—subject, audience, and purpose—to guide you, whatever your writing task.* Experienced writers may talk from time to time about "inspiration" or "good luck," but they do not depend on such mysterious forces. Effective writing emerges from effective decision making, and effective decisions are made when writers focus on the constants in every writing situation: their subject, audience, and purpose.

One of the primary aims of this book is to offer you experience, and thereby confidence, in writing. In the following chapters, you will learn and practice writing strategies. This chapter will discuss the writer's environment and habits, the four-stage division of the writing process, and the central elements—subject, audience, and purpose—that shape each piece of writing.

## The Writer's Environment and Habits

Asked to describe their writing process, students usually begin by identifying their writing habits—the conditions and tools they believe they need whenever they write. Some of these habits are formed by chance. If you completed a good paper by secluding yourself in a quiet area of the library, inscribing neatly shaped words in a spiral notebook with a Number 2 pencil, then you may be convinced that you need isolation, silence, and simple tools to write successfully. If you produced a good paper seated at your desk at home, your fish tank humming in the background, banging out your sentences on your new computer, you might believe that to write effectively you require a familiar environment, reassuring noises, and modern equipment. After a time, some writers look on their writing habits as rituals, procedures to be followed faithfully each time they write. They wear the same flannel shirt, choose the same background music, or sharpen an entire box of pencils before they begin.

Although many writing habits are formed by chance and take on the nature of ritual, most come about almost unconsciously and conform to a writer's other personal habits. If you must have a carefully organized environment to accomplish any task—from brushing your teeth to preparing dinner—then you will no doubt develop precise writing habits. You will write regularly, at approximately the same time each day, and for almost the same period, in a serene atmosphere. On the other hand, if you can tolerate disorder, then your writing habits are likely to reflect your preference for flexibility. Within reason and within the confines of your deadline, you will probably write in bursts of energy, at different hours of the day and night, for varying stretches of time, and in a number of different locations.

Most people fall somewhere in between these two extremes of working styles. You will probably experiment with several approaches before finding the environment and habits that work best for you. What matters is that you develop habits that enhance your concentration rather than interfere with it. If you try to write at an uncomfortable desk and chair where the light is too dim and the temperature too high, where friends or family members are likely to interrupt, you are sabotaging your chances for success. Find a comfortable, quiet, well-lit spot where you are as free as possible from internal and external distractions.

Consider, finally, that writing is both a *solitary* and a *social* act. At times you need isolation and silence to search for words that make meaning. At other times you need community and conversation to see if your words make sense. What matters is that you find the environment and habits that work best for you.

## EXERCISE

1. What type of physical environment do you need to write effectively? What happens when you are forced to write in a "hostile" environment?

2. What kind of writing tools do you prefer? What happens when you have to write with "alien" tools?

3. How do your writing habits match other aspects of your life and personality? How do they differ?

4. What experiences or people helped you form your writing habits?

5. a. What steps have you taken to eliminate external distractions (noise, music, talking, wrong light or temperature, uncomfortable furniture, lack of adequate supplies) from your writing environment?
   b. What steps have you taken to eliminate internal distractions (hunger, fatigue, boredom, anxiety, daydreaming, restlessness) from your writing environment?
   c. What other steps could you take to enhance your ability to concentrate?

## The Stages of the Writing Process

Whatever your writing environment and habits, they are simply the enabling conditions that allow you to enter and complete your writing process. They are the physical and psychological setting for the central action—the mental procedures you perform as you move through the stages of composition. The writing process may be divided into four stages: *planning, drafting, revising,* and *designing.* They will be discussed briefly in this chapter and at greater length, with examples, in Chapters 2, 3, 4, and 5.

### Planning

Planning is a systematic process of developing your ideas and giving them shape. As the first stage in the writing process, *planning is a series of strategies designed to find and formulate information in writing.* When you begin a writing project, you need to discover what is possible within the confines of the assignment—to explore a variety of subjects and invent alternative ways to think and write about each subject. To create and shape your text, you need to consider all the ideas, however mundane or unsettling, that come to you. In Chapter 2 you will learn

What stages in the
creative process are
revealed in the
photograph of the
River Valley Greenway?

several planning strategies for generating information you can transform into a first draft.

## Drafting

Drafting is a procedure for executing a preliminary sketch. As the second stage in the writing process, *drafting is a series of strategies designed to organize and develop a sustained piece of writing.* Once planning has enabled you to identify several subjects and gather information on those subjects from different perspectives, you need to select one subject, organize your information into meaningful clusters, and then discover the links that connect those clusters. In Chapter 3 you will learn how to use drafting techniques to produce a preliminary text. Chapters 5 through 10 will give you additional techniques for composing your preliminary draft.

## Revising

Revising is a procedure for improving a work in progress. As the third stage in the writing process, *revising is a series of strategies designed to reexamine and reevaluate the choices that have created a piece of writing.* After you have completed your preliminary draft, you need to stand back from your text and decide whether to embark on *global revision*—a complete re-creation of the world of your writing—or to begin *local revision*—a concerted effort to perfect the smaller elements in your writing. In Chapter 4, you will learn how to use global revision to rethink, reenvision, and rewrite your work. In Chapters 8 through 11, you will learn strategies for making the small rearrangements and subtle refinements that will help you produce your most effective writing.

## Designing

Designing is a process for presenting the final version of your work. As the fourth and last stage of the writing process, *designing is a series of strategies used to organize and display the choices that distinguish your completed project.* After you have planned, drafted, and revised your text, you need to create the most appropriate form for presenting your words and images. In Chapter 5, you will learn the basic principles of design that will enable you to arrange the type, position the images, and balance the color and white space in your writing project.

## Working Within the Process

The division of the writing process into four stages is deceptive because it suggests that *planning, drafting, revising,* and *designing* proceed in a linear sequence. According to this logic, you would complete all the activities in one stage and then move to the next. But writing is a complex mental activity that usually unfolds as a more flexible and "recursive" sequence of tasks. You may have to repeat the activities in one stage several times before you are ready to move on to the next, or you may have to loop back to an earlier stage before you can move forward again. For example, you may have to try a number of planning strategies until you generate enough information to work with. Or, in the middle of drafting, you may have to return to planning because you discover that the relationships you thought you saw in your material are not there after all. When you revise, you may find that your essay doesn't explain certain assumptions or illustrate important assertions, so you must return to planning or drafting. And finally, when you start designing the presentation of your final project, you may discover that you need to plan, draft, and revise some sections of your text all over again. Indeed, although planning, drafting, revising, and designing can be regarded as distinct activities, at any point in the writing process you are likely to be doing all four at once.

Experienced writers seem to perform within the process in different ways. Some spend an enormous amount of time planning every detail before they write; others prefer to dispense with planning and discover their direction in drafting or revising. The American humorist James Thurber once acknowledged that he and one of his collaborators worked quite differently when writing a play:

> Elliot Nugent . . . is a careful constructor. When we were working on
> *The Male Animal* together, he was constantly concerned with plotting

A Writer's Resources

In interviews writers often explain how they work within the writing process. A convenient site for researching such interviews is <www. writerswrite.com>. For interviews with current authors whose new books are getting attention, see <www. powells.com/ authors>; for the Associated Writing Programs website, see <www. awpwriter. org/magazine/ features>; for Poets & Writers magazines, see <www.pw.org/mag>.

the play. He could plot the thing from back to front—what was going to happen here, what sort of situation would end the first-act curtain and so forth. I can't work that way. Nugent would say, "Well, Thurber, we've got our problem, we've got all these people in the living room. Now what are we going to do with them?" I'd say that I didn't know and couldn't tell him until I'd sat down at my typewriter and found out. I don't believe the writer should know too much where he's going. (James Thurber, *Writers at Work: The Paris Review Interviews*)

Even experienced writers with established routines for producing a particular kind of work admit that each project inevitably presents new problems. Virginia Woolf planned, drafted, and revised some of her novels with great speed, but she was bewildered by her inability to repeat the process with other novels:

> . . . blundering on at *The Waves*. I write two pages of arrant nonsense, after straining; I write variations of every sentence; compromises; bad shots; possibilities; till my writing book is like a lunatic's dream. Then I trust to inspiration on re-reading; and pencil them into some sense. Still I am not satisfied . . . I press to my centre. I don't care if it all is scratched out . . . and then, if nothing comes of it—anyhow I have examined the possibilities. (Virginia Woolf, "Boxing Day 1929," *A Writer's Diary*)

Writers often discover a whole set of new problems when they are asked to write in a different context. Those writers who feel comfortable telling stories about their personal experience, for example, may encounter unexpected twists and turns in their writing process when they are asked to describe the lives of other people, explain a historical event, or analyze the arguments in an intellectual controversy. Each context requires them to make adjustments in the way they typically uncover, assess, and assert information. Calvin Trillin, an especially versatile writer, admits that he changes his writing process dramatically when he shifts from writing investigative reports to writing humorous essays or weekly columns.

> In my reporting pieces, I worry a lot about structure. Everything is there—in interviews, clippings, documents—but I don't know how to get it all in. I think that's why I do what we call around the house the vomit-out. I just start writing—to see how much I've got, how it might unfold, and what I've got to do to get through to the end. In my columns and humor pieces, I usually don't know the end or even the middle. I might start with a joke, but I don't know where it's going, so I fiddle along, polishing each paragraph, hoping something will tell me what to write next. (Personal interview)

And finally, when writers face the task of presenting their text, they understand why designer Paul Rand says, "Design is both a verb and a noun. It is the beginning as well as the end, the process and the product of the imagination." Writers must work their way through the process guided by some sense of how their final text will look. But once they see their final text, they may have to reimagine all their previous decisions. As Rand points out:

> To design is much more than simply to assemble, to order, or even to edit; it is to add value and meaning, to illuminate, to simplify, to clarify, to modify, to dignify, to dramatize, to persuade, and perhaps even to amuse.
> (Paul Rand, Design Form and Chaos)

This range of responses suggests that what appears to be a simple four-stage procedure may at times be a disorderly, contradictory procedure. But experienced writers know that disorder and contradiction are inevitable but temporary disturbances in the composition of most pieces of writing. Confusion occurs when you know too little about your writing project; contradiction occurs when you think too little about what you know. The secret to moving through temporary impasses is to keep your eye on the constants in every writing context.

## Making Decisions in the Writing Process

As you write, you discover that you are constantly making decisions. Some of these decisions are complex, as when you are trying to shape ideas; others are simple, as when you are trying to select words. But each decision, large or small, affects every other decision you make so that you are continuously adjusting and readjusting your writing to make sure it is consistent, coherent, and clear. You can test the effectiveness of your decisions by measuring them against this dictum: In every writing situation, a writer is trying to communicate a *subject* to an *audience* for a *purpose.*

Initially, think of these three elements as *prompters,* ways to consider what you want to write about and how you want to write about it. Later, as you move through planning and drafting to revising and designing, think of them as *touchstones,* ways to assess what you set out to accomplish. But mainly think of them as *guidelines,* ways to control every decision you make throughout the writing process, from formulating ideas to refining sentences.

## Selecting Your Subject

Many student writers complain that their biggest problem is finding a subject. Sometimes that problem seems less complicated because the subject is named in the writing assignment. But assignments vary in how they are worded, what they assume, and what they expect. Suppose, for example, you are asked to discuss two characters in a play. This assignment does not identify a subject; it merely identifies an area in which a subject can be found. Another version of that assignment might ask you to compare and contrast the way two characters make compromises. This assignment identifies a more restricted subject but assumes you know how to work with a specific form (the comparison and contrast essay) and expects you to produce specific information (two ways of defining and dealing with compromise). In other words, the second assignment selects your subject but requires you to select and develop the subject matter of your essay.

At the end of this chapter (and every chapter of this book) you will find a sampler of writing assignments. As you browse through each assignment, consider how the subject is defined and how you are expected to develop it. Also consider how you might respond to or reformulate each assignment in terms of your own experience. You may decide that none of the assignments strike your fancy but that part of one assignment or parts of several assignments suggest a subject that is worth pursuing.

Whether you are responding to an assignment or creating one, you need to take certain steps to find a suitable subject. First, select a subject you know or can learn something about. The more you know about a subject, the more likely you are to make it your own, shaping it to your own perspective. If, in addition, you select a subject, such as the Internet, that is familiar to most of your readers, you will know that you share an area of common knowledge that allows you more freedom to explore *your* observations, ideas, and values. Second, select a subject you can restrict. A subject such as the Internet is really a broad category that contains an unlimited supply of smaller, more specific subjects. The more you can restrict your subject, the more likely you are to control your investigation, identify vivid illustrations, and maintain a unified focus. The general category *Internet* can be divided into all sorts of subtopics, each of which can be restricted further into specific subjects.

- e-mail—the addiction to messages
- e-commerce—the simplicity of Net-shopping
- search engines—the reliability of websites
- chat rooms—the etiquette of self-expression
- e-trading—the accessibility of advice
- weather.com—the graphics of forecasting
- hypertexts—the boundaries of information
- bookmarks—the history of browsing
- print—the obsession with hard copy

Although the subjects in the right column could profit from further restriction, each one illustrates why selecting a specific subject simplifies your writing task: It helps you focus on and form judgments about a concrete topic.

Finally, as you consider possible topics, ask yourself three questions: Is it *significant?* Is it *interesting?* Is it *manageable?* A *significant* subject need not be ponderous or solemn. In fact, many significant subjects grow out of ordinary observations rather than grandiose declarations. But you need to decide whether a specific subject raises important issues (the security of electronic purchases) or appeals to the common experience of your readers (the need to send/receive daily mail). Similarly, an *interesting* subject need not be dazzling or spectacular, but it does need to capture your curiosity. If it bores you, it will surely bore your readers. You need to decide why a specific subject fascinates you (why you are attracted to the maps and symbols that predict weather) and how you can make the subject more intriguing for your readers (how electronic trading allows you to make a profit on your investments). A *manageable* subject is neither so limited that you can exhaust it in a few pages (the compulsion to print paper copies of electronic sources) nor so vast that lengthy articles or books would be required to discuss it adequately (the mass of links that complicate the reading of hypertexts).

Ultimately you must develop your own methods for answering these questions each time you examine the choice of subjects available and as you consider your audience and purpose. When you compare subjects in the context of the complete writing situation, you will naturally prefer some to others. To decide which one will enable you to produce the most suitable subject, measure it against the criteria set forth in the guidelines on page 12.

## Analyzing Your Audience

Most inexperienced writers assume that their audience is their writing teacher. But writing teachers, like writing assignments, often vary in what they teach, what they assume, and what they expect. Such variation has often prompted inexperienced writers to define their writing tasks as "trying to figure out what the teacher wants." This definition is naive and smart at the same time. Superficially, it suggests that the sole purpose of any writing assignment is to satisfy another person's whims. On a deeper level, it suggests that when writers analyze the knowledge, assumptions, and expectations of their readers, they develop a clearer perception of their subject and purpose. To make this analysis truly

# Guidelines for selecting your subject

1. **What do I know about my subject?**
   Do I know about my subject in some depth, or do I need to learn more about it? What are the sources of my knowledge—direct experience, observation, reading? How does my knowledge give me a special or unusual perspective on my subject?

2. **What is the focus of my subject?**
   Is my subject too general? How can I restrict it to a more specific subject that I can develop in greater detail?

3. **What is significant about my subject?**
   What issues of general importance does it raise? What fresh insight can I contribute to my readers' thinking on this issue?

4. **What is interesting about my subject?**
   Why is this subject interesting to me? How can I interest my readers in it?

5. **Is my subject manageable?**
   Can I write about my subject in a particular form, within a certain number of pages? Do I feel in control of my subject or confused by it? If my subject is too complicated or too simplistic, how can I make it more manageable?

effective, though, writers must remember that they are writing for multiple audiences, not for a single person.

The most immediate audience is *you*. You write not only to convey your ideas to others but also to clarify them for yourself. To think of yourself as an audience, however, you must stop thinking like a writer and begin thinking like a reader. This change in perspective offers advantages, for you are the reader you know best. You are also a fairly representative reader because you share broad concerns and interests with other people. If you feel that your writing is clear, lively, and informed, other readers will probably feel that way, too. If you sense that your text is confused or incomplete, the rest of your audience is likely to be disappointed, too.

The main drawback to considering yourself as audience is your inclination to deceive yourself. You want every sentence and paragraph to be perfect, but you know how much time and energy you invested in composing them, and that effort may blur your judgment. You may accept bad writing from yourself even though you wouldn't accept it from someone else. For that reason you need a second audience. These readers—usually your friends, classmates, and teachers—are your most attentive audience. They help you choose your subject, coach you through various stages of the writing process, and counsel you about how to improve your sentences and paragraphs. As you write, you must certainly anticipate detailed advice from these readers. But you must remember that writing teachers and even peers are essentially collaborators and thus are not your ultimate audience. They know what you

● A WRITING PROJECT

Conduct an interview with
the general reader. Create
this imaginary person's response to a range of questions such as these: What
kind of writing have you
read in the last month?
What do you say when you
recommend a piece of
writing to a friend? What
visual features in the presentation of a piece of
writing help or hinder your
ability to understand its
purpose?

have considered, cut, and corrected. The more they help you, the more eager they are to commend your writing as it approaches their standards of acceptability.

Your most significant audience consists of readers who do not know how much time and energy you invested in your writing or care about how many choices you considered and rejected. These readers want writing that tells them something interesting or important, and they are put off by writing that is tedious or trivial. It is this wider audience that you (and your collaborators) must consider as you work through the writing process.

At times this audience may seem like a nebulous creature, and you may wonder how you can direct your writing to it if you do not know any of its distinguishing features. In those cases, it may be helpful to imagine a single significant reader—an attentive, sensible, reasonably informed person who will give you a sympathetic reading as long as you do not waste his or her time. Imagine an important person whom you respect and whose respect you want. This reader, specifically imagined though often termed the "general reader," the "universal reader," or the "common reader," is essentially a fiction, but a helpful fiction. Your writing will benefit from the objectivity and sincerity with which you address this reader.

Many times, however, especially as you learn more about your subject, you discover a real-world audience for your writing. More precisely, as you consider your subject in a specific context, you may identify a number of audiences, in which case you will ultimately have to choose among them. Suppose, for example, your experience purchasing books, clothes, and tickets on the Internet suggests that "online shopping" might make an interesting subject, but you are finding it difficult to restrict your topic. You decide to identify your audience, and after some deliberation, you see that you have at least three possible audiences: (1) those who love to "shop the Net"—consumers who relish the speed and ease of electronic commerce; (2) those who refuse to "shop the Net"—customers who reject the impersonality and insecurity of electronic commerce; and (3) those who are uninformed about "shopping the Net"—people who have never explored the potential advantages and disadvantages of buying goods and services online.

Now that you have identified your audience, analyze the distinctive features of each group. What do they know? What do they think they know? What do they need to know? The more you know about each group, the more you will be able to direct your writing to their assumptions and expectations. If you have purchased stuff online, you will have little difficulty analyzing the devotees and detractors of electronic commerce. You have heard the addicts explain how quick and easy it is to

In what ways does this image suggest that Amazon.com has revised its original mission to be an online bookstore?

shop from the comfort of their homes. Similarly, you have heard the critics complain about the disappointing service and financial risks of shopping online.

At first you may have difficulty with the third group because these readers have no preconceptions about electronic commerce as either the most efficient or the most dangerous way to shop. In some ways, readers in the third group are like the "general reader"—thoughtful, discerning people who are willing to read about online shopping if you can convince them that the subject is worth their attention.

As you consider addressing each of these audiences, you should be able to anticipate their interests. As you think about the addicts, for example, you might describe how online shopping enables them to customize their shopping to avoid crowds at the mall. As you think about the critics, you might define the various procedures devised to ensure a safe and satisfactory purchase. As you think about the neutral readers, you might decide that although they may have no interest in online shopping, they may be intrigued by the astonishing growth in this section of our nation's economy.

Although this sort of audience analysis helps you visualize a group of readers, it does not help you decide which group is most suitable for your essay. If you target one group, you may fall into the trap of allowing its preferences to determine the direction of your writing. If you try to accommodate all three groups, you may waiver indecisively among them so that your writing never finds any direction. Your decision about audience, like your decision about subject, has to be made in the context of the complete writing situation. Both decisions are ultimately related to your discovery of purpose—what you want to do in your

# Guidelines for analyzing your audience

1. **Who are the readers who will be most interested in my writing?**
   What is their probable age, gender, education, economic status, and social position? What values, assumptions, and prejudices characterize their general attitudes toward life?

2. **What do my readers know or think they know about my subject?**
   What is the probable source of their knowledge—direct experience, observation, reading, rumor? Will my readers react positively or negatively toward my subject?

3. **Why will my readers read my writing?**
   If they know a great deal about my subject, what will they expect to learn from reading my writing? If they know only a few things about my subject, what will they expect to be told about it? Will they expect to be entertained, informed, or persuaded?

4. **How can I interest my readers in my subject?**
   If they are hostile toward it, how can I convince them to give my writing a fair reading? If they are sympathetic, how can I fulfill and enhance their expectations? If they are neutral, how can I catch and hold their attention?

5. **How can I help my readers read my writing?**
   What kind of organizational pattern will help them see its purpose? What kind of guideposts and transitional markers will they need to follow this pattern? What (and how many) examples will they need to understand my general statements?

essay. In the next several pages, you will learn how purpose guides your decisions in writing. But first, look at the above guidelines for analyzing your audience.

## Determining Your Purpose

The central idea of this book is that writers write most effectively when they are "writing with a purpose." Inexperienced writers occasionally have difficulty writing with *a* purpose because they see many purposes: to complete the assignment, to earn a good grade, to publish their writing. These "purposes" lie outside the writing situation, but they certainly influence the way you think about your purpose. If you want a good grade, you will define your purpose in terms of your teacher's writing assignment. If you want to publish your essay, you will define your purpose in terms of a given publisher's statement about its editorial policies.

*Purpose directs and controls all the decisions writers make. It is both the what and the how of that process.*

When *purpose* is considered as an element inside the writing situation, the term has a specific meaning: *Purpose is the overall design that governs what writers do in their writing.* Writers who have determined their purpose know what kind of information they need, how they want to organize and develop it, and why they think it is important. In effect, purpose directs and controls all the decisions writers make. It is both the *what* and the *how* of that process—that is, the specific subject the writer selects *and* the strategies the writer uses to communicate the subject most effectively.

The difficulty with this definition is that finding a purpose to guide you through the writing process *is* the purpose of the writing process. Writing is both a procedure of *discovering* what you know and a procedure for *demonstrating* what you know. For that reason, you must maintain a double vision of your purpose. You must think of it as a preliminary objective that helps illuminate the decisions you have to make. You must also think of it as a final assertion that helps you implement what you intend to do in your writing.

## Forming a Working Purpose: The Hypothesis

As you begin writing, you start to acquire a general sense of your purpose. You make tentative decisions about your subject and audience, and you begin to formulate ideas about what you want to accomplish in a given context. Suppose again that you choose to write about online shopping. You could approach this subject in many ways, but you have to start somewhere, so you decide to focus on its intent. This preliminary decision will help you gather and sort information, but as you assess it, you may see that you do not know what you want to do with it. You do not have a purpose; you have only a general notion that suggests a number of perspectives. Any one of these perspectives might provide an interesting angle from which to investigate your subject, and you can use any one of them to form a *hypothesis*—a working purpose.

Forming a hypothesis is a major step in determining your purpose. Sometimes you come to your writing certain of your hypothesis: You know from the outset what you want to prove and what you need to prove it. More often, you need to consider various possibilities; to convey something meaningful in your writing, something that bears your own mark, you need to keep an open mind and explore your options fully. Eventually, however, you must choose one hypothesis that you think most accurately says what you want to say about your subject and how you want to say it.

How do you know which hypothesis to choose? There is no easy answer to this question. The answer ultimately emerges from your temperament, experiences, and interests, and also from the requirements of the context—whether you are writing for yourself or on an assignment. Sometimes you can make the choice intuitively as you proceed. In thinking about your subject and audience, you see at once the perspective you want to adopt and how it will direct your writing. At other times you

The Evolution of Retail

KIOSK   SHOP   DEPARTMENT STORE   DISCOUNT CHAIN

MALL   INTERNET

Reprinted with special permission of King Feature Syndicate.

may find it helpful to write out various hypotheses and then consider their relative effectiveness. Which will be most interesting to write about? Which best expresses your way of looking at things? With which can you make the strongest case or most compelling assertions?

For example, as you look at the information you have gathered about the intent of online shopping, you might see several hypotheses:

▶ Online shopping provides efficient access to goods and services.

▶ Online shopping distorts the personal relationship between buyer and seller.

▶ Online shopping encourages the possibility of electronic theft.

▶ Online shopping will become a national activity as more businesses sell their goods and services online.

Any one of these or other hypotheses might guide you to the next stage of your writing. You must decide which one suits you best, and your decision must take into account the nature of your subject and intended audience.

## Testing Your Hypothesis: The Discovery Draft

After you have chosen your hypothesis, you need to determine whether this preliminary statement of purpose really provides the direction and control you need to produce an effective piece of writing. You can test your hypothesis by writing a first, or *discovery,* draft. Sometimes your discovery draft demonstrates that your hypothesis works. More often, however, as you continue the writing process, you discover new information or unforeseen complications that cause you to modify your original hypothesis. In other cases, you discover that you simply cannot prove what your hypothesis suggested you might be able to prove.

Whatever you discover about your hypothesis, you must proceed in writing. If your discovery draft reveals that your hypothesis represents what you want to prove and needs only slight modification, then change your perspective somewhat or find the additional information so that you can modify it. If, on the other hand, your discovery draft demonstrates that your hypothesis lacks conviction or that you do not have (and you suspect you cannot get) the information you need to make your case, then choose another hypothesis that reflects your intentions more accurately.

For example, if you choose the hypothesis that online shopping distorts the personal relationship between buyer and seller, you may realize in writing your discovery draft that even though you have gathered information that connects online shopping with the impersonality of customer service, you don't find the evidence overwhelming or particularly interesting. Because online shopping offers customers access to electronic catalogues, it comes as no surprise that this new form of commerce has created a more impersonal relationship between buyer and seller. You see flaws in your reasoning, holes in your draft. If you remember a study reporting that most sales exchanges are executed with credit cards, you may uncover evidence that contradicts your hypothesis—all purchases have become more impersonal. In such situations, you will need to modify your hypothesis or, more likely, find another one.

## Purpose and Thesis

Whether you proceed with your original hypothesis, modify it, or choose another, you must eventually arrive at a final decision about your purpose. You make that decision during revision, when you know what you want to do and how you want to do it. Once you have established your purpose, you can make or refine other decisions—about your organization, examples, and style. One way to express your purpose is to state your thesis. A *thesis* is a sentence that usually appears in the first paragraph of your essay and states the main idea you are going to develop. Although the thesis is often called a purpose statement, thesis and purpose are not precisely the same thing. Your purpose is both contained in and larger than your thesis: It consists of all the strategies you will use to demonstrate your thesis in a sustained and successful piece of writing.

Your thesis makes a *restricted, unified,* and *precise* assertion about your subject—an assertion that can be developed in the amount of space you have, that treats only one idea, and that is open to only one interpretation. Devising a thesis from the information that you have about your subject and stating it well are key steps in the writing process; for that reason they will be discussed in more detail in Chapter 3. For now, remember that your thesis is stated after you have determined your purpose and that it expresses your main idea about your subject. For example, if you finally determine that you want to write about the way online shopping encourages the possibility of electronic theft, your thesis might be stated this way: "The moment you send your credit-card number into cyberspace, you encourage 'lurkers' to steal it for their own purposes."

In certain situations you do not need to state your thesis explicitly. This does not mean that your writing will lack purpose, only that you do not need to compose a purpose statement. Narrating a story or describing an object, for example, does not usually require a stated thesis; the thesis is suggested, or implied.

In many ways the difference between a hypothesis (a working purpose) and a thesis (a final assertion) explains why you can speculate about your purpose *before* you write but can specify your purpose only *after* you have written. This connection between your writing process and your writing purpose requires you to pause frequently to consult the criteria set forth in the following guidelines.

# Guidelines for determining your purpose

1. **What are the requirements of my writing project?**
   If I am writing to fulfill an assignment, do I understand that assignment? If I am writing on my own, do I have definite expectations of what I will accomplish?

2. **As I proceed in this project, what do I need to know?**
   Do I have a good understanding of my subject, or do I need more information? Have I considered the possible audiences who might read my writing?

3. **What hypothesis can I use as my working purpose?**
   How many different hypotheses can I formulate about my subject? Which of them seems to direct and control my information in the most effective manner?

4. **What purpose have I discovered for this writing project?**
   Has my purpose changed as I learned more about my subject and audience? If so, in what ways? Have I discovered, by working with a hypothesis or hypotheses, what I want to do in my writing?

5. **What is my thesis?**
   How can I state my main idea about my subject in a thesis sentence? Does my thesis limit the scope of my writing to what I can demonstrate in the available space? Does it focus my writing on one specific assertion? Does it make an exact statement about what my writing intends to do?

## Coordinating Decisions in the Writing Process

You need to understand how each of the three elements—subject, audience, and purpose—helps you measure your progress through the writing process. But you must not assume that these guidelines lock you into the fixed sequence of selecting your subject, analyzing your audience, and then determining your purpose. Subject, audience, and purpose are too interconnected to allow you to follow such a simple formula. Indeed, they resemble the elements in a complex chemical formula. You can isolate the elements in the formula, but you cannot understand what they create until you combine them. And each time you alter one element, however slightly, you change the character of the other elements, setting off another chain of relationships and a new formula. To make informed and purposeful decisions about your writing, therefore, you must not only understand the separate contributions of subject, audience, and purpose but also learn to coordinate the complex and shifting relationships among them each time you write.

## EXERCISE

Describe the concepts of subject, audience, and purpose implied in each original hypothesis in the following list, and then explain how each new decision will affect the three elements. Write a new hypothesis that reflects the changes.

1. *Original hypothesis:* Online shopping has changed the way most customers purchase goods and services.

   *New decision:* You decide to discuss forms of shopping, such as catalogues, that have encouraged customers to make purchases without shopping in a store.

2. *Original hypothesis:* Online shopping is the direct result of graphically enhanced websites on the Net.

   *New decision:* You decide to address your essay to someone trying to decide whether to purchase or upgrade a connection to the Internet.

3. *Original hypothesis:* Online shopping reduces the overhead costs of maintaining expensive stores in expensive locations.

   *New decision:* You decide to prove that online shopping increases the costs of shipping and handling.

## Seeing with a Purpose

Finally, you need to see how today's visual culture has affected the relationship between words and pictures. In one sense, writing—whether it is displayed in ancient hieroglyphics or modern alphabets—is a pictorial representation of thinking. As a writer, you transform your thinking into writing by arranging visual symbols on a piece of paper or a computer screen. As a reader, you decode the meaning of these symbols by translating them back into thinking. In another sense, however, writing (the making of words) and drawing (the making of pictures) have been regarded as separate enterprises, created for different purposes, appealing to different audiences, and requiring different skills. This traditional separation is suggested by two statements about the relative merits of words and pictures:

▶ A picture is worth a thousand words.

▶ A picture takes a thousand words

Today's visual culture seems to prefer the first statement. The media—today's storytellers and argument makers—believe that the power of technology makes pictures more effective than words at illustrating ideas. Today's readers—media watchers—feel increasingly dependent on pictures to make sense of complicated issues. Words, they argue, are dense, deceptive, and designed to create hidden meanings. But pictures are not a simple substitution for words. They too conceal as much as they reveal. For that reason, pictures—particularly the accelerated flow of pictures in film and television and on the Web—take a thousand words to explain.

Instead of debating the relative merits of words and pictures, consider them as collaborators in the creative process. Words must be arranged on a page; pictures must be composed within a frame. Words can explain pictures; pictures can illustrate words. "Writing with a purpose" requires "seeing with a purpose." Or as E. M. Forster once remarked, "How do I know what I think until I see what I say?"

To see, think, and write successfully in a visual culture, you not only must learn to arrange words and compose pictures but also must create a purposeful connection between the two processes. For that reason, this textbook emphasizes *designing* (see Chapter 5) as a major stage in the writing process. The verbal texts in each chapter enable you to see how a writer focuses on a subject, anticipates an audience, and asserts a purpose. The visual texts—located throughout each chapter and especially in the Image Gallery—enable you to explain how pictures can illustrate ideas central to the writing process. And the Web Designs near the end of each chapter allow you to speculate on the subtle and significant connections between arranging words and composing pictures.

# Image Gallery

## Questions

1. Identify your favorite writing tools. What writing experience made you believe in these tools?

2. Why does Dvorak Bigelow Jr. remain loyal to his typewriter? (See "A Writer's Words," page 4.)

3. In what ways has the high-speed computer exemplified by the photo of the laptop changed the way we think about the writing tools represented in the photo of the typewriter?

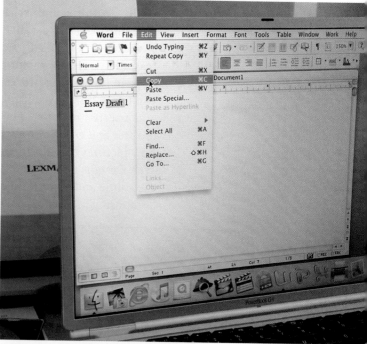

In this brief excerpt from her essay "Becoming a Writer," novelist Gail Godwin remembers the way she identified with her mother's work as a writer. She also remembers the importance of her grandmother's work as a reader. What does this selection suggest about how people choose role models? What makes her mother's work seem more interesting to Godwin than her grandmother's work?

# Becoming a Writer

## GAIL GODWIN

1 On weekend mornings my mother sat at the typewriter in a sunny breakfast nook and wrote stories about women, young women like herself, who, after some difficulty necessary to the plot, got their men. In the adjoining kitchen, my grandmother washed the breakfast dishes and kept asking, "What do you two think you could eat for lunch?" My mother and I would groan in unison. Who could imagine lunch when we'd just finished breakfast? Besides, there were more important things to do than eat.

2 Already, at five, I had allied myself with the typewriter rather than the stove. The person at the stove usually had the thankless task of fueling. Whereas, if you were faithful to your vision at the typewriter, by lunchtime you could make two more characters happy—even if you weren't so happy yourself. What is more, if you retyped your story neatly in the afternoon and sent it off in a manila envelope to New York, you'd get a check back for $100 within two or three weeks (300 words to the page, 16–17 pages, 2¢ a word: in 1942, $100 went a long way). Meanwhile, she at the stove ran our mundane life. Still new to the outrageous vulnerability of widowhood, she was glad to play Martha to my mother's Mary. In our manless little family, she also played mother and could be counted on to cook, sew on buttons, polish the piano, and give encouragement to creative endeavors. She was my mother's first reader, while the stories were still in their morning draft; "It moves a little slowly here," she'd say, or "I didn't understand why the girl did this." And the tempo would be stepped up, the heroine's ambiguous action sharpened in the afternoon draft; for if my grandmother didn't follow tempo and motive, how would all those other women who would buy the magazines?

# Brandon's Clown

## WALLACE ARMSTRONG

1  Few of those words of wisdom that are passed from father to son are followed. Most are simply acknowledged and forgotten. My father's advice about my adolescent love for painting was simple and direct: "Son, you have a special talent. Be smart. Use it to make money." With his words guiding me, I took my love to the marketplace. I began accepting commissions, painting fantasies for those who didn't have the skill or desire to paint their own.

2  Creating artwork for a client, I soon discovered, demands much more than talent and a lust for money. A friend of mine in Art History 110 was offered $175 to paint a mural in the lobby of her home-town bank. Her only direction from the bank manager was to paint "something rural looking." Obviously, rural looking can be anything from cows lapping at a sunlit pond to combines ripping the heads from a field of golden wheat. Somewhere in that wide spectrum was the painting the manager wanted. Such flexibility forces the artist to play mind reader or simply follow his own desires and hope the client likes the result. A less common, perhaps even less desirable commission is the verbal blueprint. The client knows exactly what he wants. "I want a portrait," he says, "that makes me look like General Patton. I want two American flags in the background and a Doberman at my side." Although there is some security in knowing what the client expects, most artists aren't desperate enough to follow such instructions.

3  Once the actual work begins, the question that most frequently plagues the artist is "Why am I doing this?"—especially when the commission calls for an uncharacteristic shift in creative expression. I am known on campus as "the guy who paints screaming faces," a tag I am quite happy with. I am proud of the dark maelstroms of anxiety I can create on my canvas. For hours after leaving the easel, I will walk about with my shoulders stooped and head down, frowning, lost in reflections on man's inability to overcome despair.

4  Naturally, my first commission was for a nursery painting. A young mother expecting her first child wanted an oil painting to hang in a newly remodeled nursery. Mutual friends had informed her that I was willing, able, and cheap. My father's advice prompted me to take the job and I soon found myself discussing infant tastes with the mother-to-be, a pleasant young woman whose only exposure to art was probably the Sunday comics.

5  "You know, something happy and cheery," she said between snatches of dialogue on "General Hospital." "The usual stuff for a kid's room."

6  "Is there any kind of theme to your nursery?" I asked hesitantly.

7    "Well, it's blue." she said. "If it's a boy, we're going to call him Brandon. Something like that would be nice."

8    I followed her finger to a baby stroller, decorated with circus animals. "Oh," I said, as the room began to darken and spin. "I see."

9    For the next several weeks, I had nightmares of pink giraffes and smiling zebras parading across my empty canvas. I spent hours hunched over my sketchbook, filling page after page with oddly shaped animal skeletons. Before long, the book looked like a Disneyland mortuary. The entire project seemed so pointless that I was exhausted with frustration. How would I satisfy my cheerful client and remain true to my creative vision?

10    Resolved to compromise my pride for a buck, I began gathering my paints, brushes and canvas with all the enthusiasm of the only girl in the eighth grade not chosen for the pompom squad. I reviewed my sketches hoping to find a subject and suddenly spotted a quick drawing I had made of a clown. Eureka! The answer seemed obvious: a clown. Of course. Clowns had screaming faces, even though they concealed their real pain behind their painted masks. I would mask my true intentions by painting a clown with a slightly sorrowful expression lurking behind his grease paint. He would hold the strings of two balloons, suggesting comparisons to a man behind prison bars.

11    So I began to paint. Every morning before class, I ran to my studio to re-appraise the work I had done the night before. The glistening, bright arts were so inviting. Algebra could wait. I picked out my favorite brush and dove back into the painting, detailing areas I had sketched before bedtime, making the highlights lighter and the shadows darker. Gradually, the clown's face began to emerge from the swirl of color. *Brandon's Clown* was my best work to date!

12    Feeling every bit like the proud parent myself, I carried the finished canvas home from my college studio to unveil it for my mother. As I held it up for her reaction, I was certain she would gush with glee and call the neighbors. But after a few moments of silence, she said, "It's so dark."

13    My defenses flew to Red Alert. "It's supposed to be dark. How can you emphasize light and shadow without making it dark?"

14    Leaving Mom to her *Reader's Digest,* I drove to my client's house in hopes of a better reception. Occasionally I glanced at the painting lying next to me on the seat. Perhaps it *was* a bit dark—for a nursery painting, that is. The expression on the clown's face suddenly seemed harsh and scolding. How could defenseless little Brandon lie in his crib and stare at this all day long?

15    "How do you like your painting, Mrs. Hobbs?" I asked meekly. For some reason, the canvas which had seemed so perfect that morning in my studio now looked totally out of place in Brandon's nursery. A beautiful tiny wooden rocking horse swayed peacefully on the dresser top. An 8 × 10 hospital glossy of little Brandon, looking fresh and innocent, hung on the wall. And in the corner, nearly lost in the bundle of blankets, was Brandon himself, fast asleep and completely unaware of this ugly dark thing that was about to disturb the harmony of his world.

16    "It's fine. Will you take a check?" his mother asked as she hung the painting right above Brandon's head.

17    As I left holding my first commission, I did not think about my father's advice or my artistic reputation. I thought only of poor Brandon. I will not be surprised if, twenty years from now, a deranged young man stops me on the street and smashes a clown painting over my head. I probably deserve worse.

# Web Design

Students using *Writing with a Purpose* in a composition class were asked to design a website for Wally Armstrong's "Brandon's Clown." Notice how the annotations for the two sites explain how a design can either confuse or clarify purpose.

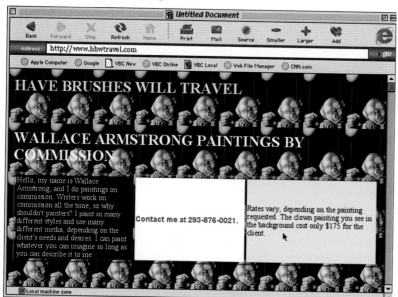

## Sample Home Page

▶ Subject is vague because words and images create clutter.

▶ Reader is confused by clash of type and color.

▶ Purpose of site is buried in small type.

## Sample Home Page

▶ Subject is clear because words and image are isolated and unified.

▶ Reader can quickly browse the brief, friendly type.

▶ Purpose of site is dramatized in the alignment of painting, headline, and text.

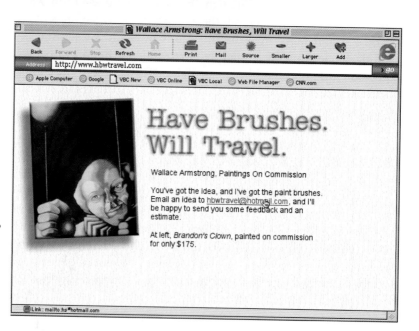

# Writing Assignments

## 1. NARRATE

Make a list of your earliest memories of writing—e.g., learning to form your letters, drafting a letter to Santa Claus, composing your first report for school. Select the memory that had the most powerful effect on you. Then write the story, dramatizing the process and explaining what you learned.

## 2. OBSERVE

Describe the habits of someone who uses writing to conduct business. The person need not be a professional writer. For example, you might describe how a family friend drafts business letters or how a former boss wrote up reports. Your purpose is to describe how writing works in the world beyond school.

## 3. INVESTIGATE

Using the questions about writing habits on page 5, interview a classmate about his or her writing habits. After you have compiled your information, write an essay addressed to the rest of the class, explaining the rituals your partner believes he or she must perform to write successfully.

## 4. COLLABORATE

Form a small writing group (three to four students) and interview each other, focusing particularly on those problems that make writing difficult in each stage of the writing process. Then write a collaborative report for each member of the group, suggesting ways he or she might solve those problems.

## 5. READ

Focus on the grandmother in Gail Godwin's "Becoming a Writer." Then construct a profile of your *first* reader. What qualities does the person possess? What do you want this reader to tell you? How do you take praise or criticism from such a reader? You may want to read the rest of Godwin's comments on "Becoming a Writer" in *The Writer on Her Work*. Ed. Janet Sternburg. New York: Norton, 2000.

## 6. RESPOND

Respond to Wallace Armstrong's "Brandon's Clown" by trying to remember some words of wisdom that your parents or a trusted friend passed on to you as guidelines for giving your life a sense of purpose. Then describe an incident in which you tried to follow those guidelines.

## 7. ANALYZE

Select a particularly creative website on the Internet—for example, a website for an art museum or a particular musical performer. Then speculate on how the sponsors of the website represent their subject, what assumptions they make about their audience, and why they choose to communicate over the Net rather than by means of more traditional media.

## 8. EVALUATE

Making use of the annotations that accompany the two versions of Wallace Armstrong's website "Have Brushes. Will Travel," explain which site has the most effective design.

## 9. ARGUE

Compare your classmates' statements about their composing process with their actual practice. Use this information to prove that readers can usually—or rarely—believe writers' testimony about their creative process.

## 10. ARGUE

Consider what you have learned in this chapter about the ways in which various professional writers work. Next, consider the differences between the writing they do and the writing you have done as schoolwork. Then develop an argument in which you demonstrate in some detail why their advice *helps* or *hinders* the "school writer." You may want to document your argument with evidence from writing assignments you had to complete in courses other than English composition.

# Planning

As we saw in Chapter 1, Ernest Hemingway testified that when he had trouble starting a new story, he would squeeze orange peels into the fire, gaze out the window, and worry about whether he would ever write again. Although they seem to have nothing to do with writing, activities like these are not a waste of time; some may even be necessary for writers to think their way into a writing project. Random thinking may seem pointless, but it often helps writers step away from the immediate problem they face and give it a chance to "cool down" so that they can think clearly again. Random thinking *is* a waste of time, however, if it encourages writers to wait for the perfect moment to begin working. Those who wait for the perfect moment usually do a lot of waiting and very little writing. Eventually, all writers must do what Hemingway recalls he did: give themselves a strong pep talk. "Stop worrying! Start writing!"

The best way to start writing is to begin planning. Inexperienced writers mistakenly regard planning as essentially a thinking activity. First, they think, they must plan inside their heads what they want to say, and then they must copy these thoughts onto a piece of paper. Unfortunately, they discover that such planning usually produces two kinds of failure: (1) They cannot think through everything they want to say before they write, and (2) they cannot simply transfer their thinking into writing. Planning, in fact, is primarily a *writing* activity, as most experienced writers can testify. Although they admit that they do some planning before they write, these writers insist that they do their most productive planning after they have begun writing. For them, planning is not so much thinking *and* writing as it is *thinking-in-writing*. Read what poet William Stafford has to say about the relationship between thinking and writing:

> When I write, I like to have an interval before me when I am not likely to be interrupted. For me, this means usually the early morning, before others are awake. I get pen and paper, take a glance out the window (often it is dark out there), and wait. It is like fishing. But I do not wait very long, for there is always a nibble—and this is where receptivity comes in. To get started I will accept anything that occurs to me. Something always occurs, of course, to any of us. We can't keep from thinking. Maybe I have to settle for an immediate impression: it's cold, or hot, or dark, or bright, or in between! Or—well, the possibilities are endless. If I put down something, that thing will help the next thing come, and I'm off. If I let the process go on, things will occur to me that were not at all in my mind when I started. These things, odd or trivial as they may be, are somehow connected. And if I let them string out, surprising things will happen.
>
> (William Stafford, "A Way of Writing," *Writing the Australian Crawl* )

## Strategies and Your Journal

As the first stage in the writing process, planning helps you uncover, explore, and evaluate a topic. Whether you are assigned a topic by your teacher or are free, like Stafford, to accept any topic that occurs to you, planning helps you locate and produce information in writing. An effective method to prompt your planning is to use one of several thinking-in-writing strategies discussed next. Used alone or in combination, these strategies help you identify familiar (or forgotten) information and create new information. These strategies are also flexible enough to use during other stages of the writing process. A strategy designed to get you started—such as listing—works equally well as a method for evaluating a draft or organizing a revision agenda.

*Those who wait for the perfect moment usually do a lot of waiting and very little writing.*

# ⊂Keeping a Journal on your computer

Open a special file on your computer called JOURNAL. Then before or after each entry, record the date and a phrase identifying the **subject** of your writing and save it. Such a procedure will enable you to (1) store and locate your writing experiments; (2) reenter your experiments to add, delete, or rework your thinking in writing; (3) combine or transfer chunks of your writing directly into a draft; (4) copy your journal onto a disk so that you can work on your writing at another computer; and (5) post interesting or troublesome sections to your writing group.

A good place to experiment with these strategies is a writer's source-book or journal. Depending on your work habits or writing context, you can use anything from a looseleaf notebook to a computer disk for your journal. In this private, no-fault environment, you can write whatever you want. But try to avoid turning your journal into a diary that simply records the clutter of your daily schedule. Instead, use it to plan writing projects—the one due next week or the one you may want to try someday.

During planning, the writing you produce in your journal will read like "one step forward, two steps back." This movement is created by your attempt to answer two questions: (1) How much information can I *produce* about this topic in writing? (2) How much of this information can I *use* to shape an interesting piece of writing? You can answer the first question after you have worked with one or more thinking-in-writing strategies. You can answer the second by evaluating the information against the guidelines produced in Chapter 1 for selecting a subject, analyzing your audience, and determining your purpose.

## Listing

Listing is a simple way to produce information in writing. If you are creating your own assignment, you can make a list of potential subjects. If you are responding to directions, you can list what you already know or need to know about the subject of the assignment. As you restrict your subject or identify its various subdivisions, you can make additional lists to help you recall more precise information. Begin by giving your list a title, a prompt that will evoke events, impressions, and ideas. Then, working down the page as quickly as possible, list any word or phrase that comes to mind. Don't stop to edit, organize, or evaluate the items in your list. Simply spill them down the page in whatever form they occur to you. Sometimes you will work in explosive bursts, producing ideas that instantly generate related ideas. At other times you will pause, probing for a new direction as you move from one isolated idea to another. Don't be discouraged by these occasional pauses or by the strange notions you jot down to keep the list going. The pauses may help you identify topics that require further consideration, and the strange notions may provoke unexpected insights into your subject.

In a sociology class, Robert Scheffel was asked to write a profile of a relative who had had an important influence on his life. Focusing on his relationship with his father, Robert selected the word *Dad* as a prompt and then produced the following list in his journal:

Dad

P.K.—preacher's kid, defensive, embarrassed, rebel-lious, special friends' fathers had normal jobs—no explanations worked at bank, factory—on weekends, slept late, played golf

```
Dad works at church—and at home
Saturday "Keep quiet! Dad's working on sermon"
Typing in study. No phone calls. Turn down T.V.
Skips lunch—dinner, glassy-eyed, distant
Sunday Morning—gone before breakfast—dress rehearsal
Mother checks our shoes, knots ties
Marches us to first pew—everybody looking
Organ, choir, congregation—processional
Dad in robe, carrying Bible—distinguished, important
Sunday voice—scripture, sermon (fidgety, sleepy)
Prayer—"Our Heavenly Father"—power, majesty
Heavenly father, my father—same words, same rules
Career day at school—doctor, lawyer, police chief
"What's your father do?"
"Nothing. He's a minister."
```

**Evaluating Lists**   After completing your list, examine your information carefully. What subject dominates your list? Can you identify other subjects or subjects you want to develop in greater detail? Circle and connect items that seem to go together. Pick a word or phrase and start another list. You may decide that you can use most of the information on your list, or you may discover that only a few fragments or sentences are worth pursuing. But one of those sentences may be what Hemingway called a "true sentence," a sentence that points the way to your subject, audience, and purpose.

Robert's list focuses immediately on his father's job. The initials *P. K.* evoke emotions he cannot easily explain. His friends' fathers have *normal* jobs, but his Dad's job is different. The weekend schedule clarifies that difference and suggests the possibility of a specific subject that is significant, interesting, and manageable. It also suggests at least three groups of readers ("normal" people, preachers' kids, and preachers) who might find the subject intriguing. But, most important, the list hints at several hypotheses about Robert's perception of his father's work that he

# ⊂listing  **on your computer**

Type your prompt at the top of your screen and begin listing all the ideas, associations, and images that come to mind. To evaluate your list, review it, highlight promising items with an asterisk or in boldface and insert additional ideas you forgot during your initial brainstorming. If you discover an image or cluster of words that provokes a new list, save the original one before creating and naming another list on a different or related subject. You may want to post your list to members of your writing group or class. Ask them to reflect on the list or suggest possible subjects for your draft.

may want to explore in greater detail, either through another list or through one of the other planning strategies described in this chapter. When he has collected enough information, he will sort through his sketchy hypotheses and select one to guide his writing during drafting.

## Freewriting

Like listing, freewriting helps you write down as quickly as possible what you can remember. But freewriting encourages you to remember in coherent blocks and to write in phrases and sentences. Freewriting is *free,* however, because you don't have to worry about writing perfect sentences. You write in your journal for a sustained period of time (usually ten to fifteen minutes) without stopping. Under these conditions, you don't have time to reflect on where you are going, where you have been, or how anything looks. You certainly don't have time to correct misspelled words, cross out awkward phrases, or reread what you have written. Once you are finished, you will have time to look it over and identify useful ideas.

You can practice freewriting as an unfocused or focused activity. In unfocused freewriting, you simply begin writing, transcribing onto the page the first ideas that pop into your head and then allowing your mind to wander to other subjects. The chief advantage of this kind of writing is that it forces you to write *immediately,* bypassing the agony of selecting the perfect topic. Its chief disadvantage is that it often forces you to write about the *immediate,* the impulses and events that have just occurred. But while you are filling up the page, you may discover a provocative idea or forgotten episode that leads to a more complex or deeply textured pattern of ideas.

Joanne Reinhardt, for example, completed the following unfocused freewriting in her journal during the confusion of the first day of her writing class:

> Here I go again. Summer's gone. September stomach back. Worry about clothes, teachers, grades. I mean how many times did I check and double-check my schedule, and then—wrong room, wrong class. Everybody's looking at blotches on my neck. Act like you're the only one who doesn't know. If you get lucky, finding this class--surprise, write an essay. Freewriting. Fat chance. First days are always a lie. I mean what do you people want? Solve the polynomial. Remember the <u>Maine</u>. Find the unknown. Never could figure out Bridgeman (Latin)—never learned to decline. My little revolt. He liked it—seemed to matter. Weird. Wonder if this matters?

What are we supposed to be doing anyway? Why not "What I did on my summer vacation" or better yet "What I didn't do on my summer vacation"?

It is often difficult to evaluate unfocused freewriting because the sentences slide from subject to subject, never stopping long enough to develop. But you can underline words that seem significant or question phrases that seem suspicious. Does your writing have a common theme? Does one sentence or phrase evoke a particularly powerful memory? Answering these questions in your journal may help you select a subject for a focused freewriting exercise. Joanne, surprised that she remembered Mr. Bridgeman's Latin class, decided to reconstruct the episode suggested by the prompt "My little revolt":

### My Little Revolt

"I'm a tough teacher. This is a tough class. Half of you will be gone in two weeks. The rest of you will love Latin." Tough love! Bridgeman paces behind desk like a caged panther. Knit shirts, no ties-pumps iron. Made Linda Thomas cry three days straight; then she was gone. Everybody got it. Even Tommy Hirschen, Latin ace. "Miss Reinhardt. Go to board. Decline fēmina." Stomach lurches. Don't cry in front of boys. Already sniffling-bad cold, no Kleenex. "Begin!" Nominative, genitive, dative . . . accusative? . . . Damn! Play with chalk. Read back of eraser. "Miss Reinhardt?" "I'm thinking." Thinking I need a Kleenex. Nose dripping, eyes watering. Should have stayed home. "Cease"-favorite word. Never "stop" or "that will be all" . . . . "Mr. Hirschen. Finish declining fēmina." Blotches on neck. Nose running all the way to desk. Ask Mary Keller for Kleenex-too loud. "Cease." Heart pounds. "What is it now, Miss Reinhardt?" "I need a Kleenex." Long sigh-"Is there a kind soul who can give Miss Reinhardt a Kleenex?" Book bags, purses, hands-six tissues. Don't look up. Stack them slowly in pile. Reshuffle them. Make him wait. Peel off top tissue and blow. Crumple in wad. Walk slowly toward his desk. He's still waiting. Drumming pencil. Drop wad in basket. Look him in the eye-"You can continue." Turn around . . . Hirschen's mouth open. Keller's in shock. Note on my desk. "You're dead." Bell. "Miss Reinhardt. May I see you before you leave?" Class crunches out. Hirschen whispers, "Bridgeman kills." Don't cry no matter what. We're alone. He smiles . . . "Congratulations. I've been waiting a long time for somebody to do something like that." Like

### • A WRITING PROJECT

Everyone has school memories—teachers, homework, research papers. Freewrite about the best teacher you ever had, the best course you ever took, or the most challenging writing assignment you ever attempted. As you consider this planning material, think about what kind of teaching strategy—e.g., intimidation, encouragement—helped you become an effective learner.

```
what? And that was it. Still can't figure it out. Never
told anybody. Let 'em fight their own battles with
Bridgeman. Never scared of him again. Never loved
Latin. Tough luck, Bridgeman.
```

**Evaluating Freewriting**    Like Joanne, you will need to make a number of decisions about your subject, audience, and purpose if you want to write a longer, more finished essay based on your freewriting. Reread both of Joanne's freewritings and then answer the following questions:

1. How does Joanne's decision to focus on her revolt restrict her subject? What does she find significant and interesting about this incident? What aspects has she managed effectively? What aspects need further development?

2. How might an assessment of her audience help Joanne transform her planning into a successful draft? What specific sections of her freewriting attract the sympathy of her readers? What additional information will they need to understand her revolt?

3. What is Joanne trying to prove about her subject? Is she attempting to prove more than one thing? Make a list of hypotheses she could use to clarify her intentions.

## Speculating

Speculating will help you produce different interpretations of a potential subject. The word *speculate* suggests an imaginative, hypothetical kind of seeing: You study your subject, mull over its possible meaning, and make several conjectures about its significance. Your subject might be an observed object (a computer classroom), a memory (your first attempt to find a subject on the Web), or something you read (a website

# freewriting on your computer

To experiment with unfocused freewriting, open a file and begin "fishing." For focused freewriting, type your prompt at the top of the screen and begin writing. After an initial session, review your work to find a focus, then move down the screen a few lines, type this focus as your new prompt, and begin another session. On occasion, try "invisible writing." Simply turn down the brightness control on your monitor, freewrite, and then turn up the brightness to review your work. Evaluate your freewriting by marking promising passages with asterisks or brackets. You may want to transfer them to your draft. You may also want to annotate such passages by hand on your hard copy. Finally, you may want to post your freewriting to members of your writing class. Their responses to your writing may help you anticipate the interests and needs of your audience.

that linked you to another, surprising website). As a thinking-in-writing strategy, speculating encourages you to expand your planning by seeing your subject from three different perspectives.

▶ *Speculate about your subject as an object.* This perspective suggests that you see your subject at rest, as a static object or scene that at a given moment has a fixed identity.

▶ *Speculate about your subject as an action.* This perspective allows you to see your subject in motion, as a dynamic process that changes form as it progresses.

▶ *Speculate about your subject as a network.* This perspective enables you to see your subject as a series of connections, as a complex system of relationships that extend and enhance your subject's importance.

As you think about your subject from each of these perspectives, note your speculations in your journal. If one perspective does not produce provocative information, move on to the next. Write what you see and make guesses about what you don't see. Don't try to write perfect sentences: You are still *planning*. You are looking for something interesting and significant about your subject that you can reveal to an audience for a purpose.

Speculating both generates information (if you have at least some notion of your subject) and interprets information you have already collected. One assignment in Joni Leisure's writing class called for her to observe a major meeting place and compose its profile. Armed with her journal, she prowled around her normal haunts, looking for a suitable subject. She considered several possibilities—her dormitory lounge, the snack bar, the registration office—but settled on a computer classroom. Although she and her fellow writing students met in the class three days a week, she had never really studied this room. Here are her speculations:

### Computer Classroom as an Object

```
At the front of the room, in the left corner, is the
teacher's "station"-a sort of star command that houses
a computer and the panels for the projection system. To
the right, on the front wall, is a large screen and in
the right corner is the printer—WARMING UP, READY. The
three remaining walls are lined by adjoining work
tables that support monitors, hard drives, keyboards,
and mouses. Students sit in swivel chairs, backs turned
to the teacher, staring at the soft glow of their moni-
tors, waiting. In the center of the room are four pod-
shaped tables. When they are not typing and clicking,
students can swing around to these tables for human
contact and conversation. And hanging from the center
of the ceiling is the eye in the sky—the counterpart
```

to the projection system at the teacher's console. This is the classroom of the future. It's supposed to be user friendly, but it looks like educational war games. GROUND CONTROL TO MAJOR TOM. . . .

## Computer Classroom as an Action

So this is the computer classroom. Students, with their backs to the teacher, check their email and surf the Net waiting for instructions from Dr. Web at mission control. Several students roll to pods and start gabbing. One student downloads a file and runs to the printer to retrieve it just as Dr. Web scans the room for absentees: "Today we're going to work on our hypertexts. Suzanne and I will be walking around to answer your questions. So, swing around to your computer and. . . ." The students shove away from the pods and hunch over their keyboards. Dr. Web and Suzanne stroll in different directions. "Why isn't this link working? I've tried changing the address twice." "Click on EDIT, scroll down to INSERT LINK." "How can I get this image to duplicate for a background?" "The sound on this was working yesterday. Now it's not even here." "Why can't I open this?" "I'm not sure it's on your disk. Did you save it on your hard drive or on your disk?" New terms. New tools. New steps. The process is fraught with confusion and anxiety. Finally, a sigh of relief. "Hey. It worked. I made a link."

## Computer Classroom as a Network

The whole class is connected to one another—the nontraditional student quivering at her computer to the Internet junkie rolling his mouse; the guy who writes all his papers about ultimate fighting to the girl who writes her papers about motherhood—they're all connected by the icons on the screen. "Click on *Writers Commons* and let's talk about ideas for our narratives. Help each other. Suggest what someone might want to do with a topic." Clicking, Chatting, Responding. "How about 'my first kiss'?" "Sounds lame." "No, really, listen. . . ." "I've already written a couple of pages. About my eviction." "Have you checked the Web for Renter's Rights?" The network expands to other "rooms"— webpages, moos, muds, and other computer classrooms. "I found a policy statement on *Renter's Rights* from Oregon." "Why not check out our distance learning site in Portland? See what students there have to say about your paper. . . ." "Hey, Dr. Web. Can we project my

**How does this photograph suggest that a networked classroom encourages collaborative learning?**

screen onto the big screen? Somebody in Portland wants to write about their first kiss."

**Evaluating Speculation**  Joni's speculations have yielded a wealth of information about the computer classroom. Before she drafts an extended profile of this special place, she needs to reconsider her information in terms of her potential subject, audience, and purpose. Reexamine her speculation exercises. Then write out your answers to the following questions. Your instructor may want to discuss your answers in class.

1. How many specific subjects can you identify in the three speculations?

2. Which speculation produces the most interesting perspective on the computer classroom? How does that perspective define a significant and manageable subject?

3. What potential audience could Joni assume for her profile? What different audiences does she assume in each of her speculations?

4. What hypotheses can you find in Joni's speculating exercises?

5. What purpose might Joni choose for writing an essay about a computer classroom? Compose a thesis statement she could use to organize an essay.

## Interviewing

Interviewing someone is the most direct way to investigate a subject, but the process is never as simple or spontaneous as it appears on television. To use the strategy effectively, you must learn how to *prepare* for an interview, how to *manage* and *record* an interview, and how to *evaluate* the results.

**How to Prepare for an Interview**  Begin by compiling a list of people who may know something about your subject. The list could include *experts* (people who have studied your subject), *participants* (people who have *lived* your subject), and *information brokers* (people who may know nothing about your subject but know how to put you in touch with people who do). Contact the people on your list and ask for an interview, stating in general terms what you are trying to find out and why you think they may be able to help. Ask to talk to them for a specific amount of time—no longer than an hour—and don't overstay your welcome. As you schedule your interviews, anticipate how your subjects may respond to your questions. Are they likely to be friendly, hostile, or merely puzzled when you arrive? Sometimes you can anticipate their attitudes because you know them or because you have heard them express their opinions on your subject. At other times you can anticipate their attitudes by imagining yourself in their position. How would you feel about being interviewed on this subject? What topics would you want to be asked about? What topics would you want to avoid? What questions would you have about the interviewer's motives and methods?

Next, ask yourself what you want to learn from each subject. To feel prepared and to avoid getting sidetracked, write out a list of questions in your journal following the journalist's formula: *who? what? where?*

# Speculating on your computer

Speculate on your computer by composing a series of three focused freewritings. (Or create a three-column grid that will enable you to compose your speculations side by side.) Explore the information in each freewriting for connections that enlarge or enrich your subject. If your columns aren't evenly matched, save your file, review it at some later date, and push yourself to produce more information that will make your speculations more balanced. Such writing will allow you to hop around, adding, deleting, and annotating your planning. If you like this planning strategy, name and save the pattern so that you can call it up whenever you want to use it. Post your speculations to other students in your writing class or to students in other writing classes (near and far). Ask them to respond to your writing using the evaluation questions (1–5) listed on page 37.

*when? why?* and *how?* Although these questions will help you organize what you want to learn, most interviews are dynamic, disorganized conversations. For that reason, you must remind yourself that your questions are likely to provoke surprising answers that will inspire new questions. The best interviewers prepare to discover things they need to know and plan to uncover things they had not expected to learn.

**How to Manage and Record an Interview**   Interviews can be formal occasions in which the interviewer acts like an attorney grilling witnesses and the interviewee acts like a jittery suspect. Or interviews can be informal occasions—pleasant and productive conversations among friends. Sometimes you cannot control the mood of an interview because the person you are talking to is suspicious before you arrive. But most of the time you can put yourself and your subject at ease by following a few basic tips:

▶ *Don't feel that you must apologize for your interview.* You may want to say something about how much you appreciate your subject's willingness to talk to you. Such remarks are part of the etiquette of interviewing. But someone who has agreed to be interviewed is probably flattered that you are there and has already made time for you in the day's schedule.

▶ *Tape recorders can supply a valuable record of your conversation, but they make some people uncomfortable.* Try your journal. Keep it out of sight as much as possible, and write in it as little as possible. When you do write, jot down words and phrases rather than complete sentences. Keep your eyes on the person you are talking to, not on your journal.

▶ *Begin your interview by talking about interesting and safe topics.* If you are conducting the interview in the subject's home or office, ask about some object or photograph you have noticed in the room. Even if you don't ask about these props, try to list them in your journal because they may help you interpret what your subject thinks is important in his or her life.

▶ *Don't tell your subject everything you want to know before your subject tells you what he or she knows.* You are trying to learn what other people think, not prove what you think. The best strategy is to encourage the interviewee to act like an expert: Ask your subject to help you understand the topic at hand by answering your questions. And then LISTEN.

▶ *Use prepared questions only when the conversation drifts far away from the designated topic.* For the most part, allow the conversation to develop naturally. Before you end the interview, however, review your prepared questions as a final check.

▶ *Save two questions for the end of the interview:* (1) What should I have asked that I didn't ask? (2) Whom else do I need to interview (or what do I need to read) to understand the topic we've been discussing?

**How to Evaluate an Interview**  Once you have completed the interview, return to your room and immediately reconstruct the conversation. Describe the atmosphere of the room where the interview took place, the appearance of your subject, and the varying attitudes (eager, evasive, expansive) he or she displayed during the discussion. Transform your words and phrases into complete sentences. If your notes seem incomplete or if you want to be sure you are quoting your subject accurately, call the person to double-check your information. Such follow-up calls are not invitations to censor. People often want to revise what they said during an interview, but only you can decide whether their second thoughts should be yours. Your follow-up call is simply an effort to make the first version complete and accurate.

After you have reproduced the interview in writing, talk to yourself in your journal about what you learned. Did your subject provide useful answers to your prepared questions? What answers confirmed your assessment of his or her biases? What answers surprised you? What new questions did you ask? If you were to draft an essay based on this interview, could you identify a subject, anticipate an audience, and formulate a hypothesis? This last assessment suggests the degree to which even the most informal interview can propel you into further planning activities. Once you try to evaluate what other people have told you, you will discover that you are making lists of questions you should have asked, people you want to talk to next, and material you think you'd better read.

Susan Reidenbach decided to write about the set design in Arthur Miller's *Death of a Salesman* for a short research paper for her literature class. The university theater was scheduled to produce the play the next semester, and she decided to interview the theater's set designer.

```
10/25  Decided on my research paper—"Set Design in
Arthur Miller's Death of a Salesman." Theater is
producing it next semester. John knows the set
designer—D. C. Schawger. Says he's easy to talk to—
real creative. Got an interview Thursday at 1:30.
Wonder what he'll do with Salesman. Better think up
some questions so I don't look dumb.

1. Who designed the original set for Salesman?
2. What kind of problems will you have to solve in
   designing the set?
3. Where will you find props for the play—trophy, tape
   recorder, flute?
```

4. When will you have to start building the set to complete it on time?
5. How will you create the set for the play—follow Miller's instructions or your own intuitions?
6. Why do some playwrights provide more information than others about the significance of the set?

10/28   Notes from Interview with D. C. Schawger

Just back from Schawger interview. First question blew my topic. Since Jo Mielziner's prize-winning design for the original production, nobody has done much with Salesman. Schawger says all you need is three rooms for the house and open space (apron) for other scenes—restaurant, hotel, garden. He's more interested in sets he's designing for Tartuffe and Waiting for Godot. Need to write down what happened.

Sign above office door: "The Miracle Worker." Room filled with props (mostly swords), drawings of sets (renderings), awards (Outstanding Creative Achievement). Next to Schawger's desk is a drafting table stacked with blueprints (working drawings). Sign behind the table: "It's a small world, but I wouldn't want to paint it." Behind his desk Schawger looks small, unimpressive—until he starts talking about his work. Real dynamo.

Designing set for one play, building set for another, tinkering with another in performance—complicated schedule. Set designer has to be organized. Reads play, researches how other designers staged it, then looks at history books to see what a formal ballroom should look like in a specific time (Tartuffe). Next collaborates with director about initial ideas—sometimes there is disagreement, but director is always in charge. Next step, makes a rendering or scale model to illustrate things like space, mood, symbolism. Then the working drawings—15-20 pages of blueprints for each play. Designer has to be architect, historian, artist, draftsman, engineer, carpenter, plumber, electrician, upholsterer. Turns drawings over to shop foreman for construction but may have to change everything in rehearsal. Too much furniture. Lights change color of paint. Audience can't see props.

New challenge with every play. Historical plays like Tartuffe you have to be accurate. Modern plays like Godot you have to be creative. Strange—less set—i.e., Godot—frees you to be more creative with what you have—tree. Each play requires you to learn something new. With Equus, weld metal masks. With Miracle Worker, get water to the pump.

Schawger blew my paper, but fired me up about the
whole process. Volunteered to work for him next semester. I could still do Salesman, but I'd rather pick
another play or maybe write about several plays that
present different design problems. Wonder if I could
write about the job of set designer and use different
plays as examples? Audience doesn't know how complicated a job it is. Just sit there and watch the actors.
Never think about plumbing or electricity unless it
doesn't work. Maybe I could interview some other
designers. Read textbooks or something by Mielziner.

Susan's interview produced much information on the world of set
design. Her original topic, "Set Design in Arthur Miller's *Death of a
Salesman*," is still feasible, but it no longer seems interesting or significant. Read through her notes, and then try to answer these questions:

1. To what extent did Susan's list of questions *prepare* her for her interview?
2. How does she *manage* Schawger's replies to her questions?
3. Why does the interview change the focus of Susan's research paper?
4. What kind of audience does she anticipate for the new essay she is
   planning?
5. What hypothesis does she start to formulate about this new subject?

## Reading

Reading what other people have written about your subject is probably
the most common strategy for gathering information for writing. But
merely consuming other people's words will not help you compose your

# Interviewing on your computer

Set up a file and write down your questions
before you conduct your interview. Write up
your interview notes or transcribe your interview tape into that file after the interview. Make
a duplicate copy of the file so that you can speculate about or rearrange your subject's comments to reveal the patterns and themes that
emerged during the interview. Although interviews are most successful face-to-face, the computer provides the option of an electronic interview. If you and your subject have access to
e-mail, exchange letters over the network. You
will be able to submit carefully composed questions, and your subject will be able to draft long,
thoughtful answers. You can also ask follow-up
questions while your subject can revise his or her
responses. Each exchange should probably be
recorded as a separate interview, but you may
want to combine and file them under one
heading to suggest the electronic conversation
you are having about your subject.

own. You must be a critical consumer—*selecting, analyzing,* and *evaluating* what you read for one purpose: to help you write. Chapters 12 and 13 will help you perform these activities according to the more formal requirements of the research paper: checking bibliographies, quoting evidence, documenting sources. In this chapter, you will use reading as an informal procedure for exploring different approaches to your subject.

The easiest way to keep track of your reading is to write about it in your journal. Think of reading as another form of interviewing—a way of talking to people who have already thought and written about your subject. So, just as you did in interviewing, start by making a list of material you want to read. Be sure to look for variety in your reading material: Skim magazines in a bookstore; interview local experts about what they read; consult with a reference librarian about possible sources; or, using several key search words, browse the Web. Once you start reading, each selection will refer you to others; then your problem will be deciding when you have read enough. There is no way to make that decision—you can *always* read more—but usually you know that you have read enough when the same names, ideas, and issues begin to pop up in everything you read.

On most subjects, reading material falls into three broad categories: eyewitness accounts (printed in popular magazines), expert studies (documented in technical journals or official reports), and advocates' opinions (expressed in editorial or promotional pamphlets). Although these categories suggest the kind of material you need to read, they may not help you classify a specific selection. Indeed, many selections combine the features of all three categories. An editorial, for example, may cite personal anecdotes and statistical data to advance its argument. To sort out the material on your list, you need a set of questions to help you interpret what you are reading. These questions are similar to the guidelines you follow as you write, but in this case you are deciding how another writer, writing in a specific format and context, selects a subject, analyzes an audience, and determines a purpose.

1. Who is the author? What makes the author an expert on the subject? What might have formed the author's point of view?

2. Where and when was the article or book published? You may know little about the author, but you may know something about the magazine *(Scientific American)*, how it was published (in print or online), and whether the date of publication makes the information current and reliable.

3. What is the author's general subject? What is the restricted subject? What does this perspective contribute to your understanding of

## A WRITER'S WORDS

A reader learns what he or she does not know from books, what has passed and yet is forever present through print. The mating rituals of the Trobriand Islanders. The travails of the Donner Party. The beaches at Normandy. The smoke from the stacks at Auschwitz. . . . The eyewitnesses die; the written word lives forever.

—Anna Quindlen,
*How Reading Changed My Life*

*your* subject? Does it confirm your perception, raise new and confusing questions, or lead you into detours and dead ends?

4. To whom is the writing addressed? What attitudes does the author assume in his or her audience? What knowledge does he or she expect these readers to possess or want to obtain?

5. What is the author's purpose? Does the author state a specific thesis, or does the author imply one? How does the thesis, stated or implied, control the direction of the writing?

These questions not only help you select the most intriguing reading material from your list; they also help you analyze and evaluate it. Keep your journal with you so you can write about your reading as you *preview, read,* and *review.*

▶ *Preview:* Before you read each selection, try to anticipate the kinds of information and the point of view you will find. Annotate each entry on your list, indicating what you expect to find when you read it.

▶ *Read:* As you read each selection, write a few notes in your journal. Comment on the major points, copy memorable sentences or important data, and write out short answers to your reading questions. You will also want to write any questions the author raises that you have not considered.

▶ *Review:* Put the material aside and write about the most vivid and thought-provoking things you remember. Thumb back through your reading notes. What did you discover that contributes to your view of the subject? Evaluate what the selection said and what it didn't say.

Jim Jones follows this three-part procedure as he does some preliminary reading for a history essay on the Holocaust. He begins by skimming through some major studies—political interpretations, personal accounts, historical analyses—but eventually decides to restrict his subject to the United States Holocaust Memorial Museum in Washington, D.C. He is particularly interested in the amount of information he finds about the museum on the Web—everything from documents in the museum's archives to a collection of journal responses to the museum written by high school history students.

```
        Reading List on Holocaust Memorial

Preview: 1. "The Doctors' Trial." United States Holocaust
            Memorial Museum. <http://atom.ushmm.org/
            research doctors/index. html> (12/5/98). Museum's
            "homepage." Documents from museum's archives
            about trial of German doctors involved in Holo-
            caust. What did they do? What was the verdict?
```

Most museums have websites. For example, the United States Holocaust Memorial Museum provides links to all sorts of valuable information. Use search words, such as *The Doctors' Trial* mentioned in Jim Jones's reading notes, and then explore the site's archives at <http://www.ushmm.org>. You could also read Timothy Luke's analysis, "Memorializing Mass Murder: The United States Holocaust Memorial Museum," in *Museum Politics: Power Plays at the Exhibition* (Minneapolis: University of Minnesota Press, 2002).

2. "Hagerstown Students React to the United States Holocaust Memorial Museum." <http://www.fred.net/nhhs/html/holoreac.html> (20 Jan 1997). Collection of student reactions to their visit to the museum. Teacher encourages readers to e-mail responses to his students' writing. What did they know before they went to the museum? What were they supposed to learn from seeing "all this evil stuff"?

3. Gourevitch, Philip. "Behold Now Behemoth." Harper's 287 (July 1993): 55-62. Behemoth from Bible. Great Beast. Author—cultural editor of Jewish newspaper. Calls museum "one more American theme park." Why does he criticize museum?

Finally, Jim reads and reviews each selection, evaluating what the article contributes to his own planning.

Reading Notes

1. "The Doctors' Trial" Just one of many items on museum's "homepage." Documents commemorate fiftieth anniversary of trial of leading German physicians who planned and enacted the "Euthanasia" program. Conducted all sorts of pseudo-scientific medical experiments. Sixteen doctors found guilty. Seven were sentenced to death. Trial: Opening statements; Indictment: Testimony; Sentences.

Review: Good example of how museum exhibits its archives to tell a story. Powerful data about experiments. (pictures). What will museum do with this information once it "commemorates" the "anniversary"?

2. "Hagerstown Students React ..." Students had one-week interdisciplinary unit on the Holocaust entitled "The Beast Within" before they visited museum. Most of the students seem to approve of the museum—"the world needs to know what happened"—and its "mission"—to "make sure that something like this never happens again." Some students made connections to Bosnia, China, and racial situations in U.S. Others connected with the ID Card—"the card showed me that ordinary kids like me and my friends were killed." Still others were overpowered by what they saw. "I would not bring a young child to the museum. Some of the exhibits were too graphic."

Review: Most of the reactions sounded "canned"—writing what they knew their teacher wanted them to say about their field trip. But what can you say about a museum that exhibits horrible things? "It's horrible!" One student wrote that seeing exhibits on pain "was a very positive experience." Is that what the museum wants visitors to think?

3. "Behold Now Behemoth" Begins with stories about his parents (survivors) and his nightmares about Nazis. Switches to controversy about museum: 1. memorialize victims v. 2. preach American ideals. Is denouncing evil the same as doing good? Roles for visitor: victim, hero, bystander. Films and other gimmicks—grotesque. Does exposure to barbarism prevent it? Museum just another show on the Mall. The Air and Space Museum.

Review: Essay challenges idea of museum, and Americans claim that they did not know what Hitler was doing until after they freed the camps. First plan for "Holocaust Museum" was drawn up by Nazis—as "a triumphant memorial to [Jewish] annihilation." (62) "Didn't these people suffer enough the first time their lives were taken from them?" (62) How can anyone answer such questions?

**What do the man's attire and manner suggest about his relationship to the men in the Holocaust photos?**

**Evaluating Reading**    Jim has come a long way since he decided to restrict his paper topic to the United States Holocaust Memorial Museum in Washington, D.C. His view of the subject has widened so that he doubts his ability to cover it. He is astonished at how much he (and his readers) will have to learn about the history of the Holocaust to understand the controversy prompted by the museum. But as he reads this material and searches for additional information, he discovers a working hypothesis: "The memorial to the victims of the Holocaust dramatizes racial hatred but does not help its visitors understand why this horror happened." When he composes his discovery draft, Jim will have to refine this hypothesis into a thesis.

## A Final Word About Planning

The most important thing to learn about planning is to know when to stop. You probably know people who spend their lives making plans. If they have to study for a test, they make lists of what to study, map out a schedule for studying each item on the list, and then talk about their study plans to everyone else taking the test. Somewhere in the midst of all their planning, they lose sight of the project—the test. Planning as a part of the writing process has a specific and limited purpose: thinking-in-writing. Once you have completed this thinking, you must come to some conclusion about what you have written. You must make choices about your *subject, audience,* and *purpose.* And you must be willing to try out those choices in a fuller, more sustained piece of writing. You must begin drafting.

# Reading on your computer

Consult the computer databases in your library or the search engines on the Web for information on your subject. Use a keyword to identify the topic you wish to locate (Holocaust) and then add other "descriptors" (United States Holocaust Memorial Museum) to refine your search. Many sources now come in two formats: (1) in print and (2) online. In the second case, you can locate *and* read your source on the computer screen and then transfer important passages into your journal. Copy the complete bibliographic entry so that you can transfer it to the "works cited" page (see Chapters 12 and 13). If you are browsing the Web, make sure you print the text after you read it. Sources travel quickly along the "information highway": What you discovered today, you may not find tomorrow. Record the date you accessed your electronic source, and record it at the end of your citation. As you read through your reading notes, insert questions, make comments, and place asterisks next to the quotations and paraphrases you wish to transfer into your draft.

# Image Gallery

## Questions

1. How do the items in the first photo represent the stages in D. C. Shawger's planning process for the set design of *Tartuffe*?

2. Select one detail in the plan, such as the central doorway or the parquet floor. How does it evolve from pencil sketch to final production?

3. How do the props, costumes, and lighting in the photo of the final production of *Tartuffe* enhance the effect of Shawger's planning?

The following observations about keeping a journal were made by three important writers: Henry David Thoreau, nineteenth-century American philosopher and essayist; Virginia Woolf, twentieth-century British novelist and essayist; and Joan Didion, twentieth-century American novelist. How would you characterize the different ways these writers use their journals? Which writer's remarks seem to approximate best how you feel about keeping a journal?

# On Keeping a Journal

## *Journal*
### —HENRY DAVID THOREAU

1 To set down such choice experiences that my own writings may inspire me and at last I may make wholes of parts. Certainly it is a distinct profession to rescue from oblivion and to fix the sentiments and thoughts which visit all men more or less generally, that the contemplation of the unfinished picture may suggest its harmonious completion. Associate reverently and as much as you can with your loftiest thoughts. Each thought that is welcomed and recorded is a nest egg, by the side of which more will be laid. Thoughts accidentally thrown together become a frame in which more may be developed and exhibited. Perhaps this is the main value of a habit of writing, of keeping a journal—that so we remember our best hours and stimulate ourselves. My thoughts are my company. They have a certain individuality and separate existence, aye, personality. Having by chance recorded a few disconnected thoughts and then brought them into juxtaposition, they suggest a whole new field in which it was possible to labor and to think. Thought begat thought. (1852)

## *A Writer's Diary*
### —VIRGINIA WOOLF

2 I have just re-read my year's diary and am much struck by the rapid haphazard gallop at which it swings along, sometimes indeed jerking almost intolerably over the cobbles. Still if it were not writtken rather faster than the fastest typewriting, if I stopped and took thought, it would never be written at all; and the advantage of the method is that it sweeps up accidentally several stray matters which I should exclude if I hesitated, but which are the diamonds of the dustheap. (January 20, 1919)

## *On Keeping a Notebook*
### —JOAN DIDION

3 So the point of my keeping a notebook has never been, nor is it now, to have an accurate factual record of what I have been doing or thinking. That would be a different impulse entirely, an instinct for reality which I sometimes envy but do not possess. At no point have I ever been able successfully to keep a diary; my approach to daily life ranges from the grossly negligent to the merely absent, and on those few occasions when I have tried dutifully to record a

day's events, boredom has so overcome me that the results are mysterious at best. What is this business about "shopping, typing piece, dinner with E, depressed"? Shopping for what? Typing what piece? Who is E? Was this "E" depressed, or was I depressed? Who cares? . . .

4    *How it felt to me:* that is getting closer to the truth about a notebook. I sometimes . . . imagine that some thrifty virtue derives from preserving everything observed. See enough and write it down, I tell myself, and then some morning when the world seems drained of wonder, some day when I am only going through the motions of doing what I am supposed to do, which is write—on that bankrupt morning I will simply open my notebook and there it will all be, a forgotten account with accumulated interest, paid passage back to the world out there: . . . I imagine, in other words, that the notebook is about other people. But of course it is not.

In this passage from *Information Anxiety* (1989), Richard Saul Wurman classifies five types of information. What type(s) of information are missing from your planning? Why does the omission of this kind of information cause information anxiety? How can you use one of the thinking-in-writing strategies described in this chapter to overcome this anxiety?

# The Five Rings

## RICHARD SAUL WURMAN

1    We are all surrounded by information that operates at varying degrees of immediacy to our lives. These degrees can be roughly divided into five rings, although what constitutes information on one level for one person may operate on another level for someone else. The rings radiate out from the most personal information that is essential for our physical survival to the most abstract form of information that encompasses our personal myths, cultural development, and sociological perspective.

2    The first ring is **internal** information—the messages that run our internal systems and enable our bodies to function. Here, information takes the form of cerebral messages. We have perhaps the least control over this level of information, but are the most affected by it.

3    The second ring is **conversational** information. It is the formal and informal exchanges and conversations that we have with the people around us, be they friends, relatives, coworkers, strangers in checkout lines, or clients in business meetings. Conversation is a prominent source of information, although we tend to play down or ignore its role, perhaps because of the informality of its nature. Yet this is the source of information over which we have the most control, both as givers and receivers of information.

4    The third ring is **reference** information. This is where we turn for the information that runs the systems of our world—science and technology—and, more immediately, the reference materials to which we turn in our own lives. Reference information can be anything from a textbook on quantum physics to the telephone book or dictionary.

5    The fourth ring is **news** information. This encompasses current events—the information

*Source:* Richard Saul Wurman. *Information Anxiety* (New York: Doubleday, 1989), 42–45.

that is transmitted via the media about people, places, and events that may not directly affect our lives, but can influence our vision of the world.

6    The fifth ring is **cultural** information, the least quantifiable form. It encompasses history, philosophy, and the arts, any expression that represents an attempt to understand and come to terms with our civilization. Information garnered from other rings is incorporated here to build the body of information that determines our own attitudes and beliefs, as well as the nature of our society as a whole.

7    Although there are specific characteristics inherent to the transmission of information at each of these levels, their systems are remarkably similar and often they are fraught with the same problems and pitfalls. Within each is the potential for anxiety. And, cumulatively, the grappling with information at each of these levels can weigh us down and induce a state of helplessness. It can paralyze thinking and prevent learning.

8    *Information anxiety* can afflict us at any level and is as likely to result from too much as too little information.

9    There are several general situations likely to induce *information anxiety:* not understanding information; feeling overwhelmed by the amount of information to be understood; not knowing if certain information exists; not knowing where to find information; and, perhaps the most frustrating, knowing exactly where to find the information, but not having the key to access it. You are sitting in front of your computer which contains all of the spread sheets that will justify the money you are spend-

ing to develop a new product, but you can't remember the name of the file. The information remains just out of your grasp.

10    You are trying to describe yourself as a lover of wine, but you have no idea how to spell the word "oenophile." Now dictionaries are quite useful if you know how to spell, but if you can't remember how the word starts, you're in trouble. This is the nightmare of inaccessibility—trying to find something when you don't know what it is listed under. How do you ask for something if you don't know how to spell it or you don't know what it's called? This is *information anxiety.*

11    We are surrounded by reference materials, but without the ability to use them, they are just another source of anxiety. I think of them as buddhas, sitting on my shelf with all that information and a knowing smile. It's a challenge for me to get access to them and to make them more accessible to others.

# Web Design

Students using *Writing with a Purpose* in a composition class were asked to design a website for Joni Leisure's speculations about a computer-networked classroom. Notice how the annotations for the two sites explain how a design can either confuse or clarify your purpose.

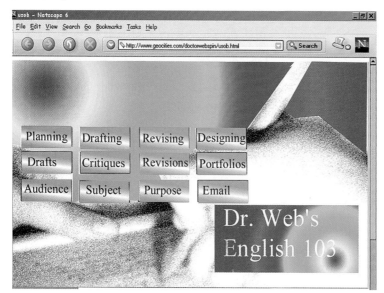

**Sample Homepage #1: Dr. Web's English 103**

▶ Subject is vague because the image of the writing hand is unclear and clashes with the rainbow colors.

▶ Reader is confused by the arrangement of the links—i.e., do they suggest a vertical or horizontal sequence?

▶ Purpose of site is not restricted by the design.

**Sample Homepage #2: Dr. Web's English 103**

▶ Subject is vague because the image of the web plays with the professor's name rather than referencing his course.

▶ Reader is confused by the arrangement of links—i.e., there is no logical sequence suggested by the links scattered across the page.

▶ Purpose of site is not unified by the design.

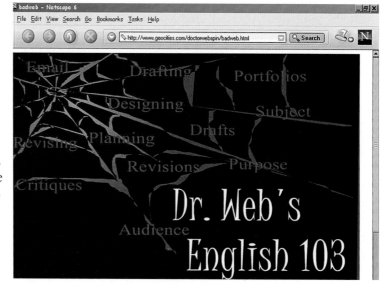

# Writing Assignments

### 1. NARRATE
Find some photographs of a close relative in an old family album or, better yet, a letter or journal written when he or she was your age. In your journal, make a list of those features you find most familiar and those you find most unsettling. Use this information to compose a narrative from your relative's perspective about "how it felt to be *me* at that age."

### 2. OBSERVE
Select a place in your neighborhood that had an important influence on your life—a garden, a playground, a movie theater. Speculate on how this place functioned in your life as you were growing up. Then, in an essay addressed to your writing class, compare the way this place used to be with the way it is now.

### 3. INVESTIGATE
Interview someone on your campus or in your community who is involved in managing information—a reference librarian, a newspaper writer, an advertising designer. Ask your subject to describe the procedures he or she uses to discover, store, and reproduce information. Then write a profile of this information manager, focusing on the procedures he or she uses to overcome the anxieties certain types of information induce.

### 4. COLLABORATE
Your writing group has been asked to design a museum to commemorate the history of the people (or a group of people) in your college community. Ask each member to list possible exhibits for the museum. Then ask each member to freewrite about one of these exhibits, focusing on ways it could be made interactive for visitors.

### 5. READ
Browse through some of your family's "texts"—such as journals, diaries, or letters. Next, fill in the gaps by studying your family photo albums or conducting interviews with relatives. Then write one of your family's stories.

### 6. RESPOND
Respond to Richard Saul Wurman's essay "The Five Rings" by describing how you overcame a case of information anxiety.

### 7. ANALYZE
Compare what your parents were taught about a particular historical event such as the Holocaust and what you were taught. For example, you may want to compare the way your college textbooks present the event and the way the event was presented in the textbooks used by your parents.

### 8. EVALUATE
Evaluate the way Henry David Thoreau, Virginia Woolf, and Joan Didion use their journals. What kind of information does each writer save? How does each use this information as a resource for writing? Use your evaluation as the basis for an essay advising beginning writing students on the purposes of a journal. Use these three writers to illustrate your recommendations.

### 9. ARGUE
As you consider drafting an essay on a specific subject, consult Richard Saul Wurman's "The Five Rings." Determine the kind of information that would be most persuasive to use in analyzing your subject. Then write a prospectus for your teacher, arguing the merits of using *one* of these rings as the *only* source of information for your essay.

### 10. ARGUE
Demonstrate that one of the versions of Dr. Web's English 103 website is a more promising candidate for development and revision than the other. First, reread Joni Leisure's speculations on pages 35–37. Then use the annotations to help make your case.

# Drafting 3

**ARRANGING FLOWERS IS LIKE WRITING**

**IN THAT IT IS AN ART OF CHOICE.**

—MAY SARTON

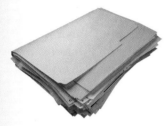

Through drafting, you determine whether the information you discovered in planning can be shaped into successful writing. In Chapter 2, you learned to apply thinking-in-writing strategies to explore likely topics and to assess the potential of each topic by using the guidelines for selecting a subject, analyzing an audience, and determining a purpose. Now you will learn to work the most promising of these topics into a draft.

Although drafting requires you to make specific choices about your subject, audience, and purpose, you should resist the temptation to think of these choices as final. It's tempting to assume, when you are starting out in writing, that composing the first draft is virtually the last stage in the writing process. You might believe that a little quick repair work transforms a first draft into a final draft. Experienced writers, however, know that their first draft is only a very preliminary attempt at producing a sustained piece of writing. Planning allows them to examine possible topics; drafting enables them to experiment with possible arrangements of thoughts on a topic. They expect this experiment to lead to new discoveries, some of which emerge in the first draft, but most of which will emerge in some subsequent draft. Experienced writers try several drafts. With each one, they come closer to what they want to say and how they want to say it.

In the following passage, May Sarton indirectly comments on the experienced writer's view of drafting when she compares the art of flower arranging to the art of writing:

> After breakfast I spend an hour or more arranging and rearranging seven or eight bunches of flowers for the house. There are flowers indoors here all the year around—in winter, bowls

of narcissus, geraniums brought in from the windowboxes in the autumn, cut flowers from a local florist when all else fails. But from late May on I have a variety to play with, and the joy becomes arduous and complex. Arranging flowers is like writing in that it is an art of choice. Not everything can be used of the rich material that rushes forward demanding utterance. And just as one tries one word after another, puts a phrase together only to tear it apart, so one arranges flowers. It is engrossing work, and needs a fresh eye and a steady hand. When you think the thing is finished, it may suddenly topple over, or look too crowded after all, or a little meager. It needs one more note of bright pink, or it needs white. White in a bunch of flowers does a little of what black does in a painting, I have found. It acts as a catalyst for all the colors. After that first hour I have used up my "seeing energy" for a while, just as, after three hours at my desk, the edge begins to go, the critical edge.                    (May Sarton, *Plant Dreaming Deep*)

You may be relieved to learn that drafting gives you additional opportunities to discover your subject, audience, and purpose, but you cannot lapse into inactivity. You must continue to exercise the "art of choice," evaluating your information, arranging and rearranging it, until you compose a coherent draft. The first section of this chapter presents three approaches to creating that draft: making a *scratch outline,* drafting a *hypothesis,* and composing a *discovery draft.* The second section of this chapter presents three strategies for measuring the success of that draft: constructing a *descriptive outline,* composing an *effective thesis,* and preparing a *formal outline.*

## The Scratch Outline

To make a scratch outline you will need to study the information you created in planning. The scratch outline is not designed to impose a rigorous pattern on this material. Its main purpose is to get you started, to help you see how you might arrange the major portion (*body*) of your draft. Later, as you draft several hypotheses about this pattern, you will see how you might compose the opening section (*introduction*) that identifies your subject and explains why you are writing about it.

Begin by assembling whatever lists or reading notes you produced during planning. Then read through your material several times, looking for recurrent patterns and any unusual ideas or phrases. Use any system you like—marking key words, using numbers or circles—to identify the related information you discover. Once you have established these groups of information, connect and arrange them into a meaningful pattern, sketching the pattern onto another sheet of paper. Don't discard your planning materials: You may need to consult them again.

Sometimes you will discover that your planning has already evinced a simple pattern, such as Joanne Reinhardt's narration about Mr. Bridgeman's Latin class or Joni Leisure's analysis of the activity in the computer classroom. More often, your information suggests several inconsistent methods of arrangement or none at all. Such confusion usually indicates that your information is too meager to work with (in which case you will have to do more planning) or that your information is too varied to work with (in which case you will have to make some tough choices). All the cherished items you found during planning will rush forward in drafting, "demanding utterance." But if you give everything equal attention, your essay is likely to "topple over." Some information may be significant enough to form a major division in your outline; other information may be less significant, useful only as minor subdivisions or illustrative examples. Still other information—wonderful, colorful, delightful information—may have to be eliminated because it does not fit into your scheme. As you arrange and rearrange various sections of your scratch outline, you may change your mind about the status of your information. You may want to condense or eliminate significant information or expand or reshape insignificant information. All the choices you make ultimately depend on one question: "What arrangement best enables me to communicate my *subject* to an *audience* for a *purpose*?"

Ellen Haack's assignment was to write an essay about *taste*—about how people decide what to eat, what to wear, what to read. During planning, she explored several ways to approach this assignment (the type of people she saw at the health food store, the problems she had selecting a necktie for a gift, and the kind of books she purchased for her personal library), but each time she tried out a thinking-in-writing strategy, she found herself thinking about her friend Barry and his habit of offering elaborate explanations for his choices. Ellen decided that Barry's behavior provided an interesting case study of "taste." Using *Barry* as her prompt, she produced the following list.

Barry

```
Drives me nuts
Type A—always busy, can't seem to relax
Discipline—routine, schedules, lists
Right way to do everything—always giving advice
Making granola—the right spoon, bowl
No junk food—Big Macs, doughnuts
Health nut—what's good for me
Salad bars, yogurt (?)
Sneaks ice cream—Heavenly Hash
Burns it off with exercise—but no jogging
```

```
Shin splints, tendons, new study
Rebounder—bounces to old time rock 'n' roll
Says he likes opera and ballet—improves his taste
Never listens, falls asleep—the sleep of the tasteless
Books—looks at diet books, buys classics
Impress himself, never reads—dust—"I'll get around
    to it someday"
Movies—Critics vs. Revenge of the Nerds
Always has his reasons—getting out of the house
Naps, wine, avoiding work
Good for me
```

Ellen is ready to begin drafting, but she needs to find a pattern in her information. Reading through her list, she begins to circle and number certain topics. She uses arrows to suggest how something from one part of her list belongs in another and question marks and asterisks to indicate problems she needs to solve or explore in greater detail.

Barry

1. Reasons
2. Food
3. Exercise
4. Culture

```
? Drives me nuts
1. Type A—always busy, can't seem to relax (3.)
1. Discipline—routine, schedules, lists
1. Right way to do everything—*always giving advice
2. Making granola—the right spoon, bowl
2. No junk food—Big Macs, doughnuts
2. Health nut—(1.)what's good for me
2. Salad bars, yogurt (?)
2. Sneaks ice cream—Heavenly Hash
3. Burns it off with exercise—but no jogging
3. Shin splints, tendons, (1.)new study
3. Rebounder—(4.)bounces to old time rock 'n' roll
4. Says he likes opera and ballet—improves his taste 1.*
4. Never listens, falls asleep—the sleep of the tasteless
4. Books—looks (2.)at diet books, buys classics
4. Impress himself, never reads—dust—"I'll get around
    to it someday" 1.*
4. Movies—Critics vs. Revenge of the Nerds
1. Always has his reasons—getting out of the house
3. Naps, (2.)wine, avoiding (3.)work
*1. Good for me
```

By circling and numbering, Ellen identifies and labels several information groups. Some groups evolve from the pattern of associations on the list (*food*); others form incomplete but potentially useful categories (*exercise*); still others are so cluttered that they will require additional planning to make them coherent (*culture*). Many of the items on Ellen's list could prompt the creation of new lists that relate to her assignment ("Type A," "sneaks ice cream," "sleep of the tasteless"). But Ellen decides that a phrase appearing intermittently throughout her list (*good for me*) provides the most promising topic for her first draft, one that might explain the concept of taste and pull together most of the information on her list. She continues her thinking-in-writing in a scratch outline.

                          Good for Me

    1. Food
       you are what you eat
       health food—granola, complex carbohydrates
       junk food—Whoppers, doughnuts
       cancer—new studies—yogurt (?), salad bars (?)
    2. Exercise
       keep in shape
       aerobics—jogging, swimming, rebounder (heart)
       isometrics—pumping iron, violent sports (competition,
          stress)
       serious injuries (shin splints), marathons—
          dehydration
    3. Culture
       improve your mind
       novels, classics, history, philosophy
       romances, trash, junk magazines ("inquiring minds
          want to know")
       big tomes—fall asleep
       some reading better than none

Through her scratch outline, Ellen has discovered some new information ("you are what you eat," "pumping iron," "junk magazines") and has deleted other information that does not seem to fit into her plan ("movies," "wine," "opera"). Her outline has helped her restrict her subject to three categories of things *good for me.* Although still sketchy, they suggest an emerging pattern that is potentially significant, interesting, and manageable. Some potential audiences have also emerged: people interested in food, exercise, or culture, and people who define *taste* in terms of what is "good for me." Before she can convert this outline into an essay, however, Ellen needs to draft a preliminary hypothesis.

*"Guilty of flaunting it without having it. Sixty days."*

## Drafting a Hypothesis

A hypothesis states a possible purpose for your writing. Unlike the thesis, which formally asserts what you will prove in your essay, the hypothesis expresses a tentative purpose. You should certainly try to make your hypothesis restricted, unified, and precise, but you may discover that writing your first draft modifies rather than demonstrates your purpose. Once you have completed your first draft, in fact, you may decide to revise your purpose completely. The first draft is like a laboratory experiment. It gives you an opportunity to test one possible explanation (*hypothesis*) for the pattern you derived from your planning.

To draft a hypothesis, read through your scratch outline and then write out answers to these questions:

1. What do I want (what am I expected) to accomplish in this writing project?

2. What is my attitude toward the material I have gathered?

3. What hypotheses could I prove by writing about it?

4. Which hypothesis seems the most restricted, unified, and precise?

Your answers to the first two questions may be lengthy and provisional because you are trying to clarify your aims and analyze your assignment.

You may not use this information in any direct way in your essay, but you may use it to determine your point of view toward your material and the ultimate effect you hope to achieve. Your answers to the second two questions should be simple and direct. These questions are designed to produce conditional theses, one of which you can use in your introduction to help keep your writing on track and to alert your readers to the main idea you are trying to develop.

When Ellen started to draft her hypothesis, she was confused about what she wanted to say about taste and what she wanted to prove about Barry's preoccupation with what is "good for me." Her answers to the first two questions exhibit her uncertainty, and her answers to the second two illustrate her attempt to resolve her confusion by proposing several provisional theses.

1. What do I want to accomplish with this project? I am supposed to be writing about taste. Why people prefer one thing over another. Or at least, the reasons people give for choosing one thing instead of another. Sounds pretty abstract. All I can think about is Barry. Drives me nuts with his explanations. Everything is either good or bad. I guess I wanted to show him that things aren't that simple. There are lots of Barrys in the world. Just like parents, always telling you what's good for you—body, mind, and soul. That's what I tried to do with my categories—<u>food</u>, <u>exercise</u>, and <u>culture</u>. It's not exact, but it might work. The interesting things in each group are the ones that don't fit or that change. What used to be good for you now gives you cancer. Maybe I could make something out of that.

2. I think my attitude toward this material is weird. I started out thinking about Barry. He's so compulsive, he's funny. Maybe not so funny. People who think things have to be good or bad are always changing their minds or cooking up new explanations. They could be devious, dangerous. How do other people react to the Barrys of the world? Maybe they're just like me. I mean I'm always trying to figure out whether <u>he's</u> good for me. I change my mind everyday—weird.

3. Possible hypotheses:

   a. Everybody wants to know what's "good for me."

   b. Most people try to divide the world into two categories—what's good for me and what's bad for me.

   c. The most interesting things in the world cannot be classified as absolutely good or bad.

4. I'm still not sure any of these will work, but if I had to pick one, I'd probably go with c.

As Ellen tries to draft her hypotheses, she struggles to clarify her subject, anticipate her readers, and define her purpose. She knows that this material is interesting and that she is raising significant issues that will appeal to most readers. Her scratch outline is simple enough to guide her through her first draft. As she tinkers with various ways to word her hypothesis, she feels confident enough to begin writing.

## The Discovery Draft

Novelist Dorothy Canfield Fisher once compared writing the first draft to skiing down a slope she wasn't sure she was clever enough to manage. Although you have compiled a large body of information during planning, organized that information into a scratch outline, and drafted several hypotheses about its significance, you cannot stand at the top of the hill forever. You must push off and see if your preparation has made you clever enough to manage the long white slope of blank paper in front of you.

*Most discoveries—even negative ones—help you to learn more about what you want to say and how you want to say it.*

This first draft is called a *discovery draft* because you should expect as you write to discover something new about the subject, audience, and purpose of your essay. Some of what you discover will be disappointing. Sections of your essay that you felt certain were complete suddenly seem sketchy. Connections that you saw between sections disappear or appear in forms you had not anticipated. And individual sections may not prove useful because certain items cannot be developed in any detail or because these items duplicate others or detract from your working hypothesis.

Most discoveries—even negative ones—help you to learn more about what you want to say and how you want to say it. As you convert notes into sentences and group sentences into paragraphs, your writing will talk to you—telling you things you had forgotten, making unexpected connections, pointing toward things you need to find out. Sections of your scratch outline will expand and contract before your eyes; your hypothesis may reshape itself into a more subtle statement. Your discovery draft gives you something to work with—a text, a core of information that you can rearrange or refine in a subsequent draft.

Ellen's discovery draft illustrates some of these changes as she struggles to say what she means.

Good for Me

Most people divide the world into two categories:                1
(1) things that are good for me and (2) things that are
bad for me. This system works as a general rule, but
the most interesting things do not fit easily into one
of the two categories.

**How will this man's choice of books help him find things that are "Good for me"?**

First, there is food. Everybody knows that raw vegetables, whole grain cereals, and fresh fruit are nutritious, and that French fries, doughnuts, and Whoppers are junk. But what about yogurt? Most advertisements claim it is a health food, but a recent study points out that one 8-ounce serving of flavored yogurt contains 9 teaspoons of sugar. And what about salad bars? They are supposed to be good for you—better than a slab of red meat or a basket of deep-fried shrimp—but recent studies charge that dangerous chemicals are sprayed on salad bar vegetables to keep them looking good. What's supposed to be good for you might give you tooth decay or cancer.

Next, there is exercise. Doctors are always telling you to stay fit. Exercise, particularly aerobic exercise like jogging, is supposed to be good for you because it controls your weight, lowers your cholesterol, and strengthens the efficiency of your heart muscle. But there is a trade-off. Jogging can cause serious injuries such as sprained ankles, pulled tendons, and shin splints. And there is a recent study that says severe physical exertion may actually accelerate the causes of coronary heart disease. One doctor says "jog," another says "don't," and another says "it all depends." How can people know for certain whether jogging will be "good for me"?

Finally, there is reading. Teachers, parents, and politicians are always saying that reading improves your mind. But what kind of reading leads to improvement? Books that are supposed to help you—diet books or pop-psychology books—don't really improve your mind. They are stacked next to the candy near the cash register, and everybody knows they are trash. But some of the books that are supposed to be good for you—the classics—many people find too long and boring. If they can't finish the books that are supposed to be good for them, how can people improve their minds?

The world is really too complex for a simple good-for- 5
me/bad-for-me system. Take ice cream, for example. On one
level it is bad for me because it contains large amounts
of sugar and cholesterol. On another level, however, it
is really good for me. After a long day of dieting, exercising, and reading, what could be better for me than a
few scoops of Heavenly Hash?

## The Descriptive Outline

A descriptive outline helps you assess what you have accomplished
during drafting. In it you report what you have done with the discovery
draft and speculate about how to compose your next draft.

To construct a descriptive outline, place your discovery draft on one
side of your desk and some blank paper on the other. Do not look at
your scratch outline; your objective is to make a new outline that
describes your draft. Counting the introductory paragraph as *1*, number
in sequence each paragraph, and then list those numbers on your blank
piece of paper. For each number, write down as briefly as possible (a)
what each paragraph *says,* and (b) what each paragraph *does.*

There is a subtle but significant difference between what a paragraph *says* and what it *does.* When you identify what a paragraph *says,*
you are concerned with subject matter, with the major topic discussed
in the paragraph. When you identify what a paragraph *does,* you are
concerned with writing strategies, with the development of each paragraph and its function within the larger design of the essay. A paragraph can do many things: It can tell a story, describe a scene, list
examples, compare evidence. You will learn more about what paragraphs can do individually and collectively in Chapters 6, 7, and 8. For
the moment, use your own words to describe what each paragraph in
your discovery draft *says* and *does.*

After you complete the descriptive outline, read through your discovery draft again. Then record your planning and drafting material.
Now return to your descriptive outline. What kind of draft does it
describe? Are you delighted or disappointed by what you see? Does the
outline reveal an interesting progression of carefully developed ideas? Or
does it show a fairly predictable pattern of underdeveloped notions?

All this rereading should force you to assess what you have already
achieved and what you still need to do. Being as honest as you can, list at
the bottom of your descriptive outline your conclusions about the effectiveness of your draft's introduction, working hypothesis, body, and
closing. Ellen's conclusions show that she realizes that she could do a
number of things to improve her essay. After you have examined her

descriptive outline, reread her discovery draft on pages 61–63, and then study her conclusions.

1. a. People divide world into two categories.
   b. Introduces hypothesis: Most interesting items don't fit easily into one of two categories.

2. a. Although most people know good from bad, some items cause confusion.
   b. Identifies two examples of food whose classification has been challenged by recent studies.

3. a. Although exercise is considered good for you, it can be dangerous.
   b. Compares benefits of exercise with possible risk factors.

4. a. Reading improves your mind—if you read.
   b. Compares not reading trash with not reading classics.

5. a. The world is too complex for a simple system of good/bad.
   b. Illustrates how ice cream can be both bad and good.

Conclusions

1. Everything goes wrong in first sentence when I replace <u>Barry</u> with <u>People</u>. Sounds more scholarly, but I'm not really interested anymore. Anybody can write about people; I want to write about Barry.

2. The hypothesis is probably all right. What does <u>interesting</u> mean? It would be more interesting if it introduced Barry's explanations.

3. Three sections—food, exercise, and reading—are really predictable. This is good. This is bad. Here's a problem. If I used Barry, I could include more examples under each category—or create some new categories—and show how Barry tries to deal with the problems.

4. The conclusion is good, but it doesn't sound like me. Heavenly Hash is really Barry talking.

5. Mainly, I need to get back to Barry and develop more examples from his point of view.

Ellen's descriptive outline has helped her identify what she has done right, what she has done wrong, and what she needs to do next. Her conclusions form an *agenda* for the next stage in the writing process—*revising*. But before Ellen revises her discovery draft, she decides to transform her hypothesis into an effective thesis and construct a formal outline.

# Composing an Effective Thesis

A thesis asserts the main idea you will develop in your writing. In a sense, it summarizes your ideas about your subject and suggests your point of view toward it. You cannot make such an assertion with any confidence until you understand your purpose. You will seldom succeed if you try to compose your thesis first and then write an essay that meets its specifications. It is more efficient to work by testing various hypotheses in drafts, selecting the one that best controls your material, and refining it into a thesis.

An effective thesis, then, derives from and makes a compelling statement about your writing. But once you have selected a thesis, you must word it properly if it is to be effective.

## Making Your Thesis Restricted, Unified, and Precise

*Restricted, unified,* and *precise* theses were defined in Chapter 1. The definitions are worth amplifying here, for the more fully your thesis reflects these qualities, the better it will control your writing in your remaining drafts.

To be *restricted,* a thesis must limit the scope of an essay to what can be discussed in detail in the space available. A thesis such as "The United States has serious pollution problems" might be suitable for a long magazine article, but using it for a three-page essay would force you to make statements so broad that your readers would find them superficial and uninformative. A better thesis about pollution might be one of the following:

▶ The government has not been sufficiently aggressive in enforcing the regulations that control the disposal of chemical wastes.

▶ In Toledo, industrial expansion has created severe air and water pollution.

▶ Widespread use of agricultural pesticides threatens the survival of certain species of wildlife.

A good thesis is *unified* if it expresses only one idea. The thesis "The use of drugs has increased significantly in the last fifteen years; hard drugs are admittedly dangerous, but there is considerable disagreement about marijuana" commits the writer to three topics: (1) the increase in drugs, (2) the dangerous effects of hard drugs, and (3) the controversy about marijuana. Each of these topics could form the thesis of a separate essay. To try to develop all three would almost surely result in an unfocused essay consisting of three unrelated, skimpy sections.

Lack of unity most often arises when a thesis contains two or more coordinate parts. The thesis "Compared with other languages, English has a relatively simple grammar, but its spelling is confusing" could lead to separate treatments of grammar and spelling. If you wanted to relate the two topics—for example, by contrasting the ease of learning grammar with the difficulty of learning spelling—the relationship has to be implied in your thesis: "In learning English, foreigners usually have less trouble with grammar than with spelling." If your chief interest is spelling, it would be safer to ignore grammar: "Foreigners have a hard time with English spelling." Sometimes one part of a two-part thesis can be embedded in the other: "The amateur ideal of the Olympic Games is being threatened; professionalism is on the increase" can be rewritten as "Increased professionalism threatens the amateur ideal of the Olympic Games."

Finally, a thesis is *precise* when it can have only one interpretation. The thesis "My home town is one of the most unusual in the state" does not indicate the content of your essay because *unusual* is vague and can mean many things. Readers will want to know in what way the town is unusual. If they have to read the whole essay to find out, the thesis does not help them. Moreover, because the wording is vague, the thesis does not help you see what you need to develop in your essay.

Words such as *unusual, inspiring,* and *interesting* are too vague for a thesis. So are metaphors. The thesis "Where instructors are concerned, all that glitters is not gold" may seem clever, but what does it mean? That the best scholars are not always the best teachers? That the instructors who are good classroom performers do not always help students master the subject? Or does it mean something else? The precise meaning of a thesis should be immediately clear. Metaphors may be effective in the text of your essay, but they can cause trouble in your thesis.

Throughout her drafting, Ellen has had difficulty composing an effective thesis. Her first hypothesis is imprecise because it relies on the vague word *interesting:* "The most interesting things in the world cannot be classified as absolutely good or bad." A second, even more imprecise version appears in the first paragraph of her discovery draft: "The system works as a general rule, but the most interesting things do not fit easily into one of the two categories." This version also suggests two subjects—a system and things that do not fit into it—that could destroy the unity of her essay. In her conclusions to her descriptive outline, Ellen recognizes the problem word and hints that she might be able to draft a more effective thesis if she restricted it to Barry's difficulties with explaining what is "good for me." This insight allows Ellen to restate her thesis. She might begin writing another draft immediately, but she decides instead to reevaluate and organize her material by constructing a formal outline.

Some of the following statements would make acceptable theses; others, because they lack restriction, unity, or precision, would not. Explain your reasons for rejecting those that are unacceptable.

1. Foods with high fiber content are very important for your diet.

2. It's not how you start; it's how you finish.

3. Social historians agree that the American Dream is no more than the snows of yesteryear.

4. Although the average person thinks of gorillas as ferocious, chest-beating monsters, they are actually gentle creatures who live at peace with other animals.

5. Workout tapes have enjoyed an enormous success, and they have proved that self-help videos are now a major consumer item.

## Preparing a Formal Outline

A formal outline can serve as an additional writing tool, helping you to discover the need for more information and enabling you to organize a more precise design before you begin another draft. It breaks your topic into major units, marked by Roman numerals, and subdivides these into minor units, marked by capital letters; the next subdivision is marked by Arabic numerals; and a still smaller subdivision is marked by lowercase letters. One warning about this format: If you make any subdivision in your outline, you must have at least *two* subdivisions. You cannot divide something into only one part.

If it seems helpful, give your outline a title. Then begin to construct the formal outline by laying out the major, Roman numeral headings first; then break each Roman numeral heading into capital letter entries, and so on, completing each level of division before starting on the next lower level. This procedure keeps you in control of your outline: You will not distort your organization by developing some headings too much and others too little. As you work your way through each division, you may discover new structural patterns that will require you to revise all the headings in your outline. Such discoveries will help you prepare a consistent outline and compose a coherent draft.

When Ellen looks at her two previous outlines, she decides that she wants her formal outline to follow the same order. When she starts to work her way through each subdivision, however, she starts reclaiming information from her initial planning that applies directly to Barry. As a result, her organization—and outline—change dramatically. She drops one major division ("exercise") and adds two new divisions ("movies" and "wine"). In the lower subdivisions, she rearranges information ("ice cream" is moved from the conclusion to the first major division) and develops new information (all the items on "movies" and "wine").

It is not always necessary to construct a formal outline to produce a new draft. Your discovery draft, descriptive outline, and reformulated thesis may give you all the direction you need. But Ellen's formal outline shows why it is such a powerful tool.

A Man with All Reasons

<u>Thesis</u>: Barry admits that he has difficulty explaining what's "good for me."

I. Barry has difficulty defending his eating habits
   A. He knows the foods that are nutritious
   B. He knows the foods that are junk
   C. He is attracted to foods that are both
      1. Yogurt has become a problem
      2. Ice cream presents a dilemma

II. Barry has difficulty explaining his reading habits
   A. He knows how to select good books
      1. He reads reviews
      2. He talks to friends
      3. He consults lists
   B. He resists his fascination with self-help books
   C. He buys classics
      1. He believes in the value of owning such books
      2. He never reads them

III. Barry has difficulty justifying his choice of movies
   A. He attends critically acclaimed movies
   B. He also attends "junk" movies
   C. He contrives elaborate justifications to explain such inconsistency

IV. Barry has difficulty rationalizing his preference for wine
   A. Wine enhances his appetite
   B. Wine relaxes him
   C. Wine is served to French and Italian children
   D. Wine is a health risk
      1. Its high sugar content could induce diabetes
      2. Its high alcohol content could induce chemical dependency

## A WRITING PROJECT

Like Barry, you may have trouble deciding whether a certain movie will be "good for me." Write an essay in which you explain the various factors you consider before making your choice. Do you read reviews? Do you talk to people who have seen the movie? Do you see any movie that features certain stars—Meg Ryan, Tom Hanks—or that has been shaped by a certain director—John Sayles, the Coen brothers? Or do you always go to certain types of movies—action, science fiction, or feel-good movies?

## Evaluating Outlines

Ellen can evaluate the usefulness of her formal outline as a stage in her writing process and as a completed product. For the first assessment, she compares her new outline with her previous writing on Barry's "good for me" justifications.

1. How much of the new outline derives from the original planning?

2. How many of the conclusions following the descriptive outline have been incorporated into the outline?

3. How effectively does the outline indicate possibilities for controlling *subject, audience,* and *purpose* in a final draft?

To make the *second* evaluation, Ellen considers the following criteria:

1. ***Is the thesis satisfactory?*** Because the thesis controls the whole outline, a faulty thesis invites trouble all along the way. A vigorous checking of the thesis is therefore the first and most important step in testing an outline.

   "Barry admits that he has difficulty explaining what's 'good for me'" is certainly more restricted, unified, and precise than Ellen's earlier hypotheses. It seems to control the whole outline, but does it say everything Ellen wants to say about her purpose? Ellen considers how she might open up her thesis to assert more about the information she is trying to present. She thinks, too, about why she feels this information is significant.

2. ***Is the relationship among the parts clear and consistent?*** In a good outline it should be clear how each main heading relates to the thesis and how each subdivision helps develop its main heading. If there is any doubt about the relation of any heading to the thesis, that heading is either poorly stated or indicates an inconsistency in the outline.

   Ellen's decision to focus on Barry's explanations has helped her establish a clearer connection among the four major divisions of her next draft.

3. ***Does the order of the parts provide an effective progression?*** Just as the sentences within each paragraph must follow a logical order, so must the parts of an outline. If any of the parts is out of order, the disorder will be magnified in the essay.

   Ellen's major divisions—*food, reading, movies,* and *wine*—suggest a progression different from the divisions of her earlier draft—*food, exercise,* and *reading.* She examines this new progression to determine if it is logical and then does the same with the material she has grouped under her capital letters and Arabic numerals.

4. ***Is the outline complete?*** This is not one question but two:

  a. Are all the major units of the subject represented?

  b. Is each major unit subdivided far enough to guide the development of the essay?

  The first question is especially important for essays that classify something or explain how something is done; all classes or steps must be included. The second question depends on the scope of the essay. For short papers, the outline may not need to go beyond the main headings. For longer papers, the outline needs to be developed in greater detail so that you can balance and control the information you group under each heading.

  Ellen's four major divisions do not represent every issue on which Barry has an opinion. She has omitted Barry's feeling about what kind of exercise is "good for me" to focus on the more interesting new subjects—movies and wine. She needs to

# ⊂Drafting⟍ on your computer

The fluid nature of composing on a computer counteracts the problems many writers have as they begin drafting. Make a scratch outline, print it out, and then begin composing those sections for which you feel you have enough information. For the moment skip those sections about which you feel uncertain.

Breaking up your draft into smaller composing units not only helps you get started, but it also helps you keep going when you hit a trouble spot. Try one of the following strategies: (1) place an asterisk in your text to mark the spot that is causing you trouble and then come back to it when you have found the information you need; (2) insert a bracketed note in your text, telling yourself what you need to find out; or (3) switch from drafting complete sentences and paragraphs to one of the planning strategies discussed in Chapter 2—that is, stop drafting and start listing, freewriting, or speculating about a particular section of your text—then

continue writing once you have worked your way through the problem.

You can also use the special features of your computer program to help you evaluate your draft. Create a split screen, composing your draft on one side and using the other to comment on your text or compose a descriptive outline. You can also split the screen horizontally. Use the bottom of the screen to draft alternative versions of the same passage after you have composed at the top.

A valuable drafting strategy is to solicit responses from the members of your writing group or class: (1) Do their scratch outlines agree with yours about the sequence of major topics in your draft? (2) Do their descriptive outlines agree with yours about what your paragraphs *say* and *do*? (3) Can they identify your thesis? (4) Can they see ways to make your thesis more *restricted*, *unified*, and *precise*?

consider whether these changes make her outline more or less complete. The other subdivisions will require the same consideration to ensure the completeness of her essay.

5. ***Can each entry be developed in detail?*** Each entry in the outline should be developed when the essay is written. There is no rigid rule about how much development each entry should receive. Sometimes a single entry will require two or three paragraphs; occasionally several minor entries may be dealt with in a single paragraph.

   In her discovery draft, Ellen devoted one paragraph to each of her three major divisions. She must consider whether her formal outline suggests the same coverage. The secondary divisions in Ellen's outline (those marked with capital letters) appeared singly as sentences in her discovery draft. Ellen must consider whether these, and the entries she marks with Arabic numerals, contain enough information to be developed into separate paragraphs or will remain single, supporting sentences.

## A Final Word About Drafting

The most important thing to learn about drafting is to expect frustration. You certainly know people who give up on a project if their effort fails to measure up. They think that additional effort is a punishment for failing to succeed on the first try. But writing, like any other valuable work, requires effort. For that reason, think of drafting as an opportunity rather than an ordeal. Remember May Sarton's comparison of arranging flowers and drafting a piece of writing. Both processes are arduous and complex, but they are also a joy. They require a fresh eye and a steady hand, and after a while they use up your seeing energy. In Chapter 4, you will study strategies that will help you recover that energy. Revising helps you *see* your material *again;* it helps you find a catalyst to restore your creative ingenuity and critical edge.

# Image Gallery

*While Mozart's rapidly produced scores seldom contained erased passages—and indeed were practically of "camera-ready" quality—Beethoven's sketchbooks chronicled painful, even tormented sieges of creation. —Howard Gardner*

**Questions**

1. The popular myth suggests that for Beethoven (top), the drafting (composing) process was painful, impetuous, and messy while for Mozart (bottom), the process was fluent, skillful, and seamless. How do the markings on Beethoven's and Mozart's drafts support this myth?

2. Listen to some recordings of works by Beethoven and Mozart. How do their drafting styles anticipate the styles of their final compositions?

3. Interview someone in your school's music department to determine how technology has altered the process of musical composition. For example, how have digital production and computer software changed composers' drafting process?

In this essay, Calvin Trillin speculates on several research studies that are supposed to comfort him. As he considers each hypothesis, he sounds like Barry, looking for reasons to justify his behavior. Construct a descriptive outline of his essay. Then reread Trillin's comments on page 8 about how he writes his humorous columns. To what extent does your descriptive outline conform to Trillin's description of his drafting process?

# Comforting Thoughts

## CALVIN TRILLIN

### February 29, 1988

1 First I read about a study in Meriden, Connecticut, which indicated that talking to yourself is a perfectly legitimate way of getting comfort during a difficult time. Then I saw an item about research at Yale demonstrating that stress seems to be reduced in some people by exposing them to the aromas of certain desserts. Then I started talking to myself about desserts with aromas I find soothing. Then I felt a lot better. Isn't science grand?

2 I didn't feel perfect. One thing that was bothering me—this is what I decided after I was asked by myself, "Well, what seems to be the trouble, guy?"—was that the ten most popular methods of comforting yourself listed in the Meriden study didn't mention sniffing desserts, even though Yale, where all the sniffing research was going on, is only about twenty miles down the road. Does this mean that some of these scientists are so busy talking to themselves that they don't talk to each other? It got me so upset that I went to the back door of a baker in our neighborhood to sniff the aroma of chocolate chip cookies. I was talking to myself the whole time, of course.

3 "What the Yale people think," I said to myself, "is that a person's soothed by the smell of, say, chocolate chip cookies because it brings back pleasant memories, like the memory of his mother baking chocolate chip cookies."

4 "What if his mother always burned the chocolate chip cookies?" I replied.

5 "Are you talking about my mother?"

6 "Whose mother do you think I'm talking about?" I said. "We're the only one here."

7 "Were those cookies burnt?"

8 "What do you think all that black stuff was?"

9 "I thought that was the chocolate chips."

10 "No, she always forgot the chocolate chips."

11 I wasn't finding the conversation very comforting at all. I don't like to hear anyone make light of my mother's chocolate chip cookies, even me. I must have raised my voice, because the next thing I knew, the baker had come out to see what was going on.

12 Even though the Meriden study had shown that being with someone else was the most comforting thing of all—it finished ahead of listening to music and even watching TV—I saw right away that being with the baker wasn't going to be much more comforting than talking to myself. He said, "What are you, some kind of nut case, or what?"

13 I told him that I was engaging in two therapies that had been scientifically proven effective:

Calvin Trillin. *Enough's Enough (and Other Rules of Life)* (New York: Ticknor & Fields, 1990), 76–79.

**How does the woman suggest that she is eating something "Good for me"? Is she?**

sniffing chocolate chip cookies and talking to myself. He told me that I owed him two dollars and fifty cents. "For sniffing, we charge a buck and a quarter a dozen," he explained.

14 "How do you know I sniffed two dozen?" I asked.

15 "We got ways," he said.

16 I told him that according to the research done at Yale, certain odors caused the brain to produce alpha waves, which are associated with relaxation. I told him that in my case the odor of chocolate chip cookies—particularly slightly burnt chocolate chip cookies—was such an odor. I told him that he ought to be proud to confirm the scientific research done at one of the great universities of the English-speaking world. That alone, I told him, ought to be payment enough for whatever small part of the aroma of his chocolate chip cookies I had used up with my sniffing.

17 He thought about it for a moment. Then he said, "Take a walk, buddy."

18 I was happy to. As it happens, going for a walk finished tenth in the Meriden study, just behind recalling pleasant memories. Naturally, I talked to myself on the way.

19 "Maybe I can find someplace to smell what the Yale people call 'spiced apple,'" I said to myself. "They found that the smell of spiced apple is so effective that with some people it can stop panic attacks."

20 "But I don't know what spiced apple smells like," I replied. "Spiced with what?"

21 That was bothering me enough that my walk wasn't actually very soothing. I thought about bolstering it with some of the other ac-

tivities on the list, but reading or watching TV seemed impractical. Prayer was also on the list, but praying for the aroma of spiced apple seemed frivolous.

22    I walked faster and faster. It occurred to me that I might be getting a panic attack. Desperately I tried to recall some pleasant memories.

I recalled the time before I knew about the Meriden list, when I talked to myself only in private. I recalled the time before I knew about the Yale research and didn't have to worry about finding any spiced apple. Then I felt a lot better. I didn't feel perfect, but you can't always feel perfect.

# Student Essay

Student Ellen Haack's final draft of her essay on "taste" focuses on Barry and his motives for choosing what he eats, reads, watches, and drinks. Compare this draft with her formal outline on page 68. In what ways do the divisions of her outline identify the paragraphs in her essay?

# A Man with All Reasons

## ELLEN HAACK

1    Barry's in the kitchen making granola. His long, narrow frame moves deftly around the work area, pausing to scan the recipe book on the counter or search the shelves for the ingredients—wheat germ, bran, rolled oats, sunflower seeds, raisins, honey—he plans to mix in a large, gray earthenware bowl. While he works, he hums a vaguely recognizable version of "Blue Moon," drumming on the top of the counter or the edge of the bowl with a wooden spoon. He's happy. Making granola always has this effect on him. He doesn't like to make granola—it's messy and time-consuming. He doesn't like to eat granola—it's too crunchy without milk and too mushy with it. But he likes to contemplate his reasons for eating granola— "it's good for me."

2    Barry moves through the world like he moves through the kitchen, carefully sorting everything into two categories: (1) things that are "good for me" and (2) things that are "not good for me." Although he is attracted to the simplicity of this system, he often has difficulty explaining what's "good for me."

3    Since he is a health nut, Barry seems most adept at sorting food. His first category includes nutritious foods such as raw vegetables, whole grains, and fish, while his second includes junk food such as French fries, doughnuts, and Whoppers. But not all food can be classified so easily. For example, Barry is currently in a quandary over yogurt. For years, he ranked it close to granola as a major "good for me." But recent reports on the sugar content of flavored yogurt have made its position shaky. Ice cream presents another dilemma. It contains too much sugar and cholesterol to be "good for me," but Barry loves it. Whenever he does something that is "good for me," he likes to reward himself with a large bowl of Heavenly Hash—which is obviously "not good for me."

4    Barry is also dedicated to improving his mind and is constantly looking for books that will be "good for me." He reads reviews, talks to

his more literary friends, and consults an old mimeographed list of "150 Great Novels Every Well-Educated Person Should Read" that was given to him by his high school English teacher. Armed with such advice, he can work his way through a book store, sorting titles into his two categories. The cash register provides the ultimate test, however. He may be attracted to *Jane Fonda's Workout Book,* justifying his interest by saying that a strenuous exercise program would be "good for me." But despite his attraction to Jane and his dedication to health, he does not buy the book; exercise books are trash. Instead, he purchases *Milton Cross' Complete Stories of the Great Operas,* explaining that knowing more about opera would be "good for me." Unfortunately, the book gathers dust next to one of his other carefully chosen purchases, H. G. Wells' *The Outline of History.* Although he has never opened these books, he believes he will get around to them eventually because they are "good for me."

5    Movies present a similar difficulty. Barry believes that only critically acclaimed films about significant subjects are "good for me." Following the critics' advice, he rented *My Dinner with Andre,* only to fall asleep during the first course. He blinked awake during the credits, saying the nap had been "good for me." On the other hand, he rented *The Revenge of the Nerds,* knowing that the critics did not think it would be "good for me." He managed to stifle his laughter and maintain his disdain throughout the film. But he announced that taking a break from studying for his physics test had been "good for me."

6    And finally there's wine. Barry assigns wine a high position in his ranking of things "good for me," and he has his reasons. Foremost among these is wine's appetite-enhancing properties. He is slightly underweight and views anything that encourages him to eat as "good for me." Wine is also a relaxant. Barry leans toward the Type A personality and so considers anything that helps him slow down as "good for me." And then there are the French and Italian children. He has read that French and Italian parents give even very young children wine on a regular basis. Parents couldn't possibly give their own children something that isn't good for them. He worries about wine, however, because sugar and alcohol are not "good for me."

7    Recently, as he was fretting about the onset of diabetes or alcoholism, he visited a friend in the hospital. When his friend's dinner tray arrived, he spotted a plastic glass of clear liquid between the Jello and the peas.

8    "Do they serve wine *here*?" he asked.

9    "Yeh, pretty nice, huh?" the friend replied, not realizing the cause of Barry's sudden elation.

10    "See, I told you it was good for me."

# Web Design

Students using *Writing with a Purpose* in a composition class were asked to design a website for Ellen Haack's essay, "A Man for All Reasons." Notice how the annotations for the two sites explain how a design can either confuse or clarify your purpose.

## Sample Homepage #1: Barry's Guide

▶ Subject is unclear because everything on the page is blurred into one yellow block.

▶ Reader has difficulty reading text because of the juxtaposition of green type and yellow background.

▶ Purpose is too general as stated in the opening sentence.

## Sample Homepage #2: Barry's Guide

▶ Subject is clarified by large type and vivid graph.

▶ Reader can follow explanation in text by referring to graph.

▶ Purpose is restricted to sorting food according to one principle— "which foods cause sudden increases in blood glucose levels."

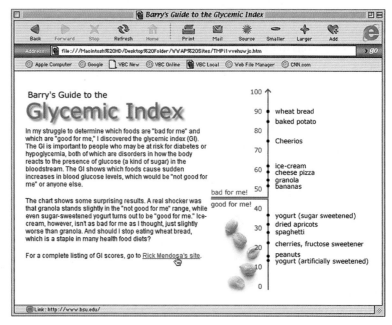

# Writing Assignments

### 1. NARRATE

Use the "Drives me nuts" note on Ellen Haack's list (pp. 56–57) to start a list of your own. Choose a person (roommate or boss) or a policy (your parents' or teachers' rules) that drove you nuts. Compose a narrative that focuses on one event that reveals the maddening inconsistency in the person's behavior or rules for your behavior.

### 2. OBSERVE

Select a public place where people are supposed to obey certain rules of etiquette—the checkout line at the grocery store, the traffic signals at a busy street corner, the ticket booth at the local theater. Observe people's behavior for an extended period, paying particular attention to their willingness to take turns or their readiness to break the rules. Then write a column for the local paper, using your observations to comment on the status of public courtesy.

### 3. INVESTIGATE

Interview someone who collects *unusual* artifacts—old records, fountain pens, ceramic animals. Pose some of the following questions: What prompted you to start this collection? Where did you buy your first *X*? How have you organized your collection? Who has the best collection? Why do you think you collect *X*? Use your interview material to write a profile of this person and his or her collection.

### 4. COLLABORATE

Your writing group has been asked to prepare a section of a student handbook on "stress." Interview one another about what causes you to feel stress, how stress affects you, and what you do to relieve it. Expand your research by interviewing people at the health center or counseling center about their experiences helping stressed-out students. Consult self-help manuals or the appropriate sections in your psychology book. Pool your information and then write the section, offering students advice about how to deal with stress.

### 5. READ

Consult the Web for explanations of *one* method of stress management—exercise, meditation, biofeedback. Consider, in particular, the testimony of people who have tried the method. How much time did it take them to learn and practice the method? How long did they remain "stress-free"? You may want to test the method yourself. Then write a "how-to" essay in which you explain the benefits of this method in particular detail.

### 6. RESPOND

Respond to the "character" revealed in Calvin Trillin's column *or* described in Ellen Haack's essay. Imagine him as your roommate or date. Describe some of the difficulties you might have communicating with someone who talks to himself or is constantly explaining why something is "good for me."

### 7. ANALYZE

Analyze the various outlines and drafts of Ellen Haack's essay. Which do you like best and why? Return to Ellen's original assignment—to write something on the issue of *taste*. Although the assignment is vague, it contains certain assumptions and expectations. Write an essay to Ellen explaining why her final essay does or does not satisfy those assumptions and expectations.

### 8. EVALUATE

Assess the relative merits of the two versions of Barry's website. Use the annotations to focus on those features that make one site more effective and informative.

### 9. ARGUE

Use your answers to questions 1 and 2 in the Image Gallery to draft an essay in which you argue that either Mozart or Beethoven was a more gifted composer. Read Howard Gardner's essay "The Compositions of Mozart's Mind," *Art, Mind and Brain.* (New York: Harper, 1982, pages 358–360), for additional information.

### 10. ARGUE

Write your own essay on the issue of *taste*—who has it, who doesn't, and why. Consider various kinds of taste—physical, aesthetic—or argue that one's taste (in food, books, or people) is a matter of education or social conditioning. Like Ellen Haack, you may want to select a case study to illustrate your thesis.

# Revising

THERE'S . . . A STRANGE MOMENT . . . WHEN I MOVE
FROM THE POSITION OF WRITER TO THE POSITION OF
READER, AND I SUDDENLY SEE MY WORDS WITH
THE EYES OF THE COLD PUBLIC.

—EUDORA WELTY

Revising is the process of *seeing again,* of discovering a new vision for the writing you produced in planning and drafting. In a sense, you have been revising from the moment you began writing. As you experimented with thinking-in-writing strategies in planning, you revised your decisions about subject, audience, and purpose. As you tried to apply those decisions in drafting, you revised again when you saw a better thesis or a more effective outline. Now that you are ready to revise, you must try to gain a new perspective on writing you have already looked at several times. One thing is certain: You will not see much that is new if you think of revising simply as taking one last look.

Nothing identifies experienced writers more dramatically than the way they look at revision. For beginners, revision means *fixing* the first draft—rearranging a few phrases, substituting one word for another, correcting spelling and punctuation. For experienced writers, revision means *creating* the final draft—redefining their purpose, reshaping their draft, and reworking the transitions between and the connections among their examples. They know they have overlooked minor trouble spots, but before they begin polishing and proofreading, they want to be sure they are looking at a final text.

Revision is a two-stage process. During the first stage (the focus of this chapter), you use various reading strategies to help you rethink, reorder, and rewrite substantial portions of your draft. When you are satisfied with this *global revision,* you can focus your attention on the second stage, *local revision,* and begin repairing individual paragraphs, sentences, and words. (Strategies for implementing local revision are presented in Chapters 8 through 11.) Work in this second stage may propel you back to the first stage, however, as your revision of individual parts may prompt you to revise a section or even the entirety of your essay.

Revision has been made easier by the wonders of word processing. But revision is more than a mechanical command. It is an intellectual choice that emerges from a creative attitude toward change. In the days before *delete* and *format*, novelist Eudora Welty expressed that attitude in her comments on revision:

> My ideal way to write . . . is to write the whole first draft through in one sitting, then work as long as it takes on revisions, and then write the final version all in one, so that in the end the whole thing amounts to one long sustained effort. . . . [Using a typewriter] helps give me the feeling of making my work objective. I can correct better if I see it in typescript. After that, I revise with scissors and pins. Pasting is too slow, and you can't undo it, but with pins you can move things from anywhere to anywhere, and that's what I really love doing—putting things in their best and proper place, revealing things at the time when they matter most. Often I shift things from the very beginning to the very end. . . .
>
> [Writing] is so much an inward thing that reading the proofs later can be a real shock. . . . [T]here's . . . a strange moment with every book when I move from the position of writer to the position of reader, and I suddenly see my words with the eyes of the cold public. It gives me a terrible sense of exposure, as if I'd gotten sunburned.                 (Eudora Welty, *Writers at Work: The Paris Review Interviews*)

## Looking to Revise

Once you consider revising a creative rather than a cleaning-up activity, you will look at yourself, your readers, and your text with more objectivity.

### How You Look at It

Revision is always hard work, especially since you have already invested considerable effort in your writing. But try to look objectively at what you have accomplished. Rethink, don't merely glance over, every aspect of your writing from your most abstract assumptions to your most concrete assertions. Do not fall in love with your words, no matter how clever or inspiring they seem. Your real concern is effectiveness, not eloquence. Like Welty, you should look forward to making changes—to achieving coherence and clarity—by moving "things from anywhere to anywhere . . . putting things in their best and proper place, revealing things at the time when they matter most."

*Do not fall in love with your words, no matter how clever or inspiring they seem to you. Your real concern is effectiveness, not eloquence.*

## How Someone Else Looks at It

When you are ready to revise, you may welcome the perspective of another reader—a teacher, editor, or friend. Your readers may ask about the larger elements in your writing (its subject, audience, or purpose) or its smaller elements (sentence structure, diction, or punctuation); they may talk about their general impression (whether your writing is interesting, funny, or dull). As you revise, you must consider all reactions to your work—even if they seem threatening or trivial. You must consider what your readers saw, why they liked or disliked what they saw, and how you might use *their* observations to strengthen *your* writing. Various readers may give you confusing or contradictory advice, making it difficult for you to decide what to do next. You will have to decide which readers you trust—and which of their recommendations you want to consider or resist. Remember, you are the *author* of your text and therefore must act as the final *authority* for deciding how it will be revised.

## How It Looks

Once you start revising, your writing will often look unfamiliar. If you have composed your messy, handwritten draft on your computer screen and then printed your text, it may look compact and complete, as if a clean page had somehow solved your writing problems. But you must look beneath this seductive surface to uncover problems that still require rethinking and rewriting.

If you have put your writing aside for a few days—or even a few hours—the mere passage of time will make your text look unfamiliar. You have been doing other things—talking, reading, thinking—while your writing has been incubating in your unconscious. Now, as you look at it again, you may see flaws that were not apparent before. Perhaps you have not restricted your subject, anticipated your audience, or defined your purpose effectively. This new perspective compels you to look for solutions that will make your writing stronger and sharper.

But mainly your writing will look unfamiliar when you revise because, like Welty, you have changed positions—from writer to reader. As a writer, your task was to create ideas; as a reader, your task is to judge the clarity of those ideas. And just as you used a set of guidelines for writing, so now you may use a set of guidelines for reading and revising what you have written.

# Reading to Revise

When you are reading to revise, you are still actively involved in the writing process. You are *not* proofreading. Proofreading presumes the existence of a completed manuscript. When you proofread, you are merely checking your writing one last time to prove that you have not mangled sentences, misplaced punctuation, or misspelled words. Reading to revise, by contrast, assumes the presence of an evolving manuscript. As you read, you are trying to identify the strengths and weaknesses of your subject. You are sharpening your perception of what your audience knows (what *is* on the page) and speculating about what your audience needs to know (what is *not* on the page). You are determining whether your purpose controls your essay and the connections among its parts.

Each of the following reading strategies suggests that you read your writing as though you were someone else—a fictitious person in a special situation who is "reading" for a particular reason. Each strategy will highlight a different facet of your work. Used jointly, they will lead to a complete revision.

## Reading for Subject

Imagine you are seated in the waiting room of your dentist's office, flipping though several magazines, looking for something to read to pass the time. What subjects attract and sustain your attention? Now pick up your writing and skim through it as quickly as possible. Then put it aside and, maintaining your identity as an "impatient patient," jot down your general reactions using the following questions as a guide:

1. *Why was I attracted to this essay?* How did the title or the first few sentences—the lead—convince me that the essay was worth reading?

2. *What is the specific subject of the essay?* Did the essay focus on the subject immediately, or did I have to read a lot of preliminary material or prolonged digressions?

3. *What is significant about the subject?* Is it a subject I like reading about, one that I need to know about, or one I ought to think about?

4. *What makes the subject interesting*—the attitude of the writer, the nature of the subject, or the way the subject is presented?

5. *Does the essay seem the right length?* Is it long enough to answer all my questions yet short enough to keep my mind from wandering?

## Reading for Audience

Now imagine you are seated in a large banquet hall listening to an after-dinner speech. You cannot avoid listening to the speech, so you decide to see how it's going over—how effectively the speaker has read the needs and expectations of the audience. One way to simulate this situation is to read your writing out loud to anyone who will listen—the important thing is to *hear* your writing. An excellent way to accomplish this objective is to read into a tape recorder; then, with your manuscript in hand, play back the "speech" with you as its audience. As you listen, use the following questions to identify passages that need revision. Stop the recorder each time your annotations become too detailed to keep up with the tape. Once you have written down your comments, push *Play* and resume listening to your writing being read.

1.  ***What kinds of people does the speaker expect to find in the audience?*** Does the speech acknowledge their values, assumptions, and prejudices?

2.  ***What role does the speaker invite the members of the audience to take (for example, that of dedicated, discerning people)?***

3.  ***What are the members of the audience likely to know about the subject of the speech?***

4.  ***Does the speaker ask questions that the audience would ask about the subject?*** Does the speaker answer those questions when they need to be answered? Does the speaker anticipate challenging or hostile questions?

5.  ***Does the speaker help the audience focus on the subject and follow the development of the parts?*** Where might the audience get bored, confused, or annoyed? Does the end echo and fulfill the promise of the beginning?

## Reading for Purpose

Imagine you are seated in an attorney's office about to sign a contract that will have an enormous impact on your life. You must determine what the thesis of this contract promises and whether the various sections and subsections deliver on that promise. Read your writing slowly and deliberately, underlining your thesis and tracing its connection to each major topic in your essay. If there are sections that need to be rewritten, rearranged, or deleted, now is the time for renegotiation. The following guidelines will remind you of the purpose of the "contract" and call your attention to how that purpose is carried out in its various "clauses."

1.  ***Does the essay rest on hidden and undocumented assumptions?*** How can these assumptions be introduced into the wording of the essay?

2.  ***What is the purpose of the essay?*** Is that purpose expressed openly, or must it be inferred from the text?

3.  ***What is the thesis of the essay?*** What specific promise does it make to its readers? Is the thesis sufficiently restricted, unified, and precise that it can be demonstrated?

4. ***Does the body of the essay fulfill the promise of the thesis?*** Is there a direct, logical, and dramatic connection among the various parts?

5. ***Is each part of the essay sufficiently developed with evidence that is germane, reliable, and verifiable?*** Does new evidence need to be introduced to clarify the thesis?

## Revision Agenda

The detailed analysis produced by the reading-to-revise questions will help you compose a *revision agenda,* a plan for rethinking, rearranging, and rewriting the next draft of your essay.

▶ You may find that the subject, audience, and purpose are so intertwined that you cannot undertake three separate readings. For you, the easiest procedure may be to keep the three imaginary readers in your head simultaneously and, after one "combined" reading, to prepare a single revision agenda.

▶ You may prefer considering each element—subject, audience, and purpose—singly and thoroughly. If so, read through the text three times, answering the sets of questions that accompany each reading. After completing all three readings, prepare one revision agenda.

▶ A complex or difficult-to-formulate subject may invite three complete revisions. After you "read for subject," prepare a revision agenda and then a new draft. Use this text to "read for audience" and the text generated then to "read for purpose."

You will have to decide which procedure helps you produce the most effective agenda and the most polished revisions. You may discover, in fact, that each writing project you undertake requires its own procedure. If you have to write under pressure on a fairly straightforward subject, then you may be able to work with one revision agenda. If, on the other hand, you have time to allow a complex subject to evolve, then you may want to generate several revision agendas to identify and solve the problems in your writing.

Organize your revision agenda by asking yourself three questions:

1. What did I try to do in this draft?

2. What are its strengths and weaknesses?

3. What revisions do I want to make in my next draft?

Answer the third question by writing yourself prescriptions containing action verbs—for example, "Collapse section on . . ."; "Expand paragraph on . . ."; "Reword sentences in. . . ." Group the larger problems (subject, audience, purpose) at the top of the list and the smaller problems (style, mechanics, usage) at the bottom.

● **A WRITER'S WORDS**

I can't stress enough the importance of revision. The first draft is wonderful and exciting—that's when you fall in love. The revision is more like the marriage. You take what you love and come to terms with the practical, domestic life. For me, the revision is when you really sink the roots. You take what can be pure, raw emotion and figure out how it works, how it fits together.

—Jill McCorkle, interview in *The Writer's Chronicle*

Remember, revision is an *intuitive* process: You may decide to relocate a paragraph or realign the parts of a sentence because a sudden impulse tells you it looks or sounds better. And revision is a *recursive* process: You are constantly stepping back from your writing to see the big picture, moving forward to touch up some detail, and stepping back again to see how the altered detail changes the composition of the whole. But revision is also a *logical* process. In any piece of writing, you will discover large problems of form and focus and smaller problems of syntax and usage. You may be tempted to fix the simple problems first and the more difficult problems later. But the logical way to proceed is to work on the difficult problems first, for in solving them you may eliminate the simple problems or at least discover an efficient method for dealing with them.

## Revising: A Case Study

Early in their writing class, Sarah Penning and her classmates were challenged to write their final paper on how the economy had a direct impact on their lives. Some students explored the impact of a local business' "down-sizing" or relocating. Other students wrote about the job skills they would need to succeed in a changing economy. Still others speculated on the products American business would have to create to keep the economy healthy.

But Sarah was in a dither. The standard topics sounded too much like those discussed on the nightly business report. None seemed to have a *direct impact* on her life. Then, one Sunday morning, as she was sorting through the inserts in the local paper, she saw her subject—COUPONS! They were everywhere. Where did they come from? Who used them? Why did people spend so much time designing, distributing, collecting, and trading them? And why—most of all—did the subject both fascinate and infuriate her? Amidst her colorful clutter on the kitchen counter, Sarah suspected she had uncovered a mystery worth exploring.

Sarah began by *planning*. She listed what she already knew about coupons, what she needed to know about them, and where she might go to confirm her suspicions and answer her questions. She interviewed shoppers, cashiers, store managers, and newspaper sales personnel. She read several articles in sales and marketing magazines. During *drafting*, however, Sarah decided to write about her personal experience with coupons. Using a scratch outline, she organized the experience under three chronological headings: *Buying Stuff, Checking Out, Saving Face*. She used the following hypothesis to begin her discovery draft: *Although I have become a skillful shopper, I would rather save my dignity than my money.*

# NOT ME
## (Discovery Draft)

Since I have moved out of the dorm into my apartment, I have learned that the secret to successful living is successful shopping. If I am going to save time for studying, then I must make my shopping trips effective. If I am going to save money for rent, I must make my shopping trips efficient. Although I have learned the strategies of a skillful shopper, I have also learned that at the checkout counter, I would rather save my dignity than my money.

Learning how to buy stuff at the supermarket is not hard. I think about what I want to eat, check the cabinets and refrigerator to see what I have, and then make a list. I go to the store after my eight o'clock class to avoid the crowds, and I go to the same store every time, so I know where things are. I grab an empty cart, cruise the aisles, compare prices, and check items off my list. I never pick up anything that's not on my list, unless it's absolutely necessary. My mother used to drive me crazy using these strategies, but I can see now that they save time and money.

The only flaw in my strategy is picking the right checkout counter. I seem to make the same mistake every time I go to the store. I round the last aisle and head toward the counters. Bingo! A register with only one person in line. I wheel behind a middle-aged mom unloading her cart and smile in a slightly superior way at the guy in the next line who has four people in front of him. My cashier begins sorting the woman's stuff, and I congratulate myself on getting it right this time. I'll be putting my bags in the car before Number 5 gets out his wallet.

Then it happens. The cashier lets out a sigh. I try not to look, hoping the sigh doesn't mean what I think it means. But it always does. COUPONS! Mom is pulling them out of her purse and peeling them off her packages. When she begins sorting and stacking them, they slide off the counter and flutter into her cart, onto the floor, and under the gum rack. I look at my watch. Number 5 is checking out. Mom and the cashier are on their hands and knees groping after the elusive coupons. Mom looks up for help, but I look at Number 5 pushing his cart through the electric door. Finally, they are standing again—Mom smiling like she won the lottery, the cashier smiling because she has to. Then they start over again. The cashier scans the groceries,

How does this photograph illustrate Sarah's problem in picking the shortest line?

scans the coupons, checks the expiration dates, and slides each coupon into her cash drawer. I see Number 5 pushing his empty cart back through the parking lot.

Mom stares at the tape as the cashier totals her bill, and then beams blissfully, "Saved five bucks!" Right, lady! And wasted twenty minutes of my time. As I start to unload my cart, a guy wheels in behind me with a six-pack of Cokes, a bag of chips, some toothpaste, and a vaguely familiar smile. The cashier starts scanning my stuff. The moment arrives. Do I or don't I? I know there are coupons in my wallet. I could probably save some money. I watch Mom marching through the electric door, then glance at the smiling cashier in front of me and the happy guy behind me. No way! I'd rather save face than money. I pay up, bag my stuff, and head toward the parking lot—a few pennies poorer but my dignity intact.

Revision Agenda

1. <u>What did I want to do in this draft?</u>
   Tell a story about my personal experience with coupons.

2. <u>What are its strengths and weaknesses?</u>
   I like some parts of the story. Mom on her hands and knees. Number 5 pushing his cart through the parking lot. But the story doesn't focus on coupons. Why does Mom use them and I don't? What's all that stuff about saving dignity? What does that mean? Most of the essay is about saving time.

3. <u>What revisions do I want to make in my next draft?</u>
   a. Cut personal stuff—my shopping skills.
   b. Focus on shoppers who use coupons.
   c. Classify them into different categories.
   d. Speculate about why each group uses them.
   e. Identify shoppers by the products in their carts.

## Revising for Subject

Sarah's narrative about her supermarket excursion is an entertaining narrative, but she realizes that it focuses more on her shopping behavior than on coupons. She never deals with the issue of who uses them and why. She consults some of the notes she made during planning—her observations of shoppers, her interviews with cashiers and store personnel—and decides to broaden her subject. She writes a new hypothesis— "Depending on how much they participate in the system, coupon users can be classified into three categories"—and then tries to implement her revision agenda in a second draft.

HOW MUCH DO YOU SAVE?
(2nd Draft)

```
    As you cruise the aisles in the supermarket, you will
discover an interesting cultural phenomenon—COUPONS!
Shoppers seem obsessed with these slippery little pieces
of paper—saving, swapping, and spending them as if they
were cash. To the casual observer, these shoppers form
a cohesive economic community. But closer inspection
```

reveals that not all coupon users are alike. Depending on how much they participate in the system, coupon users can be classified into three different categories.

The reluctant coupon user rarely uses coupons by choice. You can spot him rushing down the aisle searching for items on a list written in a circular feminine hand. His cart looks fuller than it should, given his list, because he has picked up a frozen pizza and some cookies on impulse. But he doesn't clip coupons. In fact, he protests that the whole system is a fraud and that only the misguided believe they can save by clipping. Despite such protests, he is not coupon clean. Somewhere—folded neatly in his wallet—he has a coupon for his favorite cereal or shaving cream. He will use it when he has to, but for now he scowls at the cashier as she peels a coupon off his pizza. Reluctantly, he pulls out a coupon for the box of Kleenex on his list. The cashier smiles patiently and tells him he doesn't understand—the coupon said he has to buy two boxes.

The occasional coupon user trades coupons when she remembers to sort through her stash before she comes to the store. You can spot her in the middle of an aisle, coupon in one hand, product in the other, mumbling. She's usually got it half right—coupon, cake mix—but "this won't work without frosting and sprinkles." She believes in the system and, when she remembers, clips her own coupons—although most of those in her stash expired three months ago. She likes the idea of using coupons because it gives her an excuse to try new products. Unfortunately, although she may save as much as a dollar or two on these occasional splurges, she is always surprised when the cashier rings up a total that is a few dollars higher than she expected.

Compulsive coupon users use coupons for every shopping occasion. You can spot them clustered in little groups by the special displays, comparing their portfolios where they arrange their coupons alphabetically by aisle. These people not only clip coupons; they also attend weekly coupon-club meetings where they do some down-and-dirty swapping. You'll also hear them talking about driving from store to store, saving a few cents on Peter Pan here and a few cents on Pepto Bismol there. Their main concern is to make it to the cashier with a coupon for each item in their carts. They are less concerned about whether they actually need or want the items. In a few weeks, they will have trouble remembering why they bought a box of Tuna Helper Cheesy Noodles, but they will remember that they saved 55 cents.

1. <u>What did I want to do in this draft?</u>
   Classify three kinds of coupon users.

2. <u>What are its strengths and weaknesses?</u>
   Got to my subject—coupons and the people who use them.
   I liked describing people's behavior and purchases.
   "Nobody is coupon clean." But what do I do next? No
   conclusion. Still don't say what the coupon system is
   all about.

3. <u>What revisions do I want to make in my next draft?</u>
   a. Tell readers something about the coupon system.
   b. Look over notes from interview at newspaper.
   c. Reread articles on "double coupons" and "cashier
      coupons."
   d. Track delivery system—tell readers where coupons
      come from.
   e. Fix thesis so I can have a conclusion.

## Revising for Audience

Sarah is beginning to know more about her subject. She is also beginning to recognize the difference between *recounting* her experience and
*using* her experience to create a subject. But her major reaction to her
second draft concerns her audience. She wants to separate herself from
the shoppers in the store and tell her readers how the system works.
Sarah thinks her interviews and reading will help her, in her next draft,
to draw some conclusions about this system. This decision, made
because she wants to enlighten her audience, also enlarges her subject
and redefines her purpose.

THEY KNOW HOW TO GET TO US
(3rd Draft)

Coupons! What are they? Everywhere we look we see
those shiny little slips of paper decorated with bright
pictures, bar codes, and dotted lines. And whether we
admit it or not, all of us have clipped or used a coupon
at least once. None of us is coupon clean. But where do
they come from? Once we start tracking them, we discover
that they come to us through a complex delivery system.

A popular coupon distributor is the local newspaper,
especially the Sunday edition. In fact, we probably spend
as much time separating coupons from the newspaper as we
do reading the news. Most of these colorful eye-catchers
are called FSIs or Free Standing Inserts. The coupons or

ads that are actually printed on the pages of the newspaper are called ROPs or Run of Press ads.

The difference between FSIs and ROPs suggests the complexity in the coupon system. Although ROPs are less detailed and less colorful, they cost more than FSIs because printing them supposedly replaces valuable news space. For that reason, most national companies bypass the cost and hassle of ROPs. Instead, they print FSIs in bulk and pay local newspapers to insert them. Unfortunately, newspapers must invest as much money in the machinery to insert FSIs as they do in the machinery to print the news. And they must also invest in storage space. Inserts start arriving in semis on Monday and must be stored on large flats until they are ready to be stuffed into Sunday's paper.

Another popular coupon distributor is the U.S. Postal Service. How many times have we opened our mailboxes, expecting an important letter, only to see a logjam of envelopes filled with coupons encouraging us to buy everything from birdseed to toilet paper? These envelopes used to be addressed to "Occupant," but direct mail companies are getting smarter. By purchasing mailing lists from our credit-card companies, coupon distributors can chart our demographics, select an appropriate sample of coupons, and then insert them in an envelope addressed directly to us. Because these "manufacturer's coupons" have bar codes and expiration dates, they can be used in any store in America.

So, let's not forget the obvious. The most effective coupon distributor is the local supermarket. In-store coupons, coupons designed for a particular store, are stacked near the entrance doors where we pick up a shopping cart. In some stores, there are coupon machines at the end of each aisle. And in some areas of the country, stores use these devices to offer double coupons, where the value of a single coupon is doubled up to, but not exceeding, one dollar.

Even if we avoid these temptations, we still see coupons everywhere. On the shelf where we reach for a box of cereal, some elf has left an unused coupon. The box we place in our cart often has a pull-off coupon on its side. And at the checkout register we discover the ultimate delivery system. The cashier smiles, says, "Thank you. Come again," and hands us our receipt. When we flip over the receipt, we discover a coupon printed on the tape—not just any coupon but a coupon for the product we

just bought or an invitation from its competitor to try
it next time and save $1.00.

Home at last. Only mildly tainted by the system that
seems to find us wherever we are, we pause for a snack.
We open a box of cereal and start pouring. Surprise! Surprise! Mixed between the raisins and the bran is a
COUPON!

Revision Agenda

1. <u>What did I try to do in this essay?</u>
   Track how different kinds of coupons are delivered
   to consumers.

2. <u>What are its strengths and weaknesses?</u>
   Good information on the delivery system—how coupons
   get to us. Good stuff from notes on machinery at
   newspaper and cash-register coupons. But I'm still
   not answering main question. Why? Why coupons? Why
   not cheaper prices, better commercials? Check interview notes on "the mix."

3. <u>What revisions do I want to make in my next draft?</u>
   a. Reduce information on delivery system to one
      section.
   b. Revise thesis to focus on <u>why</u> advertisers use
      coupons.
   c. Hook reader with opening—maybe use cereal bowl
      from last draft.
   d. Suggest ways to respond to system—now that you
      know, what are you supposed to do?
   e. Put people and products back into essay.
   f. Make sure paragraphs connect to thesis.

## Revising for Purpose

Sarah's revisions are helping her discover her *purpose* for this project.
She has written about her own experience with coupons, how others
use coupons, and how coupons get to consumers, but she realizes that
she still has not answered her fundamental question: Why do
advertisers—given all the sophisticated strategies available in the
American marketplace—use coupons? She suggests that her fascination
with (and anger about) coupons is prompted by the feeling that the
system controls what she buys.

She decides to revise her purpose so that she can demonstrate how
coupons control consumer behavior. This revised purpose will allow her
to use some of the information from her last draft but will require her to

present more significant and interesting information about why advertisers use coupons. Finally, she wants to hook her readers by planning some way to insert herself (and her mixed feelings about coupons) into her analysis of how to respond to the system. Consult Sarah's "last" revision, "The Coupon Conspiracy," on page 97.

# Revising on your computer

The chief advantage of composing on a computer is the simplicity of revision. With a simple click, you can delete words, rearrange sentences, and move paragraphs. But remember, substantial revision, unlike editing and proofreading, involves reseeing and reshaping the ideas and information in a draft. In Chapter 4, this chapter, this process is called global revision. Chapters 8 through 11 illustrate the more restricted process of local revision, suggesting strategies for revising the paragraphs, sentences, diction, and style you see on your screen.

Global revision encourages you to think through the purpose of your planning and drafting in complete texts. Save and print each text. Assess its success in a revision agenda. Then compose the new text you prescribe. As you move on to the new text, reread your previous drafts and agendas to see if there is anything you can use or rework.

If you are uncertain about a draft, post your text to your writing group or the members of your writing class. Ask different students to assume the different roles described in "Reading to Revise." Then ask them to use the questions provided for their role to respond to your text. They can mark sections they like and comment on sections that surprise or confuse them. They can even insert questions or additional information into or in a space beside your text, like this: [CAN YOU ILLUSTRATE HOW THIS WOULD WORK? or HAVE YOU EVER CONSIDERED WHAT COUPONS TEACH US, INDIRECTLY, ABOUT THE QUALITY OF PRODUCTS?] After your readers have read and annotated your text, invite them to compose their own revision agenda for your next draft. You may even want to ask them to rewrite portions of your text—create a new introduction, fix a dull spot in the middle, or rework your conclusion.

A personal conference with your instructor will certainly help you think about global revision, but an electronic conference will also prove useful. Send a copy of your draft first so that your instructor has time to think about the way you defined your subject, audience, and purpose. You may want to include your revision agenda to indicate what you are thinking about doing next. Then the two of you can exchange comments about what you are attempting to discover and what you have already accomplished. Your instructor may decide to send you an alternative revision agenda to point you in a new direction.

No matter who initiates your revision, remember that global revision often requires a completely new text. Occasionally, modifying your thesis or repositioning certain examples will solve your problems. More often, you must start from scratch. Open a new file, reread all your notes and reader responses, and begin, again.

What does this photograph say about the temporary appeal of advertising campaigns? What are S&H Green Stamps?

## A Final Word About Revising

There is no final word about revising. You can revise endlessly, rearranging information, rewriting paragraphs, substituting new words. The more you look, the more you will see. But at some point, revising becomes rationalizing—an excuse for idle tinkering. The test of global revision is whether it produces significant improvement. Sometimes additional revision actually destroys good writing, replacing spontaneous, original insights with self-conscious, overwrought commentary. You have to know when to say, "I'm done." Strategies for local revision to help you polish and perfect your last draft are contained in Part Two of this text.

# Image Gallery

**Questions**

1. How do the butterflies in the "Absolut Citron" ad define or disguise the ad's subject?

2. What do the designers of both ads assume their audience knows about the product and its advertising campaign?

3. In what ways does the spoof ad, "Absolute on Ice," revise the purpose of the product's original advertising campaign.

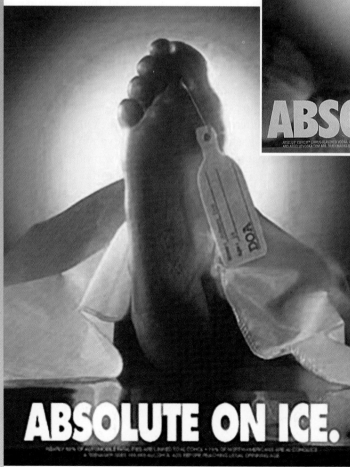

# Readings

In this brief essay, television commentator Andy Rooney asks if new products are necessarily better products. What evidence does Rooney use to distinguish between genuine innovation and cosmetic change? If the subject were writing rather than manufacturing, how would you characterize the difference between a *revised* text and a *changed* text?

# New Products

## ANDY ROONEY

1  Money is not my game, so I don't often read the *Wall Street Journal,* but someone on the train I take got off at the stop before mine the other night and left the paper on the seat next to me, so I looked through it. The *Wall Street Journal* gives you sort of a digest of the news you get on television.

2  One small story in there said that the companies that make things are coming up with fewer new products this year than last. The paper suggested this was bad, but I thought it was good. You can carry freedom of choice too far in a grocery store, for example. I don't want all the big companies squeezing out all the little upstart companies, but I don't want to be faced with ten different brands of what is substantially the identical product, either.

3  Our kitchen sink got stopped up last Saturday and I went to the grocery store for a can of Drano. I don't know why Drano. I'm just familiar with what the can looks like, and I was surprised to find a whole shelf filled with products that were supposed to free a clogged sink. There were powders, liquids and pellets. They came in cans, tubes, bottles and plastic. All of them said that if they didn't work, call your plumber. That always makes me suspect that they probably won't work on my problem. I found myself wishing the grocer had taken it upon himself to test the products for me

so that he could have become expert enough to narrow my choices to just two or three.

4  I ended up with a can of Drano, as always. I don't know whether any of those new, improved products were any better or not. I figured they were all more or less the same.

5  Genuine innovation is something we all like. That's what we mean by the line "Build a better mousetrap and the world will beat a path to your door."

6  The trouble is, too many big companies have been making the same old mousetrap and trying to get us to come to their door by painting it a different color or calling it the Official Mickey Mousetrap. That's not innovation, but that's what too often passes for a new product.

7  The automobile manufacturers of America are in trouble because we wanted something genuinely different and they gave us the same old mousetrap with electrically operated windows. The Japanese came up with some really new ideas in cars and people are buying them. When Volkswagen switched from the Bug to the Rabbit, the difference was more than new bumper stickers. You can tell a Saab from a Toyota, but you can't tell a Chevrolet from an Oldsmobile unless you own one.

8  Too many "new" products are coming from the sales departments of companies rather than

Andy Rooney, "New Products," *And More by Andy Rooney.* (New York: Atheneum, 1982), 26–28.

from the engineering division. I hope Americans are tired of being tricked. A lot of good U.S. companies spend big money on product development, on good design, on engineering or improved chemistry. They have good, serious professionals working to make real improvements, not cosmetic changes, but for all the effort that is put into making the product better, it is hardly ever as much money as is put into selling it.

9    It has always seemed to me that, over the long run, we do one thing about as well or as poorly as we do something else in America. We have some national traits that show through our work no matter what our work is. Sometimes it's good, sometimes it isn't.

10    For instance, take two products as different as those produced by Detroit and the television industry. Our cars and our television, for all my complaints, are in many ways the best in the world, but they both suffer from the same things. They're big, fluffy and tend to imitate the other products in their market. Two situation comedies on competing networks are apt to be as much alike as an Oldsmobile and a Chevrolet.

11    Putting the same product in a new package isn't what I call a new product. When an advertisement tells me what I'm buying is "new and improved," I always wonder exactly what the improvement is and whether I was a sucker for having bought the product last year before they fixed whatever was wrong with it.

12    I don't care what the *Wall Street Journal* says, I like the idea of fewer new products on the market. What we ought to do is keep making the old ones until we get them right.

# S t u d e n t  E s s a y

Student Sarah Penning's final revision, "The Coupon Conspiracy," demonstrates how coupons control consumer behavior. Read her essay. Then examine her Revision Agenda on page 99. Finally, answer the questions about her revising process in the Exercises on page 99.

# The Coupon Conspiracy (4th Draft)

## SARAH PENNING

1    In the beginning, I'd be furious. I'd start to pour my 2% over my Raisin Bran and suddenly I'd spot one—another brightly colored coupon, folded in thirds, mixed with my raisins and bran. How did it get there? Why was it there? Was the competition so cutthroat that they expected me to eat their advertising? Slowly, I'd relent, unfolding the paper and beaming at my good fortune: a picture of Raisin Bran and an invitation to "Save $1.00." All right, I'd confess. I'm hooked, but I'm not hoodwinked. I've pushed my cart around the supermarket enough times to know that coupons are not gifts. Indeed, most skillful shoppers know that coupons are part of a complex conspiracy to control what they buy.

2    Coupons are actually part of a larger conspiracy advertisers call "the mix." To sell any product, advertisers concoct a mixture of strategies ranging from television commercials to

highway billboards. But coupons play an important part in this conspiracy because they supply a valuable currency in the marketplace—information. If advertisers want to introduce a new product, increase the market share for an established product, or test the price range for a particular line of products, they flood the market with coupons. Some consumers buy. Some don't. Either way, advertisers study their reactions carefully, collecting information and projecting hypotheses about what sells.

3 Such studies have led to the careful design of coupons. They may be printed alone or marked by dotted lines at the bottom of a large ad, but they must resemble the size and shape of dollar bills to encourage consumers to think of them as money. They must also contain some basic information: (1) a colorful picture of the product to create brand recognition, (2) a simple headline to encourage savings and proclaim the amount saved, (3) an expiration date to set limits on their use, (4) a bar code for cashiers to scan and researchers to track, and (5) special information about the purchasing and redemp-

tion agreements to control and interpret the advertiser's purpose.

4 The subtle strategies of coupon design are matched by the elaborate systems of coupon distribution. Advertisers study the purchasing patterns of certain communities and neighborhoods to determine what kinds of coupons to insert into newspapers, stuff into mailboxes, or affix to products in the stores. In some areas of the country, there are coupon machines at the end of each aisle or cash register designed to print coupons on the back of receipts, encouraging consumers to buy the same product or one of its competitors the next time they shop.

5 Of course, advertisers have developed all sorts of theories about how to place and time coupon distribution. They are convinced that a coupon for Campbell's chicken noodle soup is more tempting when placed next to a coupon for Ritz crackers than next to a coupon for Puppy Chow. Their research also convinces them that a coupon for Taster's Choice coffee produces a larger response if it is inserted in the Sunday paper rather than the Wednesday paper.

6 If shoppers think all this effort is the result of good will, well . . . they had better think again. If they clip a coupon to save a dollar on a new box of cereal, they should realize that <u>that</u> dollar has already been calculated into the four-dollar price. The dollar off looks terrific until the coupon expires. Then consumers must decide whether they like the new cereal well enough to pay the inflated price. If they discover a new coupon for an old standby, forty cents rather than thirty cents off a box of Kleenex, they had best check the redemption agreement, where they will no doubt discover that the new coupon requires them to buy two boxes instead of one. And as long as they are checking, con-

**What does this image reveal about the complicated process of shopping on television? What does "S&H" mean in this process?**

sumers should remember that the only price that matters is the one posted on the shelf. Supermarkets often raise the price on a particular product to cover the cost of handling its coupons.

7    Where does this leave me and my one-dollar coupon for Raisin Bran? I could pitch it, protest that the whole system is a fraud, and refuse to participate. But the coupon conspiracy is too pervasive. If I don't use my coupon, I'll simply pay an inflated price for Raisin Bran (and every-thing else I buy). I'm not that naive. On the other hand, I'm not nuts. I refuse to obsess about the conspiracy, calculating how I can use coupons to save pennies on every purchase. I don't have that kind of time, and I'm not sure what I'd win if I could actually figure out a way to win. So . . . I guess I'll hang around the middle of the aisle, coupon in one hand, product in the other, at once fascinated by and furious at the fine mess they've got me in.

Revision Agenda

1. <u>What did I try to do in this draft?</u>
   Demonstrate how advertisers use coupons to control what consumers buy.

2. <u>What are its strengths and weaknesses?</u>
   I like the "inside" information about the coupon conspiracy—why and how advertisers use them. I also like the opening and closing paragraphs. Didn't think I'd turn out to be "the mumbler." Not sure about 3rd paragraph. List seems dull.

3. <u>What revisions do I want to make in my next draft?</u>
   a. I'm done. I never want to think about coupons again!
   b. If I must . . . Revise 3rd and 5th paragraphs.
   c. Decide if intro and conclusion match up.
   d. Add more "conspiratorial tone" to explanation.
   e. Question #1: Are advertisers really conspirators?
   f. Question #2: Does any other culture use coupons?

## Exercises

**Consider the following questions about Sarah's four revision agendas:**

1. How does Sarah's *subject* change from her discovery draft to her final draft?

2. How does Sarah's concern about her *audience* affect her decision making?

3. What is Sarah's *purpose* for each draft? How does she try to embody that purpose in a thesis statement?

4. How effectively does Sarah follow Eudora Welty's notion of revising? For example, how does she move things around in her last draft? Which draft do you like best? Explain your answer.

# Web Design

Students using *Writing with a Purpose* in a composition class were asked to design a website for Sarah Penning's essay, "The Coupon Conspiracy." Notice how the annotations for the two sites explain how a design can either confuse or clarify purpose.

## Sample Homepage #1: Coupons

▶ The subject is defused by the clutter of information presented on the site.

▶ Readers find the site difficult to read because of the mixture of type fonts and garish colors.

▶ The purpose of the site is buried in the small type.

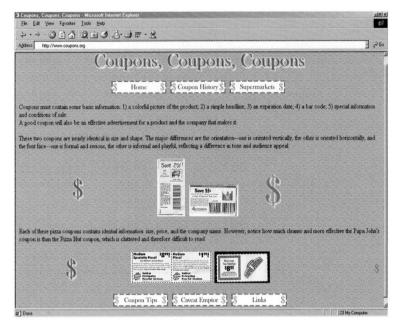

## Sample Homepage #2: Coupons

▶ The subject is identified by the repetition of the word *Coupons* across the top of the site.

▶ Readers can follow the navigational system presented in the sequence of "coupon" links.

▶ The purpose of the site is established by the logical grouping of words and images.

# Writing Assignments

### 1. NARRATE

Compile a list of sales ventures you have encountered—for example, selling door-to-door, shopping for a special present, negotiating the terms of a warranty. Select one that raised your expectations. Then write a narrative that reveals how your experience caused you to revise your expectations.

### 2. OBSERVE

Visit a shopping mall or large discount store. Find a store or a particular section of a store where you can observe shoppers. Then write an essay in which you describe the behavior of three kinds of shoppers: reluctant, recreational, and relentless.

### 3. INVESTIGATE

Interview the people in charge of your college or university website. Ask them how they sell the university. For example, ask them about design issues: What colors do they use? When do they use text, and when do they use graphics? How do they arrange the page—especially the links to other pages? Use your interview information to write a feature revealing how your university uses technology to inform old customers or attract new ones. This assignment is particularly interesting if your university (or one of its departments/programs) recently *revised* its website.

### 4. COLLABORATE

Convert your writing group into a coupon club for a month. Develop an investment strategy for collecting, trading, and redeeming coupons. Keep a record of what you save. Then write a guide for students on how to use coupons effectively.

### 5. READ

Search the business journals in your library for articles directed toward readers who want to work in some unusual form of marketing—infomercials, for example. Read one article carefully. Write a brief analysis of its projected audience. Then speculate about a completely different audience— for example, consumer advocates who want to eliminate such marketing strategies. Revise the information in the article so that you can present it effectively to this new audience.

### 6. RESPOND

Look through mail-order catalogues for products that support or refute Andy Rooney's claim that "too many companies have been making the same old mousetrap." Then write a letter to Rooney presenting your findings as evidence that he is correct or that the products you have found are indeed better.

### 7. ANALYZE

Study the design of the two websites for coupons. Use the annotations to focus on important details in each site. Then analyze how the grouping of information and the use of white space make the second site more effective than the first.

### 8. EVALUATE

Consult your responses to the exercises on page 99. Then write an essay reassessing the strengths and weaknesses of one of Sarah Penning's four essays on coupons. Begin by revising her assessment of the essay's strengths and weaknesses. Then compose a new set of directions for how she might improve her essay.

### 9. ARGUE

Speculate about the impact of the two Absolut ads. Then argue that in addition to spoofing all Absolut ads, the "Absolute on Ice" ad makes its readers revise their attitude toward the product.

### 10. ARGUE

Argue that creative deception is essential to the free-enterprise system. Support your claim with examples of successful advertising campaigns.

# Designing

**IT DOESN'T TAKE MUCH TO CLEAN UP**

**A SLIGHTLY MESSY DESIGN.**

—ROBIN WILLIAMS

Designing—arranging words and images on a page—enables you to present your writing in an effective, memorable, and persuasive pattern. It is similar to the other stages of the writing process because much of your initial activity involves "playing around" with the arrangement of words and ideas—mixing and matching visual patterns to determine which ones demonstrate your purpose most effectively. Indeed, as you experiment with different arrangements, you may have to return to *planning, drafting,* and *revising* to develop information and discover images to complete the designing process.

Designing differs from the other stages in the composing process because it is both a process and a product. You may try out several patterns for your writing, but once you select the most effective one, you will need to make decisions to craft and control the final look of your design. Robin Williams, author of several valuable books on design, explains how the designing process creates the need for such decisions:

> Design beginners tend to put text and graphics on the page wherever there happens to be space, often without regard to other items on the page. What this creates is the slightly-messy-kitchen effect—you know, with a cup here, a plate there, a napkin on the floor, a pot in the sink, a spill on the floor. It doesn't take much to clean up the slightly messy kitchen, just as it doesn't take much to clean up a slightly messy design. (Robin Williams, *The Non-Designers Design Book*)

Knowing how to clean up a mess or create a memorable effect requires that you know the conventions of your writing situation,

the elements and principles of design, and when it is possible and appropriate to modify them.

## Conventions of MLA and APA Style

In most composition classes, you are required to follow either the MLA or APA style for designing writing assignments. You will learn more about these two styles in Chapter 12, "Planning the Research Paper," and Chapter 13, "Writing the Research Paper." But, in simple terms, if you are required to present your writing in one of these two styles, you will *not* have to make many decisions about design. Every feature in your composition—from the arrangement of your title page to the format of your Works Cited page—is specified in the MLA or APA style manual.[1] However, both style books work with the same *elements* and *principles* of design.

## Elements of Design

The basic elements of any design are created with *typeface, graphics*, and *color* and *white space*. Before the invention of the personal computer, these elements were the special concern of printers and graphic designers. However, since most software programs provide you with an array of capabilities, you can now select different sizes and styles of typeface,

1. Joseph Gibaldi, *MLA Handbook for Writers of Research Papers*, 6th ed. (New York: MLA, 2003); *Publication Manual of the American Psychological Association*, 5th ed. (Washington, D.C.: APA, 2001).

display all sorts of graphics, and experiment with various patterns of color and white space. And by using the latest printers, scanners, and digital cameras, you can transfer your designs onto paper documents.

## Typeface

Although your word processing program gives you access to all sorts of typefaces, you still need to consider your subject, audience, and purpose before you select a particular size and style. Typeface size is measured in *points*. Type set in a small point, like "fine print," is difficult to read whereas type set in a large point, like a headline, can overpower your reader. For that reason, academic papers, especially those designed to follow MLA or APA style, are set in a midsized typeface.

If you are selecting text for a different kind of writing situation—for example, a brochure, a webpage or a PowerPoint slide presentation—you will want to work with a small or large type size. For some complicated projects, you may want to use several different type sizes. For example, the main body of this text is set in 11 point type, but other features—headings, captions, sidebars—are set in smaller or larger type sizes.

Your word processing program enables you to present typeface in four different forms:

1. Roman is the standard presentational form in which letters stand straight up and down.

2. *Italics* is a special presentational form in which letters are *slanted* and appear in a thinner stroke.

3. **Bold** is another special form in which the stroke of the letters' lines are darkened and thickened.

4. <u>Underline</u> or <u>underscore</u> is a special form in which a line appears under the letters.

You can select one of these presentational forms for any typeface size with a simple click of your mouse. But your choice should be appropriate for the purpose of your writing. Roman should be used for most documents. *Italics* should be used for emphasis in special situations. For example, APA style requires that all book titles be presented in *italics*. By contrast, MLA style requires that all book titles be <u>underlined</u>. **Bold** should be used sparingly for features such as headings that mark sections within your text.

Since the invention of the printing press, type—the standardized style of letters and characters—has evolved into thousands of typefaces, or fonts. Your word processing program allows you to use many of these fonts, most of which fit into two broad categories—*serif* and *sans serif*. You can distinguish between these two families of typefaces by looking for the *serif,* or the small horizontal line marking the top or bottom of individual letters. *Sans* (the French word for *without*) *serif* fonts do not have any horizontal markings. Notice how the presence or absence of the serif distinguishes the following fonts.

|  | *Serif* | *Sans Serif* |  |
|---|---|---|---|
|  | Clarendon | Arial |  |
| Serif on l → | Palatino | Gill Sans | ← no serif on l |
|  | Times | Helvetica |  |

In addition to standard fonts—many of which differ from one another in small and subtle ways—your software may provide you with display or decorative fonts. Like the lettering on a billboard or birthday cake, decorative fonts should be used for special purposes or occasions.

Notice how each of the following fonts defines the subject differently, appeals to a different audience, and suggests a different purpose. The first font asserts a polished subject, appeals to a contemporary audience, and implies that the product it names has a compelling professional value:

PalmPilot

The second font, however, suggests a clunky subject, appeals to an audience with old-fashioned tastes, and implies that the product it names may be out of date:

𝕻𝖆𝖑𝖒𝕻𝖎𝖑𝖔𝖙

The last font is so informal that it suggests a frivolous subject, appeals to a casual audience, and implies that the product it describes may be a toy:

**PalmPilot**

## Mixing Fonts

In any design, you may mix sizes, forms, and styles of typefaces. But before doing so, consider three effects that mixing fonts will have on the way that you present your subject, appeal to your audience, and assert your purpose.

1. If you select one font, even if you vary its size and present some portions of it in italics, you create the impression of *uniformity.* Uniformity evokes a sedate subject, has a calming effect on your audience, and suggests a formal purpose. This does not mean that uniformity is undesirable; it simply means that you need to understand the effect you are creating, as the following example illustrates.

   The telephone is at once one of the most *public and private* communication devices in our culture.
   [Because the capital letter *T* and the italics are in the same font, the passage looks uniform.]

Andrew Gaub, the student whose writing is featured in this chapter, is writing an essay about how the different designs of the telephone have affected our notions of public and private communication. Respond to his project by analyzing a television or print advertising campaign for cell phones that raises questions about privacy. For example, consider what Verizon's "Can You Hear Me Now?" campaign suggests about private and public communication.

2. If you select fonts that are similar but slightly different in size, form, and style, you create the impression of *discord*. Discord evokes conflicting messages about the unity of the subject, has a disorienting effect on your audience, and suggests an uncertain purpose. Uniformity is a solid, useful effect; discord is not and should be avoided. Notice how the different typeface sizes, forms, and styles disrupt the readability in the following example.

The telephone is at once one of the most *public and private* communication devices in our culture.
[Because the large letter *T* and the italics are in slightly different fonts, the passage is disorienting.]

3. If you combine fonts that are clearly distinct from each other, you create the impression of *contrast*. In the "language" of design, contrast evokes a visually appealing subject, excites your audience, and suggests an engaging, energetic purpose. This does not mean that you should use contrast constantly; it simply means that in special situations, you can use it effectively and purposefully to counterbalance the impression of uniformity, as in the following example.

The telephone is at once one of the most **public and private** communication devices in our culture.
[Because the difference between the two type fonts is clear, the contrasting passage has more visual energy and is more exciting.]

## Graphics

In the early days of printing, the term *graphics* referred to various lines and markings within the text. But recently, especially with the development of digital media, the term's meaning has been expanded to include all sorts of visuals from bullets and boxes to maps and photographs. Your software provides you with access to all these visuals, but before you use them, consider what purpose you hope to accomplish by including them in your design.

- *Decoration*: If you use graphics to adorn your text with a lot of "eye-candy," you might distort your subject and distract your reader.
- *Demonstration*: If you use graphics to explain a specific idea or the major thesis of your text, you will define your subject and engage your reader.

You can use any of the graphics discussed next to make your text more effective, memorable, and persuasive.

### Textual Graphics

You see the following textual graphics every day in newspapers and magazines. And you are certainly seeing them featured in this book. You may want to use them in your writing to organize your subject, guide you audience, and advance your purpose

▶ *Bullets.* A bullet is a little marker used before an item in a list instead of a number. You can use this device to mark a series of related ideas in your writing, break up large chunks of text to assist your reader's comprehension, or call attention to the connection among concepts.

▶ *Boxes.* A box is a device used to set off and frame a portion of your text. Often such boxes are "screened" with a contrasting color to dramatize further the special significance of the information. You can use this device to focus on a specific feature of your subject, separate and shape information for your reader, or frame a portion of your argument to clarify your purpose.

▶ *Sidebars.* A sidebar is a section of text placed in the margin *beside* the body of your text. You can use this device to provide complimentary information to enrich your subject or advance your purpose. You can also use this device to direct your readers to other information that will help them understand the context for your writing.

▶ *Pull Quotes.* A pull quote extracts a key phrase or sentence from the main body of the text. The quotation is usually presented in a contrasting font, displayed in the middle of the text (or inserted into the side of the text), and framed by lines. You can use a pull quote to help your readers identify the main ideas in your text.

Although each of these textual graphics can add visual interest and energy to your text, you should use them sparingly to keep your design clean, coherent, and free from clutter.

## Exercise

Select any chapter of this textbook.

1. Identify the textual graphics—bullets, boxes, sidebars, pull quotes, and other lines and markings—that distinguish its design.

2. Explain whether these graphics *decorate* the text or *demonstrate* the ideas presented in the chapter.

## Representational Graphics

The following representational graphics provide a pictorial method for displaying information. As with textual graphics, representational graphics can add visual interest to your subject, illustrate complicated ideas with shapes and images, and provide powerful and dramatic evidence to support your purpose. But these graphics, like textual graphics, should be used sparingly and carefully so that you don't dilute your subject, distract your reader, or derail your purpose.

## TABLE 1 ATTITUDES TOWARD CELL PHONES

| | |
|---|---|
| 41% | Cell phones are a great convenience and time-saver. |
| 29% | Cell phones are a necessary evil for busy people. I only take it when I need to use it. |
| 3% | I am addicted to my mobile phone. I find myself making calls that I don't really need to make. |
| 26% | I have a mobile phone, but I don't really use it. |

SOURCE: "Cell Phone Bill of Rights" at <http://www.Let'sTalk.com/company/bill_study.htm>.

**Tables and Charts** A *table* presents words and numbers in rows and columns. Such a device restricts your subject, organizes information in a logical sequence, and evokes the power of "hard data" to advance your purpose. For example, LetsTalk.com conducted an opinion poll in 2002 to find out what Americans think about cell phone usage. One of the tables presented in this survey appears above.

A chart or graph enables you to transform the data presented in the previous table into a pictorial image. By using the *Table* function on your word processor, you can convert words and numbers into one of several kinds of charts and graphs. Figure 5.1 is an example of a *bar graph*.

Figure 5.2 is an example of a *pie chart*.

The overall design of your text will help you decide which kind of chart best suits your purpose. Indeed, you may decide that too many tables and charts distract the reader from your text. For example, the cleanest way to introduce the preceding data might be simply to summarize it in a few sentences and cite the source.

If you use a table or create a chart, remember to provide a *caption*. Use the title from the original source or one that you want to use in your text. In most academic papers, captions are placed *above* the table and *beneath* the chart, preceded by a label and a number, as in the following examples.

**Figure 5.1**

Attitudes Toward Cell Phones

*Source:* "Cell Phone Bill of Rights" <http://www.Let'sTalk.com/company/bill_study.htm>.

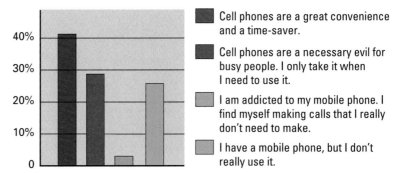

**Figure 5.2**

Attitudes Toward Cell
Phones

*Source:* "Cell Phone Bill of Rights"
<http://www.Let'sTalk.com/com-
pany/bill_study.htm>.

Cell phones are a great convenience
and a time-saver.

Cell phones are a necessary evil for
busy people. I only take it when
I need to use it.

I am addicted to my mobile phone. I
find myself making calls that I really
don't need to make.

I have a mobile phone, but I don't
really use it.

**TABLE 1  ATTITUDES TOWARD CELL PHONES**
**Figure 1.**  Attitudes Toward Cell Phones

You should also provide a *source*. The information about the source is usually placed beneath the table or chart. It is preceded by the word *Source*, as in the following example:

*Source:* "Cell Phone Bill of Rights" at <http://www.Let'sTalk.com/company/bill_study.htm>.

**Diagrams and Maps**    Diagrams and maps are drawings that represent some aspect of reality. *Diagrams* outline, label, and identify various parts of an object, structure, or process. For example, Figure 5.3 illustrates how the Internet is connected and routed through various switches to individual computers. Although this diagram will require explanation, it provides a vivid picture of the interrelated stages in a complex process. Your software will allow you to draw your own diagrams, but if you use one from another source, provide a caption and cite the source.

**Figure 5.3**

Wireless Network

*Source:* <http://www.verniernet-
works.com/products.html>.

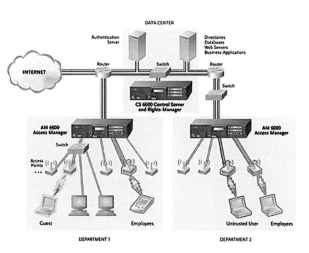

**Figure 5.4**

U.S. Cell Phone
Operator Coverage

*Source:*
<http://wireless.fcc.gov/reports/
documents/fc99136.pdf>

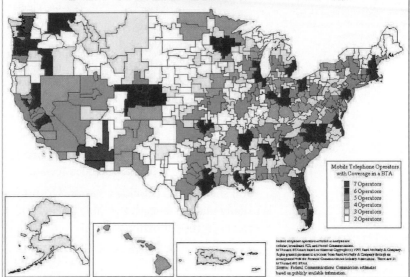

Estimated Mobile Telephony Service Deployment: Number of
Operators in Each BTA with Some Level of Coverage

Maps represent the features of an area by illustrating their form, size, and relationships. Most maps are designed to inform users about an aspect of the area being shown, such as a weather map or a highway map. Maps have a *legend*—a key that explains the colors or symbols used. In Figure 5.4, the legend explains how the colors on the map indicate the number of mobil telephone operators that are available in particular basic trading areas (BTAs) in the United States. You can use your computer to create a map, imposing your own legend on some geographical area. If you borrow a map from another source, provide a caption and cite the *complete* source.

## Artwork: Drawings, Paintings, Photographs

Artwork that contains blacks and whites—a pen-and-ink drawing, a cartoon—is usually called a *drawing*. The tools in many software programs enable you to create your own drawings. But if you borrow a drawing from another source, you need to identify that source. A cartoon's caption is provided by the artist. Cartoons—particularly those that appear on the editorial page of a newspaper—provide interesting and memorable commentary on issues and ideas (see page 103). But such artwork rarely will provide essential data for your writing. You must decide whether drawings would distract your readers or enrich your purpose.

In the language of design, artwork that contains significant shading—a painting or a photograph—is called a *halftone*—a term that refers to the way in which such images are reproduced in print. But since the development of scanners, digital cameras, and computer software, you now can reproduce and position your own photographs in your text with relative ease. Most search engines also contain an *Image* function that enables you to find all kinds of *clip art* that you may find useful to illustrate your ideas. But be careful since most clip art tends to be decorative (general) instead of illustrative (specific). And most museums and art galleries require you to pay a fee to reproduce their art.

If you decide to include such artwork, you need to revisit the criteria for including any representational graphics in your writing. That is, does the inclusion of a photograph *decorate* or *demonstrate* your purpose? You also need to ask yourself some tough questions about whether *your* photographs, or some simple *clip art*, is really worth including in your writing. If you are considering reproducing artwork—such as images of photographs or paintings from a museum site—remember that such images are covered by copyright. Even though they may look available on a website, you can't use them without permission—which usually means obtaining and paying for reprint rights.

**Figure 5.5**
Satellites and Cell Phones

*Source:* <http://www.Qualcomm.com/globalstar/about/satellites.html>.

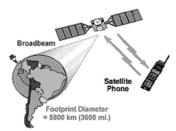

## Infographics

*Infographics* is a relatively new term that refers to the combination of art and information. For example, how would you classify Figure 5.5? Is it a diagram, a drawing, a map, or a chart? Using the term *infographics* is a simple way to describe how the convergence of visual categories blurs traditional boundaries—creating a new category.

You can use your computer to create your own infographics, but if you borrow such artwork, provide a caption and cite the source.

## EXERCISE

Browse through your hometown newspaper or favorite magazines and look for tables, charts, diagrams, maps, drawings, photographs, and infographics that are visually effective. Then explain whether these compelling images *decorate* or *demonstrate* the ideas that they illustrate.

## Color and White Space

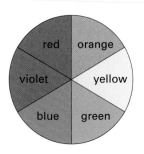

**Figure 5.6**
A Color Wheel

The development of the personal computer, high-speed printers, and the World Wide Web has opened a door to a world full of color. In the past, most writing students never had the opportunity to reproduce their work in color. Now it's easy to do so. But if you are like most people, you have not studied the fine points of color theory. You may like certain colors. However, before you start including color in your design, you should understand some basic ideas about its use.

In simple terms, colors can be warm (reds, oranges) and cool (blues, greens). See Figure 5.6. As you think about your subject, audience, and purpose, experiment with different colors in this spectrum to reinforce the overall design of your writing project. For example, assign specific colors for headings, subheads, and other navigational markers. Doing this helps to give each page a consistent look and feel.

Selecting colors for your text is like selecting fonts. In other words, as you mix and match colors, you need to think about *uniformity, discord,* and *contrast.*

▶ If you select similar hues of one color, your text will look *uniform,* but it will also look monochrome. There is nothing wrong with a monochromatic design—if it suits your purpose—but if you can use color, why use only one? Notice how the use of different shades of purple typefaces and background creates a monochromatic effect in the following box.

### Exercise

Select any chapter in this book. Identify the representational graphics—table and charts; diagrams and maps; drawings, paintings, and photographs; and infographics. Then explain whether each graphic *decorates* or *demonstrates* the information in the chapter.

▶ If you select several colors—all from the same part of the color spectrum (reds, oranges)—your text will look *discordant,* or garish. You should avoid selecting similar colors for your design, especially if you are planning on placing them closely together. Notice how the red typeface and yellow background in the following box clash—creating a garish look.

### Exercise

Select any chapter in this book. Identify the representational graphics—table and charts; diagrams and maps; drawings, paintings, and photographs; and infographics. Then explain whether each graphic *decorates* or *demonstrates* the information in the chapter.

> If you select colors that are from different parts of the color spectrum, the visual component of your text will have *contrast*. Contrast is an important, but complicated, concept in color selection—particularly when you are considering the background. Strong, dark, warm colors should be used for typefaces. Pale, light, cool colors should be used for background. Notice that the dark red background and the light green type in the following box create contrast. However, using a dark instead of a pale background makes the text difficult to read.

> ### Exercise
>
> Select any chapter in this book. Identify the representational graphics—table and charts; diagrams and maps; drawings, paintings, and photographs; and infographics. Then explain whether each graphic *decorates* or *demonstrates* the information in the chapter.

## White Space

*White space* is the space on a page that is not occupied by text or graphics. You might think of it as blank space, but designers think of it as a negative shape—a box, a bar, a frame—that contrasts with the shape of the text or the graphic. You can also think of white space as a color—a background color that contrasts with the color of the typeface or graphic. You use white space as a shape when you create the columns that form your margins or the bars that produce the spacing between the lines of your text. You use white space as a color when you contrast the headings and the body of your text. Notice how in the following box the white space creates a negative shape—a box on the left that contrasts with the text on the right. Also, notice how the heading *Exercise* is set in a larger, boldface font; arranged in lowercase letters; and presented in a dark red to counterbalance the dark blue of the text.

> **e x e r c i s e**  Select any chapter in this book. Identify the representational graphics—table and charts; diagrams and maps; drawings, paintings, and photographs; and infographics. Then explain whether each graphic *decorates* or *demonstrates* the information in the chapter.

Andrew Gaub is working on an essay about how the designs of the telephone—as an object and as a network—have changed our attitudes about public and private communication. Since his essay is about design, he decides to experiment with several design features, hoping to present his ideas in a more effective and persuasive pattern. As he tries each feature, evaluate his experiments. Which ones merely decorate his text? Which ones help to demonstrate his purpose?

## Principles of Design

Four principles of design enable you to use typeface, graphics, color, and white space to plan an overall design for your document: *proximity, alignment, repetition,* and *contrast.* Each of these principles focuses on a particular feature of design, but inevitably they interact with and reinforce one another. Therefore, whether you are following a stylebook's rules or creating your own design, you need to understand how the four principles work.

## Proximity

*Proximity* requires that you group related units of information together. Such grouping creates a logical pattern that your readers can identify and remember. Andrew Gaub experiments with several presentational formats. Notice how the information on the first draft for his title page appears scattered, forcing your eyes to jump around the page.

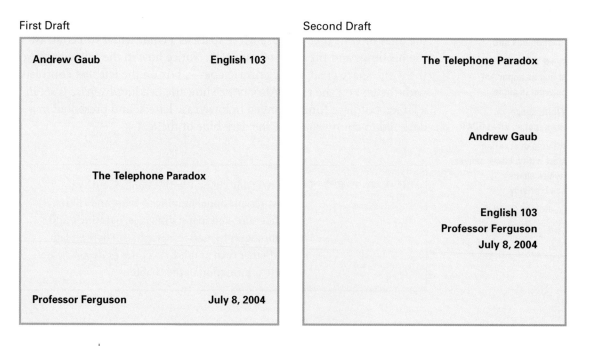

First Draft

> **Andrew Gaub**                    **English 103**
>
>
> **The Telephone Paradox**
>
>
> **Professor Ferguson**              **July 8, 2004**

Second Draft

> **The Telephone Paradox**
>
>
> **Andrew Gaub**
>
>
> **English 103**
> **Professor Ferguson**
> **July 8, 2004**

If you, like Andrew, are given the opportunity to design your own text, follow the principle of proximity. Group related items together. Separate groups of information that don't belong together. Call attention to the different categories of information by presenting them, consistently, in different font sizes or colors and by separating them with appropriate amounts of white space. In his second draft (page 114), notice how Andrew uses proximity to revise his title page.

## Alignment

*Alignment* requires that every item on the page has a visual connection to something else on the page. You can create this connection by establishing an invisible line—in your mind and on the page. This line can be created down the center of the page (*centered*), on the left (*flush left*), or on the right (*flush right*). You can also create this line by establishing an imaginary axis in the middle of the page and then projecting an imaginary diagonal line through the axis—for example, from a graphic on the top left to a graphic on the bottom right.

Alignment enables you to unify your design. The invisible line suggests that even though the items on a page may be separated from one another, they form a cohesive pattern. For that reason, make sure that you use only one text alignment on a page. Notice how Andrew's decision to use two different alignments creates a "messy" design in the first draft. Also, notice how in the fourth draft he shifts clusters of information to form a clear diagonal alignment.

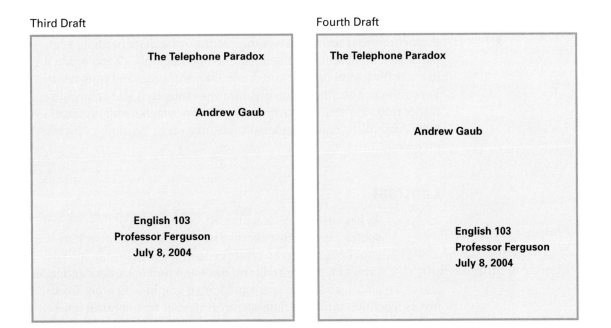

Third Draft

The Telephone Paradox

Andrew Gaub

English 103
Professor Ferguson
July 8, 2004

Fourth Draft

The Telephone Paradox

Andrew Gaub

English 103
Professor Ferguson
July 8, 2004

Given the potential for its various purposes, alignment is particularly useful for expressing an individual style. Centering, the most common method of alignment, is so predictable that some designers try to avoid it unless the occasion requires a formal (and some designers would say dull) text. A flush left (with breaks or indents to mark paragraphs) is the most common method for establishing the left margin on a page of type. But designers disagree about the right margin. Depending on your purpose and audience, some designers would suggest that the right margin be *justified,* or blocked, while others would suggest that the right margin be *unjustified,* or ragged. Andrew experiments with both a justified-right and a ragged-right design. Which style do you prefer?

Flush Left, Paragraph Breaks, Justified Right

The network for this telephone has also become wireless. Regional hubs connected by fiber optics, and more recently, satellites responding to high frequency radio waves can transmit private voice messages or digital data from anywhere--an office, a restaurant, a golf course--to anywhere--the mall, the airport, the beach.

Flush Left, Paragraph Indents, Ragged Right

The network for this telephone has also become wireless. Regional hubs connected by fiber optics, and more recently, satellites responding to high frequency radio waves can transmit private voice messages or digital data from anywhere--an office, a restaurant, a golf course--to anywhere--the mall, the airport, the beach.

## Repetition

*Repetition* suggests that you try to repeat some aspect of your design throughout your text. Whatever the feature—a boldface heading, a certain bullet, or a particular alignment for a photograph—if you repeat it in a visually logical pattern, you create a sense of order and consistency. Repetition not only helps you organize your subject; it also helps your reader read your text. Notice how Andrew experiments with typeface form and bullets in his text to mark the three major divisions in his essay on page 117.

## Contrast

*Contrast is the most effective way to add visual interest to your design.*

As has already been mentioned several times in this chapter, contrast is the most effective way to add visual interest to your design. You can create contrast by juxtaposing such features as type size and font, thick and thin lines, dark and light colors, and white space and text or graphics. In other words, just as repetition unifies various elements in your text, contrast illustrates their differences. However, by evoking difference, you also demon-

Ragged right with bulleted list

---

### The Telephone Paradox

The telephone is at once one of the most public and private communication devices in our culture. The three stages in its development as an object and as a network clarify this curious paradox. They also demonstrate how the changes in its design have influenced the behavior designated as public and private.

- **In the beginning,** the telephone was a large wooden box, featuring a mouthpiece and an ear cup, that was operated by a crank handle. . . .

- **During the next stage** in its development, the telephone emerged as a small, black, plastic console that cradled and was wired to a hand piece. . . .

- **In our time,** the invention of the cell phone has liberated callers from the wires that tethered them to a room or a booth. . . .

---

A pull quote creates contrast

---

- **During the next stage in its development, the telephone emerged as a small, black, plastic console that cradled and was wired to a hand piece. Because callers could listen and speak into this hand piece, their conversations seemed more private. But soon this simple black phone was augmented by extension phones in various private rooms in the house. These customized phones, eventually designed in many shapes and colors, expressed the tastes of their individual users. Even "public phones" were designed to cater to privacy and individual tastes. Phones were placed in a booth where doors could be closed or were positioned in special public spaces where soundproof panels protected individual conversations.**

> *"Public phones" were designed to cater to privacy and individual tastes.*

---

strate the pattern of your design. The features you present as different contrast with the features you present as similar—thereby suggesting that they are logically related.

Notice how Andrew experiments with a pull quote to create contrast. This device gives his readers a break in a page of type and also highlights an important section of his argument.

## Headings

The elements and principles of design govern the way you use headings to organize your text. Titles, headings, and subheadings are designed to contrast with the rest of your text. If you have constructed an outline for your text, then you have already established a series of headings that mark the subdivisions of your text. By consulting your outline, you can create a system that distinguishes different kinds of headings by using different type. For example:

### LEVEL-ONE HEADING

### Level-Two Heading

### *Level-Three Heading*

Whatever system you create, use it consistently. Also, make sure that you follow the principle of alignment by positioning your headings in the same places throughout your text.

## Breaking the Rules

Now that you understand the basic elements and principles of design, you can risk creating your own design—if it suits your purpose. In other words, once you understand what's inside the box, you can think outside the box. Notice how David Carson plays with the visual logic of proximity and alignment in the following image.

```
MIS-   DON'T
LEGI-  TAKE
F OR   BILITY
ICATIO N.  CO MMUN
```

Breaking the rules is risky. You want to present your writing in an effective, memorable, and persuasive pattern. And you want to avoid confusing, distracting, or overpowering your reader. Although Carson's design may be a memorable stunt, you may wonder whether it is persuasive writing.

## Designing with Your Computer

A WRITER'S RESOURCES

An excellent place to view how designers follow or break the rules is <http://www.webbyawards.com>—a resource that lists the year's best websites according to categories ranging from *Activism* to *Weird*.

Throughout this chapter, the computer has been cited as the primary reason that writers can serve as their own designers. There is so much to play with in most software—text, graphics, color—and so much available on the Web—designs, photographs, infographics—that beginning designers usually feel as though they have been let loose in a toy shop. In this space, rather than provide you with more advice about how to design with your computer, it might be wiser to caution you against the design excesses that can occur when you are playing with all the new toys. Remember, your primary task is to write with a purpose about a subject for an audience. If you can create a design that enhances and enriches that job, then by all means use it. However, if your computer tempts you to decorate or disguise your primary task, then designing with a computer may be a counterproductive effort.

## Questions

1. How do these two images support Michael Rock's argument that some texts are designed for "reading" while others are designed for "looking"?

2. What does the design of each newspaper suggest about the culture that shaped its readers?

3. How does the technology available to the designer determine how each newspaper was designed?

# Readings

In his essay, Michael Rock, an art professor and professional designer, argues that the graphic style of *USA Today* has created a new design ideal that "has the look of information but no content." What examples does Rock use to illustrate his objection to "LITE" design? Why do you think he avoids using graphics to demonstrate his argument that graphics are overtaking meaning?

# Since When Did *USA Today* Become the National Design Ideal?

## MICHAEL ROCK

1 In a recent *New York Times* Sunday magazine article on school textbooks, writer Robert Reinhold described California's new history series as "filled with colorful charts, graphs, time lines, maps and photographs in a format suggestive of the newspaper *USA Today*." There it is again. Since when did *USA Today* become the national design ideal? Everywhere you look you find *USA Today* used as an analogy to describe a noteworthy design format. Making ideas "accessible" is the operative term for the information age. But too often information is drained of its significance in the name of accessibility.

2 Some things are designed for reading: scholarly journals, literary reviews, financial pages, and their ilk are fairly impenetrable to the casual page flipper. Other objects like *USA Today,* annual reports, fashion magazines, and so on are for looking. (Haven't you heard in the course of a design project someone say, only half in jest, "No one actually reads the copy, just make it look good.") Then there are the gray areas. These include news magazines and textbooks, which imply reading but are increasingly about looking. If you compare *Time* or *Newsweek* or a fifth grade schoolbook of twenty years ago to their present incarnations, the change is remarkable. The headlines are bigger, the captions are bigger, the photographs, charts, and call-outs are all bigger. Something had to go, someone must have decided, and what went was the text.

3 The trend in typography is clearly towards a destruction of narrative text, with images increasingly responsible for carrying the content. Running copy is being replaced with exaggerated hierarchies, charts, graphs, sidebars, boxes, captions, and call-outs that reduce the "story" to a collection of visualized pseudo-facts. It is the design equivalent of the video sound-bite, with complex ideas boiled down (in the words of Nigel Holmes, *Time's* design director) to "manageable chunks."

## How to Compete Against TV

4 The resulting designs often have the look of information, but without real content. Beyond its stylistic implications, this new typographic sensibility represents a change in the consumer's relationship to information, the author's authority, and the significance of the form. There is a fragmentation of communication, with the model of contemporary typography no longer being the linear argument but the simultaneous slogan. For instance, a *Newsweek* story may now open with an image that takes up as much as ninety percent of the spread, with only a small introductory paragraph of text as accompaniment. We are rapidly approaching the critical point where the graphics overtake the meaning.

Michael Rock, "Since When Did *USA Today* Become the National Design Ideal?" *I.D.* (March/April 1992).

5    The rationale behind the accessibility movement is that information is easier to absorb in small pieces. Prodded along by marketing data, publishers and designers feel the need to compete with television and video for consumer attention. We have all heard that newspaper readership is down and that television has surpassed reading as the information source-of-choice for the majority of Americans. In response, publishers seem inclined to apply the TV info-tainment format to newspapers, and magazines. The logic is something along the lines of "TV is fast, vapid, and unbelievably successful. Publications should employ the same techniques as TV."

6    This perhaps makes sense in mass market magazines like *Entertainment Weekly* or *Spy* or even in corporate annual reports, where the message is not necessarily crucial; those products are not intended to challenge your intellect. When the same stylistic formats are applied to news-magazines, newspapers, and school books, the implication may be more troubling. The distinction between what is news, opinion, entertainment, and propaganda is blurry enough. The turn toward graphic oversimplification may make the boundaries even more obscure. U.S. Education Secretary T. H. Bell referred to this phenomenon as part of the "dumbing down" of American textbooks that removes all complex information in an attempt to capture the reader's attention. But if students are unable to read and to grasp complex subjects, is the problem in the book? Is simplifying the content to fit into "exciting" *USA Today* formats going to solve the problem?

## Designing Fictional Facts

7    Publications made for looking rather than for reading can suggest entire themes with carefully composed photographs or coded design forms that avoid the kind of supporting evidence demanded in expository writing. (Consider the photograph from *People* of November 1991 showing Clarence and Virginia Thomas curled up on their couch reading the Bible. How can you respond to that image? How can you reason against it?) These formats emphasize the incredible power of the art-directed image, buttressed by the decontextualized quotation, the boldface caption, the "scientific" diagram, and the brightly colored map. Charts and diagrams are certainly useful for offering general, relational explications of an issue but they necessarily shave away the ambiguous, nuanced, or obscure aspects of any idea. The information has been preprocessed, prechewed; it can only lead to one conclusion. And so the design of these pages controls the reading, siphoning off all complexity and presenting a slyly fictional "fact."

8    At the most fundamental level, the spread of the *USA Today* style represents a destruction of traditional narrative ideals. Narrative implies an author as well as a reader. The reader negotiates the process of the rational argument, checking any specific point against the entire premise. The credibility of the content is measured against the author's authority. The argument set forth is understood to be limited by the perspective inherently implied in the narrative voice. But images and charts seem to not imply an inherent point-of-view. They radiate a kind of false objectivity because the concept of the image-as-opinion is difficult for most people to grasp.

9    Cultural critics may see this shift toward the fragmented layout as an example of the continuing decline of textual authority, with the author's intention giving way to the reader's interpretation. They may praise this impulse. "Design becomes a provocation to the audience to construct meaning, consider new ideas, and reconsider preconceptions," says Cranbrook's Katherine McCoy. The philosophy of deconstruction may indeed serve as a tool to describe the original move toward fragmentation. But when the concept becomes codified and adopted as mainstream style, when the devices of mass culture adopt "deconstructed" typographic mannerisms, you can be sure it is not done to put greater interpretive power into the hands of the audience.

Fighting to grab one second from the harried, over-informed consumer, the makers of the mass media have concluded that messages must be instantaneous, offering about the same content level as a fifteen-second television commercial. (As Nigel Holmes puts it, "The dentist may well get through his first appointment sooner than you thought.") If a chart with a picture of Uncle Sam and a Russian bear on a seesaw balanced over an oil barrel can replace several paragraphs of text, all the better. No one has time to think about a rational argument; it takes too long, it's too boring. A sharp image and a few well-chosen words can produce the same idea without the nuances but with a kind of prefabricated logic.

11   Setting aside the more sinister interpretations of this trend, one could argue that it actually relates to basic shifts in the way typography and design are produced. The Macintosh opened up to designers a vast array of new graphic possibilities, giving them access to what is the equivalent of sophisticated typesetting terminals. Intricate settings, overlapping or run-around type, complex charts and graphs that were once too costly and time-consuming to design are now within the scope of even the smallest studio. Similarly, book and magazine publishers have greater digital composition possibilities and more four-color printing forms.

Or maybe the best explanation for the spread of *USA Today* look-alikes is that it is an inevitable extension of the LITE phenomenon. If beer or mayonnaise or individually wrapped slices of American cheese make you fat, then a) stop eating and drinking so much or b) remanufacture the products with fewer calories. We are more comfortable with the idea of changing our products than with changing our habits. Maybe publication design is under the same pressure. Maybe we want the "experience" of reading without all that heavy, annoying thinking. Maybe it's LITE design; it tastes great and it's less filling.

# Student Essay

Andrew Gaub experimented with several design features as he considered how to present his essay on the evolving design of the telephone. But after several drafts, he decided those features overpowered his compact text. Compare his final presentation with some of his experiments, which you examined earlier in the chapter. In what ways does his clean design contribute to his argument about effective communication?

# The Telephone Paradox

## ANDREW GAUB

1   The telephone is at once one of the most public and private communication devices in our culture. The three stages in its development as an object and as a network clarify this curious paradox. They also demonstrate how design can influence the behavior designated as public and private.

In the beginning, the telephone was a large wooden box, featuring a mouthpiece and an ear cup, that was operated by a crank handle. The box was placed in the most public room in the house—the central hall, the kitchen—and callers had to talk loudly into the mouthpiece to be heard at the other end of the line. And, inevitably, callers were overheard by anyone in the room or surrounding rooms.

3      Two features in the telephone's network also contributed to the public behavior associated with its use. The box was connected to the local switchboard operator, who could be counted on to supply information, pass on group gossip and, of course, connect local callers. Also, since most phones were hooked up on "party lines," they created a new form of entertainment—eavesdropping. Although callers intended to make "private" calls, other callers could listen in and even join in the conversation among people they did not know.

4      During the next stage in its development, the telephone emerged as a small, black, plastic console that cradled and was wired to a hand piece. Because callers could listen and speak into this hand piece, their conversations seemed more private. But soon this simple black phone was augmented by extension phones in various private rooms in the house. These customized phones, eventually designed in many shapes and colors, expressed the tastes of their individual users. Even "public phones" were designed to cater to privacy and individual taste. Phones were placed in a booth where doors could be closed, or positioned in special public spaces where soundproof panels protected individual conversations.

5      Revolutions in the design of the telephone network added to this promise of privacy. The local switchboard operator was replaced by automatic switching stations that enabled callers, first with a rotary dial and then with an electronic pad, to place their calls directly. And with the creation of a menu of country and area codes, callers could place these direct calls anywhere in the world. Similarly, the party line was replaced by the private line. But with the addition of extension phones, private conversations were often compromised by the possibility of someone listening in on one of the extensions. So, to guarantee privacy, families often invested in several private lines—one for the parents and one for each of the children.

6      In our time, the invention of the cell phone has liberated callers from the wires that tethered them to a room or a booth. The design of this compact device, smaller than a human hand, enables people to travel anywhere—by foot, by car, by plane—with their wireless phones strapped to their belts, stuffed in their purse, or, in the latest manifestation, swinging by a slight wire from their ear. This latest design enables callers to carry on their conversations with their hands free to multitask in many directions—parking their car, carrying their luggage, or checking their email.

7      The network for this telephone has also become wireless. Regional hubs connected by fiber optic cables and, more recently, satellites responding to high-frequency radio waves can transmit private voice messages or digital data from anywhere—an office, a restaurant, a golf course—to anywhere—the mall, the airport, the beach.

8      The difficulty with this latest development in private communication is that the efficiency of its design has, paradoxically, made calling behavior more public. Callers making calls on cell phones in public places often talk loudly enough so that anyone within ten to twenty feet can hear virtually every spoken word, making what appears to be a private call an annoying public event.

9      Finally, the telephone has become such an invisible part of our daily public and private behavior that we often forget the purpose of its design and development. The phone was designed for one person to communicate information to another person for a purpose. But if the phone has become simply a toy, where callers talk simultaneously to the person on another phone and anyone within hearing distance, one begins to wonder about the value of such communication. Indeed, one is reminded of the nineteenth-century writer Henry David Thoreau, who said in *Walden*, "We are in a great haste to construct a magnetic telegraph from Maine to Texas; but Maine and Texas, it may be, have nothing to communicate."

# Web Design

Students using *Writing with a Purpose* in a composition class were asked to design a website for Andrew Gaub's essay, "The Telephone Paradox." Now that you understand the basic elements and principles of design, answer the questions about the effectiveness of the two sites.

**Sample Homepage #1:**
**The Telephone Paradox**

1. How does running the text all the way across the screen make the design easier or harder to read?

2. How does placing the photos in the middle of the text interrupt or enhance your reading of the essay?

3. How does this layout deal with the source of the photos?

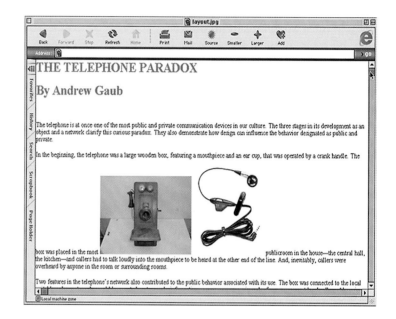

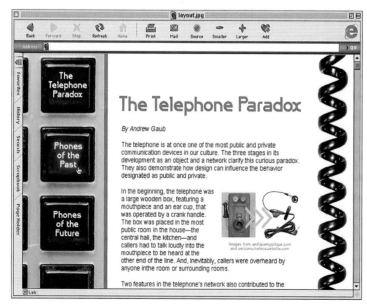

**Sample Homepage #2:**
**The Telephone Paradox**

1. Do the images for this layout decorate or demonstrate the ideas in Andrew's essay?

2. How does the alignment of graphics and text contribute to the readability of this design?

3. How would you characterize the colors in this design—unified, conflicting, or contrasting?

# Writing Assignments

### 1. NARRATE

Make a list of the things that you have tried to design—a poster, a room, a piece of clothing. Select an item to describe what you have learned about the successes and failures of the designing process.

### 2. OBSERVE

Examine your local or campus newspaper to determine whether it has been affected by what Michael Rock describes as the *USA Today* design ideal. Then write a letter to the editor using your information to compliment or criticize the paper's design.

### 3. INVESTIGATE

Conduct an opinion poll to determine how students in your class or on campus use cell phones. Write up your research and illustrate your findings with a compelling table or graph.

### 4. COLLABORATE

Work with the students in your writing group to draft a document describing the appropriate cell phone etiquette for your university's students and faculty.

### 5. READ

Browse the Design section of the stacks in your university library to locate two books that seem to take radically different approaches to design—Robin Williams's *The Non-Designer's Design Book* and David Carson's *The End of Print.* Then write a review explaining what the views of the two designers have in common.

### 6. RESPOND

In the end, design is a matter of personal taste. Select a design that appeals to you and one that appalls you from a magazine or the Web. Using the guidelines in this chapter, justify your personal choices.

### 7. ANALYZE

Analyze the type fonts in the various books on your bookshelf or in your book bag. Then explain why the fonts produce either a good match or a mismatch for the information they are trying to communicate.

### 8. EVALUATE

Evaluate the textbooks that you are reading in your current courses. Pay particular attention to the ways in which they use representational graphics. Use your research to classify the graphics that provide mere decoration or effective demonstration.

### 9. ARGUE

Take on Michael Rock. Argue that the *USA Today* design creates a visual style that enriches rather than diminishes the reading experience.

### 10. ARGUE

Make a case for the cell phone as the most essential communication tool in our culture. Consider such issues as mobility, accessibility, and safety.

# PART II

# *Writing Structures*

**Common Methods of Development** 6

**Argument** 7

**Paragraphs: Units of Development** 8

**Sentences: Patterns of Expression** 9

**Diction: The Choice of Words** 10

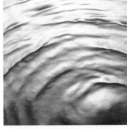

**Tone and Style** 11

# Common Methods of Development

In Part One you learned how working through the stages of the writing process enables you to discover your subject, audience, and purpose. You also learned how these discoveries suggest various structures for shaping your writing. Once Joanne Reinhardt decided to write about Mr. Bridgeman, she began telling a story about her "little revolt" in his Latin class. Once Ellen Haack decided to explain Barry's preoccupation with "what's good for me," she began to think of illustrative examples that would engage her audience. Once Sarah Penning decided to write about the "coupon conspiracy," she reformulated her purpose to demonstrate how advertisers use coupons to control what consumers buy. And once Andrew Gaub experimented with several decorative features for his essay on the telephone, he decided to clean up his mess and present his brief essay in a simple, uncluttered design. In each case, the method of development—the structure of the writing—emerged from the material the writer discovered in planning, drafting, revising, and designing.

In Part Two you will learn how and when to use various structures to express your ideas more effectively. Nonfiction writer John McPhee asserts that "everything in writing is a structure within a structure within a structure down to the simple sentence, which, of course, is also a structure" (personal interview). As you work your way through particular writing assignments, you need to decide whether to impose a structure on your information or look for a structure within your information.

McPhee explains that selecting a method (or methods) of developing his writing is probably the most important decision he makes, but one he can make only after immersing himself in the writing process:

> The structure of a piece of writing arises from within the material I have collected. When I go out to gather information on a subject, I am observing, asking questions, constantly scribbling notes. Then I go to the library, read, and make more notes. I end up with this great pile of miscellaneous notes that don't reveal their important relationships. It's at this point that I go over my notes again and again, looking for a couple of things that might illuminate each other. When I find them, I think, "Well, that makes sense. I could put these two things side by side." So I put them there. Once these two go together, gradually, slowly, the other segments work themselves out until I have a beginning, middle, and end. It's sort of the way the structure of some kind of mineral might get itself together. (Personal interview)

Like McPhee, you will uncover various patterns for developing your ideas throughout the writing process. In *planning,* these patterns often emerge as answers to the basic questions you might ask about any body of information: *What is it? How does it work? Why does it matter?* These questions are like the different lenses you attach to your camera: Each lens gives you a different picture of your subject. If you decide to write about women artists, for example, you might formulate a series of questions such as Why are comparatively few women ranked among the world's great artists? What historical forces may have discouraged women from becoming artists? Who is in charge of the "ranking" process, and how does it work? Do the ways women look at the world differ from the ways men look at it, and if so, what implications does this difference have for women's art and its reception? As you can see, each question not only shifts your perspective on your subject but also suggests a different method for developing your information about it.

*These patterns often emerge as answers to the basic questions you might ask about any body of information: What is it? How does it work? Why does it matter?*

If planning gives you the opportunity to envision your subject from a variety of perspectives, then *drafting* encourages you to develop the pattern (or patterns) that appears to you most effective for demonstrating your purpose. In some writing projects, a pattern may seem to emerge naturally from your planning. If you decide to write about your observation of a game of lacrosse, your choice seems obvious: to tell what happened. In attempting this, however, you may need to answer other questions about this unfamiliar sport: What do the field and equipment look like? How is it played? How is it similar to or different from other sports? Developing this new information may require you to develop new patterns that challenge your ability to advance your purpose without distorting your structure.

Logically, this judgment is best made during *revising*. As you look over your draft, you will need to make two decisions. First, you must decide whether individual segments or patterns of information develop or distort your original structure. The history of lacrosse—its creation by Iroquois Indians, its discovery by French explorers, and its development by Canadians—is an interesting body of information, but it may need to be reshaped, relocated, or even eliminated in revision to preserve the purpose of your original design: to tell what happened. Second, you must decide whether your original design, often mirroring the method by which you discovered the structure of your essay, is still the best method for presenting your information to your audience. Instead of using this organic structure, telling what happened, you may decide that you can best express your ideas by choosing a more formal structure, comparing lacrosse to games with which your readers are already familiar, such as soccer or hockey.

Finally, when you consider *designing*—creating a pattern to display your information—you will need to rethink the whole issue of structure. When Andrew started his essay on the telephone, he considered using all sorts of design elements—bullets, pull quotes, charts, and photographs—to illustrate his purpose. But once he tried to embed these features in his essay, he decided that the graphics overpowered the linear structure of his text. His essay required a more straightforward design. However, once he started thinking about his essay as a hypertext on the Web, he decided to include some design elements in his three-dimensional structure.

Whatever you decide, you need to understand each pattern's purpose, strategies, and effect if you are going to use it successfully to develop a paragraph, a section of your essay, or your whole essay. The remainder of this chapter presents and analyzes the most common methods of development, except for building arguments, which, because of its complexity, is given extended explanation in Chapter 7.

## Narration: What Happened?

*Narration* tells a story to make a point. It can be used in an anecdotal, abbreviated way to introduce or illustrate a complicated subject or in an extended way to provide a detailed, personal account of "what happened." An effective narrative has a *plot* —a meaningful and dramatic sequence of action—that may or may not follow the order in which events actually occurred and usually focuses on some tension or conflict within the writer, between the writer and others, or between the writer and the environment.

A narrative depends on pace to effect its purpose. *Pace* means the speed at which events are narrated. Sometimes you need to slow the pace to describe one aspect of an event in great detail; at other times several related events can be quickly summarized in a few sentences. By making such decisions about pace, you control the development of your narrative to dramatize its purpose for your readers.

A narrative requires the selection of a *point of view*, that is, establishing the person and position of the narrator. If you tell the story as "I" or "we," you are writing in the *first person;* if you recount what "he," "she," or "they" did, you are writing in the *third person*. In addition to identity, *person* refers to the attitude and personality of the narrator. *Position* is the narrator's closeness to the action in both space and time: The narrator may be a participant or an observer and may be telling the story as it happens, shortly thereafter, or much later.

In the following passage, Francine duPlessix Gray narrates a scene that illustrates what happens when tourists invade an animal habitat.

<table>
<tr><td>Introduces context and intended conflict.</td><td>Driving one evening through Amboseli, at the foot of Kilimanjaro, we see twenty-one minibuses gathered near a clearing to observe three cheetahs stalking. The first cheetah curtly moves through the thicket toward a small herd of impalas, occasionally twitching her ears as a signal for her companions to move on. There is an exaggerated stylishness about these animals' features—extravagantly long, elegant forelegs, outlandishly small, heavily marked faces. These most endangered animals of East Africa—champion runners but unskilled at camouflage, their temperament as open as the plains they frequent—seem only too willing to be movie stars, and cock their heads photogenically toward the tourists.</td></tr>
<tr><td>Climax of narrative produces reversal of action.</td><td>After we have watched them for several minutes the cheetahs have approached to about a hundred and fifty yards of their prey, coming close to the distance from which they make their famous sixty-mile-per-hour dash for the kill. But as they reach the critical moment minibuses start crashing about them; tourists lean on the open rooftops of their vehicles, cameras poised, and urge their drivers to get the closest possible view of the kill. Startled by the commotion, the impalas race about in circles and cough out their warning message, the baboons' terrierlike barking comes sloughing off the trees. The cheetahs must know better than we that they have lost their chance for dinner, but they go on stalking for a few minutes, as if to finish their pose. And then, amid the clicking of some fifty cameras, the head scout abruptly turns away from the impalas. The three cheetahs slink off into the plain. Their fragile rib cages seem terribly thin in the dusk, the black markings of their cheeks—like rivulets of black tears—seem to express their frustrated hunger.</td></tr>
<tr><td>Concludes by establishing point of narrative.</td><td>We are going to kill these animals with sentiment. Having slain and trapped wild creatures for food, domesticated them for our</td></tr>
</table>

amusement, and hunted them for sport, we are now decimating them by our fantasies of wilderness. How curious that photographic "shooting" is becoming deadlier to game than the ancient pastime of sport shooting. How regrettable that the tourists' most intrusive drivers tend to be Africans. The ancient code of hunting is past, a new etiquette of viewing has yet to be elaborated if the animals are to survive. I turn to Big Hunter, who, along with two other European drivers, respectfully kept his vehicle still during the cheetahs' attempted hunt. "Looking at game may become more dangerous to them than hunting," I say. "Worse than that," he remarks laconically, "it's so bloody rude to the animals."   (Francine duPlessix Gray, "On Safari")

Like Gray, Jane Graham wants to write about a journey to an animal habitat, her first whale watch. Although she was only at sea for a few hours, she was overwhelmed by events, information, and insights. She decides that one way to explore her ideas is to transcribe the sequence of events in a narrative.

1. How does Jane establish the position and attitude of the narrator?

2. What conflicts does she introduce to characterize her narrative?

3. How does the conclusion resolve conflicts and confirm the purpose of the narrative?

It was mist upon mist. The <u>Portuguese Princess</u> plowed out of Provincetown harbor toward Stellwagen Bank where the humpbacks had been feeding for several months. I was seated forward so that the gasoline fumes would not combine with the rolling swell to make me sick. Nothing was going to spoil this long-anticipated adventure. My insistence chased away the mist, and we chugged along in the hot sun for about an hour. Some people tried to talk above the sound of the engine: "I've watched all the Cousteau specials." "Have you seen the skeletons at the Museum of Natural History?" Others checked their camera lenses or scanned the horizon through binoculars. "Thar she blows!" yelled our tour guide. "Off the port bow. There!" I followed his finger, straining to see what he saw in the dark blue sea. Nothing. Then, suddenly, against the skyline, I saw it. A definite vertical spray. Then a pause. Then another. A whale. At last, a whale.

## EXERCISES

1. Freewrite in your journal about an experience in which you intruded on some group's privacy. How did you disrupt its behavior? How did you feel? What alternative did you consider before you intruded?

2. List the events that contributed to your achievement of a long-anticipated goal. Then draft a narrative in which you help your readers appreciate the conflicts, large and small, you had to overcome to reach your goal.

Who has invaded whose environment?

## Description: What Does It Look Like?

A WRITING PROJECT

Venture into a storm—
wind, rain, snow—and
describe how it feels to be
in an uncomfortable or
even hostile environment.

*Description* presents a verbal portrait of a person, place, or thing. It can be used to enrich other forms of writing or as a dominant strategy for developing a picture of a subject. A successful description does not depend solely on visual effects, however, but attempts to identify the subject's significant features by evoking all the senses. Impressions and observations are arranged in an appropriate pattern designed to capture both detail and wholeness. Specific, vivid detail makes your readers see what you see, and arranging those details in an appropriate sequence helps your readers understand why your subject is interesting and significant. Description is not merely a catalogue of facts or a collection of ornaments; like narration, it must make a point.

In the following passage from "The Courage of Turtles," Edward Hoagland describes the unique physical behavior of turtles

Evokes senses.

Arranges details in sequence.

Turtles cough, burp, whistle, grunt and hiss, and produce social judgments. They put their heads together amicably enough, but then one drives the other back with the suddenness of two dogs who have been conversing in tones too low for an onlooker to hear. They pee in fear when they're first caught, but exercise both pluck and optimism in trying to escape, walking for hundreds of yards within the confines of their pen, carrying the weight of that cumbersome box on legs which are cruelly positioned for walking. They don't feel that the contest is unfair; they keep plugging, rolling like sailorly souls—a bobbing, infirm gait, a brave, sea-legged momentum—stopping occasionally to study the lay of the land. For me, anyway, they manage to contain the rest of the animal world. They can stretch out their necks like a giraffe, or loom underwater like an apocryphal hippo. They browse on lettuce thrown on the water like a cow moose which is partly submerged. They have a penguin's alertness, combined with a build like a Brontosaurus when they rise up on tiptoe. Then they hunch and ponderously lunge like a grizzly going forward. (Edward Hoagland, "The Courage of Turtles")

Jane saw and photographed so many whales on her voyage that she has trouble sorting out her impressions. She decides that a description of a whale will concentrate and enrich her narrative. She describes the last whale she saw—the one that saw her.

How does she arrange details
to create a dominant
impression?

```
     The biologist hushed us. A finback, the world's
second largest whale, had been spotted swimming toward
the boat. He was way off course from the usual pattern
of his species. Finbacks are shy, solitary creatures,
and, because they are still hunted, usually stay clear
of boats. The boat, its engine cut, rolled on four-
foot swells. The smell of oil and gas hung in the air,
making my head ache and my throat tighten as I tried
to swallow. Soon, we saw him—a sea-green monolith,
silhouetted several feet beneath the water. His color
was uneven. The small distinguishing dorsal fin was
speckled with white and gray spots. He was silent. We
were silent. He swam purposefully toward the boat. Then
under. More silence. I crossed to the other side in
time to see his huge greenish head explode through the
surface. One watery eye looked back at me before he
arched his body and sounded. We did not see him again,
but we knew we had seen something rare.
```

## EXERCISES

1. Look up a description of some mythical beast—a dragon, griffin, or unicorn—in an encyclopedia. Then describe your own impressions of one of these beasts. You may want to describe the way such beasts have been portrayed in film.

2. Interview people who have extensive contacts with animals—veterinarians, zookeepers, park rangers. For them, what animal "contains the rest of the animal world"? How would they describe it?

# Process Analysis: How Do You Do It?

A *process* is a sequence of actions or changes that bring about a result. The development of the human embryo from conception to birth is one process; the procedure by which citizens of the United States elect the president is another. To *analyze* a process effectively, you must know it thoroughly or learn as much as you can about it, and then you must divide it into steps or stages. A careful division will help you see the best way to describe the process: Several small steps may be combined into one large step; certain steps may be suspended while others are completed; still other steps may require special emphasis so that they are not overlooked or reversed. After you have established an effective pattern of steps, you must explain each step, acknowledging how it connects to the next and what special knowledge or tools will be needed to complete it.

You must also make a careful assessment of your audience to determine whether you want to provide them with information about *how something works or happens* or to give them instructions on *how to do something.* In the first case, your readers may be interested in the stages and operation of a particular process even though they have no direct involvement in it. In the second case, they will want to know enough about the process so they can actually perform it.

In the following selection, humorist H. Allen Smith asks an expert, "Mr. Buttolph," to analyze the proper process for killing a wasp.

Introduces need for "campaign."

Describes "necessary" tools and strategies.

Analyzes steps—and advises additional steps.

"Don't ever think," Mr. Buttolph explained, "that you can handle a wasp the way you handle a fly. You've got to plan a campaign—figure out just exactly how you're going to proceed against him, and hope he doesn't get you while you're mapping your plans. Keep your eye on him, *but don't let him know you're looking at him.* Quietly assemble your equipment. A rubber fly swatter. Thick gloves. Put a hat on. Turn your shirt collar up and button it. Keep a ball peen hammer handy. Then go after him—but don't go directly at him. Sidle up to him. . . . Say something to throw him off guard, like 'Now, I wonder what I did with those glasses.' Watch him out of the corner of your eye, and if he starts to wiggle or flap his legs ease away from him, back off, and wait a while. Give him a chance to settle down. Go outdoors and practice with the rubber swatter. . . . [D]evelop your aim, because that's important. God help you if you ever swing at a wasp and miss him. Now, go back in and locate him again and see what sort of a mood he's in. If he's at ease, sidle up to him and when you're . . . certain that you've got the proper range, bust him one as hard as you can. If he falls to the floor, jump on him, stomp him—even then he may get up off the floor and stab you. Hit him with the hammer. Don't take your eye off him. No matter that he's lying there like a corpse. He may be playing possum. Get a newspaper and wrap him up in it and then set fire to it. After that it *may* be that he won't bother you again."

(H. Allen Smith, "How to Kill a Wasp")

One of the real dangers Jane faced when she went on the whale watch was her susceptibility to seasickness. She had been at sea enough and sick enough to qualify as an expert on the illness. In her draft, she composes a section in which she provides instructions about how to avoid the whale-watcher's curse.

1.  How does Jane establish the need for an effective procedure?

2.  What are the stages in the prevention process?

3.  What is the effect of not following the process?

A person who suffers from motion sickness and loves whale watching has a problem. Whales do not fit under microscopes. They must be watched at sea, atop rolling four-foot swells. I have solved this problem by developing a procedure to combat the sickness that attacks me when "I go down to the sea in boats." Several hours before boarding, I eat a mild meal: toast, tea, mashed potatoes. An hour later, I take two Dramamine tablets. Then, I dress warmly, knowing that I will not be able to go below when I get cold. When I board the ship, I stay away from the engine, which spews gas and oil fumes into the air. Once underway, I stand forward, always to windward, so that I can feel the cold, salty breeze on my face. When we finally encounter some whales, I try to avoid looking too quickly from whale to whale. Finally, on the way back to port, I avoid the green tourist who has not taken these precautions. The next "Thar she blows" might be her.

## EXERCISES

1.  Map the steps in a familiar process. Divide the process into major stages and then smaller steps. Consult with an expert to see if you have overlooked some hidden steps or failed to provide the appropriate cautions.

2.  Analyze a process that confuses, intimidates, or terrifies most people. Use your personal experience to demystify the process: "I did this and survived to tell the tale. So can you."

## Comparison: How Is It Similar or Different?

A WRITER'S WORDS

To be in relation to everything around us, above us, below us, earth, sky, bones, blood, flesh, is to see the world whole, even holy.

—Terry Tempest Williams, *The Erotic Landscape*

A *comparison* systematically analyzes and evaluates the similarities of two or more things. (A *contrast* is a comparison that emphasizes differences rather than similarities.) An effective comparison demonstrates one of three general purposes: (1) Two things thought to be different are shown to be quite similar; (2) two things thought to be similar are shown to be quite different; or (3) two things, although comparable, are shown to be not equal (that is, one is shown to be better than the other). To demonstrate one of these purposes, you will need to develop your comparison according to either the divided (A + B) pattern or the alternating (A/B + A/B) pattern.

## The Divided Pattern of Comparison: *A + B*

The *divided pattern,* the most common of the two strategies, divides the comparison into two sections, the first devoted to a discussion of *A* and the second to a discussion of *B.* Linking the examples in *A* to those in *B* —for example, by making three points about *A* and three similar points about *B* —unifies the two contrasting parts. The points should be in the same sequence and, where possible, paired points should be treated in the same amount of space. Although such exact pairings are not always necessary, in working out your purpose you should demonstrate that *A + B* are inextricably bound.

The two main parts of an *A + B* comparison should develop cumulatively. A simple description of two unlike houses, for example, becomes a contrast only when its thesis points out the significance of the differences. In some cases, as when one side of the contrast is so well known to readers that it need not be stated, the comparison is *implied.* If you are contrasting American football (*A*) with English rugby (*B*) for an American audience, the details of *A* are already in the mind of your audience and need only be mentioned in passing to explain the significant details of *B.*

From an interview with Richard, the marine biologist on the *Portuguese Princess,* and from her reading, Jane gathers information on two of the world's largest creatures—the diplodocus and the blue whale. Then she develops this information in a divided pattern that contrasts their enormous size with their gentle behavior.

Thesis contrasts perception with reality.

A. Diplodocus
1. Enormous size
2. Small brain
3. Gentle behavior
4. Eating habits

B. Blue whale
1. Enormous size
2. Large brain
3. Gentle behavior
4. Eating habits

The creatures that seem to threaten man most with their size and power have often been quite gentle. They have banded together to care for their young, to protect one another, and to provide each other with company. Consider the big, dumb diplodocus—his huge body laboring with a slow, steady drumbeat through the prehistoric forest. Although his body was enormous, his brain was small, so small that it did not generate enough power to control his weighty tail. He needed a separate ganglion to control that end of his body. His size promised danger, but Big D spent most of his day grazing harmlessly on vegetation with his pals. When a meat-eating enemy approached, he lumbered into knee-deep water and munched on a soggy plant.

Similarly, the blue whale, the largest creature ever to exist, is as gentle as a golden retriever. One hundred feet long, he glides soundlessly through the ocean, his enormous head concealing his fifteen-pound brain. Like Big D, Big Blue was once a pack animal, but his numbers have been so depleted by hunters that he is rarely seen alone, much less in groups. He feeds on

**How does the skeleton of "Big D" and the photograph of "Big Blue" support Jane's comparison and contrast?**

krill and other microscopic marine life. Instead of teeth, he has baleen, long strands that form a kind of sieve in his upper jaw. He sifts his food through this sieve by swimming, mouth open, through tons of water. When he closes his mouth, the water strains back through the baleen, and he swallows the remaining food in gigantic gulps.

## The Alternating Pattern of Comparison: *A/B + A/B*

The *alternating pattern* develops your material through matched pairs of *A* and *B*, expressed either in the same paragraph or in the same sentence. The divided pattern is perhaps easier to organize and control, particularly in short essays, but unless you connect the two subjects with a clear thesis, you may discover that you have written two separate essays. The alternating pattern requires you to organize your material more precisely than the divided pattern, especially in a longer essay, but the pattern is often more interesting and accessible for your reader because the point-by-point development can be written in balanced sentences that reinforce the comparison with every pair of matched details. Gretel Ehrlich uses the alternating pattern in the following passage to compare the romanticized conception (*A*) and the real character (*B*) of the American cowboy:

How does Ehrlich use the Marlboro man to introduce the two terms in her comparison?

How does she use parallel sentence structure to contrast A and B?

What does the comparison of cowboys with rocks contribute to her thesis?

> When I'm in New York but feeling lonely for Wyoming I look for the Marlboro ads in the subway. What I'm aching to see is horseflesh, the glint of a spur, a line of distant mountains, brimming creeks, and a reminder of the ranchers and cowboys I've ridden with for the last eight years. But the men I see in those posters with their stern, humorless looks remind me of no one I know here. In our hellbent earnestness to romanticize the cowboy we've ironically disesteemed his true character. If he's "strong and silent" it's because there's probably no one to talk to. If he "rides away into the sunset" it's because he's been on horseback since four in the morning moving cattle and he's trying . . . to get home to his family. If he's "a rugged individualist" he's also part of a team: ranch work is teamwork and even the glorified open-range cowboys of the 1880s rode up and down the Chisholm Trail in the company of twenty or thirty other riders. Instead of the macho, trigger-happy man our culture has perversely wanted him to be, the cowboy is more apt to be convivial, quirky, and softhearted. To be "tough" on a ranch has nothing to do with conquests and displays of power. More often than not, circumstances—like the colt he's riding or an unexpected blizzard—are overpowering him. It's not toughness but "toughing it out" that counts. In other words, this macho, cultural artifact the cowboy has become is simply a man who possesses resilience, patience, and an instinct for survival. "Cowboys are just like a pile of rocks—everything happens to them. They get climbed on, kicked, rained and snowed on, scuffed up by wind. Their job is 'just to take it,'" one old timer told me.
>
> (Gretel Ehrlich, *The Solace of Open Spaces*)

## EXERCISES

1. Speculate in your journal on some of the similarities you have observed between two apparently different activities—eating and sleeping, talking and listening, reading and running. Arrange the points of your comparison in a list and then freewrite about the specific advantages and disadvantages of presenting your information according to one of the two patterns.

2. Read through several popular magazines looking for common comparisons between people and animals: The lawyer is as sly as a fox, the doctor is as busy as a beaver, the tennis player moves like a gazelle, the two political candidates are in a real dogfight, and so on. Develop an extended comparison to show how the comparison to animals may elevate or demean the true character of the two subjects.

# Classification: What Kind of Subdivision Does It Contain?

*Classification* organizes information into groups and categories. An effective classification begins by defining a subject and then dividing it into major categories based on a common trait. The categories are then arranged in a sequence that shows that the division is *consistent* (the same principle is used to classify each category), *complete* (no major categories are omitted), and *significant* (categories and subcategories are arranged in an order that demonstrates some purpose).

Classification, like comparison, builds on your readers' expectations for precision, balance, and order. Call your readers' attention to the principle you have used to classify each category, or clearly imply it, and devote approximately the same amount of space to each category. Finally, arrange your categories and subpoints clearly and logically so that your reader is able to follow your system.

In the following excerpt Desmond Morris employs these strategies to establish three kinds of territories people define and defend:

**Establishes three kinds of territory.**

**Arranges categories in logical sequence (largest to smallest).**

A territory is defended space. In the broadest sense, there are three kinds of human territory: tribal, family and personal. . . .

First: the Tribal Territory. We evolved as tribal animals, living in comparatively small groups, probably of less than a hundred, and we existed like that for millions of years. It is our basic social unit, a group in which everyone knows everyone else. Essentially, the tribal territory consisted of a home base surrounded by extended hunting grounds. Any neighbouring tribe intruding on our social space would be repelled and driven away. As these early tribes swelled into agricultural super-tribes, and eventually into industrial nations, their territorial defence systems became increasingly elaborate. The tiny, ancient home base of the hunting tribe became the great capital city, the primitive war-paint became the flags, emblems, uniforms and regalia of the specialized military, and the war-chants became national anthems, marching songs and bugle calls. Territorial boundary-lines hardened into fixed borders, often conspicuously patrolled and punctuated with defensive structures—forts and lookout posts, checkpoints and great walls, and, today, customs barriers. . . .

Second: the Family Territory. Essentially, the family is a breeding unit and the family territory is a breeding ground. At the centre of this space, there is the nest—the bedroom—where, tucked up in bed, we feel at our most territorially secure. In a typical house the bedroom is upstairs, where a safe nest should be. This puts it farther away from the entrance hall, the area where contact is made, intermittently, with the outside world. The less private reception rooms, where intruders are allowed access, are the next line of defence. Beyond them, outside the walls of the building, there is often a symbolic remnant of the ancient feeding grounds—a garden. Its symbolism often extends to the plants and animals it contains, which cease to be nutritional and become merely decorative—flowers and pets. But like a true territorial space it has a conspicuously displayed boundary-line, the garden fence, wall, or railings. . . .

Third: the Personal Space. If a man enters a waiting-room and sits at one end of a long row of empty chairs, it is possible to predict where the next man to enter will seat himself. He will not sit next to the first man, nor will he sit at the far end, right away from him. He will choose a position about halfway between these two points. The next man to enter will take the largest gap left, and sit roughly in the middle of that, and so on, until eventually the latest newcomer will be forced to select a seat that places him right next to one of the already seated men. Similar patterns can be observed in cinemas, public urinals, aeroplanes, trains and buses. This is a reflection of the fact that we all carry with us, everywhere we go, a portable territory called Personal Space. If people move inside this space, we feel threatened. If they keep too far outside it, we feel rejected. (Desmond Morris, "Territorial Behaviour," *Manwatching*)

Presents the same kind of information to distinguish each territory.

Jane was fascinated by the many types of whales. The books she read emphasized their physical differences, and Richard, who had studied many individual whales, helped her understand their behavioral idiosyncrasies. During planning, Jane tries to combine her sources to classify whales according to their "personalities."

1. How does Jane attempt to establish the completeness of her classification?

2. How does she avoid the apparent contradiction in her system?

3. What is significant about the sequence in which she presents her categories?

```
Although there are over one hundred kinds of whales
in the world (and even more names to designate each
kind), most whales can be classified into three major
categories. The gregarious whales are outgoing,
curious, and friendly toward people. This category
includes extroverts, like the humpback, who have
baleen and feed off microscopic marine life, and acro-
bats, like the porpoises, who have teeth and eat small
fish. The aggressive whales are formidable, ornery,
and dangerous. This category includes killer whales,
who hunt in packs, stalking all sorts of marine life
from penguins to baby blue whales, and sperm whales,
who hunt alone, devouring such impressive prey as
octopi, and who have been known to ram ships. The shy
whales are solitary, enigmatic, and unpredictable.
This category includes whales like the finback, who
seem indifferent to other whales as well as to people,
and the blue whale, who has been hunted to near
extinction by those eager to kill the world's largest
creature.
```

1. Interview friends or family members about their behavior in certain types of territory—tribal, family, personal. What special techniques have they discovered for claiming and defending space with "signals rather than fists"?

2. Read about an established method for classifying information, such as categories for rating films or the procedure for naming plants. Then devise a principle that will enable you to simplify and streamline the system.

## Definition: How Would You Characterize It?

**A WRITER'S RESOURCES**

An excellent source on the environment is <http:www.enature.com>. eNature is a project of the National Wildlife Federation, the nation's largest conservation group. You may also want to check the websites for the Sierra Club, the Audubon Society, and *National Geographic*.

Definition provides a necessary explanation of a word or concept. The explanation may be a simple substitution of a familiar for an unfamiliar word, as when you substitute *cancer* for *carcinoma*. It may be the addition of a phrase, as when you follow *vintage* with "the yield of wine or grapes from a particular vineyard or district during one season." It may be a single sentence: "In the theater, a *prompter* is a person who provides cues for the actors or singers on stage." Or a definition may consist of one or more paragraphs, or even a whole essay, in which you explain your subject, such as *tradition* or *excellence*, in some depth.

Definitions may be short, stipulative, or extended. *Short* definitions, like the definition of *carcinoma, vintage,* and *prompter,* provide brief explanations similar to those in your dictionary. *Stipulative* definitions specify the exact meaning or sense of a word as you intend to use it in your writing. Some words may have favorable or unfavorable connotations, depending on the audience. In a political election, for example, a candidate, on being called *liberal,* might reply, "Yes, I am a liberal, but only in the true sense of the word. It originally meant *free,* and I believe in the freedom of individuals to think, speak, and act according to their consciences." The candidate is emphasizing one meaning and excluding others. Such definitions enable your readers to see the purpose of your words. The definition of *purpose* on page 15 is another example of a stipulative definition.

*Extended* definitions, usually long pieces of writing, explain a writer's view of a subject, sometimes using short or stipulative definitions but going far beyond both. The writer adds to, modifies, and illustrates the basic definition. Any pattern of development may be used: comparison of a word's synonym, for example, or an analysis of changes in its meaning. Cultural geographer Yi-Fu Tuan combines different strategies in his extended definition of *fear*.

*Introduces two short definitions to answer a question that prompts an extended definition.*

What is fear? It is a complex feeling of which two strains, alarm and anxiety, are clearly distinguishable. Alarm is triggered by an obtrusive event in the environment, and an animal's instinctive response is to combat it or run. Anxiety, on the other hand, is a diffuse sense of dread and presupposes an ability to anticipate. It commonly occurs when an animal is in a strange and disorienting milieu, separated from the supportive objects and figures of its home ground. Anxiety is a presentiment of danger when nothing in the immediate surroundings can be pinpointed as dangerous. The need for decisive action is checked by the lack of any specific circumventable threat.

Alarm and anxiety are exhibited in all higher animals. Human beings have much in common with other primates both in the causes of these sensations and in their subsequent behavioral response. Where humans differ from other species, the reason lies in their greater emotional range and superior mind.

Explains that fear depends on emotional capacity.

Emotional range is a gauge of the nervous system's complexity and hence, indirectly, of the mind. A jellyfish's repertoire of emotions is very limited compared with that of a complex animal like the rabbit, and the rabbit's range of feeling is narrow compared with that of a human being. An animal perhaps knows anger and sadness, but can it be wistful or melancholic? It shows alarm and signs of anxiety, but does it stand in dread of humiliation, of being shamed by its peers? A capacity for shame and guilt adds greatly to the scope of human fear. Can an animal living in its natural setting experience the macabre and the uncanny? Awareness of preternatural evil, unique to the human species, enables a person to see and live in phantasmagorical worlds of witches, ghosts, and monsters; these figures embody a weight of dread unknown to other animals. Fear of betrayal by a relative or friend is very different from fear of an enemy outside the familiar circle. Imagination adds immeasurably to the kinds and intensity of fear in the human world. (Yi-Fu Tuan, *Landscapes of Fear*)

Explains how imagination adds to the capacity to experience fear.

During Jane's whale-watching experience, she encountered many unusual words. She had heard some of them before (*breeching, spouting*) but did not appreciate their true significance until she saw the actions they identified. Others she heard for the first time on the *Portuguese Princess (krill, baleen)*, grasping their meaning as Richard explained them. But one term, *gam*, was used without explanation. In reviewing her notes, she found the word popped up again, prompting her to research and meditate on its meaning in the following definition:

1. How does the quotation from Melville add credibility to her definition?

2. How does she use substitution to clarify the meaning of the word?

When Herman Melville used the word <u>gam</u> in <u>Moby Dick</u>, he was certain he was the first writer to define it: "You might wear out your index finger running up and down the columns of dictionaries and never find the word." But he was equally certain that the word needed an official definition because it "has now for many years been in constant use among fifteen thousand trueborn Yankees" (Herman Melville, "The Gam," <u>Moby Dick</u>). Perhaps because of Melville, the word now appears in most dictionaries. <u>Gam</u>, like its equally unusual synonyms <u>pod</u> and <u>school</u>, refers to a herd of whales. By extension, <u>gam</u> refers to a meeting of two or more whaling ships at sea. Its precise origin is unknown, but some speculate that the word derives from <u>gammon</u>, a little-used word for talk or chatter. And that's what whales and whalers do when they <u>gam</u>. They socialize. Whales seem to enjoy each other's company as they feed. And whalers, once they meet at sea, stop the hunt, visit between ships, and settle down to food and conversation.

**3. How do her closing examples extend the definition?**

## EXERCISES

1. Select a common word, such as *stress,* that seems to have many subtle meanings. Freewrite a few simple definitions: "Stress is . . ." Next, try a few negative definitions: "Stress is not . . ." Then look up the word in a dictionary to determine its precise meaning.

2. Select an unusual word that puzzled you when you first heard or read it. Interview several "authorities" about what the word might mean. Check the word in several dictionaries (especially a historical dictionary such as the *Oxford English Dictionary*). Then prepare your own extended definition.

## Causal Analysis: Why Did It Happen?

*Causal analysis,* like process analysis, details a sequence of steps that produce a result. But rather than describing these steps, causal analysis examines them for *causes* and *effects*. Such an analysis can be developed in three ways: by describing an action or event and then demonstrating the effect, by describing an action or event and then determining its cause, or by examining two related actions or events and proving a cause-and-effect connection between them.

In each case, you must be careful not to exaggerate or oversimplify the cause-and-effect relationship. You may mistake coincidence for cause, or you may identify one cause as *the* direct cause when any number of complex causes (working independently or in combination) could have produced the same effect. In the following passage Alan Devoe analyzes the many causes of hibernation:

**Suggests possible causes:**

**1. cold**

**2. diminishing food supply**

**3. increased darkness**

**4. silence**

The season of hibernating begins quite early for some of the creatures of outdoors. It is not alone the cold which causes it; there are a multiplicity of other factors—diminishing food supply; increased darkness as the fall days shorten; silence—frequently decisive. Any or all of these may be the signal for entrance into the Long Sleep, depending upon the habits and make-up of the particular creature. Among the skunks, it is usually the coming of the cold that sends them, torpid, to their root-lined underground burrows; but many other mammals (for instance, ground squirrels) begin to grow drowsy when the fall sun is still warm on their furry backs and the food supply is not at all diminished. This ground-squirrel kind of hibernating, independent of the weather and the food supply, may be an old race habit, an instinctual behavior pattern like the unaccountable migrations of certain birds. Weather, food, inheritance, darkness—all of these obscurely play their parts in bringing on the annual subsidence into what one biologist has called "the little death." Investigation of the causes will need a good many years before they can be understood, for in captivity, where observation is more easy than in the wild, the hibernators often do not sleep at all.          (Alan Devoe, *Lives Around Us*)

Her first whale watch had a profound effect on Jane, and as she read more about whale watching, she realized that many other people had had similarly significant experiences. In fact, she speculates that whale watching has produced three important effects.

1. How does Jane account for the origin of whale watching?

2. What have been the three main effects of this popularity?

3. Why is the third effect potentially the most important?

```
        Since its inception over a decade ago, whale watching
has become a major industry. It began as a scientific
enterprise as marine biologists, concerned about
extinction, attempted to chart the feeding and migrat-
ing patterns of whales. The biologists soon became so
adept at sighting whales and so enthusiastic about what
they saw that they offered the experience to the
public, producing three significant effects. First,
whale watching has become an enormously popular recre-
ational experience. The exhilarating voyage out to sea,
the spectacular acrobatics of the whales, and the sen-
sation of seeing something extraordinary rivals the
best rides at Disneyland. Second, whale watching has
increased public awareness about preservation. Once
people have seen the power, grace, and agility of
whales, they can never again be indifferent to their
wholesale slaughter. Third, whale watching in America
has become so profitable that entrepreneurs are trying
to convince the nations that still hunt whales, such as
Japan and the Soviet Union, that there is more money to
be made in watching whales than in killing them.
```

## EXERCISES

1. Analyze the possible causes for one of your common problems, such as occasional insomnia or headaches. Read a general reference work, such as *The Columbia Medical Encyclopedia*, to identify some probable causes. Then interview others who are afflicted by the same problem to see how they explain its causes.

2. Speculate on the possible effects that some dramatic change might have on your life. For example, how would one of the following events affect your life?

   a. Purchasing an expensive camera
   b. Studying in another country (such as Kenya or New Zealand) for a semester
   c. Acquiring a new pet
   d. Working in a zoo

# EXploring methods of development on your computer

Use your subject as a prompt to explore various methods of discovering and arranging information in your draft. Begin with the question (What is it? How do you do it? Why did it happen?) that got you started, and develop your writing according to the method it suggests (definition, process analysis, causal analysis). Save this first draft, and then study it for questions your readers might have about various aspects of your subject (What does it look like? How is it similar or different? What kind of subdivision does it contain?). Mark the passages that prompt these questions. Then move down the screen and draft your answer to each question by using the appropriate pattern (description, comparison, classification). Insert each block of new information into the draft at the spot where you marked the question. Determine whether this additional text—or some revised version of it—helps or detours your readers. Another way to use this new material is to print all your answers, shuffle them, and then read them several times as different texts. If one of these answers seems to reshape the purpose of your essay, compose another draft, using the new method to develop a dominant plan for your essay.

Once you have drafted and revised your text, send a copy to your writing group or the members of your writing class. Ask them to investigate your subject with the questions described in this chapter. For example, they may encounter terms they want defined or effects they need analyzed. Indeed, they may discover a portion of your essay they would like to see developed into a completely new essay. Although you may not be able to accommodate all your readers' requests for new material or different structures, you will discover the substructures in your text that need reinforcement.

# Image Gallery

**Questions**

1. How do the tree rings illustrate John McPhee's observation that "structure" can emerge from within the material?

2. How does the framing of a house illustrate that structure is imposed upon material?

3. How do the two photographs document McPhee's assertion that "Everything . . . is a structure within a structure within a structure"?

# Readings

Reread John McPhee's comments on how he organizes his writing (page 129) then read this passage from *Coming into the Country.* As you read this selection, identify McPhee's predominant pattern and the way he employs other patterns to enhance his purpose. Which pattern seems to emerge naturally from the material? Which pattern seems to be imposed on the material?

# Grizzly

## JOHN MCPHEE

1 We passed first through stands of fireweed, and then over ground that was wine-red with the leaves of bearberries. There were curlewberries, too, which put a deep-purple stain on the hand. We kicked at some wolf scat, old as winter. It was woolly and white and filled with the hair of a snowshoe hare. Nearby was a rich inventory of caribou pellets and, in increasing quantity as we moved downhill, blueberries—an outspreading acreage of blueberries. Fedeler stopped walking. He touched my arm. He had in an instant become even more alert than he usually was, and obviously apprehensive. His gaze followed straight on down our intended course. What he saw there I saw now. It appeared to me to be a hill of fur. "Big boar grizzly," Fedeler said in a near-whisper. The bear was about a hundred steps away, in the blueberries, grazing. The head was down, the hump high. The immensity of muscle seemed to vibrate slowly—to expand and contract, with the grazing. Not berries alone but whole bushes were going into the bear. He was big for a barren-ground grizzly. The brown bears of Arctic Alaska (or grizzlies; they are no longer thought to be different) do not grow to the size they will reach on more ample diets elsewhere. The barren-ground grizzly will rarely grow larger than six hundred pounds.

2 "What if he got too close?" I said.

3 Fedeler said, "We'd be in real trouble."

4 "You can't outrun them," Hession said.

5 A grizzly, no slower than a racing horse, is about half again as fast as the fastest human being. Watching the great mound of weight in the blueberries, with a fifty-five-inch waist and a neck more than thirty inches around, I had difficulty imagining that he could move with such speed, but I believed it, and was without impulse to test the proposition. Fortunately, a light southerly wind was coming up the Salmon valley. On its way to us, it passed the bear. The wind was relieving, coming into our faces, for had it been moving the other way, the bear would not have been placidly grazing. There is an old adage that when a pine needle drops in the forest the eagle will see it fall; the deer will hear it when it hits the ground; the bear will smell it. If the boar grizzly were to catch our scent, he might stand on his hind legs, the better to try to see. Although he could hear well and had an extraordinary sense of smell, his eyesight was not much better than what was required to see a blueberry inches away. For this reason, a grizzly stands and squints, attempting to bring the middle distance into focus, and the gesture is often misunderstood as a sign of anger and forthcoming attack. If the bear were getting ready to attack, he would be on four feet, head low, ears cocked, the hair above his hump muscle standing on end. As if that message were not

John McPhee, *Coming into the Country.* (New York: Farrar, 1976), 58–65.

clear enough, he would also chop his jaws. His teeth would make a sound that would carry like the ringing of an axe.

6    One could predict, but not with certainty, what a grizzly would do. Odds were very great that one touch of man scent would cause him to stop his activity, pause in a moment of absorbed and alert curiosity, and then move, at a not undignified pace, in a direction other than the one from which the scent was coming. That is what would happen almost every time, but there was, to be sure, no guarantee. The forest Eskimos fear and revere the grizzly. They know that certain individual bears not only will fail to avoid a person who comes into their country but will approach and even stalk the trespasser. It is potentially inaccurate to extrapolate the behavior of any one bear from the behavior of most, since they are both intelligent and independent and will do what they choose to do according to mood, experience, whim. A grizzly that has ever been wounded by a bullet will not forget it, and will probably know that it was a human being who sent the bullet. At sight of a human, such a bear will be likely to charge. Grizzlies hide food sometimes—a caribou calf, say, under a pile of scraped-up moss—and a person the bear might otherwise ignore might suddenly not be ignored if the person were inadvertently to step into the line between the food cache and the bear. A sow grizzly with cubs, of course, will charge anything that suggests danger to the cubs, even if the cubs are nearly as big as she is. They stay with their mother two and a half years. . . .

"I'd like to hear less talk about animal rights and more talk about animal responsibilities."

7    If a wolf kills a caribou, and a grizzly comes along while the wolf is feeding on the kill, the wolf puts its tail between its legs and hurries away. A black bear will run from a grizzly, too. Grizzlies sometimes kill and eat black bears. The grizzly takes what he happens upon. He is an opportunistic eater. The predominance of the grizzly in his terrain is challenged by nothing but men and ravens. To frustrate ravens from stealing his food, he will lie down and sleep on top of a carcass, occasionally swatting the birds as if they were big black flies. He prefers a vegetable diet. He can pulp a moosehead with a single blow, but he is not lusting always to kill, and when he moves through his country he can be something munificent, going into copses of willow among unfleeing moose and their calves, touching nothing, letting it all breathe as before. He may, though, get the head of a cow moose

between his legs and rake her flanks with the five-inch knives that protrude from the ends of his paws. Opportunistic. He removes and eats her entrails. He likes porcupines, too, and when one turns and presents to him a pygal bouquet of quills, he will leap into the air, land on the other side, chuck the fretful porpentine beneath the chin, flip it over, and with a swift ventral incision, neatly remove its body from its skin, leaving something like a sea urchin behind him on the ground. He is nothing if not athletic. Before he dens, or just after he emerges, if his mountains are covered with snow he will climb to the brink of some impossible schuss, sit down on his butt, and shove off. Thirty-two, sixty-four, ninety-six feet per second, he plummets down the mountainside, spray snow flying to either side, as he approaches collision with boulders and trees. Just short of catastrophe, still going at bonecrushing speed, he flips to his feet and walks sedately onward as if his ride had not occurred.

8   His population density is thin on the Arctic barren ground. He needs for his forage at least fifty and perhaps a hundred square miles that are all his own—sixty-four thousand acres, his home range. Within it, he will move, typically, eight miles a summer day, doing his travelling through the twilight hours of the dead of night. To scratch his belly he walks over a tree—where forest exists. The tree bends beneath him as he passes. He forages in the morning, generally; and he rests a great deal, particularly after he eats. He rests fourteen hours a day. If he becomes hot in the sun, he lies down in a pool in the river. He sleeps on the tundra—restlessly tossing and turning, forever changing position. What he could be worrying about I cannot imagine.

His fur blends so well into the tundra colors   9 that sometimes it is hard to see him. Fortunately, we could see well enough the one in front of us, or we would have walked right to him. He caused a considerable revision of our travel plans. Not wholly prepared to follow the advice of Andy Russell, I asked Fedeler what one should do if a bear were to charge. He said, "Take off your pack and throw it into the bear's path, then crawl away, and hope the pack will distract the bear. But there is no good thing to do, really. It's just not a situation to be in."

# Student Essay

Jane Graham's final essay incorporates much of the writing she developed during planning and drafting. Read her essay and then review her experiments with various patterns throughout the chapter. What patterns has she reshaped, relocated, or eliminated during revising? Is the dominant structure of her essay the most effective method for accomplishing her purpose? Explain your answer.

# Watching Whales

## JANE GRAHAM

1   The problem with whales is that they don't fit under a microscope. As a small girl, I walked around and around the large skeleton of a blue whale on the first floor of the American Museum of Natural History, trying to compare its size to the skeletons of the brontosaurus and

diplodocus I had seen on the fourth floor. Like those creatures from another time, whales challenged and held my imagination. I could never see enough of them. The drawings in textbooks outlined their shape but reduced their enormous size to a few inches. The photographs in magazines suggested their magnificence but usually focused on their parts—the head rising to breech, the tail arching to dive. Last summer, hoping to see more, I booked passage on the *Portuguese Princess* out of Provincetown, Massachusetts, for my first whale watch.

2   A motley crowd assembled on MacMillan Pier in the early morning mist. Seasoned whale watchers checked their binoculars, cameras, and lens cases. Casual tourists chased after wayward children, counted their supply of Dramamine, and looked anxiously at the *Princess* as it creaked and groaned against its moorings. Various members of the crew, dressed in T-shirts and cutoffs, peered into the engine hole or studied the sighting charts stacked on the elevated table behind the wheel house. The haunting sounds of whale songs were piped through the mist by the boat's loud-speaker system. Soon, Richard, a marine biologist, dressed like the crew but wearing a Red Sox cap, walked out of the mist and jumped aboard. He checked the charts for a few minutes and then picked up a clipboard to call the seventy names on his new manifest.

3   I crossed the gangplank and took a position forward, away from the engine, knowing that the combination of gasoline fumes and rolling seas could make me sick. The engine sputtered to life, drowning out the whale songs and the nervous chatter of passengers. As the *Princess* plowed out of the harbor, I looked back to watch Provincetown disappear. The streets crowded with gawking summer people blurred, and the silhouette of the old fishing village—shacks resting on huge pilings, seagulls diving behind weathered boats—lingered briefly on the horizon.

"We're headed for Stellwagen Bank," Richard   4 announced from his perch behind the wheel house. "This is an area of shallow water and undersea crags that attracts microscopic marine life, plankton, and krill, the staple diet of many whales, especially the humpbacks. Humpbacks are baleen whales. They do not hunt, kill, and devour. Instead of teeth, they have baleen, long strands of tissue that hang from their upper jaws. They sift their food through this tissue by swimming, mouth open, through tons of water. When they close their mouths, the water strains back through the baleen, and they swallow the remaining food in gigantic gulps."

The mist had cleared, the sun burned my   5 neck, and a cold, salty spray occasionally splashed my face as the *Princess* headed into the wind for the next half hour. The passengers talked, gestured, and looked for signs. "I've watched all the Cousteau specials," a New Hampshire bride was telling me when Richard yelled, "Thar she blows! Off the port bow! There!" We followed his finger, focusing binoculars, twisting telephoto lenses, straining to see what he had seen in the dark blue swells. Against the skyline, I saw it. A definite vertical spray. Then a pause. Then another.

I was actually seeing two sprays, one from   6 each of the whale's spouts or nostrils. Whales are mammals and so, like us, cannot breathe under water. They store air in their lungs before they dive and then blow it out their spouts when they surface. This whale was diving and blowing steadily, heading away from Stellwagen Bank. Richard tried to identify its flukes, the large flippers at the end of its tail. The patterns and notches on a whale's flukes are like fingerprints, enabling expert whale watchers to identify individual whales. But this whale, swimming intently toward some destination, was too far away for even Richard to see its colors.

The *Princess* churned on for another thirty   7 minutes. Suddenly, the captain killed the engine.

"We're here." And so were they. As we drifted, several sets of feeding humpbacks swam into view. A mother, her calf beside her, dived, surfaced, and waved her flukes in a perfect vertical before diving again. Her calf, eager to imitate, tried the same maneuver over and over, but his tail and flukes flopped sideways at the last minute like a sloppy cartwheel. At our stern, an obstreperous male leaped totally out of the water and then fell sideways with an impressive clap. I could see his huge, vulnerable underbelly and the white undersides of his long flippers. When he burst out of the water, he held his flippers at a slight angle to his side. As he descended, he moved them gracefully away from his body like the arms of a ballerina finishing a pirouette.

8     After an hour of dashing around the deck, elbowing my way to the rail, and snapping pictures of everything I could see, I thought I had seen enough. Other excursion boats and private craft had slowly encircled the feeding whales. Shortwave radios crackled: "Look to the west. A male is breeching." "Over to the south. Two bachelors are gamming." "In the center. The mother and calf are resting." The noise prompted thoughts of other messages delivered on distant seas: "Finback, south, southwest. Lower the boats. Aim the harpoon." Richard had apparently seen enough as well. The engine erupted, and the *Princess* began to turn. I looked forward, trying to sort it all out—the graceful, powerful gentleness of the whales; the curious, careless intrusiveness of the whale watchers. Why couldn't we simply watch? Why did people have to hunt, kill, and destroy?

9     The engine stopped. Richard's voice came over the loud-speaker in an excited, controlled whisper. "There's a finback heading toward us. He's way off course. Finbacks are shy and solitary. They're still hunted and so usually stay clear of boats. If we're quiet, we may see something rare." Seventy watchers became still. The *Princess* rolled on four-foot swells. Soon we saw him—a sea-green monolith, his huge bulk silhouetted several feet beneath the surface. His distinguishing fin was mottled in patterns of white and gray. He was swimming purposefully toward us. We were obviously in his path, but not in his way. He was silent. We were silent. Closer, closer, and then under. More silence. I rushed to the other side. His green head exploded through the surface twenty feet away. One large, watery eye looked back at me before he arched his body into the sea. He swam in a straight line for a couple of hundred yards, blew, and then sounded.

10    Although we watched eagerly for him to surface again, we looked in vain. Soon we began to look at one another. We smiled, but we did not talk. Neither did Richard. No explanation was necessary. We had watched a whale. A whale had watched us. Finally, the engine coughed, and the *Portuguese Princess* resumed her journey back to Provincetown.

# web Design

Students using *Writing with a Purpose* in a composition class were asked to design a website for Jane Graham's essay, "Watching Whales." Consult the elements and principles of design in Chapter 5 to help you answer the questions about the effectiveness of each site.

## Sample Homepage #1: Whale Watching

▶ What do the graphics contribute to your understanding of the subject of this site?

▶ Why do the background and text color make this site difficult to read?

▶ Why does the text at the bottom of this site limit your understanding of the purpose of the site?

## Sample Homepage #2: Whale Watching

▶ How do the typeface of the heading and the single pair of binoculars clarify the subject of this site?

▶ How does the use of white space for a background color make this site easier to read than the first?

▶ How does the alignment of the three graphics clarify the purpose of this site?

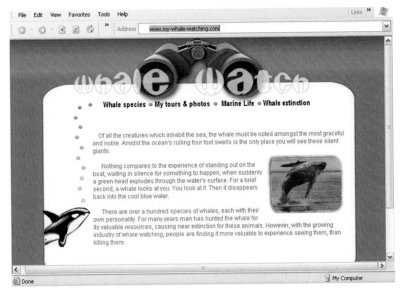

# Writing Assignments

### 1. NARRATE

Freewrite in your journal about your memories of a specific animal that you remember from books (*Curious George*), films (*Seabiscuit*), or television ("The Muppets"). List features that encouraged you to identify with the animal. Then write a narrative that records your adventures with this imaginary companion.

### 2. OBSERVE

Check the categories (and links) listed on conservation websites (e.g., the Audubon Society, the Orion Society, or the Sierra Club). Observe how each organization describes a hot topic such as *habitat* or *species loss.* Then write an opinion piece for your local paper in which you describe how such information enables your community to "think globally and act locally."

### 3. INVESTIGATE

Interview faculty and students who work with laboratory animals. You may want to contrast those who simply observe animal responses with those who dissect animals. Develop your interview notes into a profile that documents the use of laboratory animals on your campus.

### 4. COLLABORATE

Most universities have a formal policy governing the use of animals in laboratory experiments. Your writing group has been asked to revise that policy. Read the policy carefully; then ask members of your group to conduct more interviews (with faculty researchers and animal rights advocates) and to read more documents (policies from other research institutions and criticism from activists like Peter Singer). Then revise or defend your university's policy.

### 5. READ

Read some articles and books on the history (and philosophy) of zoos (e.g., H. Hediger, *Man and Animal in the Zoo,* or Virginia McKenna et al., eds., *Beyond the Bars*). Visit a zoo in your area. Talk to attendants and visitors. Finally, write an analysis, based on personal experience and historical documentation, that speculates on the causes and effects of zoos in our culture.

### 6. RESPOND

Read Peter Singer's analysis of the "process that provides people with their meat" in *Animal Liberation.* You may want to interview ranchers who raise cattle or doctors who recommend vegetarian diets. In either case, you are looking for information that will help you understand your response toward eating meat.

### 7. ANALYZE

Analyze the way Jane Graham expands, contrasts, or relocates her experiments with the common patterns of development in her essay. Jane's essay seems to be driven by a narrative question: What happened? What other questions emerge as the result of her attempt to tell what happened? How do those questions affect Jane's overall purpose? You may want to alter this assignment by using one of Jane's experiments as a prompt to write a longer essay of your own.

### 8. EVALUATE

Compare and contrast the attitudes expressed by Jane Graham and Francine duPlessix Gray toward animal watching. What motivates each of them to watch? Why does Gray (and her guide) object to the watching? Why does Jane (and her guide) savor it? Evaluate each writer's perspective in relation to that of the other or write an essay suggesting a third.

### 9. ARGUE

Compare John McPhee's comments on structure (p. 129) and his commentary on the grizzly bear. Then argue that McPhee's comments do or do not help explain the method(s) of development he uses in the selection.

### 10. ARGUE

Using the information gathered from your reading or experience, argue for or against a "wilderness ethic" that forbids people from studying, managing, and altering the behavior of animals.

# 7 Argument

IN A TRUE CONTROVERSY, THE DEBATE IS TAKING
PLACE ON SO MANY LEVELS—EMOTIONAL, ETHICAL,
SOCIAL—I CAN'T CHOOSE SIDES. I SWITCH BACK AND
FORTH AND USUALLY WIND UP SOMEWHERE IN THE
MIDDLE.

—ANNA QUINDLEN

Argument, in a sense, underlies all writing. In expressing your ideas, no matter what method or combination of methods you use, you are "arguing" some point about your subject. In Chapter 6, for example, each of Jane Graham's writing ventures attempts to demonstrate a certain thesis: Whales can be understood best when seen at sea; whales may seem threatening but are really gentle; whale watching has helped increase public support for whale preservation. Jane uses these informal arguments to advance her primary purpose—explaining her impressions of a whale watch.

Formal arguments, too, commonly employ expository patterns to convey information. But because their primary purpose is to convince others—to accept a proposal, to challenge a situation, to support some cause—formal arguments must be developed according to rules of evidence and logical reasoning. These demands may seem formidable, but in many ways they are simply extensions of what you have learned about those elements that govern the writing process.

You begin composing an argument by planning, by investigating a variety of sources so that you can discover a subject. Next, you organize your argument into a draft so that it most effectively and fully expresses your subject to persuade your audience. Then you examine your text to revise those features that obscure the clarity or weaken the credibility of your purpose. Finally, you

Public discourse requires *making* an argument for a point of view, not *having* an argument—as in having a fight.

—Deborah Tannen,
*The Argument Culture: Moving from Debate to Dialogue.*

create an appealing design for your text so that it catches your readers' attention and persuades them to take a careful look at your argument.

As you move through these stages, you will expand your appreciation of other arguments (particularly those of the opposition), develop your authority to present those features of your argument that matter most, and increase your understanding of those aspects of your argument or your opponent's argument that might be negotiated or that might never be resolved.

## Planning: Investigating the Argument

In planning an argument, you *select a subject, collect and use evidence,* and *consider the opposition.*

### Selecting a Subject

Not every subject can be treated in a formal argument. Common sense tells you that there is no point in arguing about *facts.* You may like to argue about when the Red Sox last won the World Series or how many times Katharine Hepburn has won an Oscar, but such trivial disputes can be settled quickly by looking up the correct answer in an almanac. You may like to argue that chocolate chocolate chip is the best flavor of ice cream in the world or that all politicians are corrupt—but these assertions are merely *opinions,* based on preference (or prejudice) rather than evidence.

*A formal argument must focus on a subject that can be debated.* Such subjects are open to interpretation because opposing opinions can be supported with evidence, and the audience is free to consider both claims and to choose sides.

*What you know about a subject (or what you can find out about it) will lead you to take a side. But to convince your readers that yours is the right side (or at least the better side), you will need to support your position.*

As you think about possible subjects for an argument, review "Guidelines for Selecting Your Subject" in Chapter 1. Your subject should be one you know something about, consider interesting and significant, and can restrict to a manageable size. When you develop your subject into an argument, you will need to view it as a controversy with at least two contending sides. What you know about a subject (or what you can find out about it) will lead you to take a side. But to convince your readers that yours is the right side (or at least the better side), you will need to support your position.

Jon Seidel is enrolled in an advanced journalism course that involves much discussion of First Amendment rights. While doing some preliminary research, he discovers a major controversy about freedom of the press and national security. Read his list of potential subjects and identify those that are a) facts, b) opinions, and c) open to debate.

1. All journalists who cover the military endanger our troops.

2. Almost half of the Americans surveyed believe that the press has been too aggressive in covering the war on terrorism.

3. The military's control of information about its operations results in a public that is ignorant of them.

4. Interviewing soldiers in combat is illegal.

5. Competition among news networks results in hasty reporting and the presentation of inaccurate news.

## Collecting and Using Evidence

Once you have selected a subject, start gathering evidence. You might begin by making lists or freewriting in your journal. Such activities help you identify what you already know (or think you know) about your subject, but eventually you will need to expand and deepen your knowledge by conducting some research. Anna Quindlen, a novelist and *Newsweek* columnist, suggests that an effective investigation requires several planning strategies:

> I begin by reading, reading, reading. I have to understand my subject before I interview people, otherwise I won't understand the terms they use or the issues they raise. Also, I have to understand where they're coming from. You need to watch out for those red flags, those people on one side of an argument who distort issues by making highly inflammatory statements. Sometimes you can catch their bias when you ask other people to comment on their remarks. So much of reporting is bouncing from one person to another, trying to get all sides of the story. You never get it all. You simply run out of time. (Personal interview)

Whatever planning strategy you use, follow Quindlen's advice and collect information from all sides of the issue, not just your side. The most common kinds of evidence are *facts, judgments,* and *testimony.*

**Facts**   Facts are a valuable ally in building an argument because they cannot be debated. It is a fact that the stock market crashed on October 29, 1929. It is a fact that at the close of the week following September 11, 2001, the Dow Jones Industrial Average fell 1,370 points. But not all facts are so clear-cut, and some statements that look like facts may

● A WRITER'S RESOURCES

For information on First
Amendment controversies,
check the website for the
American Civil Liberties
Union. For information
about censorship of the
media, check the websites
for the Society of Professional Journalists and the
Canadian Association of
Journalists.

not be facts. A stock analyst who announces a company's projected earnings for the next five years is making an estimate, not a statement of fact.

**Judgments**  Judgments are conclusions inferred from facts. Unlike opinions, judgments lend credibility to an argument because they result from careful reasoning. A doctor considering a patient's symptoms reaches a tentative diagnosis of either tuberculosis or a tumor. If a laboratory test eliminates tuberculosis, then the patient probably has a tumor that is either malignant or benign, questions that can be settled by surgery. The doctor's judgment emerges from the following chain of reasoning:

1. *The patient's symptoms are caused by tuberculosis or a tumor.*
   This diagnosis is based on knowledge of the symptoms of or facts about the two conditions.

2. *The patient does not have tuberculosis.*
   This is a judgment based on the results of a laboratory test that produces certain factual information.

3. *The patient has a tumor.*
   This judgment is inferred from the facts of statements 1 and 2.

4. *The patient does not have cancer.*
   This judgment is determined after surgery, which reveals the fact that the tumor is benign.

**Testimony**  Testimony affirms or asserts facts. A person who has had direct experience (an *eyewitness*) or who has developed expertise in a subject (an *expert witness*) can provide testimony based on fact, judgment, or both. An eyewitness is asked to report facts, as when an observer reports seeing a man drown in strong current. An expert witness is asked to study facts and render a judgment, as when a coroner reports that an autopsy has shown that the victim did not drown but died of a heart attack.

Both kinds of testimony can constitute powerful evidence. Eyewitness testimony provides authenticity. Expert testimony provides authority. Each has its limitations, however. An eyewitness is not always trustworthy; eyewitness testimony can be distorted by faulty observation or biased opinion. An expert witness is not infallible or always unbiased; expert testimony, though often difficult for the nonexpert to challenge, can be disputed by other experts employing a different method of investigation. Each type of testimony can be abused. An eyewitness account of an event may be convincing, but it should not be used to draw parallels to unrelated events. And expert credentials in one field, whatever eminence they convey, do not automatically carry over to other (even related) fields.

**Using the Evidence**   Evaluate your evidence by determining whether it is *pertinent, verifiable,* and *reliable.* A stock analyst who uses the success of the polio vaccine as a reason for investing in a drug company researching a vaccine for the common cold is not presenting evidence *pertinent* to the argument. A historian who claims that Amelia Earhart's flying ability was impaired by Alzheimer's disease is using an argument that is not *verifiable.* And an attorney who builds a case on the eyewitness testimony of a person who has been arrested several times for public intoxication is not using the most *reliable* evidence (see "Evaluating Sources," in Chapter 12).

As you collect your evidence, be careful to identify and record its source. Your readers will want to know where you found the information important to your argument. If you cannot identify your source, your reader may question your knowledgeability. If your information comes from dubious sources, your readers may doubt your credibility. Identify information from printed and other sources in the text of your paper (see "Documenting Sources," in Chapter 13).

## EXERCISES

Jon has decided to write about the conflict between the military and the media over how to cover military operations during a time of national crisis. He gathered information from many sources. Examine the following items from his notes and determine 1) whether each is a **fact,** a **judgment,** or an **eyewitness** or **expert testimony.** Then determine 2) whether each is likely to be **pertinent, verifiable,** and **reliable** evidence.

1. "A survey of some 2,000 officers and 350 journalists found that 6 of 10 officers said their leaders could lie to the press in order to deceive the enemy. Not surprisingly, 9 of 10 journalists thought that was unacceptable." Wood, David. "Pentagon to Begin Training War Correspondents." Newhouse News Service, 2002.

2. "The military tends to be secretive. The media [tends] to be intrusive. . . . The media [are] liberal. The military is usually conservative." Lt. General Bernard Trainor, former director of the National Security Program at Harvard University. Qtd. in "Journalists Debate Role in Terror War." *Yale Daily News* 6 December 2002.

3. "The reporter on the news last night was wearing an American flag on his lapel. I doubt anything he had to say about the war in Afghanistan was free from the bias of American propaganda." Warren, Charles. Personal Interview. 6 March 2002.

4. "Fewer than 30 reporters landed with the troops on the beaches of Normandy on D-Day. In contrast, more than 1,600 journalists showed up to cover Desert Storm." Wood, David. "Pentagon to Begin Training War Correspondents." Newhouse News Service, 2002.

5. "Acceptance of these ground rules is an agreement between you and the granting commands. You agree to follow the ground rules and the command will provide support, access to military members, information and other privileges. Violation of ground rules, however, may result in the revocation of your credentials." "Ground Rules Agreement." Qtd. in Vernon, Mike. "The War We Couldn't Report." Canadian Broadcasting Corporation, 13 August 2002.

**How does this photo-graph support the media's criticism of how the military provided information about the Gulf War?**

## Considering the Opposition

If you have selected a debatable subject and collected a broad range of evidence, you have discovered that controversies are tricky. You may remain convinced that your side is the right side; you may be tempted, given your discovery of new information, to change sides; or you may feel confused as you try to balance the evidence on both sides of the debate. To complete your investigation and test your original position (or to write your way out of your current confusion), you must give serious consideration to the opposition.

Assume the identity of your opposition and draft an argument enti-tled "Their Side." This planning exercise will enable you to understand the important evidence that makes your opponents' position credible— evidence that you may have to concede when you present your side of the argument. The exercise will also help you to uncover the weak spots in their argument—points that you will have to disguise when you write "Their Side," but points that you can dispute when you write "My Side." And finally, this exercise will encourage you to identify the points, often overlooked in the heat of argument, on which both sides agree.

If you are going to compose an effective "Their Side," you have to be *knowledgeable* and *fair*. You must present your opponents' best argument in such a way that they would recognize it as a thorough and accurate statement of their position. If you set up a "straw man," presenting your opponents' weakest evidence in the most unfavorable light with the intention of knocking it down, the exercise will not be useful to you. Knowledge of your opponents' best arguments and a sincere effort to avoid bias will help you avoid an unfair, unproductive effort. Common signs of such unfairness are *distortion, slanting,* and *quoting out of context.*

**Distortion**   You distort your evidence if you intentionally exaggerate your opponents' views. Councilwoman Jones supports Planned Parenthood because the agency provides valuable information on birth control. Councilman Smith distorts his opponent's position by claiming that support for Planned Parenthood is an endorsement of an extreme form of birth control, such as abortion.

**Slanting**   If you select facts favorable to your position and suppress those unfavorable to it, you are slanting the evidence. A business executive who says there can be no real poverty in a country where the average annual income is $30,000 ignores two facts: (1) the average includes incomes of $1 million or more, and (2) a great many incomes fall far below the average.

**Quoting Out of Context**   If you remove words deliberately (or carelessly) from their original context and reuse them in a new context that changes their meaning, you are quoting out of context. In reviewing a play, a critic writes: "The plot is fascinating in a strange way: You keep waiting for something to happen, but nothing does. The characters never come close to greatness, and the few witty lines are out of place among the predictable dialogue." An advertisement based on this review quotes out of context if it reads: "Fascinating plot . . . characters close to greatness . . . witty lines."

---

## Exercises

When Jon began his investigation, he was opposed to any form of military censorship. But as he collected more research on the historical relationship between the military and the media and considered the consequences of hasty or inaccurate reporting, he tried to assess the military's point of view by drafting a "Their Side" argument. After reading Jon's analysis, discuss whether the military would see Jon's presentation of its position as knowledgeable and fair. Answer these questions: 1) What types of evidence does he present? 2) Does this evidence seem to be the best evidence— most *pertinent, verifiable,* and *reliable*? 3) In what sections of this essay might Jon be accused of misrepresenting the opposition's major argument?

Imagine the following: Your brother enlists in the army to fight the war on terrorism. While traveling to the site of his first military operation, his unit is ambushed and he is killed. Later you learn that the press had discovered the details of the mission and published them several days before the operation began. The enemy read the story and then plotted its ambush. Whom do you blame for your brother's death—the army that sent him on the mission, the enemy who killed him, or the press that leaked the story?

This scenario illustrates the tension that exists between the media and the military. The Constitution protects the freedom of the press, but the military protects the Constitution and the freedoms it guarantees. In a time of national crisis, who sits at the head of the table? One answer plays itself out in our example. Such tragedies are now possible and are likely to increase the more the press insists on its freedom to obtain and publish information about military operations. Another answer seems more reasonable: In times of national crisis, freedom of the press must defer to national security.

When the framers of the Constitution drafted the Bill of Rights, their intention was to protect the people from a despotic government. Freedom of the press would enable an "objective" source to keep the government in check by informing the people about its policies and procedures free from the spin of propaganda. Although this is still the press's job, the definition of the press has changed dramatically in the last fifty years. It now includes multiple news channels and thousands of websites, all thirsty for instant and constant information. This information travels so fast that it is rarely checked for accuracy or discussed in terms of its potential consequences. Thus, it puts all sorts of damaging news in the hands of both friends and foe.

Some argue for a return to the systems of World War II and Vietnam in which the press was put in uniform and allowed to travel with the military and report from the front lines. But as David Wood points out, the size of the press has increased exponentially since World War II: "Fewer than 30 reporters landed with the troops on the beaches of Normandy on D-Day. In contrast, more than 1,600 journalists showed up to cover Desert Storm." And the nature of reporting has changed since Vietnam: The critical coverage of that controversial war created "mistrust and misunderstanding between the military and the news media."

The military protects the ability of the press to operate. In return, the press should protect the ability of the military to operate. Freedom of the press is not, and has never been, as important as our country's survival. Indeed, the incessant, intrusive behavior of the press in recent years seems a national disgrace. A recent survey of the "state of the First Amendment" reveals that almost half of the American population thinks the press has been too aggressive in asking government officials for information about the war on terrorism.

Indeed, the war on terrorism is a new kind of war. As James W. Carey, journalism professor at Columbia University, explains, "World War II was unambiguous. The Nazis were obviously the danger. This whole thing is shrouded in vagueness. Who are we fighting? Is this a real threat? How much of a threat is it?" (qtd. in Barton). Thus, Peter Clark, senior scholar at the Poynster Institute for Media Studies, suggests that this new kind of war will require "a new kind of behavior from the press" (qtd. in Barton). An unfettered press that demands daily, detailed information about military operations will likely endanger our national security and lead to the deaths of many of our brothers and sisters.

Works Cited

Barton, Gina. "Patriotism and the News." Society of
    Professional Journalists. 3 March 2002.

"New 2002 'State of the First Amendment' Survey."
    Freedom Forum. 29 August 2002.

Wood, David. "Pentagon to Begin Training War
    Correspondents." Newhouse New Service, 2002.

*"And this one is for being wounded by the media."*

# Drafting: Organizing the Argument

Once you have completed your preliminary investigation, you need to develop, organize, and draft your argument, following the procedures you learned in Chapters 3, 4, and 5. Anna Quindlen points out that organizing an effective argument is terribly important and terribly difficult:

> Structure is a slippery subject. I usually like to lead with an anecdote, particularly if I can use a quote that works like a punch in the stomach. Also, up front, in what I call my *nut paragraph,* I like to spell out the issues I've discovered. "Where are we going? Where have we been? Have we gone too far?" Then I'll get into an "on the one hand, on the other hand" pattern where I present the sides in the debate. But in a true controversy, the debate is taking place on so many levels—emotional, ethical, social—that I can't choose sides. I switch back and forth and usually wind up somewhere in the middle.
> (Personal interview)

The final shape of an argument depends, as Quindlen suggests, on a series of interrelated decisions. To make *informed* decisions, you need to *analyze the audience, arrange the evidence,* and *monitor the appeals.*

## Analyzing the Audience

In the preceding chapters you learned that knowing your audience helps you discover and demonstrate your purpose. This is particularly true in argument because you are attempting to convince your audience to believe in your purpose. To do this, you must assess what potential audiences are likely to know about your subject, what they believe is important in the controversy, and what kind of evidence will influence their judgment.

As Quindlen points out, arguments take place in a context that contains "many levels—emotional, ethical, social." To help you clarify this context and to sort out how your readers might be affected by it, use the advice that follows in conjunction with "Guidelines for Analyzing Your Audience" in Chapter 1 (page 15).

**Identify Specific Readers**  You need to identify the specific groups of readers who form the potential audience for your argument. Some may seem in the thick of things—friendly or hostile to your position. Others may seem on the edge—skeptical about any proposal or merely uncommitted. Unfortunately, the sides in controversies are rarely that clear-cut, and your potential audience usually contains many people with uncertain or conflicting views. Identify these specific groups of potential readers for your argument. Then acknowledge their conflicting opinions and anticipate their various objections to your draft.

**Identify with Your Readers**    The "Their Side" exercise helped you see the debate from the perspective of your opponent. Now, as you identify other readers who have only partial or passing interest in the controversy, place yourself in those positions and assess the issues from those viewpoints. Who are the "friendlies"? What do they know? Who are the skeptics? What makes them resist? Who are the uncommitted? What will make them decide? Such imaginative identification helps you establish the points of conflict and areas of agreement among the various readers in your audience.

**Establish Your Identity for Your Readers**    In drafting your argument, you inevitably establish an identity (or a *persona*) that reveals to your readers your attitude toward your subject. You should be alert to strategies that strengthen your bond with your readers and avoid tactics that distance you from them. As the "Their Side" exercise helped demonstrate, the most effective arguments consider all sides of a controversy. In arguing, your identity should be that of a "reasonable citizen" who follows a balanced discussion with a thoughtfully rendered judgment. You must consider your readers, too, to be reasonable citizens. However indignant you are about the situation you are writing about, you cannot be indignant with your readers—not if you want their agreement. You can concede or refute certain points, but you cannot flatter or talk down to your readers, or neglect to provide logical proof of your argument—not if you want their respect. You are trying to establish a partnership of mutual inquiry. Anything that distorts your identity in that partnership will destroy your credibility.

**Provide Your Readers with Appropriate Evidence**    If you respect your readers, you will not ask them to accept unsupported assertions. A business executive would not ask her partners to accept her unsupported word that investing in another company will be profitable. She would provide detailed evidence for their review and would address the particular concerns (management, labor, debt, productivity, competition) of individual partners with appropriate evidence. She may believe the investment is sound, but if she wants to convince her partners, she must supply the right kind of evidence. As a writer of argument, you have an obligation to spell out in detail why you think your readers should accept your conclusion. And you must provide the specific kinds of evidence your readers will find compelling.

**Draft an Argument Your Readers Can Read**    You are asking your readers to agree with you, so make their job as easy as possible. Highly complex arguments, technical terminology, abstract diction, confusing statistics—all these obstructive elements make communication difficult. You want to convince your readers that you are knowledgeable, but you do not want to clutter your argument with arcane or unnecessary information that confuses and annoys them. Anticipate your readers' needs and try to fulfill them to obtain the response you seek.

---

## EXERCISE

As Jon thinks about drafting his argument about the media and the military, he identifies the following list of readers as potential members of his audience. Examine his list. Has he overlooked any group that has a stake in the controversy? Identify readers who might belong to more than one group. Then discuss how each group of readers might see the issue.

1. War correspondents
2. Military officers
3. Citizens from another country (allies)
4. Citizens from another country (enemies)
5. War widows

6. Conservative columnists
7. Liberal historians
8. Members of the American Legion
9. Member of the American Civil Liberties Union
10. Producers of evening news programs

---

## Arranging the Evidence

Because every controversy creates its own problems and possibilities, no one method of arrangement will always work best. Sometimes you may even have to combine methods to make your case. To make an informed decision, you need to consider how you might adapt your evidence to the four common methods of arrangement: *induction, deduction, claims and warrants,* and *accommodation.*

**Induction**    Often called the scientific method, induction begins by presenting specific evidence and then moves to a general conclusion. This arrangement reflects the history of your investigation. You began your research with a hypothesis about what you wanted to find out and where you needed to look. You collected a cross-section of examples until a pattern emerged. At this point, you made what scientists call an "inductive leap": You determined that although you had not collected every example, you had examined enough examples to risk proposing a probable conclusion.

To incorporate this arrangement into a draft, begin by posing the question that prompted your research:

> Why is our company losing so many valuable data processors to other companies?

Then arrange your individual pieces of evidence in such a way that they help your readers see the pattern you discovered. You need not list all the false leads or blind alleys you encountered along the way unless they changed your perspective or confirmed your judgment.

> 1. Most data processors are women who have preschool children. (Provide examples.)
> 2. A nearby day-care center used by employees has closed because it lost federal funding. (Provide examples.)
> 3. Other day-care centers in the area are inconvenient and understaffed. (Provide examples.)
> 4. Other companies provide on-site day care for children of employees. (Provide examples.)
> 5. On-site day care is beneficial to the emotional well-being of both preschool children and their mothers because of the possibility of contact during the workday.

Finally, present the conclusion that seems warranted by the evidence you have presented.

> Therefore, our company needs to provide on-site day care to retain valuable employees.

**Deduction**   Usually identified with classical reasoning, deduction begins with a general statement or *major premise* that, when restricted by a *minor premise,* leads to a specific conclusion. Unlike induction, which in theory makes an assertion only in its conclusion, deduction does make initial assertions (based on evidence) from which a conclusion is derived.

To use this organization in your draft, consider the pattern of this three-step syllogism.

> Retention of data processors who have preschool children is promoted by on-site day care.

> Our company wants to retain data processors who have preschool children.

> Our company should establish on-site day-care centers.

To gain your audience's acceptance of your major and minor premises, you must support each assertion with specific evidence. Demonstrate that retaining data processors who have preschool children is promoted by on-site day-care centers and that "our company" wants to retain computer operators who have preschool children. If your readers accept your premises, then they are logically committed to accepting your conclusion.

**Claims and Warrants**   Claims and warrants is often called the Toulmin argument after Stephen Toulmin—the legal philosopher who analyzed the process and defined its terminology. Like deduction, claims and warrants argues from a general principle to a specific example, but it presents a more complex arrangement than the simple major premise/minor premise/conclusion pattern illustrated in deduction.

You begin by asserting a *claim* (or general assertion about the argument you intend to make), then provide *evidence* to support your claim. The statement that links the claim to the evidence is called a *warrant.* In some arguments the warrant is implied; in others, you need to state it directly. Additional parts of the claims and warrants arrangement include *support* to strengthen your argument, *qualifiers* to modify or limit your claim, and *reservations* to point out instances in which your claim may not apply.

To use this organization in your draft, consider how it complicates and empowers the argument about data processors and day-care centers:

Claim

Retention of data processors who have preschool children is promoted by on-site day-care centers.

Evidence

Many of our data processors have preschool children.
These employees have difficulties arranging and paying for day-care services.
Mothers are more effective employees when they don't have to worry about their children.

Warrant

Our company should establish on-site day-care centers.

Support

Competitors who provide on-site day care for their employees have a high retention rate.
Data processors at such companies have a lower absentee rate.
The cost of training new data processors is expensive.

Qualification

Some of our data processors do not have preschool children or will soon be able to send their children to school.

> Because our company wants to retain a qualified
> work force, we don't want to add expenses to the work-
> place that will penalize data processors who don't
> have children.

Claims and warrants is an effective arrangement because, like induction, it enables you to present your evidence systematically, and, like induction, the inclusion of qualifiers and reservations suggests that you are considering your data objectively. But, like deduction, claims and warrants enables you to provide a clear and cogent link (warrant) between your general assertion (claim) and the data you have collected (evidence).

**Accommodation** Sometimes called "nonthreatening argument," accommodation arranges evidence so that all parties believe their position has received a fair hearing. Induction reveals how a chain of evidence leads to a conclusion. Deduction demonstrates why certain premises demand a single conclusion. Although both procedures work effectively in specific situations, they occasionally defeat your purpose. Readers may feel trapped by the relentless march of your argument; though unable to refute your logic, they are still unwilling to listen to reason. Accommodation takes your audience's hesitations into account. Instead of trying to win the argument, you try to improve communication and increase understanding.

To employ this strategy, begin by composing an objective description of the controversy: Women data processors who have preschool children are leaving the company. Then draft a complete and accurate statement of the contending positions, supplying the evidence that makes each position credible.

**Corporation board**

> We need a qualified work force, but we are not in
> business to provide social services. (Provide evidence.)

**Fellow workers
(Single, male, etc.)**

> We understand their problem, but providing an on-
> site day-care center is giving expensive, preferential
> treatment to a small segment of the work force.
> (Provide evidence.)

**Competitors**

> We need better data processors if we are going to
> compete, and we will provide what is necessary to hire
> them. (Provide evidence.)

Next, show where and why you and the various parties agree: The corporation should not be in the day-care business; providing a center is preferential treatment; women data processors have the right to market their skills in a competitive market. Then present your own opinion, explaining where it differs from other positions and why it deserves serious consideration: We have invested a large amount of money in training our work force; child care is an appropriate investment in view of the long-term contribution these people will make to the corporation. Finally, present a proposal that might resolve the issue in a way that recognizes the interests of all concerned: Suggest that the corporation help fund the nearby day-care center that was previously supported by government money.

## EXERCISE

Jon Seidel decides to make a scratch outline to organize his evidence against military censorship. What method of arrangement does he use? What sections of his outline suggest the potential for combining several methods?

I. Military and the Media
   World War II
   Vietnam

II. Gulf War
   Ground Rules
   Sanitized War

III. Information and Democracy
   Access to Policies and Strategies
   Peace of Mind vs. Ignorance

## Monitoring the Appeals

In organizing your draft, you must keep track of how you are using the three basic appeals of argument: the *emotional* appeal, the *ethical* appeal, and the *logical* appeal. These three appeals are rarely fully separate; they all weave in and out of virtually every argument. But to control their effects to your advantage, you must know when and why you are using them.

**The Emotional Appeal**   Readers feel as well as think, and to be thoroughly convinced, they must be emotionally as well as intellectually engaged by your argument. Some people think that the emotional appeal is suspect; because it relies on the feelings, instincts, and opinions of readers, they link it to the devious manipulations of advertising or politics. The emotional appeal is often used to stampede an audience into thoughtless action, but such abuses do not negate its value. The emotional appeal should never replace more rational appeals, but it can be an effective strategy for convincing your readers that they need to pay attention to your arguments.

The greatest strength of the emotional appeal is also its greatest weakness. Dramatic examples, presented in concrete images and connotative language, personalize a problem and produce powerful emotions. Some examples produce predictable emotions: An abandoned puppy or a lonely old woman evokes pity; a senseless accident or recurring incompetence evokes anger; a smiling family or a heroic deed evokes delight. Some examples, however, produce unpredictable results, and their dramatic presentation often works against your purpose. It would be difficult to predict, for instance, how all your readers would respond to a working mother's fears for and guilt about her preschool child in day care. Some might pity her; others might disdain her inability to solve her problems. Because controversial issues attract a range of passions, use the emotional appeal with care.

**The Ethical Appeal**    The character (or *ethos*) of the writer, not the writer's morality, is the basis of the ethical appeal. It suggests that the writer is someone to be trusted, a claim that emerges from a demonstration of competence as an authority on the subject under discussion. Readers trust a writer such as Anna Quindlen and are inclined to agree with her arguments because she has established a reputation for informed, reasonable, and reliable writing about controversial subjects.

You can incorporate the ethical appeal into your argument either by citing authorities, such as Quindlen, who have conducted thorough investigations of your subject, or by following the example of authorities in your competent treatment of evidence. There are two potential dangers with the ethical appeal. First, you cannot win the trust of your readers by citing as an authority in one field someone who is an authority in another. Bill Gates is an established authority on computers, but he should not be cited as an authority on nuclear disarmament. And second, you cannot convince your readers that you are knowledgeable if you present your argument exclusively in personal terms. Your own experience in trying to find reliable, convenient day-care services may make your argument for providing on-site day care more forceful, but you need to consider the experience of other people to establish your ethical appeal.

**The Logical Appeal**    The rational methods used to develop an argument constitute a logical appeal. Some people think that the forceful use of logic, like the precise use of facts, makes an argument absolutely true. But controversies contain many truths, no one of which can be graded simply true or false. By using the logical appeal, you acknowledge that arguments are conducted in a world of probability, not certainty; by offering a series of reasonable observations and conclusions, you establish the most reliable case.

The logical appeal is widely used and accepted in argument. Establishing the relationships that bind your evidence to your proposition engages your readers' reasoning power, and an appeal to their intelligence and common sense is likely to win their assent. But the logical appeal is not infallible. Its limit is in acknowledging limits: How much evidence is enough? There is no simple answer to this question. The amount of evidence required to convince fellow workers that your company should provide on-site day care may not be sufficient to persuade the company's board of directors. On the other hand, too much evidence, however methodically analyzed, may win the argument but lose your audience. Without emotional or ethical appeal, your "reasonable" presentation may be put aside in favor of more urgent issues. Accurate and cogent reasoning is the basis for any sound argument, but the logical appeal, like the emotional and ethical appeals, must be monitored carefully during drafting to make sure it is accomplishing your purpose.

## EXERCISE

In his ongoing investigation of the media and the military, Jon Seidel has collected evidence, considered the position of his opponents, and analyzed the claims of various readers. Now he wants to turn off these other voices and rediscover his own: He is ready to write "My Side" of the argument. As you read his discovery draft, identify the various appeals he has used to accomplish his purpose. Note the places that were probably strengthened by his decision to write "Their Side" first. Finally, point to the sections that would probably be weaker had he written "My Side" first.

### My Side

A back issue of *The Onion,* the satiric magazine "not intended for readers under eighteen," announced, "Congress Passes Freedom From Information Act." According to this spoof of real news, America's peace of mind has been destroyed by newspaper accounts of the threats of war. To give the American people "the emotional comfort and well-being" they deserve, Congress voted to restrict free-flowing information, especially information about our government's policies and military operations. In the current national crisis, such satire hits home because it strikes close to the truth. Our government and the military want to control information. Similarly, the press wants to investigate and disclose information. Some Americans may well want to be protected from "bad news." But in order for our democracy to work, Americans must be informed about what its government and its military are doing in their name.

The battle over who controls information in a time of crisis has an interesting history. During World

War II, correspondents collaborated with the military. The Nazis were clearly the enemy, and reporters donned fatigues and traveled with the troops so they could report on the heroic deeds of "our boys." Later, in Vietnam, the press was critical of the military. The war was controversial, and reporters packed their television cameras through the jungle to document the hopeless and often ugly behavior of our troops.

During the Gulf War, the media was controlled by the military. The lesson learned from Vietnam was that when a war is controversial, correspondents cannot have unlimited access to information. Reporters were organized into "pools" and then given official "briefings" by military public relations personnel. In "The War We Couldn't Report," Canadian correspondent Mike Vernon explains how this policy continued during the war in Afghanistan. In both wars, reporters had to obey an intricate list of "ground rules" to retain their credentials. Those few reporters who were able to venture outside the official briefings could do so only in certain areas and only when accompanied by military personnel. Virtually every word and image they collected on these ventures was subject to military censorship.

The military argued that these ground rules were essential to protect the security and safety of the Armed Forces. The press argued that these ground rules forced them to accept carefully sanitized information that misrepresented what was actually happening. The military's presentation of the Gulf War may have protected our troops, but it also protected American citizens from the truth. According to the official version, the Gulf War was fought by "smart" weapons, and during it both faceless and named enemies, but few Americans, died. Because reporters were forced to report this version of the Gulf War, they could not investigate the complexities of the actual war, complexities that in many ways anticipated the attack on the World Trade Center, the potential for the war against terrorism, and the war against Iraq.

As Roy Peter Clark, a senior scholar at the Poynter Institute for Media Studies, points out, "Journalism is the oxygen of democracy. One cannot exist without the other" (qtd. in Barton). If the government controls information, then we will never know what "facts" prompted our leaders to go to war or what "intelligence" prompted them to adopt certain military strategies.

Most importantly, we will never know what facts were suppressed or what other strategies were available.

In a time of crisis, the temptation is to rally behind the flag and support the troops. But such behavior is a form of self-censorship that creates an uninformed public. French journalist Alexandre Levy argues that journalists have to resist such simplistic reporting shaped by nationalistic propaganda. They must "continue to do their job in covering all sides of the war" (qtd. in Barton). We don't want to trade peace of mind for ignorance. The truth may not always be pleasant, but the truth will keep us free.

Works Cited

Barton, Gina. "Patriotism and the News." Society of Professional Journalists. 3 March 2002.

"Congress Passes Freedom From Information Act." The Onion. 2 April 1998.

Vernon, Mike. "The War We Couldn't Report." Canadian Broadcasting Corporation. 13 August 2002.

## Revising: Eliminating Fallacies

Once you have organized your argument, reexamine your draft to see if it accomplishes your purpose. Revision, as you learned in Chapter 4, can mean *global revision* —the rethinking, reordering, and rewriting of your text—or *local revision* often necessitated by a small problem: a faulty thesis, an undeveloped paragraph, or an unclear sentence. In argument, many local problems are the result of errors in reasoning known as *fallacies*. Some fallacies are unintentional, created in the haste of composition. Others are intentional, created to deceive readers. In either case, they oversimplify or distort evidence, thus making an argument unreliable. Read the following list as a guide to finding and eliminating fallacies from your writing during revision or to detecting fallacies in the writing of others.

▶ *Faulty analogy* attempts to argue that because two things are alike in some ways, they are alike in all ways. Attending school may be analogous to working at a factory in that both require long hours to complete specific tasks for a supervisor. School work and factory work are not the same, however. An analogy can be useful in helping your readers understand how something complex or unknown is similar to something simple and familiar, but such illustrations should not be confused with proof. Arguments by analogy are particularly suspect when an insignificant resemblance is proposed as evidence for a more relevant (but unsupportable) comparison.

- **Hasty generalizations** are conclusions drawn from inadequate or atypical evidence. Suppose there are twelve women and ten men in your section of business law. On the final exam, the four highest scores are made by women and the four lowest scores by men. On the basis of the evidence, you conclude that men are unqualified for business law. There is no justification for that generalization because ten men in one section are not typical of all men, and ten is hardly an adequate sample to justify such a sweeping conclusion. To avoid hasty generalizations, make sure you provide sufficient and appropriate evidence to support your conclusions.

- **Post hoc, ergo propter hoc** (Latin for "after this, therefore because of this") asserts that one event caused another because it preceded it. Lowering the drinking age in your state should not be claimed as the direct cause of the increased crime rate. The first event may have contributed in some way to the other, but the two events may also be merely coincidental. Because direct cause-and-effect relationships are difficult to establish, do not overstate your claims for events that may have many plausible explanations.

- **Begging the question** occurs when part of what has to be proved is assumed to be true. When a lawyer seeks to use as evidence the results of a polygraph test because such tests verify the truth, he begs the question: Are polygraph tests reliable? Sometimes begging the question can produce a *circular argument* that restates in different words what you are trying to prove: "Polygraph tests do not provide reliable evidence because their results cannot be trusted." As you revise, check each of your claims to make sure you advance your argument with evidence; do not assume a claim is credible because you have used "new and improved" language.

- **Either-or** states a position in such categorical terms—either *A* or *B*—that it ignores (or denies) the possibility of other alternatives. An economist who argues that "the United States must either adopt a new industrial policy or face financial ruin" does not see (or prefers not to see) that there are many possible ways to solve our economic difficulties and that financial ruin does not inevitably follow from the failure to adopt one policy. If you have conducted a thorough investigation, you know that there are more than two sides to the issue.

- **Ad hominem** (Latin for "to the man") distorts an argument by attacking the character of the opponent to arouse the emotions or prejudices of the audience. This strategy attempts to discredit an opponent by using labels (or stereotypes) with highly unfavorable connotations: "Senator Hoover is an avowed feminist. Her antidiscrimination bill just expresses her radical political views." As you have seen, an expert witness's trustworthiness is always on trial. If Senator Hoover's opinions are not supported by evidence, then her credibility should be discounted. But as long as she presents evidence for her case, you should resist calling her names and address her argument.

▶ **Red herring** is a smoked fish that has a reddish color and strong odor. A hunter may drag a red herring across a trail to distract the hounds and trick them into following a new scent. In argument, a *red herring* is an unrelated issue introduced to divert attention from the real issue: "As long as we are discussing whether women should receive equal pay, we should also discuss whether women still want to retain preferred treatment on social occasions, as when men open doors for them and pay for their meals. It seems to me that women want equal and preferred treatment at the same time." Such diversions confuse the issue by introducing irrelevancies. Economic equality and social courtesy are two different issues.

## EXERCISE

While checking through his planning notes and preliminary drafts, Jon found several assertions that looked like fallacies. In the following list, identify the probable fallacies and then discuss how they might be revised to avoid oversimplification or distortion.

1. We must control the media or lose the war on terrorism.

2. Many Islamic countries claim that the American media want to control the minds of their people.

3. The American military must have something to hide. What other reason does it have for being so secretive?

4. Controlling the media will guarantee our victory over terrorism.

5. All reporters are biased against the military.

6. Allowing reporters access to American soldiers is like giving terrorists the key to your back door.

7. Americans deserve peace of mind. The media are always reporting bad news.

# Composing

As you work your way through the argument assignment, you may wish to arrange the three drafts ("Their Side," "My Side," "Our Side") in columns. In this way you can compare the openings in each draft—measuring each one's ability to restrict its subject, assess its audience, and determine its purpose. You can also compare the way you arrange and develop the evidence you use in each essay. Do you cite the same evidence, different evidence, or the same evidence with a different slant? Read your final text carefully, marking assertions that may rest on unstated or shaky assumptions. If you find logical fallacies, mark those and then rework the thought patterns that trapped you into slanting or oversimplifying your evidence.

Once you have completed your revision, post it to your writing group or the members of your writing class. Invite them to critique your essay. For example, do they understand your main proposition? Can they determine how your argument is structured, the kinds of evidence you use, and the appeals you make? Then ask your peers to offer evidence that helps you find alternative solutions to the contending positions you cite in your argument.

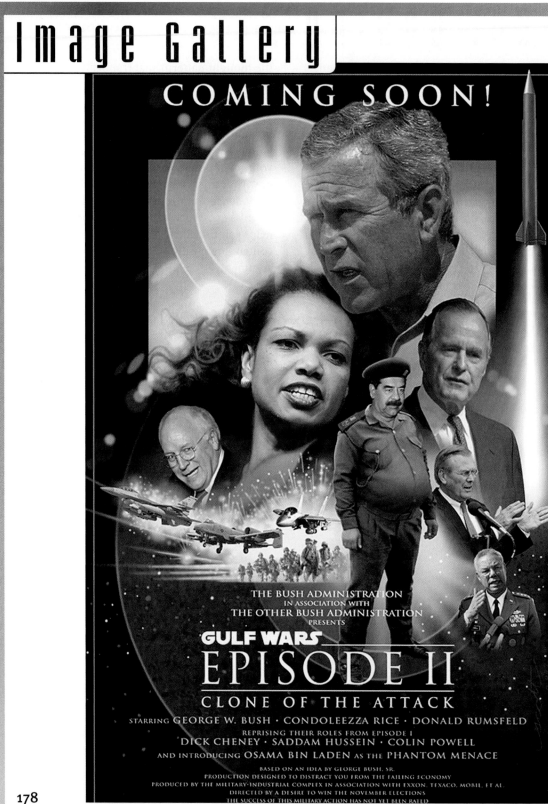

**Questions**

1. How does the representation of the central actors in these spoof movie posters, *Vietnam* and *Gulf Wars: Episode II,* create an argument about the wars they depict?

2. How do these posters use textual features of authentic movie posters (reviewers' quotes, special appearances, special techniques) to criticize the wars they presumably celebrate? How would the veterans of these wars or their families respond to these posters?

3. How do these posters compare with the posters for classic war films—e.g., *Saving Private Ryan, Apocalypse Now,* and *Star Wars?*

# Readings

Reread Anna Quindlen's comments on the difficulties she encounters when she tries to organize an argument on a controversial subject (page 164). Then read her essay on the emotionally charged issue of capital punishment. How does she present the evidence for the contending positions? How does she accommodate the opposing positions? Explain your answer.

# Execution

## ANNA QUINDLEN

1 Ted Bundy and I go back a long way, to a time when there was a series of unsolved murders in Washington State known only as the Ted murders. Like a lot of reporters, I'm something of a crime buff. But the Washington Ted murders— and the ones that followed in Utah, Colorado, and finally in Florida, where Ted Bundy was convicted and sentenced to die—fascinated me because I could see myself as one of the victims. I looked at the studio photographs of young women with long hair, pierced ears, easy smiles, and I read the descriptions: polite, friendly, quick to help, eager to please. I thought about being approached by a handsome young man asking for help, and I knew if I had been in the wrong place at the wrong time I would have been a goner. By the time Ted finished up in Florida, law enforcement authorities suspected he had murdered dozens of young women. He and the death penalty seemed made for each other.

2 The death penalty and I, on the other hand, seem to have nothing in common. But Ted Bundy has made me think about it all over again, now that the outlines of my sixties liberalism have been filled in with a decade as a reporter covering some of the worst back alleys in New York City and three years as a mother who,

like most, would lay down her life for her kids. Simply put, I am opposed to the death penalty. I would tell that to any judge or lawyer undertaking the voir dire of jury candidates in a state in which the death penalty can be imposed. That is why I would be excused from such a jury. In a rational, completely cerebral way, I think the killing of one human being as punishment for the killing of another makes no sense and is inherently immoral.

3 But whenever my response to an important subject is rational and completely cerebral, I know there is something wrong with it—and so it is here. I have always been governed by my gut, and my gut says I am hypocritical about the death penalty. That is, I do not in theory think that Ted Bundy, or others like him, should be put to death. But if my daughter had been the one clubbed to death as she slept in a Tallahassee sorority house, and if the bite mark left in her buttocks has been one of the prime pieces of evidence against the young man charged with her murder, I would with the greatest pleasure kill him myself.

4 The State of Florida will not permit the parents of Bundy's victims to do that, and, in a way, that is the problem with an emotional response to capital punishment. The only reason for a

Anna Quindlen, *Thinking Out Loud* (New York: Random, 1988), 220–23.

death penalty is to exact retribution. Is there anyone who really thinks that it is a deterrent, that there are considerable numbers of criminals out there who think twice about committing crimes because of the sentence involved? The ones I have met in my professional duties have either sneered at the justice system, where they can exchange one charge for another with more ease than they could return a shirt to a clothing store, or they have simply believed that it is the other guy who will get caught, get convicted, get the stiffest sentence. Of course, the death penalty would act as a deterrent by eliminating recidivism, but then so would life without parole, albeit at greater taxpayer expense.

5    I don't believe deterrence is what most proponents seek from the death penalty anyhow. Our most profound emotional response is to want criminals to suffer as their victims did. When a man is accused of throwing a child from a high-rise terrace, my emotional—some might say hysterical—response is that he should be given an opportunity to see how endless the seconds are from the thirty-first story to the ground. In a civilized society that will never happen. And so what many people want from the death penalty, they will never get.

6    Death is death, you may say, and you would be right. But anyone who has seen someone die suddenly of a heart attack and someone else slip slowly into the clutches of cancer knows that there are gradations of dying.

7    I watched a television reenactment one night of an execution by lethal injection. It was well done; it was horrible. The methodical approach, people standing around the gurney waiting, made it more awful. One moment there was a man in a prone position; the next moment that man was gone. On another night I watched a television movie about a little boy named Adam Walsh, who disappeared from a shopping center in Florida. There was a reenactment of Adam's parents coming to New York, where they appeared on morning talk shows begging for their son's return, and in their hotel room, where they received a call from the police saying that Adam had just been found: not all of Adam, actually, just his severed head, discovered in the waters of a Florida canal. There is nothing anyone could do that is bad enough for an adult who took a six-year-old boy away from his parents, perhaps tortured, then murdered him and cut off his head. Nothing at all. Lethal injection? The electric chair? Bah.

8    And so I come back to the position that the death penalty is wrong, not only because it consists of stooping to the level of the killers, but also because it is not what it seems. Just before one of Ted Bundy's execution dates was postponed pending further appeals, the father of his last known victim, a twelve-year-old girl, said what almost every father in his situation must feel. "I wish they'd bring him back to Lake City," said Tom Leach of the town where Kimberly Leach lived and died, "and let us all have at him." But the death penalty does not let us all have at him in the way Mr. Leach seems to mean. What he wants is for something as horrifying as what happened to his child to happen to Ted Bundy. And that is impossible.

# Who Controls Information? (Our Side)

## JON SEIDEL

1    In the Information Age, it is not surprising that America's biggest dilemma is deciding who controls information. This is particularly true during a time of national crisis. The military argues that its job is to protect the public and the rights guaranteed by the Constitution. To do this job effectively, the military must maintain a certain level of secrecy to protect the security of its missions and the safety of its personnel. The media argue that their job is to inform the public by exercising the freedoms guaranteed by the Constitution. To do this job effectively, the media must have unlimited access to information about government policies and military strategies and be allowed to report what they discover as quickly as possible to keep the public informed. These competing claims often put the military and the media at cross-purposes. But particularly in a time of national crisis, they must find a way to work together if we are to preserve our democracy.

2    The antagonism between the military and the media has a complicated history. During World War II, correspondents traveled with the army, reporting the heroic deeds of "our boys" as they battled the Germans and the Japanese. But their reporting was hardly free from censorship. Reporters at the front lines had to have their stories "cleared" by a series of military personnel before they could mail or wire them to their papers for publication. However, because reporters agreed with the purpose of the military campaign, they accepted military censorship. Also, because the technology of reporting was slower, correspondents realized that their stories would not be read until long after the events they had witnessed had taken place.

3    During the Vietnam War, correspondents also traveled with the army. But because the mission of the war was controversial, reporters often regarded their job as an opportunity to reveal the pointless skirmishes our soldiers had with the Vietnamese. Also, the technology of reporting was quicker and more visual than it had been in previous wars. Correspondents could bypass official briefings and military censorship and transmit graphic film footage of our troops at war to television sets in American living rooms. As a result, the once collaborative relationship between the military and the media became combative. The military blamed the media for poisoning American public opinion against the war. The media blamed the military for trying to deceive the American people.

4    The military tried to solve the Vietnam War era's media problem during the Gulf War and the battles against terrorism in Afghanistan by drafting a complicated list of "ground rules." In part, these rules were created to deal with the increasing size of the media: "Fewer than 30 reporters landed with the troops on the beaches of Normandy on D-Day. . . . [while] more than 1,600 journalists showed up to cover Desert Storm" (Wood). This notion of organizing reporters into smaller "pools" who heard briefings and then passed the information on to their col-

leagues seemed like a logical solution. But, in part, these rules were also created to deal with the technological changes in both reporting and warfare. The briefings could control the information that would be instantly broadcast by satellite all over the world. The military could also use these briefings to outline the grand strategy of fighting a war with "smart" bombs rather than with individual soldiers.

The media reacted to these solutions by ⁵ claiming that they were not being allowed to cover the war. They complained that the carefully edited briefings were misleading, if not downright deceptive. And if they ventured outside the briefings, they could not conduct independent investigations if they had to be constantly escorted by military personnel. If reporters violated any of the "ground rules,"

**How do these images support Jon's assertion that "the war against terrrorism is, in essence, a war of information"?**

their credentials would be revoked. As a result, the reporting of the Gulf War and the campaign in Afghanistan seemed simplistic—contributing to Americans' ignorance about the new enemies and the kind of war that they were likely to conduct against the United States.

6    The military and the media will have to rethink their relationship because the war against terrorism is, in essence, a war of information. American soldiers and reporters are not the only players in this new kind of war. Osama bin Laden's messages have been broadcast on the Arab satellite television network, Al Jazeera. And Saddam Hussein's pronouncements are designed to counter what he calls American imperialistic propanganda. If America is to respond to these "disinformation" campaigns, it will have to demonstrate that its reporting is fair and balanced—and free from military manipulation.

7    A step toward a solution may grow out of a recent announcement of the Pentagon's decision to conduct "boot camp" for American reporters covering the war with Iraq (Wood). This new strategy, officials admit, is a "concession that the post-Vietnam arrangement for war coverage hasn't worked for either journalists, or, in a sense, the military" (Neuman). There will still be "pools" and "briefings," but training reporters in the rigors of war will help correspondents and the general public to understand the problems and possibilities inherent in the jobs of both reporters and soldiers. It will also mean that the military will "put more reporters with troops in battle than in any other war since World War II" (Neuman). These "embedded" reporters will still have to follow certain "ground rules," and military personnel will still be concerned about the potential for reporters to reveal information that might compromise their missions. But by working together, military and media will help tell a "truer" story of the war with Iraq to Americans, Arabs, and the rest of the world. Such stories should go a long way to demonstrating the value of a free press in a democracy.

### Works Cited

Neuman, Johanna. *Gulf News.* 6 December 2002.

Wood, David. "Pentagon to Begin Training War Correspondents," Newhouse News Service. 6 December 2002.

# Web Design

Students using *Writing with a Purpose* in a composition class were asked to design a website for Jon Seidel's essay "Who Controls the Information?" Consult the elements and principles of design presented in Chapter 5 to help you answer the questions about the effectiveness of each design.

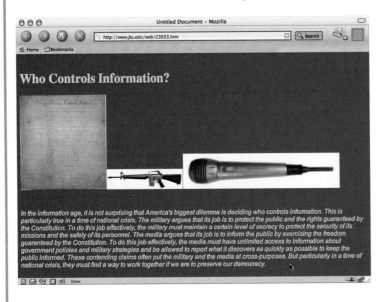

## Sample Homepage #1: Who Controls Information?

1. How does the alignment of the title and the three images confuse rather than clarify the subject of the site?

2. How do the background and text color make the site difficult to read?

3. How does the image of the Bill of Rights complicate the purpose of this site?

## Sample Homepage #2: Who Controls Information?

1. How does the design of the banner suggest that the subject of this site deals with the press?

2. How does the contrast between the dark colors in the banner and the white space for the text make the site more readable?

3. How do the subtitles clarify the purpose of the site?

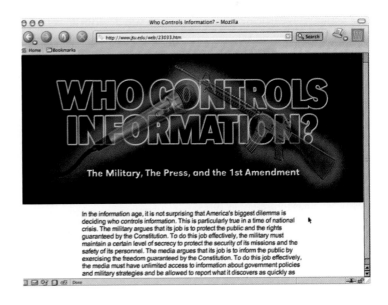

# Writing Assignments

## 1. NARRATE

Select an occasion when you (or one of your fellow workers) felt as though your civil rights were abused by an employer's policy. Write a narrative about that occasion in a way that will make your readers understand why the events influenced you to select "My Side" in the controversy.

## 2. OBSERVE

Keep track of how the females and males participate in the often "adversarial" format of your classes. How many times do male students speak? How many times do female students speak? How often do male and female students participate in classroom discussions that are framed as arguments between opposing sides? Then write an essay for the college newspaper speculating on the topic "Who Participates in Class Discussion (and Why)?"

## 3. INVESTIGATE

Interview someone who has to make arguments in public for a living—a lawyer who has to make a case to jurors, a minister who has to preach to a congregation, a college president who has to address alumni groups, a professor who has to present lectures to other scholars. Ask about the special "tricks of the trade" that he or she uses in difficult situations. Then write a profile about the person entitled "Speaking My Mind and Getting My Way."

## 4. COLLABORATE

Your writing group has been asked to draft a letter to the newspaper editor about a controversial campus practice such as library fees, preferential parking, or distribution of birth-control information. An initial poll reveals that your group is undecided or perhaps even strongly divided about the issue. Discuss ways to reach accommodation so that you can collaborate on a text whose purpose is to increase your audience's understanding of the issue.

## 5. READ

Examine the headlines from the major online newspapers (such as *USA Today*) to determine those that use the language of war to characterize various events—politics, sports, entertainment. Write an essay in which you describe how replacing these military metaphors might modify readers' expectations about the story they read.

## 6. RESPOND

Select a news story reported on the website for the Guerrilla News Network. Then respond by constructing your own argument that challenges its assertions.

## 7. ANALYZE

Analyze the types of evidence that Anna Quindlen uses in her essay "Execution." Identify what is fact, judgment, eyewitness testimony, and expert testimony. Sort out the kinds of evidence that make it

difficult for Quindlen to decide where she stands on the issue. Then analyze why this approach makes an effective argument.

## 8. EVALUATE

Evaluate each of Jon Seidel's drafts. Write him a letter to convince him which draft he should place in his writing portfolio for final assessment. Your purpose is to convince him to submit his "best" essay. Your problem is to determine which of these essays is the "best" argument.

## 9. ARGUE

Select an issue that is provoking discussion on the editorial page of your community newspaper but about which you have no strong opinion. Collect editorials and letters to the editor that represent the range of disagreement on the issue. Interview people who are involved in the controversy or who are reporting on it for the local paper. After you have completed your investigation, compose a historical analysis explaining the issue.

## 10. ARGUE

In *The Argument Culture: Moving from Debate to Dialogue*, Deborah Tannen argues that American education is based on "attacking" those with whom you disagree rather than trying to find common ground. Argue that "attack learning" is either the most challenging or the most dispiriting form of education.

# Paragraphs: Units of Development

A paragraph is a set of related sentences that express or develop a topic. A paragraph is usually part of an extended piece of writing, although in some situations you may need only one paragraph to fulfill your purpose. In narration or description, a new paragraph usually signals a shift in time, scene, or speaker. In exposition or argument, a new paragraph adds information or announces another point supporting your thesis. This chapter discusses two kinds of paragraphs: *topical paragraphs,* those that develop a topic or idea; and *special paragraphs,* those that introduce or conclude a piece of writing or provide a transition between major parts.

Paragraphs serve several purposes for you and your readers. You can use them to divide your subject into manageable units of information: By grouping ideas into paragraphs, you show the relationship of ideas to one another and their significance to your overall purpose. You can also use paragraphs to control emphasis: By placing a paragraph in a particular position, you demonstrate the relative importance of an idea in your essay. Finally, you can use paragraphs to establish rhythm: By interrupting a series of long paragraphs with a short paragraph, or creating a series of brief paragraphs, you fix and vary cadence in your writing.

Readers use your paragraphs to grasp key points and follow your reasoning. Extended, uninterrupted passages tax their attention. They expect and need to see the regularly spaced indentations that signal a new paragraph. This visual cue tells them that they have completed one topic and are about to take up another. Because the new paragraph promises new information, they refocus their attention to see how this change alters or advances your essay.

Like so many other writing procedures, making paragraphs depends on your subject, your audience, your purpose—and your own composing process. Some writers like to plan every detail of a project before they begin, assigning each subdivision of their subject to a specific paragraph. Such a procedure usually produces a blueprint for an orderly essay, but it may box the writer into a pattern that forces connections and discourages discoveries. Other writers prefer a more open-ended procedure. They know what they want to accomplish but realize that when they start writing they will discover ideas and associations that will call for paragraphs they could not have anticipated. Bill Barich, a contributor to *The New Yorker,* admits that he prefers this more organic approach to creating paragraphs:

> When I am planning an essay or a piece of reporting, I usually have a sense of the beginning and ending, but my paragraphs tend to arrange themselves during the writing. The process is instinctive and often surprising. I have general ideas grouped together in my notes—facts and information I want to include. But I don't know where I will put them until the piece begins to unfold. Information gathers around a center and becomes a paragraph. It's a thought unit, an energy unit. When the energy runs out, I move on, establishing a rhythm that tells me how much information I can use in the next paragraph.
>
> This sounds a little disorderly, but for me a piece becomes lifeless if I know from the beginning what goes where. I am less interested in getting the information in the right place the first time through than I am in finding the rhythm that will carry the information. I like the structure to be organic, to flow naturally. Once I have finished writing, I can check for things like sequence and fullness of statement. Maybe there is something in my notes that I can insert in a phrase or use in a new paragraph. I may push myself to shorten everything, just to see what that does to the energy of the work. I'll shift, compress, and strip away extraneous material, hoping that what remains is diamond bright. (Personal interview)

Whether you chart every paragraph before you write or form paragraphs intuitively as you compose, once you have made them, you must be sure, as Barich suggests, that they meet certain criteria. The following pages discuss the four characteristics of effective topical paragraphs, the primary functions of special paragraphs, and strategies for revising paragraphs.

# The Requirements of Topical Paragraphs

● A WRITER'S WORDS

**More can probably be found out about a writer from a single paragraph of work than any interview or essay.**

—Joy Williams, "Shifting Things," *The Writer and Her Work, Volume II.*

An effective topical paragraph must meet four requirements. First, it must discuss one topic only—that is, its statements and illustrations must display a *unity* of subject matter, often expressed in a topic sentence. Second, it must say all that your readers need to know about the topic; it must be *complete* enough to do what it is intended to do. Third, the sentences within the paragraph must exhibit an *order* that your readers can recognize and follow. Fourth, the sentences within the paragraph must display *coherence*, allowing readers to move easily from one sentence to the next without feeling that there are gaps in the sequence of your ideas.

## Unity

Paragraph unity requires the considered development of the idea in your paragraph. To achieve this, each sentence must show a clear connection to the topic. In the following paragraph, the first sentence introduces Middletown, the topic the paragraph intends to develop.

> (1) Middletown is not an actual place but an assortment of principles—the democratic ideal, the golden mean, the common citizen—central to our sense of the American experience. (2) We have located it in a middle landscape, somewhere between the desolation of the wilderness and the debauchery of the city, and we have envisioned it as a middle-sized community, large enough to provide everything its citizens want and small enough to preserve everything they need. (3) Our culture contains many Middletowns. (4) Although their names change—Winesburg, Main Street, Mayberry—their image remains the same. (5) Their courthouse squares, tree-lined streets, and warm-hearted people represent our desire for stability in a century of bewildering change.

Notice that each succeeding sentence casts light on the topic; all the sentences together focus on the distinguishing characteristics of Middletown. This close relationship among individual sentences gives the paragraph unity.

Any sentence that digresses or drifts away from the topic blurs the focus of the paragraph and obscures your purpose. Consider the following paragraph:

> (1) The legend of the Old South has a certain timeless beauty. (2) On the veranda of stately mansions, courtly gentlemen and charming ladies talked quietly of family, land, and cotton. (3) Even the slaves, who worked the fields, were said to be content. (4) The poor whites were barely visible until the vigilante movement after the Civil War.

(5) They formed secret societies such as the Klan to terrorize the black community and to acquire political power. (6) Political power led to economic power, and by the turn of the century the poor whites were no longer poor.

The first three sentences deal with the legend of the Old South, and the reader assumes that this "timeless beauty" will be the topic for the rest of the paragraph. In sentence 4, however, the writer shifts to poor whites, a topic that is "barely visible" in the legend. The remaining sentences build on the allusion to the vigilante movement and shift the focus of the paragraph to the Ku Klux Klan and its use of violence to acquire political and economic power. Most readers can follow this digression, but as they proceed past the first few sentences, they become less sure about the main topic of the paragraph and more certain that the paragraph lacks unity.

## EXERCISE

Read the following paragraph, checking for unity by marking shifts in focus. Each sentence should clearly refer to the topic of Oregon as an ideal place to live. Suggest revisions where you think they are needed.

(1) With its seaside beaches, snowcapped mountains, and extensive forests, Oregon is an ideal place to live. (2) Its magnificent forests alone, covering more than 30 million acres, make it a natural paradise. (3) The National Park Service protects 17 million acres in national forests, but the rest is used for Oregon's lumber industry. (4) Loggers "harvest" trees with chain saws and then send their "crop" to the mill on trucks. (5) Many sawmills that used to employ 100 or more people are now closed because of the decline in the lumber business. (6) But loggers are not like steelworkers. (7) They don't go on relief and wait for their factory to reopen. (8) Self-reliant, eccentric, and impatient, loggers simply move to other parts of the country to look for work.

## The Topic Sentence

A *topic sentence* is a statement that presents the main idea to be developed in the paragraph. It is often a single sentence, although sometimes you will need two sentences to state the topic. By beginning a paragraph with a topic sentence, you immediately tell your readers what main idea you are going to develop. In turn, they expect that the remaining sentences in your paragraph will elaborate on that idea. The following example shows how an opening topic sentence controls a paragraph.

There is no simple formula for describing the intricate logic of the Pawnee people's lives. One thing is clear—that no one is caught within the social code. Against the backdrop of his natural environment, each individual stands as his own person. The Old World design for the human personality does not apply to this New World Man. The Pawnee child was born into a community from the beginning, and he never acquired the notion that he was closed in "within four walls." He was literally trained to feel that the world around him was his home—*kahuraru,* the universe, meaning literally the inside land, and that his house was a small model of it. The infinite cosmos was his constant source of strength and his ultimate progenitor, and there was no reason why he should hesitate to set out alone and explore the wide world, even though years should pass before he returned. Not only was he not confined within four walls but he was not closed in with a permanent group of people. The special concern of his mother did not mean that he was so closely embedded with her emotionally that he was not able to move about. (Gene Weltfish, *The Lost Universe*)

Gene Weltfish begins his paragraph with a simple declarative sentence: "There is no simple formula for describing the intricate logic of the Pawnee people's lives." His purpose is to explain the complexity of that logic, and the remaining sentences in the paragraph advance that purpose by showing how the Pawnees imagined the universe and their place in it.

Not all topical paragraphs begin with topic sentences. If you begin composing and don't discover the main point of your paragraph until you reach the end, you must decide whether to move the topic sentence to the beginning, place it somewhere else, or leave it where you found it—at the end. In most cases, you will probably want to place it at the beginning to cue your readers about the significance of the sentences to come. On a few occasions, you may want to place it midparagraph, where it serves as a commentary on the sentences that come before or after it.

In the following paragraph, Richard Rodriguez uses his first sentence to make a flat statement of fact: Two nuns come to visit. He uses his second sentence to explain the reason for their visit: They suggest that the family speak English more often. But he defers his actual statement of topic until the third sentence, where he confirms the significance of the preceding sentences and points a direction for the rest of the paragraph.

I remember when, 20 years ago, two grammar-school nuns visited my childhood home. They had come to suggest—with more tact than was necessary, because my parents accepted without question the church's authority—that we make a greater effort to speak as much English around the house as possible. The nuns realized that my brothers and I led solitary lives largely because we were barely able to comprehend English in a school where we were the only Spanish-speaking students. My mother and father complied as best they could. Heroically, they gave up speaking to us in Spanish—the language that formed so much of the family's sense of intimacy in an alien world—and began to speak a broken English. Instead of

Spanish sounds, I began hearing sounds that were new, harder, less friendly. More important, I was encouraged to respond in English.

(Richard Rodriguez, "On Becoming a Chicano," *Saturday Review*)

Sometimes you will want readers to follow the path that led to your discovery. On such occasions, build your paragraph toward a topic sentence that provides an appropriate conclusion. Ralph Ellison uses this technique skillfully in the following paragraph:

To live in Harlem is to dwell in the very bowels of the city; it is to pass a labyrinthine existence among streets that explode monotonously skyward with the spires and crosses of churches and clutter under foot with garbage and decay. Harlem is a ruin—many of its ordinary aspects (its crimes, its casual violence, its crumbling buildings with littered area-ways, ill-smelling halls and vermin-invaded rooms) are indistinguishable from the distorted images that appear in dreams, and which, like muggers haunting a lonely hall, quiver in the waking mind with hidden and threatening significance. Yet this is no dream but the reality of well over four hundred thousand Americans; a reality which for many defines and colors the world. Overcrowded and exploited politically and economically, Harlem is the scene and symbol of the Negro's perpetual alienation in the land of his birth.

(Ralph Ellison, "Harlem Is Nowhere," *Shadow and Act*)

Not every paragraph needs a topic sentence. Sometimes your readers will be able to infer your purpose from the way you express your thoughts. On such occasions a topic sentence would be gratuitous, out of place. In the following paragraph, for example, E. B. White, one of America's master stylists, evokes a summer place without composing a formal topic sentence.

Summertime, oh, summertime, pattern of life indelible, the fade-proof lake, the woods unshatterable, the pasture with the sweetfern and the juniper forever and ever, summer without end; this was the background, and the life along the shore was the design, the cottages with their innocent and tranquil design, their tiny docks with the flag-pole and the American flag floating against the white clouds in the blue sky, the little paths over the roots of the trees leading from camp to camp and the paths leading back to the outhouses and can of lime for sprinkling, and at the souvenir counters at the store, the miniature birch-bark canoes and the postcards that showed things looking a little better than they looked. This was the American family at play, escaping the city heat, wondering whether the newcomers in the camp at the head of the cove were "common" or "nice," wondering whether it was true that the people who drove up for Sunday dinner at the farmhouse were turned away because there wasn't enough chicken.

(E. B. White, "Once More to the Lake," *Essays of E. B. White*)

As a rule, you should reserve paragraphs without topic sentences for special occasions. When used for effect, they can be powerful and memorable, but you risk misleading your readers and yourself if you routinely decline to write topic sentences.

Remember, your readers are most disoriented and most alert at the beginning of a paragraph. They look to your first sentences for help. They expect you to tell them how to interpret the new group of sentences they are about to read. Although you don't have to place your topic sentence at the beginning of a paragraph, or even use a topic sentence, be aware that your readers will scrutinize your first sentence for a clue to the unity of your paragraph. If that opening sentence does not declare the topic of your paragraph, it must at least point your readers toward the sentence or group of sentences that does identify or evoke the main topic.

> *Readers are most disoriented and most alert at the beginning of a paragraph. They look to your first sentences for help. They expect you to tell them how to interpret the new group of sentences they are about to read.*

## Completeness

Completeness, the second major requirement of an effective paragraph, is relative. The amount of explanation an idea requires depends on the amount your readers need. You must decide this based on your knowledge of your subject and of your audience. Too much information can overwhelm readers; too little can annoy them. Inexperienced writers tend to supply too little detail. Consider this example:

> American Sign Language is a language unto itself. It has its own rules that determine the meaning and significance of each gesture. Experts familiar with these rules can use their hands to communicate extremely complex thoughts.

If that is all the writer is going to say about American Sign Language, this paragraph is incomplete for most readers because the first two sentences merely state the topic. This paragraph would only "satisfy" readers who were already familiar with the intricacies of American Sign Language—but such readers would not even need this brief paragraph. For those who do need it, the writer must provide further explanation:

> American Sign Language—ASL—is a language unto itself, with its own syntax and grammar. Adjectives follow nouns, as in Romance languages. In sign, one says "house blue," establishing a picture of what is being described and then embellishing on that. Many sign language "sentences" begin with a time element and then proceed with what happened, thereby conjugating the verbs. The movement of the shoulders, the speed of the hands, the facial expression, the number of repetitions of a sign, combine with the actual signs to give meaning to the language. Signing is precise. The casual gestures hearing people make when talking have no meaning in sign language. Hearing people who

do learn sign usually practice "signed English," a word-for-word coding of English into signs, but that translation sorely limits the language. In some hands, signing is an art equal to an actor's rendering of Shakespeare. It is not just swoops and swirls but an enormous variety of expression, just as a great actor's delivery is completely different from some ham's idea of haughty speeches.   (Lou Ann Walker, *A Loss for Words*)

Detailed information is necessary to make the meaning of the short paragraph clear. Of course, you can begin with a short paragraph, if your purpose is to state the idea and then develop the topic in greater detail in a subsequent paragraph. In that case, the second paragraph would complete the first.

Here is another example of an incomplete paragraph:

A child understands far more than we suspect. She may not understand words too well, but she senses what they mean by how they are spoken.

If the writer stops there, the reader is left with only a topic sentence and a brief statement that barely begins to develop the main idea. The reader needs to know how a child can "sense" the meaning of words she does not understand. The complete version of the paragraph supplies the answer:

There is also a sense in which a child understands far more than we suspect. Because a child doesn't understand words too well (and also because his nervous system is not yet deadened by years spent as a lawyer, accountant, advertising executive, or professor of philosophy), a child attends not only to what we say but to everything about us as we say it—tone of voice, gesture, facial expression, bodily tensions, and so on. A child attends to a conversation between grown-ups with the same amazing absorption. Indeed, a child listening is, I hope, like a good psychiatrist listening—or like a good semanticist listening—because she watches not only the words but also the nonverbal events to which words bear, in all too many cases, so uncertain a relationship. Therefore a child is in some matters quite difficult to fool, especially on the subject of one's true attitude toward her. For this reason many parents, without knowing it, are to a greater or lesser degree in the situation of the worried mother who said to the psychiatrist to whom she brought her child, "I tell her a dozen times a day that I love her, but the brat still hates me. Why, doctor?"   (S. I. Hayakawa, "Words and Children," *Through the Conversation Barrier*)

The additions to the paragraph clarify the process children use to understand words: They pay attention to tone of voice, gestures, facial expressions, and so on. The final example illustrates that children see beyond the words we use and understand what we really mean.

These examples demonstrate that you need to spell out the implications of a topic sentence with facts, illustrations, explanations—whatever is needed. Unless you give your readers the necessary information, they will have difficulty grasping your purpose. You can easily flesh out incomplete paragraphs once you realize that every generalization must be developed with supporting details.

## EXERCISES

The following paragraphs are incomplete. Complete them by adding several examples or a sustained illustration from your own experience.

1. You cannot and should not try to eliminate all anger from your life. If you react mildly to everything, you will often suppress your true feelings. You must learn to recognize situations where expressing anger is counter-productive.

2. Most families have a private set of signs that enable them to communicate with one another without having to say a word. Family members use these signs in public to warn each other about a potential problem.

## Order

The third requirement of effective paragraphs is consistent *order*. You saw in the paragraph on the Old South (pages 189–190) that when sentences point in various directions, readers are likely to have trouble following the writer's line of reasoning.

Order in a paragraph is like organization in an essay, but because paragraphs are smaller in scope, it may be easier to consider order as *direction of movement*. Four directional patterns in expository paragraphs are from *general to particular*, from *particular to general*, from *whole to parts*, and from *question to answer* or *effect to cause*.

**General to Particular**  A common pattern in expository paragraphs moves from a general statement, often a topic sentence, to specific explanations or illustrations of that statement. The purpose of the paragraph is to help the reader understand the general statement. That meaning becomes increasingly clear as the paragraph progresses. You saw this kind of clarification in the paragraphs on American Sign Language and children's ability to make sense of nonverbal language. Here is another example:

> It is easy to produce examples of the many ways in which Americans attempt to minimize, circumvent, or deny the interdependence upon which all human societies are based. We seek a private house, a private means of transportation, a private garden, a private laundry, self-service stores, and do-it-yourself skills of every kind. An enormous technology seems to have set itself the task of making it unnecessary for one human being ever to ask anything of another in the course of going about his daily business. Even within the family Americans are

unique in their feeling that each member should have a separate room, and even a separate telephone, television, and car, when economically possible. We seek more and more privacy, and feel more and more alienated and lonely when we get it. What accidental contacts we do have, furthermore, seem more intrusive, not only because they are unsought but because they are unconnected with any familiar pattern of interdependence. (Philip Slater, *The Pursuit of Loneliness*)

**Particular to General**   A particular-to-general pattern reverses the preceding pattern. It begins with specific information and leads to a general conclusion, as in this example:

We look at old family photographs in which we stand next to black, boxy Fords and are wearing period costumes, and we do not gaze fascinated because there we are young again, or there we are standing, as we never will again in life, next to our mother. We stare and drift because there we are . . . historical. It is the dress, the black car that dazzle us now and draw us beyond our mother's bright arms which once caught us. We reach into the attractive impersonality of something more significant than ourselves. (Patricia Hampl, *A Romantic Education*)

Had Hampl chosen, she could have followed a general-to-particular order by beginning with her last sentence and then illustrating its significance with details about family photographs.

The direction of movement within an individual paragraph is often determined by the direction of movement within an extended passage. As Bill Barich points out, paragraphs develop a rhythm for carrying various kinds of information. In the paragraphs that precede the quoted example, Hampl uses several general-to-particular patterns to discuss the search for a family past. In the example, she reverses the order to emphasize the particulars—family photographs. She returns to the general-to-particular order in the next paragraph, when she explores the impersonality of history.

**Whole to Parts**   Sometimes the purpose of a paragraph is to show the parts or divisions of a topic, as in this example:

There are medium friends, and pretty good friends, and very good friends indeed, and these friendships are defined by their level of intimacy. And what we'll reveal at each of these levels of intimacy is calibrated with care. We might tell a medium friend, for example, that yesterday we had a fight with our husband. And we might tell a pretty good friend that this fight with our husband made us so mad that we slept on the couch. And we might tell a very good friend that the reason we got so mad in that fight that we slept on the couch had something to do with that girl who works in his office. But it's only to our very best friends that we're willing to tell all, to tell what's going on with that girl in his office. (Judith Viorst, "Friends, Good Friends—and Such Good Friends," *Redbook*)

This order is also called *partitive* or *enumerative.* The opening statement announces the divisions of the topic, often indicating their number; the rest of the paragraph identifies and defines each of the parts. The partitive or enumerative paragraph is often used in argument, either to introduce the issues to be considered or to summarize a discussion. In exposition, it is used to introduce the categories to be analyzed. Such paragraphs are usually less detailed than Viorst's paragraph because succeeding paragraphs supply information about the categories.

**Question to Answer, Effect to Cause**    A paragraph may begin with a question and give the answer or begin with an effect and explain the cause. Such a paragraph may have no specific topic sentence beyond the opening question or statement of the effect. This paragraph begins with a question which it proceeds to answer:

> So what are we to do, those of us whose habit and pleasure and doom is our tendency, as a Georgia lady put it, to "fly off at every other whipstitch"? Think in terms of movable feasts, for a start. Live here, wherever here may be, as if we were going to belong here for the rest of our lives. Learn to hallow whatever ground we happen to stand on or land on. Like medieval knights who took their tapestries along on Crusades, like modern Afghanis with their yurts, we must pack such totems and icons as we can to make short-term quarters feel like home. Pillows, small rugs, watercolors can dispel much of the chilling anonymity of a sublet apartment or motel room. When we can, we should live in rooms with stoves or fireplaces or anyway candlelight. The ancient saying still is true: Extinguished hearth, extinguished family. Round tables help, too, and as a friend of mine once put it, so do "too many comfortable chairs, with surfaces to put feet on, arranged so as to encourage a maximum of eye-contact." Such rooms inspire good talk, of which good clans can never have enough. (Jane Howard, *Families*)

The next paragraph begins with an effect and then considers some of the causes of that effect.

> There is something very wrong with an institution that so often disintegrates at the very point it is supposed to be the most useful. It is obviously absurd that we should marry, have children, get divorced, and then start the whole thing over in an even more difficult and complicated way. The "reconstituted" families of remarriage give statistical stability to the big picture. But the clue to what is wrong with the big picture lies in the "transition period to new family life," which

is likely to be three or four years when a woman is caring for very small children. Nearly half the children born today will spend a significant part of their lives in a single-parent home. Raising a child or—worse—children, alone, is the wrong way to do it. It is too hard, not on the children—if recent studies mean anything—but on the mother. Of American women divorced and separated, only 4 percent receive alimony, and only 23 percent with children receive child support. Women earn, on the average, fifty-nine cents for every dollar men earn. And of all female-headed families, 41.8 percent live below the poverty level.                    (Jane O'Reilly, *The Girl I Left Behind*)

### Summary of Main Orders of Movement Within Paragraphs

1. *General to particular*
   Opening general statement or topic sentence followed by illustration or details of explanation or proof. The paragraph may conclude with a restatement of the topic sentence.

2. *Particular to general*
   From a series of detailed statements to a conclusion drawn from them. If there is a topic sentence, it occurs at or near the end of the paragraph.

3. *Whole to parts*
   Paragraph begins with an introductory statement about the number of parts and then explains each part: often a first, second, third order.

4. *Question to answer, or effect to cause*
   Paragraph begins with question or effect, then answers the question or shows the cause.

## Coherence

● A WRITER'S RESOURCES

For information about the laws and regulations that control immigration, check the website for America's Immigration and Naturalization Services (INS).

A paragraph is coherent when the sentences are woven together in such a way that readers move easily from one sentence to the next and read the paragraph as an integrated discussion rather than as a series of separate sentences.

If you have a sense of purpose when you begin writing, then you are not likely to have trouble with coherence. Lack of coherence often results if you think about your topic one sentence at a time: You write one sentence, stop, think a minute, write a second sentence, stop, and continue in a series of spurts and pauses. Paragraphs written in this way are likely to lack coherence because your ideas do not flow from one sentence to the next and continuity is lost.

A paragraph can exhibit unity, completeness, and order but still lack coherence. The writer of the following paragraph is composing a paper to describe the ordeals of the immigration experience. Here he tries to illustrate the processing procedure at Ellis Island in New York Harbor, the official place of entry for most European immigrants from 1892 until 1943.

**How does this photograph illustrate the physical and psychological ordeal of Ellis Island?**

> The immigrants were herded off the boat onto Ellis Island. Inspectors talking in a strange language pushed them into a building where metal railings divided them into lines. They waited as the doctors examined them for diseases and defects. Some were separated from their families and sent to other parts of the building. The rest moved on to the next test. They were asked about their relatives, their politics, their work, their money. The questions were confusing, and they were never sure they gave the right answers.

Although this paragraph moves in an orderly sequence, it requires revision. Consider the following points:

▶ What is the purpose of the paragraph? You know from the description of the paper that the writer wants to describe the ordeal of immigration. The information does illustrate this experience, but its significance would be clearer if the paragraph possessed a topic sentence that bound the individual sentences together. Without such a sentence, a reader may not see the writer's purpose in describing the activity on Ellis Island.

▶ What is the relationship between this paragraph and the one that preceded it? The reader is told that the immigrants were on a boat, but there is no introductory statement that explains the transition from boat to island.

▶ Although the repetition of *they* provides some coherence, the sentence structure becomes monotonous, emphasizing the paragraph's disjointedness.

Now consider this revised version:

    Although the immigrants endured many physical hard-
ships during the crossing, they were not prepared for
the psychological ordeal of Ellis Island. They had come
so far, and now they realized that they could be sent
back. Inspectors shouting strange words herded them
into a massive building where metal railings divided
them into lines. There they waited in silent humiliation as one doctor after another poked at their bodies,
looking for diseases and defects. Occasional screams
followed family members who were pulled out of line and
led off to another part of the building. The rest moved
on to the next test. Interpreters asked them about
their relatives, their politics, their work, their
money. Every question seemed like a trap. If they told
the truth, they might be turned away. If they lied,
they might be caught. If they said nothing, they might
be marked dumb and sent back where they came from.

*"And yet __another__ headache for the Immigration and Naturalization Service!"*

The revision was improved in the following ways:

▶ The topic sentence states the purpose of the paragraph, gives significance to all the details that follow, and connects this paragraph to preceding paragraphs.

▶ The more detailed and evocative explanation of the psychological ordeal of the inspection process helps bind the sentences together more effectively than in the unsatisfactory version, in which sentences were connected only by a common subject.

▶ The concluding sentences dramatize the anxiety of those waiting for clearance and sum up the content of the whole paragraph.

This contrast of the original and revised paragraphs shows how an unsatisfactory piece of writing can better express the main idea by providing the links that reveal the relationship among the sentences. Other connective devices that increase paragraph coherence are *pronouns, contrast, repetitive structure,* and *transitional markers.*

**Coherence Through Pronoun Reference**    Because it refers to an antecedent, a pronoun points back (or forward) to create a simple, natural connection. Notice in the following paragraph how the pronoun *they* links the whole paragraph to the antecedent *emigrants.* Pronoun repetition reinforces the purpose of this paragraph: to illustrate that emigrants "shared certain characteristics."

> Most of the emigrants shared certain characteristics as a group: they were men and women who had already made one or more moves before in a restless search for better lands. They were children of parents who themselves had moved to new lands. If ever a people could be said to have been "prepared" for the adventure of the Overland Trail, it would have to be these men and women. They possessed the assortment of skills needed to make the journey and to start again. They had owned land before, had cleared land before, and were prepared to clear and own land again. And they were young. Most of the population that moved across half the continent were between sixteen and thirty-five years of age.    (Lillian Schlissel, *Women's Diaries of Westward Journey*)

**Coherence Through Contrasted Elements**    When a topic sentence calls for a comparison or contrast, the pairing of the contrasted elements enhances coherence. In the following paragraph, the middle sentences illustrate the contrast between the lives of generals Grant and Lee—a contrast that is announced in the topic sentence and summarized in the concluding sentence.

> So Grant and Lee were in complete contrast, representing two diametrically opposed elements in American life. Grant was the modern man emerging; beyond him, ready to come on the stage, was the great age of

steel and machinery, of crowded cities and a restless, burgeoning vitality. Lee might have ridden down from the old age of chivalry, lance in hand, silken banner fluttering over his head. Each man was the perfect champion of his cause, drawing both his strengths and his weaknesses from the people he led. (Bruce Catton, "Grant and Lee: A Study in Contrasts," *The American Story*)

**Coherence Through Repetitive Structure** Purposeless repetition should be avoided, but deliberate repetition of key words, phrases, or sentence patterns can make sentences flow into a coherent paragraph. In the following example, every sentence after the first has the same structure and the same opening words, "There is nothing." This kind of repetition (discussed as *parallel structure* in Chapter 9) ties the sentences together in a coherent development of the topic sentence.

● A WRITING PROJECT

**Write a paragraph presenting the qualifications you would require for American citizenship.**

America, the richest and most powerful nation in the world, can well lead the way in this revolution of values. There is nothing to prevent us from paying adequate wages to schoolteachers, social workers and other servants of the public to insure that we have the best available personnel in these positions, which are charged with the responsibility of guiding our future generations. There is nothing but a lack of social vision to prevent us from paying an adequate wage to every American citizen whether he be a hospital worker, laundry worker, maid or day laborer. There is nothing except shortsightedness to prevent us from guaranteeing an annual minimum—and *livable* income for every American family. There is nothing except a tragic death wish, to prevent us from reordering our priorities so the pursuit of peace will take precedence over the pursuit of war. There is nothing to keep us from remolding a recalcitrant status quo with bruised hands until we have fashioned it into brotherhood. (Martin Luther King Jr., *Where Do We Go from Here: Chaos or Community?*)

**Coherence Through Transitional Markers** *Transitional markers* are words or phrases often placed at or near the beginning of a sentence or clause to signal the relationship between the new sentence or clause and the one before it. The most common markers are the conjunctions *and, or, nor, but,* and *for.* Others—sometimes called *transitional connectives*—indicate the direction a new sentence is about to take and prepare the reader for what is to follow. The most common transitional connectives are used as follows:

▷ *To introduce an illustration:* for example, for instance, to illustrate

▷ *To add another phrase of the same idea:* second, in the second place, then, furthermore, next, moreover, in addition, similarly, again, also, finally

▷ *To point out a contrast or qualification:* on the other hand, nevertheless, despite this fact, on the contrary, still, however, conversely, instead

▷ *To indicate a conclusion or result:* therefore, in conclusion, to sum up, consequently, as a result, accordingly, in other words

Coherence is necessary not only within a paragraph but also between the paragraphs of an essay so that your readers can see how each paragraph is related to those that precede or follow it. The following passage begins with an assertion. At the end of the first paragraph, the writer notes a change, thus providing the transitional link to the next paragraphs and giving coherence to the whole passage.

Those of us who grew up in the fifties believed in the permanence of our American-history textbooks. To us as children, those texts were the truth of things: they were American history. It was not just that we read them before we understood that not everything that is printed is the truth, or the whole truth. It was that they, much more than other books, had the demeanor and trappings of authority. They were weighty volumes. They spoke in measured cadences: imperturbable, humorless, and as distant as Chinese emperors. Our teachers treated them with respect, and we paid them abject homage by memorizing a chapter a week. But now the textbook histories have changed, some of them to such an extent that an adult would find them unrecognizable.

One current junior-high-school American history begins with a story about a Negro cowboy called George McJunkin. It appears that when McJunkin was riding down a lonely trail in New Mexico one cold spring morning in 1925 he discovered a mound containing bones and stone implements, which scientists later proved belonged to an Indian civilization ten thousand years old. The book goes on to say that scientists now believe there were people in the Americas at least twenty thousand years ago. It discusses the Aztec, Mayan, and Incan civilizations and the meaning of the word "culture" before introducing the European explorers.    (Frances FitzGerald, *America Revised*)

# Special Paragraphs

So far in this chapter you have examined topical paragraphs, the main paragraphs in an essay that develop your topic or some aspect of it. Special paragraphs are used to *introduce* or *conclude* an essay and to *mark transitions* from one unit to another.

## Introductory Paragraphs

Readers want to know what you are writing about and whether they will find your subject interesting and significant. Your introductory paragraph leads into your essay, giving your readers a preview. Most introductions contain attention-getting statements that engage the readers'

Read the following passage excerpted from "The Crazy Life," Bill Barich's article on youth gangs in Los Angeles. The passage is presented without its original paragraphing. Reread Barich's comments on paragraphing (page 188), review the four requirements of effective topical paragraphs, and then discuss how you would break this passage into manageable units.

The landmark work in the sociology of gangs is Frederic M. Thrasher's "The Gang," which was published in 1927. Thrasher was a founder of the Chicago school, a methodology that stressed the importance of interviews and direct observation. In pursuing his study, he observed more than a thousand Illinois gangs before arriving at his well-known theory that gangs are largely a phenomenon of immigrant communities. According to Thrasher, they represent an ethnic group in transition, waiting out its adolescence until it can be assimilated into the mainstream. The underlying assumption is that the attractions of a so-called "normal" life—a job, a family, a house in the suburbs—far outweigh the attractions of a life of crime. Over the years, Thrasher's ideas would be repeated, with variations, in many other studies, monographs, and books, and they still echo in current sociological theory, coloring the way youth-gang members are perceived, making them seem distant, opposite, always somewhat less than human. In Los Angeles County, there are Hispanic youth gangs whose histories go back almost a century, involving three and sometimes four generations of men. There are black gangs of such size, sophistication, and economic well-being that they put many small corporations to shame. There are gangs of Chinese teenagers who run gambling emporiums as skillfully as old Vegas hands. When immigrants, legal or illegal, come to Southern California, their children form gangs—Korean, Vietnamese, Filipino, Honduran, Salvadoran, Nicaraguan, Guatemalan. There are Somoan gangs in Los Angeles County, and gangs from Tonga, and they feud with each other just as their ancestors did on the islands. Increasingly, in affluent suburban towns, there are gangs of white teen-agers, kids from decent homes, who—the saying goes—"have everything," and still take to the streets.

(Bill Barich, "The Crazy Life," The New Yorker)

interest or statements that suggest the organization or indicate the scope, focus, or thesis of your essay. Notice how Bill Barich blends these in his introductory paragraph to "The Crazy Life."

> The first time I met Manuel Velazquez, he greeted me awkwardly, unable to shake hands. He had cut himself on a broken bottle while crawling around in a tunnel to read a new graffito, and a doctor at a local clinic had sewed him up with seventeen stitches and then wrapped the wound in cotton, gauze, and tape. Manuel was stoical about his injury, seeing it as an unfortunate but perhaps necessary consequence of his job, which is to keep teen-age gang members in the San Fernando Valley, in California, from killing one another in wars. In Los Angeles County, of which the valley is a part, there are an estimated fifty thousand youth-gang members, and about three hundred of them are expected to be murdered this year. In the old days of youth-gang warfare, the days of "Blackboard Jungle" and "West Side Story," a boy might arm himself with a knife or a home-made zip gun, but now in times of trouble he has access to .357 magnum pistols, hunting rifles with pinpoint scopes, and Uzi semi-automatics from Israel. (Bill Barich, "The Crazy Life," *The New Yorker*)

You can utilize many strategies in your introductory paragraph to suggest your intentions. The writers whose essays appear in previous chapters have used the following techniques.

**Direct Statement**   Andrew Gaub uses direct statement to introduce his essay on the public-private paradox of the telephone in Chapter 5.

> The telephone is at once the most public and private communication device in our culture. The three stages in its development as an object and a network clarify this curious paradox. They also demonstrate how design can influence the behavior designated as public and private.

**Factual Information**   In her essay "Only Child Policy," Yili Shi attempts to establish an objective tone by informing her readers about the *facts* of one of China's most controversial public policies (See Part Four, pages 451–452).

> The biggest problem facing the People's Republic of China in its attempt to build a modern socialist state is its own population. One of every four people in the world lives in China. This enormous population of over one billion people causes incredibly complex difficulties in virtually every aspect of daily life. In 1979, the Chinese government made a dramatic step to control the growth of this population by declaring that each family could produce only one child. Given the size of the population, the speed at which it was growing, and the strains it was placing on any attempt to chart China's future, the "only child policy" seemed logical and necessary. But implementing it has

caused a wide range of social and psychological problems for China's families and their children.

**Quotation**   Wallace Armstrong uses his father's "words of wisdom" to set up his essay about painting *Brandon's Clown* (see Chapter 1, page 24). The quotation guides the reader through the narration and serves as an ironic commentary on Wally's subject and purpose.

> Few of those words of wisdom that are passed from father to son are followed. Most are simply acknowledged and forgotten. My father's advice about my adolescent love for painting was simple and direct: "Son, you have a special talent. Be smart. Use it to make money." With his words guiding me, I took my love to the marketplace. I began accepting commissions, painting fantasies for those who didn't have the skill or desire to paint their own.

**Dramatic Episode**   Ellen Haack's description of Barry making granola dramatizes the unique features of Barry's personality (see Chapter 3, page 75). She concludes the episode with his infamous words, "it's good for me"— words with which Barry, as the reader soon discovers, justifies everything:

> Barry's in the kitchen making granola. His long, narrow frame moves deftly around the work area, pausing to scan the recipe book on the counter or search the shelves for the ingredients—wheat germ, bran, rolled oats, sunflower seeds, raisins, honey—he plans to mix in a large, gray earthenware bowl. While he works, he hums a vaguely recognizable version of "Blue Moon," drumming on the top of the counter or the edge of the bowl with a wooden spoon. He's happy. Making granola always has this effect on him. He doesn't like to make granola—it's messy and time-consuming. He doesn't like to eat granola—it's too crunchy without milk and too mushy with it. But he likes to contemplate his reasons for eating granola—"it's good for me."

**Anecdote**   After her attention-getting first sentence, Jane Graham uses an anecdote about her trip to the American Museum of Natural History to introduce her reasons for her whale-watching trip (see Chapter 6, page 150). The purpose of her allusions to textbooks and magazines is to arouse the curiosity of her readers, making them want to "see more."

> The problem with whales is that they don't fit under a microscope. As a small girl, I walked around and around the large skeleton of a blue whale on the first floor of the American Museum of Natural History, trying to compare its size to the skeletons of the brontosaurus and diplodocus I had seen on the fourth floor. Like those creatures from another time, whales challenged and held my imagination. I could never see enough of them. The drawings in textbooks outlined their

shape but reduced their enormous size to a few inches. The photographs in magazines suggested their magnificence but usually focused on their parts—the head rising to breech, the tail arching to dive. Last summer, hoping to see more, I booked passage on the *Portuguese Princess* out of Provincetown, Massachusetts, for my first whale watch.

## Transitional Paragraphs

A transitional paragraph signals a change in content. It tells your readers that they have finished one main unit and are moving to the next, or it tells them that they are moving from a general explanation to specific examples or applications. A transitional paragraph is often as brief as one sentence:

So much for the parents. We come now to the children.

Let us see how this theory works in practice.

And this brings us to the final ordeal of the crossing: Ellis Island.

A few examples will make this explanation clear.

Sometimes you will need to supplement such signals with a concise summary of what has been covered or with a suggestion of what is to come, as Jon Seidel did in this paragraph from "Who Controls Information (Our Side)" (see Chapter 7, page 182).

The military and the media will have to rethink their relationship because the war against terrorism is, in essence, a war of information. American soldiers and reporters are not the only players in this new kind of war. Osama bin Laden's messages have been broadcast on the Arab satellite network, Al Jazeer. And Saddam Hussein's pronouncements are designed to counter what he calls American imperialistic propaganda. If America is to counter these "disinformation" campaigns, it will have to demonstrate that its reporting is fair and balanced, free from military manipulation.

## Concluding Paragraphs

Not every essay needs a concluding paragraph. If you have adequately demonstrated your thesis, nothing more is necessary. You do not need to add a paragraph that mechanically restates the obvious: "Thus I have shown. . . ."

A good concluding paragraph does not necessarily sum up the ideas in an essay. Bill Barich concludes "The Crazy Life" with a quotation from Manuel, the man he introduced at the beginning of the essay. This paragraph echoes the introduction, but it also opens up the essay by suggesting that Manuel will always have more work to do.

"You can't get depressed about it," he said. "You know, with the people on my team, I tell them they have to make their job fun—even though it's a crummy job. It's got lots of negatives, but lots of positives, too. Once you start an input into somebody's life, you begin to influence them, you break the monotony. Some kids, they don't know any other kind of life. What we do, it's like throwing a wrench inside an engine. It screws up the structure. Suddenly, you're a part of their lives. That's good to feel. Sometimes it's like I can almost control what's going on. It's like having a sixth sense. Like seeing into the future and controlling it. That's when you know you're doing your job." (Bill Barich, "The Crazy Life," *The New Yorker*)

An effective concluding paragraph leaves the reader with a sense of completeness, a conviction that the point has been made, that nothing else needs to be said; it contributes something significant to the essay that could not have been accomplished by a "Thus I have shown . . ." conclusion.

The following examples, taken from essays in previous chapters, show various strategies for concluding paragraphs.

**Restatement and Recommendation**   Andy Rooney summarizes the main points he has made about advertising and emphasizes the need to perfect existing products instead of increasing the number of new products (see Chapter 4, page 97):

Putting the same product in a new package isn't what I call a new product. When an advertisement tells me what I'm buying is "new and improved," I always wonder exactly what the improvement is and whether I was a sucker for having bought the product last year before they fixed whatever was wrong with it.

I don't care what the *Wall Street Journal* says, I like the idea of fewer new products on the market. What we ought to do is keep making the old ones until we get them right.

**Prediction**   Wallace Armstrong begins his conclusion by drawing on the information he has discussed in other paragraphs—his father's advice, his artistic reputation. But he ends by predicting that in twenty years Brandon may pay him back for his creation (see Chapter 1, page 25):

As I left holding my first commission, I did not think about my father's advice or my artistic reputation. I thought only of poor Brandon. I will not be surprised if, twenty years from now, a deranged young man stops me on the street and smashes a clown painting over my head. I probably deserve worse.

**Resolution**   Jane Graham presents a chronological windup to her narrative and a final, climactic insight into her experience (see Chapter 6, page 152):

> Although we watched eagerly for him to surface again, we looked in vain. Soon we began to look at one another. We smiled, but we did not talk. Neither did Richard. No explanation was necessary. We had watched a whale. A whale had watched us. Finally, the engine coughed, and the *Portuguese Princess* resumed her journey back to Provincetown.

**Quotation**   Sometimes a single line of dialogue makes an effective ending, especially when the words resonate like Ellen Haack's (see Chapter 3, page 76):

> "See, I told you it was good for me."

At other times, a carefully chosen statement from an expert can strengthen the authority of your conclusion. Jill Taraskiewicz uses this strategy to make her final point about the recycling controversy (See Part Four, page 462).

> Finally, we need to develop other environmental policies such as waste reduction. Anne Magnuson reports that some communities encourage their citizens to precycle—that is, to buy products in bulk rather than in many small containers that require recycling. Other communities discourage the accumulation of waste by charging a flat fee for every trash bag. And some encourage citizens to use preprinted postcards to remove their names from junk mailing lists (30–37). Such policies discourage the introduction of more waste into the system. Unless we develop such waste reduction policies, all the recycling, landfills, and incinerators in the world will not save us from our own garbage.

## Revising Topical Paragraphs

As you learned in Chapter 4, there are two types of revision: global revision, employed while you are still creating your final draft, and local revision, in which you fine-tune your final draft. Local revision of paragraphs ensures that each paragraph in your essay not only works externally, to advance the purpose of your essay, but also works internally, to create a sensible sequence of thought. The discussion of topical paragraphs in this chapter has shown you some ways to think about local revision, especially in the case of the paragraph about Ellis Island (pages 199–200). To identify problems in your own paragraphs, you must view your paragraphs as your readers will. In other words, after you have refined your subject, audience, and purpose through global revision, and after you have established a reasonably firm organization, you must give your work a sentence-by-sentence reading, concentrating on the relation of sentences to each other and to the topic sentence.

One helpful technique in such close reading is creating a descriptive outline (see Chapter 3, page 63). As you recall, in a descriptive outline you describe what each paragraph in an essay says (that is, its main idea) and does (that is, how the paragraph supports the main idea). You should be able to state succinctly the main idea of every topical paragraph you write. If in reading a paragraph you find that you cannot succinctly state its main idea, you probably need to reconsider your topic sentence—or create one in the first place. If you find that you cannot determine what a paragraph does, the problem may be that it does nothing: It may fail to support the topic sentence or fail to relate any particular meaning.

You need then to consider the paragraph's internal qualities: unity, completeness, order, and coherence. A paragraph that does not exhibit each of these qualities will not effectively advance your purpose. It will leave questions unanswered, details unsupported, transitions incomplete; and your readers will receive less from your writing than you intended. You must question both the meaning and function of each sentence in your paragraph and the overall effect of all the sentences.

In the following example a writer reports a series of impressions:

(1) On Bourbon Street in the French Quarter of New Orleans there are a 50-cent peepshow and a theater that shows pornographic movies. (2) Pictures painted by talented artists are for sale in a shop down the street. (3) Canned music blares through doors held partly open by hustlers of strip joints. (4) There is a concert hall with no doors and no admission fee, where the crowd is entertained by jazz musicians. (5) In some places there are "dancing girls" who just walk across the stage and do "bumps" in what is supposed to be a dancer routine. (6) Sometimes there is a young woman who dances gracefully. (7) She has mastered the techniques that the better burlesques made popular in earlier years.

This paragraph does not lack detail; it is a series of details that try to capture the confusion of Bourbon Street. But the paragraph is all detail and no pattern: It has no unifying idea, no recognizable order, and no semblance of coherence.

The details in the paragraph fall into two groups: sentences 1, 3, and 5 show an unfavorable impression of Bourbon Street; sentences 2, 4, 6, and 7 suggest a more favorable impression. By classifying the details in this way, you can discern that the writer probably intends to contrast the two impressions. This purpose, stated in a topic sentence, is "Bourbon Street in the French Quarter of New Orleans is a contrast of vulgarity and art." With that topic sentence as the controlling idea of the paragraph, you can revise its order in one of two ways:

▸ Use an *A+B* contrast in which all the details suggesting vulgarity (*A*) are placed in the first half of the paragraph and all those suggesting art (*B*) are placed in the second half, with a transitional marker (*but* or *on the other hand*) to mark the change.

▸ Use an *A/B+A/B* contrast in which matched details of vulgarity and art alternate within each sentence.

For this paragraph, the second arrangement is better because it is truer to the frequent contrasts the writer is trying to describe. Here is a revised version:

> Bourbon Street in the French Quarter of New Orleans is a contrast of vulgarity and art. Just a few doors down the street from a 50-cent peepshow and a theater that presents pornographic movies is a shop displaying and selling paintings by talented artists. At strip joints canned music blares out from doors kept ajar by hustlers seeking to entice passers-by; yet not far away is a concert hall with no admission fee, where musicians play first-rate jazz. Even the "dancing girls" offer a sharp contrast: most limit themselves to a slow walk across the stage, interrupted by exaggerated "bumps"; but a few gracefully demonstrate the techniques that once made burlesque at its best an art form.

## Revising Special Paragraphs

Because introductory, transitional, and concluding paragraphs are used for special purposes, they require a somewhat different approach in revision. In judging how well they do what they are meant to do, you should focus less on method than on effect.

Be sure that your introductory paragraph clearly states the thesis you intend to develop and that the thesis is advantageously positioned within the paragraph. Or, if you have used an attention-getting device, you need to look carefully at this "hook" to see that it entices rather than confuses your readers.

Check to see that your opening paragraph fits your final draft. An introductory paragraph written before the final draft was completed may no longer be appropriate. Does your opening seem misleading, flat, or simply uninspiring? View it with an open mind, and do not hesitate to revise it completely if your other revisions make a different opening necessary.

As you revise, pay particular attention to transitional paragraphs, the structural seams of your essay. Significant revisions elsewhere may require you to revise your transitional paragraphs or to delete them and use a concluding sentence or an opening phrase in existing paragraphs. Or you may discover that changes in your essay require you to add a transitional paragraph to clarify the movement from one unit to another. Such decisions require you to reexamine the connections between your ideas to be certain that you have chosen the most effective strategy for communicating those connections to your readers.

When you revise a concluding paragraph, consider whether your essay needs a formal conclusion. You do not want to belabor the obvious. If your conclusion merely repeats what you have already said, delete it. If you decide that your essay does need a conclusion, consider

# Composing paragraphs on your computer

The size of your computer screen limits the amount of text you can see at one time. To evaluate all the paragraphs in your essay, you will have to print out your entire text and read the hard copy. You can make a quick check on your screen, however, by marking the first sentence in every paragraph and transferring it to another file on your computer. This new file should then contain an outline of your essay. Read this sequence of sentences to determine if it organizes and advances the purpose of your text in a logical and coherent way.

Next, return to your original text and evaluate each individual paragraph. If a paragraph needs additional development, add appropriate examples to make it *complete.* If a sentence distracts from your purpose or destroys the *unity* of your paragraph, delete it. If other sentences are out of *order,* use the cut-and-paste feature of your word-processing program to move them to a logical position. You can also use the copy-and-paste feature to compare the original passage with the new one you have created.

After you have checked individual paragraphs, reread the hard copy to assess the visual and dramatic features of your paragraphs. If your introduction seems too long, condense it so that your readers can easily locate your subject and purpose. If you need to add a transitional paragraph, or a transitional marker within a paragraph, do so at the appropriate spot. If your concluding paragraphs seem undramatic, delete them and compose another ending. If you want to change your emphasis, mark your paragraphs and move them to another place in your text.

One way to test the effectiveness of your paragraphs is to eliminate the indentations marking paragraphs in your text. Then post your draft—represented as one continuous paragraph—to your writing group or the members of your writing class. Ask them to mark up your text, determining where they think you should chunk your information into paragraphs. Also, ask them to suggest new paragraphs, or transitional paragraphs to establish greater coherence or completeness in your text. Compare their divisions and suggestions with your original plan, and decide which ones merit your consideration.

the impression you want to leave in closing. You will sometimes discover that other revisions—both global and local—have weakened the effectiveness of your original conclusion. After revising the other parts of your essay, you will know what you must do to round off your work effectively, perhaps even memorably.

## EXERCISES

**Identify the problems in the following paragraphs and then revise each paragraph.**

1. The front porch was once a doorsill. It became a square platform large enough to hold two chairs. It lengthened and began to expand around the sides of the house. At one time, it was long and narrow, just wide enough for a row of chairs. People sat there watching and talking about their neighbors. Porches were a status symbol of economic prosperity and social prominence. Architects complained that they were too ornate. Cars created dust and fumes, so families went inside. The car also gave young lovers more privacy than the porch swing. Air conditioning made it unnecessary to go outside for air. People built backyard patios so the family could have some privacy.

2. It is unusual for one family to live in the same community for more than two generations. The average American family moves once every five years. Americans want to look for their roots. Many have complex ties to different parts of the world and are proud of their heritage. It's hard to trace the effects of immigration. Most families are scattered all over the country. Parents or grandparents who used to bring everyone together for Christmas spend December in trailer parks in Florida.

3. The Gateway Arch in St. Louis is a 630-foot stainless-steel arch. It marks the most prominent point of embarkation for those who traveled into the new territories. A Museum of Westward Expansion, near the arch, commemorates the frontier experience. Inside the steel structure is a contraption like a Ferris wheel that travels to the apex of the arch. The small windows provide a thirty-mile view in any direction. On the Mississippi River, tied to a dock near the arch, is a fast-food restaurant designed to look like a riverboat.

4. The people whose ancestors built the Great Wall of China made one of the most widely acclaimed contributions to American history. Over thirteen thousand Chinese built the western half of the transcontinental railroad. Digging tunnels through mountains and track beds across deserts, they laid 10 miles of track a day. On May 10, 1869, when a golden spike was driven at Promontory Point, Utah, no Chinese were visible. Americans resented the strength and skill of the "little yellow men." Anti-Chinese resentment was so high that Congress passed a series of Exclusion Acts that prohibited Chinese immigration. These laws were repealed in 1943, and Chinese were admitted under a strict quota system.

# Image Gallery

### Questions

1. How would you describe the way that the families are posed in each photograph?

2. What assumptions about culture, cuisine, and etiquette are represented in each photograph?

3. Three of the photographs depict sumptuous meals. One of them depicts a small meal. How does the small meal suggest a cultural stereotype? What other explanations can you suggest to interpret this picture?

# Readings

In her syndicated newspaper column, Ellen Goodman takes occasion to comment on a variety of social issues. In this column her subject is the American family, the "only place where we remember we're all related." How do you account for the difference in length between Goodman's and Barich's paragraphs? How do the size and sequence of Goodman's paragraphs contribute to her purpose?

# Family: The One Social Glue

## ELLEN GOODMAN

1 They are going home for Thanksgiving, traveling through the clogged arteries of airports and highways, bearing bridge chairs and serving plates, Port-a-Cribs and pies. They are going home to rooms that resound with old arguments and interruptions, to piano benches filled with small cousins, to dining-room tables stretched out to the last leaf.

2 They no longer migrate over the river and through the woods straight into that Norman Rockwell poster: Freedom from Want. No, Thanksgiving isn't just a feast, but a reunion. It's no longer a celebration of food (which is plentiful in America) but of family (which is scarce).

3 Now families are so dispersed that it's easier to bring in the crops than the cousins. Now it's not so remarkable that we have a turkey to feed the family. It's more remarkable that there's enough family around to warrant a turkey.

4 For most of the year, we are a nation of individuals, all wrapped in separate cellophane packages like lamb chops in the meat department of a city supermarket. Increasingly we live with decreasing numbers. We create a new category like Single Householder, and fill it to the top of the Census Bureau reports.

5 For most of the year, we are segregated along generation lines into retirement villages and singles' complexes, young married subdivisions and college dormitories, all exclusive clubs whose membership is defined by age.

6 Even when we don't live in age ghettos, we often think that way. Those who worried about a generation gap in the sixties worry about a generation war in the seventies. They see a community torn by warring rights: the Elderly Rights vs. the Middle-Aged Rights vs. the Children Rights. All competing for a piece of the pie.

7 This year, the Elderly Rights fought against mandatory retirement while the Younger Rights fought for job openings. The Children Rights worried about money to keep their schools open, while the Elderly Rights worried about the rising cost of real estate taxes.

8 The retired generation lobbied for an increase in Social Security payments, while the working generation lobbied for a decrease in Social Security taxes. The elderly wanted health care and the children wanted day care and the middle-aged were tired of taking care. They wanted the right to lead their own lives.

9 At times it seemed as if the nation had splintered into peer pressure groups, panthers of all ages. People who cried, not "Me First" but, rather, "My Generation First."

10 But now they have come home for Thanksgiving. Even the Rights are a family who come

Ellen Goodman, *Close to Home* (New York: Simon, 1979), 150–51.

together, not to fight for their piece of the pie this day, but to share it.

11    The family—as extended as that dining-room table—may be the one social glue strong enough to withstand the centrifuge of special interests which send us spinning away from each other. There, in the family, the Elderly Rights are also grandparents and the Children Rights are also nieces and nephews. There, the old are our parents and the young are our children. There, we care about each other's lives. There, self-interest includes concern for the future of the next generation. Because they are ours.

12    Our families are not just the people (if I may massacre Robert Frost) who, "when you have to go there, they have to let you in." They are the people who maintain an unreasonable interest in each other. They are the natural peacemakers in the generation war.

13    "Home" is the only place in society where we now connect along the ages, like discs along the spine of society. The only place where we remember that we're all related. And that's not a bad idea to go home to.

*In this opening section of a much longer essay, Bill Barich describes the movement across the "most heavily travelled border in the world." Reread his comments on composing paragraphs on page 188. Then examine the* unity, completeness, order, *and* coherence *of his paragraphs. How do the size and sequence of his paragraphs contribute to his purpose?*

# La Frontera

## BILL BARICH

1    The most heavily travelled border in the world is a strip of scrubby California desert that runs for fifteen miles between the United States and Mexico, starting at the Pacific Ocean and ending at a thriving yet isolated spot called Otay Mesa. A chain-link fence follows the border for much of its course, but it is torn in many places and trampled in many others, and in some places it has fallen down. Where the fence is still standing, you find litter on both sides of it which illegal aliens have left behind—beer and soda cans, cigarette packs, diapers, syringes, candy wrappers, and even comic-book *novelas* that feature cautionary tales about the perils of a trip to *El Norte*. These *novelas* tell of dishonest employers, horrible living conditions, and the corruptive power of American dollars. In their most dra-

matic stories, families come apart, brothers murder brothers, and lovers' hearts are broken beyond mending. The stories offer a liberal blend of truth and fiction, but that is an accurate reflection of the border, where nothing is ever absolute.

2    Between the ocean and the mesa, the only town of any size is San Ysidro, California, just across from Tijuana. About forty-three million people pass through its legal port of entry every year, in vehicles, on bicycles, and on foot, but nobody knows for certain how many undocumented migrants slip illegally over *la frontera*. An educated guess would be about five thousand every day. They come primarily from Mexico and Central America, and they carry their most precious belongings with them in

Bill Barich, "La Frontera," *The New Yorker* 17 Dec. 1990: 72–74.

knapsacks or plastic supermarket bags. The Border Patrol, in its San Diego Sector—a territory roughly as big as Connecticut—apprehends about a third of them, logging almost fifteen hundred arrests every twenty-four hours, but the others drift on to Los Angeles or San Francisco or Sacramento, or to farms in the great Central Valley, staying with relatives and friends while they look for work. If they fail to be hired anywhere, they go farther north, to Oregon and Washington, ready to pick fruit or to gut salmon in a packing-house, willing to do anything to earn their keep.

3    Like many border towns, San Ysidro is conducive to paranoia. Set in the midst of sagebrush and dry, brown mountains covered with chaparral, it has the harmless look of an ordinary suburb, but this is deceptive and does not hold up under close inspection. For instance, there is a blood bank on the edge of its largest mall, and all day you can watch donors come out the door with balls of cotton pressed to their forearms, bound for a shopping spree at a nearby K mart before going home to Tijuana. The sky above San Ysidro is often full of ravens and buzzards, and skulls of small animals turn up in its playgrounds. Its population is mostly Hispanic, but more and more Anglos—retired people, and people who commute to San Diego—are buying property in the tile-roofed housing tracts that are devouring the last farms and ranches, and they get very angry the first time some illegal aliens dash through their back yards, trampling the shrubbery and pausing to drink from garden hoses.

4    The Border Patrol is the uniformed arm of the Immigration and Naturalization Service, and it is supposed to control the flow of uninvited foreigners into the States. In California, as in Texas, its stations are understaffed and underfunded, and are asked to perform a nearly impossible task. In the San Diego Sector, agents must police all of San Diego County, as well as substantial parts of Orange and Riverside Counties, scouring not only the canyons and the backwoods but also the teeming barrios in cities, where aliens frequently seek shelter. Although the sector captures more illegal aliens than any other sector in the country—more than four hundred and seventy thousand in fiscal year 1990, almost half the United States total—this record does little for the morale of the agents, since there is no real penalty imposed on those who are apprehended, unless they have some contraband or resist arrest. Mexicans are given a brief interview, then returned to Tijuana, sometimes so quickly that they get caught crossing again on the same night.

5    The law isn't the only obstacle that the Border Patrol faces in dispatching its duty. It used to be easy for agents to spot new arrivals because they dressed like field hands and looked dirty and frightened, but now the aliens disguise themselves in clothes fresh off the rack, relying on such items as bluejeans, Reeboks, and L.A. Dodgers caps for protective coloration. The business of providing goods and services to migrants has grown enormously, forming a closed economy worth millions, and they have an elaborate network of support, which often involves extended families and functions in the manner of an underground railroad. Then, too, illegal aliens are always testing agents by devising new tricks for sneaking into California. On a hot summer day, they like to put on bathing suits and wander up the coast, or they dive from a boat and swim to shore. They wade through raw sewage in the Tijuana River and slip into Imperial Beach, just north of San Ysidro. They jam themselves into car trunks and into boxcars, and they ride across the border spread-eagled on top of freight trains. The boldest ones merely sprint through the backed-up traffic at the port of entry, defying the Border Patrol to chase them.

6    Once illegal aliens get by this first line of defense, they can relax and blend into the crowd of

legal Hispanics in San Ysidro. They treat the town as a sort of flea market, making connections and buying Stateside necessities, usually on the sly. If they require fake documents—anything from birth certificates to green cards—they seek out a dealer in such papers and begin negotiations. A high-quality document might cost more than a thousand dollars. Only an expert can detect that it's a forgery, while a so-called "fifty-footer" looks bad even at that distance and can be bought without much haggling. If migrants have some pesos to be laundered, they speak to the fellows hanging around the pay phones by the United States Customs gate. Those phones, supplied by half a dozen different companies, are the conduit through which a fortune in drug profits—from the sale of cocaine, marijuana, and methamphetamines—is annually rerouted. The men who smuggle in aliens use the phones, too, arranging transportation for their customers. The smugglers are known as *coyotes,* on account of their predatory habits, and they flourish on the border, where expediency is the rule of thumb.

7    In San Ysidro, there are also safe houses, where, for a price, a migrant can hole up for a while. The safe houses look like the houses around them, but everybody on a given block can point them out. As it happens, secrecy tends to play a very limited role in illegal immigration. Anyone who wants to see how openly aliens cross the border, even in broad daylight, can take a drive on Dairy Mart Road, which winds from the outskirts of town through beanfields, pastures, and fallow land scattered with junked farm machinery. On any morning or afternoon, in any season, you'll have to brake to a halt as people streak by in front of your car, speeding from one hiding place to another. For the most part, they are young men in their late teens and early twenties, and they never seem the slightest bit afraid. They emerge from arroyos, from stands of bamboo and pampas grass, from copses of trees, and from vacant buildings. One morning as I cruised on Dairy Mart Road, I counted twenty-two people in a two-hour period.

The action at night is even more spectacular,    8 and it occurs on a much larger scale. At dusk, you start hearing sirens and whistles all over San Ysidro, as if several robberies were in progress, and then comes the chopping sound of helicopter blades slashing up the clouds. Step outside your motel room and you notice beams from above shining down on a Carl's, Jr., restaurant, on kids in baseball uniforms and elderly folks out for an evening stroll. Sometimes a beam illuminates a drainage ditch, and a human form scampers away, like a rabbit rousted from its burrow. It's disconcerting to find normal life going on in what appears to be a suburban war zone. If you walk to a weedy field near the blood bank, you can look toward the concrete levee of the Tijuana River, where, in the glare of I.N.S. floodlights and in full view of the Border Patrol, more than five hundred people will be congregated in little bands, waiting for an opportune moment to begin their journey to the United States.

# Web Design

Students using *Writing with a Purpose* in a composition class were asked to design a website for Bill Barich's essay, "La Frontera." Consult the elements and principles of design in Chapter 5 to help you answer the questions about the effectiveness of each design.

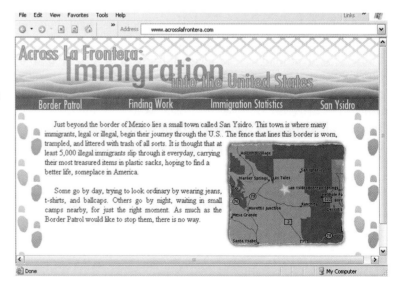

**Sample Homepage #1: La Frontera**

1. How do you react to the footprints in this design?

2. What is the dark brown line dividing the text supposed to represent?

3. In what ways do the graphics distract from the text and its links?

**Sample Homepage #2: La Frontera**

1. How do the chainlink fence and the word *Immigration* clarify the title, "La Frontera"?

2. In what ways does the map help readers understand the subject of this site?

3. How does the alignment of graphics and text focus on the purpose of this design?

# Writing Assignments

### 1. NARRATE

Your family, like most, probably has a relative about whom you like to tell stories. Freewrite about this person without stopping to divide your information into paragraphs. Then reread your material to determine how you might group and sequence your information into paragraphs that present a coherent biographical sketch of your family's favorite hero or villain.

### 2. OBSERVE

Examine old pictures in a family photograph album. Select a photograph taken during a significant or revealing occasion. Reread Patricia Hampl's comments on old family photographs on page 196, then write a letter to a member of your family describing the photograph and your interest in this historical moment.

### 3. INVESTIGATE

Interview a student or someone in your university's office of student affairs who is concerned about the status of minority students on your campus. Inquire about the social, intellectual, and emotional difficulties specific minority students face as they acquire an education with students (and faculty) from the dominant culture. Then write a profile for your student newspaper on "A Day in the Life" of a minority student on your campus.

### 4. COLLABORATE

Your writing group has been asked to compile a group portrait that describes its ethnic diversity. Pair up with a member of your group. Interview one another. Then talk to relatives to explore your family's ethnic history. When did the first member of your family immigrate to the United States? What advantages or difficulties did members of your family face because of their ethnicity? Is your family in touch or out of touch with its ethnic heritage? Use such questions to collect information that can be transformed into topical paragraphs. Then write a collaborative portrait of your group in which you select a similar sequence of paragraphs to present the biographical profile for each member of your group.

### 5. READ

Select a cultural group with which you are unfamiliar—for example, Amish, Lithuanian, or Zuni—and then read several articles about how that group has been treated in the United States. Draft several topic sentences that advance an explanation for this treatment. Then compose an essay by developing those sentences into topical paragraphs. Experiment with each paragraph by placing the topic sentence in a different position.

### 6. RESPOND

Respond to the following assertion about how immigration will change the face of America: Those who appear today to be *alien* will in a generation be *us*.

### 7. ANALYZE

Compare and contrast the size and complexity of the paragraphs written by Ellen Goodman and Bill Barich. The most obvious difference, size, can be explained by the context for their essays—a short newspaper column (Goodman) and a long magazine feature (Barich). You may want to analyze the effectiveness of these conventions. For example, are Goodman's paragraphs *complete?* Are Barich's paragraphs *unified?* You may also want to consider the appropriateness of form and purpose—short paragraphs about the social fragmentation (Goodman); long paragraphs about social crowding (Barich). Write an analysis explaining these concepts, using examples from these sources.

### 8. EVALUATE

Surf the Web looking for sites dedicated to genealogy. Evaluate the tools at these sites by entering your family name and starting a search. Then evaluate the degree to which your family has kept track of its history. Finally, write an essay—addressed to members of your family on your Christmas card list or to family members who might come to a reunion—evaluating the status of your family history. To what extent does it seem complete, orderly, and coherent? What branches of your family tree seem to create difficulties for a writer/researcher?

## 9. ARGUE

Reread the paragraphs about Ellis Island on pages 199 and 200. You may want to read additional material on immigration in the 1890s. (Some good sources are Oscar Handlin's *Uprooted: The Epic Story of the Great Migrations That Made the American People* and Wilson Tifft and Thomas Dunne's *Ellis Island*.) Reread Bill Barich's description of *La Frontera*. You may want to read the whole essay (*The New Yorker* 17 December 1990: 72–92). Then argue that (a) there is no real difference between the way immigrant groups were treated at Ellis Island and the way they are treated along the Mexican border, or (b) specific issues—economic, social, legal—account for contemporary attitudes toward those who want to cross America's borders.

## 10. ARGUE

Examine your university catalogue and reading lists for courses. What opportunities are available in your college curriculum for studying the history and culture of various ethnic groups? Use this information to compose an open letter to the faculty and administration, arguing that (a) such opportunities already exist, but students need better advice about why they should study such material, or (b) such opportunities do *not* exist in the current curriculum, but faculty can enrich existing courses or create new ones that would meet this need.

# 9 Sentences: Patterns of Expression

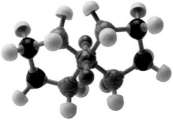

**I TRY TO RESPOND TO THE MARVELOUS ELASTICITY OF THE LANGUAGE BY CONSTANTLY OPENING UP OR COMPRESSING MY SENTENCES.**

—RICHARD SELZER

As you saw in Chapter 8, the sentences in a well-written paragraph are not isolated statements; they exist in complex interrelationships with each other. Although traditionally called units of composition, sentences are units chiefly in the grammatical sense that each sentence has its own subject and predicate and is not part of another sentence. Beyond these basic attributes, however, sentences vary widely in style—and therefore in the effect they create. By varying the arrangements of words, phrases, and clauses in sentences, writers reveal emphasis, shade meaning, and create various kinds of movement in their writing.

Richard Selzer, surgeon and writer, composes sentences in two stages:

> The *first* propels me across the page with an armful of language. It's like the technique of the abstract painter. He will make a brush stroke on a bare canvas. That stroke leads to another and the combination to a third until the canvas is done and he realizes what he has made. The *second* is the fully conscious tinkering that goes on. The artist is always blacking out parts of his canvas and correcting small details until the painting is done in his mind. So one of my essays isn't finished until I cross out half of it and revise its individual parts. I try to respond to the marvellous elasticity of the language by constantly opening up or compressing my sentences. When I am done, they possess a distinctive rhythm and resonance. I can pick them out immediately on any page of prose. They're like my signature. (Personal interview)

This chapter will take a close look at how writers such as Selzer express their purpose by expanding, combining, and revising their sentences.

223

# Expanding and Combining Sentences

Like a brush stroke, a basic sentence moves across the page in a simple line. It consists of a subject and a predicate. The predicate may be a complete verb or a verb that needs something to complete it. For example, the sentence "The doctor smiled" consists of the subject *doctor* and the complete verb *smiled.* But in the following two sentences the verb requires completion:

> The doctor + *examined* + the patient. [Subject, verb, and object]

> The doctor + *was* + courteous. [Subject, verb, and complement]

A *basic sentence,* then, is a main clause consisting of subject and verb and any object or complement required to complete the verb.

Any element in a basic sentence may be modified by adjectives, adverb phrases, or clauses that describe or limit the words being modified. Or the whole main clause rather than one of its elements may be modified. For example, in the sentence "If you can't do it, I'll ask Dr. Helena," the introductory *if* clause modifies the whole main clause and is called a *sentence modifier.*

In the following examples the basic sentence is underscored; the modifiers are italicized and are connected by arrows to the words they modify.

Many <u>students</u> *enrolled in the pre-med curriculum* <u>find</u> *organic* <u>chemistry</u> *extremely* <u>difficult</u>.

*To prepare for a test,* <u>they study</u> *for hours with incredible concentration.*

<u>Some</u>, *recognizing their limitations in math,* <u>hire</u> *private* <u>tutors</u> *to help them prepare for each exam.*

<u>Others study</u> *alone because they are driven to master the material in seclusion.*

*If their study habits predict how they will behave as doctors,* <u>some will consult with colleagues</u>, *while others will insist on making their own diagnosis.*

As these examples show, modifiers may be single words or phrases (*many, private, for hours*) or subordinate clauses (*because they are driven to master the material in seclusion*). The modifiers may come before, after, or within the main clause. In the last two sentences, the subordinate clauses modify the whole main clause and are therefore sentence modifiers.

Distinguish between basic sentences and modifying words or phrases in the following passage from Richard Selzer's "An Absence of Windows." First underline the basic sentence, then circle the modifiers.

(1) Part of my surgical training was spent in a rural hospital in eastern Connecticut. (2) The building was situated on the slope of a modest hill. (3) Behind it, cows grazed in a pasture. (4) The operating theater occupied the fourth, the ultimate floor, wherefrom high windows looked down upon the scene. (5) To glance up from our work and see lovely cattle about theirs, calmed the frenzy of the most temperamental of prima donnas. (6) Intuition tells me that our patients had fewer wound infections and made speedier recoveries than those operated upon in the airless sealed boxes where we now strive. (7) Certainly the surgeons were of gentler stripe.

## Expanding Sentences by Modification

In effective writing, details communicate specific information and hold the reader's interest. Any sentence can be enriched by modification. Notice how much detail is added by the italicized modifiers in the following sentences.

My father kept his own books, *in a desk calendar that recorded in his fine Spencerian handwriting the names of the patients he had seen each day, each name followed by the amount he charged, and that number followed by the amount received.*

(Lewis Thomas, "Amity Street," *The Youngest Science: Notes of a Medicine Watcher*)

I debated whether I should major in zoology *so early in the term before I knew whether my high-school science courses had prepared me for the difficult challenges of the college curriculum.*

The drug companies, *usually operating through private physicians with access to the prisons,* can obtain healthy human subjects *living in conditions that are difficult, if not impossible, to duplicate elsewhere.*

(Jessica Mitford, *Kind and Unusual Punishment*)

In this portion of the chart, *after all the histories are taken, after the chest has been thumped and the spleen has been fingered, after the white cells have been counted and the potassium surveyed,* the doctor can be seen *to abandon the position of recorder and assume that of natural scientist.*

(Gerald Weissman, "The Chart of the Novel," *The Woods Hole Cantata: Essays on Science and Society*)

In sentences like these, the effect comes not from the main clause, which provides no details, but from the specific information provided by the modifiers. You can easily see that this is so by isolating the main clauses from the modifiers:

My father kept his own books.

I debated whether I should major in zoology.

The drug companies can obtain healthy human subjects.

In this portion of the chart, the doctor can be seen.

Effective modifiers such as the ones shown in the full sentences above have two qualities. First, they are not tacked on as afterthoughts but are essential parts of the writers' purposes. A significant portion of Thomas's recollection of his father's books focuses on the shape of the handwriting and the pattern of the accounts; the student's debate about majoring in zoology is occasioned by her doubts about her high-school preparation in science; Weissman's description of a doctor's writing process is based on the details he has to record. In each case the modifying details are necessary to express the writer's complete thought.

Second, effective modification is grounded in observation or experience. Weissman knows from experience how to keep a patient's chart. Mitford has researched her subject and knows about the doctor's cooperation and the conditions that made prisoners ideal subjects for experiments. In each example, the writer has used modification to get his or her observations into the sentences.

Suppose you were asked to expand these three sentences by modification:

I am uncomfortable in my doctor's office.

My doctor always seems impatient.

Doctors study the human body.

To complete the assignment, you need to know the context in which the writer is working and his or her purpose for composing the sentences. Without that knowledge, asking you to expand them is asking you to supply a context and purpose. By drawing on your own experience, you can describe why doctors' offices make you uncomfortable, what makes your doctor appear impatient, and how doctors study the human body. You might expand the first sentence this way:

I am uncomfortable in my doctor's office because while I sit in the posh chairs of the waiting room, I imagine that my body is being secretly afflicted with all sorts of life-threatening diseases.

## EXERCISE

Drawing on your own experience, expand the following basic sentences to make them fuller expressions of the ideas they suggest to you.

1. My doctor always seems impatient.

2. I don't like to read reports about medical studies.

3. I always get sick on vacations.

4. Doctors study the human body.

5. I don't know if an ache is a symptom or something that will just go away.

## Combining Sentences by Coordination

Coordination is combining or joining similar elements into pairs or series. As in the following pairs of examples, sentences can be combined by using a common subject or predicate and compounding the remaining element:

Medical technology contributes to the high cost of health care. Medical liability insurance is also extremely expensive.

**Compound subject/ Common predicate**

Medical technology and medical liability insurance both contribute to the high cost of health care.

Doctors must complete their charts under pressure. They also must carefully think through their comments and notations.

**Compound predicate/ Common subject**

Doctors completing their charts must carefully think through their comments and notations and must write under pressure.

---

### EXERCISE

**By combining parts through coordination, compress the sentences in each group into a single sentence.**

1. Coronary heart disease is the major cause of death in this country.
   Cancer also causes many deaths.

2. My doctor warned me about trying to lose weight too fast.
   My coach reminded me of the danger involved.
   My mother told me the same thing.

3. The first documented case of AIDS within the United States occurred in 1977.
   The AIDS crisis continues to grow.

   The number of newspaper and magazine articles on AIDS has declined in the last few years.

4. Breakfast cereals contain fiber.
   Oat bran may reduce cholesterol.
   Advertisers stress the health benefits of their products.

5. The cost of running shoes is escalating.
   Most people are very selective about the kind of running shoes they buy.

---

## Using Parallel Structure

When two or more coordinate elements have the same form, they are said to have *parallel structure*. Such structures may be unnoticed in any sentence, but when the parallelism is conspicuous, the whole sentence may be called a *parallel sentence*. Thus, "He was without a job, without money, without opportunity, and without hope" is a parallel sentence in which the four phrases have the same form (they all start with *without*) and the same grammatical function (they all complete the verb *was*).

Both science and art have a habit of waking us up, turning on the lights, grabbing us by the collar and saying, *Would you please pay attention!*

—Diane Ackerman,
*A Natural History of the Senses*

Consider these contrasted sentences:

| | |
|---|---|
| I am in favor of equal economic rights for women. Women should be able to compete with men for jobs for which they are both qualified. The pay should be the same for the same jobs. There should be the same opportunities for advancement. | I am in favor of equal economic rights for women: the right to compete with men for jobs for which they are both qualified, the right to get the same pay for the same job, and the right to equal opportunities for advancement. |

Both versions assert the same three rights. The version on the left advances the assertions in four sentences, each using a different subject. The version on the right states all three rights in one sentence and focuses the reader's attention by the repetition of the phrase "the right to." The parallel structure of the second version gives it the unity, coherence, and emphasis that the first version lacks.

Parallel elements may be single words, phrases, clauses, or sentences (contributing to a paragraph with parallel structure); they may act as subjects, objects, verbs, or adverbial or adjectival modifiers. But for elements in a pair or a series to be parallel, all members must have the same form and serve the same grammatical function. You cannot coordinate nouns with adjectives, verbs with infinitives, or phrases with clauses. Any attempt to do so disrupts parallelism, disappoints your readers, and produces awkwardness.

In each of the following sentences, the italicized element disrupts parallelism by switching from one grammatical form to another:

The children were laughing, squealing, and *danced*. [To restore parallelism, *danced* should be changed to *dancing*.]

My two ambitions are to become a doctor and *having* enough money to give my children a good education. [Parallelism requires that *to become* must be matched with *to have*.]

My parents taught me such things as honesty, faith, *to be fair,* and *having patience*. [Parallelism with the two nouns would be sustained by replacing the infinitive and participial phrases with the nouns *fairness* and *patience*.]

The following diagrams show the similarity in form and function of various parallel structures:

***Parallel predicates***

| | |
|---|---|
| He | walked past the information desk, followed the signs to obstetrics, selected a seat in the waiting room, and watched the other expectant fathers pace the floor. |

*Prepositional phrases in a series*

Fat people know all about about the mystery of life. They are the ones acquainted

with the night, with luck, with fate, with playing it by ear.

(Suzanne Britt Jordan)

*Participial phrases in a series*

This was the American family at play

escaping the city heat,

wondering whether the newcomers in the camp at the head of the cove were "common" or "nice,"

wondering whether it was true that the people who drove up for Sunday dinner at the farmhouse were turned away because there wasn't enough chicken.

(E. B. White)

## EXERCISES

1. Identify and diagram the parallel elements in the following sentences:
   a. We hold these truths to be self-evident: that all men are created equal, that they are endowed by their Creator with certain unalienable Rights. . . .
   b. Berton Roueche's narratives of "medical detection" are full of patients with unusual symptoms, of laboratory technicians with specialized knowledge, and of doctors with extraordinary diagnostic powers.

2. The following are lists of the distinguishing characteristics of people who exhibit Type A and Type B behaviors. Organize the items into parallel lists, and then write a parallel sentence coordinating the information in the two series.

   *Type A behavior*
   Obsessed with deadlines
   Intense need to win at all costs
   Conversation dominated by numbers
   Harshly critical of others

   *Type B behavior*
   Evokes serenity in others
   Enjoys creating images and metaphors
   Secure sense of self-esteem
   Rarely wears a watch

3. List characteristics of the brain suggested by the following list for the computer. Then compose a parallel sentence contrasting the advantages of the brain with those of the computer as a "thinking machine."

   | *Computer* | *Brain* |
   |---|---|
   | Circuits | |
   | Blank disk | |
   | Storage | |
   | Program | |

When parallelism is extended through a paragraph, each sentence becomes an element in a series. An example of a series of parallel sentences appears on page 202 in the paragraph by Martin Luther King Jr., in which each sentence begins with the clause "There is nothing." Such deliberate repetition binds individual sentences into a coherent paragraph. Consider the features of conspicuous parallelism in the following paragraph:

> H. G. Wells continues to be a biographer's dream and book reviewer's waltz. His life stretches very nearly from Appomattox to Hiroshima. He was one of the world's great storytellers, the father of modern science fiction, an autobiographic novelist of scandalous proportions, a proselytizer for world peace through brain power, an unsurpassed popular historian, a journalist and inexhaustible pamphleteer, the friend and worthy adversary of great men and the lover of numerous and intelligent women. (R. Z. Sheppard, *Time*)

## Combining Sentences by Subordination

Subordination reduces one sentence to a subordinate clause or to a phrase that becomes part of another sentence. Consider the following basic sentences:

> We left early. We had work to do.

The second of these sentences may be embedded in the first as a subordinate clause.

> We left early *because we had work to do.*

In the next example, a basic sentence is reduced to a phrase.

> The man was evidently in great pain. He was taken to a hospital.
> The man, *evidently in great pain,* was taken to the hospital.

As these examples show, when two sentences are combined by subordination, the information in one sentence is embedded in the other. Using subordination, a writer can pack a great deal of information into a sentence and still emphasize what is most important. This does not mean that short, basic sentences are always inappropriate. Often they are useful to create variety and achieve emphasis. But consistent use of basic sentences in a sustained piece of writing can make the writing seem repetitive and dull.

In the following example, a complex sentence is created through the subordination of four basic sentences.

1. Last weekend I saw a science fiction film.
2. Three friends went with me.
3. The film focused on the experiments of a mad doctor.
4. He altered his patients' lives by manipulating their dreams.

Last weekend three friends and I saw a science fiction film in which a mad doctor altered his patients' lives by manipulating their dreams.

The original four sentences contain thirty-two words. Using subordination to embed sentences 2, 3, and 4 in sentence 1 creates a denser sentence in which the same information is expressed economically, in twenty-four words, and the monotony of the original sentences is eliminated.

## EXERCISES

**Practice creating denser sentences through subordination by reducing each of the following sets of sentences to a single sentence without omitting any of the information.**

1. Scientists use guinea pigs in their laboratory experiments.
   They inject them with a disease.
   They observe their behavior.
   They dissect them.
   They examine the effect of the disease on their organs.

2. Michelangelo studied anatomy.

He dissected cadavers.
Such gruesome work helped him understand human bones and muscles.
His sculpture celebrates the human body.

3. X-rays can penetrate the human body.
   They produce images on photographic film.
   Shadows on the picture reveal changes in body tissue.

4. The early history of medicine is filled with guesswork.
   Doctors did not know what caused disease.

They developed cures through trial and error.
Most of the cures did not work.
Cures that worked were considered magical.

5. People went to spas to restore their health.
   Most spas were located in beautiful settings.
   They featured special mineral waters.
   The waters were supposed to purge the body of disease.
   These watering spots were developed into vacation resorts.

## Combining for a Purpose

When you combine basic sentences into denser structures through coordination and subordination, you should choose the sentence pattern that best suits your purpose. If you are writing a paper on the latest developments in frozen foods for a nutrition class, you might collect the following information:

1. Frozen food has long been part of the American way of life.

2. Frozen dinners once consisted of such dull items as lima beans, gooey potatoes, and mystery meat.

3. Currently available frozen dinner entrées include beef bourguignon with glazed carrots, asparagus crepes with Mornay sauce, and vegetarian lasagna.

4. Some frozen-food companies have even developed gourmet dietetic dinners.

5. Americans have fast-paced, busy lifestyles these days.

6. They are also more concerned than they were before about eating healthful, interesting, and balanced meals.

Strung together in this order, these sentences have little meaning. They trace a sequence, to be sure, but what is significant about that sequence and what are its implications? The answer, of course, depends on your purpose. If you have a purpose, you can combine the sentences through coordination or subordination to achieve focus and establish relationships among the facts.

For example, if you want to propose a cause-and-effect relationship between the change in American lifestyles and the change in frozen food, you can reduce sentence 1 to a subordinate clause and embed it in sentence 2.

Frozen dinners, long part of the American way of life, once consisted of such dull items as lima beans, gooey potatoes, and mystery meat.

Through a similar process you can combine sentences 5 with 6 and 3 with 4.

To satisfy busy Americans' concern for healthy, interesting, and balanced meals, today's frozen-food companies have developed more sophisticated fare: beef bourguignon with glazed carrots, asparagus crepes with Mornay sauce, vegetarian lasagna, and even gourmet dietetic dinners.

With a coordinating conjunction you can combine the two sentences into one.

Frozen dinners, long part of the American way of life, once consisted of such dull items as lima beans, gooey potatoes, and mystery meat, but to satisfy busy Americans' concern for healthy, interesting, and balanced meals, today's food companies have developed more sophisticated fare: beef bourguignon with glazed carrots, asparagus crepes with Mornay sauce, vegetarian lasagna, and even gourmet dietetic dinners.

If you want to say that those who once found frozen dinners unappetizing now have a reason to try them, you can combine the original sentences for this purpose.

Busy Americans once identified frozen dinners with such dull items as lima beans, gooey potatoes, and mystery meat, but today those same consumers are tempted by a new variety of healthy, interesting, and balanced frozen meals: beef bourguignon with glazed carrots, asparagus crepes with Mornay sauce, vegetarian lasagna, and even gourmet dietetic dinners.

The last version focuses on the customer rather than on the company, but the focus is still achieved by subordination and coordination.

The three devices you have been studying—modification, coordination, and subordination—allow you to combine and present information in complex sentences. Organizing ideas into an effective form is just as important in a sentence as it is in a paragraph or essay. In a series of simple sentences, each idea is stated separately; the statements lack coherence, and relationships among the ideas are not clear. Moreover, such sentences lack emphasis; all information appears to be of equal importance. By subordinating the less important to the more important or by showing the equality of ideas through coordination, you can revise such sentences so that they have variety, clarity, and emphasis.

*Organizing ideas into an effective form is just as important in a sentence as it is in a paragraph or essay.*

## EXERCISES

For each of the following clusters, combine as many of the items as you need (you may not need or want to use them all) into a sentence that fulfills each of the two purposes specified. Combine any remaining items into a second, supporting sentence.

### Cluster A

1. Clothes reveal an individual's personality and attitudes.
2. Clothes like blue jeans and T-shirts make a statement.
3. Dark blue suits and white laboratory jackets also make a statement.
4. Certain occasions, situations, or jobs require appropriate attire.
5. "Appropriate" attire is often formal: a dress, suit, tie.
6. People should be free to dress as they please.
7. In many professional situations, people judge others by their appearance.

*Purpose 1:* You want to assert that people should be free to dress as they please.

*Purpose 2:* You want to argue that people should dress appropriately in professional situations.

### Cluster B

1. Hospitals are often the setting for television soap operas.
2. Characters spend more time discussing their personal problems than their professional responsibilities.
3. Doctors are seen making rounds; nurses are seen keeping charts.
4. Soap operas rarely show medical procedures.
5. Characters conveniently develop illnesses to complicate the plot.
6. Doctors use vague medical terminology to discuss cases.

*Purpose 1:* You want to demonstrate that soap operas treat the topic of illness superficially.

*Purpose 2:* You want to illustrate that soap operas use hospitals as a convenient setting for dramatic conflict.

### Cluster C

1. Many of today's sports injuries are treated with arthroscopic surgery.
2. Major surgery requires doctors to cut through the muscle to find the damaged area.
3. Such surgery requires many months of rehabilitation.
4. An arthroscopic surgeon punctures the muscle with a catheter carrying a microscopic television camera and another catheter carrying appropriate surgical tools.
5. He locates the injury with the camera and uses the tool to repair it.
6. Players can often return to action within several weeks.
7. Any injury requires sufficient recuperation.
8. Reinjury of damaged areas can result in disability.

*Purpose 1:* You want to argue that arthroscopic surgery is a major medical breakthrough.

*Purpose 2:* You want to suggest that the availability of arthroscopic surgery can give players a false sense of security.

## Types of Sentences and Their Effects

In this section you will learn to use to good effect three important sentence types: the *balanced* sentence, the *periodic* sentence, and the *cumulative* sentence.

### The Balanced Sentence

In a balanced sentence, two coordinate but contrasting structures are set off against each other like the weights on a balanced scale. In each of the following sentences the underlined parts balance each other:

> <u>Many are called</u> but <u>few are chosen</u>.                (Matthew 22:14)

> <u>I come to bury Caesar</u>, not <u>to praise him</u>.    (William Shakespeare, *Julius Caesar*)

> <u>Where I used to suture the tissue of the body together,</u>
> <u>now I suture words together.</u>                (Richard Selzer)

When you read a balanced sentence aloud, you tend to pause between the balanced parts. That pause is often marked by a coordinating conjunction (*but, or, nor, yet, and*), sometimes by *not* (as in the second sentence), and sometimes by punctuation alone (as in the third sentence). Whatever the marker, it serves as a fulcrum, the point at which the contrasted parts balance against each other, as the following diagram illustrates:

|  | but |  |
|---|---|---|
| When a man dies on shore, his body remains with his friends, and the "mourners go about the streets," | | when a man falls overboard at sea and is lost, there is a suddenness in the event . . . which gives it an air of awful mystery. |

(Richard Henry Dana)

The balanced structure points up the contrast in thought. It is effective when two subjects are to be contrasted within the same sentence.

---

### EXERCISE

Compose a sentence about each item in each pair. Then combine the two sentences into a balanced sentence.

jogging—swimming
pain—stress
doctors—dentists
painting—photograph
smokers—nonsmokers
mural—miniature

---

## Periodic and Cumulative Sentences

A *periodic* sentence builds to a climactic statement in its final main clause. The writer withholds the main idea until the end of the sentence. Here is an example:

> Just before I went away to college, my father took me aside, as I had expected, and said, as I had not expected, "Now, Son, if a strange woman comes up to you on a street corner and offers to take your watch around the corner and have it engraved, don't do it." (Eric Lax)

The father's remarks lead up to the advice given in the final main clause—"don't do it"—which provides a climax, like the punch line of a joke. All the rest of the sentence has been a preparation for that statement.

*Cumulative* sentences, also called *loose sentences,* reverse the order of periodic sentences. Instead of withholding the main idea until the last clause, the writer states it immediately and then adds examples and details. Compare the style and effect of the cumulative and periodic sentences in these two examples:

> I fought migraine then, ignored the warnings it sent, went to school and later to work in spite of it, sat through lectures in Middle English and presentations to advertisers with involuntary tears running down the right side of my face, threw up in washrooms, stumbled home by instinct, emptied ice trays onto my bed and tried to freeze the pain in my right temple, wished only for a neurosurgeon who would do a lobotomy on house call, and cussed my imagination. (Joan Didion, "In Bed," *The White Album*)

> For doctors, who confront death when they go to work in the morning as routinely as other people deal with balance sheets and computer print outs, and for me, to whom a chest x-ray or a blood test will never again be a simple routine procedure, it is particularly important to face the fact of death squarely, to talk about it with one another.
>
> (Alice Trillin, "Of Dragons and Garden Peas: A Cancer Patient Talks to Doctors," *The New England Journal of Medicine*)

Both writers could have reversed the order of their sentences. Didion could have listed her agonies first, building to her main clause, "I fought migraine." But by announcing her struggle first and then providing the details, she exhausts the main idea and forces her reader to experience some of the exhaustion she feels. Similarly, Trillin could have begun with a clause that states her main idea—that doctors and patients talk squarely to each other about death—and then added the details to illustrate her assertion. But by suspending her assertion until she establishes the contrasting perspectives of doctors and patients, she gains the reader's sympathy and interest. In each example the style and effect of the sentence advance the writer's purpose.

## EXERCISE

1. Write a periodic sentence describing the most frustrating, fulfilling, or comic day you have had recently. Use your opening clauses to build suspense and reveal your final assertion in the last clause.

2. Reverse this order and write a cumulative sentence. Make your assertion first and then accumulate detailed examples.

3. Which pattern is more effective? Explain your answer.

## Revising Sentences

You have been examining the structure of different types of sentences and techniques for increasing the density of sentences through modification, coordination, and subordination. The process of shaping ideas into sentences is a learning process, and as you grope toward a satisfactory statement of your meaning, you will try out different sentence structures, revising your sentences while you write them. But in this section you will be trying, through local revision, to make your sentences more effective expressions of the ideas you intend them to convey, to improve sentences that have already been written—to "tinker," as Richard Selzer suggests, with your completed draft—by revising for *clarity, emphasis, economy,* and *variety.*

### Revising for Clarity

A WRITER'S RESOURCES

For interesting comparisons between art and medicine, check the following websites: Art and Medicine, the National Library of Medicine (Exhibits and Public Programs), and the Literature, Arts, and Medicine Database.

This section is concerned only with revising confusing sentence structure, even though lack of clarity can also result from faulty grammar or punctuation, misleading pronoun reference, or vague or ambiguous wording. Unclear sentence structure sometimes occurs when a writer tries to pack too much information into one sentence. The following sentence illustrates this problem:

Last month while I was visiting the federal buildings in Washington on a guided tour, we went to the National Gallery of Art, where we had been for an hour when the rest of the group was ready to move on to the Treasury Building, and I told a friend with the group that I wanted to stay in the art gallery a while longer and that I would rejoin the group about a half an hour later, but I never did, even though I moved more quickly than I wanted to from room to room, not having seen after about four more hours all that I wanted to see.

As written, this sentence of 108 words consists of three main clauses and eight subordinate clauses. This involved structure is hard going for both writer and reader. The goal of revision should be to simplify the structure by reducing the number of clauses. This can be done by (1) distributing the clauses into two or more sentences, or (2) omitting material irrelevant to the writer's purpose.

Here is a revision that employs the first strategy:

> While I was visiting the National Gallery of Art with a tour group last month, I decided to stay longer when the group left after an hour, and so I told a friend that I would rejoin the group at the Treasury Building in about half an hour. I moved from room to room much more quickly than I wanted to, but after four more hours I had not seen all I wanted to see. I never did rejoin the tour group that day.

This revision distributes all the original material into three sentences and makes the passage easier to read. In addition, the revision uses 25 fewer words, a reduction of more than 23 percent.

Here is a revision that employs the second strategy, cutting the original drastically by leaving out irrelevant material.

> While visiting the National Gallery of Art with a tour group last month, I stayed four hours after the group left. Even then I did not see all that I wanted to.

This version reduces the original eleven clauses to four and compresses the 108-word paragraph to 31 words in two sentences.

Both revisions are clearer than the original. The first revision is minor since it makes little change in content. The second is major since it both selects and reorganizes the content. In addition to these revisions, others are possible. Try a few variations to see which you prefer.

Notice that the previous revisions reduce the amount of information in the original sentence. This may seem to contradict what was said earlier about combining sentences to increase their density. But in fact there is no contradiction. Some sentences should be combined to achieve greater density; others should be separated into several sentences to achieve greater clarity. The decision to combine or to separate, to enrich or to simplify, depends on your material and your best judgment about your audience and purpose.

*"I understood each and every word you said but not the order in which they appeared."*

**Simplify the structure of the following sentences to make them easier to read.**

1. For centuries artists have known that the paint that they keep in their studios and that they allow to collect on their clothing and that they are constantly touching and breathing, so that it penetrates their skin and gets into their bloodstream, contains lead, which can poison them, causing them to have convulsive cramps, fatigue, and making them look sickly by comparison to the portraits of the healthy subjects they paint.

2. In the movies, artists are often portrayed as tormented and anguished people who live in poverty and squalor that causes them to contract all sorts of strange diseases that make them suffer so that they become more sensitive than normal people, which enables them to create beautiful art in the midst of their illness, even though they have to die for their art and only become famous once they are dead.

3. One of the conceptions not founded in fact that many people have about abstract painters is that they don't possess the skills necessary to draw a landscape or a face. In fact, most abstract painters have developed the ability to be extremely adept at drawing objects and people with photographic accuracy. Instead of painting such realistic portraits, however, they design thickly woven textures of paint that enable them to create more universal symbols that express aspects of all human experience. Some of these symbols are called "biomorphic" because they appear to resemble organic forms or fragments of human anatomy sandwiched into densely packed spatial landscapes. These symbols are often interpreted to express the abstract painter's sense of fragmentation in modern society.

## Revising for Emphasis

Emphasis reflects your purpose and helps you convey that purpose to your readers. Among the numerous ways available to express any idea, the most effective are those that underscore your purpose—that best achieve the effect you have in mind. You can create purposeful emphasis by means of *emphatic word order, emphatic repetition, climactic order,* and *emphatic voice.*

**Emphatic Word Order**     To employ emphatic word order, you must know what you want to emphasize and which positions in a sentence provide the most emphasis. In an English sentence the positions of greatest emphasis are the beginning and the end. The most important material should be placed in those positions; less important material, in midsentence. Unimportant details piled up at the end of a sentence get more emphasis than they deserve and make your readers feel that the sentence is "running out of gas."

Notice the difference between the following statements.

*Unemphatic order*
From 1904 to 1914, Americans built the fifty-mile Panama Canal, which caused over five thousand workers to die of malaria in the jungles of Central America.

*Emphatic order*

Over five thousand workers died of malaria in the jungles of Central America when Americans labored from 1904 to 1914 to build the fifty-mile Panama Canal.

The most important information in this sentence is that over five thousand workers died of malaria to build a fifty-mile canal—about one hundred workers per mile. The first version puts the number of deaths and the size of the canal in the least important position, lessening the impact. The second version puts this information where it will get the most emphasis, relegating the less important information to the middle of the statement.

## EXERCISES

**Revise the order of each sentence to emphasize the points you think most important.**

1. It is entirely possible that longevity depends on the luck of your genes, I sometimes think.

2. A proposal that has caused much discussion about our national health policy is the one about insurance for catastrophic illness that is now before Congress.

3. Dr. Albert Schweitzer, even when he was ninety, worked in his clinic all day and played his piano at night because he believed that a sense of purpose and creativity was the best medicine for any illness he might have.

4. Thomas Eakins, in his painting *The Gross Clinic* (below), reveals his extensive knowledge of anatomy by portraying Samuel Gross, the famous surgeon, standing next to the operating table with a scalpel in his hand, lecturing to his students as his assistant probes the patient's open wound.

5. One of America's leading authors and child psychiatrists, Robert Coles, learned about sickness when he was a medical student from the stories he heard from the patients he met as he went on rounds with poet and physician William Carlos Williams.

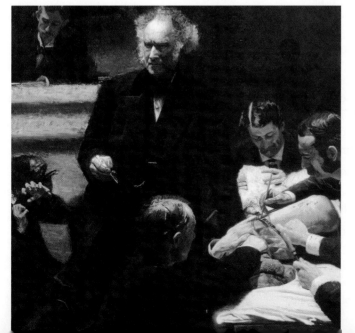

**What details on Thomas Eakins' *The Gross Clinic* are similar to or different from the details in Richard Selzer's "The Knife"(pages 252–253)?**

Source: Thomas Eakins (1844–1916), *The Gross Clinic,* oil on canvas (1875). From the Jefferson Medical College of Thomas Jefferson University, Philadelphia.

**Emphatic Repetition**    Unintentional repetition generally weakens a sentence, as the following examples show:

> The disappointing results were all the more disappointing because we were sure that the experiment would be a success, and so were disappointed in the results.

> The writer who wrote the novel that won the award for the best novel of the year did not attend the awards ceremony.

Deliberate repetition, by contrast, can produce a desired emphasis. You have seen how the repetition of words can help unify a paragraph and how the use of parallel and balanced structures creates coherence. The following examples show the effective use of deliberate repetition:

> If we *write* about our scientific *observations,* our *observations* inevitably color our *writing.*  (Leigh Hafrey, "Write About What You Know: Big Bang or Grecian Urn")

> And this hell was simply, that he had never in his life owned anything—*not his* wife, *not his* house, *not his* child—which could *not,* at any instant, be taken from him by the power of white people.                         (James Baldwin)

**Climactic Order**    Climactic word order achieves emphasis by building to a major idea. The effect of a periodic sentence depends on climactic order, but climax may be used in other sentences as well. The following example contrasts anticlimactic and climactic order. Study both versions of the sentence to determine what changes were made in revision.

*Anticlimactic order*
Paul Gauguin, near the end of his life, painted *Where Do We Come From? Who Are We? Where Are We Going?* in the hopes of glimpsing the life we live from infancy to our last years.

*Climactic order*
Near the end of his life, in the hopes of glimpsing the life we live from infancy to our last years, Paul Gauguin painted *Where Do We Come From? Who Are We? Where Are We Going?*

**Emphatic Voice**    Although it is commonplace that writers should use verbs in the active rather than passive voice, this sound advice is worth repeating. The active voice creates natural, vigorous sentences; the passive voice encourages awkward shifts in structure and anemic, evasive wordiness.

| *Weak passive* | *More emphatic active voice* |
| --- | --- |
| Fantasies of the self are created by modern artists. | Modern artists create fantasies of the self. |
| Real people afflicted by real diseases have been helped by medical science. | Medical science helps real people afflicted by real diseases. |

How do the figures in Paul Gauguin's *Where Do We Come From? Who Are We? Where Are We Going?* suggest a climatic order?

Source: Paul Gauguin (1848–1903), *Where Do We Come From? Who Are We? Where Are We Going?*, oil on canvas (1897). Thompkins Collection. Reproduced with permission. (c) 2000 Museum of Fine Arts, Boston. All rights reserved.

## EXERCISES

Revise the following sentences by changing passive verbs to the active voice.

1. Changing the criteria for what people consider ugly has been proposed by critics as the goal of much modern art.

2. It must surely be recognized by the American Hospital Association that such costs cannot be afforded by many families.

3. The critic said that the winners in the photographic competition would be announced by her within three days.

4. Once the danger was gone, the safety precautions that had been so carefully observed by us were abandoned.

But in some cases, the passive voice may provide greater emphasis than the active voice. Passive constructions can be used to bypass a sentence's grammatical subject in order to emphasize a more important element, such as a significant action or object of an action. For example:

| *Active voice* | *Passive voice* |
| --- | --- |
| A person may not smoke in the museum. | Smoking is prohibited in the museum. |
| The doctor performed the emergency surgery under battery-operated lights. | The emergency surgery was performed under battery-operated lights. |

Choosing active or passive voice is like any other choice you make in the writing process. You must judge by results: Which form provides the emphasis you want? But to avoid the awkward or ungrammatical sentences that can result from misuse of the passive, use the active voice unless the passive advances your purpose more effectively.

## Revising for Economy

Economical prose achieves an equivalence between the number of words used and the amount of meaning they convey. A sentence is not economical because it is short, or wordy because it is long. Consider these two statements:

| | |
|---|---|
| I should like to make it entirely clear to one and all that neither I nor any of my associates or fellow workers had anything at all to do in any way, shape, or form with this illicit and legally unjustifiable act that has been committed. | I want to make it clear to everyone that neither I nor any of my assciates had anything to do with this illegal act. |

The version on the left takes 46 words to say what is more clearly said on the right in 24. The 22 additional words do not add significant information: They merely make reading more difficult and annoy the reader with useless repetition.

Now contrast the following statements:

| | |
|---|---|
| His defense is not believable. | His defense is not believable: At points it is contradicted by the unanimous testimony of other witnesses, and it offers no proof that that testimony is false; it ignores significant facts about which there can be no dispute or evades them by saying that he does not recollect them; it contains inconsistencies that he is unable to resolve, even when specifically asked to do so. |

The version on the right contains over twelve times more words than the one on the left, and its greater length is justified by the greater information it provides. Both versions express the same judgment, but the second presents the reasons for that judgment. If the writer believes these reasons must be stated, it would be foolish to omit them simply to compose a shorter sentence. Decisions about economy must always be made in relation to meaning and purpose.

Wordiness—the failure to achieve economy—is a common writing problem. Essays can be wordy because of scanty planning (corrected through global revision) or a monotonous style (corrected through better use of coordination and subordination). To eliminate wordiness *within* a sentence entails local revision. The two most common methods are deleting useless words and phrases and substituting more economical expressions for wordy ones.

## Cutting Out Useless Words and Phrases

~~It seems unnecessary to point out that~~ the purpose of chemistry lab is to give students ~~the kind of~~ practical experience ~~they need~~ in testing chemical formulas.

~~I would say in response to your question that~~ the task of the art teacher is to help students ~~develop the ability~~ to understand the function of shape, line, color, and light.

Picasso ~~was an artist who~~ took ~~everyday~~ common objects such as a ~~bicycle~~ seat and the handlebars of an old bicycle and ~~through the process of his imagination~~ transformed them into ~~a work of art called~~ *Bull's Head.*

## Substituting an Economical Expression for a Wordy One

*Contemporary researchers in*
~~The forward-looking thinking of those working in the area of~~ coronary
*emphasize*
artery disease ~~tends to place a great deal of emphasis on~~ the potential of

laser technology.

*an international*
The Armory Show, ~~a famous~~ exhibition of painting and sculpture ~~that~~

~~brought together the works of artists from throughout the world and~~
*held*
~~displayed them~~ in the Armory of the 69th Regiment in New York City
*introduced*
in 1913, ~~enabled~~ the American public to ~~see for the first time artistic~~

~~movements such as~~ Cubism and Expressionism.

*Over* *ago* *argued that*
~~It has been more than~~ thirty years ~~since~~ C. P. Snow ~~presented his argu-~~
*our*
~~ment that the~~ world ~~we live in~~ is divided into *two cultures*—one ~~of~~
*dedicated to* *to*
~~these cultures was preoccupied with~~ the humanities; the other ~~was~~

~~interested only in~~ the sciences.

**Eliminate wordiness in the following sentences:**

1. As far as the average citizen is concerned, it is probable that most people are not greatly concerned with the latest critical reaction to the new fads in the world of art.

2. When we studied the parts of the human face, which we did in our art class, I discovered that I knew most of the parts that were discussed in the textbook.

3. Concerning the question of whether there are more gifted men artists than women artists, it seems to me that the answer is variable depending on how one interprets the word *gifted*.

4. When, after much careful and painstaking study of the many and various problems involved, the administrators in charge of the different phases of the operation of the hospital made the decision to build a rehabilitation center for patients with all sorts of disabilities, a completely new staff of doctors, nurses, and physical therapists had to be hired.

5. Many doctors, after trying many different methods of relaxing, have discovered that taking up a pleasurable pastime or hobby such as painting calms them down and reduces the amount of stress in their lives.

## Revising for Variety

Variety is a characteristic not of single sentences but of a succession of sentences, and it is best seen in a paragraph. But variety is achieved through modification, coordination, subordination, and changes in word order, as shown in the following example:

1. Maxwell Perkins was born in 1884 and died in 1947.

2. He worked for Charles Scribner's Sons for thirty-seven years.

3. He was the head editor for Scribner's for the last twenty of those thirty-seven years.

4. He was almost certainly the most important American editor in the first half of the twentieth century.

5. He worked closely with Thomas Wolfe, F. Scott Fitzgerald, and Ernest Hemingway.

6. He also worked closely with a number of other well-known writers.

The sentences are of similar length (10, 9, 15, 17, 11, and 11 words, respectively) and structure (subject + predicate). Their lack of variety becomes monotonous.

Now contrast the same passage revised for variety:

Maxwell Perkins (1884–1947), head editor of Charles Scribner's Sons for the last twenty of his thirty-seven years with that company, was almost certainly the most important American editor in the first half of the twentieth century. Among the many well-known writers with whom he worked closely were Thomas Wolfe, F. Scott Fitzgerald, and Ernest Hemingway.

The revision combines the original into two sentences of 37 and 18 words, respectively, and results in greater economy (57 words instead of 73), greater density, and more variety. The following operations produced the revision.

▶ Sentences 1, 2, 3, and 4 of the original were combined into a new sentence by (a) making *Maxwell Perkins* the subject of the new sentence, (b) placing his dates in parentheses, (c) reducing sentences 2 and 3 to a phrase in apposition with the subject of the new sentence, and (d) making sentence 4 the complement of the new sentence.

▶ Sentences 5 and 6 of the original were combined into a new sentence by (a) having them share a common verb, *were,* and (b) making sentence 6 the subject of *were,* and sentence 5 the complement.

## EXERCISE

Consider the possible revisions listed after this paragraph about Nathaniel Hawthorne's story "The Birthmark." Decide which of those procedures you want to use to revise the paragraph. You do not need to use them all; just use those that will give you the best paragraph.

(1) Nathaniel Hawthorne's "The Birthmark" is one of his most famous short stories. (2) It is essentially a story about the limits of science and human perfectibility. (3) Aylmer has conducted many previous experiments in the attempt to improve nature, but all of them have failed. (4) Even so, he decides to perfect his wife Georgiana's beauty by removing a tiny birthmark on her cheek. (5) At the beginning of his experiment, Aylmer is confident he will succeed. (6) He secludes Georgiana in a private chamber. (7) Then he doctors her with strange medicines concocted in his laboratory. (8) He soon discovers that the birthmark is stronger than he thought. (9) He tries to avoid another failure by giving Georgiana an extremely powerful potion. (10) At the climax of the story, Aylmer sees his experiment succeed. (11) Unfortunately, it does so at a price. (12) Georgiana loses her birthmark. (13) She also loses her life.

Consider these revisions:

▶ Combine 1 and 2 by omitting everything after *is* in 1 and adding everything after *essentially* in 2. Write the revised sentence.

▶ Reduce most of 3 to a subordinate clause, "whose previous attempts to improve nature have failed," and insert it after *Aylmer* in 3 and before *decides* in 4. Write the revised sentence.

▶ Leave 5 as it is.

▶ Combine 6, 7, and 8 into a parallel structure using *but* to separate 7 and 8. Write the revised sentence.

▶ Change the pattern of 9 by beginning the sentence with an introductory phrase, "To avoid another failure," and converting "by giving" to "he decides to give." Write the revised sentence.

▶ Join 10 and 11 by adding a dash after *succeed* and then inserting the phrase "at a price." Write the revised sentence.

▶ Combine 12 and 13 with coordinating conjunction *and*. Write the revised sentence.

Using any of those revised sentences, or any revisions of your own, rewrite the complete paragraph.

## Three Pieces of Advice on Sentence Variety

1. *Don't overdo it.* It is neither necessary nor effective to give every sentence a different structure. Within a paragraph, try to have *some* variety in the pattern of your sentences. Most of your sentences will probably be basic sentences containing about 20 words. Individual sentences will range from 10 words or fewer to 30 words or more and will include balanced, periodic, or cumulative structures.

2. *Postpone revising for variety until you have written your first draft.* As Richard Selzer suggests, the process of *tinkering*, of opening up and compressing sentences, takes place after you have a number of sentences on the page. As you rework your completed sentences, read them aloud, listening for the variations in sound and rhythm that Selzer says are essential to effective writing. You can even *see* recurring structures in sentences, just as Bill Barich sees unvaried patterns in paragraphs, by noticing that they all occupy about the same number of lines.

3. *Be aware of the effect that sentence length has on your readers.* In general, long sentences slow down reading, and short ones speed it up. Short sentences are often effective as topic sentences because

they state the general idea simply; longer sentences are often needed to develop the idea. Short sentences are excellent for communicating a series of actions, emotions, or impressions; longer sentences are more appropriate for analysis and explanation. Short sentences are closer to the rhythms of speech and are therefore suitable when you want to adopt an intimate tone and a conversational style. The more formal the tone and style, the more likely you are to use long and complex sentences.

Keep in mind that these statements are relative to the particular material and perspective you are trying to present to your readers. As in all writing, your choices should reflect your purpose.

# Composing sentences on your computer

The computer enables you to expand, combine, and delete sentences with great speed. Indeed, you can compose them almost as fast as you can think them. If you are stuck in an individual sentence, compose other versions of it, one after another. Determine which one works best and delete the others. You can also use the cut-and-paste feature of your word-processing program to rearrange the order of parts of sentences. For example, you can mark a subordinate clause at the beginning of a sentence and move it to the end to achieve more variety.

The editing feature of your word-processing program may also call your attention to sentences that appear wordy. As you look at these sentences, you may determine that, although they are long, they fulfill your purpose. A computer editor does not know your subject, audience, and purpose—much less the context for each sentence. It simply compares your sentences to standard formulas and points out those that seem different. But this does give you the opportunity to reexamine your sentences to see if they are concise and cogent and contribute to your overall purpose.

Post your text to your writing group or the members of your writing class. Ask them to use the information in this chapter to "tinker" with your sentences. Invite them to expand, combine, and revise your sentences to make them more effective. In particular, encourage them to mark those sentences that they have difficulty reading or understanding. They may not know how to solve the problem, but they may alert you to areas of possible confusion that you can diagnose and cure.

# Image Gallery

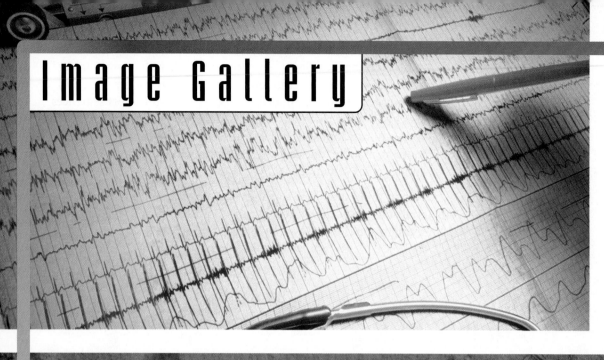

Vital signs (top); Tibetan writing on red rock (middle); and painting (right).

**Shadows of people standing in line (above); Satellite photo of Belgrade (below).**

**Questions**

1. Sentences, as Richard Selzer suggests, are like brush strokes or lines (p. 223). What kind of line is represented in each photograph?

2. How do the first three photographs illustrate Selzer's comparison of painting, medicine, and writing?

3. How do the last two photographs expand the concept of "line"?

# Readings

In these excerpts from her "studio notes," Pam Smith comments on her creative process in progress. What kinds of sentences does she use to describe different stages of her process? How might her sentences be compared to brush strokes?

# Excerpts from a Painter's Studio Notes

## PAM SMITH

### June 1981

1    When confusion visits me these days, I tell myself it is the blur of growth.

2    Suggestion is too coy for the real meaning of a painting. I struggle with whether my images are complete or incomplete, not with what they may suggest.

### July 1981

3    It is color, color, color that moves me.

4    I am an ambassador for the color green, a spy for the color red, and a surgeon sent to insert the color blue.

5    In private life, I am white's lover. And gray's.

6    No painting I have ever painted has ended up being the same painting I started.

7    Some days, I feel like I'm a dictionary in reverse, cataloguing all the possible meanings, and then coming up with a word.

8    I'm concerned about showing my work. I feel this is forced on me, to "prove" my serious intentions. But when I finish a painting, I am only interested in what I am going to paint next.

9    I had a dream last night. I kept saying in this dream, "I am in love with a green painting." Then I would paint it. This happened over and over, each time the painting was different and beautiful.

### October 1981

10    The point of a painting is not to say, "This way, and only this way." That's fascism. The point of a painting is, "There's something extra here because it is done this way."

11    My paintings these days are renegades. Such unruly things. Each painting is its own world. I try to rework a problem from another painting, and I end up getting a completely different painting. These paintings slip away from my understanding, like baffling children, they elude me. I listen for them to speak to me.

12    Some days, in my studio, I feel like a plumber who's always fixing leaks. Which is to say, I don't approach a canvas with solemn ceremony, I squint and gyrate in front of a canvas, to see what needs to be fixed.

13    Art is adjustment.

Pam Smith, "Powerful Red Dogs: Excerpts from a Painter's Studio Notes," *Georgia Review 34* (Spring/Summer 1990): 184–86.

## November 1982

14     My new paintings are pretty good. They may even be still lifes and landscapes, it's possible.

15     Some of these new paintings are all gray, some of them have new color.

16     They are sassy. I love that.

17     You can look in, but some of them just roar off the wall.

18     I think it's wonderful, because the painting goes from being a view of something, a canvas window with a set scene, to BEING something.

19     When I paint, my colors are a shape and a placement. I paint their boundaries. Just this much I paint. Here. And how.

20     Sometimes I enhance the boundaries by painting them as lines. Sometimes I let the boundaries be where two areas bump into each other.

21     The way to become an artist is to apprentice yourself and make a thousand stupid mistakes from the heart.

22     When I paint, the world is malleable. It is up to some definition the paint and I work out.

## February 1983

23     I started a new painting today. Large, silky, sexy, lush geometry. I am doing this painting from a casual sketch in an old notebook. I have lifted the bones of the sketch intact and put it on the canvas, but painting this painting is a battle between chaos and control.

24     There is such texture to this experience, the painting comes into and out of focus all the time. Possibilities flash by, and each one of them dictates a completely different painting. Literally every stroke affects this large painting. I understand the original image which spawned the sketch, but I want to do more to it. I simultaneously curse myself for not having planned the whole painting out beforehand, and feel exhilarated by the discoveries that are made.

25     I believe that a painting reveals itself. It reveals itself while it is being painted.

26     I believe the motion of my right hand, drawing or painting, is another form of thought.

# The Knife

## RICHARD SELZER

1 One holds the knife as one holds the bow of a cello or a tulip—by the stem. Not palmed nor gripped nor grasped, but lightly, with the tips of the fingers. The knife is not for pressing. It is for drawing across the field of skin. Like a slender fish, it waits, at the ready, then, go! It darts, followed by a fine wake of red. The flesh parts, falling away to yellow globules of fat. Even now, after so many times, I still marvel at its power— cold, gleaming, silent. More, I am still struck with a kind of dread that it is I in whose hand the blade travels, that my hand is its vehicle, that yet again this terrible steel-bellied thing and I have conspired for a most unnatural purpose, the laying open of the body of a human being.

2 A stillness settles in my heart and is carried to my hand. It is the quietude of resolve layered over fear. And it is this resolve that lowers us, my knife and me, deeper and deeper into the person beneath. It is an entry into the body that is nothing like a caress; still, it is among the gentlest of acts. Then stroke and stroke again, and we are joined by other instruments, hemostats and forceps, until the wound blooms with strange flowers whose looped handles fall to the sides in steely array.

3 There is sound, the tight click of clamps fixing teeth into severed blood vessels, the snuffle and gargle of the suction machine clearing the field of blood for the next stroke, the litany of monosyllables with which one prays his way down and in: *clamp, sponge, suture, tie, cut.* And there is color. The green of the cloth, the white of the sponges, the red and yellow of the body. Beneath the fat lies the fascia, the tough fibrous sheet encasing the muscles. It must be sliced and the red beef of the muscles separated. Now there are retractors to hold apart the wound. Hands move together, part, weave. We are fully engaged, like children absorbed in a game or the craftsmen of some place like Damascus.

4 Deeper still. The peritoneum, pink and gleaming and membranous, bulges into the wound. It is grasped with forceps, and opened. For the first time we can see into the cavity of the abdomen. Such a primitive place. One expects to find drawings of buffalo on the walls. The sense of trespassing is keener now, heightened by the world's light illuminating the organs, their secret colors revealed—maroon and salmon and yellow. The vista is sweetly vulnerable at this moment, a kind of welcoming. An arc of the liver shines high and on the right, like a dark sun. It laps over the pink sweep of the stomach, from whose lower border the gauzy omentum is draped, and through which veil one sees, sinuous, slow as just-fed snakes, the indolent coils of the intestine.

5 You turn aside to wash your gloves. It is a ritual cleansing. One enters this temple doubly washed. Here is man as microcosm, representing in all his parts the earth, perhaps the universe.

6 I must confess that the priestliness of my profession has ever been impressed on me. In

Richard Selzer, *Mortal Lessons* (New York: Simon, 1976), 92–97.

the beginning there are vows, taken with all solemnity. Then there is the endless harsh novitiate of training, much fatigue, much sacrifice. At last one emerges as celebrant, standing close to the truth lying curtained in the Ark of the body. Not surplice and cassock but mask and gown are your regalia. You hold no chalice, but a knife. There is no wine, no wafer. There are only the facts of blood and flesh.

7 And if the surgeon is like a poet, then the scars you have made on countless bodies are like verses into the fashioning of which you have poured your soul. I think that if years later I were to see the trace from an old incision of mine, I should know it at once, as one recognizes his pet expressions.

8 But mostly you are a traveler in a dangerous country, advancing into the moist and jungly cleft your hands have made. Eyes and ears are shuttered from the land you left behind; mind empties itself of all other thought. You are the root of groping fingers. It is a fine hour for the fingers, their sense of touch so enhanced. The blind must know this feeling. Oh, there is risk everywhere. One goes lightly. The spleen. No! No! Do not touch the spleen that lurks below the left leaf of the diaphragm, a manta ray in a coral cave, its bloody tongue protruding. One poke and it might rupture, exploding with sudden hemorrhage. The filmy omentum must not be torn, the intestine scraped or denuded. The hand finds the liver, palms it, fingers running along its sharp lower edge, admiring. Here are the twin mounds of the kidneys, the apron of the omentum hanging in front of the intestinal coils. One lifts it aside and the fingers dip among the loops, searching, mapping territory, establishing boundaries. Deeper still, and the

womb is touched, then held like a small muscular bottle—the womb and its earlike appendages, the ovaries. How they do nestle in the cup of a man's hand, their power all dormant. They are frailty itself.

9 There is a hush in the room. Speech stops. The hands of the others, assistants and nurses, are still. Only the voice of the patient's respiration remains. It is the rhythm of a quiet sea, the sound of waiting. Then you speak, slowly, the terse entries of a Himalayan climber reporting back.

10 "The stomach is okay. Greater curvature clean. No sign of ulcer. Pylorus, duodenum fine. Now comes the gallbladder. No stones. Right kidney, left, all right. Liver . . . uh-oh."

11 Your speech lowers to a whisper, falters, stops for a long, long moment, then picks up again at the end of a sigh that comes through your mask like a last exhalation.

12 "Three big hard ones in the left lobe, one on the right. Metastatic deposits. Bad, bad. Where's the primary? Got to be coming from somewhere."

13 The arm shifts direction and the fingers drop lower and lower into the pelvis—the body impaled now upon the arm of the surgeon to the hilt of the elbow.

14 "Here it is."

15 The voice goes flat, all business now.

16 "Tumor in the sigmoid colon, wrapped all around it, pretty tight. We'll take out a sleeve of the bowel. No colostomy. Not that, anyway. But, God, there's a lot of it down there. Here, you take a feel."

17 You step back from the table, and lean into a sterile basin of water, resting on stiff arms, while the others locate the cancer.

# Web Design

Students using *Writing with a Purpose* in a composition class were asked to design a website for Richard Selzer's essay, "The Knife." Consult the elements and principles of design in Chapter 5 to help answer the questions about the effectiveness of each design.

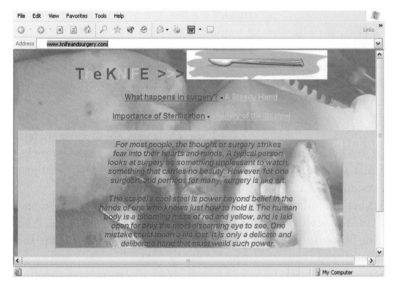

## Sample Homepage #1: The Knife

1. Why does the alignment of Selzer's title and the image create confusion about the subject?

2. Why does the mixture of colors in the headings make the text difficult to read?

3. What does the image in the background contribute to the purpose of the site?

## Sample Homepage #2: The Knife

1. How does the juxtaposition of the photo and the bulleted list clarify the subject?

2. How do the photo, the knife, and Selzer's quotation create an effective alignment?

3. How do the selection and presentation of the excerpt from Selzer's essay explain the purpose of the site?

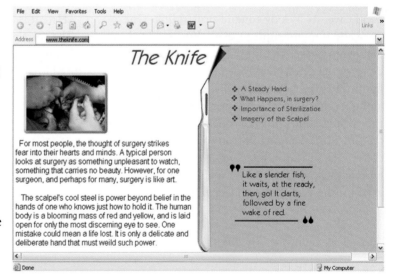

# Writing Assignments

### 1. NARRATE

Compose a freewriting exercise about your most memorable experience with an illness. Follow Richard Selzer's advice and make one "brush stroke" after another until you have painted a fairly complete portrait of your experience. Then check out the Web for "support groups" where people "chat" about their experience with the same illness. Compare your sentences and their sentences for clarity, emphasis, economy—and purpose.

### 2. OBSERVE

Visit your local art museum or look through the virtual gallery on the website for an art museum. Select a particular painting that "speaks to you." *Study* the way the painter arranges the subject for your observation. Then write a letter to a close friend describing the painting and speculating about why it has had such a powerful impact on you.

### 3. INVESTIGATE

Visit the studio of a local artist or the studios in your university's art department. Ask for permission to observe a painter at work. Watch the way he or she uses different techniques— applying paint with fingers, brushes, spray devises, or palette knives—to "compose" the painting. Ask a few questions, but encourage the painter to talk about his or her work as it is being created. You may have to visit the studio several times to see the project through to completion. Then write a "biography of the painting" to introduce it to the students in your writing group.

### 4. COLLABORATE

Your writing group has been asked to draft a program for an exhibit of student paintings. Assign each member of your group to write the copy for one painter. Study previous programs to see how many and what kinds of sentences have been used to describe the painters and their work. Decide if you want to *expand* or *modify* that pattern. Then interview the student painters, study their work, design the layout for the program, and collaborate on creating the final copy.

### 5. READ

Read selections from some of Richard Selzer's other books about surgery, *Rituals of Surgery* (1974), *Confessions of a Knife* (1979), and *Letters to a Young Doctor* (1982). Compose a series of sentences on the reasons why you *would* or *would not* want to become a surgeon. After you have compared one set of reasons with the other, subordinate one group to the other in an essay entitled "I Want to Be a Surgeon" or "I Don't Want to Be a Surgeon."

### 6. RESPOND

Study one of Cezanne's paintings. See <http://www.artcyclopedia.com/artists/cezanne_paul.html>. Then respond to the following revelation from Diane Ackerman: "When one thinks of the masses of color and shape in his paintings, perhaps it won't come as a surprise to learn that Cezanne was myopic."

### 7. ANALYZE

Analyze the sentences in Pam Smith's "Excerpts from a Painter's Studio Notes." Reread Richard Selzer's comparison of sentences and brush strokes on page 223. Then write an essay, citing specific sentences from Smith's "studio notes," to demonstrate the appropriateness of Selzer's comparison of painting and writing.

### 8. EVALUATE

Richard Selzer uses many comparisons in "The Knife" to illustrate the process he is describing. Analyze each of these comparisons—the surgeon is like a priest, a poet, a traveler in a dangerous country. Then select one—for example, the artistry of the surgeon is similar to the artistry of the writer—and evaluate the points of the comparison that Selzer leaves out, the points that suggest that the two processes are radically different.

### 9. ARGUE

You have been asked by a friend or your employer to select a painting by a local artist to be hung in a special location. Visit local galleries or art shows, looking for the *right* painting. Consider your immediate audience (the person who asked you to select the painting), your ultimate audience (the people who will see the painting), and the context (where the painting will be hung). Compose a series of sentences (or reasons) explaining why you think a particular painting is the *right* painting. Then write a letter recommending your choice to your friend or employer. (You may want to reread Wallace Armstrong's "Brandon's Clown" in Chapter 1 to remind yourself of how such purchases affect the painter.)

### 10. ARGUE

As an experiment in revising sentences, work with the following sentences by expanding, modifying, or combining them into an effective argument. Add other sentences to fill out your portrait and fulfill your purpose.

a. Surgeons are revered as medical priests.
b. They are cloaked and masked in green vestments.
c. They have acquired a secret knowledge.
d. They are given absolute authority over life and death.
e. They cut the human body with special tools.
f. They eliminate disease.
g. They stitch the body together.
h. They wash their hands after the ritual.
i. The people they restore to health view the process as a miracle.

# Diction: The Choice of Words

I LEARN WORDS BY LEARNING WORLDS.

—ANNIE DILLARD

As you think your way through a sentence, you inevitably search for the best words to convey your thoughts. Sometimes, especially when you are quite clear about what you want to say, the words come so easily that you are hardly aware of choosing them. At other times, especially when you are trying to discover what you want to say, you find yourself scratching out one choice after another as you search for the exact word to express your meaning. Such revisions are not necessarily a sign of indecision. The best writers worry constantly about diction—the selection and use of words for effective communication. Perhaps they are the best writers partly because they take pains to choose the best word.

Words are not right or wrong in themselves. What makes a particular word right is the effect it creates in the context of your sentence or paragraph. Annie Dillard, celebrated for her evocative descriptions of nature, explains how she chooses words.

> I learn words by learning worlds. Any writer does that out of simple curiosity. When I choose words, I think about their effect—of course I like to create a rich prose surface that pommels the reader with verbs and images. I think of them as jabs. Jab, jab, jab, left. Jab, jab, jab, right. That's the vigor I want. (Personal interview)

To create vigor in your writing and to advance your purpose, you must, like Dillard, learn the words that represent the "worlds" you want to write about and learn to use words for their effect. You must learn the denotations and connotations of words.

*Wordsmiths*

## Denotation and Connotation

The most familiar use of words is to name things—plants, people, oceans, stars. When words are used in this way, the things they refer to are called their *denotations*. The word *molecule* most commonly denotes small structures of atoms. The denotation of *Mars* is the fourth planet from the sun. The denotation is a word's explicit meaning.

But some words acquire connotations as well as denotations. A connotation is an *implicit* meaning, an implied or suggested attitude that is not stated outright. When you label theories about life on Mars "improbable" or "preposterous," you are not only describing them; you are also expressing, and inviting your readers to share, an attitude toward them.

In each of these sentences, the writer implies a different attitude toward similar events.

> My wife asked me why I was *slashing* the shrubbery. I told her I was merely *pruning* it.

> The difference between *childish pranks* and acts of *vandalism* depends on whose child does the mischief.

> Although most bathers thought the high surf looked *threatening,* a few thought it looked *challenging.*

When our team of scientists traveled across the crater to *collect samples,* they encountered another team *stealing evidence.*

The contrast in each example is not between denotations and connotations but between favorable and unfavorable connotations. *Slashing* and *pruning* refer to similar actions, but the first implies destructive recklessness, and the second suggests careful cutting.

The words you choose should support your purpose. If you wish to report objectively, select words that suggest a neutral attitude: *collect samples* not *stealing evidence.* If you wish to convey a tolerant or approving attitude, use words that invite a tolerant or approving response: *pruning, childish pranks, challenging.* If you wish to suggest disapproval, select words with unfavorable connotations: *slashing, act of vandalism, threatening.*

## EXERCISE

In the following sentences the blank may be filled with any of the words in parentheses, but each choice creates different connotations. Discuss how each choice affects the writer's intention and the reader's interpretation of the sentence.

1. The roses _____ the trellis. (climbed, adorned, strangled)

2. She was a _____ reader. (compulsive, critical, perceptive)

3. The children were _____. (sleepy, exhausted, weary)

4. The reef _____ beneath the surface. (appeared, loomed, glimmered)

5. The comet _____ across the night sky. (shot, blinked, blazed)

## Three Qualities of Effective Diction

Choice of diction is always made with reference to a particular sentence and to the total context of your writing. For this reason no dictionary or thesaurus will give you *the* right word. A dictionary presents a word's various meanings, and a thesaurus provides a list of synonyms, words with slightly varying meanings. You must decide which word and meaning meet your needs. To make this decision, consider the qualities of effective diction: *appropriateness, specificity,* and *imagery.*

### Appropriateness

Words are appropriate when they are suited to your subject, audience, and purpose. Imagine an astronomer reporting the discovery of a new star to a convention of scientists and then to the viewers of a morning television show. The subject is the same, but the audience and purpose are so different that the speaker alters the content, style, and language of the report. Choices to accommodate audience and purpose affect not only diction, the subject of this chapter, but tone and style, the subjects of the next chapter. Diction, tone, and style are alike in requiring you to make important decisions about the degree of formality appropriate for a given context. Jeans and a T-shirt are not appropriate for a formal dance; an evening gown or tuxedo is conspicuously inappropriate for the classroom; in the same way, some words inappropriate in some situations are perfectly acceptable in others. The best way to understand this distinction is to consider four types of words: *learned, popular, colloquial,* and *slang.*

**Learned and Popular Words**   Most words in English, as in other languages, are common to the speech of educated and uneducated speakers alike. These words are the basic elements of everyday communication. They are called *popular words* because they belong to the whole populace.

By contrast, there are words that you read more often than you hear, write more often than you speak—words used more widely by educated than by uneducated people, and more likely to be used on formal than on informal occasions. Such words are called *learned words.*

The following list contrasts pairs of popular and learned words that have similar denotations.

| *Popular* | *Learned* | *Popular* | *Learned* |
|---|---|---|---|
| agree | concur | help | succor |
| begin | commence | make easy | facilitate |
| clear | lucid | secret | esoteric |
| disagree | remonstrate | think | cogitate |
| end | terminate | wordy | verbose |

**Colloquialisms**   The term *colloquial* is defined by the *American Heritage Dictionary* as "characteristic of or appropriate to the spoken language or writing that seeks its effect; informal in diction or style of expression." Colloquialisms are not "incorrect" or "bad" English. They are the kinds of words people, educated and uneducated alike, use when they are speaking together informally. Their deliberate use in writing conveys the impression of direct and intimate conversation. To achieve this effect you might use contractions *(don't, wasn't, hasn't)* or clipped words *(taxi, phone).* Other typical colloquialisms are

| | | |
|---|---|---|
| awfully *(for* very) | fix *(for* predicament) | movie *(for* film) |
| back of *(for* behind) | it's me | over with *(for* completed) |
| cute | kind of *(for* somewhat) | peeve *(for* annoy) |
| exam | a lot of; lots of | plenty *(as an adverb)* |
| expect *(for* suppose) | mad *(for* angry) | sure *(for* certainly)* |

**Slang**   The *Oxford English Dictionary* defines slang as "language of a highly colloquial type." Notice that the adjective used is *colloquial,* not *vulgar* or *incorrect.* Slang is used by everyone. The appropriateness of slang, however, depends on the occasion. A college president would probably avoid slang in a public speech but might use it at an informal gathering.

Slang satisfies a desire for novelty of expression. It is often borrowed from the vocabularies of particular occupations or activities: *input* (computer technology), *on the beam* (aerial navigation), *behind the eight ball* (pool), *dunk* (basketball). Some slang words are from the insider languages of those who commit crimes or take drugs: *sting, torch, grass, stoned.* Much slang is borrowed from the popular vocabulary and given new meanings: *cool, crib, fly, spam, sweet, whack.* Some slang proves so imaginative and useful that it becomes part of the popular vocabulary but then quickly becomes dated, obscure, and loses its impact.

In most of your writing, words from the middle of the following formality scale will be appropriate. Unfortunately, some inexperienced writers think that formality is a virtue and that big, fancy words are more impressive than short, common ones. If writers cannot maintain an appropriate level of formality, their diction becomes strained and inconsistent.

| Learned | Popular | Colloquial | Slang |

*Most formal*                                         *Least formal*

The following passage provides a humorous illustration of such inconsistency. In this scene from Bernard Shaw's play *Pygmalion* (from which the musical *My Fair Lady* was created), Eliza Doolittle, a cockney flower girl who is being taught by Professor Higgins to speak like a lady, meets her first test at a small party at the home of Mrs. Higgins, the professor's mother. Notice the contrast between Eliza's first speech and her last.

MRS. HIGGINS:  Will it rain, do you think?
ELIZA:  The shallow depression in the west of these islands is likely to move slowly in an easterly direction. There are no indications of any great change in the barometrical situation.
FREDDY:  Ha! Ha! How awfully funny!
ELIZA:  What is wrong with that, young man? I bet I got it right.
FREDDY:  Killing!
MRS. EYNSFORD HILL:  I'm sure I hope it won't turn cold. There's so much influenza about. It runs right through our whole family regularly every spring.
ELIZA:  My aunt died of influenza: so they said. . . . But it's my belief they done the old woman in. . . . Why should *she* die of

influenza? She come through diphtheria right enough the year before. I saw her with my own eyes. Fairly blue with it, she was. They all thought she was dead; but my father he kept ladling gin down her throat 'til she came to so sudden that she bit the bowl off the spoon. . . . What call would a woman with that strength in her have to die of influenza? What become of her new straw hat that should have come to me? Somebody pinched it; and what I say is, them as pinched it done her in.

The obvious switch from formal to highly colloquial speech is justified by Shaw's purpose, which is to show Eliza in a transitional stage at which she cannot yet consistently maintain the pose of being a well-educated young woman. Eliza does not see that her learned comment on the weather is inappropriate in this situation, and therefore has no idea why Freddy is laughing. When the subject changes to influenza, she forgets she is supposed to be a lady and reverts to her natural speech—which is much more expressive and colorful than her phony formality. Her inconsistency is amusing, as Shaw meant it to be.

But in the compositions of inexperienced writers, most inconsistencies are not intended for humorous effect. They slip in when the writer is not in control of *how* to say *what* he or she wants to say. The writer may start off like Eliza, hoping to make a good impression, but the writer's natural voice asserts itself, and the result is neither formal nor informal diction but an embarrassing mixture. Try to choose words consistently appropriate to your purpose throughout the writing process, and, of course, in revision, stay alert for unintentional shifts in diction.

---

## EXERCISE

The following paragraph does not maintain a consistent level of diction. Identify the words and phrases that seem too formal or too informal. Then rewrite the paragraph, substituting more appropriate diction to make the language of the paragraph consistent.

In my perusal of the morning paper, I often pause to take a gander at my horoscope. This stuff is supposed to be figured out on a chart of the heavens, which manifests the positions of the sun, moon, and the signs of the zodiac at the honest-to-goodness time and location of your birth. These configurations are then juxtaposed to the twelve hours of the celestial sphere. The signs are presumed to hold sway over certain parts of the body, and the houses are supposed to tell you what's happening in the various conditions of life. The degree of influence attributed to these houses depends on a bunch of factors. Sometimes my horoscope predicts the orb of my daily activities with confounding accuracy. But most of the time it's just hogwash.

## Specificity

*General* and *specific* are opposite terms. Words are general when they refer not to individual things but to groups or classes: *mother, flowers, hurricane.* Words are specific when they refer to individual persons, objects, or events: *Joe's mother, the flowers in the vase near the window, Hurricane Bob.* A general term may be made more specific with a modifier that restricts the reference to a particular member of the group or class.

    *Specific* and *general* are also relative terms: A word may seem specific in one context and general in another, as the diagram shows.

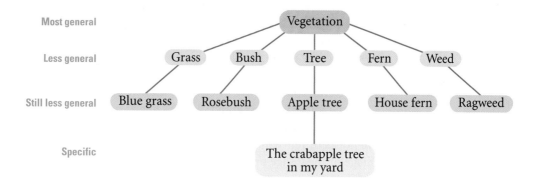

---

### EXERCISE

For each set of terms, show the gradation from general to specific. Place the most general term at the left and the most specific at the right, as in this example:

    matter, food, fruit, citrus fruit, orange

1. Labrador retriever, quadruped, bird dog, animal, dog

2. protons, molecule, electrons, atom, nucleus

3. bush, rosebush, plant, decorative bush, Tropicana rosebush

4. Jupiter, Milky Way, sun, solar system, galaxy

5. Scientist, chemist, Marie Curie, Nobel Prize winner

---

Your context determines whether a specific or a general word is required. Some purposes require generalities. A president's inaugural address, for example, does not deal with specifics; it states general policies and intentions. The best policy is to be as specific as the situation permits. Notice how the specific language in the examples on the right communicates meaning that is not conveyed by the general diction on the left.

| | |
|---|---|
| A drop of water contains particles. | A drop of water contains microscopic strands of algae and multicellular aquatic organisms. |
| Saturn has rings. | Saturn is surrounded by a vast swarm of meteoric fragments revolving in various orbits. |

The term *concrete* is used to describe some kinds of specific diction. *Concrete* is the opposite of *abstract*. Concrete words refer to particular things or qualities that can be perceived by your senses: details of appearance, sounds, smells, textures, tastes. Abstract words refer to qualities shared by many people or things: newness, width, size, shape, value, joy, anger. Abstract qualities cannot be perceived directly by observation; they are concepts that you infer from what you see.

In the following paragraph, Annie Dillard uses concrete, sensory detail to illustrate her abstract opening sentence. The image of successive flocks of red-winged blackbirds materializing from the dense, green foliage of the Osage orange tree remains in the mind in a way impossible for concepts such as *nature* or *revelation*.

> For nature does reveal as well as conceal; now-you-don't-see-it, now-you-do. For a week this September migrating red-winged blackbirds were feeding heavily down by Tinker Creek at the back of the house. One day I went out to investigate the racket; I walked up to a tree, an Osage orange, and a hundred birds flew away. They simply materialized out of the tree. I saw a tree, then a whisk of color, then a tree again. I walked closer and another hundred blackbirds took flight. Not a branch, not a twig budged: the birds were apparently weightless as well as invisible. Or, it was as if the leaves of the Osage orange had been freed from a spell in the form of red-winged blackbirds; they flew from the tree, caught my eye in the sky, and vanished. When I looked again at the tree, the leaves had reassembled as if nothing had happened. Finally I walked directly to the trunk of the tree and a final hundred, the real diehards, appeared, spread, and vanished. How could so many hide in the tree without my seeing them? The Osage orange, unruffled, looked just as it had looked from the house, when three hundred red-winged blackbirds cried from its crown. I looked upstream where they flew, and they were gone. Searching, I couldn't spot one. I wandered upstream to force them to play their hand, but they'd crossed the creek and scattered. One show to a customer. These appearances catch at my throat; they are the free gifts, the bright coppers at the roots of trees. (Annie Dillard, "Sight into Insight," *Pilgrim at Tinker Creek*)

What aspects of Momaday's description of the prairie landscape (Exercise 1 on page 266) are included in and missing from this photograph?

Words that refer to sensory experiences—to what you see, hear, touch, taste, and smell—call up sensory images (particularly when they are embedded in strong verbs) and create the "rich prose surface" Dillard uses to "jab" her reader. The following is a list of additional examples (some words fit into more than one sensory category):

*Touch*   chill, clammy, cold, grainy, gritty, jarring, knobby, moist, numb, rough, smooth, sting, tingle

*Taste*   bland, bitter, brackish, metallic, minty, peppery, salty, sour, spicy, sweet

*Smell*   acrid, fetid, greasy, musky, musty, pungent, putrid, rancid, rank, reek, stench

*Sound*   bellow, blare, buzz, chime, clang, clatter, clink, crackle, crash, creak, gurgle, hiss, hum, murmur, pop, purr, rattle, rustle, screech, snap, squeak, whine, whisper

*Sight*   blaze, bleary, bloody, chalky, dappled, ebony, flame, flicker, florid, foggy, gaudy, glare, glitter, glossy, grimy, haze, inky, leaden, muddy, pallid, sallow, shadow, smudged, streak, tawny

1. Read the following passage and note the words or phrases that seem most concrete. Then copy the passage over without those words or phrases. In what ways is the meaning of the second version diminished?

A single knoll rises out of the plain in Oklahoma, north and west of the Wichita Range. For my people, the Kiowas, it is an old landmark, and they gave it the name Rainy Mountain. The hardest weather in the world is there. Winter brings blizzards, hot tornadic winds arise in the spring, and in summer the prairie is an anvil's edge. The grass turns brittle and brown, and it cracks beneath your feet. There are green belts along the rivers and creeks, linear groves of hickory and pecan, willow and witch hazel. At a distance in July or August the steaming foliage seems almost to writhe in fire. Great green and yellow grasshoppers are everywhere in the tall grass, popping up like corn to sting the flesh, and tortoises crawl about on the red earth, going nowhere in plenty of time. Loneliness is an aspect of the land. All things in the plain are isolate; there is no confusion of objects in the eye, but *one* hill or *one* tree or *one* man. To look upon that landscape in the early morning, with the sun at your back, is to lose the sense of proportion. Your imagination comes to life, and this, you think, is where Creation was begun.
(N. Scott Momaday, "The Way to Rainy Mountain")

2. The following contrasted statements deal with the same subject. From each pair, choose the statement that you think is more concrete. Explain the specific reasons for your choice.

In the past, girls in rural communities had no facilities for bathing except those offered by some neighboring stream. In such circumstances a bathing suit was not always a necessity, but if one was worn it was likely to consist of nothing more than some discarded article of clothing tailored to fit the occasion.

Forty years ago, if the farmer's daughter went swimming she swam in the crick below the pasture, and if she wore a bathing suit, which was not as customary as you may think, it was likely to be a pair of her brother's outgrown overalls trimmed with scissors as her discretion might suggest.

Suddenly I felt something on the biceps of my right arm—a queer light touch, clinging for an instant, and then the smooth glide of its body. I could feel the muscles of the snake's body slowly contract and relax. At last I saw a flat, V-shaped head, with two glistening, black, protruding buttons. A thin, pointed, sickening yellow tongue slipped out, then in, accompanied by a sound like that of escaping steam.

Suddenly I felt the snake moving over my arm. I felt the contraction of its muscles as it moved. Then I saw its ugly head and its evil looking eyes. All the time its tongue kept moving in and out, making a kind of hissing noise.

## Imagery

*Imagery* has two general meanings when applied to diction: The images or pictures that concrete words sometimes suggest and figures of speech such as similes and metaphors. The first meaning includes the pictorial quality of phrases such as *an anvil's edge, green belts, popping up like corn*. In this section you will learn about the second meaning—the use of figurative language.

The chief element in all figures of speech is an imaginative comparison in which dissimilar things are described as having a meaningful similarity. The writer, by thus linking the unfamiliar with the familiar, creates a context in which the reader may more easily or clearly understand a new aspect of the subject or new information and ideas. Here is an example:

> The moon was a ghostly galleon tossed upon cloudy seas.   (Alfred Noyes)

The line of poetry compares the moon to a sailing ship. Now in most ways the moon is quite unlike a ship. But as the poet watches it alternately emerging from behind the clouds and disappearing into them again, he thinks of a ship alternately emerging and disappearing from view as it rides the troughs and crests of the waves. In his imagination the moon is being tossed by the clouds as a ship is tossed by the waves.

The most commonly used figures of speech are *simile, metaphor, analogy, personification,* and *allusion.* Each figure makes a comparison, but each has its own characteristic form and use.

**Simile**   A simile compares two things—*A* and *B*—by asserting that one is like the other. A simile usually contains the word *like, as,* or *so* and is used to transfer to *A* the qualities or feelings associated with *B.* Thus, when Annie Dillard in "Total Eclipse" describes a solar eclipse, she imagines that the sky *(A)*—or more precisely the moon—functions like the lens cover *(B)* on a camera, covering the lens and shutting out all the light:

> The sky snapped over the sun like a lens cover.

Here are some other similes:

> Insects in the first frosts of autumn all run down like little clocks.
> (Loren Eiseley, "How Flowers Changed the World," *The Star Thrower*)

> When, as you approach, [the iguanas] swish away, there is a flash of azure, green and purple over the stones, the colour seems to be standing behind them in the air, like a comet's luminous tail.
> (Isak Dinesen, *Out of Africa*)

> Floating on one's back is like riding between two skies.
> (Edward Hoagland, "Summer Pond")

> Laverne wasn't too bad a dancer, but the other one, old Marty . . . was like dragging the Statue of Liberty around the floor.
> (J. D. Salinger, *Catcher in the Rye*)

**How do the lamps and the sunset create a metaphor?**

**Metaphor**    A metaphor compares two things by identifying one with the other. It does not say that *A* is like *B* but instead states that *A* is *B*. Lewis Thomas is using metaphor when he suggests that the sky encloses the earth just as a membrane surrounds an organ or cell.

> Aloft, floating free beneath the moist, gleaming membrane of bright blue sky, is the rising earth, the only exuberant thing in this part of the cosmos.    (Lewis Thomas, "The World's Biggest Membrane," *The Lives of a Cell*)

Here are other metaphors:

> Time is but a stream I go a-fishing in.    (Henry David Thoreau, *Walden*)

> Suddenly the whole room broke into a sea of shouting, as they saw me rise. Waves of rejoicing swept the place.    (Langston Hughes, *The Big Sea*)

Each rich nation is a lifeboat full of comparatively rich people. In the ocean outside each lifeboat swim the poor of the world who want to get in, or at best to share some of the wealth.

(Garrett Hardin, "Lifeboat Ethics: The Case Against Helping the Poor")

Many words and phrases no longer thought of as figures of speech were originally metaphors or similes. "At bay" originally described a hunted animal cornered by pursuers and forced to turn and fight the baying hounds. "Crestfallen" first described a cock that had been humbled in a cockfight. Many other expressions can be analyzed as metaphors even though you no longer think of them as figures of speech—expressions such as the "mouth" of a river, the "face" of a clock, the "brow" of a hill. Such expressions are often called, metaphorically, *dead* or *frozen metaphors.* They are so common in the language that it is hard to write a paragraph without them, but you should try to avoid those (such as "rosy red," "dirt cheap," and "face the music") that have become clichés.

• A WRITER'S RESOURCES

For an interesting new-media version of the traditional thesaurus, check <http://www.visualthesarus.com>.

**Analogy**   An analogy is an extended metaphor that, through several sentences or paragraphs, explains an abstract idea or seeks to persuade readers that because two things are alike, a conclusion drawn from one suggests a similar conclusion can be drawn from the other. In the following passage, Robert Jastrow uses analogy to explain the shape of our galaxy:

The Galaxy is flattened by its rotating motion into the shape of a disk whose thickness is roughly one-fifth of its diameter. Most of the stars in the Galaxy are in this disk, although some are located outside it. A relatively small, spherical cluster of stars, called the nucleus of the Galaxy, bulges out of the disk at the center. The center structure resembles a double sombrero with the gigantic nucleus as the crown and the disk as the brim. The sun is located in the brim of the sombrero about three-fifths of the way out from the center of the edge. When we look into the sky in the direction of the disk we see so many stars that they are not visible as separate points of light, but blend together into a luminous band stretching across the sky. This band is called the Milky Way.

(Robert Jastrow, "The Size of Things," *Red Giants and White Dwarfs*)

**Personification**   Personification is a figure of speech by which inanimate objects or abstractions are given human or animal characteristics. Thus winds are said to "roar" or "bite"; flames "eat hungrily" at a burning house and may even "devour" it; a tree may "bow" before a gale or in fair weather "stretch" its branches; truth or virtue emerges "triumphant"; and justice is "blind." In these examples, the writer imagines a resemblance between the acts observed and the actions of an animal or person.

Such implied comparisons are often effective, but they should be used with restraint. If they seem exaggerated ("the waves roared their threat to the listening clouds while the palm trees nodded their approval"), your reader is likely to reject them as far-fetched or as an unsuccessful attempt to be "literary."

**Allusion**   An allusion is a comparison between a historical, literary, or mythological event or person and the subject under discussion. When a scientific discovery is said to possess Copernican significance, it is being associated with Copernicus's theory that revolutionized the way we saw the universe (the Earth rotating around the sun rather than the sun rotating around the Earth). Or when a film is called another *Star Wars,* it is being likened to one of the most extraordinary films ever made about outer space.

A successful allusion provides a flash of wit or insight and gives your readers the pleasure of recognition. But you must be reasonably sure that an allusion is suited to your audience; if your readers do not recognize or understand the allusion, they will be confused and not appreciate its effect. Calling writing a research paper a "Sisyphean task" is amusing only if your audience remembers that Sisyphus was condemned forever to roll a huge stone up a steep hill in Hades, only to have it roll back down just as it neared the top.

## EXERCISES

1.  **In the following selections, underline effective examples of specificity and imagery.**

When wild ducks or wild geese migrate in their season, a strange tide rises in the territories over which they sweep. As if magnetized by the great triangular flight, the barnyard fowl leap a foot or two into the air and try to fly . . . and a vestige of savagery quickens their blood. All the ducks on the farm are transformed for an instant into migrant birds, and into those hard little heads, till now filled with humble images of pools and worms and barnyards, there swims a sense of continental expanse, of the breadth of seas and the salt taste of the ocean wind. The duck totters to the right and left in its wire enclosure, gripped by a sudden passion to perform the impossible and a sudden love whose object is a mystery.

(Antoine de Saint Exupéry, *Wind, Sand and Stars*)

The word is terracide. As in homicide, or genocide. Except it's terra. Land.

It is not committed with guns and knives, but with great, relentless bulldozers and thundering dump trucks, with giant shovels like mythological creatures, their girded necks lifting massive steel mouths high above the tallest trees. And with dynamite. They cut and blast and rip apart mountains to reach the minerals inside, and when they have finished there is nothing left but naked hills, ugly monuments to waste, stripped of everything that once held them in place, cut off from the top and sides and dug out from the inside and then left, restless, to slide down on houses and wash off into rivers and streams, rendering the land unlivable and the water for miles downstream undrinkable.

Terracide. Or, if you prefer, strip-mining.

(Skip Rozin, "People of the Ruined Hills," *Audubon*)

"On nights like that," Raymond Chandler once wrote about the Santa Ana, "every booze party ends in a fight. Meek little wives feel the edge of the carving knife and study their husbands' necks. Anything can happen." That was the kind of wind it was. I did not know then that there was any basis for the effect it had on all of us, but it turns out to be another of those cases in which science bears out folk wisdom. The Santa Ana, which is named for one of the canyons it rushes through, is a *foehn* wind, like the *foehn* of Austria and Switzerland and the *hamsin* of Israel. There are a number of persistent malevolent winds, perhaps the best known of which are the mistral of France and the Mediterranean sirocco, but a *foehn* wind has distinct characteristics: it occurs on the leeward slope of a mountain range and, although the air begins as a cold mass, it is warmed as it comes down the mountain and appears finally as a hot dry wind.

Whenever and wherever a *foehn* blows, doctors hear about headaches and nausea and allergies, about "nervousness," about "depression." In Los Angeles some teachers do not attempt to conduct formal classes during a Santa Ana, because the children become unmanageable. In Switzerland the suicide rate goes up during the *foehn,* and in the courts of some Swiss cantons the wind is considered a mitigating circumstance for crime. Surgeons are said to watch the wind, because blood does not clot normally during a *foehn.* A few years ago an Israeli physicist discovered that not only during such winds, but for the ten or twelve hours which precede them, the air carries an unusually high ratio of positive to negative ions. No one seems to know exactly why that should be; some talk about friction and others suggest solar disturbances. In any case the positive ions are there, and what an excess of positive ions does, in the sim-

plest terms, is make people unhappy. One cannot get much more mechanistic than that.

(Joan Didion, "Los Angeles Notebook,"
*Slouching Towards Bethlehem*)

2. Evaluate the effectiveness of the following figures of speech from the student writing used in previous chapters. Discuss how each figure contributes to the writer's purpose.

a. Wallace Armstrong, "Brandon's Clown" (Chapter 1):

   Before long, the book looked like a Disneyland mortuary.

b. Jane Graham, "Watching Whales" (Chapter 6):

When he burst out of the water, he held his flippers at a slight angle to his side. As he descended, he moved them gracefully away from his body like the arms of a ballerina finishing a pirouette.

## Revising Diction

In considering the qualities of effective diction, you evaluated ways of expressing ideas, and your evaluation included a great deal of revision. In this stage of local revision, you need to change your emphasis from expressing yourself effectively to rooting out the ineffective. Work through your text slowly, looking for words that don't fully express your purpose. Four major weaknesses to watch for are *vagueness, jargon, triteness,* and *ineffective imagery.*

### Eliminating Vagueness

Words are vague when, in context, they do not convey a single, specific meaning to your readers. Consider this sentence:

I could tell by the funny look on her face that she was mad.

*Funny* and *mad* can have quite specific meanings, but not in this sentence. What does *funny* mean here—a purposeful attempt to provoke laughter? What does *mad* mean—"insane," as it might in another sentence? Certainly not. "Angry," then, or "annoyed" or "irritated" or "offended"? A reader cannot be sure. The writer can remove doubt by using more specific diction.

I could tell by the *way her face stiffened* that she was *offended.*

Words like *funny* and *mad* belong to a group called *utility words.* Such words, as their name implies, are useful. In ordinary conversation, which does not usually permit or require deliberate choice and offers little chance for revision, utility words are common and often pass unnoticed. In writing, they may be adequate if the context limits them to a single, clear interpretation. But because their meaning is often left vague, they should be used with caution. The following is a list of some of the most common utility words:

| | | | |
|---|---|---|---|
| affair | funny | marvelous | regular |
| awful | gadget | matter | silly |
| business | glamorous | nature | situation |
| cute | goods | neat | stuff |
| fantastic | gorgeous | nice | terrible |
| fierce | great | outfit | terrific |
| fine | line | peculiar | weird |
| freak | lovely | pretty | wonderful |

Usually the simplest way to clarify a vague utility word or phrase is to substitute a specific word or phrase, as in the following examples:

*puzzling*
It was a ~~peculiar~~ statement.

*alarming*
The news is ~~terrible~~.

*clear, sunny, and in the low 80s.*
The weather will be ~~fantastic~~.

Vagueness is not limited to unclear utility words. Any word or phrase that is more general than the intended meaning should be revised. The substitutions in these sentences make the information more specific.

*Annie Dillard's "Total Eclipse."*
The class was discussing ~~an essay~~.

*how this winter's storms eroded the sand dunes on Cape Cod.*
Professor Jones is studying ~~erosion~~.

1. Assume that the italicized words are not made clear by context. Substitute more specific diction to give a precise meaning.

   a. She is a scientist, but I don't know what her *line* is.
   b. Our *group* thought the *samples* were *peculiar*.
   c. One *aspect* of the *project* is its *effect* on prices.
   d. What a *terrific* surprise to meet so many *important* people at the same *affair*.
   e. The lab fees for this course are *something else*.

2. Circle the more specific expression in each parenthetical set.

   The whole surface of the ice was *(a chaos—full)* of movement. It looked like an enormous *(mass—jigsaw puzzle)* stretching away to infinity and being *(pushed—crunched)* together by some invisible but irresistible force. The impression of its *(titanic—great)* power was heightened by the unhurried deliberateness of the motion. Whenever two thick *(pieces—floes)* came together, their edges *(met—butted)* and *(moved—ground)* against one another for a time. Then, when neither of them showed signs of yielding, they rose *(uncertainly—quiveringly)*, driven by the *(implacable—tremendous)* power behind them. Sometimes they would stop *(altogether—abruptly)* as the unseen forces affecting the ice appeared mysteriously to lose interest. More frequently, though, the two floes—often ten feet thick or more—would continue to rise *(rearing up—tenting up)*, until one or both of them toppled over, creating a pressure ridge.

## Eliminating Jargon

*The only way to revise jargon is to get rid of it. When readers have to rewrite your jargon mentally, they may not be sure what you meant.*

*Jargon* originally meant meaningless chatter. Later it meant the specialized language of a group or profession, as in *habeas corpus* (law) and *cursor* (computer technology). There is no reason not to use learned and technical terms for audiences and situations for which they are appropriate, but to use them unnecessarily when addressing a general audience is a violation of the basic rule that your style should fit your purpose and audience. Jargon in informal writing is pretentious and frustrating to your audience. The following contrast shows inappropriate jargon that results in vague, indirect writing. The version on the left comes from the King James translation of the Bible; the version on the right is George Orwell's "translation" of the same material into modern jargon.

I returned and saw under the sun, that the race is not to the swift, nor the battle to the strong, neither yet bread to the wise, nor yet riches to men of understanding, nor yet favor to men of skill; but time and chance happeneth to them all.

Objective considerations of contemporary phenomena compel the conclusion that success or failure in competitive activities exhibits no tendency to be commensurate with innate capacity, but that a considerable element of the unpredictable must invariably be taken into account.

Although the Biblical version first appeared in 1611, it makes more sense and is easier to read than the "translation," which smothers simplicity and clarity under a blanket of vague, polysyllabic words. As Orwell points out:

> The first contains forty-nine words but only sixty syllables, and all of its words are those of everyday life. The second contains thirty-eight words of ninety syllables; eighteen of its words are from Latin roots, and one from Greek. The first sentence contains six vivid images, and only one phrase ("time and chance") that could be called vague. The second contains not a single fresh, arresting phrase, and in spite of its ninety syllables it gives only a shortened version of the meaning contained in the first. ("Politics and the English Language," *Shooting an Elephant and Other Essays*)

● A WRITING PROJECT

**Compose a narrative essay about the consequences of your inability to select the right word(s) to explain your behavior on an important occasion.**

Jargon has three chief characteristics:

▷ Highly abstract, often technical, diction that shows a fondness for learned rather than popular words: *have the capability to* for *can*, *maximize productivity* for *increase production*, and *utilization of mechanical equipment* for *use of machinery*.

▷ Excessive use of the passive voice. If machines break down, they "are found to be functionally impaired." If a plan does not work, "its objectives were not realized." If management failed to consider the effects of certain changes on the workers, the error is reported like this: "With respect to employee reactions, management seems to have been inadequately advised."

▷ Conspicuous wordiness, as illustrated in the previous examples.

Jargon combines inappropriateness, vagueness, and wordiness into one consistently unintelligible style. Writers who lapse into jargon do so because they believe that ordinary language is not good enough. Like Eliza Doolittle, they are trying to make a good impression. But the best way to make a good impression with your writing is to have something to say and to say it clearly.

The only way to revise jargon is to get rid of it. When readers have to rewrite your jargon mentally, they may not be sure what you meant. Notice how the following passage creates ambiguity for the reader.

> (1) Rigorous comprehension and innermost instincts are the features of collaborative inquiry that spelunkers must engage when they delve into the unexplored terrain of a new cave. (2) They must scrutinize the formation of the rocks and the current of the river, establish their directional movement with the assistance of a compass, and maintain a precise topographical record so that they can renegotiate their expedition to its inception. (3) But since they have no established record, they must still commit their full confidence to their instincts when

they reach an intersection. (4) At that juncture they must contemplate whether traversing one passageway will bring them into contact with a chamber enlarged by a high ceiling or with a corridor that narrows into a cul-de-sac.

The writer probably consulted a thesaurus to dress up the language of that needlessly "learned" paragraph. If you rewrite the paragraph, reducing each sentence to a summary of what the writer was trying to say, you get this:

1. Spelunkers use knowledge and instincts to explore a new cave.
2. They study rock formations and river currents; they use a compass; and they need to find their way out.
3. Since they have no maps, at intersections they must rely on their instincts.
4. They may turn into big chambers or dead ends.

If you join the revised sentences, you get a paragraph that says all the original was trying to say, but says it more clearly and in fewer words— 51 words instead of 119. You might get a still better revision by tinkering with the sentence structure, adding or subtracting words where appropriate:

> When they explore a new cave, spelunkers rely on educated guesswork. They study the rock formation and river current, chart their movement with a compass, and mark their trail so that they can find their way out. But since they have no map, they must trust their instincts at each intersection. They may select a passage that turns into a vaulted chamber or a dead end.

The revised paragraph says nothing that was not said in the previous passage. But it sharpens the focus by beginning with a clear topic sentence and then explaining that sentence. The pomposities of the original version have been eliminated, and the meaning is conveyed in half the space.

## EXERCISE

**Using the procedure just shown, revise this paragraph.**

Last month as I was perambulating through the stacks, I happened to encounter a book filled with photographs of volcanoes. Not yet having realized my latent interest in such geological formations, I was surprised at the manner in which this book enthralled my attention. The color displays of the spectacular discharge of Washington's Mount St. Helens and the florid lava flows of Hawaii's Kilauea I found to be particularly disquieting. It was these photographs which led me to the decision to espouse volcanoes as the subject of my research paper.

## Eliminating Triteness

The terms *trite, hackneyed,* and *clichéd* are used to describe expressions, once colorful and apt, that have been used so often that they have lost their freshness and force. Like outdated slang, trite expressions once evoked images and conveyed a sense of discovery through language. Striking when new, such phrases become meaningless when they are overused. Note these examples:

| | |
|---|---|
| apple of her eye | hook, line, and sinker |
| birds of a feather | lock, stock, and barrel |
| black sheep | mountains out of molehills |
| blind as a bat | sober as a judge |
| budding genius | teeth like pearls |
| diamond in the rough | thick as thieves |
| fly in the ointment | water over the dam |

Trite diction blocks thought. Writers who use ready-made phrases instead of creating their own soon find it difficult to think beyond stereotyped expressions: Any change in personnel becomes a "shakeup"; all hopes become "fond," "foolish," or "forlorn"; defeats are "crushing"; changes in the existing system are "noble experiments" or "dangerous departures"; unexpected occurrences are "bolts from the blue"; and people who "sow wild oats" always have to "pay the piper" even though they are "as poor as church mice."

When you spot triteness in your writing, you should remove it. The way to learn to detect and avoid triteness in your writing is to learn to recognize triteness in the speech and writing of others. Notice the italicized clichés in this paragraph.

> *Money doesn't grow on trees,* and how well I've learned that. What a *rude awakening* when I realized that the odd change I used to ask for at home was not available at school. I had thought my allowance was enormous but, before I knew it, it had *trickled through my fingers.* College has taught me that *"A penny saved is a penny earned."* I have learned to live within my allowance and even to *save something for a rainy day.* What I have learned in college is *not all in the books.* I have learned to *shoulder my responsibilities.*

How many of those phrases do you recognize as prefabricated units that can be inserted into any sentence? If you can identify triteness in another writer's work, you can identify it in your own.

1. Politics, television, popular music, and sports seem to encourage the use of trite expressions. Although some writers interpret these subjects with originality and insight, most seem to type their texts on a cliché machine. Examine the following paragraph to determine whether it provides any insights into football or simply repeats clichés.

Whenever the gridiron game is played in the United States—on a sandlot, a high school field, or in a college or professional stadium—the players learn through the school of hard knocks the invaluable lesson that only by the men's blending together like birds of a feather can the team win. It is a lesson they do not forget on the gridiron. Off the field, they duly remember it. In society, the former player does not look upon himself as a lone wolf on the prowl who has the right to do his own thing—that is, to observe only his individual social laws. He knows he is a part of the big picture and must conduct himself as such. He realizes that only by playing as a team man can he do his share in making society what it should be—the protector and benefactor of all. The man who has been willing to make the sacrifice to play football knows that teamwork is essential in this modern day and age and that every citizen must pull his weight in the boat if the nation is to prosper. So he has little difficulty in adjusting to his roles in family life and in the world of business and to his duties as a citizen in the total scheme of things. In short, his football training helps make him a better citizen and person, better able to play the big game of life.

2. Rewrite the previous paragraph to eliminate the major objections made about it during class discussion.

3. Choose as a general subject a current issue in the world of politics, television, or popular music. Restrict that general subject to a topic that you think is important to students, and write a letter to the campus newspaper expressing your opinion. Then reread your letter to catch any trite language you may have used.

## Eliminating Ineffective Imagery

An effective figure of speech can make your writing concrete; a figure that is trite, far-fetched, obscure, or confused mars your writing and distracts your readers. *Mixed metaphors*—metaphors that combine two or more incompatible images in a single figure—are especially ineffective. Consider the following:

> The scientist decided to gauge the political water by throwing his hat into the ring as a trial balloon.

This sentence mixes three overused, equally unimaginative images. "Testing the water" has a literal meaning in cooking and bathing. "Throwing one's hat into the ring" was a conventional way of issuing a challenge in the days of bare-knuckle prize fights. Trial balloons were once used to determine wind direction and velocity. Each of these images can be used in a political context, but fitting all three into one consistent figure of speech is impossible. And because the subject of the sentence is "the scientist," these figures distract the reader by suggesting that the sentence is about science rather than politics. The writer of the sentence should abandon metaphor and simply say, "The scientist tried to evaluate his chances of being nominated by announcing his intention to seek the position."

A poor figure of speech is worse than none at all. Imagery is ruined if the picture it conveys is preposterous or dull. If the figure with which you intended to strengthen your writing weakens it, then delete or revise it. Test every figure of speech by *seeing* the picture it represents. If you visualize what your words are saying, then you will see and be able to eliminate ineffective or mixed images during revision.

## EXERCISE

These sentences try unsuccessfully to combine discordant elements in the same figure of speech. Visualize the images they suggest, and then revise each sentence by creating an acceptable figure or restating the idea without a figure.

1. A host of music fans flocked into the arena like an avalanche.

2. The president's ill-advised action has thrown the ship of state into low gear, and unless the members of Congress wipe out the party lines and carry the ball as a team, it may take months to get the country back on the track.

3. When I try to focus my microscope, I do something that throws a monkey wrench into the ointment.

4. NASA expressed confidence that the hearing would allow the real facts of the case to come out in the wash.

5. Although the members of our writing group have difficulty forgetting where the hatchet is buried, we decided that was water over the dam.

# Correcting diction

As you compose, you may often be unable to think of the *right* word. Use the thesaurus function of your word-processing program to identify a word that is similar to the one you want. Call up that word and see if any of the synonyms listed suggest the word you are looking for.

Although the thesaurus in some word-processing programs provides a brief definition of every word, don't depend on such definitions when you are making your final choice. Look up words in a standard dictionary to determine their various meanings and connotations. Words that have similar meanings are not interchangeable. For example, only a dictionary will tell you why the underlined word in the second sentence makes the sentence ludicrous: (1) The studio was <u>cluttered</u> with easels. (2) The studio was <u>choked up</u> with easels.

Perhaps the most valuable feature in most word-processing programs is the spellchecker. But you must know what it will and will not do. It *will* flag every word that does not appear in its dictionary. It will suggest alternatives and enable you to correct your mistakes quickly. But many of the words you may use in your text—proper nouns, for example—will not be in the spellchecker and so will be flagged as misspelled. You can fix this problem by adding such words to your computer's dictionary. The spellchecker will *not* catch words that are correctly spelled but misused in the text. For example, it will not catch a common error such as the use of *their* for *there.*

The spellchecker can function as a kind of thesaurus. If it flags a word as misspelled, it will suggest a list of other words—one of which you may actually prefer to the one you have misspelled. Again, check your dictionary first. If the new word works, use it instead of your original choice.

When you have completed your draft, post it to your writing group or the members of your writing class. Ask them to mark the words that seem ineffective or inappropriate. Then ask them to insert [in brackets] other words, that they think might sharpen or clarify your purpose. As you read their suggestions, you may discover that you have misread your audience. For example, some members of your writing group will tolerate slang or will encourage difficult jargon. You should not alter your diction to satisfy every member of your audience, but you can use this network exercise to locate your readers on the diction scale (page 261). Once you know more about their vocabulary skills, you can tailor your diction to their knowledge and expectations.

# Image Gallery

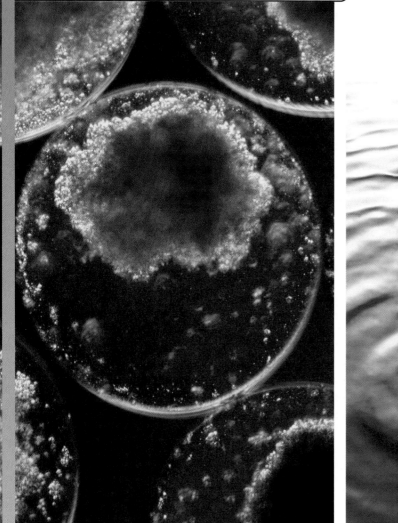

## Questions

1. Annie Dillard says that she "learns words by learning worlds" (p. 257). What words would you use to describe the "world" depicted in each picture?

2. What words would you use to describe the pattern presented in the sequence of photos?

3. How do the worlds in the first photograph and last photograph illustrate the words *microcosm* and *macrocosm*?

# Readings

In this episode from his classic essay "University Days," humorist James Thurber explains his frustration in trying to see through a microscope. How would you characterize the *appropriateness* of Thurber's diction? On the scale of most formal to least formal, where would you place Thurber's choice of words? Select specific examples to support your choice.

# The Microscope

## JAMES THURBER

1 I passed all the other courses that I took at my university, but I could never pass botany. This was because all botany students had to spend several hours a week in a laboratory looking through a microscope at plant cells, and I could never see through a microscope. I never once saw a cell through a microscope. This used to enrage my instructor. He would wander around the laboratory pleased with the progress all the students were making in drawing the involved, and so I am told, interesting structure of flower cells, until he came to me. I would just be standing there. "I can't see anything," I would say. He would begin patiently enough, explaining how anybody can see through a microscope, but he would always end up in a fury, claiming that I could *too* see through the microscope but just pretended that I couldn't. "It takes away from the beauty of flowers anyway," I used to tell him. "We are not concerned with beauty in this course," he would say. "We are concerned solely with what I may call the *mechanics* of flars." "Well," I'd say, "I can't see anything." "Try it just once again," he'd say, and I would put my eye to the microscope and see nothing at all, except now and again a nebulous milky substance—a phenomenon of maladjustment. You were supposed to see a vivid, restless clockwork of sharply defined plant cells. "I see what looks like a lot of milk," I would tell him. This, he claimed, was the result of my not having adjusted the microscope properly, so he would readjust it for me, or rather for himself. And I would look again and see milk.

2 I finally took a deferred pass, as they called it, and waited a year and tried again. (You had to pass one of the biological sciences or you couldn't graduate.) The professor had come back from vacation brown as a berry, bright-eyed, and eager to explain cell-structure again to his classes. "Well," he said to me, cheerily, when we met in the first laboratory hour of the semester, "we're going to see cells this time, aren't we?" "Yes, sir," I said. Students to right of me and to left of me and in front of me were seeing cells; what's more, they were quietly drawing pictures of them in their notebooks. Of course, I didn't see anything.

3 "We'll try it," the professor said to me, grimly, "with every adjustment of the microscope known to man. As God is my witness, I'll arrange this glass so that you see cells through it or I'll give up teaching. In twenty-two years of botany, I—" He cut off abruptly for he was beginning to quiver all over, like Lionel Barrymore, and he genuinely wished to hold onto his temper; his scenes with me had taken a great deal out of him.

4 So we tried it with every adjustment of the microscope known to man. With only one of

James Thurber, "University Days," *My Life and Hard Times* (New York: Harper, 1961), 88–90.

them did I see anything but blackness or the familiar lacteal opacity, and that time I saw, to my pleasure and amazement, a variegated constellation of flecks, specks, and dots. These I hastily drew. The instructor, noting my activity, came back from an adjoining desk, a smile on his lips and his eyebrows high in hope. He looked at my cell drawing. "What's that?" he demanded, with a hint of a squeal in his voice. "That's what I saw," I said. "You didn't, you didn't, you *didn't*!" he screamed, losing control of his temper instantly, and he bent over and squinted into the microscope. His head snapped up. "That's your eye!" he shouted. "You've fixed the lens so that it reflects! You've drawn your eye!"

Compare Annie Dillard's comments (page 257) on choosing and using words with her diction in this excerpt from "Total Eclipse." Select specific examples where her word choice exhibits the three qualities of effective diction—appropriateness, specificity, and imagery. How does each example advance her purpose?

# Total Eclipse

## ANNIE DILLARD

1 The hill was five hundred feet high. Long winter-killed grass covered it, as high as our knees. We climbed and rested, sweating in the cold; we passed clumps of bundled people on the hillside who were setting up telescopes and fiddling with cameras. The top of the hill stuck up in the middle of the sky. We tightened our scarves and looked around.

2 East of us rose another hill like ours. Between the hills, far below, was the highway which threaded south into the valley. This was the Yakima valley; I have never seen it before. It is justly famous for its beauty, like every planted valley. It extended south into the horizon, a distant dream of a valley, a Shangri-la. All its hundreds of low, golden slopes bore orchards. Among the orchards were towns, and roads, and plowed and fallow fields. Through the valley wandered a thin, shining river; from the river extended fine, frozen irrigation ditches. Distance blurred and blued the sight, so that the whole valley looked like a thickness or sediment at the bottom of the sky. Directly behind us was more sky, and empty lowlands blued by distance, and Mount Adams. Mount Adams was an enormous, snow-covered volcanic cone rising flat, like so much scenery.

3 Now the sun was up. We could not see it; but the sky behind the band of clouds was yellow, and far down the valley, some hillside orchards had lighted up. More people were parking near the highway and climbing the hills. It was the West. All of us rugged individualists were wearing knit caps and blue nylon parkas. People were climbing the nearby hills and setting up shop in clumps among the dead grasses. It looked as though we had all gathered on hilltops to pray for the world on its last day. It looked as though we had all crawled out of spaceships and were preparing to assault the valley below. It

Annie Dillard, *Teaching a Stone to Talk* (New York: Harper, 1982), 88–93.

looked as though we were scattered on hilltops at dawn to sacrifice virgins, make rain, set stone stelae in a ring. There was no place out of the wind. The straw grasses banged our legs.

4     Up in the sky where we stood the air was lusterless yellow. To the west the sky was blue. Now the sun cleared the clouds. We cast rough shadows on the blowing grass; freezing, we waved our arms. Near the sun, the sky was bright and colorless. There was nothing to see.

5  It began with no ado. It was odd that such a well-advertised public event should have no starting gun, no overture, no introductory speaker. I should have known right then that I was out of my depth. Without pause or preamble, silent as orbits, a piece of the sun went away. We looked at it through welders' goggles. A piece of the sun was missing; in its place we saw empty sky.

6     I had seen a partial eclipse in 1970. A partial eclipse is very interesting. It bears almost no relation to a total eclipse. Seeing a partial eclipse bears the same relation to seeing a total eclipse as kissing a man does to marrying him, or as flying in an airplane does to falling out of an airplane. Although the one experience precedes the other, it in no way prepares you for it. During a partial eclipse the sky does not darken—not even when 94 percent of the sun is hidden. Nor does the sun, seen colorless through protective devices, seem terribly strange. We have all seen a sliver of light in the sky; we have all seen the crescent moon by day. However, during a partial eclipse the air does indeed get cold, precisely as if someone were standing between you and the fire. And blackbirds do fly back to their roosts. I had seen a partial eclipse before, and here was another.

7     What you see in an eclipse is entirely different from what you know. It is especially different for those of us whose grasp of astronomy is so frail that, given a flashlight, a grapefruit, two oranges, and fifteen years, we still could not figure out which way to set the clocks for Daylight Saving Time. Usually it is a bit of a trick to keep your knowledge from blinding you. But during an eclipse it is easy. What you see is much more convincing than any wild-eyed theory you may know.

8     You may read that the moon has something to do with eclipses. I have never seen the moon yet. You do not see the moon. So near the sun, it is as completely invisible as the stars are by day. What you see before your eyes is the sun going through phases. It gets narrower and narrower, as the waning moon does, and like the ordinary moon, it travels alone in the simple sky. The sky is of course background. It does not appear to eat the sun; it is far behind the sun. The sun simply shaves away; gradually, you see less sun and more sky.

9  The sky's blue was deepening, but there was no darkness. The sun was a wide crescent, like a segment of tangerine. The wind freshened and blew steadily over the hill. The eastern hill across the highway grew dusky and sharp. The towns and orchards in the valley to the south were dissolving into the blue light. Only the thin river held a trickle of sun.

10     Now the sky to the west deepened to indigo, a color never seen. A dark sky usually loses color. This was a saturated, deep indigo, up in the air. Stuck up into that unworldly sky was the cone of Mount Adams, and the alpenglow was upon it. The alpenglow is that red light of sunset which holds out on snowy mountaintops long after the valleys and tablelands are dimmed. "Look at Mount Adams," I said, and that was the last sane moment I remember.

11  I turned back to the sun. It was going. The sun was going, and the world was wrong. The grasses were wrong; they were platinum. Their every detail of stem, head, and blade shone

lightness and artificially distinct as an art photographer's platinum print. This color has never been seen on earth. The hues were metallic; their finish was matte. The hillside was a nineteenth-century tinted photograph from which the tints had faded. All the people you see in the photograph, distinct and detailed as their faces look, are now dead. The sky was navy blue. My hands were silver. All the distant hills' grasses were finespun metal which the wind laid down. I was watching a faded color print of a movie filmed in the Middle Ages; I was standing in it, by some mistake. I was standing in a movie of hillside grasses filmed in the Middle Ages. I missed my own century, the people I knew, and the real light of day.

12      I looked at Gary. He was in the film. Everything was lost. He was a platinum print, a dead artist's version of life. I saw on his skull the darkness of night mixed with the colors of day. My mind was going out; my eyes were receding the way galaxies recede to the rim of space. Gary was light-years away, gesturing inside a circle of darkness, down the wrong end of a telescope. He smiled as if he saw me; the stringy crinkles around his eyes moved. The sight of him, familiar and wrong, was something I was remembering from centuries hence, from the other side of death: yes, *that* is the way he used to look, when we were living. When it was our generation's turn to be alive. I could not hear him; the wind was too loud. Behind him the sun was going. We had all started down a chute of time. At first it was pleasant; now there was no stopping it. Gary was chuting away across space, moving and talking and catching my eye, chuting down the long corridor of separation. The skin on his face moved like thin bronze plating that would peel.

13      The grass at our feet was wild barley. It was the wild einkorn wheat which grew on the hilly flanks of the Zagros Mountains, above the Euphrates valley, above the valley of the river we called *River*. We harvested the grass with stone sickles, I remember. We found the grasses on the hillsides; we built our shelter beside them and cut them down. That is how he used to look then, that one, moving and living and catching my eye, with the sky so dark behind him and the wind blowing. God save our life.

From all the hills came screams. A piece of sky beside the crescent sun was detaching. It was a loosened circle of evening sky, suddenly lighted from the back. It was an abrupt black body out of nowhere; it was a flat disk; it was almost over the sun. That is when there were screams. At once this disk of sky slid over the sun like a lid. The sky snapped over the sun like a lens cover. The hatch in the brain slammed. Abruptly it was dark night, on the land and in the sky. In the night sky was a tiny ring of light. The hole where the sun belongs is very small. A thin ring of light marked its place. There was no sound. The eyes dried, the arteries drained, the lungs hushed. There was no world. We were the world's dead people rotating and orbiting around and around, embedded in the planet's crust, while the earth rolled down. Our minds were light-years distant, forgetful of almost everything. Only an extraordinary act of will could recall to us our former, living selves and our contexts in matter and time. We had, it seems, loved the planet and loved our lives, but could no longer remember the way of them. We got the light wrong. In the sky was something that should not be there. In the black sky was a ring of light. It was a thin ring, an old, thin silver wedding band, an old, worn ring. It was an old wedding band in the sky, or a morsel of bone. There were stars. It was all over.

14

# Web Design

Students using *Writing with a Purpose* in a composition class were asked to design a website suggested by Annie Dillard's essay, "Total Eclipse." Consult the elements and principles of design in Chapter 5 to help you answer the questions about the effectiveness of each design.

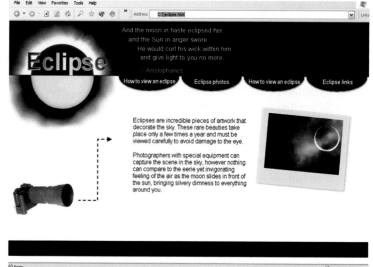

## Sample Homepage #1: Eclipse

1. How does the use of mixed colors in the title clash with the black and white in the text?

2. How does the juxtaposition of the black sky (background) and the white ornate fonts make the text difficult to read?

3. How do the clashing typefaces destroy the unity the design tries to establish with centered alignment?

## Sample Homepage #2: Eclipse

1. How does overlapping the title *Eclipse* on the image of an eclipse clarify the subject?

2. How does the alignment of title, image, and camera on one side and of the photo of the eclipse on the other side help focus your eye on the text in the middle?

3. How does the use of black and white add to Dillard's description of how the world looks during an eclipse?

# Writing Assignments

## 1. NARRATE

Write a narrative essay about the difficulties you encountered when you used a word you didn't know in a context that was inappropriate.

## 2. OBSERVE

Select several students and observe their use of certain words in conversation. Make a list of the words they use most often to describe certain social events on campus. Pay particular attention to their use of slang. Then compile a dictionary of slang for next year's freshman class. Ask your friends to help compose definitions.

## 3. INVESTIGATE

Interview an expert on your campus (botany professor) or in your community (car mechanic) about some aspect of his or her job. As you conduct the interview, make a list of all the words you don't understand. Ask your expert to help you with your list. Which words would he or she classify as popular, learned, or jargon? Ask your expert to define the words on the jargon list. Then write an essay for uninformed readers explaining some of the jargon they need to know to understand this area of expertise.

## 4. COLLABORATE

Each month *The Atlantic* concludes with a page called "Word Watch." The four or five words presented each month are being tracked by the editors of the *American Heritage Dictionary* to see if they exhibit sustained use over time and therefore merit inclusion in a future edition of the dictionary. In the August 1987 issue, for example, one of the words presented was *dink,* an acronym for "double income, no kids" couples. Your writing group has been asked to conduct a "Word Watch" using four or five words that you see used on the Web—for example, *flame*—with some regularity. Consider the origin, definitions, and synonyms for your words. Then collaborate on a letter to the *American Heritage Dictionary* arguing for the inclusion of your words in the next edition of the dictionary.

## 5. READ

Select a troublesome word you have encountered in your reading about science—such as *entropy, refraction,* or *void.* Examine the history of the word in the *Oxford English Dictionary.* See if the word is given an expanded definition in a general or specialized encyclopedia such as *Encyclopedia Britannica* or the *McGraw-Hill Encyclopedia of Science and Technology.* Look up some of its synonyms in *Roget's Thesaurus.* Then compose an extended definition of the word, pointing out its denotative and connotative meanings.

## 6. RESPOND

Respond to James Thurber's essay by describing your own experiences seeing what you are supposed to see. You may want to describe your difficulties seeing a microscopic world (a cell) or a cosmic world (a constellation). You may want to expand this assignment to include the "lab report"—that is, to describe the difficulty you had describing *in writing* what you saw to a professor who knew exactly what you were supposed to see.

## 7. ANALYZE

Analyze the process of *code switching*—a speaker's switching from using the words of one language (e.g., English) to using the words of another language (e.g., Spanish) in one sentence. How do strange words from one language slowly become familiar words in another language?

## 8. EVALUATE

Evaluate Annie Dillard's diction in the selection from "Total Eclipse." Begin by finding words that document the range of her word choice (from *popular* to *learned*). Next, assess her use of imagery (see in particular her comparison of a partial eclipse with a total eclipse). Then evaluate how Dillard's diction deepens and extends her description of the event.

### 9. ARGUE

In an essay designed for a popular nature magazine (or the "Lifestyle" section of your Sunday newspaper), argue that physical events create certain psychological reactions. You may want to select an extraordinary event, such as a solar eclipse, tornado, or flood, and speculate on why it produces extreme reactions. Or you may want to select a more common event, such as sunshine, rain, or humidity, and set up correlations between external and internal weather.

### 10. ARGUE

When the emperor asked Confucius what could be done to restore harmony to his troubled land, the wise man replied, "Purify the language." Select an example of language that needs purifying from, for example, a political speech or a product warranty. Identify those places in the text that need revision. Then write a letter to the appropriate authority using your revisions to illustrate how effective diction can create social harmony.

# 11

# Tone and Style

YOU CAN DEAL WITH ONLY SO MUCH OPERATIC TRUTH.

THEN YOU HAVE TO ACKNOWLEDGE THE POPCORN STAND

AND THE PEANUT GALLERY.

—PATRICIA HAMPL

In Chapters 9 and 10, you examined sentence structure and diction separately, but you must also consider their joint impact on the tone and style of a piece of writing. You are generally familiar with the words *tone* and *style,* of course. When someone says, "Don't speak to me in that tone," or "The style of that book is difficult," you know what is meant. In this chapter, however, you will learn that *tone* and *style* are technical concepts that you need to understand and control to improve your writing.

As you work your way through the stages of the writing process, you try to sort out what you think about your material and how you want your readers to think about it. For example, Ellen Haack's initial planning draft (in Chapter 3) captured much of Barry's quirkiness, but her scratch outline reduced his behavior to abstractions *(food, exercise,* and *culture).* This led her to eliminate Barry as a subject and adopt an academic tone for her working hypothesis and discovery draft. She discovered this problem through her descriptive outline and concluded that her draft sounded scholarly but wasn't very interesting. By returning to Barry in her new outline and subsequent draft, she achieved a more entertaining tone and engaging style and revealed Barry's quirkiness to her readers.

## Tone

Essayist Patricia Hampl, like Ellen, finds that the right tone is essential for an effective writing style.

> The issue of tone is central to me because I want my readers to know that another human being is speaking to them. I've never had much interest in the objective tone of the godlike narrator. It's supposed to give your writing a kind of neutral authority, but I don't think it exists. Even God has a personality. There's the God of light. The God of mercy. The philosophical issue at stake here is how to maintain the middle position, the position of a human being who possesses both authority and reliability. I try to create that balance by mixing a formal tone with a more conversational tone. You can deal with only so much operatic truth. Then you have to acknowledge the popcorn stand and the peanut gallery. (Personal interview)

*"When I say 'Please pass the butter,' why do you say 'Hey, no problem'?"*

## Range of Tone: Informative to Affective

As Patricia Hampl suggests, writers can adopt an objective or a subjective tone. You adopt the first when your purpose is to give your readers authoritative information. You adopt the second when your purpose is to affect or influence your readers in some way. The following excerpt exemplifies one of these two extremes of tone.

> The United States was the first nation in history so many of whose citizens could go so far simply in quest of fun and culture. The size of this phenomenon made international travel, for the first time, a major element in world trade, a new problem for the American economy and for American balance of payments, and a new opportunity for the destination countries. In 1970 the Department of Commerce estimated that the expenditures of American travelers overseas had reached $2 billion each year. In the United States, economists began to count foreign travel as a major import, and other countries began to plan for tourism by Americans as a principal export.
>
> (Daniel Boorstin, *The Americans: The Democratic Experience*)

Notice the following characterisitics of this passage:

- Boorstin is principally concerned with giving readers information about his subject. He assumes that they will be interested in the historic and economic significance of travel.

- Boorstin's writing is informative and objective—he does not show his personal feelings. He supports his judgment about America's preoccupation with travel by citing experts: the Department of Commerce and economists.

- As a result of Boorstin's purpose and strategies, his tone is informative, factual, and impersonal.

Contrast Boorstin's passage with this one:

> I don't know where we got the idea we have to go away for a vacation. I suppose the travel industry sold it to us. The travel business is the second largest industry in the United States. It's always trying to get us to go someplace *else* to spend our money when most of us don't have any trouble spending it right here where we are. The industry tries to make us feel cheap if we don't go on an expensive trip.
>
> Well, I've got my plans all made for my vacation. I'm not going *anywhere.* How do you like that, travel industry? Show me all the luxurious accommodations you want, tempt me with pictures of bikini-clad girls with windswept hair on pearl-white beaches—I'm not going. I'm staying put is what I'm doing. We've been tourists, and none of us likes being a tourist, so this summer I'll be somewhere I've never been on vacation—right where I live. (Andy Rooney, *A Few Minutes with Andy Rooney*)

The sample is quite different from Boorstin's.

▶ Rooney's purpose is to offer his opinion, not to give information. He does tell his readers that the travel industry is the second largest in the United States, but he tells them little more about it—except how it makes him feel.

▶ Rooney's writing is affective and *subjective*. Rooney writes almost exclusively about how *he* feels about the subject of vacations: "I've got my plans," "I'm not going *anywhere*," "I'm staying put." His language reveals his defiant attitude: "How do you like that, travel industry?"

▶ As a result of Rooney's purpose and strategies, his tone is affective, opinionated, and personal.

These two passages represent the extremes of tone on a scale ranging from informative to affective.

Boorstin passage         Rooney passage

*Informative*         *Affective*

Between the extremes, you could place other samples that show varying degrees of objectivity and subjectivity; those in the middle would be equally balanced between the two.

Each time you write, you will have to decide how informative or affective your writing should be. Certain assignments—laboratory reports, summaries of books or events, essay examinations—usually require an informative tone. Persuasive essays, intended to convince a reader to believe or do something, are usually affective. But, as Hampl indicates, a balance of informative and affective elements produces the most flexible and natural tone. The balance in your essays will depend on your subject and purpose.

Inexperienced writers sometimes believe that the way to be objective is to avoid writing in the first person. When you are writing about your own experience, ideas, and feelings, however, you need to use the pronoun *I*. Moreover, a third-person account is not necessarily an objective treatment of the subject. The statement "I saw the car run through a red light" is more objective than "The crazy fool drove through a red light," even though the first sentence contains *I* and the second does not.

**Where on the informative/affective scale would you place the following passages? Examine each passage closely so that you can support your judgment by reference to specific details.**

Passage 1

Why is it almost impossible to gaze directly at the Grand Canyon under these circumstances and see it for what it is—as one picks up a strange object from one's back yard and gazes directly at it? It is almost impossible because the Grand Canyon, the thing as it is, has been appropriated by the symbolic complex which has already been formed in the sightseer's mind. Seeing the canyon under approved circumstances is seeing the symbolic complex head on. The thing is no longer the thing as it confronted the Spaniard; it is rather that which has already been formulated—by picture postcard, geography book, tourist folders, and the words *Grand Canyon.* As a result of this preformulation, the source of the sightseer's pleasure undergoes a shift. Where the wonder and delight of the Spaniard arose from his penetration of the thing itself, from a progressive discovery of depths, patterns, colors, shadows, etc., now the sightseer measures his satisfaction *by the degree to which the canyon conforms to the preformed complex.* If it does so, if it looks just like the postcard, he is pleased; he might even

say, "Why it is every bit as beautiful as a picture postcard!" He feels he has not been cheated. But if it does not conform, if the colors are somber, he will not be able to see it directly; he will only be conscious of the disparity between what it is and what it is supposed to be. He will say later that he was unlucky in not being there at the right time. The highest point, the term of the sightseer's satisfaction, is not the sovereign discovery of the thing before him; it is rather the measuring up of the thing to the criterion of the preformed symbolic complex.

(Walker Percy, "The Loss of the Creature," *The Message in the Bottle*)

Passage 2

Everything comes onto the island: nothing much goes off, even by evaporation. Once it was a gateway to a New World, now it is a portal chiefly to itself. Manhattan long ago abandoned its melting-pot function. Nobody even tries to Americanize the Lebanese or the Lithuanians now, and indeed the ethnic enclaves of the island seem to me to become more potently ethnic each time I visit the place. Nothing could be much more Italian than the Festival of St. Anthony of Padua down on Mulberry Street, when the families of Little Italy stroll here and there through their estate, pausing often to greet volatile contemporaries and sometimes munching the soft-

shelled crabs which, spread-eagled on slices of bread like zoological specimens, are offered loudly for sale by street vendors. Harlem has become almost a private city in itself, no longer to be slummed through by whities after dinner, while Manhattan's Chinatown is as good a place as anywhere in the world to test your skill at that universal challenge, trying to make a Chinese waiter smile.

(Jan Morris, "Manhattan: The Islanders," *Destinations: Essays from Rolling Stone*)

Passage 3

The next day when I was already in full flight—aboard a northward bound train—I could not have accounted, if it had been demanded of me, for all the varied forces that were making me reject the culture that had molded and shaped me. I was leaving without a qualm, without a single backward glance. The face of the South that I had known was hostile and forbidding, and yet out of all the conflicts and the curses, the blows and the anger, the tension and the terror, I had somehow gotten the idea that life could be different, could be lived in a fuller and richer manner. As had happened, when I had fled the orphan home, I was now running more away from something than toward something. But that did not matter to me. My mood was: I've got to get away; I can't stay here.

(Richard Wright, *Black Boy*)

## Distance

Another element of tone is the impression of distance between writer and reader.

Consider a professor lecturing to a large class. She is separated from her listeners by her position on a platform; she cannot speak to each student in the audience individually. The situation requires her to speak more slowly, more loudly, and more formally than if she were conferring with a student in her office. The lecture room produces both physical and stylistic distance. Consider the distance in a statement in a printed syllabus that says, "Students are expected to hand in assignments on the date stipulated," and an instructor's after-class remark, "Joe, you've got to get your papers in on time." In the first statement the writer is impersonal and remote; in the second the speaker is personal and close.

The following selections illustrate the difference between writing that tries to get close to the reader and writing that addresses the reader from a distance.

Example 1

Did you ever wonder, looking at a map or whirling a globe, how the intricate shape of continents, shorelines, rivers and mountains came to be mapped, and who designed the system of parallels and meridians? Or how people found out, in the first place, that the earth is shaped like a globe? If we had not been told so I am not even sure that you or I would have found it out for ourselves. (Erwin Raisz, *Mapping the World*)

Here the distance between writer and reader is very slight. By using the second person, Raisz gives the impression of speaking personally to each reader. His conversational and questioning tone and his diction suggest that he identifies with his readers.

Example 2

The map predates the book (even a fairly ordinary map may contain several books' worth of information). It is the oldest means of information storage, and can present the most subtle facts with great clarity. It is a masterly form of compression, a way of miniaturizing a country or society. Most hill-climbers and perhaps all mountaineers know the thrill at a certain altitude of looking down and recognizing the landscape that is indistinguishable from a map. The only pleasure I take in flying in a jet plane is the experience of matching a coastline or the contour of a river to the corresponding map in my memory. A map can do many things, but I think its chief use is in lessening our fear of foreign parts and helping us anticipate the problems of dislocation. Maps give the world coherence. It seems to me one of man's supreme achievements that he knew the precise shape of every continent and practically every river-vein on earth long before he was able to gaze at them whole from the window of a rocketship. (Paul Theroux, "Mapping the World," *Sunrise with Seamonsters*)

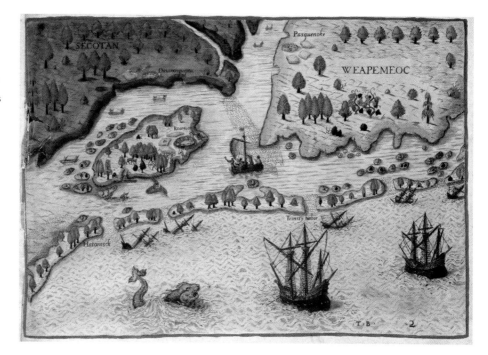

What information about the early settlers' perception of the language of the landscape is "stored" in this old map of Roanoke Island and the North Carolina coast?

● A Writer's Resources

Check the popular travel websites such as Orbitz, Expedia, and Yahoo.travel for information about how to get from where you are to where you want to go. For more detailed information about the place you want to visit, check the website for a country's or city's board of tourism or the websites for specific categories—museums, restaurants, hotels, or tours. Popular travel guides such as Fodor's, Frommer's, and the Rough Guide series have online guides to virtually any place in the world.

This paragraph is addressed not to any particular reader but to all readers. Theroux does not address his readers as "you" or try to appeal to their special interests. He is more interested in what he has to say than in his audience. His tone establishes greater distance between writer and reader than existed in the passage by Raisz.

The impression of distance comes chiefly from sentence structure and diction, the linguistic bases of tone, discussed next under "Style." Remember that the tone of your writing depends in part on decisions you make about the distance, or degree of separation, you want to maintain between yourself and your readers. The decision is not arbitrary; it is related to decisions about your attitude toward your subject, and it should be consistent with your purpose.

## Style

The *American Heritage Dictionary* defines *style* as "the way in which something is said or done, as distinguished from its substance." In writing, *style* refers to *how* something is said—the way a writer arranges sentences and words; *substance* means *what* is said—the ideas or message that the writer wishes to convey. The difficulty with the dictionary definition is that it assumes that what is said can somehow be examined apart from how it is said. In writing, however, the *what* and the *how* are virtually indistinguishable. The most subtle changes in sentences or diction can change the ideas or message. A simple, though more accurate definition, then, would be "Style is the way something is written."

How do you describe the way something is written? Consider the following passage from *The Adventures of Huckleberry Finn* by Mark Twain. Huck, staying with the Grangerfords after his raft has been wrecked, has been reading a poem written by the youngest daughter, now dead. The poem, intended to be a sad story about a young man who fell into a well and drowned, is so maudlin and so badly written that it is funny. Huck thinks it is very good. After reading it, he says:

> If Emmeline Grangerford could make poetry like that before she was fourteen, there ain't no telling what she could a done by-and-by. Buck [her younger brother] said she could rattle off poetry like nothing. She didn't ever have to stop and think. He said she would slap down a line, and if she couldn't find anything to rhyme with it she would just scratch it out and slap down another one, and go ahead. She warn't particular; she could write about anything you choose to give her to write about just so it was sadful. Every time a man died, or a woman died, or a child died, she would be on hand with her "tribute" before he was cold. She called them tributes. The neighbors said it was the doctor first, then Emmeline, then the undertaker—the undertaker never got in ahead of Emmeline but once, and then she hung fire on a rhyme for the dead person's name, which was Whistler. She warn't ever the same, after that; she never complained, but she kinder pined away and did not live long.

Notice the following things about this passage:

▶ Mark Twain is having fun with the subject. He knows the poem is sentimental to the point of being ridiculous, and he expects the reader to see that, too.

▶ Huck himself is serious. Huck, the narrator, says what a boy like him, but not a man like Twain, would say. Even though Twain is the writer, the *voice* you hear is that of Huck Finn. Twain creates an ironical situation in which everything Huck says about Emmeline's poetry confirms a different judgment in his readers.

▶ The diction is appropriate to the speaker. The humorous effect would be lost if Huck were made to speak like a sophisticated adult. He must speak in his own voice.

▶ All these elements are so interrelated that a change in any one of them would spoil the total effect.

Even this brief sample suggests that when you write something, you must consider your attitude toward your subject, your relationship with your readers, and the language you use to express your ideas. The tone of your writing reveals the decisions you have made about the first two. The third is expressed in the choices you make as you develop your purpose. As you have seen throughout this text, a clear sense of purpose guides you through all the choices you make from planning through revision. If these choices are consistent, your writing will exhibit a distinctive *style* that will express your attitude toward and embody your understanding of your purpose.

## Range of Style: Sentence Structure, Diction, and Tone

Style, of course, rests finally on language. Look closely at the sentence structure, diction, and tone of the following passages to see what generalizations you can make about them.

Example 1

Airplanes are invariably scheduled to depart at such times as 7:54, 9:21 or 11:37. This extreme specificity has the effect on the novice of instilling in him the twin beliefs that he will be *arriving* at 10:08, 1:43 or 4:22, and that he should get to the airport on time. These beliefs are not only erroneous but actually unhealthy, and could easily be dispelled by an attempt on the part of the airlines toward greater realism. Understandably, they may be reluctant to make such a radical change all at once. In an effort to make the transition easier I offer the following graduated alternatives to "Flight 477 to Minneapolis will depart at 8:03 P.M.":

a.  Flight 477 to Minneapolis will depart oh, let's say, eightish.
b.  Flight 477 to Minneapolis will depart around eight, eight-thirty.
c.  Flight 477 to Minneapolis will depart while it's still dark.
d.  Flight 477 to Minneapolis will depart before the paperback is out.

(Fran Leibowitz, "Fran Leibowitz's Travel Hints," *Social Studies*)

Analysis of Example 1: Sentence Structure

The nine sentences in this passage average only seventeen words in length, and almost half of them are set apart in a list of brief announcements. Most of the sentences consist of one or two independent clauses. Only the second sentence has a slightly inverted construction. The rest of the sentences follow a subject-verb-object order.

Diction

In the whole passage there are proportionately few words more than two syllables long. *Invariably, specificity,* and *graduated* are the most notable. Except for *novice* and *erroneous* there are no learned words. There are a few contractions *(let's, it's)* and one example of slang *(eightish).*

Tone

Leibowitz's attitude toward her subject is humorous and ironic. Supposedly informative—after all, she is offering advice—her attitude is really affective because she wants to exploit her readers' exasperation over airline schedules. The distance between writer and reader is slight. Leibowitz writes as a fellow sufferer commenting on a common frustration. You hear the voice of a world-weary crank, slightly angry about a situation over which she has no control.

With simple sentences and diction, Leibowitz establishes her tone and creates a style that achieves ease and clarity. The diction and the pace of her sentences are those of informal conversation, creating an impression of talking in print. In Chapter 10 the word *colloquial* was used to describe diction of this sort. That term can apply to a style as well. A colloquial style is not common in college writing, but it is by no means inappropriate when it is used—as it is here—to fulfill the writer's purpose.

Now contrast the next example with Leibowitz's writing. Read the following passage aloud, slowly, to hear how it sounds.

Example 2

What a fierce weird pleasure to lie in my berth at night in the luxurious palace-car, drawn by the mighty Baldwin—embodying, and filling me, too, full of the swiftest motion, and most resistless strength! It is late, perhaps midnight or after—distances join'd like magic—as we speed through Harrisburg, Columbus, Indianapolis. The element of danger adds zest to it all. On we go, rumbling and flashing, with our loud whinnies thrown out from time to time, or trumpet-blasts, into the darkness. Passing the homes of men, the farms, barns, cattle—the silent villages. And the car itself, the sleeper, with curtains drawn and lights turn'd down—in the berths the slumberers, many of them women and children—as on, on, on, we fly like lightning through the night—how strangely sound and sweet they sleep! (They say the French Voltaire in his time designated the grand opera and a ship of war the most signal illustrations of the growth of humanity's and art's advance beyond primitive barbarism. Perhaps if the witty philosopher were here these days, and went in the same car with perfect bedding and feed from New York to San Francisco, he would shift his type and sample to one of our American sleepers.) (Walt Whitman, *Specimen Days*)

The paragraph has only eight sentences. Although there are two short sentences (one a fragment), most of the sentences are long. The average sentence length is 26 words, against 17 in the Leibowitz passage; the last three sentences are 42, 32, and 39 words long. The sentences are not simple. Subjects and verbs are often separated—sometimes widely—by modifiers. Several of the sentences exhibit extremely complicated punctuation. Throughout the paragraph, parallel and periodic structures are used for rhythmic and other effects.

About 27 percent of the words in the passage are more than two syllables long, and it contains a smaller proportion of monosyllables than the Leibowitz example. Whitman's diction is sprinkled with learned words—*resistless, slumberers, barbarism.* Several phrases have a lofty, poetic ring— "embodying, and filling me, too, full of the swiftest motion, and most resistless strength!"

Whitman is celebrating the mythic adventure of train travel, and his attitude toward his subject is clearly subjective. The distance between writer and reader is great; the emphasis is on the subject, not on the reader. The affective tone is impersonal, dignified, eloquent.

*Summary*

As in the Leibowitz example, all the components blend into a consistent style. But what a different style! Whitman aims at eloquence, not ease or familiarity. You would not use this style to give directions, explain a process, answer an examination question, or report a story in a newspaper. Whitman's style shares many of the characteristics of nineteenth-century prose, characteristics still found in prose seeking similar effects. It could be called a *grand* style, but the usual name for it is *formal*.

*Example 3*

In those days differences in vegetation between a main highway and a side road were even greater than now. There weren't many state highways but the best of them stretched straight ahead with mathematical perfection, even though just of gravel. These rights-of-way were usually wide and from the road edge to the boundary fences were mowed pretty much as now, though road building had not been preceded by earth moving. As a result, there were more native plants in among the grass and fewer of those cosmopolitan tramps which take so readily to disturbed habitats. But the side roads, those fascinating side roads, they are mostly gone and there is nothing in the modern road system to compare with them. The wheel track wound here and there, depending upon the slope and the vegetation and the character of the land. Sometimes it was straight for a little way; frequently it wobbled. There was often grass in the roadway outside the actual wheel tracks; shrubs like sumac and elderberry pressed so close to the road that you could smell them as you drove by and children snatched at the flowers. Accommodating drivers of the local stage-line learned to snip off small twigs with a snap of the buggy whip and present them to lady passengers.

(Edgar Anderson, "Horse-and-Buggy Countryside," *Landscape*)

*Analysis of Example 3: Sentence Structure*

This paragraph has nine sentences, all following the standard pattern: subject-verb-object with modifiers and subordinate clauses appearing in predictable places. There are no conspicuous periodic sentences. Sentences do vary in length, from 11 to 38 words, but most fall between 19 and 26, averaging 21 (between the 17-word Leibowitz average and the 26-word Whitman average).

*Diction*

In this 214-word passage, only 15 words (or about 7 percent) are more than two syllables long. There are a few learned words such as *cosmopolitan* and *habitat,* but they are counterbalanced by popular words such as *snip* and *snap.*

*Tone*

Anderson's attitude toward his subject is both informative and affective. He wants to inform his readers about country roads, and he wants to describe how it must have looked and felt to ride down one of these roads in a horse-and-buggy. His choice of details—children

## SUMMARY OF THE FORMAL, MODERATE, AND COLLOQUIAL STYLES

| | Formal | Moderate | Colloquial |
|---|---|---|---|
| **SENTENCES** | Relatively long and involved; likely to make considerable use of parallel, balanced, and periodic structures; fragments rare. | Of medium length, averaging between 15 and 25 words; mostly standard structure but with some use of parallel, balanced, and periodic sentences; fragments occasional | Short, simple structures; mainly subject-verb-object order; almost no use of balanced or periodic sentences; fragments common. |
| **DICTION** | Extensive vocabulary, some use of learned and abstract words; no slang; almost no contractions or clipped words. | Ranges from learned to colloquial but mostly popular words; both abstract and concrete diction; occasional contractions and clipped words; may contain some inconspicuous slang. | Diction limited to popular and colloquial words, frequent contractions, and clipped words; frequent use of utility words; more slang than in moderate style. |
| **TONE** | Always a serious attitude toward an important subject; may be either subjective or objective and informative or affective; no attempt to establish closeness with reader, who is almost never addressed as "you"; personality of the writer often inconspicuous; whole tone usually dignified and impersonal. | Attitude toward subject may be serious or light, objective or subjective, informative or affective; relationship with reader close but seldom intimate; writer often refers to himself or herself as "I" and to reader as "you"; the range of moderate style is so broad that tone can vary from semiformal to semicolloquial. | Attitude toward subject may be serious or light but is usually subjective; close, usually intimate, relation with reader, who is nearly always addressed as "you"; whole tone is that of informal conversation. |
| **USES** | A restricted style used chiefly for scholarly or technical writing for experts, or for essays and speeches that aim at eloquence or inspiration; a distinguished style, but not one for everyday use or practical affairs. | The broadest and most usable style for expository and argumentative writing and for all but the most formal of public speeches; the prevailing style in nontechnical books and magazines, in newspaper reports and editorials, in college lectures and discussions, in all student writing except some fiction. | Light, chatty writing as in letters to close friends; a restricted style that is inappropriate to most college writing except fiction. |

snatching flowers, stage drivers snipping off flowers with their buggy whips—helps establish his informal, familiar tone. The distance between writer and reader is greater than in the first example but less than in the second example.

**Summary**

Anderson's style is neither as simple as Leibowitz's nor as involved as Whitman's. It has none of Leibowitz's chattiness and none of the poetry or exaltation that pervades Whitman's writing. Its balance of sentence length, diction, and tone produces a *moderate* style.

| Whitman passage | Anderson passage | Leibowitz passage |
|:---:|:---:|:---:|
| *Formal* | *Moderate* | *Colloquial* |

The diagram suggests three things:

▶ *The scale indicates degree of formality, from most to least.* It does not measure degree of excellence; no one style is better than another. All three are standard styles, and each is appropriate in some situations—although the moderate style is appropriate for most writing situations.

▶ *Each classification embodies a range.* A particular sample may be more or less formal than others. For example, a legal contract is more formal than Whitman's paragraph.

▶ *There is no clear division between styles.* The overlapping in the diagram is intended to suggest that the moderate style has such a broad range that it may include some formal and colloquial elements. Such inclusions, however, must be consistent with the writer's purpose. Edgar Anderson's use of *habitat,* for example, was justified because his purpose was to identify the characteristics of a particular landscape.

---

## EXERCISE

Analyze the sentence structure, diction, and tone of each of the following passages, using supporting details. Then rate each passage on the scale provided.

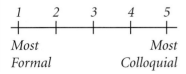

1   2   3   4   5
*Most*                *Most*
*Formal*          *Colloquial*

Competitors in conquest have overlooked the vital soul of Africa herself, from which emanates the true resistance to conquest. The soul is not dead, but silent, the wisdom not lacking, but of such simplicity as to be counted non-existent in the tinker's mind of modern civilization. Africa is of an ancient age and the blood of many of her peoples is as venerable and as chaste as truth. What upstart race, sprung from some recent, callow century to arm itself with steel and boastfulness, can match in purity the blood of a single Masai Murani whose heritage may have stemmed not far from Eden? It is not the weed that is corrupt; roots of the weed sucked first life from the genesis of earth and hold the essence of it still. Always the weed returns; the cultured plant retreats before it. Racial purity, true aristocracy, devolve not from edict, nor from rote, but from the preservation of kinship with the elemental forces and purposes of life whose understanding is not farther beyond the mind of a Native shepherd than beyond the cultured fumblings of a mortar-board intelligence.

(Beryl Markham, *West with the Night*)

We were sitting in a restaurant called Orchid Garden, in the Wanchai district, beginning our first meal in Hong Kong, and I had just sampled something called fish-brain soup. I was about to comment. Alice was looking a bit anxious. She was concerned, I think, that over the years I might have created a vision of Hong Kong in my mind that could not be matched by the reality—like some harried businessman who finally arrives in what he has pictured as the remote, other-worldly peace of a Tahiti beach only to be hustled by a couple of hip beach-umbrella salesmen wearing "Souvenir of Fort Lauderdale" T-shirts. Even before we had a meal,

she must have noticed my surprise at discovering that most of the other visitors in Hong Kong seemed to be there for purposes other than eating. That's the sort of thing that can put a visionary off his stride. How would the obsessed mountain climber feel if he arrived in Nepal after years of fantasizing about a clamber up the Himalayas, and found that most of the other tourists had come to observe the jute harvest? It appeared that just about everyone else had come to Hong Kong to shop. Hong Kong has dozens of vast shopping malls—floor after floor of shops run by cheerfully competitive merchants who knock off 10 percent at the hint of a frown and have never heard of sales tax. There are restaurants in some of the shopping malls, but most of the visitors seemed too busy shopping to eat. It was obvious that they would have come to Hong Kong even if it had been one of those British colonies where the natives have been taught to observe the queen's birthday by boiling brussels sprouts for an extra month. That very morning, in the lobby of a hotel, we had noticed a couple in late middle age suddenly drawing close to share some whispered intimacy in what Alice, the romantic, took to be

a scene of enduring affection until one of the softly spoken phrases reached her ears— "customs declaration."

(Calvin Trillin, "Hong Kong Dream," *Third Helpings*)

If you want to get something done, here is a professional secret: don't try to rush it by laying down the law that it *must be done* within a given time, but come back, each day if need be, and ask again, and do it with a smile. While evidences of irritation are fatal, persistence is never resented if it is clothed in good manners and good temper. When you can't wait any longer, the thing to do is to take an unfair advantage of your Brazilian friend—appeal to him to arrange matters for you because, first, you are in trouble with your principals; second, you are embarrassed by your own failure; third, you are obliged to leave by a given boat and will be humiliated if matters have not been arranged—anything to put it on a personal basis. When you do this your Brazilian is lost. He feels that you have been reasonable and patient and that he cannot throw you to the wolves. And in arranging matters for you he probably has to make a series of appeals more or less similar to yours.         (Hugh Gibson, *Rio*)

# Some Practical Advice About Style

● A WRITING PROJECT

**Using a specific example from your own experience, respond to James Gorman's assertion that "the Web can be seen as one vast travel magazine, a catalogue to the outdoors, and just as it is easier to read books about Everest than to climb it, it is much easier to plan hikes than to take them."**

—James Gorman, "Getting Away, on the Web and from It," *New York Times,* 13 June 2002.

You have examined the elements of style in passages by other writers. Now you are ready to apply what you have learned to your own writing. As you revise your writing, keep these stylistic considerations in mind:

1. *Let your purpose be your guide.* A clear sense of purpose controls all the choices you make at every stage in writing. Style results from that control.

2. *Generally, choose a moderate style.* There is nothing wrong with a formal or a colloquial style when it is appropriate. Unnecessary formality, however, often leads to pretentiousness and wordiness. The writer tries too hard to be impressive or literary when it would be enough to express his purpose clearly. The colloquial style, if used for serious treatment of a serious subject, can undermine the writer's purpose. The best policy, as Patricia Hampl suggests, is to maintain the middle position, "the position of a human being who possesses both authority and reliability." You can then mix objective and subjective—informative and affective—as your purpose demands.

3. *Keep your style consistent.* Probably the worst stylistic defect is inconsistency. An inconsistent style is not the same as a moderate style in which formal and colloquial elements are balanced for a purpose. Writing that is totally inconsistent has no discoverable purpose and therefore no discoverable style. The inconsistencies in tone and diction that often occur in individual paragraphs, sentences, or words can be removed in revision.

   a. *Inconsistency in tone.* Conspicuous inconsistency in tone is likely to jar a reader. It is most obvious when colloquial elements appear in a formal style or formal elements in a colloquial style. Because a moderate style can range from semiformal to semi-colloquial, it can tolerate usages that would be conspicuous in the extreme styles.

   b. *Inconsistency in diction.* As you begin planning and drafting your essay, you gradually commit yourself to a recognizable approach to both your subject and your reader. Your choice of words will either contribute to stylistic consistency or obscure the pattern in your writing. You are most likely to confuse readers by choosing words that are close but not close enough to your meaning. Do you want to say that your traveling companions are *insensitive, naive, or undiscriminating*? Your purpose determines the "best" choice of words.

4. *Try to see your writing as your readers will see it.* This advice may be the hardest to follow. People assume that what is clear to them will

be clear to others, but common experience demonstrates that this assumption is not always true. In everyday conversation, a frequently asked question is "What do you mean by that?" Because your readers will not have the opportunity to ask you that question, try to anticipate their need for clarity and completeness.

5. *Be as specific as you can.* Writing is a difficult medium because it is abstract. The word *apple* is more abstract than any apple you ever ate because it leaves out your actual experience with apples—their shape, size, color, texture, and taste. The problem all writers face is how to make abstractions concrete. The two common solutions are to (a) illustrate the meaning of general statements with examples and (b) choose words that are specific.

6. *Revise for style.* You revise for style when you undertake global revision. Your style is dependent on your purpose, so if you revise your purpose, you must revise your style. Likewise, if you change your subject or audience, you must make new decisions about sentence structure, diction, and tone.

Local revision—arranging your sentences, selecting your words, and adjusting your tone—involves the nuts and bolts of style. In fact, the changes you make in local revision will probably make the most improvement in your style. Follow your local revision with one last reading—just for style. Read the text aloud, or, better yet, listen to it read aloud, and concentrate on its overall effect. Imagine yourself listening to a band or a singer performing a piece of music. As you listen to your own writing, concentrate on the style of the piece and keep alert for any false notes. The following guidelines provide some basic questions to ask yourself when you revise for style.

The best policy, as Patricia Hampl suggests, is to maintain the middle position, "the position of a human being who possesses both authority and reliability."

Once you have completed all your revisions and have typed your final draft, you should proofread your writing very carefully. Proofreading is a close reading of the final version to catch errors in grammar, spelling, and punctuation, as well as typographical errors, that survived your revisions or crept into the final copy. Proofreading should be done slowly, preferably aloud. If possible, you should allow some time to elapse between your final typing and your proofreading. In that way you are more likely to read with a fresh eye.

# Guidelines for revising your style

1. **What is my general impression of my writing?**

   Do I find my writing clear, unambiguous, and likely to engage my readers? Have I carried out my purpose at every level; that is, am I satisfied that the *how* of my writing—its attitude, organization, and language—conveys the *what* of my ideas?

2. **What tone have I established in my writing?**

   Is my tone informative, affective, or a blend of both? How much distance have I maintained between myself and my readers? Is my tone appropriate for my subject and audience? Is it maintained consistently?

3. **How can I characterize the overall style of my writing?**

   Have I written this essay in a moderate style, opting for more or less colloquialism or formality as my purpose requires? Does my purpose in fact require me to be overtly colloquial or formal?

4. **Are my sentences well constructed and easy on the ear?**

   Have I written sentences varying in length and style so that they hold my readers' interest? Have I avoided the choppiness that comes from too many basic or loosely coordinated sentences? Have I avoided the density that comes from too many complicated sentences with multiple subordinate clauses?

5. **Have I used words as effectively as possible?**

   Do the connotations and denotations of my words support my purpose? Have I avoided unnecessary formalities and slang? Is my language specific and, when appropriate, vivid? Have I inadvertently mixed metaphors? Have I used imagery successfully to *heighten* effects, not merely to strive after them?

# Checking your tone and style on your computer

Most word-processing programs have a feature that will check your style, that is, keep track of the length and variety of your sentences, put an asterisk next to phrases that seem wordy, and mark constructions—such as "There are . . ." or "to be . . ."—that it identifies as ineffective.

You may also want to solicit opinions on your style by posting your text to your writing group or the members of your writing class. Ask them to analyze *your* style according to the strategies used to analyze the writers' styles on pages 295–301.

You may want to consider these points as you edit and revise. But a computer can make choices between only two existing options. It cannot analyze subtle nuances or be creative about solving the problem that appears on the screen. And your classmates' opinions may clash with yours on the relative formality of sentences, diction, tone, and style. *Style* is a matter of personal choice. Your imagination and judgment remain the best tools for evaluating your tone and style.

# Image Gallery

**Questions**

1. What do the travel posters (circa 1930–1950) suggest about the tone and style of travel in another time?

2. What do the photographs (circa 2000) suggest about the tone and style of travel in our time?

3. How has your attitude toward travel changed since September 11, 2001?

307

# Readings

In this selection from *Holidays in Hell,* P. J. O'Rourke demonstrates the particular style that he has exhibited as an editor for *The National Lampoon* and as International Affairs Desk Chief at *Rolling Stone.* The title of the essay suggests that its purpose is to inform. At what point in the essay do you realize that O'Rourke's purpose is to entertain? How does his purpose affect his tone?

# Third World Driving Hints and Tips

## P. J. O'ROURKE

1 During the past couple of years I've had to do my share of driving in the Third World—in Mexico, Lebanon, the Philippines, Cyprus, El Salvador, Africa and Italy. (Italy is not technically part of the Third World, but no one has told the Italians.) I don't pretend to be an expert, but I have been making notes. Maybe these notes will be useful to readers who are planning to do something with their Hertz #1 Club cards.

## Road Hazards

2 What would be a road hazard anywhere else, in the Third World is probably the road. There are two techniques for coping with this. One is to drive very fast so your wheels "get on top" of the ruts and your car sails over the ditches and gullies. Predictably, this will result in disaster. The other technique is to drive very slowly. This will also result in disaster. No matter how slowly you drive into a ten-foot hole, you're still going to get hurt. You'll find the locals themselves can't make up their minds. Either they drive at 2 m.p.h.—which they do every time there's absolutely no way to get around them. Or else they drive at 100 m.p.h.—which they do coming right at you when you finally get a chance to pass the guy going 2 m.p.h.

## Basic Information

3 It's important to have your facts straight before you begin piloting a car around an underdeveloped country. For instance, which side of the road do they drive on? This is easy. They drive on your side. That is, you can depend on it, any oncoming traffic will be on your side of the road. Also, how do you translate kilometres into miles? Most people don't know this, but one kilometre = ten miles, exactly. True, a kilometre is only 62 per cent of a mile, but if something is one hundred kilometres away, read that as one thousand miles because the roads are 620 per cent worse than anything you've ever seen. And when you see a 50-k.p.h. speed limit, you might as well figure that means 500 *m.p.h.* because nobody cares. The Third World does not have Broderick Crawford and the Highway Patrol. Outside the cities, it doesn't have many police at all. Law enforcement is in the hands of the army. And soldiers, if they feel like it, will shoot you no matter what speed you're going.

P. J. O'Rourke, *Holidays in Hell* (New York: Atlantic Monthly Press, 1988), 78–82.

## Traffic Signs and Signals

4  Most developing nations use international traffic symbols. Americans may find themselves perplexed by road signs that look like Boy Scout merit badges and by such things as an iguana silhouette with a red diagonal bar across it. Don't worry, the natives don't know what they mean, either. The natives do, however, have an elaborate set of signals used to convey information to the traffic around them. For example, if you're trying to pass someone and he blinks his left turn signal, it means go ahead. Either that or it means a large truck is coming around the bend, and you'll get killed if you try. You'll find out in a moment.

5  Signalling is further complicated by festive decorations found on many vehicles. It can be hard to tell a hazard flasher from a string of Christmas-tree lights wrapped around the bumper, and brake lights can easily be confused with the dozen red Jesus statuettes and the ten stuffed animals with blinking eyes on the package shelf.

## Dangerous Curves

6  Dangerous curves are marked, at least in Christian lands, by white wooden crosses positioned to make the curves even more dangerous. These crosses are memorials to people who've died in traffic accidents, and they give a rough statistical indication of how much trouble you're likely to have at that spot in the road. Thus, when you come through a curve in a full-power slide and are suddenly confronted with a veritable forest of crucifixes, you know you're dead.

## Learning to Drive Like a Native

7  It's important to understand that in the Third World most driving is done with the horn, or "Egyptian Brake Pedal," as it is known. There is a precise and complicated etiquette of horn use. Honk your horn only under the following circumstances:

1.  When anything blocks the road.
2.  When anything doesn't.
3.  When anything might.
4.  At red lights.
5.  At green lights.
6.  At all other times.

## Road-Blocks

8  One thing you can count on in Third World countries is trouble. There's always some uprising, coup or Marxist insurrection going on, and this means military road-blocks. There are two kinds of military road-block, the kind where you slow down so they can look you over, and the kind where you come to a full stop so they can steal your luggage. The important thing is that you must *never* stop at the slow-down kind of road-block. If you stop, they'll think you're a terrorist about to attack them, and they'll shoot you. And you must *always* stop at the full-stop kind of road-block. If you just slow down, they'll think you're a terrorist about to attack them, and they'll shoot you. How do you tell the difference between the two kinds of road-block? Here's the fun part: you can't!

9  (The terrorists, of course, have road-blocks of their own. They always make you stop. Sometimes with land mines.)

## Animals in the Right of Way

10  As a rule of thumb, you should slow down for donkeys, speed up for goats and stop for cows. Donkeys will get out of your way eventually, and so will pedestrians. But never actually stop for either of them or they'll take advantage, especially the pedestrians. If you stop in the middle of a crowd of Third World pedestrians, you'll be there buying Chiclets and bogus antiquities for days.

11  Drive like hell through the goats. It's almost impossible to hit a goat. On the other hand, it's almost impossible *not* to hit a cow. Cows are immune to horn-honking, shouting, swats with sticks and taps on the hind quarters with the bumper. The only thing you can do to make a cow move is to swerve to avoid it, which will make the cow move in front of you with lightning speed.

12  Actually, the most dangerous animals are the chickens. In the United States, when you see a ball roll into the street, you hit your brakes because you know the next thing you'll see is a kid chasing it. In the Third World, it's not balls the kids are chasing, but chickens. Are they practising punt returns with a leghorn? Dribbling it? Playing stick-hen? I don't know. But Third Worlders are remarkably fond of their chickens and, also, their children (population problems notwithstanding). If you hit one or both, they may survive. But you will not.

## Accidents

13  Never look where you're going—you'll only scare yourself. Nonetheless, try to avoid collisions. There are bound to be more people in that bus, truck or even on that moped than there are in your car. At best you'll be screamed deaf. And if the police do happen to be around, standard procedure is to throw everyone in jail regardless of fault. This is done to forestall blood feuds, which are a popular hobby in many of these places. Remember the American consul is very busy fretting about that Marxist insurrection, and it may be many months before he comes to visit.

14  If you do have an accident, the only thing to do is go on the offensive. Throw big wads of American money at everyone, and hope for the best.

## Safety Tips

15  One nice thing about the Third World, you don't have to fasten your safety belt. (Or stop smoking. Or cut down on saturated fats.) It takes a lot off your mind when average life expectancy is forty-five minutes.

In this excerpt from her memoir *A Romantic Education*, Patricia Hampl tries to explain why she revised her intention to visit her grandparents' birthplace. Reread Hampl's comments on tone and style at the beginning of this chapter. Identify the specific passages in Hampl's essay where you sense that "another human being is speaking to" you. Where does Hampl use a formal tone? Where does she use a more conversational tone? How does this mixture help her readers understand the conclusions she forms in the last paragraph?

# Prague

## PATRICIA HAMPL

1  In May 1975, during the spring music festival that opens every year with a performance of Smetana's "Ma Vlast" ("My Homeland"), I went to Prague for the first time. The lilacs were in bloom everywhere: the various lavenders of the French and Persian lilac, and the more unusual—except in Prague—double white lilac. Huge flat red banners with yellow lettering were hoisted everywhere too, draped across homely suburban factories and from the subtle rose and

Patricia Hampl, *A Romantic Education* (Boston: Houghton, 1981), 145–148, 149–152.

mustard baroque buildings of Staré Město (the Old City).

2     The banners were in honor of the thirtieth anniversary of the liberation of Prague by the Soviet Army in May 1945. 30 *Let,* "30 years," it said everywhere, even on the visa stamp in my passport. Many offices and stores had photographs in their windows, blowups from 1945 showing Russian soldiers accepting spring bouquets from shy little girls, Russian soldiers waving from tanks to happy crowds. For the first time, I was in a city where the end of the Second World War was really celebrated, where history was close at hand. Prague was the first Continental European city I had seen (I had come from London) and it was almost weirdly intact, not modern. On the plane from America to London I had reminded myself that London would be modern; *my* England was so much a product of the nineteenth-century novels and poetry I'd been reading all my life that I knew I would be shocked to see automobiles. And in fact, nothing could prepare me for the slump I felt in London: I wanted the city of Becky Sharpe, of Daniel Deronda, even of Clarissa Dalloway, not the London of Frommer's guidebooks and the thrill of finding lunch for 5 pence.

3     Prague stopped my tourism flat. The weight of its history and the beauty of its architecture came to me first as an awareness of dirt, a sort of ancient grime I had never seen before. It bewitched me, that dirt, caught in the corners of baroque moldings and decorative cornices, and especially I loved the dusty filth of the long, grave windows at sunset when the light flared against the tall oblongs and caused them to look gilded.

4     I had arrived in a river city, just as I had left one in St. Paul. But the difference . . . On the right bank of the Vltava (in German, the Moldau) the buildings were old—to me. Some of them were truly old, churches and wine cellars and squares dating from the Middle Ages. But the real look, especially of the residential and shopping areas of Nové Město (New City—

new since the fourteenth century when Charles IV founded it), was art nouveau, highly decorative, the Bohemian version of the Victorian. Across the river, in Malá Strana (Small Side— Prague's Left Bank), the city became most intensely itself, however; it rose baroquely up, villa by villa, palace crushed to palace, gardens crumbling and climbing, to the castle that ran like a great crown above it on a bluff.

5     The city silenced me. It was just as well I didn't know the language and was traveling alone. There was nothing for me to say. I was here to look.

6     My original intention in going to Prague was simple: to see the place my grandparents had come from, to hear the language they had spoken. I knew Prague was Kafka's city, I knew Rilke had been born here, and I had read his *Letters to a Young Poet* many times. I was a young poet myself. But my visit wasn't for them. Mine was the return of a third generation American, the sort of journey that is so inexplicable to the second generation: "What are you going to *do* there?" my father asked me before I left Minnesota.

7     That spring, the lines at the Prague Čedok office (the government agency that runs tourism in Czechoslovakia) were dotted here and there with young Americans looking for family villages. The young couple in front of me in the line had come from Cleveland. The man was asking a young travel agent, who was dressed in a jeans skirt and wore nail polish the color of an eggplant, how he and his wife could get to a village whose name he couldn't manage to pronounce.

8     "There does not seem to be such a place," she told him. She couldn't find a name on the map with a spelling that corresponded to the one the young man had brought from Cleveland on the piece of paper he was holding out to his wife. ("It's *his* family," she said to me. "I'm Irish.")

9     They decided to set out, anyway, for a village in Moravia that had a similar spelling. "I guess

that's the place," the young man said, without much conviction.

10     I asked my father's question: "What are you going to *do* there?"

11     "Look around," he said. "Maybe somebody"—he meant a relative—"will be there."

12     My own slip of paper, which I'd brought from St. Paul, had the name of my grandmother's village ("spelling approximate," my cousin had written next to the name when he gave it to me) which was supposed to be near Třeboň, small town in southern Bohemia. On the map, Třeboň was set among lakes (like Minneapolis, I had thought); here, the guidebook said, "the famous carp" were caught.

13     Suddenly, just then, as my turn came up, I had no heart for the approximate name of the village, for the famous carp, the kind of journey the Cleveland couple had set for themselves. ("We're going to do the same thing in Ireland," the wife said.) I stepped out of the line, crumpled up my piece of paper, and left it in an ashtray. The absurdity of trying to get to Třeboň, and from there to wherever this village with the approximate spelling was supposed to be, lay on me like a plank. I felt like a student who drops out of medical school a semester before graduation; I was almost there and, suddenly, it didn't matter, I didn't want what I'd been seeking. Apparently I wanted something else.

14     "Do you want to get something to eat?" I asked the couple from Cleveland.

15     But they didn't have time. "We have to split," she said.

16     "Yeah," said her husband. "It's a long way. . . ."

17     I put Třeboň out of my mind and spent the rest of the week walking aimlessly around Prague. If I had answered my father's question—what was I *doing*—I would have said I was sitting in coffeehouses, in between long, aimless walks. A long trip for a cup of coffee, but I was listless, suddenly lacking curiosity and I felt, as I sat in the Slavia next to the big win-

dows that provide one of the best views of the Hradčany in the city, that simply by staring out the window I was doing my bit: there it was, the castle, and I was looking at it. I had fallen on the breast of the Middle European coffeehouse and I was content among the putty- and dove-colored clothes, the pensioners stirring away the hours, the tables of university students studying and writing their papers, the luscious waste of time, the gossip whose ardor I sensed in the bent heads, lifted eyebrows—because of course I couldn't understand a word.

18     In Vienna the coffeehouses—not all of them, thank God—lose their leases to McDonald's and fast-food chains. But in Prague the colors just fade and become more, rather than less, what they were. The coffeehouse is deeply attached to the idea of conversation, the exchange of ideas, and therefore, to a political society. In *The Agony of Czechoslovakia '38/'68*, Kurt Weisskopf remembers the Prague coffeehouses before the Second World War.

19     You were expected to patronize the coffeehouse of your group, your profession, your political party. Crooks frequented the Golden Goose, or the Black Rose in the centre of Prague. Snobs went to the Savarin, whores and their prospective clients to the Lind or Julis; commercial travelers occupied the front part of Cafe Boulevard, while the rear was the traditional meeting place of Stalinists and Trotskyites, glaring at each other as they sat around separate marble tables. The rich went to the Urban, "progressive" intellectuals to the Metro. Abstract painters met at the Union, and surrealists at the Manes where they argued with impressionists. You were still served by the black-coated waiters if you did not belong, but so contemptuously that you realized how unwelcome your presence was. The papers in their bamboo frames and the magazines in their folders, an essential part of the

Central European coffeehouse service, were regrettably not available to intruders. If you went to the wrong coffeehouse you were just frozen out.

20      But if you fitted in, socially, politically, philosophically, artistically or professionally, well, then the headwaiter and the manager treated you almost as a relative and you were even deemed worthy of credit.

21      "Rudolf, switch on the light over the Communists, they can't read their papers properly," old Loebl, manager of the Edison, used to instruct the headwaiter. "And see that the Anarchists get more iced water." Once you had ordered your coffee you were entitled to free glasses of iced water brought regularly by the trayload; this was called a "swimming pool."

22      The water was still brought, as I sat at the marble table of the Slavia though not by the trayload. Perhaps there were political conversations, even arguments: I couldn't tell. But the newspapers were the official ones of the Communist Party, including, in English, the *Daily Worker*. When I asked someone I'd struck up a conversation with, who was quoted as a source on American news, I was told, "Gus Hall," the president of the American Communist Party. "As a typical American?" I asked incredulously. "As the voice of the people," I was told. It struck me as funny, not sinister, although later I realized I was annoyed.

23      I walked around Prague, hardly caring if I hit the right tourist spots, missing baroque gems, I suppose, getting lost, leaving the hotel without a map as if I had no destination. I just walked, stopping at coffeehouses, smoking unfiltered cigarettes and looking out from the blue wreath around me to other deep-drawing smokers. Everyone seemed to have time to sit, to smoke as if smoking were breathing, to stare into the vacancy of private thought, if their thoughts were private. I was in the thirties, I'd finally arrived in my parents' decade, the men's soft caps, the dove colors of Depression pictures, the acquiescence to circumstance, the ruined quality. For the first time I recognized the truth of beauty: that it is brokenness, it is on its knees. I sat and watched it and smoked (I don't smoke but I found myself buying cigarettes), smoked a blue relation between those coffeehouses and me. For this sadness turned out to be, to me, beautiful. Or rather, the missing quality of beauty, whatever makes it approachable, became apparent in Prague. I could sit, merely breathing, and be part of it. I was beautiful—at last. And I didn't care—at last. I stumbled through the ancient streets, stopped in the smoke-grimed coffeehouses and added my signature of ash, anonymous and yet entirely satisfied. I had ceased even to be a reverse immigrant—I sought no one, no sign of my family or any ethnic heritage that might be mine. I was, simply, in the most beautiful place I had ever seen, and it was grimy and sad and broken. I was relieved of some weight, the odd burden of happiness and unblemished joy of the adored child—or perhaps I was free of beauty itself as an abstract concept. I didn't think about it and didn't bother to wonder. I sat and smoked; I walked and got lost and didn't care because I couldn't get lost. I hardly understood that I was happy: my happiness consisted of encountering sadness. I simply felt *accurate*.

# Web Design

Students using *Writing with a Purpose* in a composition class were asked to design a website suggested by Patricia Hampl's memoir "Prague." Consult the elements and principles of design in Chapter 5 to help you answer the questions about the effectiveness of each design.

**Sample Homepage #1: Prague**

1. How do the placement of the title of the website and its contrast with the background colors make the subject of the site unclear?

2. In what ways does the positioning of the photograph of the coffeeshops overpower the text?

3. How does the alignment of the links, photograph, and text confuse the purpose of the site?

**Sample Homepage #2: Prague**

1. How does the revised version of the title, "Prague," help you focus on the subject?

2. How does the clock—a centerpiece in the city of Prague—help establish the unity of the website about Prague?

3. How does the alignment of the pull quote and the bulleted list of links clarify the purpose of the site?

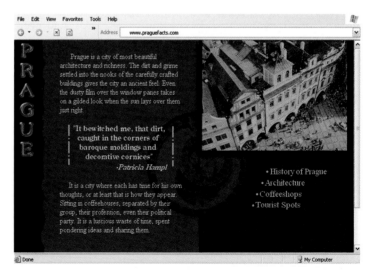

# Writing Assignments

## 1. NARRATE

Write a brief guidebook to a place you remember well and with great affection. Provide a map, a brief (informative) history, and the kind of information your readers will want—how to get there, where to stay, what to see, how much things cost. Reserve a section to explain why this place has special, personal significance for you.

## 2. OBSERVE

Select a place you have visited on several occasions and compare how two means of travel—driving a car or flying in a plane—affected what you saw on your way and altered your attitude toward your destination. Consider why you prefer one style of travel to the other. Then draft an essay, "The Best Way to Get There," describing your observations and the reasons for your choice.

## 3. INVESTIGATE

In "Girl Talk—Boy Talk," *Science 85* (January/February 1985), John Pfeiffer reports that researcher "Sally McConnell-Ginet of Cornell finds that women's voices are more colorful—they vary their pitch and change pitch more frequently than do men's voices. In one experiment, women immediately assumed a monotone style when asked to imitate men's speech. McConnell-Ginet regards speaking tunefully as an effective strategy for getting and holding attention, a strategy used more often by women than men." Use McConnell-Ginet's research as a starting point for developing your own investigation of the way gender, class, profession, or place may affect the tone of speech of the people you talk with during your daily travels.

## 4. COLLABORATE

Your writing group has been asked to write and produce a series of language/culture tapes for a group of exchange students visiting your campus for a semester. Make a list of the kinds of information you think they should have about America, your region, and campus. Interview other exchange students who are already on your campus from that country to see what specific difficulties they have encountered. Ask these students to evaluate the sentence structure, diction, and tone in your scripts. Then audition members of your group, and select those people with the most engaging *voices* to read the scripts on tape.

## 5. READ

Select a place people commonly visit for vacations—the Caribbean, Europe, California, Florida. Check out various websites that provide basic information on that place. Compare and contrast the tone and style of these sites in a review for the "Travel and Leisure" section of your newspaper. Focus on one specific spot—such as Key West or Stratford-on-Avon—so that you can restrict the terms of your comparison.

## 6. RESPOND

Write a response to P. J. O'Rourke's "Third World Driving Hints and Tips." Your experience driving in other countries or particular sections of our country, for example, may encourage you to imitate O'Rourke's essay, detailing the many comic aspects of driving in a strange place. On the other hand, you may wish to take issue with O'Rourke's attitude toward the people of the Third World. In that case, you may want to use specific driving experiences to demonstrate why good guests should learn and respect the customs of their hosts.

## 7. ANALYZE

Analyze the reasons that people in another country often treat Americans as "ugly tourists." Or, conversely, analyze the reasons that Americans treat travelers from certain foreign countries as "ugly tourists."

# Writing Assignments

### 8. EVALUATE

Evaluate Patricia Hampl's style (sentence structure, diction, tone) in those sections in which she is talking about the history of Prague and those sections in which she is talking about herself. Use the information to explain how Prague "silenced" Hampl, "stopped my tourism flat." Then write an essay illustrating how her decision to stop touring and get lost helped her understand this alien culture, helped her feel "accurate."

### 9. ARGUE

Reread Walker Percy's description of the Grand Canyon in this chapter (page 293). Then, using a specific experience to illustrate your case, write an opinion column arguing that tourists adopt a particular style of touring. For example, some tourists see what they expect to see, some see something less than what they were led to believe they would see, and some see something no one else has ever seen.

### 10. ARGUE

Using your own experience, your knowledge of American history, and the readings in this chapter, write a speech about America's fascination with travel for the travel lecture series at your local public library. You could argue, for example, that such fascination is a deficiency: Americans are continually traveling because we are unable to find happiness in any one place. Or you could argue that such fascination is a virtue: Americans are flexible, capable of change, and tolerant of other lifestyles.

# PART III

# Writing Research

**Planning the Research Paper** 12

**Writing the Research Paper** 13

# Planning the Research Paper

THE STACKS AT WIDENER [LIBRARY] . . . WERE MY

ARCHIMEDES' BATHTUB, MY BURNING BUSH.

—BARBARA TUCHMAN

You will probably write a number of research papers (also called library or term papers) during your formal education, papers that will figure prominently in your course grades but also provide you with an opportunity to discover new ways of thinking and writing. Noted historian Barbara Tuchman remembers researching her undergraduate honors thesis as "the single most formative experience of my career. . . . It was not a tutor or a teacher or a fellow student or a great book or the shining example of some famous lecturer. . . . It was the stacks at Widener [library]. They were *my* Archimedes' bathtub, my burning bush, my dish of mold where I found my personal penicillin" (Barbara Tuchman, "In Search of History," *Practicing History*).

The assignment to write a research paper is similar to other writing assignments in that you must discover information to fulfill a specific purpose. But it differs from other writing assignments in that your major source of information is not memory, observation, or informal reading (as in most personal essays), your textbook or lecture notes (as in the essay examination), or one or more literary texts (as in the critical essay) but—as Tuchman suggests—the books, articles, and documents housed in your university library or accessed on the Internet. Locating the information you need and then using it in your paper requires skills in thinking, reading, and writing that you do not draw on in other assignments.

Chapter 12 introduces the stages you must work through in *planning* a research paper:

- Understanding the assignment
- Making a schedule
- Selecting a subject
- Finding sources
- Evaluating sources
- Taking notes
- Filling gaps

Chapter 13 discusses the stages involved in *writing* the paper. In these chapters you will follow Erin McMullen, a student writer, as she plans, drafts, and revises her paper on the value of online education. Erin's final paper appears fully annotated at the end of Chapter 13 so that you can see how she made important decisions about her sources and used those sources to clarify her own position in the controversy.

## Understanding the Assignment

Before you begin working, you need to determine the kind of paper you are to write. There are two basic kinds of research papers. In one you are expected to compile a *survey;* in the other you are expected to conduct an *argument.*

### The Survey

The survey is a factual review of what other researchers have written about a subject. When you select a subject for a survey, focus on an issue or problem that has provoked extensive commentary or controversy, such as the causes of acid rain, the effects of gun control, or the merits of educational reform. Imagine that your readers are curious about your subject but uncommitted to any particular position. They expect you to examine all sides of the subject objectively and to document your sources accurately so that they can read more about the subject. Your purpose is not to present your own argument about the subject but to identify and summarize the major arguments of others.

### The Argument

The argument presents your analysis of a subject that has been researched by others; you interpret the information you uncovered in your research. You work from the perspective you have chosen, and you devise your own method of organizing and analyzing sources. Imagine that your readers are curious and uncommitted but ready to be convinced by a compelling argument. They expect you to acknowledge opinions that do not support your own, but they also expect you to present a forceful analysis, citing the proper authorities to support your viewpoint. Your purpose is not to compile a neutral summary of what others have written but to make your own contribution to a growing body of knowledge. (See Chapter 7, "Argument.")

## Making a Schedule

Your instructor will specify when your paper is due and may require you to submit your work in stages so that both of you can track your progress. If your instructor does not provide a timetable, make one yourself. Start with the deadline and then work backward through the process, assigning a specific amount of time to each stage. Be cautious; allow yourself plenty of time to complete each activity. Be conscientious; work in the library or at your computer for a certain number of hours each week. And be pragmatic; produce some kind of written material (journal entries, note cards, drafts) at the end of each stage. Post your schedule in a prominent place and consult it often. A schedule for a research paper might look like this:

| Time | Activity | Written Product |
|---|---|---|
| Week 1 | Study assignment. Make out schedule. Use journal to assess subject, audience, and purpose. Pick general subject. Identify key concepts. Read background material. | Schedule, journal entries, general subject, notes on background reading |
| Week 2 | Select a specific subject. Formulate several hypotheses. Begin compiling bibliography of possible sources. | Specific subject, several hypotheses |
| Week 3 | Locate and evaluate print and electronic sources. Begin reading and taking notes. | Computer notes |
| Week 4 | Restrict subject. Analyze most valuable sources. Identify gaps in research. | Restricted subject in computer notes |
| Week 5 | Locate and read additional sources. Take notes. | Computer notes |
| Week 6 | Select hypothesis. Develop outline. | Hypothesis, outline |

| Week 7 | Write first draft. Prepare revision agenda for next draft. New outline. | First draft, revision agenda, new outline |
| Week 8 | Write final draft. Check quotations. Complete documentation. Compile works-cited list. Type and proofread final manuscript. | Completed assignment |

Even if you start planning your paper the day you receive your assignment and follow a schedule like this one, inevitably you will have to adjust your timetable as your work proceeds. A good rule of thumb is to add two weeks to your schedule for unexpected difficulties. You may need this time for situations like these:

▶ *Some things take more time than you planned.* Because the article you must read by Friday has to be ordered through interlibrary loan, you have to wait two weeks to complete your background reading.

▶ *Some stages prove more difficult than you expected.* Because your search strategy turns up only a few sources that deal directly with your subject, you have to find new sources or a new angle on your subject.

▶ *Deadlines on your schedule have to be adjusted, making it more difficult to meet subsequent deadlines.* Difficulties composing the final draft cut into time set aside for designing, typing, and proofreading.

Writers who start promptly, map out a reasonable timetable, make allowances for setbacks, and work efficiently can produce a research paper on time. Those who leave everything until the last minute will discover too late that they cannot throw together a satisfactory paper overnight. You need to live with your project for several weeks, reading and assimilating sources. A realistic schedule is a written reminder of your goal and encourages you to work at a steady pace, committing your discoveries and ideas to writing as soon as possible.

## Selecting a Subject

Selecting a subject for a research paper is like staking a prospector's claim. You *hope* the claim will produce gold, but you won't *know* until you begin digging. Some instructors, therefore, ask students to select a subject from a pretested list. If your instructor instead asks you to select your own subject, assess potential subjects according to the following criteria of successful research subjects. (Review "Guidelines for Selecting Your Subject" in Chapter 1 on page 12.)

1. ***Select a subject you can research.*** This may seem an obvious requirement, but many subjects cannot be easily researched.
    a. ***Some subjects are too autobiographical.*** A paper that draws primarily on your own experience—"Growing Up in Oklahoma City"—does not require you to search for information in other sources.
    b. ***Some subjects are too subjective.*** No amount of research will resolve a question of personal taste, such as "Which is the better poet—Yeats or Eliot?"
    c. ***Some subjects are too restricted.*** A mechanical process—"How to Operate a DVD Player"—that can be explained by only one source does not require significant research.
    d. ***Some subjects are too current.*** Events that produce today's headlines—"Scandal at the State House"—have not been studied in sufficient depth for you to find enough information about them.
    e. ***Some subjects are too specialized.*** A subject such as "Reactions of German-American Pacifists to the Great Sioux Massacre of 1864" cannot be researched if your library does not own or have online access to the required special documents.

2. ***Select a subject you can restrict.*** Before you begin your research, you may worry that you will not be able to find enough information. Once you begin, however, you are likely to find that nearly every source reveals new aspects of your subject. Instead of feeling overwhelmed, take control of your subject and reduce it to a manageable size. Two factors will help you:
    a. ***The time you scheduled for planning your paper.*** Whether you select a subject that you already know something about or one that is new to you, be realistic about how much you can learn in the time available. A subject such as heart disease, for example, will lead to more sources than you will have time to read, analyze, and understand. Restrict your subject to a specific aspect of heart disease, such as one of its suspected causes. Restricting your subject even further, to one method used to control a cause of heart disease, might lead to an even better focus for your paper.
    b. ***The space available to develop your paper.*** If your assignment restricts the length of your paper, be realistic about how much you can cover in the specified number of pages. A subject such as websites, for example, will have more sources than can be listed in ten pages, let alone usefully developed into an argument. Restricting your subject to advertising on the Web or how *one* corporation has revised its website will be more manageable.

3. ***Select a subject you can live with.*** Writing a research paper requires you to work with one subject for a long time. If this subject does not

fascinate you, if you do not care about the questions it poses or the answers you can provide, you will become bored; your planning will be careless, and your writing uninspired. Be sure to select a subject that holds your interest.

4. ***Select a subject that will appeal to other readers.*** Although the immediate audience for your research paper is your instructor, imagine at least two other audiences. One is the authors you have come to know while doing your research. In a sense, you are carrying on an extended conversation with these writers about a new direction in an area familiar to them. The other audience is the intelligent general reader, who is always interested in new information or new approaches. You are asking this reader to consider your thesis. As you select your subject, strike a balance between the expectations of these two audiences. Previous researchers should consider your work substantive, not trendy; the general reader should find it innovative, not shopworn.

5. ***Select a subject you can prove something about.*** If you are writing an *argument,* not a *survey,* the purpose of your paper is to use sources to support a thesis. You must be sure to select a subject that will yield a thesis, not a summary of other researchers' arguments. Your subject must be focused, so that you can control your evidence to support your argument, and complex, so that you can develop and sustain your argument throughout your paper.

## EXERCISE

One way to discover a subject is to explore, in your journal, what you think you already know about related subjects. Erin tries this approach as she thinks about possible topics for her research paper. Read her journal, and then discuss how she applies the five criteria for selecting a subject, described previously.

I knew we'd get to it—
the dreaded research
paper assignment.
Johnson says we should
pick a topic that inter-
ests us, maybe something

about our majors. Sigh.
I don't have a major
yet, so that doesn't
help much. What should I
write about? Can't
decide. Would rather
procrastinate and check
my email.... So much
junk mail in my account.
I was getting ready to
delete it all when one
subject line caught my
eye. Online degree.
Get your bachelor's in
a year without ever
setting foot in a class-
room. Sounds interesting

but impossible. I wonder
if this is legitimate?
Are there a lot of these
programs? How do they
work? Hmmm ... seems
like an interesting
topic. Should search
Google and other places
for info on online
degree programs. A uni-
versity without build-
ings? The next step in
education or another
technology-driven fad?
This topic could hold my
interest.

# Finding Sources

Once you have selected your general subject, begin the formal process of researching it in the library. Most libraries, like most cities, try to help visitors by providing tours, publishing maps and online directories, and hiring guides (librarians) to work at specific locations throughout the building. Because no two libraries are organized exactly alike, even the most experienced researchers depend on this kind of assistance to help them work in an unfamiliar library.

One reason you will need this advice is that in the last ten years libraries, like most other institutions in our culture, have undergone a technological revolution. They still provide traditional resources, but more and more libraries also are providing computerized versions of nearly every reference tool mentioned in this chapter. The card catalogue has been replaced by the online catalogue, and many periodical indexes are available electronically. Most libraries provide a battery of terminals and printers at convenient locations throughout the building to access these electronic resources. In addition, these resources can be accessed from computer ports in other buildings (including faculty offices and student dormitory rooms) all over campus.

Clearly such technological devices have changed the way researchers track and compile their sources. But not every library has the same technological capacity. And every technological wonder has built-in limitations that can frustrate rather than facilitate your research. You will save yourself much needless confusion at the outset if you realize that your best allies are librarians. No matter how difficult or ridiculous your question seems, the librarians have probably heard it or one like it before. They can show you where and how to look for answers or refer you to someone who can help. Indeed, they can direct you to many more sources than are mentioned in this chapter. You have already considered how to select a subject. Reference librarians will help you formulate a *search strategy*—a systematic procedure for finding information on your subject. The "Search Strategy" diagram shows you the sequence of steps in a search strategy.

## Background Information in the Library

Read several overviews of your general subject so that you can learn about its history, major themes, key concepts, and principal figures. Such background information can be found in general and specialized encyclopedias located in the reference collection of the library.

General Encyclopedias   These reference works, written for a general audience and covering a wide variety of subjects, are available in both print and electronic formats. The entries, generally arranged in alpha-

● A WRITER'S WORDS

[R]esearch . . . [is] rarely
dull, for the further one
goes in the pursuit, the
more fascinating it
becomes, like being on
a detective case.

—David McCullough,
*Brave Companions:
Portraits in History*

**SEARCH STRATEGY**

```
                    ┌─────────────┐
                    │   Subject   │
                    └──────┬──────┘
                           │
                    ┌──────▼──────┐
                    │ Background  │
                    │ Information │
                    └──────┬──────┘
                           │
                    ┌──────▼──────┐
                    │  Keywords   │
                    └──────┬──────┘
                           │
                    ┌──────▼──────┐
                    │   Indexes   │
                    └──────┬──────┘
              ┌────────────┼────────────┐
              ▼            ▼            ▼
     ┌──────────────┐┌──────────────┐┌──────────────┐
     │ Online/Card  ││ Online/Print ││  Web/Search  │
     │  Catalogues  ││  Periodical  ││   Engines    │
     │              ││   Indexes    ││              │
     └──────┬───────┘└──────┬───────┘└──────┬───────┘
            ▼               ▼               ▼
     ┌──────────────┐┌──────────────┐┌──────────────┐
     │    Books     ││   Articles   ││   Websites   │
     └──────────────┘└──────────────┘└──────────────┘
```

betical order, are not technical or scholarly, but they often contain a brief list of sources that do treat the subject in depth. You can find the main entry about your general subject by looking in the appropriate volume. To locate every reference to your subject in the encyclopedia, you can consult the index, which is usually the last volume. The latter method enables you to see how your subject is subdivided and cross-referenced, and reading the additional entries may give you a perspective that will help you restrict or revise your subject. Online encyclopedias provide a search function that enables you to use keywords to search their databases. General encyclopedias include

> *Encyclopedia Britannica*
> *New Columbia Encyclopedia*
> *Encyclopedia Americana*
> *Britannica Online*

**Specialized Encyclopedias**  These works are usually devoted to one or two disciplines or to specific subject areas. They provide narrow, detailed coverage of particular topics. The entries tend to be more technical than those in a general encyclopedia, with longer lists of sources. Because specialized encyclopedias are available on a wide range of academic and general interest subjects, you will need to use the online or the card catalogue to locate them. Look up your general subject, and then look for the subheading "Dictionaries." The *Encyclopedia of Philosophy*, for example, is listed under the subject heading "Philosophy—Dictionaries." The following brief list of specialized encyclopedias shows the variety of material available:

> *International Encyclopedia of Higher Education*
> *McGraw-Hill Encyclopedia of Science and Technology*
> *Webopeida.com*

**Biographical Sources**   These works give brief accounts of notable figures, listing such information as family history, educational background, major accomplishments, and significant publications. A short list of additional sources is often included. If your background reading points to one or two people significant in the development of your general subject, you should research these figures in a biographical source. Some examples are

> *Dictionary of American Biography*
> *International Who's Who*
> *American Men and Women of Science*

## Background Information on the Internet

Many students, like Erin, start their research paper by surfing the Internet. Although this method may lead to instant results, it may also mislead you because you have no context for your topic. You may misinterpret what you find or waste a good deal of time looking for something that isn't there—or isn't there in the way you expect it to be. For that reason, conduct your search for background information in the library *first*. Once you understand some of the ways your general topic is indexed and connected, you can work more productively on the Internet.

A WRITER'S RESOURCES

To learn how to search better and how major search engines work from a researcher's point of view, see <http://searchenginewatch.com>.

Pay particular attention to the subtle but significant differences between a *subject archive* (such as Yahoo!) and a *search engine* (such as Google). As the following lists suggest, these Internet research tools work differently and often yield different results:

| *Subject Archive* | *Search Engine* |
| --- | --- |
| 1. Groups links by topic area | 1. Allows searching by keyword |
| 2. Allows hierarchical browsing | 2. Allows analytical searching by using *and, or, not* |
| 3. Is assembled by humans | 3. Is generated by software utilities |
| 4. Usually links to a site's homepage | 4. Provides links to all the pages of a site |

5. Use when searching a broad topic

6. Use for general subject exploration

7. Generates more *relevant* results

8. Examples: Yahoo!, InfoMine

5. Use when looking for a specific item, such as a name or title

6. Use for complex search queries

7. Generates more *comprehensive* results

8. Examples: Google, Lycos

**SEARCH STRATEGY ON THE INTERNET**

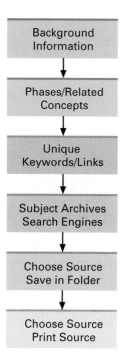

Background Information

↓

Phases/Related Concepts

↓

Unique Keywords/Links

↓

Subject Archives Search Engines

↓

Choose Source Save in Folder

↓

Choose Source Print Source

Although the ever-expanding World Wide Web seems like a vast databank, be aware of its built-in limitations. For example, 82 percent of the sites on the Web are commercial, as suggested by the tag *.com* on their electronic addresses. Sites you might commonly consult for academic research—science/education marked by the tag *.org*, government marked by the tag *.gov*—compose less than 10 percent of the Web. Research tools such as subject archives and search engines search only a small portion of the Web. For example, Yahoo! searches about 7 percent, Lycos 15 percent. Also, the sources listed by an electronic search are ranked on the basis of popularity. This may mean that the most authoritative and pertinent sources that you need to complete your research will not even appear on a web search.

If you are unfamiliar with the Internet, consult a friendly text such as Eric Crump and Nick Carbone's *Online: A Student's Guide to the Internet*

*"We have lots of information technology. We just don't have any information."*

© 2002 Sid Harris. Reprinted by permission.

*and World Wide Web Writing* (Boston: Houghton, 2000). Such texts will get you started and provide explanations for terms that seem to be used interchangeably—*Internet, Net, World Wide Web, the Web,* and so on. Such texts will also help you understand how some of the essential processes in this search strategy work.

## EXERCISE

Erin uses her journal to take notes on the information she has discovered about online education in reference books and encyclopedias and on the Internet. Read her notes and consider how her background reading helps her to shape her subject.

Looked on Google under "Online University Degrees" and got 559,000 hits. Found <u>.com</u> sites and <u>.edu</u> sites, so it seems like these programs are run through companies or colleges. A few sites really summed up the content of most of the more relevant hits: "online-masters-degrees-programs.org/" and "online-college-degree.com." The second site has several links to government sites that discuss online/distance education, but they give a rosy picture of online degrees. They talk about how liberating these programs are. Seems like these sites are really caught up in how the programs are innovative, but no one is looking at how students, profs, and universities benefit or suffer from them. Bookmarked those two sites on my computer. I think I'll return to them for sure. As for which university sites will be most valuable, I think I'll look through reports on online degrees (in newspapers and magazines probably) and see which ones the experts mention. That should help make my research time more efficient. Interesting meeting of business world and university world in the online degree topic.

I wonder if there are clashes between the two? Seems like I should have some other search terms. This one is so big, and I'm not finding much reporting on how effective or ineffective the programs are. Every site talks about how great an online degree is, but I'm not finding any criticism of them yet. Seems like I should look for some info that has evaluated these programs to see if they are legit. Also, searched Lycos under "Online University Degrees" (154,113 hits) and got universities advertising degree availability. Will wait until I've done some reading to venture into those sites.

## Subject Headings

When you have done some background reading, you will discover that there are many ways to classify, subdivide, and cross-reference your topic. This cluster of categories should tell you three things:

1. You must restrict your general subject (in Erin's case, online education) to the specific subject you want to write about (benefits and drawbacks).

2. You may find your specific subject listed under several headings (distance education, open learning).

3. You may have to read material that does not deal directly with your subject in order to develop a perspective that will help you to organize your information (university extension).

The best way to discover subject headings related to your subject is to consult the reference book entitled *Library of Congress Subject Headings.* This guide, usually located near the card catalogue and online terminals, shows you how your subject is classified and cross-referenced in the library's various databases. Many databases use their own headings and subject terms, so you will have to use some ingenuity to determine how your subject might be listed. For example, Erin found the following in the *Library of Congress Subject Headings:* "Distance Education," "Education," "Open Learning: Telecommunications in Education," "Copyright and Distance Education," "Correspondence Schools and Courses," "Libraries and Distance Education," "Telephone in Education," and "Television in Education; University Extension."

Throughout your research you will revise your subject headings. You will eliminate some because the information on them is not related to your subject. You will add others because they lead you to sources that give you valuable insights. In fact, one of the most powerful features of the computerized systems is the *keyword,* a feature that encourages you to strike out in a new direction, using a word or combination of words to find a new angle on your subject. If the keyword is listed in a publication's title, subject headings, description, or abstract, the publication will appear on your computer screen in a list of possible sources.

Although Erin found several keywords that she could plug into her search, she thought the following terms had the most potential: *distance learning, open learning,* and *university extension.* Erin is actually developing several hypotheses about the controversy on the value of online learning. The hypothesis she selects will help her shape her draft.

## Bibliographies

When you have compiled a preliminary list of subject headings or keywords, you are ready to begin building your bibliography. You begin with a *working bibliography,* a list of books and articles you intend to consult as you plan your paper. (When you finish writing your research paper, you will have a *final bibliography,* a list of *works cited.*) Consult a reference guide to reference books, such as the American Library Association's *Guide to Reference Books* (11th ed., 1996), compiled by Robert Balay. These guides will tell you if there is a specialized bibliography on your subject. Specialized bibliographies not only save you time but also ensure that you consult the most significant sources. Such bibliographies are often *annotated,* providing a brief description (and sometimes an evaluation) of each book and article listed. However, specialized bibliographies may not cover recent works. A bibliography on computers published in 1950, for example, will not cover much about the "computer revolution" in our time.

Two other sources of information on specialized bibliographies are the

▶ *Bibliography Index,* a reference work that lists articles, parts of books, and pamphlets devoted in whole or in part to bibliographies

▶ Online catalogue under one of your keywords and bibliography

Erin's search for "distance education" produced the following source:

---

**LC5800.W55 1993**

| | |
|---|---|
| Personal Author: | **Willis, Barry Donald, 1952–** |
| Title: | **Distance education : a practical guide / Barry Willis.** |
| Publication info: | **Englewood Cliffs, NJ: Educational Technology Publications, c1993.** |
| Physical descrip: | **x, 138 p. : ill. ; 24 cm.** |
| Bibliography note: | **Includes bibliographical references (p. 125–131) and index.** |
| Subject: | **Distance education—Handbooks, manuals, etc.** |

---

| Call Numbers for: BRACKEN | Copy | Material | Location |
|---|---|---|---|
| 1) LC5800 . W55 1993 | 1 | GEN_BOOK | due:4/26/2003 |

---

After locating a specialized bibliography or books that contain a bibliography, begin constructing your bibliography with the two major research tools in the library—the *online catalogue* and *periodical indexes.*

## Online Catalogue

The online catalogue lists books and other material in the library by subject, keyword, author, and title.

**Subject**　If you know only your subject or several related subjects, enter a subject search. The catalogue will create a list of books on that subject arranged in order of date of publication (most recent first). Select the book you want, and click on "View." You will see the complete catalogue entry. The subject list will also provide links, or cross-references, that will allow you to broaden or narrow your search.

**Keyword**　If you are working with a group of keywords, enter a keyword search. Combining terms with *and, or, adj,* and *not* will give you cross-references to limit or broaden your search and provide you with additional lists of sources.

**Author**  If you know the author of a book on your subject, or if you suspect that a certain author might have written about the subject, initiate an author search.

**Title**  If you know the title of the book you want to consult but have forgotten the author, or if you suspect one of your keywords might be included in the title, start a title search.

SEARCH RESULT — BASIC SEARCH

1. Viewing record **1** of **21** from catalog **title "distance training."**
   ☐ Check here to mark this record for Print/Save. Then click on the Print/Save button.

2. **LC5800.K42 2000**
3. Personal Author: **Keegan, Desmond.**
4. Title: **Distance training : taking stock at a time of change / Desmond Keegan.**
5. Publication info: **London; New York : Routledge/Falmer, c2000.**
6. Physical descrip: **xiv, 152 p. : ill. ; 24 cm.**
7. Bibliography note: **Includes bibliographical references (p. [147]–149) and index.**
8. Subject: **Distance education.**
   Subject: **World Wide Web.**
   Series: **Routledge/Falmer studies in distance education.**

9. **Call Numbers for: BRACKEN**      **Copy**     **Material**      **Location**

   1) LC5800 . K42 2000                          1        GEN_BOOK     due:4/26/2003

The following items explain the features in the record just illustrated.

1. *Search result.* The record indicates how many sources owned by the library are listed under this search word (1 of 21) and that useful cross-references are available.

2. *Call number and location number (plus publication date).* These letters and numbers, in the exact order in which they appear, constitute the *call number,* which indicates the book's location on the library shelves. The publication date identifies its place on the list. This information is repeated several times to ensure proper identification.

3. *Personal author.* The last name appears first, followed by the first name and middle initial (if any), depending on how the name appears on the title page.

4. *Title.* The title is given as it appears on the title page.

5. *Publication information.* This line includes the place of publication, the publisher, and year of publication.

6. *Physical description.* This line describes the size and length of the book and indicates whether there are any maps or illustrations.

7. *Bibliography note.* This line indicates the length of the bibliography.

8. *Content/subject:* This line provides a brief abstract of the contents and various aspects of the subject discussed in the source.

9. *Copy material location.* This section repeats the call number of the book in the library where you are working and indicates its location in a specific collection and its current status—whether it is in the library or has been checked out. In the latter case, it will also tell you when the book is due to be returned or whether it is overdue.

After you locate the book you want in the catalogue, print out your data on the printer connected to your terminal; then locate the book on the shelf. Most libraries are arranged according to the Library of Congress classification system:

*Library of Congress Classification*

| | | | |
|---|---|---|---|
| **A** | General works | **N** | Fine Arts |
| **B** | Philosophy, Psychology, Religion | **P** | Language and Literature |
| **C–D** | History and Topography (except America) | **Q** | Science |
| | | **R** | Medicine |
| **E–F** | America | **S** | Agriculture and Forestry |
| **G** | Geography, Anthropology, Sports and Games | **T** | Engineering and Technology |
| **H** | Social Sciences | | |
| **J** | Political Science | **U** | Military Science |
| **K** | Law | **V** | Naval Science |
| **L** | Education | **Z** | Bibliography and Library Science |
| **M** | Music | | |

## Periodical Indexes

Periodicals (magazines and journals) exist on almost every conceivable subject. Their value in research is their currency and specificity, and back issues can show the ways your subject was treated in the past. Indexes to periodicals are of two types, general and subject, and are available in print or electronic format. Some periodical indexes provide an abstract or the full text of the articles cited.

*General indexes* list articles from hundreds of nontechnical and scholarly magazines. Individual articles are classified by author, subject, and keywords. In print, the most commonly used general index is *Readers' Guide to Periodical Literature.* The *Readers' Guide* is bound in individual volumes and organized by year. A useful online general index is *LexisNexis Academic.* It works like most online services: You provide a search word (or words), and it provides a list of sources.

DISTANCE EDUCATION
>*See also*
>>Virtual schools
>>Virtual universities

Brave new world for higher education. M. Schrage. il *Technology Review* (Cambridge, Mass.: 1998) v104 no8 p90-1 O 2001

College@home. J. Spayde. il *Modern Maturity* v44R no4 p60-2 Jl/Ag 2001

Digital diplomas [cover story] E. Press and J. Washburn. il *Mother Jones* v26 no1 p34-9, 82-3 Ja/F 2001

Distance learning in postsecondary education: learning whenever, wherever [cover story] M. Mariani. il *Occupational Outlook Quarterly* v45 no 2 p2-10 Summ 2001

Get smart [technology investments to make this year] D. De Myer. il tab *Ziff Davis Smart Business for the New Economy* v14 no2 p92-9 F 2001

Going the distance [online distance education] J. Lichtenberg. *Publishers Weekly* v248 no26 p37-40 Je 25 2001

Learning online [special section] il *U.S. News & World Report* v131 no 15 p43-78 O 15 2001

Live and E-learn [on-line learning for professionals] K. Morrione. il *Working Woman* v26 no4 p34-5 Ap 2001

Next frontiers [educational forecasting for the wired state of South Dakota] D. Johnson. graph il *Newsweek* v 138 no18 p54-8 O 29 2001

Each of these general indexes has advantages and disadvantages. *Readers' Guide* covers a long historical period (volume 1 was published in 1900), but checking each volume is time-consuming and cumbersome. *LexisNexis Academic* is quick and efficient, but it covers a relatively short time period.

*Subject indexes* list articles on specific subjects. The articles tend to be more detailed and scholarly than those listed in general indexes. Here is a brief sampling of subject indexes available in both print and online formats:

| | |
|---|---|
| Art Index | General Science Index |
| Business Periodical Index | ERIC |

Most periodical indexes are located in the reference area of the library or can be accessed online through your university library's homepage. When you have selected the best indexes for your subject, look under your subject headings to find major listings and then check subheadings or cross-references for any additional information. When you find your entry, you will see that it contains (1) the title of the article, (2) the name of the author, (3) the title of the periodical (or an abbreviated version of the title), (4) the volume of the periodical, (5) the date of publication, and (6) the page numbers. This information is essential when you compile your list of works cited. For that reason, you will need to copy the information from print sources into your computer notes or print the information from online sources (See "Taking Notes," pages 341–344).

## General Index: LexisNexis Academic (Online)

## LexisNexis Academic (Online)—Full Text of Article

## Internet Sources

The most effective way to find sources on the Internet is to use a *subject archive* or *search engine* (see the explanation of these two tools on pages 326–327). There are many such tools on the Net, and you will discover more everyday. Each one has its own special features, methods for classifying information, and links to other systems. The best way to determine how to use a specific tool is to check its "Help" documentation. The Help page will outline the design of the tool and help you determine if it is the appropriate one for your search. Depending on the capacities of your computer and printer, subject archives and search engines can find sources that include text, graphics, and sound and video. Here are some of the most common subject archives and search engines:

| *Subject Archives* | *Search Engines* |
|---|---|
| InfoMine | Google |
| Yahoo! | Lycos |

Like most online databases, subject archives and search engines perform a Boolean search. Once you find a keyword, you can use *and, or,* and *not* to refine your search. For example,

**AND** reduces results by including only "hits" with both terms present.

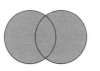

**OR** increases results by including "hits" with either term present.

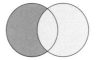

**NOT** reduces results by excluding "hits" containing the specified term.

When you identify a possible source, print it or save it in a computer folder so that you will avoid the two most common problems students encounter when doing research on the Internet:

1. If you have no record of your source, you will not remember how you found it. Surfing is a quick and impulsive process that is hard to duplicate unless you have a trail.

2. If you have no record of your source, you will not know how to find it again. Accurate addresses are essential on the Internet. Every slash (/) or dot (.) counts. If you create a paper trail, you can provide an accurate address for the citation in your works-cited list.

When Erin started surfing the Web, she linked various words to see what she could find out about degrees at online universities. Using the search engine Lycos, she produced the following results:

```
Distance education--1,190,054 hits
Open learning--1,765,412 hits
University extension--839,942 hits
```

As you can see, these search words produced a wealth of information. Erin tried using the words with the library's specialized reference tools to restrict her list of sources. Then, as she reports in her journal, she began reading the summaries and abstracts of these sources to restrict her list of sources even further.

Erin next tried to link several ideas—*online degrees* and *student satisfaction*—to search Google again.

> The search words <u>Distance education</u> and <u>university extension</u> were helpful with the online catalogue, LexisNexis Academic, and ERIC digest resources. By looking at the summaries and abstracts, I found about thirty-seven relevant articles, plus books—good start! Internet sources are only giving me one side, but online periodicals are more balanced. They provide arguments for all sides of the issue--lots of positive results for administration (more money from tuition fees) but not-so-great results for teachers (lots of work keeping up with correspondence). Seems like there are other issues such as who really ends up teaching the course and how teaching even happens. Mixed results for students as well. I need to narrow my focus to look at student benefits and drawbacks. What do they get out of an online degree? Is it comparable to a traditional degree? What kinds of students pursue online degrees?

This second search still gave her too much information:

1. A series of additional categories to extend her search—*Advanced Search, Images, News*

2. The number of sites found

3. Each site's name and description

4. The site's electronic address (enabling immediate linking)

5. Links to related issues (embedded in sidebars)

Think of library research as giving you *vertical power*—the ability to dig into a subject in depth. Internet research gives you *horizontal power*—the ability to skim across the surface of many related subjects. As you plan your paper, you probably will use a mixture of research tools. But your job is to understand the possibilities and limitations of each tool as it applies to the subject and purpose of your research paper.

## Government Documents and Publications

The U.S. government publishes an enormous amount of information on a wide variety of subjects. These publications are housed in a separate area of the library and catalogued according to a separate classification system. There are print and computer disk indexes and websites for this information, such as *American Statistics Index* and the *Monthly Catalogue of United States Government Publications*. But to use the collection effectively, you will need help from someone familiar with government documents. A documents librarian or a member of your library's reference staff will be able to provide this guidance.

## Microforms

Most libraries do not have space for all the documents they wish to keep. Thus many periodicals and other materials are photographically reduced in size and stored on *microfilm* (reels of film), *microfiche* (transparent sheets of film), or *microcard* (opaque prints). With the aid of mechanical viewers, you can enlarge and read these documents easily or make photocopies of the enlarged images. Librarians can tell you which books and periodicals are stored in microform and show you how to operate the microreaders.

## Evaluating Sources

To compile a working bibliography of books, articles, and websites that might pertain to your subject, you must decide which items are likely to prove most useful. The best way to make this decision is through careful reading, but you will *never* have time to read every

# Guidelines for evaluating sources

1. **The source should be relevant.**
   Whether a particular source is relevant is not always apparent. When you begin your research, your lack of perspective on your subject may make every source seem potentially relevant. Titles of sources may be misleading or vague, prompting you to examine a source unrelated to your subject or to dismiss a source as too theoretical or general when it actually gives you vital perspective on your subject. The status of your sources will also change as you restrict your subject. A source that seemed irrelevant yesterday may appear more important today.

2. **The source should be authoritative.**
   The author of a particular source should have the necessary expertise or experience to speak authoritatively about your subject. Most print sources enable you to judge the credentials (and bias) of the author. The book has been reviewed, or the article has

   been evaluated by the journal's editorial board. But you have no way to evaluate the authority of many of the sources on the Internet. A source that you assume is authoritative may have been posted by an adolescent hacker or crackpot.

3. **The source should be current.**
   You want sources that are reliable and up-to-date. A paper on the latest cures for cancer should not rely on research conducted in 1945. On the other hand, if you are analyzing the public's attitude toward cancer in different historical periods, the source based on 1945 research may be "current." And remember, not all old works are dated. Experts in many subjects acknowledge classic, or standard, sources that have advanced major interpretations of a subject. A major advantage of Internet sources, however, is that they are absolutely current. Many provide information that is only minutes old—like news on the weather or

possible source. The computer can be frustrating to use simply because it produces so many sources. If Erin attempts to read everything she finds about online degrees, she will never finish reading, much less begin writing. If she decides to read, in addition, all the books and articles she can find on distance learning, she will spend her life trying to keep up with an ever-growing reading list.

All researchers need guidelines and shortcuts to help them make intelligent guesses about the potential value of the sources they uncover. Following such guidelines will help you eliminate some sources immediately, discard others after determining that they do not focus on your subject, and concentrate on the ones that will make the most significant contribution to your research.

## Shortcuts for Evaluating Sources

**Locate Annotated Bibliographies**  If you are lucky enough to find an annotated bibliography on your subject or if the notes in an article

stock market quotations. Unfortunately, much of this information may not be useful for research papers.

4. **The source should be comprehensive.**
Some sources will focus on an extremely narrow aspect of your subject; others will cover every feature and many related topics as well. Begin reading the most comprehensive source first because it will cover the essential information in the more specialized sources and give you a context for understanding how to see the related subtopics within your subject. Most books, for example, are comprehensive sources whereas most websites provide only "bits" of information.

5. **The source should be stable.**
There is nothing more stable than a book. You can depend on reference books, scholarly books, and even popular books to remain fairly permanent. Even if your library does not own a source or a source

goes out of print, your librarian can find a copy through interlibrary loan. The same is true for most articles. But the sources on the Internet are not stable. The source you stumble on today may not be there tomorrow because it may have been renamed, reclassified, or often simply deleted. If your readers want to check your sources, you should cite sources they can find.

6. **The source should provide links.**
The best sources are often those that lead you to other sources. The subject headings on a source provide an excellent system for linking up with other sources. Annotated bibliographies not only link you to other sources but also provide you with an assessment of their value. And, of course, the chief advantage of the Internet and its various search engines is that they allow you to link up with thousands of sources simply by pointing and clicking.

*"I can't explain it—it's just a funny feeling that I'm being Googled."*

contain extensive annotations, you can determine quickly whether the sources they describe are worth reading.

**Read Book Reviews**    If you want to determine whether a particular book is reliable, see how it was reviewed when it was first published. Reference guides, such as the *Book Review Digest* and the *New York Times Index,* contain either summaries of or references to book reviews that should help you evaluate the book's content and critical reception.

**Obtain the Advice of Experts**    Many people on your campus or in your community are experts on certain subjects. A quick phone call or visit to these people can help you identify the "must-reads" or classic treatments of your subject. They can also direct you to annotated bibliographies and special indexes. And, finally, they can refer you to unusual sources that you would not find by using a normal search strategy. Such books and articles, often dealing with related subjects, may introduce you to new ideas or new methods of interpretation.

**Review the Table of Contents**    To determine the way a book develops its major ideas, study the table of contents. The chapter titles and subheadings work like an outline, giving you a general sense of the author's understanding, treatment, and organization of the subject.

**Read the Introduction**    To discover the particular focus of a source, read its introduction—the preface and often the first chapter of a book, the first few paragraphs of an article. A few pages is usually enough to detect the author's thesis and to decide whether it is relevant and the source is valuable.

**Browse Through the Index**  An index works like a miniature card catalogue, helping you see whether a source has information on your subject, how it classifies and cross-references your subject, how much information it devotes to each of your subject's features, and precisely where that information is located.

## EXERCISE

The following titles come from Erin's working bibliography for her paper on the value of on-line degrees. (Erin is using the Modern Language Association's documentation style described in Chapter 13 on pages 362–377). Using the "Guidelines for Evaluating Sources" on pages 338–339, what guesses would you make about the usefulness of these sources to Erin's project?

Boyd, W., and E. King. The History of Western Education. London: Black, 1969.

Mannix, Margaret. "Buyers, Be Wary." U.S. News and World Report 15 October 2001: 68–70.

Dubin, R., and T. Taveggia. The Teaching-Learning Paradox: A Comparative Analysis of College Teaching Methods. Eugene: U Oregon P, 1968.

Normile, D. "Online Science is a Stretch for Asia." Science 31 August 2001: 1623.

Paulsen, M. F. "Courses on the World Wide Web." 10 February 2002. <http://www.nettskolen.com/kurs/0000-spice.homeside.html>.

Maddux, C. D. Distance Education: A Selected Bibliography. Englewood Cliffs, NJ: Educational Technology Publications, 1992.

## Taking Notes

The old system of taking notes—(1) making a source card and then (2) creating a note card for each piece of information you summarize, paraphrase, or quote—is still useful but no doubt appears archaic to a generation raised on computer games and e-mail. However, the old system and the electronic one recommended here share many of the same procedures. The new tools are different, faster, and more efficient, but they must be used carefully if you are to avoid the major difficulties encountered by every researcher. (See "Plagiarism" in Chapter 13 on pages 361–362.)

As you find your sources and select those that you suspect will prove most useful, start saving them in a folder that you have created for your research paper on the hard drive of your computer or on a special disk that you have labeled for this project. (See "Planning Your Research Paper on Your Computer" on page 347.)

Several pieces of information will help you during your research. If the item is a book, the call number (a number that appears at the top of the screen) will enable you to locate the book in the library. If the source is an article, the name and date of the publication will help you find the article in the stacks or online. If the source is a website, the electronic address will help you find it on the Internet. Make sure that you save this information in your computer folder, print a hard copy, or transcribe it onto a source card.

As you read through your sources, create a coding system that allows you to establish subcategories for your topic. Assign each topic a *source number* (a number you create to code the major divisions of your topic). These numbers and the subjects that they identify may change as you conduct your research, but they will help you sort through your information or rearrange it into meaningful clusters.

After you have selected your sources, use the "Guidelines for Evaluating Sources" on pages 338–339 to establish some priorities for your reading. What sources seem most crucial? What sources will take the most time to read? What sources are likely to help you find other sources? Sort through your information and plan your reading to make the best use of your time.

*Source Record with Source Number*

---

**LC5800.T42 2003**

| | |
|---|---|
| Title: | **Teaching and learning at a distance : foundations of distance education / Michael R. Simonson ... [et al.].** |
| Edition: | **2nd. ed.** |
| Publication info: | **Upper Saddle River, N.J. : Merrill Prentice Hall, c2003.** |
| Physical descrip: | **xvii, 302 p. : ill. ; 24 cm.** |
| Bibliography note: | **Includes bibliographical references and index.** |
| Contents: | **Foundations of distance education — Definitions, history, and theories of distance education — Research and distance education — Distance education technologies — Copyright and distance education — Instructional design for distance education — The distance education student — Teaching at a distance — Handouts, study guides, and visuals — Distance education, the World Wide Web, and the Internet — Assessment for distance education — Evaluating teaching and learning at a distance.** |
| Subject: | **Distance education.** |
| Series: | **Simonson, Michael R.** |

---

| Call Numbers for: BRACKEN | Copy | Material | Location |
|---|---|---|---|
| 1) LC5800 . T42 2003 | 1 | GEN_BOOK | General Collection, Bracken Library |

---

## Note-taking Process

Note taking is the most critical stage of research because it demands that you read, select, interpret, and evaluate the information that will form the substance of your paper. When you return the books and articles to the library or turn off your computer, your notes will be your only record of your research. If you have taken notes carelessly, you will be in trouble when you begin writing. Many students inadvertently plagiarize because they work from inaccurate notes. The wise procedure is to take notes very carefully from the beginning.

Begin by recasting the information in your library record into the documentation style you will use in your works-cited list. Then read and compose notes on note cards or on the computer screen. The citation serves to identify the source of all the notes composed beneath it, but you still will need to enter the page number for each note and compose subheadings to help yourself organize the material.

• A WRITING PROJECT

**Reconstruct your work as a researcher-detective. Describe the search strategy you used to solve a mystery or resolve a problem.**

When composing notes on the computer, you can create your own database on a subject, using the keyword function to re-search your notes for information on particular subheadings. You can also use your word processor's cut-and-paste feature to collect information on each subheading from different sources and place it in a new file, thus performing the traditional step of shuffling note cards with various subheadings. The disadvantage of this method is that you must read and take notes at your computer terminal. Sometimes it is easier (or even necessary) to take notes the traditional way—as you read a book in the study lounge or examine a document in a special collection of the library.

No matter which method you use, begin by reading quickly through your source to determine if it contains any worthwhile information. If it does, then during a second, more careful reading, use one of these three methods to take notes: *quoting, summarizing, paraphrasing.* At the end of each note leave some room for a personal comment—for example, ideas on how you might make use of this information in your paper.

To understand how to read, react, and write during the note-taking process, consider Erin's response to the following passage from Rachel Hartigan Shea's article, "So Where's the Beef?"

> Still, throughout the history of distance education, critics have questioned whether students could really be taught well from far away. Those concerns have been revived with online education. Detractors worry that online courses sacrifice intellectual sophistication for convenience, that they foster isolation among students, and that they dehumanize the process of learning. E-learning may "inhibit rather than promote good education," charges the American Federation of

Teachers. Faculty fret that online education forces them to surrender control of their academic work to administrators and business people, who will warp it into something profitable. And with the continuing shakeout among e-learning companies and universities, students could be left in the untenable position of paying for classes at a school that no longer exists.

*Computer Notes*

> Shea, Rachel Hartigan. "So Where's the Beef?" <u>U.S. News and World Report</u> 15 October 2001: 44–50.
>
> Shea says that critics have always questioned the value of distance education. They have argued that such programs "foster isolation among students, and that they dehumanize the process of learning" (55)
>
> Powerful argument about the disadvantages of "online education" from students' point of view.

## Quoting Sources

Quoting an author's text word-for-word is the easiest way to record information, but you should use this method selectively. Quote only the passages that deal directly with your subject in particularly memorable language. When you write a quotation on your note card or computer screen, place quotation marks at the beginning and end of the passage to indicate that you are quoting. If you decide to leave out part of the text, use *three* ellipsis points (. . .) to indicate that you have omitted words from the beginning or middle of the sentence and *four* ellipsis points (. . . .) to indicate that you have omitted the end of a sentence or one or more sentences. (See discussion of ellipsis points in Section 28 of the "Handbook of Grammar and Usage.") Finally, proofread your quotation against the original to confirm that every word and mark of punctuation is in its proper place.

## Summarizing Sources

Summarizing an author's views is an effective way to record the essence of a text. Use this method when the author states a thesis or analyzes evidence in a way that either anticipates or contradicts your emerging perception of your argument. Use key words or two or three phrases to restate briefly the author's principal points.

## Paraphrasing Sources

Paraphrasing an author's views is both the most useful and the most misused method of note taking. It is *not* simply a casual way for you to reproduce the author's views nearly word-for-word without using quotation marks. Rather, paraphrasing requires you to think through what the author has said and then restate the information *in your own words*. To accomplish this objective, you must understand what the author has said and then reformulate her or his opinion without adding or deleting significant information and without distorting the intent of the original passage. The paraphrase combines the advantages of quoting and summarizing because it allows you to reproduce the essence of the author's argument and adapt it to the flow of your own argument.

### EXERCISE

Read the following passage by Rachel Hartigan Shea and then, following the procedures discussed earlier, compose three types of notes. First, quote a few important sentences; second, summarize the major point of the passage; and third, paraphrase a major section of Shea's argument. At the bottom of each note, indicate why it is significant and how you might use it in a paper.

It seems fair to say that distance education has had a checkered past. The correspondence courses at the turn of the 20th century promised the equivalent of "anytime, anywhere" education but instead delivered shoddy lessons and slapdash instruction, driving dropout rates through the roof. But people still wanted to learn from a distance. Indeed, in the early 1960s, two DC-6 airplanes flew over Indiana beaming lessons by satellite into Midwestern classrooms. With each new technological innovation—telephone, film, radio, audiotapes, and television—distance education rebounded. By the 1980s, many colleges were offering courses and programs that taught through correspondence, teleconferencing, videotaped lectures, or some combination of all three. But by the late 1990s, most schools had moved to take the entire experience online. Schools rushed to the Web for a slew of reasons: Some found the possibility of reaching thousands of new students intoxicating, while others wanted to take the lead in developing new educational technology. More than a few thought the dotcom mirage would become a pool of cold, hard cash. Some universities set up their online operations in separate, hoped-for, profit centers. Many were just afraid of being left behind.

## Photocopying

Photocopying print sources and printing (downloading) online sources have had a great impact on research. When you discover a particularly valuable source, copying all of it (if it is an article) or major portions of it (if it is a book) may seem to be the most efficient thing to do. You can cut out appropriate passages and paste them onto individual note cards, thus ensuring that you have precise quotations. You can even review the pertinent information in the original when you begin to write.

But if you decide to photocopy or download every source you uncover, you will waste a lot of time, paper, and money. The purpose of reading and note taking is to extract the essence of an article or book, to identify the information most pertinent to your argument. Photocopying is not an alternative to evaluating your sources. Compiling a large stack of paper only postpones your examination, reading, and assessment of the material.

## Copy-Paste Trap

The chief advantage of using computer software in your research is that you can **copy** important passages from online sources you have found and then **paste** them into your research folder. But this quick and easy way of "saving" information can also get you into a lot of trouble. If you don't take notes on the original information, and you instead just "save" the material that you have found, then you may later assume that you composed the sentences that you see in your notes and present them as your own writing. In other words, *copying* and *pasting* can trap you into committing plagiarism. (See "Plagiarism," pages 361–362.)

## Filling Gaps

Planning the research paper is like planning any other paper. As you evaluate your information, you discover that you need more or different kinds of material. As you conduct your research, you constantly refine and restrict your subject. By the time you finish taking notes on the sources you first discovered and the sources you have uncovered along the way, you know where the holes in your research are and what gaps you have to fill if you are to present a thorough and coherent argument.

The research process, like the writing process, is recursive. You must loop back to the beginning to devise additional subject headings and to check specialized bibliographies and other references to find the sources to fill the gaps in your information. When you begin writing your paper, you may have to make yet another loop to discover information that forges missing connections. Because you have worked through the process once and know what you are looking for, however, these further efforts should be quick and to the point.

# Planning your research paper on your computer

As you read this sentence, the advances in computer technology have changed much of the information in this chapter on how to find sources both in the library and on the Internet. Despite these changes, however, the job of *planning* your research paper remains the same. Online databases may help you locate 10,000 sources on your subject, but you will never have time to read them all, much less cite them. You need a few basic strategies to find, organize, and assess the sources that will support or refute the arguments you are making in your research paper.

Begin by creating a single file on the subject of your paper (online degrees). Rather than open a file for each source you consult, create a single database of sources, notes, and comments. As you discover additional descriptors that restrict your subject or lead to promising sources (student satisfaction), add them to your notes. Similarly, as you see your notes begin to cluster around certain topics (accreditation), insert these keywords into your data.

Once you have created your database, use the search feature to locate all references to a particular topic. Then use your copy-and-paste feature to collect information from a variety of sources and to create a new file, which you may want to consider a section of your paper. Keep track of each source's web address, or URL, so that you can cite each chunk of information correctly.

If you discover new information on a subject, enter it into your main file and then copy it into the smaller file you have created for that subtopic. If you decide to rename one of your smaller files, consider using the global search feature to find all references to your old heading in your database (teaching), and then revise the heading (online teaching strategies).

The purposes of this planning are to (1) create your own library of information on your subject and (2) construct your own subject heading index so that you can find the information you want once you begin drafting. Indeed, the subheadings in your index may well end up representing major sections of your paper.

Many computer networks enable you to post citation abstracts and full texts to a variety of places. For example, some databases allow you to mail your sources to your e-mail address so that you can open and print them at some future time. You can also send sources to your teacher or writing groups so that you can solicit their opinions about the sources' relative value to your emerging paper. In turn, your teacher, classmates, or experts whom you have interviewed can send you commentary on your sources and add attachments that contain sources (abstracts or full text) that they feel will advance the purpose of your paper.

# Writing Assignments

### 1. NARRATE

Freewrite in your journal about some special childhood experiences you had in your school or public library. Make a list of the sights and smells you remember, the books you read, the people you met. Then compose a narrative about how the library introduced you to new worlds.

### 2. OBSERVE

Study the research behavior of the students in your writing class. How many of them go to the Web first? How many go to the library first? How much paper do they create by photocopying or downloading? Write an essay (perhaps a comic one) for your student newspaper on the various *styles* of research you observed.

### 3. INVESTIGATE

Interview the head reference librarian at your university library. Ask him or her to discuss how computer technology has changed library research in the last five years and to speculate on what new technologies will become available in the next five years. Then write a profile of the reference librarian for your university's alumni magazine, explaining to graduates how things have changed since they thumbed their way through the card catalogue and the *Readers' Guide*.

### 4. COLLABORATE

Your writing group has been asked to update your university library's guide. Assign each member of the group to a specific area—circulation, reference, periodicals, special collections, and so on. Ask librarians about how the area is supposed to function and students about the problems they encounter when they try to work in the library. Then ask them both what improvements they would like to see implemented. Collect your evidence and then revise the guide.

### 5. READ

Read selected passages from a book such as Robert D. Altick's *The Scholar Adventurers* (New York: Macmillan, 1965). Then write an essay in which you comment on one of these adventurers or in which you discuss your own adventures tracking down and interpreting some piece of evidence. Consider as your audience students about to begin their first research paper and as your purpose convincing them that research is *adventurous*.

### 6. RESPOND

Read Robert Weber's speculations about the future of library research in "Library Without Walls" (*Publisher's Weekly* 8 June 1990: S20–S22). Respond to his description of the computerized library from one of two positions: as someone who is overwhelmed by the advances in technology, or as someone who is excited by these new advances.

### 7. ANALYZE

Consider the various sources you used in your research. What did you learn from interviewing people? What did you learn by reading books? What did you learn by surfing the Net? Then write a letter to your writing teacher analyzing the benefits of *real-world* research as a strategy for enriching *library-based* research.

### 8. EVALUATE

Read the statements on plagiarism in your university's catalogue or student manual. Evaluate the degree to which these statements explain the conventions of citation and documentation you need to learn to write a successful research paper.

# Writing Assignments

## 9. ARGUE

Argue that your library needs to provide more systematic instruction on how to use its new computer technology. Acknowledge that such explanations seem abstract unless the researcher has a specific problem to solve. For that reason, argue that instruction in the library's computer technology should be linked in some official way with instruction in a basic writing course in which students are writing their first college research paper. Address your argument to the directors of the library and the freshman writing program.

## 10. ARGUE

In a letter addressed to the chair of the English Department, argue that students should be required to complete two kinds of research assignments: (1) the library research paper (based on secondary sources) and (2) the field research paper (based on observations, interviews, questionnaires, and other kinds of primary sources).

# Writing the Research Paper

**WRITING, BEING A CREATIVE PROCESS, IS MUCH HARDER AND TAKES TWICE AS LONG.**

—BARBARA TUCHMAN

For the research paper, as for any writing project, eventually you must stop planning and start writing. The large stack of note cards or the computer folders you have prepared point to two accomplishments: (1) you have learned a systematic procedure for gathering information (a procedure you can apply to other subjects), and (2) you have learned a great deal about the research that has already been published on your subject. But, as Barbara Tuchman suggests, most people are "overimpressed by research. People are always saying to me in awed tones, 'Think of all the *research* you must have done!' as if this were the hard part. It is not; writing, being a creative process, is much harder and takes twice as long" (Barbara Tuchman, "Problems in Writing the Biography of General Stilwell," *Practicing History*).

Your sources will guide you through the hard part of research—writing your paper. But they can also present two problems: (1) you have probably gathered more information than you can use in one paper, and (2) you have become so immersed in what other researchers have written about your subject that you may no longer know what *you* want to write about it. The most effective way to overcome these difficulties is to settle down and write a first draft.

This chapter will discuss the basic steps in writing that first draft. It will also show you some of Erin McMullen's initial difficulties with getting started on her first draft. And further, it will give you detailed advice about how to quote and document sources in the final draft. Read Erin's final draft and accompanying annotations at the end of the chapter to see how she resolved her difficulties and integrated her research into her writing.

The major topics discussed in this chapter are

▸ Organizing a preliminary outline

▸ Developing a thesis

▸ Writing the first draft

▸ Creating the introduction

▸ Quoting sources

▸ Documenting sources

▸ Listing sources

▸ Designing the final draft

## Organizing a Preliminary Outline

To organize a preliminary (or *scratch*) outline, read through your notes, collecting information that deals with specific subdivisions of your subject. If you have created subheadings, then you can search your database for chunks of information to copy and paste into small files. If you discover that some divisions (1) focus on similar aspects of your subject, (2) do not contain enough information, or (3) deal with subject headings no longer appropriate to the emerging design of your paper, then relabel, combine, or eliminate these divisions so that they begin to form a logical and coherent sequence.

Before drafting your paper, try several preliminary outlines to determine the most effective pattern for presenting your information. After you have completed your first draft, use a *descriptive* outline (or *revision agenda*) to evaluate what you have written. Once you are ready to write the final draft of your research paper, prepare a *formal* outline to guide your composing process. (You may want to review the types, formats, and purposes of these strategies as they are described in Chapters 3 and 4). Your instructor may require you to submit your formal outline with your paper as a kind of table of contents.

Once you have established your categories, arrange them into various patterns to find the one that seems most effective. (You may wish to review the patterns in Chapter 6, "Common Methods of Development," or in Part Four, "Readings with a Purpose.") Some of your subject headings may suggest a simple pattern (a *definition* of online education); others may point to a more complicated pattern (a *causal analysis* of why students are attracted to online learning). Erin's research, for example, led her to study good and bad aspects of online degrees. Because Erin understood the pros and cons of this controversy, she considered organizing her paper as a *comparison and contrast* essay. But she was perplexed about how to arrange her material. Which side should she analyze first—pro-online degrees or anti-online degrees? What was her purpose in comparing the two positions? She sorted her notes again and discovered that she needed to be more precise about her purpose.

PRELIMINARY OUTLINE

University Degrees: On-campus vs. Online Education

1. Introduce online degrees
        Case studies
        Virtual universities
        Brick-and-mortar universities that offer online
            degrees
        Combination for-profit organizations and tradi-
            tional universities

2. Pros of online degrees
        Convenience—students can access class from any-
            where, anytime
        Comfortable communication—chat room environment
        Career-specific degrees—sometimes designed by
            corporations

3. Pros of on-campus degrees
        Support—student services, financial aid ser-
            vices to help students
        Communication—more dimensional, varied communi-
            cation can improve course content/pace
        More degrees—degrees offered in wide variety
            of disciplines, clear understanding of who
            teaches courses

A preliminary outline reveals at a glance the kind of paper your sources will allow you to write. As Erin looks at her outline, she sees that her planning has uncovered several interesting issues. Her reading has helped her measure the pros and cons of on-campus and online education. Each side presents a convincing argument, but Erin is bothered by the either/or nature of this controversy. Does she have to decide, absolutely, whether on-campus or online learning is best? That question prompts her to resist any absolute statements—preferring instead to reply, "It all depends on where you live and how you learn." Erin suspects that if she reviews her research, she may have some additional insights about this controversy that will help her revise her preliminary outline so that it demonstrates a thesis.

# Developing a Thesis

Developing a thesis is the most difficult task in composing the research paper. Your notes, even when they are sorted and arranged in a compelling pattern, represent the voices of authority. It is easy to be intimidated by your own research, to let your sources speak for you. But remember that your main aim is to advance your own argument—to discuss and analyze a topic from your own point of view. Like all other writing assignments, the research paper requires you to write with a purpose.

To find that purpose, review the comments you wrote about your notes. If you consistently commented on or posed questions about the ideas in your notes, then you have already established a degree of independence from your sources. As you reread your comments, look for common denominators in your thinking. What fascinated you about your subject? What connections did you see among the various sources you read?

Once you have identified some common themes, convert each into a hypothesis and try to match it with some point in your preliminary outline. Some of your hypotheses may match up easily, leading to assertions that explain each subdivision and pointing toward a thesis. Others may require you to revise the subdivisions or expand the range of categories you need to consider. Still others may suggest that you reorganize your outline completely. The thesis you try to advance in your first draft depends on a number of factors: your personal preference, your understanding of the information you have gathered, and your confidence in your ability to demonstrate what you propose to prove.

As Erin looked back through her comments, she discovered that she had uncovered a significant controversy. Rachel Hartigan Shea convinced her that the newest form of technology has always created a new form of *distance learning*. Each "next new thing" may have tried to duplicate traditional education programs, but it has also created its fair share of ill-conceived or even fraudulent programs. However, as she looked at the descriptions of these new programs on the Web, she understood their appeal—particularly to students who live in remote settings or who have to balance work and school.

Erin formulated three hypotheses that she hoped would unblock the gridlock she had discovered in her research:

1. Online degrees are the newest form of distance education, but there are many fraudulent online degree programs that easily mislead students.
2. Online education can be really valuable for students with specific goals and with lifestyles that make regularly commuting to a campus difficult.
3. Many facets of campus education cannot be replicated online.

## EXERCISE

Discuss how each of Erin's hypotheses matches up with her preliminary outline (page 352).

In what ways will each hypothesis require Erin to change the major headings and subdivisions

of her outline? What information will she need to add, eliminate, or relabel?

## Writing the First Draft

Writing the first draft of your research paper is like writing the first draft of any other paper—it is a discovery exercise. You have to discover whether your planning will enable you to communicate a subject to an audience for a purpose. Some of your discoveries will seem familiar because they are common in every writing situation: The information that seemed so complete in your notes now seems sketchy; and the overall purpose of your paper, so clear in your mind when you began, now strikes you as confused or inconsistent. Other discoveries may prove unsettling because they seem unique to the research paper: Your first draft may follow your preliminary outline and support your thesis, but it may seem stiff, mechanical, and dull.

For most inexperienced writers, first-draft dullness derives from the inability to compose a simple, straightforward introduction that asserts a thesis and the inability to weave quoted material gracefully and naturally into the body of the paper. The following sections will illustrate and discuss some methods for solving these problems.

## Creating the Introduction

Do not be surprised if you have to struggle with the introduction to your research paper. You have learned a great deal about your subject and are eager to display that learning in the body of your paper. But in order to do that you have to write an introduction that establishes the focus of your subject, attracts the attention of your readers, and asserts the purpose of your paper. Some writers cannot write such an introduction until they have discovered precisely what they are going to say in the body of the paper. For that reason, they prefer to write the introduction after they have drafted the rest of the paper—when they know exactly what they want to introduce. Other writers cannot develop the body of the paper until they have defined its exact direction. For that reason, they draft several versions of the introduction, hoping to learn what they want to introduce. Either method will require you to make a series of adjustments—some large, some small—to the introduction and to the body when you revise the final draft.

Erin is intrigued by her first hypothesis because it suggests that although online education seems attractive, it presents its own share of problems. She is particularly concerned about what students actually get when they receive an online education. Certain students may buy into the notion of virtual education (hypothesis #2), but they may not realize what a "real/traditional" education can offer (hypothesis #3). Her attempts to work out the implications of these issues and to find a purpose for her paper produce two different introductions. Her revision agendas reveal her dissatisfaction with them because each fails to establish her subject and clarify her thesis. Here are both introductions and the revision agendas.

FIRST DRAFT: Introduction

Everybody's online these days. From checking e-mail, stock quotes, and credit card balances to shopping, renting apartments, and planning vacations-- everyone is taking care of business on the Net. So why not get your education on the Internet, too? It's not just for computer geeks anymore. Lots of professionals and working adults with families are switching online for their degrees. Sometimes they succeed--get a great degree and a promotion--and sometimes they get swindled--waste thousands of dollars and don't get a legit degree at all. Online students never waste their time in a classroom; they never meet other students or professors--except through e-mailing biographies. Luddites may be wary of online degrees, but students, universities, and corporations all heartily approve of the switch to virtual universities and online degrees.

REVISION AGENDA

1.  What did I try to do in this draft?
    I tried to be casual and "hip" when I wrote about the Internet so that it would seem attractive, fresh, and really useful in all facets of a person's life.
2.  What are its strengths and weaknesses?
    I like the way I show how much people depend on the Internet, but I think I'm not serious enough about the issues of online education. I only say that students, universities, and businesses like the idea of online degrees. As a result, I don't address the problems with online education.
3.  What revisions do I want to make in my next draft?
    a. Write a more accurate and direct thesis.
    b. Present both sides of the issue.
    c. Give the specific pros and cons of online education.

SECOND DRAFT: Introduction

The Internet makes communicating, banking, and shopping more convenient for many people. In today's busy world, many adults who work and have families would like to go back to school and get a college degree, but traditional universities do not meet their needs. As a result, these busy and successful adult learners are turning to online degree programs for their education. Online degree programs offer convenience and specific programs for these finicky adult learners, but they also come with a variety of problems. However, more students every year are seeking out online degree programs instead of traditional university programs.

REVISION AGENDA

1. <u>What did I try to do in this draft?</u>
   I tried to present a more balanced picture of online degrees and a more specific description of adult learners who prefer online degrees.
2. <u>What are its strengths and weaknesses?</u>
   I think taking out a lot of the slang makes the introduction sound more serious. I also think it was a good idea to present the possibility that there are problems with online degrees. I don't think I'm specific enough about what those problems are, and I've omitted the mention that some students are successful and others get swindled. I think that part helped show that online degrees aren't always good.
3. <u>What revisions do I want to make in my next draft?</u>
   a. Be more specific and complete in my descriptions of the pros of online degrees and on-campus degrees.
   b. Include two different experiences of students who try to get online degrees--maybe case studies from my research would work here.
   c. Offer research for the "pro" positions for both online and on-campus education.
   d. Give a better explanation of what online education can be.
   e. Construct a thesis that can be proven, and state it directly.

When she finished her second revision agenda, Erin was confident that her third hypothesis might lead to a good thesis and purpose for her paper. She reworked the introduction and drafted her paper, encountering and solving a number of tricky problems. She decided, for example, how to weave her source material into her text and how to prepare her list of works cited. You will see how Erin handled these problems when you read her paper and the annotations that accompany it on pages 380–393.

### Exercise

Compare Erin's two introductions (pages 355 and 356) with the introduction she uses in her final paper (pages 382–383). How do her revision agendas help her expand her introduction and sharpen her thesis? What specific decisions seem to produce the most important changes in her final draft?

## Quoting Sources

The most persistent challenge posed by the research paper is deciding *when* and *where* to cite your sources to support your argument. For every division of your outline, you have notes that contain the words and ideas of other writers. If you use this material, you must acknowledge the sources of your information (see "Documenting Sources," pages 362–368, and "Listing Sources," pages 368–376). It's a common beginner's error, however, not just to use sources but to let the sources write the paper for you. Excessive quoting distorts the balance between your writing and the writing of others and makes your paper seem to be a scrapbook of other people's opinions. And it can disrupt the flow of your argument by introducing ideas and images that may not deal directly with your thesis.

To avoid these problems, you should be selective when you quote. Because each quotation creates a special effect, ask yourself the following questions when you are deciding whether to quote a passage:

1. *Will the substance of the passage make a significant contribution to my subject?* Sometimes a passage may seem significant because it provides extensive evidence for its conclusions. But you may be able to make the same point more effectively by summarizing or paraphrasing rather than by quoting the passage.

2. *Will the phrasing of the passage seem memorable to my readers?* You do not want to blur the effect of a quotation by quoting too much material. Nor do you want to quote uninspired or unintelligible writing. You should quote only key sentences or phrases—those that convey the author's meaning in especially vivid language.

3. *Will the reputation of the author give credibility to my argument?* The mere mention of certain "experts" produces controversy or distorts your argument. If the authorities of your sources are suspect, there is no point in quoting them.

When you determine that you want to use a particular quotation, you have to decide how to incorporate it into your own writing. There are several methods for quoting material; the one you choose depends on why you are quoting the passage and how much you intend to quote.

## Introducing Quotations

All quotations must be placed within quotation marks or set off from your text in a block quotation. They must be documented in a parenthetical reference that includes the exact page numbers from which they were taken and, if necessary, the authors' names or other words or phrases that identify the sources. A lead-in phrase or sentence identifying the person you are quoting and the reason he or she is being quoted helps your readers follow your reasoning and prepares them for the special effect conveyed by a quotation.

There are at least three ways to introduce a quotation. Here is the most common method:

> In <u>Distance Training: Taking Stock at a Time of Change</u>, Desmond Keegan, editor of studies in distance education, points out that research studies published over the last fifty years conclude that "there is no significant difference between distance education and on-campus provision" (76).

The author to be quoted (Desmond Keegan), his credentials (editor of studies in distance education) and the source of his quotation (*Distance Training: Taking Stock at a Time of Change*) are all identified. But the purpose for which Keegan is being quoted is not explained; presumably, this passage will appear in a paragraph in which the context or reason for the quotation has been established. Introductory phrases such as the one used here help your readers see how authority advances your argument.

In the second way of introducing a quotation, the author being quoted and the reason that he is being quoted are both identified in a sentence that concludes with a colon; the quotation follows, as in this example:

> Educational researcher Desmond Keegan, in <u>Distance Training: Taking Stock at a Time of Change</u>, explains the results of over fifty years of studies conducted on students taught in a variety of settings: "The almost invariable result of these studies is that there is no significant difference between distance education and on-campus provision" (76).

The third method of identifying a quotation rests on the assumption that you introduced the author's full name and credentials earlier in the paper.

```
        Research studies, Keegan reminds us, have found "no
        significant difference between distance education and
        on-campus provision" (76).
```

Compare these quotations with Erin's treatment of the source on page 391 [McMullen 10].

## Length of Quotations

The length (and look) of your quotation will determine its effect. Working a brief, pointed quotation into the syntax of your sentence is often the best way to advance your argument. But on rare occasions (perhaps no more than two or three times in a ten-page research paper), you may want to quote a long passage that expresses the main ideas you are trying to present.

*Long quotations* (five or more lines of prose, four or more lines of poetry) are usually introduced by a colon or comma, begun on a new line, and indented ten spaces or one inch from the left margin. This special placement identifies the passage as a quotation, so do *not* enclose it in quotation marks. In such block quotations, the final period goes *before* rather than *after* the parenthetical page reference. Here is an example:

```
        Distance education expert Barry Willis explains the
        subtleties of face-to-face teaching:

            Whether they realize it or not, effective classroom
            teachers rely on a number of visual and unobtrusive
            cues and clues from their students. A quick glance,
            for example, reveals who is attentively taking
            notes, pondering a difficult concept, or enthusias-
            tically preparing to make a comment. The student who
            is frustrated, confused, tired, or bored is equally
            evident. The attentive teacher consciously and sub-
            consciously receives and analyzes these visual cues.
            As a result, the delivery of information, and often
            the course content itself, is adapted to meet the
            unique characteristics and needs of the class during
            any particular lesson. (6)
```

*Short quotations* (fewer than five lines of prose, fewer than four lines of poetry) are usually run into your text, unless they deserve special emphasis. You can introduce a short quotation by using one of the three methods described previously. Or, as in the example that follows, you can work brief phrases from your source into the syntax of your sentence, using quotation marks and identifying the source in a parenthetical reference. See how Erin uses this passage in her paper on page 387 [McMullen 6].

In his book <u>Distance Education: A Practical Guide</u>, researcher Barry Willis explains that effective teachers rely on visual cues to adapt the course content "to meet the unique characteristics and needs of the class during any particular lesson" (6).

## Integrating Quotations

Sometimes, to make a quoted passage fit smoothly into the flow of your sentences, you will have to use *ellipsis points* and *brackets*. Use ellipsis points when you want to omit part of the quoted passage to make it conform to your sentence. Use three points (. . .) to indicate omission of material within the sentence. Use four points (. . . .) to indicate the omission of a whole sentence or more. Use brackets when you need to add your own words to a quotation to make the passage complete or grammatically correct or, on occasion, when you need to make an editorial comment. (See Sections 27 and 28, on brackets and ellipses, respectively, in Part 5, "Handbook of Grammar and Usage.")

Here is a lengthy passage from Rachel Hartigan's article "Smart New Degrees Take Center Stage":

> Both students and employers are clamoring for degrees. "Employers need more in the bank than general intellectual skills," explains Clifton Conrad, a professor of higher education at Wisconsin and the lead author of <u>A Silent Success: Master's Education in the United States</u>. Doctoral graduates are often too narrowly focused for corporate tastes, while recruiters complain that undergraduate education barely compensates for the inadequacies of high school
>
> Students are seeking master's degrees because they have become the passport to entry-level jobs in many fields or at least the key to moving up the ladder. Meanwhile, working professionals just want to keep their jobs. With business and technology seeping into nursing, education, science, public policy, and diplomacy, employees must learn new skills or risk being passed over.

Notice how Erin uses ellipses and brackets to incorporate Rachel Hartigan's phrasing into one of the early drafts of her paper:

> "Students are seeking master's degrees because they have become the passport to entry-level jobs. . . . [E]mployees must learn new skills or risk being passed over" (7).

See pages 388–389 [McMullen 7–8] to see how Erin uses this passage to advance the argument in her paper.

## Using Summary and Paraphrase

Often the most efficient way to work your sources into your own writing is to summarize or paraphrase them. As you remember from Chapter 12, a summary states the thesis or outlines the principal points of an author's argument; a paraphrase is a restatement of the author's ideas in *your own words* (see pages 344–345). Because the words of a summary or paraphrase are yours, they do not have to be enclosed in quotation marks. But because the ideas come from someone else, you do need to cite the source in your text and document the passage in a parenthetical reference.

Erin paraphrases Rachel Hartigan's words this way:

> As Rachel Hartigan points out, employers want to hire people with advanced degrees, and employees want advanced degrees to keep their jobs (7).

## Plagiarism

● A WRITER'S WORDS

**To some extent every writer's desk top is like a Ouija board, his pen pushed across it by whatever literary ghost he's just entertained.**

—Thomas Mallon,
*Stolen Words: Forays into the Origins and Ravages of Plagiarism*

Plagiarism is the use of someone else's writing without giving proper credit—or perhaps without giving any credit at all—to the writer of the original. Whether plagiarism is intentional or unintentional, it is a serious offense that you can easily avoid by adhering scrupulously to the following advice. You should document your sources whenever you

▶ Use a direct quotation

▶ Copy a table, chart, or other diagram

▶ Construct a table from data provided by others

▶ Summarize or paraphrase a passage in your own words

▶ Present specific examples, figures, or factual information that you have taken from a specific source and used to explain or support your judgments

The following excerpt from Mark Pendergrast's *Uncommon Grounds: The History of Coffee and How It Transformed Our World* and three examples of students' use of it illustrate the problem:

*Original version*

> Experts in fact don't agree on much when it comes to coffee and caffeine intake, partly because individuals exhibit remarkably different reactions. Some people are wired for hours with a mere sip; others can drink a double espresso right before falling into a sound sleep. Thus, every coffee lover should determine his or her level of comfortable consumption, preferably no more than two or three cups a day.

*Version A*

> Experts in fact don't agree on much when it comes to coffee and caffeine intake, partly because individuals exhibit remarkably different reactions. Some people are

```
wired for hours with a mere sip; others can drink a
double espresso right before falling into a sound
sleep. Thus, every coffee lover should determine his
or her level of comfortable consumption, preferably no
more than two or three cups a day.
```

This is plagiarism in its most blatant form. Because the writer of Version A does not indicate in the text or in a parenthetical reference that the words and ideas belong to Pendergrast, his readers will believe that the words are his. He stole Pendergrast's words.

Version B

```
     Mark Pendergrast points out that experts don't agree
about coffee and caffeine intake, partly because indi-
viduals exhibit remarkably different reactions. Some
people are wired for hours after a mere sip; others can
drink a double espresso and fall asleep. Thus every
coffee lover should determine his or her level of com-
fortable consumption, preferably no more than two or
three cups a day (415).
```

Version B is also plagiarism, even though the writer acknowledges his source and documents the passage in a parenthetical reference. Obviously, the writer copied the original almost word-for-word but has supplied no quotation marks to indicate the extent of the borrowing. As written and documented, the passage masquerades as a paraphrase when in fact it is nearly a direct quotation.

Version C

```
     In his Uncommon Grounds: The History of Coffee and
How It Transformed Our World, Mark Pendergrast explains
why experts can't agree on coffee and caffeine:
"[I]ndividuals exhibit remarkably different reactions.
Some people are wired for hours ... ; others can drink
a double espresso right before falling into a sound
sleep" (415).
```

Version C represents one, although not the only, satisfactory way of handling this source material. The writer identifies his source at the beginning of the sentence, letting his readers know who is being quoted. He then uses an introductory phrase and a colon to characterize and set up the material he plans to quote. He marks the original passage in quotation marks. Finally, he provides the parenthetical reference. By following this procedure, he makes perfectly clear which words are his and which belong to Pendergrast.

## Documenting Sources

The purpose of documenting each source with a parenthetical reference is twofold: (1) to avoid the appearance of representing somebody else's work as your own and (2) to refer your readers to your list of works cited, where they will find a complete citation on your source. Although there is general agreement about the purpose of documentation, different fields of learning, periodicals, and publishers prefer different styles.

The two most commonly used styles are those recommended by the Modern Language Association in its *MLA Handbook for Writers of Research Papers, Sixth Edition*, and by the American Psychological Association in its *Publication Manual of the American Psychological Association, Fifth Edition*. The two styles differ:

| *MLA Style* | *APA Style* |
|---|---|
| Sources are documented by parenthetical reference to author's last name and to page number. No punctuation separates these elements, and no abbreviation for *page* or *pages* is used. | Sources are documented by parenthetical reference to author's last name, publication date, and page number. Commas separate these elements, and the abbreviations *p.* and *pp.* are used. |

Here is the same source documented according to each style:

MLA style

```
Coffee, the drink that keeps "the industrialized world
alert, is grown in regions that know how to enjoy a
siesta" (Pendergrast 409)
```

WORKS CITED

```
Pendergrast, Mark. Uncommon Grounds: The History of
    Coffee and How It Transformed Our World. New York:
    Basic, 1999.
```

APA style

```
Coffee, the drink that keeps "the industrialized world
alert, is grown in regions that know how to enjoy a
siesta" (Pendergrast, 1999, p. 409).
```

REFERENCES

```
    Pendergrast, Mark. (1999). Uncommon grounds: The
history of coffee and how it transformed our world.
New York: Basic Books.
```

Different departments in your college or university may require a particular style; your instructors will tell you which documentation style they require. If you are writing a research paper in the social sciences, your instructor is likely to require APA style. If you are writing a research paper in the humanities, your instructor is likely to require MLA style. Because this chapter is designed to help you write a research paper in a composition class, its examples, including Erin's research paper, follow MLA style.

## Sample Citations

Frequently you will need to cite sources that are not as straightforward as the Pendergrast example, such as a book written by more than one author or several works by the same author. In these cases, follow the specific styles given here. Each example of a citation is followed by the entry that would appear in the works-cited list.

**Citing One Work by an Author of Two or More Works**   If you are citing two or more titles by the same author, place a comma after the author's last name, add a shortened version of the title of the work, and then supply the relevant page numbers. Another solution is to cite the author's last name and title in your sentence and then add the page numbers in a parenthetical reference.

> Once society reaches a certain stage of industrial growth, it will shift its energies to the production of services (Toffler, <u>Future</u> 221).
> Toffler argues in <u>The Third Wave</u> that society has gone through two eras (agricultural and industrial) and is now entering another—the information age (26).

WORKS CITED

Toffler, Alvin. <u>Future Shock</u>. New York: Random, 1970.
- - -. <u>The Third Wave</u>. New York: Morrow, 1980.

**Citing One Work by an Author Who Has the Same Last Name as Another Author in Your List of Cited Works**   When you are citing two or more authors with the same last name, avoid confusion by supplying each author's first name in the parenthetical reference or in your sentence. In the list of cited works, the two authors should be alphabetized by their first names.

> Critics have often debated the usefulness of the psychological approach to literary interpretation (Frederick Hoffman 317).
> Daniel Hoffman argues that folklore and myth provide valuable insights for the literary critic (9-15).

WORKS CITED

Hoffman, Daniel G. <u>Form and Fable in American Fiction</u>. New York: Oxford, 1961.
Hoffman, Frederick J. <u>Freudianism and the Literary Mind</u>. Baton Rouge: Louisiana State UP, 1945.

**Citing a Work by More Than One Author**   If you are citing a book by two authors, you have the option of naming them in your sentence or of putting their names in a parenthetical reference. If you are citing a book by three or more authors, you should probably place their names in a parenthetical reference to sustain the readability of your sentence. The authorship of a work by three or more authors can be given in a shortened form by using the first author's last name and "et al." (an abbreviation for the Latin phrase *et alia*, meaning "and others").

> Boller and Story interpret the Declaration of Independence as Thomas Jefferson's attempt to list America's grievances against England (58).
> Other historians view the Declaration of Independence as Jefferson's attempt to formulate the principles of America's political philosophy (Norton et al. 124).

WORKS CITED

Boller, Paul, and Ronald Story. <u>A More Perfect Union: Documents in U.S. History</u>. Boston: Houghton, 1984.
Norton, Mary Beth, et al. <u>A People and a Nation: A History of the United States</u>. Boston: Houghton, 1984.

**Citing a Multivolume Work**   If you are citing one volume from a multivolume work, indicate in your parenthetical reference the specific volume you used.

> William Faulkner's initial reluctance to travel to Stockholm to receive the Nobel Prize produced considerable consternation in the American embassy (Blotner 2: 1347).

WORKS CITED

Blotner, Joseph. <u>Faulkner: A Biography</u>. 2 vols. New York: Random, 1974.

**Citing a Work by Title**   If you are citing a source for which no author is named, use an abbreviated version of the title—or the whole title, if it is short—either in the text citation or in a parenthetical reference. If you abbreviate the title, be sure to begin with the work by which the source is alphabetized in the list of cited works.

> The recent exhibit of nineteenth-century patent models at the Cooper-Hewitt Museum featured plans for such inventions as the Rotating Blast-Producing Chair, an Improved, Creeping Doll, and the Life Preserving Coffin: In Doubtful Cases of Actual Death ("Notes").

Notice that page numbers are omitted from the parenthetical reference when a one-page article is cited.

WORKS CITED

"Notes and Comments: The Talk of the Town." <u>New Yorker</u>
16 July 1984: 23.

**Citing an Illustration**   Place the illustrative material as close as possible to the part of the text it illustrates. The illustration—a photograph, advertisement, map, drawing, or graph—should be labeled "Figure" (often abbreviated "Fig."), assigned an Arabic number, and, if appropriate, given a caption and complete citation. In your text, use a parenthetical reference to guide the reader to the illustration: "(see Fig. 1)." Place all necessary information below the illustration:

Fig. 1. "Your Gateway to Tomorrow." Advertisement.
<u>Money</u> Mar. 1983: 1-2.

**Citing Literary Works**   Because some literary works—novels, plays, poems—are available in several editions, MLA recommends that you give more information than just a page number so that readers who are not using the same edition as you are can locate in their books the passage you are citing. After the page number, add a semicolon and other appropriate information, using lowercase abbreviations such as *pt., sec.,* and *ch.* (for *part, section,* and *chapter*).

Although Flaubert sees Madame Bovary for what she
is—a silly, romantic woman—he insists that "none of
us can ever express the exact measure of his needs or
his thoughts or his sorrows" and that all of us "long
to make music that will melt the stars" (216; pt. 2,
ch. 12).

WORKS CITED

Flaubert, Gustave. <u>Madame Bovary: Patterns of Provin-
cial Life</u>. Trans. Francis Steegmuller. New York:
Random-Modern Library, 1957.

When you cite classic verse plays and poems, omit all page numbers and document by division(s) and line(s), using periods to separate the various numbers. You can also use appropriate abbreviations to designate certain well-known words. For example, "*Od.* 8.326" refers to book 8, line 326, of Homer's *Odyssey*. Do not use the abbreviations "l" or "ll" to designate lines because they can be confused with numbers. Once you have established in your text which numbers indicate lines, you may omit the words *line* and *lines* and simply use the numbers.

Also, as shown in the *Odyssey* citation just given, use Arabic numbers rather than Roman numerals for division and page numbers. Some teachers prefer Roman numerals for designating acts and scenes in plays (for example, "*Mac.* III.iv"), but if your instructor does not insist on them, use Arabic numbers: "*Mac.* 3.4."

**Citing More Than One Work in a Single Parenthetical Reference**   If you need to mention two or more works in a single parenthetical reference, document each reference according to the normal pattern, and use semicolons to separate the citations.

```
(Oleson 59; Trimble 85; Hylton 63)
```

WORKS CITED

```
Hylton, Marion Willard. "On the Trail of Pollen:
    Momaday's House Made of Dawn." Critique 14.2 (1972):
    60-69.
Oleson, Carole. "The Remembered Earth: Momaday's House
    Made of Dawn." South Dakota Review 2 (1973): 59-78.
Trimble, Martha Scott. N. Scott Momaday. Western
    Writers Series. Boise, ID: Boise State College,
    1973.
```

Although the MLA style provides this procedure for documenting multiple citations within parenthetical references, that kind of documentation is often the result of "scholarly" padding and may be disruptive for readers. If multiple citations are absolutely necessary, MLA recommends that they be placed in a bibliographical endnote or footnote.

## Using Notes with Parenthetical References

A *superscript numeral* (a number raised above the line) placed at an appropriate place in the text—usually at the end of a sentence—signals a note. The note itself, identified by a matching number, may appear at the end of the text (as an endnote) or at the bottom of the page on which its superscript appears (as a footnote).

In MLA style, notes (preferably endnotes) are reserved for two specific purposes.

## Notes Containing Additional Commentary

```
    Thurber's reputation continued to grow until the
1950s, when he was forced to give up drawing because of
his blindness.[1]
```

```
    [1]Thurber's older brother accidentally shot him in
the eye with an arrow when they were children, causing
the immediate loss of that eye. He gradually lost the
sight of the other eye because of complications from
the accident and a cataract.
```

## Notes Listing or Evaluating Sources or Referring to Additional Sources

> The argument that American policy in Vietnam was on the whole morally justified has come under attack from many quarters.[2]

> [2]For a useful sampling of opinion, see Buckley 20; Draper 32; Nardin and Slater 437.

Notice that the sources cited in note 2 are documented like parenthetical references. Complete citations would be given in the works-cited list.

WORKS CITED

Buckley, Kevin. "Vietnam: The Defense Case." <u>New York Times</u> 7 Dec. 1978: 19–24.

Draper, Theodore. "Ghosts of Vietnam." <u>Dissent</u> 26 (1979): 30–41.

Nardin, Terry, and Jerome Slater. "Vietnam Revisited." <u>World Politics</u> 33 (1981): 436–48.

## Listing Sources: Sample Entries

In the MLA documentation style readers can locate complete information about your sources in a list of cited works. The list goes at the end of your paper and, as its title, "Works Cited," suggests, contains only the sources you have *cited* in your paper. Occasionally, your instructor may require a list of the works you *consulted*. Such a list would include not only the sources you cited in your paper but also the sources you consulted while conducting your research. (If you have questions about the kind of list you are to prepare, ask your instructor.)

Even though the list of cited works appears at the end of your paper, you must compile it *before* you begin writing. The bibliographic information on your sources cards will eventually constitute your works-cited list. In order to create the list, you must alphabetize your sources, being careful that each entry is complete according to the appropriate format. As you write, you may need to add or delete sources. Be sure to identify your sources clearly and accurately in your text and to provide complete bibliographic information about each source in your list of cited works.

When you type your final list, adhere to the instructions that follow. For an illustration of this format, see Erin's works-cited list on page 393.

1. Paginate the works-cited list as a continuation of your text. If the conclusion of your paper appears on page 9, begin your list on page 10, unless there is an intervening page of endnotes.

● A WRITER'S RESOURCES

Check <http://www.noodletools.com> for an interactive website that enables you to generate, edit, and print MLA and APA source lists for your works-cited page.

2. List all entries in alphabetical order according to the last name of the author.

3. Double-space between successive lines of an entry *and* between entries.

4. After the first line of an entry, indent successive lines five spaces or one-half inch.

5. If you are listing more than one work by the same author, alphabetize the works according to title (excluding any initial articles—*a, an, the*). Instead of repeating the author's name with each citation, for the second and additional works, type three hyphens and a period or a long underscore, skip a space, and then give the title:

```
Lanham, Richard A. Literacy and the Survival of Human-
    ism. New Haven: Yale, 1983.
- - -. Style: An Anti-Textbook. New Haven: Yale,
    1974.
```

The form of each entry in your works-cited list will vary according to the type of source you are citing. The major variations are illustrated next. If you need additional information, consult the *MLA Handbook for Writers of Research Papers, Sixth Edition.*

## Books

Citations for books have three main parts—author, title, and facts of publication. Separate each part with a period followed by one space. (The first sample entry is described completely; significant variations in subsequent entries are noted in marginal annotations.)

### A Book by a Single Author or Agency

```
Tuchman, Barbara W. A Distant Mirror: The Calamitous
    Fourteenth Century. New York: Knopf, 1978.
```

▷ The author's last name comes before the given name or initial to facilitate alphabetizing. Use the name exactly as it appears on the title page of the source.

▷ If the book is the work of an agency (committee, organization, or department) instead of an individual, the name of the agency takes the place of the author's name.

▷ If no author or agency is given, the citation begins with and is alphabetized by the title of the source.

▷ The title and subtitle of the book are underlined.

▷ The place of publication, the publisher, and the date of publication are named in that order and are punctuated and spaced as in the preceding Tuchman citation. A colon separates the place of publication from the name of the publishing company, and a comma separates the publisher's name from the date.

▶ If more than one place of publication is given on the title page, mention only the first.

▶ If the place of publication might be unfamiliar or unclear to your readers, add an abbreviation identifying the appropriate state or country: Cambridge, MA.

▶ Shorten the publisher's name if the shortened form is easily identifiable: *Houghton Mifflin* can be shortened to *Houghton*; *Harvard University Press*, to *Harvard UP*.

▶ When you cannot locate one or more pieces of information concerning the facts of publication, use these abbreviations in the appropriate positions:

No place:       n.p.
No publisher:   n.p.
No date:        n.d.

### A Book by Two or Three Authors

Smith, Michael W., and Jeffrey D. Wilhelm. "Reading
    Don't Fix No Chevys": Literacy in the Lives of Young
    Men. Portsmouth: Heinemann, 2002.
Booth, Wayne C., Gregory G. Colomb, and Joseph M.
    Williams. The Craft of Research, 2nd ed. Chicago:
    U Chicago P, 2003.

### A Book by More Than Three authors

Belenky, Mary Field, et al. Women's Ways of Knowing:
    The Development of Self, Voice and Mind. New York:
    Basic, 1986.

### A Book with an Editor

Jackson, Kenneth T., ed. The Encyclopedia of New York
    City. New Haven: Yale UP, 1995.

### A Book with an Author and an Editor

Emphasis on author
Ginsberg, Allen. Journals: Early Fifties, Early
    Sixties. Ed. Gordon Ball. New York: Grove,
    1977.

Emphasis on editor
Ball, Gordon, ed. Journals: Early Fifties, Early
    Sixties. By Allen Ginsberg. New York: Grove,
    1977.

## Works in an Anthology

Tyler, Anne. "Still Just Writing." <u>The Writer on Her Work</u>. Ed. Janet Sternberg. New York: Norton, 1980, 3-16.

Sternberg, Janet, ed. <u>The Writer on Her Work</u>. New York: Norton, 1980.

Walker, Alice. "One Child of One's Own: A Meaningful Digression within the Works." Sternberg 121-40.

Walker, Margaret. "On Being Female, Black, and Free." Sternberg 95-106.

## An Article in an Alphabetically Arranged Reference Book

Hayward, Jane. "Stained Glass." <u>Encyclopedia Americana</u> 2002 ed.

## A Multivolume Work

Blotner, Joseph. <u>Faulkner: A Biography</u>. 2 vols. New York: Random, 1974.

Blotner, Joseph. <u>Faulkner: A Biography</u>. Vol. 2. New York: Random, 1974.

## An Edition Other Than the First

Chaucer, Geoffrey. <u>The Riverside Chaucer</u>. Ed. Larry Benson. 3rd ed. Boston: Houghton, 1987.

## An Introduction, Preface, Foreword, or Afterword

Bernstein, Carl. Afterword. <u>Poison Penmanship: The Gentle Art of Muckraking</u>. By Jessica Mitford. New York: Random, 1979. 275-77.

## A Book in a Series

McClave, Heather, ed. <u>Women Writers of the Short Story: Twentieth-Century Views</u>. Englewood Cliffs: Spectrum-Prentice, 1980.

## A Book with a Title Usually Italicized in Its Title

Habich, Robert. D. <u>Transcendentalism and the Western Messenger: A History of the Magazine and Its Contributors, 1835-1841</u>. Rutherford: Farleigh Dickinson UP, 1985.

## A Republished Book

Malamud, Bernard. <u>The Natural</u>. 1952. New York: Avon, 1980.

Griggs, John, ed. <u>AIDS: Public Policy Dimensions. Proc. of a conference. 16–17 Jan. 1986</u>. New York: United Hospital Fund of New York, 1987.

### A Translation

Mâle, Émile. <u>Chartres</u>. Trans. Sara Wilson. New York: Harper, 1983.

### A Book with a Title Usually Italicized in Its Title

Miller, James E., Jr. <u>A Critical Guide to</u> Leaves of Grass. Chicago: U of Chicago P, 1957.

## Articles

Citations for articles in periodicals, like citations for books, contain three parts: author, title, and facts of publication. But articles include more complicated facts of publication such as the periodical title, the volume number, year of publication, and inclusive page numbers. You can usually find this information on the first page of the article and on the cover or title page of the periodical. The first entry is discussed completely; significant variations in subsequent entries are noted in marginal annotations.

Hesse, Douglas. "The Place of Creative Nonfiction." <u>College English</u> 65 (2003):237–41.

▶ Cite author (last name first).

▶ Place title of article within quotation marks.

▶ Underline title of periodical.

▶ Place volume number after title of periodical.

▶ Enclose year of publication within parentheses.

▶ Use colon to separate date of periodical from inclusive page numbers of article.

▶ If a periodical pages its issues continuously through an annual volume, as does *College English*, give only the volume number, not the issue number.

### An Article in a Journal That Pages Each Issue Separately or Uses Only Issue Numbers

Seely, Bruce. "The Saga of American Infrastructure: A Republic Bound Together." <u>Wilson Quarterly</u> 17.1 (1993): 19–39.

## An Article from a Monthly or Bimonthly Periodical

Theilheimer, Rachel. "How Publishing Can Be More Than Not Perishing." <u>Change</u> Mar./Apr. 2003: 49-53.

## An Article from a Weekly or Biweekly Periodical

Sedaris, David. "Who's the Chef?" <u>New Yorker</u> 10 Mar. 2003: 40-41.

## An Article Whose Title Contains a Quotation or a Title within Quotation Marks

Decuir, Andre L. "Italy, England and the Female Artist in George Eliot's 'Mr. Gilfil's Love-Story.'" <u>Studies In Short Fiction</u> 29 (1992): 67-75.

## An Article from a Daily Newspaper

Article with byline

Whited, Charles. "The Priceless Treasure of the Marquesas." <u>Miami Herald</u> 15 July 1973: 1.

Separately paginated sections

"Culture Shock: Williamsburg and Disney World, Back to Back." <u>New York Times</u> 21 Sept. 1975, sec. 10: 1.

Newspaper title that does not include city name

"Oliver North Faces Congress." <u>Union Star</u> [Schenectady, NY] 7 July 1987: 1.

## An Editorial, Letter to the Editor, or Review

"From Good News to Bad." Editorial. <u>Washington Post</u> 16 July 1984: 10.

Coldwater, Charles F., MD. Letter. <u>The Muncie Star</u> 17 June 1987: 4.

DeCurtis, Anthony, "Bob Dylan's Blue Highways." Rev. of <u>The Bootleg Series, Volumes 1-3 (Rare and Unreleased), 1961-1991,</u> by Bob Dylan. <u>Rolling Stone</u> 4 April 1991: 53-55.

Griswold, Charles L., Jr. "Soul Food." Rev. of <u>Statecraft as Soulcraft: What Government Does,</u> by George F. Will. <u>American Scholar</u> 53 (1984): 401-6.

## An Article Whose Title Contains a Quotation or a Title within Quotation Marks

Carpenter, Lynette. "The Daring Gift in Ellen Glasgow's 'Dare's Gift.'" <u>Studies in Short Fiction</u> 21 (1984): 95-102.

## An Abstract from Dissertation Abstracts (DA) or Dissertation Abstracts International (DAI)

Creek, Mardena Bridges. "Myth, Wound, Accommodation: American Literary Response to the War in Vietnam." Diss. Ball State U, 1982. <u>DAI</u> 43 (1982): 3593A.

## Electronic Sources

MLA style for electronic sources resembles the MLA format for books and periodicals in every respect except for including the user's date of access and the electronic address. The best way to confirm the accuracy of your citations is to click "Documenting Sources from the World Wide Web" on the "MLA Style" section of the MLA website (<http://www.mla.org>).

### A Professional Site

Date of publication

MLA Style. 4 Apr. 2002. Modern Language Association of America. 26 Mar. 2003 <http://www.mla.org>.

Date of access

### A Personal Site

Hawisher, Gail. Home page. University of Illinois Urbana-Champaign. 26 Mar. 2003. <http://www.english. uiuc.edu/facpages/Hawisher.htm>.

### A Book

Conrad, Joseph. Lord Jim. London Blackwoods, 1900. Oxford Text Archive. 12 July 1993. Oxford University Computing Services. 20 Feb. 1998 <ftp://ota.ox.ac. uk/pub/ota/english/conrad/lordjim.1824>.

### A Poem

Roethke, Theodore. "My Papa' Waltz," Favorite Poem Project. 5 May 2003. <http://www.favoritepoem.org/ poems/roethke/waltz/html>.

### An Article in a Reference Database

"Women in American History," Britannica Online Vers. 98.1.1.Nov. 1997. Encyclopaedia Britannica. 10 Mar. 1998 <http://www.britannica.com>.

### An Article in a Journal

Bieder, Robert A. "The Representation of Indian Bodies in Nineteenth-Century American Anthropology." The American Indian Quarterly 20.2 (1996). 28 Mar. 1998 <http://www/uoknor.edu/aiq/aiq202.html#beider>.

### An Article in a Magazine

Levine, Judith. "I Surf, Therefore I am." Salon 29 July 1997. 9 Dec. 1997 <http://www.salonmagazine.com/ July97/mothers/surfing.970729.html>.

### A Review

> Roth, Martha. "A Tantalizing Remoteness." Rev. of <u>Jane
> Austen: A Biography</u>, by Claire Tomalin. <u>Hungry
> Mind Review</u> Winter 1997. 10 Mar. 1998 <http://www.
> bookwire.com/HMR/nonfiction/read.review$5376>.

### A Posting to a Discussion Group

> Inman, James. "Re: Technologist." Online posting. 24
> Sept. 1997. Alliance for Computers in Writing. 27
> Mar. 1998 <acw-1@unicorn.acs.ttu.edu>.

### A Personal E-Mail Message

> Penning, Sarah. "Mentor Advice." E-mail to Rai Peter-
> son. 6 May 1995.

### CD-ROM: Periodical Publication with Printed Source or Printed Analogue

> West, Cornel. "The Dilemma of the Black Intellectual."
> <u>Critical Quarterly</u> 29 (1987): 39-52. <u>MLA Interna-
> tional Bibliography</u>. CD-ROM. Silver Platter. Feb.
> 1995.

### CD-ROM: Nonperiodical Publication

> <u>Cinemania 97</u>. CD-ROM. Redmond: Microsoft, 1996.

### CD-ROM: A Work in More Than One Electronic Medium

> <u>Mozart</u>. CD-ROM. Laser disk. Union City, CA: Ebook,
> 1992.

## Other Sources

The particular treatment of sources other than books and articles
depends on what information is available and what information needs
to be included to enable readers to locate the material.

### Government Document

> United States. Cong. House Committee on the Judiciary.
> <u>Immigration and Nationality Act with Amendments and
> Notes on Related Laws</u>. 7th ed. Washington: GPO,
> 1980.

### A Film or a Radio or Television Program

> <u>Chicago</u>. Dir. Rob Marshall. With Renee Zellweger,
> Catherine Zeta-Jones, Richard Gere. Miramax, 2002.

"If God Ever Listened: A Portrait of Alice Walker."
_Horizons_. Prod. Jane Rosenthal. Natl. Public Radio.
WBST, Muncie. 3 Mar. 1984.
"The Hero's Adventure." _Moyers: Joseph Campbell and the
Power of Myth_. Prod. Catherine Tatge. PBS. WNET, New
York. 23 May 1988.

### A Performance

_The Producers_. By Mel Brooks. Dir. Susan Stroman. With
Nathan Lane and Mathew Broderick. St. James Theater.
8 Oct. 2002.
Ozawa, Seiji, cond. Boston Symphony Orch. Concert. Symphony Hall, Boston. 30 Sept. 1988.

### A Sound Recording

Mozart, Wolfgang A. _Cosi Fan Tutte_. Perf. Kiri Te
Kanawa, Frederica von Stade, David Rendall, and
Philippe Huttenlocher. Strasbourg Philharmonic Orch.
Cond. Alain Lombard. LP. RCA, 1978.
Jones, Norah. _Come Away with Me_. Blue Note, 2002.

### A Work of Art

Botticelli, Sandro. _Giuliano de' Medici_. Samuel H.
Kress Collection. National Gallery of Art, Washing-
ton.
Rodin, Auguste. _The Gate of Hell_. Rodin Museum, Paris.

### A Map or Chart

_Sonoma and Napa Counties_. Map. San Francisco: California State Automobile Assn., 1984.

### A Published or Unpublished Letter

Fitzgerald, F. Scott. "To Ernest Hemingway." 1 June
1934. _The Letters of F. Scott Fitzgerald_. Ed. Andrew
Turnbull. New York: Scribner's, 1963. 308-10.
Stowe, Harriet Beecher. Letter to George Eliot. 25 May
1869. Berg Collection. New York Public Lib., New
York.

### A Published or Unpublished Interview

Ellison, Ralph. "Indivisible Man." Interview with James
Alan McPherson. _Atlantic_ Dec. 1970: 45-60.
McPhee, John. Personal interview. 4 Nov. 1986.

# Designing the Final Draft (MLA Style)

When you type the final draft of your research paper, follow these general guidelines:

1. Use white, 20-pound bond, 8½" × 11" paper.

2. Choose an appropriate type size and font style.

3. Double-space the text throughout—*including* quotations, notes, and the works-cited list.

4. Maintain margins of one inch at the top and the bottom and on both sides of each page.

5. Indent five spaces or one-half inch at the beginning of each paragraph.

6. Leave one space after periods and other terminal marks of punctuation.

7. Leave one space after commas and other internal marks of punctuation.

8. Do not supply a title page. Instead (unless your instructor has given you other instructions for setting up your cover page), type your name, your instructor's name, the course title, and the date on separate lines (double-spacing between lines) in the upper-left corner of the first page.

9. Double-space after the date and center the title of your paper. Double-space again and begin the first paragraph, indenting it five spaces or one-half inch from the left margin.

10. Number the pages of your manuscript consecutively. Type your last name and the page number in the upper-right corner, one-half inch from the top and flush with the one-inch right margin.

11. A formal outline, if required, should be attached to the front of the paper. Use topics or full sentences consistently, and follow the outline formats discussed in Chapter 3. Type the title of your paper at the top of the first page of the outline; then type your thesis, double-spaced below the title. Do not list your introduction or conclusion in your outline.

12. Label any illustrations. Double-space below the figure, and align the caption with the left side of the figure.

When you have finished typing, proofread every page carefully—including the title page, the formal outline, captions, endnotes, and the works-cited list. Save or make a photocopy of your paper. If your instructor asked you to hand in your notes with your paper, arrange them in a logical order and place them in an envelope.

# Writing your research paper on your computer

Writing your research paper on your computer makes the whole task more efficient. Print out from your database the subdivisions you have created. Arrange them in various patterns to create a preliminary outline. Then determine what each outline will allow you to prove. If you have difficulty constructing a thesis, read back through the notes in your database to see if some of your comments and questions will point you toward a working hypothesis that you can use to start a draft.

Before you begin drafting, set up your format (margins, line-spacing, and so on) according to the guidelines just listed. Then begin working your way through your outline, drafting each division of your paper. Examine the sources you want to use to support your argument. Determine what method for integrating them into your text is most effective. Sometimes you may want to focus on the key information in a source and incorporate it into your text (paraphrase) so that it does not interrupt your readers' train of thought. Other times, you may want to dramatize your citation by setting it off (block quotation) so that your readers understand its significance. Try to vary these strategies so that your readers follow *your* argument.

Use the various features of your word-processing program to create an attractive and effective text. Some software systems have both MLA and APA systems installed. If yours doesn't, you can construct the system you need by working with the various field divisions of your sort system. Transfer your bibliographic entries from your database into a works-cited file; your sort feature can help you accomplish this task. Then use your spellchecker to proofread your paper for spelling errors. Also proofread your paper yourself to make sure that your program did not miss words or constructions that it does not recognize. Then save your paper on a backup disk, label it, and store it in a safe place: You may need additional copies for your class, or you may want to revise it for the writing portfolio you submit for graduation or employment. Finally, print your paper and place it in an appropriate binder.

Computer networks also provide a convenient way to send your research paper—in preliminary or final draft—to your writing group or your teacher. They can respond to your text—pointing out places where you need better information, better sentences, or more precise documentation.

Some colleges and universities require students to create an electronic portfolio. This site will become an electronic résumé that lists all your accomplishments. You can add or delete papers you write throughout your college career at this site. Like Erin, you may decide to place the research paper you completed in your composition class in your electronic portfolio.

## Sample Student Research Paper

Reading the final draft of Erin McMullen's research paper will teach you many valuable lessons. You will see that an informed writer can make any subject, however unfamiliar, significant and interesting. You will see how a carefully crafted essay evolved from the writer's earlier complex and confusing attempts to discover a subject, audience, and purpose. And you will see how Erin uses the specific techniques of analyzing, quoting, and documenting sources to advance her purpose. Consider, too, as you read, how Erin positions her argument in relation to the two sides of the controversy.

Erin McMullen

English 104

Mr. Johnson

10 April 2003

THE POSSIBILITIES AND LIMITATIONS OF ONLINE LEARNING

<u>Thesis</u>: Although online degrees are convenient, they cannot replicate many of the benefits of traditional, on-campus degrees.

I.     Online education is increasing.

    A. Online learning is convenient.

    B. Traditional universities offer professional online degrees.

    C. Commercial organizations offer practical online degrees.

II.    Online education has limitations.

    A. Online learning is more expensive.

    B. Online learning systems have difficulty providing financial aid.

    C. Online learning systems provide no student services.

III.   Online education has possibilities.

    A. Online education allows students to focus on learning.

    B. Online education enables students to participate at their convenience.

C. Online education provides students with a comfortable setting for learning.

IV.    Online courses have defects.

    A. Faculty misses visual cues from students that enrich teaching.

    B. Student isolation leads to dropping out.

V.    Online courses have benefits.

    A. Online courses are designed for practical purposes.

    B. Online courses lead to jobs and promotions.

VI.    On-campus courses have benefits.

    A. On-campus courses are designed for face-to-face learning.

    B. On-campus courses provide a clearer connection between course content and instruction.

    C. Online "all star" faculty claims are deceptive.

VII.    What is the value of mixing online and on-campus learning?

    A. Online learning promotes access to education.

    B. On-campus learning promotes better relationships with classmates and instructors.

    C. Students (customers) can help shape the design of online and on-campus learning.

Double-space every line.

Indent paragraphs five spaces.

THE POSSIBILITIES AND LIMITATIONS OF ONLINE LEARNING

Getting a college degree means spending countless hours in countless classrooms, trudging across campus in winter, and strolling through it in spring. Right? Not always, thanks to the Internet and a recent increase in the number of online universities that offer a variety of degrees—without your having to set foot inside a classroom. Online degrees are both attractive and dangerous, and profiles of online students depict both aspects. For example, Will Davies is an oil-field service coordinator who has relocated internationally thirteen times in fifteen years. Someone so mobile could not be expected to complete an M.B.A. at a traditional university and still maintain his career. Completing his degree online allowed Davies

Short quotation: A quotation embedded in a quotation

"to gain a business education from anywhere in the world—in a method that's convenient for [him] and allows [him] to continue with [his] career" (Davies qtd. in McClenahen 20). Margaret Chester wanted to earn a Ph.D. in health and human services while working, raising a family, and tending a farm in Hawaii. Chester found an online degree program that matched the convenience of Davies's program, but Chester never received a legitimate degree. After experiencing communication problems with the university, Chester discovered that

Paraphrase: A source para-phrased with author and pages placed within parentheses

it had been operating without state approval while claiming to offer legitimate degrees (Mannix 68).

Online universities offer a convenient and career-specific alternative to the traditional degrees granted by brick-and-mortar institutions, and they usually attract professionals and adult learners with families who desire advanced degrees in their fields. However, buyer beware: online degrees are convenient for many professionals and adult learners, but they cannot replicate the benefits of traditional universities such as student services, multidimensional instructor-student communication, and a real, not virtual, student community.

From what kinds of institutions can a student pursue an online degree? Virtual universities, hubs of learning that exist completely on the Internet, provide online degrees to students who never set foot on a campus or in a classroom. In addition, traditional universities such as the University of California at Berkeley, the University of Michigan, Ohio State University, and Duke University have begun to create their own online degrees. And finally, some universities have teamed up with for-profit online organizations to create degree programs culled from courses at a variety of universities and managed by the for-profit organization. For example, Unext.com has created Cardean

Documentation: Information from two sources summarized with authors and pages placed within parentheses

University by blending course material and syllabi from Columbia University, Stanford University, the University of Chicago, Carnegie-Mellon, and the London School of Economics (Clayton 15; Carr A50).

No matter what kind of institution a student selects to provide his or her online education, online courses on the whole are increasingly popular. In fact, International Data Corporation, a respected research firm in Framingham, Massachusetts, claimed that in 2002, 2.2 million students would be enrolled in online courses, a number significantly higher than the 710,000 online students enrolled in 1998 (Clayton 15). Students gravitate to online learning because of the convenience of asynchronous learning. This style of education assumes that the students and instructor will not participate in the class at the same time, but the variety of schedules is not seen as a hindrance. On the contrary, students working toward online degrees usually choose courses that allow them to work asynchronously so that they can go to class when it is convenient for

Paraphrase: A source paraphrased with author and page placed within parentheses

them (Willis 119). Asynchronous learning also allows students to "go to class" from any location in the world—as long as they can access the Internet.

Although online students benefit from asynchronous communication, they find that campus life and its accompanying student benefits are missing from online programs and universities. Online classes are oftentimes more expensive than traditional ones—Duke University's online Global Executive M.B.A. costs $85,000 (Mangan A27)—and less financial aid is available to students. Taking online courses through a brick-and-mortar university does not necessarily qualify students for traditional forms of financial aid (teaching assistantships and fellowships) for graduate work (Hartigan 6). The nature of completely online universities, such as Jones International University and the University of Phoenix, has impeded their abilities to make government subsidized funding and grants available to their students (http://www.jonesinternation.edu). Students in a traditional university also benefit from a physical space in which they can solve problems that arise with funding, course work, instructors, and billing procedures. Online universities do not have corresponding student service components that can compete with the efficiency and convenience of on-site help offered at a traditional university (Shea 55).

In spite of online education's lack of student services and financial aid, many adult learners who have completed online degrees welcome the virtual environment. In a virtual classroom, they do not have to worry about negotiating the aspects of college for which they may care very little, such as sporting events and social occasions that are geared toward eighteen- to twenty-two-year-olds. In an online environment, adult learners can focus completely on their course work, and the chat-room environment is a more comfortable means of communication if they find face-to-face communication threatening. Additionally, students have found the online discussions to be more fruitful than traditional classroom discussions in which, "if you don't know the answer, you can hunker down and hope the professor doesn't call on you" (Tapley qtd. in Mangan A27). As this online student explained, in the chat-room environment, where there will be a printed-out record of who participated in discussion, students feel a greater responsibility to participate consistently and thoughtfully than they might feel in a traditional classroom. Students for whom English is a second language can also benefit from the chat-room system. If those students are not confident about their communication skills in English, sending written communications in an asynchronous environment allows them more time to prepare a remark than they would have if they were participating in a classroom discussion. Online programs foster a more comfortable communication environment, but these programs can also demand a higher level of accountability than courses taught in traditional classrooms.

Online universities and degree programs do offer the ease of communicating in a virtual, equalizing environment, but the nuances in communication that often drive a course's direction and speed are missing from an online class centered around e-mail and chat-room communication. In his <u>Distance Education: A Practical Guide</u>, Barry Willis comments on the importance of face-to-face interaction:

Long quotation: A quotation of more than four lines indented ten spaces and not placed within quotation marks

> effective classroom teachers rely on a number of visual and unobtrusive cues and clues from their students. A quick glance ... reveals who is attentively taking notes, pondering a difficult concept, or enthusiastically preparing to make a comment.... the delivery of information, and often the course content itself, is adapted to meet the unique characteristics and needs of the class. (6)

The communication techniques used in online courses do not provide a rich array of visual cues from which instructors can effectively shape their course

content and direction. The amount of online communication, or lack of it, can also be a problem. In fact,
many students drop out of their online courses because
there is not enough communication, a situation that
leaves them feeling disconnected and lost in work that
should be supported by group discussion. Programs with
courses that suffer from this communication problem
claim that 60 percent of their students drop out of the
courses before completion (Shea 46). Online courses
can reduce this drop-out rate through improved communication, but they cannot replicate the nuances and
dimensions available in classroom communication.

Online courses offer more than convenience and
comfort; they are often specifically designed on the
basis of recommendations or requests from corporations.
This means that online students can take courses that
can provide them with present, direct, and immediate
professional application. Most online students are
twenty-five or older with at least a few years of
working experience in their professions, so the lure to
earn a degree tailored to help them pursue promotion in
their field is very enticing. As Rachel Hartigan
writes, "Students are seeking master's degrees because
they have become the passport to entry-level jobs in

Documentation: Ellipsis points
used to indicate omission of
one or more words of the
quotation

many fields, or at least the key to moving up the ladder.... With business and technology seeping into nursing, education, science, public policy, and diplomacy, employees must learn new skills or risk being passed over" (6). Although these programs are infinitely valuable for some students, it is clear that many of them could not pursue an advanced degree that was not taught through the lens of business, technology, or education. Online degrees are a valuable and important innovation, but they are not for everyone. Those pursuing careers in business will benefit, but the liberal arts and sciences are generally left out of online degree programs and universities.

Students in all disciplines benefit from clear instructor and institution communication—something that online universities do not always offer. Students in traditional universities benefit from on-campus learning by having instructor support throughout a course—through e-mail, office hours, and class time. Students in brick-and-mortar universities know who provides them with information, generates class discussion, and grades their work because they physically see their instructors and teaching assistants in class. Online universities are murkier in this area. Jones

International University, the first online university to receive accreditation, claims an "all-star cast" of professors from top universities. As the university's website explains, "Courses are _designed by_ faculty and content experts from around the globe." The website goes on to claim that faculty come from twenty-five countries and from prestigious institutions such as the University of California at Berkeley, Columbia University, the London School of Economics, and Stanford University <http://www.jonesinternation.edu>, emphasis added). Although this sounds promising, a look through the names of faculty listed on the website shows that these "all-stars" do not actually teach JIU's courses. Students taking these all-star-designed courses through JIU do not interact with the academic experts who have created them. More than likely, they communicate with adjunct instructors, almost half of whom also teach classes at brick-and-mortar universities. Unclear associations between professors and course content can easily mislead students aspiring to study with those intellectual "all-stars" lauded on online university websites. Traditional universities benefit from a clearer connection between course content and instructor.

Documentation: A citation to an electronic address with an editorial comment on the source included within parentheses

The recent shift to online education, predominantly at the advanced degree level, has raised a plethora of new issues in higher education. Online degrees are more convenient for many students, with more direct relationships to their current professions or professions they are hoping to enter. Studies from the 1960s to the present, ending with one by University of North Carolina at Chapel Hill's Thomas Russell, have consistently concluded that students learn just as well in correspondence or online courses as they do in on-campus courses (Keegan 73; Willis 11; Shea 55).

However, online universities have not taken the place of traditional brick-and-mortar institutions. Fortunately, those pursuing degrees online can take advantage of a hybrid mix of traditional and online education. For example, the online M.B.A. program at Ohio University requires six weekend sessions and three one-week residencies, requirements that demand that online students come to campus and interact face to face with one another. The combination of on-campus and online education helps promote more effective team-building and a more developed relationship with one's classmates while also retaining the freedom and convenience that online courses offer. As Ohio University

Short quotation: A quotation
embedded within a quotation
professor John Stinson reflects, "It would be hard to learn how to give an effective presentation and do it all over the Web" (qtd. in McClenahen 20).

The online degree program has firmly established a new model for universities—the students are demanding consumers, and they have the freedom to shop around to find the best program for them, one that meets more of their requirements than any other program. Viewing students as consumers and the university as a business implies that universities will tailor their online programs to student demands and to the demands of companies that want their employees to be better informed in any area or skill of the company's choosing. The student population and the business world, not the faculty and administration, shape the kinds of classes and degrees offered online. This shift in higher education is more career- and consumer-driven and less concerned about learning for the sake of learning. Nevertheless, students with specific requirements that brick-and-mortar institutions cannot meet may find a haven in learning online.

WORKS CITED

Double-space every line.

Carr, Sara. "Closely Watched Unext Rolls Out Its First Courses." <u>Chronicle of Higher Education</u>. 12 May 2000: A50.

Clayton, Mark S. "Click 'n' Learn." <u>Christian Science Monitor</u>. 15 Aug. 2000: 15.

Hartigan, Rachel. "Smart New Degrees Take Center Stage." <u>U.S. News and World Report</u> 2002 Special Issue Graduate Schools: 6–10.

Sample entry: Electronic website

<http://www.jonesinternation.edu>. 1 April 2002.

Keegan, Desmond. <u>Distance Training: Taking Stock at a Time of Change</u>. London: Routledge Falmer, 2000.

McClenahen, John St. "http://www.mba.degree." 27 Feb. 2002. <u>Industry Week</u> 21 July 1997: 19–22.

Sample entry: An article in a periodical

Mangan, Katherine S. "Top Business Schools Seek to Ride a Bull Market in On-line MBAs." <u>Chronicle of Higher Education</u> 15 Jan. 1999: A27–A28.

Mannix, Margaret. "Buyers, Be Wary." <u>U.S. News and World Report</u> 15 Oct. 2001: 68–70.

Shea, Rachel Hartigan. "So Where's the Beef?" <u>U.S. News and Report</u> 15 Oct. 2001: 44–50.

Sample entry: A book by one author

Willis, Barry. <u>Distance Education: A Practical Guide.</u> Englewood Cliffs: Educational Technology Publications, 1993.

# Writing Assignments

### 1. NARRATE

Select one core subject—such as history, literature, science, or math—that you have taken several times during your educational career. In what ways did the material seem different each time you studied it? Compose a narrative that forces you to come to terms with that difference.

### 2. OBSERVE

Log on to a chat group devoted to one of your special interests—sports, film, food. Observe the conversations online. Then draft an essay about your observations for the "Sports," "Entertainment," or "Education" section of your local newspaper.

### 3. INVESTIGATE

Interview the people in your writing class who have considered or participated in online learning. Then write an article about the possibilities and limitations of such an education from the perspective of the students.

### 4. COLLABORATE

Organize other students to design a webpage for your writing class. Your purpose is to attract other writing classes around the country to join your chat group—to exchange ideas on how to find writing topics and refine writing style. Determine which students in your class have the appropriate skills—computer, graphic, sound, video—to design an attractive webpage; then design it and post it.

### 5. READ

Read sections of Barry Willis's *Distance Education: A Practical Guide*. Then speculate about why his teaching position at the University of Alaska may have influenced his analysis.

### 6. RESPOND

Respond to Desmond Keegan's assertion that "there is no significant difference between distance education and on-campus provision."

### 7. ANALYZE

Analyze the ways in which you and your writing teacher respond to each other during a writing conference. What visual cues are crucial to your communication?

### 8. EVALUATE

Evaluate the claims made on the websites of online universities about their "all-star" faculty. In what way would such faculty actually "teach" students?

### 9. ARGUE

Argue that you can create a more effective education by mixing online and on-campus courses. Make your argument specific to the possibilities in your major and the limitations on receiving credit for online courses from other universities in your school's curriculum.

### 10. ARGUE

Argue that even though you live on campus, you should be allowed to take your own university's distance learning courses. Make your argument specific to your major and to your school and work schedule.

# Readings with a Purpose

Writing
Strategies

14

# Writing Strategies

**14**

EACH OF THESE STRATEGIES WORKS LIKE THE DIFFERENT
LENSES YOU ATTACH TO YOUR CAMERA: EACH LENS GIVES
YOU A SLIGHTLY DIFFERENT WAY TO FRAME YOUR SUBJECT.

In Part Four you will study seven common strategies writers use
to select their subject, analyze their audience, and determine
their purpose. Most of this material should seem familiar. You
have already examined how these strategies evolve through the
writing process (Part One) and give structure to the expression
of ideas (Part Two). You have also examined how these strategies
emerge in the work of the student and professional writers featured in and at the end of previous chapters. Indeed, you may
have experimented with one or more of these strategies as you
planned, drafted, and revised your writing assignments. But the
collection of essays in this part places these strategies in a new
context, giving you the opportunity to learn more about how
their special features enable you to write with a purpose.

You will notice that the order of the seven strategies in this
part is the same as it was in Chapters 6 and 7, and corresponds
roughly to the order of the writing assignments at the end of each
chapter:

1. Narration and Description
2. Process Analysis
3. Comparison and Contrast
4. Division and Classification
5. Definition
6. Causal Analysis
7. Argument

In the earlier sections of this book, you were given examples to encourage you to see these strategies as ways to *develop* your writing. For example, you saw that Jane Graham used the first six strategies to discover what she observed on her whale watch and that Jon Seidel used the seventh strategy to generate information for his argument on the military and the media. Each of these strategies works like the different lenses you attach to your camera: each lens gives you a slightly different way to frame your subject.

To assist you in this project, each strategy is presented in the same format. The introduction begins with general observations about choosing your subject, audience, and purpose and ends with specific advice about using various features of the strategy effectively. The student essay (complete with annotations) and the professional essay (followed by questions) illustrate the use of those features. "A Sampler of Other Essays" refers you to additional readings in this book that illustrate the same strategy. Part Four concludes with writing assignments, each of which invites you to organize your writing using one of the strategies.

## Strategy One: *Narration and Description*

### Selecting Your Subject

Any experience can be narrated and described. In *narration,* you tell a story to make a point; in *description,* you create a picture to evoke the senses. You can select either strategy for a subject, but you will discover that most subjects require you to use them in combination. The best place to look for a subject is your own experience: You can always invent a subject or the details with which you describe it, but you will have more success writing about events and people you know. You will also have more success if you restrict your subject to manageable size—your first trip alone, your last argument with friends—and sort out what makes your story interesting and significant. What is the story in your story?

### Analyzing Your Audience

As you think about your essay, consider how much you need to tell your readers and how much you will need to show them. If you are writing from personal experience, few readers will know the story before you tell it. They may know similar stories or have had similar experiences, but they do not know your story. Because you can tell your story in so many different ways—adding or deleting material to fit your purpose—you need to decide how much information your readers need. Do they need to know every detail, only brief summaries of certain parts, or some mixture of detail and summary? You must also decide how much your readers already know and what they expect to learn. If your subject is familiar to most people (for example, working at a fast-food restaurant), your readers will need few technical details to understand your subject. But they will expect you to give them images and insights that create a fresh vision of your subject—for example, portraying the restaurant as a community center.

## Determining Your Purpose

You can use narration and description for two purposes. One, you can use them to introduce or illustrate a complicated subject: You might begin an analysis of the energy crisis by telling a story about wastefulness, or you might conclude an argument for gun control by providing a graphic description of a shooting incident. Two, you can use these strategies as the primary method for presenting or analyzing a topic. For example, you might devote an entire essay to recounting your experiences in a foreign country. Although your personal experience forms the core of your essay, your narrative purpose (what happened) and your descriptive purpose (what it looked or felt like) might be linked to larger purposes—for example, explaining how the experience altered your sense of cultural superiority.

## Using the Strategy

The key to writing effective narration and description is recognizing that an experience and an essay about that experience are not the same thing. To transform an experience into an essay, you must locate the central *conflict*. It may be a conflict between you and other people, you and the social or natural environment, or aspects of your personality.

Once you have identified the conflict, you must arrange the action so that your readers know how the conflict started, how it developed, and how it was resolved. This coherent sequence of events is called a *plot*. Sometimes you may want to arrange your plot so that it follows a simple chronological pattern, starting at the beginning and describing events as they occur. At other times, you may want to start your essay in the middle or near the end of the event you are describing. After you choose the beginning, middle, and end, you need to establish the *pace* of each section. Sometimes you can narrate events quickly by omitting details, compressing time, and summarizing experience. At other times you must pace events more slowly, adding small details, describing every movement, and using dialogue to render the experience as a fully realized scene.

You can make your scenes and summaries effective by the careful *selection of details*. Simply adding detail is not enough. You must choose those details that satisfy the needs of your reader and advance your purpose. Sometimes you will need to select *objective* or technical details to help your readers understand your subject. At other times you will want to select *subjective* or impressionistic details to appeal to your readers' senses. Occasionally, you may want to select details so that they form a *figurative image* or evoke a *dominant impression.*

Finally, you need to determine your *point of view.* Simply stated, point of view refers to the person and the position of the narrator (point) and the attitude expressed toward the narrative (view). You choose your *person* by deciding whether you want to tell your story in the first person ("I") or third person ("she" or "he"). Your *position* refers to how close you are to the action in time and space. You may be involved in the action or be viewing it as an observer. You may be telling about events as they are happening or many years after they have taken place. You create your attitude once you decide how you want to interpret the events you intend to present.

# Inside and Out

## LISA WIDENHOFER

**Introduction: Establish scene and point of view**

It was another gloomy day on my Christmas break. This particular after- 1
noon Mom and I settled down in the sewing room to search through a box
of old photographs taken from Grandma's house. So many things had been
taken from the house since she had moved into the nursing home that it was
hard to get excited about going through yet another box. In previous boxes
we had found junk jewelry, outgrown clothes, and little baubles purchased
on sale for some future Christmas.

**Plot: Introduce conflict**

This box, however, was different. Instead of sorting the pitchable objects 2
from the valuables, we were on a mission, of sorts. There was something specific that we hoped to find amidst the curling pictures of Christmases past
and New Year's Eve parties of long ago. We were looking for any photos from
Grandma and Grandpa's wedding. No one had ever seen any, not even my
father.

**Detail: Select details to advance plot**

Grandma's house always had a special wall dedicated to everyone's 3
wedding picture, everyone's except for Grandma and Grandpa's own. In all
of her trips down memory lane, Grandma never talked about her own
wedding. When my brother was married, my future sister-in-law's wedding
gown was the talk of the family. Yet no one ever talked about Grandma's
gown. And no one had really much thought about it. Until now. When we
had discovered the box full of old pictures, we hoped to find a wedding
picture. Mom now had a special wall of her own dedicated to wedding pictures. It displayed a photo of herself and Dad, my brother Gary and his wife
Marianne, Mom's parents, even her grandparents. But Dad's parents' picture
was conspicuously missing.

**Pace: Mix summary and scene**

The hours of the afternoon flew by. I shuffled through old black and 4
whites and stopped on occasion to laugh at pictures of my father as a lady-
killing six-year-old. Meanwhile, Mom stood up to get something out of the
closet, a surprise of some sort. She pulled out a black, plastic covered
hanging thing, a dress by the shape of it, and asked me to help her unwrap
it. "It's Grandma's," Mom told me. "It almost was thrown away. It was literally wadded up into a ball and jammed in some old newspapers. Your father
and I were cleaning out some junk from the attic at Grandma's house and
almost missed it hiding in the trash. We didn't even know Grandma still had
it." I stood, knees cracking from the hour of kneeling, and lifted the plastic
as Mom held the hanger. Sliding from beneath the bag was cream-colored
silk, wrinkled like an old woman's face.

It was my grandmother's wedding gown. A page torn from history, a 5 little dirty in places from newsprint and rusting snaps. But the cloth was still intact, not frayed or worn through. The dress was the most simple gown I had ever seen, but pretty in its own uncomplicated way. Even the cream color of the silk was soothing in its simplicity and held its color true. As Mom held the dress up to the light, I could see that there were tiny gathers along the neckline; long, slim sleeves; and a beautiful, wide train that hung almost four feet below the dress's hemline.

As I admired the gown, I remembered Mom telling me about her own 6 wedding dress. The dress Mom picked out for her wedding was not the one she wore. The dress she had chosen had been replaced by a different one, hand picked by an imitation of Cinderella's wicked stepmother, Mom's own stepmother. She didn't know or care what happened to that gown. My Mom's mom, gone from this world for far too many years, had no wedding gown of her own, either. Her wedding had been rushed in order to have it before World War II called my Grandpa to battle. This dress of my Dad's mother was the only wedding gown in our family.

"It still seems pretty well intact, probably even wearable if it was cleaned 7 and pressed carefully," Mom thought aloud. Her fingers glided over the silk, and she inspected the rusting snaps and hand-sewn seams with an expert eye. I returned to the box to look for a photograph even more diligently than before. I breezed by old family photos and pictures of Uncle Steve in his "difficult stage." And then, there at the bottom of the box sat two large photo savers.

"Check it out, Ma!" I called to Mom, and together we opened the binders 8 to find my grandparents on their wedding day. Grandma looked stunning. The gown hanging beside me seemed to have jumped from the picture itself. Grandma wore a long, gorgeous lace train hanging from the headpiece. It extended almost three feet past the silk train of the dress. She was so petite and young. Her arms held a full bouquet of flowers, and her big eyes were warm and deep.

And then there was Grandpa, looking dashing in his dark suit. I loved 9 him so very much, as I do still. It made my heart both happy and sad to see him so handsome, so alive. His long, thin face wore a warm smile, and his lean frame stood tall and proud. I felt that if I stared at the picture hard enough it would somehow give him back those fifty years to live again, to be with me. Gone for almost six years, however, Grandpa had passed on, and Grandma was very sick. They were both so very different from their picture now.

Grandma had moved from her house to Lutheran Home when her heart 10 muscle just couldn't take the strain of living alone anymore. Congestive heart failure had been tightening its grip on her. It seemed so odd to see the bustling, cooking, cleaning Grandma that I had always known sitting in the wheelchair waiting to go down to dinner. But somehow the discovery of the dress and the photos brought renewed life and energy where it had been once forgotten. I thought of Grandma sitting, slouched in her favorite chair brought over from the house. My memory saw her as she so often looked, framed in the open doorway of the home. I looked again at the wedding picture, her eyes full of youth and vitality, her face framed in the dark, cardboard picture trim. Different but somehow the same.

Plot: Introduce new complication

I sat lost in memories, clutching the dog-eared pictures tight while Mom 11 stood once again to examine the wedding gown. "It has held up pretty well," Mom said, as she held the dress at arm's length. Then she looked at me, kneeling there among the photos. "You know," she mused, "it might even fit you. Wanna try it on?"

Point of View: Present narrator's attitude

The thought seemed eerie. Even thinking that Grandma and I were ever 12 the same size or shape was a new idea. She sat in the home now, shoulders rounding from worry. She was also heavier now from the fluid that her heart just couldn't get rid of anymore. I looked again at the young woman in the photograph. She was so young, so alive, so real. It was a new experience to think of Grandma not only looking like I do now, but going through the same changes of growing up, through the same frustrations of being not quite a kid, but not quite a grownup either.

Pace: Focus on the details of the dress

I set down the picture, kicked off my tennis shoes and socks to reveal my 13 painted toenails, and carefully stepped into the silky folds of the dress. With deft fingers Mom buttoned up the small buttons, lined up the seams, and straightened the train behind me. And there I stood. I was not the only thing within the dress. It held Grandma, it held memories of a young couple's love, it held new discoveries and old truths. I stared at the sleeves that reached beyond where they should. My fingers glided over the silk, toying for a moment with the small newsprint stain that slightly dulled the otherwise shiny material.

I stared at my fingers peeking out of the material, imagining myself as 14 Grandma on her wedding day. Although the dress fit, the extra long sleeves reminded me that the dress was not mine, that I was still the granddaughter

Point of View: Establish narrator's position through Mother's dialogue

dressing up in her grandma's gown. "I can't get over how well it fits you. A little long in the sleeves and a tad big in length, but with heels even that isn't far off. And sleeves can be shortened." Mom was right. The gown fit me, and it was exciting but frightening as well. It was like stepping into the past and the future all at once, becoming aware of my family heritage, feeling it, breathing it as well. I discovered something new in me. Or maybe it was something very old, older than my years, finally surfacing in me.

Plot: Introduce new scene

Mom looked at me in silence for a moment. "We have to show Dad and 15 Gary. They're downstairs rummaging through the refrigerator." She snatched up the two photographs of Grandma and Grandpa and then helped me maneuver the train to the stairs and we began to descend, Mom leading the way. The stairs seemed longer than I had remembered. Each step was filled with anticipation. I concentrated on breathing and not stepping on the dress or tripping. I could feel my pulse all the way down to my toes, and my fingers aimlessly clutched that extra material on the long sleeves as a child might hold a security blanket. Mom said, "Hey, Lisa's got something to show you." I heard their footsteps come closer to the stairs. As they spotted me, the men stopped silent. At first glance they probably thought I was reverting to the old days, playing dress-up in Mommy's clothes. Nobody spoke. Suddenly Dad's eyes misted over.

"Beautiful," he whispered. I couldn't decide what he meant. Was the 16 word for me, the gown, his mother, or the captivating and swirling dance between memory and imagination?

Pace: Present and summarize actions of others

Mom smiled an old smile and handed each man a picture of Grandma 17 and Grandpa's wedding. "Just look." I imagine that Mom was busy with mixed memories of her wedding, imagining Grandma and Grandpa's wedding, and dreaming of mine. The guys looked at the pictures and then back at me. Gary smiled, suggesting he understood completely, that he had the full picture. With half a smile he said, "It looks as if it was made for you, Lis. It's almost creepy. Grandma must have been a lot like you when she was your age." Gary handed the picture back to Mom. I watched him do it through a fuzzy glaze as my eyes began to swell with tears.

Detail: Describe reactions of narrator

At that, Dad stepped toward me, put his big hands on my shoulders, and 18 gave me a light kiss on the forehead. "Just beautiful," he muttered. I smiled a half smile, clutched the sleeves with my fingertips, gathered up the gown, revealing my painted toes again, and scooted up the stairs as fast as I could, not even waiting for Mom's aid. The descent down the stairs had been prolonged by anticipation. The return was a blur. I wanted only to hide away, to get into my own clothes, and quietly to sort out my emotions.

Plot: Resolve plot

Once again in the sewing room, I paused for a moment in front of the 19 long mirror. The mirror, like the picture, framed the image of a vital young woman with her Grandma's big, warm eyes, in a simple but beautiful gown. Different but somehow the same. I unbuttoned the silken wedding dress worn so many years ago by my grandmother. Pulling it over my head I felt almost as if I were peeling myself out of a memory. I returned the dress to its hanger and stepped back into my own jeans and sweatshirt, shoes, and socks. Back in my own clothes I looked at the gown hanging once again on the back of the closet door. It hung there still wrinkled and still bursting with memories. I hugged myself and smiled, inside and out. And I shivered, inside and out. And I cried. I had put on my grandmother's wedding gown. I had worn the dress and wear still all that it encompassed. Inside and out.

Point of View: Suggest importance of experience

# Digging

## ANDRE DUBUS

That hot June in Lafayette, Louisiana, I was sixteen, I would be seventeen in
August, I weighed 105 pounds, and my ruddy, broad-chested father wanted
me to have a summer job. I only wanted the dollar allowance he gave me
each week, and the dollar and a quarter I earned caddying for him on
weekend and Wednesday afternoons. With a quarter I could go to a movie,
or buy a bottle of beer, or a pack of cigarettes to smoke secretly. I did not
have a girlfriend, so I did not have to buy drinks or food or movie tickets for
anyone else. I did not want to work. I wanted to drive around with my
friends, or walk with them downtown, to stand in front of the department
store, comb our ducktails, talk, look at girls.

My father was a civil engineer, and the district manager for the Gulf States
Utilities Company. He had been working for them since he left college, beginning as a surveyor, wearing boots and khakis and, in a holster on his belt, a
twenty-two caliber pistol for cottonmouths. At home he was quiet; in the
evenings he sat in his easy chair, and smoked, and read: *Time, The Saturday
Evening Post, Collier's, The Reader's Digest,* detective novels, books about golf,
and Book-of-the-Month Club novels. He loved to talk, and he did this at
parties I listened to from my bedroom, and with his friends on the golf
course, and drinking in the clubhouse after playing eighteen holes. I listened
to more of my father's conversations about politics and golf and his life and
the world than I ever engaged in, during the nearly twenty-two years I lived
with him. I was afraid of angering him, seeing his blue eyes, and reddening
face, hearing the words he would use to rebuke me; but what I feared most
was his voice, suddenly and harshly rising. He never yelled for long, only a
few sentences, but they emptied me, as if his voice had pulled my soul from
my body. His voice seemed to empty the house, too, and, when he stopped
yelling, the house filled with silence. He did not yell often. That sound was
not part of our family life. The fear of it was part of my love for him.

I was shy with him. Since my forties I have believed that he was shy with
me too, and I hope it was not as painful for him as it was for me. I think my
shyness had very little to do with my fear. Other boys had fathers who yelled
longer and more often, fathers who spanked them, or, when they were in
their teens, slapped or punched them. My father spanked me only three
times, probably because he did not know of most of my transgressions. My

Andre Dubus, "Digging," *Meditations from a Moveable Chair* (New York: Random, 1998).

friends with harsher fathers were neither afraid nor shy; they quarreled with their fathers, provoked them. My father sired a sensitive boy, easily hurt or frightened, and he worried about me; I knew he did when I was a boy, and he told me this on his deathbed, when I was a Marine captain.

My imagination gave me a dual life: I lived in my body, and at the same time lived a life no one could see. All my life I have told myself stories, and have talked in my mind to friends. Imagine my father sitting at supper with my mother and two older sisters and me: I am ten and small and appear distracted. Every year at school there is a bully, sometimes a new one, sometimes the one from the year before. I draw bullies to me, not because I am small, but because they know I will neither fight nor inform on them. I will take their pushes or pinches or punches, and try not to cry, and I will pretend I am not hurt. My father does not know this. He only sees me at supper, and I am not there. I am riding a horse and shooting bad men. My father eats, glances at me. I know he is trying to see who I am, who I will be.

Before my teens, he took me to professional wrestling matches because I wanted to go; he told me they were fake, and I did not believe him. We listened to championship boxing matches on the radio. When I was not old enough to fire a shotgun he took me dove hunting with his friends: we crouched in a ditch facing a field, and I watched the doves fly toward us and my father rising to shoot, then I ran to fetch the warm, dead and delicious birds. In summer he took me fishing with his friends; we walked in woods to creeks and bayous and fished with bamboo poles. When I was ten he learned to play golf and stopped hunting and fishing, and on weekends I was his caddy. I did not want to be, I wanted to play with my friends, but when I became a man and left home, I was grateful that I had spent those afternoons watching him, listening to him. A minor league baseball team made our town its home, and my father took me to games, usually with my mother. When I was twelve or so, he taught me to play golf, and sometimes I played nine holes with him; more often and more comfortably, I played with other boys.

If my father and I were not watching or listening to something and responding to it, or were not doing something, but were simply alone together, I could not talk, and he did not, and I felt that I should, and I was ashamed. That June of my seventeenth year, I could not tell him that I did not want a job. He talked to a friend of his, a building contractor, who hired me as a carpenter's helper; my pay was seventy-five cents an hour.

On a Monday morning my father drove me to work. I would ride the bus home and, next day, would start riding the bus to work. Probably my father drove me that morning because it was my first day; when I was twelve he had taken me to a store to buy my first pair of long pants; we boys wore shorts and, in fall and winter, knickers and long socks till we were twelve; and he had taken me to a barber for my first haircut. In the car I sat frightened, sadly resigned, and feeling absolutely incompetent. I had the lunch my mother had put in a brown paper bag, along with a mason jar with sugar and squeezed lemons in it, so I could make lemonade with water from the cooler. We drove to a street with houses and small stores and parked at a corner where, on a flat piece of land, men were busy. They were building a liquor store, and I assumed I would spend my summer handing things to a carpenter. I hoped he would be patient and kind.

As a boy in Louisiana's benevolent winters and hot summers I had 8 played outdoors with friends: we built a clubhouse, chased each other on bicycles, shot air rifles at birds, tin cans, bottles, trees; in fall and winter, wearing shoulder pads and helmets, we played football on someone's very large side lawn; and in summer we played baseball in a field that a father mowed for us; he also built us a backstop of wood and chicken wire. None of us played well enough to be on a varsity team; but I wanted that gift, not knowing that it was a gift, and I felt ashamed that I did not have it. Now we drove cars, smoked, drank in nightclubs. This was French Catholic country; we could always buy drinks. Sometimes we went on dates with girls, but more often looked at them and talked about them; or visited them, when several girls were gathered at the home of a girl whose parents were out for the evening. I had never done physical work except caddying, pushing a lawn mower, and raking leaves, and I was walking from the car with my father toward working men. My father wore his straw hat and seersucker suit. He introduced me to the foreman and said: "Make a man of him."

Then he left. The foreman wore a straw hat and looked old; everyone 9 looked old; the foreman was probably thirty-five. I stood mutely, waiting for him to assign me to some good-hearted Cajun carpenter. He assigned me a pickaxe and a shovel and told me to get into the trench and go to work. In all four sides of the trench were files of black men, swinging picks, and shoveling. The trench was about three feet deep and it would be the building's foundation; I went to where the foreman pointed, and laid my tools on the ground; two black men made a space for me, and I jumped between them. They smiled and we greeted each other. I would learn days later that they earned a dollar an hour. They were men with families and I knew this was unjust, as everything else was for black people. But on that first morning I did not know what they were being paid, I did not know their names, only that one was working behind me and one in front, and they were good to me and stronger than I could ever be. All I really knew in those first hours under the hot sun was raising the pickaxe and swinging it down, raising it and swinging, again and again till the earth was loose; then putting the pick on the ground beside me and taking the shovel and plunging it into dirt that I lifted and tossed beside the trench.

I did not have the strength for this: not in my back, my legs, my arms, my 10 shoulders. Certainly not in my soul. I only wanted it to end. The air was very humid, and sweat dripped on my face and arms, soaked my shirts and jeans. My hands gripping the pick or shovel were sore, my palms burned, the muscles in my arms ached, and my breath was quick. Sometimes I saw tiny black spots before my eyes. Weakly I raised the pick, straightening my back, then swung it down, bending my body with it, and it felt heavier than I was, more durable, this thing of wood and steel that was melting me. I laid it on the ground and picked up the shovel and pushed it into the dirt, lifted it, grunted, and emptied it beside the trench. The sun, always my friend till now, burned me, and my mouth and throat were dry, and often I climbed out of the trench and went to the large tin water cooler with a block of ice in it and water from a hose. At the cooler were paper cups and salt tablets, and I swallowed salt and drank and drank, and poured water onto my head and face; then I want back to the trench, the shovel, the pick.

Nausea came in the third and fourth hour. I kept swinging the pick, 11 pushing and lifting the shovel. I became my sick and hot and tired and hurting flesh. Or it became me; so, for an hour or more, I tasted a very small piece of despair. At noon in Lafayette a loud whistle blew, and in the cathedral the bell rang. I could not hear the bell where we worked, but I heard the whistle, and lowered the shovel and looked around. I was dizzy and sick. All the men had stopped working and were walking toward shade. One of the men with me said it was time to eat, and I climbed out of the trench and walked with black men to the shade of the tool shed. The white men went to another shaded place; I do not remember what work they had been doing that morning, but it was not with picks and shovels in the trench. Everyone looked hot but comfortable. The black men sat talking and began to eat and drink. My bag of lunch and jar with lemons and sugar were on the ground in the shade. Still I stood, gripped by nausea. I looked at the black men and at my lunch bag. Then my stomach tightened and everything in it rose, and I went around the corner of the shed where no one could see me and, bending over, I vomited and moaned and heaved until it ended. I went to the water cooler and rinsed my mouth and spat, and then I took another paper cup and drank. I walked back to the shade and lay on my back, tasting vomit. One of the black men said: "You got to eat."

"I threw up," I said, and closed my eyes and slept for the rest of the hour 12 that everyone—students and workers—had for the noon meal. At home my nineteen-year-old sister and my mother and father were eating dinner, meat and rice and gravy, vegetables and salad and iced tea with a leaf of mint; and an oscillating fan cooled them. My twenty-two-year-old sister was married. At one o'clock the whistle blew, and I woke up and stood and one of the black men said: "Are you all right?"

I nodded. If I had spoken, I may have wept. When I was a boy I could not 13 tell a man what I felt, if I believed what I felt was unmanly. We went back to the trench, down into it, and I picked up the shovel I had left there at noon, and shoveled out all the loose earth between me and the man in front of me, then put the shovel beside the trench, lifted the pick, raised it over my shoulder, and swung it down into the dirt. I was dizzy and weak and hot; I worked for forty minutes or so; then, above me, I heard my father's voice, speaking my name. I looked up at him; he was here to take me home, to forgive my failure, and in my great relief I could not know that I would not be able to forgive it. I was going home. But he said: "Let's go buy you a hat."

Every man there wore a hat, most of them straw, the others baseball caps. 14 I said nothing. I climbed out of the trench, and went with my father. In the car, in a voice softened with pride, he said: "The foreman called me. He said the Nigras told him you threw up, and didn't eat, and you didn't tell him."

"That's right," I said, and shamefully watched the road, and cars with 15 people who seemed free of all torment, and let my father believe I was brave, because I was afraid to tell him that I was afraid to tell the foreman. Quietly we drove to town and he parked and took me first to a drugstore with air-conditioning and a lunch counter, and bought me a 7-Up for my stomach, and told me to order a sandwich. Sweet-smelling women at the counter were smoking. The men in the trench had smoked while they worked, but my body's only desire had been to stop shoveling and swinging the pick, to be with no transition at all in the shower at home, then to lie on my bed, feeling the soft breath of the fan on my damp skin. I would not have smoked at work anyway, with men. Now I wanted a cigarette. My father smoked, and I ate a bacon and lettuce and tomato sandwich.

Then we walked outside, into humidity and the heat and glare of the sun. 16 We crossed the street to the department store where, in the work clothes section, my father chose a pith helmet. I did not want to wear a pith helmet. I would happily wear one in Africa, hunting lions and rhinoceroses. But I did not want to wear such a thing in Lafayette. I said nothing; there was no hat I wanted to wear. I carried the helmet in its bag out of the store and, in the car, laid it beside me. At that place where sweating men worked, I put it on; a thin leather strap looped around the back of my head. I went to my two comrades in the trench. One of them said: "That's a good hat."

I jumped in. 17

The man behind me said: "You going to be all right now." 18

I was; and I still do not know why. A sandwich and a soft drink had not 19 given me any more strength than the breakfast I had vomited. An hour's respite in the car and the cool drugstore and buying the helmet that now was keeping my wet head cool certainly helped. But I had the same soft arms and legs, the same back and shoulders I had demanded so little of in my nearly seventeen years of stewardship. Yet all I remember of that afternoon is the absence of nausea.

At five o'clock the whistle blew downtown and we climbed out of the 20 trench and washed our tools with the hose, then put them in the shed. Dirt was on my arms and hands, my face and neck and clothes. I could have wrung sweat from my shirt and jeans. I got my lunch from the shade. My two comrades said, See you tomorrow. I said I would see them. I went to the bus stop at the corner and sat on the bench. My wet clothes cooled my skin. I looked down at my dirty tennis shoes; my socks and feet were wet. I watched people in passing cars. In one were teenaged boys, and they laughed and shouted something about my helmet. I watched the car till it was blocks away, then took off the helmet and held it on my lap. I carried it aboard the bus; yet all summer I wore it at work, maybe because my father bought it for me and I did not want to hurt him, maybe because it was a wonderful helmet for hard work outdoors in Louisiana.

My father got home before I did and told my mother and sister the story, 21 the only one he knew, or the only one I assumed he knew. The women proudly greeted me when I walked into the house. They were also worried. They wanted to know how I felt. They wore dresses, they smelled of perfume or cologne, they were drinking bourbon and water, and my sister and father were smoking cigarettes. Standing in the living room, holding my lunch and helmet, I said I was fine. I could not tell the truth to these women who loved me, even if my father were not there. I could not say that I was not strong enough and that I could not bear going back to work tomorrow, and all summer, anymore than I could tell them I did not believe I was as good at being a boy as other boys were: not at sports, or with girls; and now not with a man's work. I was home, where vases held flowers, and things were clean, and our manners were good.

Next morning, carrying my helmet and lunch, I rode the bus to work 22 and joined the two black men in the trench. I felt that we were friends. Soon I felt this about all the black men at work. We were digging the foundation; we were the men and the boy with picks and shovels in the trench. One day the foundation was done. I use the passive voice, because this was a square or rectangular trench, men were working at each of its sides. I had been working with my comrades on the same side for weeks, moving not forward but down. Then it was done. Someone told us. Maybe the contractor was there, with the foreman. Who dug out that last bit of dirt? I only knew that I had worked as hard as I could, I was part of the trench, it was part of me, and it was finished; it was there in the earth to receive concrete and probably never to be seen again. Someone should have blown a bugle, we should have climbed exultant from the trench, gathered to wipe sweat from our brows, drink water, shake hands, then walk together to each of the four sides and marvel at what we had made.

On that second morning of work I was not sick, and at noon I ate lunch 23 with the blacks in the shade, then we all slept on the grass till one o'clock. We worked till five, said goodbye to each other, and they went to the colored section of town, and I rode the bus home. When I walked into the living room, into cocktail hour, and my family asked me about my day, I said it was fine. I may have learned something if I had told them the truth: the work was too hard, but after the first morning I could bear it. And all summer it would be hard; after we finished the foundation, I would be transferred to another crew. We would build a mess hall at a Boy Scout camp and with a black man, I would dig a septic tank in clay so hard that the foreman kept hosing water into it as we dug; black men and I would push wheelbarrows of mixed cement; on my shoulder I would carry eighty-pound bags of dry cement, twenty-five pounds less than my own weight; and at the summer's end my body would be twenty pounds heavier. If I had told these three people who loved me that I did not understand my weak body's stamina, they may have taught me why something terrible had so quickly changed to something arduous.

It is time to thank my father for wanting me to work and telling me I had 24 to work and getting the job for me and buying me lunch and a pithy helmet instead of taking me home to my mother and sister. He may have wanted to take me home. But he knew he must not, and he came tenderly to me. My mother would have been at home that afternoon; if he had taken me to her she would have given me iced tea and, after my shower, a hot dinner. When my sister came home from work, she would have understood, and told me not to despise myself because I could not work with a pickaxe and a shovel. And I would have spent the summer at home, nestled in the love of the two women, peering at my father's face, and yearning to be someone I respected, a varsity second baseman, a halfback, someone cheerleaders and drum majorettes and pretty scholars loved; yearning to be a man among men, and that is where my father sent me with a helmet on my head.

## Questions About Strategy

1. How does Dubus pace his first day at work to reveal the intensity of his efforts?
2. How does Dubus use his friendship with black workmen to teach his readers something about justice?
3. How do Dubus's speculations about what would have happened if he had gone home for lunch help clarify the purpose of the narrative?

## A Sampler of Other Essays

1. Jane Graham, "Watching Whales" (student essay), p. 150
2. John McPhee, "Grizzly," p. 148
3. Patricia Hampl, "Prague," p. 310

## Strategy Two: *Process Analysis*

### Selecting Your Subject

Because a *process* is an operation that moves through a series of steps to bring about a desired result, you could consider almost any procedure— from brushing your teeth to investing in the stock market—a possible subject. But selecting the appropriate subject for a process analysis essay requires some planning. You should know your subject thoroughly so that you can divide it into steps and analyze its movement from beginning to end. You should also select a process that you can analyze effectively in an essay—brushing your teeth is too simple; investing in the stock market is too complex. And finally, you should select a subject whose individual steps and final results require thoughtful analysis and evaluation.

### Analyzing Your Audience

When you write a process analysis essay, you must think carefully about your audience. First, you need to decide whether you are writing *to* an audience or *for* an audience. If you are writing to an audience, you can address your readers directly: "If you want to send a message by e-mail, follow these four steps." If you are writing *for* an audience, you may want to assume a more formal point of view: "Although many Americans say they are interested in computers, few know how computers work." Second, you need to determine how much your readers know about the process you intend to analyze. Your decision to write about the process suggests that you are an expert. If you suspect your readers are also knowledgeable, you can write your analysis with certain assumptions. For example, if you are writing about e-mail, you can assume that you don't need to define it or explain why someone would want to use it. On the other hand, if you think that your intended audience knows almost nothing about a process, you can take nothing for granted: You will need to define e-mail, explain its purpose, and inch your way through an analysis of how it works.

### Determining Your Purpose

Usually you write a process analysis to accomplish one of two purposes: *to give directions* or *to provide information.* In the first case you want to help your readers do something they want to do (record a television program on a VCR). In the second case you want to satisfy your readers' curiosity about some process they'd like to know about but are unlikely to perform (repair a television satellite). You might also write a process analysis to demonstrate that a task that looks difficult is really easy (operating a cellular phone) or that a task that looks easy is really complex (installing an answering machine).

### Using the Strategy

The best way to organize a process analysis essay is to follow these five steps:

1. Overview
2. Special Terms

3. Sequence of Steps

4. Examples

5. Results

The first two steps help your readers understand the process, the next two show the process in action, and the last helps them evaluate its final results.

Begin your analysis with an *overview* of the whole process. Such an overview includes (1) defining the objective of the process, (2) identifying (and numbering) the steps in the sequence, (3) grouping small steps into larger organizational units, and (4) calling attention to those steps or units that are crucial to the success of the procedure and therefore require the most detailed analysis.

Each process has its own *special terms* for tools, tasks, and methods. You can define these at the beginning so that your readers will recognize them when you use them later. Or you can define them when you introduce them. Your readers may have difficulty remembering new terminology out of context, so it's often easier to define your terms throughout the course of the essay, pausing to explain their special meaning when you use them in your analysis.

You must present your process analysis in a clear *sequence of steps*. Such a presentation interprets the reason for each step and, where appropriate, provides the following advice:

1. *Do not omit any step.* A sequence is a sequence because all steps depend on one another. Omitting a step can have disastrous consequences.

2. *Do not reverse steps.* A sequence is a sequence because each step must be performed in a necessary and logical order. Reversing steps is not an option if you want to obtain the desired result.

3. *Suspend certain steps.* Occasionally, a series of steps must be suspended, and another completed, before the sequence can resume.

4. *Do not overlook steps within steps.* Every sequence has a series of smaller steps buried within each step. Make sure your readers understand how these little, unstated steps contribute to the process.

5. *Avoid certain steps.* It is often tempting to try out steps that appear logical but are in fact harmful. As an expert, you have the task of alerting your readers to the consequences of modifying the process with such innovations.

You may want to use several kinds of *examples* to illustrate the steps in the process. You can use graphs, charts, and blueprints to outline the operation. You can clarify the process by using examples from your own experience or the experience of experts. Such testimony offers you the opportunity to suggest shortcuts or *variations* in the process you are analyzing. You can help your readers understand a complex process by *comparing* it to a similar and simpler process they already know.

Although your analysis will tend to focus on the movement of the process through its various steps, you should also try to establish criteria for evaluating the final *results*. You can move to this last step by asking two questions:

1. How do you know it's done?
2. How do you know it's good?

# Anatomy of a Garage Band

## ROB STURMA

Somebody famous once said something about music having charms to $\quad$ 1
soothe somebody, or something like that. This makes sense. If you take a
look at any community, whether it be a sprawling metropolis, a college
town, or your little neck of the woods, somebody out there is making music.

**Introduction: Establish reader's interest in process**

The reasons are varied: some people enjoy the sense of community it brings,
some find that it helps them to express their feelings, and, well, some just
think it's cool. Admit it, somewhere in your deepest, primordial urges exists
the need to hammer away on a cheap guitar and bring a basement full of
enthralled party-goers to some form of screaming frenzy. The need to satisfy
this urge is why you, my friend, must join a garage band. So let's get to it.

**Overview: Define the garage band**

For those uninitiated into the ragtag world of rock 'n' roll, some defini- $\quad$ 2
tions must be set. A garage band is a loose amalgamation of people you know
or meet who fancy themselves musicians, and with or without the incentive
of fame or fortune, choose to form a collective in which they can produce the
liberating sounds that we know homogeneously as rock 'n' roll. In layman's
terms, it's a bunch of dudes who want to jam. We'll take a look at one partic-

**Examples: Illustrate with Lovejunkies**

ular band of this ilk, the Lovejunkies, and follow them through the steps of
achieving garage-band status. The Lovejunkies play what they call "college-
pop," which ranges from alternative rock to universally embraced cover tunes
to sophomoric '70's heavy metal (this is known within the garage world as
"manly rock" for obvious lyrical reasons; see "Cooper, Alice").

**Overview: Identify and number first step**

According to these local veterans, your first step to amplified bliss is $\quad$ 3
getting your band together. Best friends and roommates are always a good
jump-off point, and from there it's a matter of filling in the musical blanks,
as it were. Enlisting the talents of a specialist is not always an easy task; when
the Lovejunkies needed a new drummer, their ideal choice was an accomplished musician, but they advertised realistically for someone "who will
show up for rehearsal." This can turn out okay, though. You may be pleas-
antly surprised by the sounds emanating from your first jam session. If not,
well, that's what rehearsal is for.

Before you delve into the rehearsal process and all that goes with it, you $\quad$ 4
must make sure that your band's name will leave its imprint on the world.
Creativity counts; no points are awarded for using another band's name.

**Sequence of Steps: Suspend one step to complete another**

Let's face it, a band called The New Beatles leave themselves little room for
creative expansion. Citing your influences is okay, though; the Lovejunkies'
lead singer Joe dug the bands Love Cowboys and the Cowboy Junkies. See

how simple it can be? He took out the "cowboy," and voila! Like the phoenix, a new band emerges. Feel free, though, to use any appropriate method to dub your ensemble. Names like Freaks of Nature, Neurotic Box, Wishful Thinking, and The Uninvited are all monickers that help to bring a clearer picture of their namesakes' stylistic contributions. Remember, if the New Fast Automatic Daffodils can nominally exist, nothing is too far-fetched.

Special Terms: Introduce and define special terminology

At this point, let's assume that your posse of players has been assembled. 5 You've got some drums, a bass, a few guitars, and somebody who likes to refer to him- or herself as a "vocal stylist" (this is the proper term as the word "singer" often has little to do with a garage band. See "Pistols, Sex"). A prudent direction to take would be to decide what type of music you'll be indulging in. The Lovejunkies, as already mentioned, play "college-pop," which is an appropriate choice for their target college audience. Go figure. Some of their tunes can range in musical style, but be warned. As exciting as stylistic fusion can be, an AC/DC drum line does not always fare well coupled with a Police guitar riff and an R.E.M. vocal (if that last sentence seems far too buried in subreference, then perhaps you should think about forming a polka band instead). As everyone's tastes will forever vary, you will learn that the term "creative differences" significantly figures into the rehearsal process. If all else fails, a rousing rendition of "Louie, Louie" is always a crowd pleaser.

Sequence of Steps: Do not omit certain steps

Let's assume, then, that your band has established their style. You might 6 do well to assemble a set list, or a list of songs that you plan to practice and practice and practice and eventually perform and then practice some more. You must, I repeat, must, love these songs, for just as your audiences begin to share your aesthetic enthusiasm, you will begin to hate them. Get used to this, as part of paying your musical dues consists of driving the same ten to twenty songs into the ground. Your audience may not know art, but they know what they like. Suffer.

Sequence of Steps: Do not overlook certain steps

Intertwined within the set list dilemma lies the age-old question: Are we 7 a cover band, or do we do originals? Well, wake up, silly. Cover bands make money. Never presume that anyone wants to hear your silly little songs when they could listen to "My Sharona" for the two-thousandth time. Nothing against "My Sharona," mind you. Songs become popular for a reason. I digress, however.

The path to garagedom, as chosen by the Lovejunkies, has been to 8 become a cover band (i.e., "gig-getters") who occasionally play an original song or two (i.e., "Hey, this ain't Free Bird"). Then, as their popularity grew, they managed to sneak more and more originals into their set. Subversive? Yes, but someone needs to enlighten the masses.

Your other option, of course, is to scrap all of that advice and just kick 9 out your own jams. It's your creative life, friend.

Okay, now let's take a little inventory. You have a band (well, most of the 10 time, y'see, because your lead guitarist can only rehearse on Wednesday and that's a bad night for your bass player), you've got a slammin' name (so maybe it's been changed a few times, but "The Pat Sajak Experience" wasn't the image you needed anyway), and you have a vast array of songs (except I guess you'll have to drop "Layla" because your drummer insists on playing it reggae style). Let's get some gigs—er, excuse me, procure some performance dates. The secret to your success? Beats the heck out of me. I've heard bands who can't play a lick get booked into every venue in town, while others with genuine talent are shoved into playing nonstop basement parties and charity shows. If it's about anything, I guess, it's about promotion.

This is the point where you or someone who fancies himself your 11 manager begins to visit every bar, restaurant, or club in town that supports and books live bands. Make sure, of course, that it's not a theme bar, as restless country music fans will not appreciate your killer interpretation of David Bowie material. So, appropriate venue established, do your best to bother the folks in charge of booking bands. Bug 'em, bug 'em, and bug 'em some more. Your only weapons are some kind of publicity package (usually a band photo and maybe a little something about yourselves) and some form of demo tape (about 4 or 5 songs, recorded any way possible. The Lovejunkies did one on a four-track mixer in Joe's living room). Ninety percent of the time, persistence pays off. If not, hey, keep trying. The only thing more important than persistence is the unrivaled ability to wear down your opponent. And who says rock 'n' roll isn't a contact sport?

Let's say, for the sake of the narrative, that you now have a place to play. 12 You've almost reached your larger goal, and I have but one word for you: flyers.

Familiarize yourself with the local copy shop, as they will be the people 13 giving you more for your advertising dollar. After you have designed your provocatively eye-catching yet chock full of all pertinent information-type 8½" × 11" flyer, you will be spending all kinds of money you don't have copying said flyer onto hundreds of once again eye-catching yet not too brightly colored so as to be distracting pieces of paper. Yes, I said hundreds. You will then proceed to tape, staple, hand out, and otherwise rid yourself of these relatively cheap advertisements. Saturation of your market is essential, as half of your flyers will be torn down and/or thrown away. Don't be offended by this; after all, you are being noticed.

Whew. You've made it through the toughest parts of your ascendance to 14 local stardom; now you need only to perform, bask in your 15 minutes of fame, and start the process all over again. At best, you will over time establish your band as a crowd-pleaser and a fresh, new talent. At worst, you'll never even hit the stage because yet another member has quit to pursue a solo career playing his unique brand of acoustic funk. Problems will inevitably occur. You may not always get paid. You may have to borrow an amplifier from that metal band that you hate. You may have a serious debate, as did Tim, the Lovejunkies' guitarist, whether or not to use your grocery money for guitar strings. Will you let these petty things drag you down? Will you be defeated? Heck, no, you shout. And well you should.

Results: How do you know it's good?

You have become part of a larger family, and the music binds you 15 together. It doesn't matter whether you've been trying to hold one band together for five years (see "Lovejunkies, The"), or whether you've been in seven different bands in the past three months (see "Former Members of the Lovejunkies, Many"). The need to play is bigger than you, than your garage band; it's bigger than you ever dreamed. I think that the rock legends KISS put it best when they made the proclamation, "God gave rock 'n' roll to you." See? It's unavoidable. You're trapped.

So, to paraphrase somebody famous who once said something some 16 time ago: it's time to plug in, turn up, and rock out. If you're really good, fantastically original, or just plain lucky, somebody who's not famous may someday recognize you as somebody who is . . . or something like that.

# Selling in Minnesota

## BARBARA EHRENREICH

So this is the home from which I go forth on Monday to begin my life as a  1
Wal-Martian. After the rigors of orientation, I am expecting a highly structured welcome, perhaps a ceremonial donning of my bright blue Wal-Mart
vest and a forty-five-minute training on the operation of the vending
machines in the break room. But when I arrive in the morning for the ten-to-
six shift, no one seems to be expecting me. I'm in "softlines," which has a
wonderful, sinuous sound to it, but I have no idea what it means. Someone
in personnel tells me I'm in ladies' wear (a division of softlines, I learn) and
sends me to the counter next to the fitting rooms, where I am passed around
from one person to the next—finally ending up with Ellie, whose lack of a
vest signals that she is management. She sets me to work "zoning" the Bobbie
Brooks knit summer dresses, a task that could serve as an IQ test for the
severely cognitively challenged. First the dresses must be grouped by color—
olive, peach, or lavender, in this case—then by decorative pattern—the leafy
design on the bodice, the single flower, or the grouped flowers—and within
each pattern by size. When I am finished, though hardly exhausted by the
effort, I meet Melissa, who is, with only a couple of weeks on the job, pretty
much my equivalent. She asks me to help her consolidate the Kathie Lee knit
dresses so the Kathie Lee silky ones can take their place at the "image," the
high-traffic corner area. I learn, in a couple of hours of scattered exchanges,
that Melissa was a waitress before this job, that her husband works in construction and her children are grown. There have been some disorganized
patches in her life—an out-of-wedlock child, a problem with alcohol and
drugs—but that's all over now that she has given her life to Christ.

Our job, it emerges in fragments throughout the day, is to keep ladies'  2
wear "shoppable." Sure, we help customers (who are increasingly called
"guests" here as well), if they want any help. At first I go around practicing the
"aggressive hospitality" demanded by our training videos: as soon as anyone
comes within ten feet of a sales associate, that associate is supposed to smile
warmly and offer assistance. But I never see a more experienced associate do
this—first, because the customers are often annoyed to have their shopping
dazes interrupted and, second, because we have far more pressing things to
do. In ladies' wear, the big task, which has no real equivalent in, say, house-
wares or lawn and garden, is to put away the "returns"—clothes that have

Barbara Ehrenreich, "Selling in Minnesota," *Nickle and Dimed* (New York: Holt, 2001).

been tried on and rejected or, more rarely, purchased and then returned to the store. There are also the many items that have been scattered by customers, dropped on the floor, removed from their hangers and strewn over the racks, or secreted in locations far from their natural homes. Each of these items, too, must be returned to its precise place, matched by color, pattern, price, and size. Any leftover time is to be devoted to zoning. When I relate this to Caroline on the phone, she commiserates, "Ugh, a no-brainer."

But no job is as easy as it looks to the uninitiated. I have to put clothes 3 away—the question is, Where? Much of my first few days is devoted to trying to memorize the layout of ladies' wear, one thousand (two thousand?) square feet of space bordered by men's wear, children's wear, greeting cards, and underwear. Standing at the fitting rooms and facing toward the main store entrance, we are looking directly at the tentlike, utilitarian plus sizes, also known as "woman" sizes. These are flanked on the left by our dressiest and costliest line (going up to $29 and change), the all-polyester Kathie Lee collection, suitable for dates and subprofessional levels of office work. Moving clockwise, we encounter the determinedly sexless Russ and Bobbie Brooks lines, seemingly aimed at pudgy fourth-grade teachers with important barbecues to attend. Then, after the sturdy White Stag, come the breezy, revealing Faded Glory, No Boundaries, and Jordache collections, designed for the younger and thinner crowd. Tucked throughout are nests of the lesser brands, such as Athletic Works, Basic Equipment, and the whimsical Looney Tunes, Pooh, and Mickey lines, generally decorated with images of their eponymous characters. Within each brand-name area, there are of course dozens of items, even dozens of each *kind* of item. This summer, for example, pants may be capri, classic, carpenter, clam-digger, boot, or flood, depending on their length and cut, and I'm probably leaving a few categories out. So my characteristic stance is one of rotating slowly on one foot, eyes wide, garment in hand, asking myself, "Where have I seen the $9.96 Athletic Works knit overalls?" or similar query. Inevitably there are mystery items requiring extra time and inquiry: clothes that have wandered over from girls' or men's, clearanced items whose tags haven't been changed to reflect their new prices, the occasional one-of-a-kind.

Then, when I have the layout memorized, it suddenly changes. On my 4 third morning I find, after a few futile searches, that the Russ shirt-and-short combinations have edged Kathie Lee out of her image. When I groaningly accuse Ellie of trying to trick me into thinking I'm getting Alzheimer's, she's genuinely apologetic, explaining that the average customer shops the store three times a week, so you need to have the element of surprise. Besides, the layout is about the only thing she *can* control, since the clothes and at least the starting prices are all determined by the home office in Arkansas. So as fast as I can memorize, she furiously rearranges.

My first response to the work is disappointment and a kind of sexist con- 5 tempt. I could have been in plumbing, mastering the vocabulary of valves, dangling tools from my belt, joshing around with Steve and Walt, and instead the mission of the moment is to return a pink bikini top to its place on the Bermuda swimwear rack. Nothing is heavy or, as far as I can see, very urgent. No one will go hungry or die or be hurt if I screw up; in fact, how would anyone ever know if I screwed up, given the customers' constant depredations? I feel oppressed, too, by the mandatory gentility of Wal-Mart culture. This is ladies' and we are all "ladies" here, forbidden, by storewide rule, to raise our voices or cuss. Give me a few weeks of this and I'll femme out entirely, my stride will be reduced to a mince, I'll start tucking my head down to one side.

My job is not, however, as genteel as it at first appears, thanks to the sheer $_6$ volume of clothing in motion. At Wal-Mart, as opposed to say Lord & Taylor, customers shop with supermarket-style shopping carts, which they can fill to the brim before proceeding to the fitting room. There the rejected items, which are about 90 percent of try-ons, are folded and put on hangers by whoever is staffing the fitting room, then placed in fresh shopping carts for Melissa and me. So this is how we measure our workload—in carts. When I get in, Melissa, whose shift begins earlier than mine, will tell me how things have been going—"Can you believe, eight carts this morning!"—and how many carts are awaiting me. At first a cart takes me an average of forty-five minutes and there may still be three or four mystery items left at the bottom. I get this down to half an hour, and still the carts keep coming.

Most of the time, the work requires minimal human interaction, of either $_7$ the collegial or the supervisory sort, largely because it's so self-defining. I arrive at the start of a shift or the end of a break, assess the damage wrought by the guests in my absence, count the full carts that await me, and plunge in. I could be a deaf-mute as far as most of this goes, and despite all the orientation directives to smile and exude personal warmth, autism might be a definite advantage. Sometimes, if things are slow, Melissa and I will invent a task we can do together—zoning swimsuits, for example, a nightmarish tangle of straps—and giggle, she in her Christian way, me from a more feminist per-spective, about the useless little see-through wraps meant to accompany the more revealing among them. Or sometimes Ellie will give me something special to do, like putting all the Basic Equipment T-shirts on hangers, because things on hangers sell faster, and then arranging them neatly on racks. I like Ellie. Gray-faced and fiftyish, she must be the apotheosis of "servant leader-ship" or, in more secular terms, the vaunted "feminine" style of management. She says "please" and "thank you"; she doesn't order, she asks. Not so, though, with young Howard—*assistant manager* Howard, as he is uniformly called— who rules over all of softlines, including infants', children's, men's, accessories, and underwear. On my first day, I am called off the floor to an associates' meeting, where he spends ten minutes taking attendance, fixing each of us with his unnerving Tom Cruise–style smile, in which the brows come together as the corners of the mouth turn up, then reveals (where have I heard this before?) his "pet peeve": associates standing around talking to one another, which is, of course, a prime example of time theft.

## Questions about Strategy

1. How does Ehrenreich reveal the steps within her job? How do these steps change or have to be adjusted for different situations?

2. What special terms does Ehrenreich define to help her readers understand her job?

3. How does Ehrenreich explain the "purpose" of her job?

## A Sampler of Other Essays

1. Wallace Armstrong, "Brandon's Clown" (student essay), p. 24

2. P. J. O'Rourke, "Third World Driving Hints and Tips," p. 308

3. Richard Selzer, "The Knife," p. 252

# Strategy Three: *Comparison and Contrast*

## Selecting Your Subject

As you shop around for subjects, you will find that you can compare anything from the trivial (regular gum with sugarless gum) to the really serious (a career as a doctor with a job in a pharmaceutical company). Technically speaking, when you *compare* you are looking for similarities; when you *contrast* you are looking for differences. In practice, the operations are part of the same process. When you look for what's similar, you will also notice what's different. The challenge in selecting a subject for such analysis is to avoid what is commonly called the "so-what" problem. You can always make a list of differences and similarities. This is blue; that's red. This is round; that's square. So what! To convert a list of comparisons into a comparison and contrast essay, you need to see your subject as part of a larger project—to demonstrate that one object is better than another or to reveal a particular relationship between two objects.

## Analyzing Your Audience

As you plan a comparison and contrast essay, think about what your readers already know and what they expect to learn. If you're confident that your readers know a lot about the items you are comparing (two television shows), you can spend less time on pointing out similarities and more time on your reasons for making the comparison. When your readers know little about the items (two Chinese folktales), you'll have to describe each, using examples they are familiar with before you can point out important contrasts. If your readers know about only one item in the pair (the American film, but not the French film on which it was based), then use the familiar item to describe the unfamiliar. As you think about what your readers expect, remember they want your essay to be fairly balanced, not 90 percent on the American film and 10 percent on the French film. When your essay is so unbalanced, you will disappoint your readers who expect to learn about both items being compared.

## Determining Your Purpose

You can take two approaches to writing comparison and contrast essays; each has a different purpose. When you write a *strict* comparison, you compare only those things in the same category—actors with actors, musicians with musicians, but not actors with musicians. Although subjects often inhabit several categories at the same time, your purpose is to find what your subjects have in common. For example, how are jazz musicians and classical musicians alike, even if their music is quite different? Often, in a strict comparison, your purpose is to make a judgment and a choice. When you write a *fanciful* comparison, you try to compare in an imaginative, illuminating way, two things that don't seem at all alike. You can use such comparisons to help your readers understand a complex idea (how a highway system and the new computer networks are alike) or to expand their concept of your subject (how the increased use of drugs is an epidemic). You may find it difficult to sustain a fanciful comparison for a whole essay. But you can construct such a comparison to help your readers see new connections between unlike things.

## Using the Strategy

You can use two basic strategies for organizing a comparison and contrast essay. With the *divided* or *subject-by-subject* pattern, you present all your information on one topic before introducing information on the other topic. With the *alternating* or *point-by-point* pattern, you work your way through the comparison point by point, giving information on one aspect of the first topic, then on the same aspect of the other topic.

Although both methods are useful, you'll discover that each has weaknesses. The divided pattern works especially well in short essays, in which your reader can easily keep track of your points. Its weakness, however, is that you can slip into writing two separate essays. The alternating pattern works well when you want to show the two subjects side by side according to their points of comparison. You'll find it particularly useful in longer essays when you want to discuss many complex points of comparison. Its weakness is that it may reduce your analysis to exercise, encouraging you to compose a simple list.

Often you can make the best of both worlds by *combining strategies*. For example, you could start with a divided pattern to give a unified, overall view of each subject, then shift to an alternating pattern to illustrate the larger purpose of your comparison. Or you could establish the points you want to make using the alternating pattern and then move on to a longer, detailed analysis of each topic.

To write a successful comparison and contrast essay, keep three guidelines in mind:

1. *balance* the various selections of your comparison;

2. *include reminders,* such as transitional phrases and sentences, to help your readers connect the points of your comparison; and

3. *supply reasons* to support your purpose and to explain why you are making the comparison.

# Same Goal/Different Plan

## KRIS MODLIN

"Bid 'em if you got 'em!" 1

**Pattern: Establish points of comparison**

My brother's exasperated encouragement rings in my ears each time we 2 play euchre. He believes in decisive action. I believe in deliberate choices.

"Don't rush me. I'm thinking." 3

My reply is as predictable as his command. I like to mull over my 4 options.

**Purpose: Contrast differences in politics and religion with similarity of objective**

Whenever my family gets together for birthdays, Mother's Day, Labor 5 Day, or Christmas, we play cards, most often doubledeck bid euchre. Once, I don't remember exactly when, we drew for partners. Somehow my brother and I, so different in our political and religious beliefs despite our similar upbringing, became a team challenging my mother and sister-in-law. To our great surprise the pairing clicked, making us an almost unbeatable twosome. When we can concentrate on winning rather than tiptoeing around our opposing opinions, my brother and I bridge our differences and recreate the closeness of our childhood.

**Pattern:**
**A. Politics**
**1. Brother**

Sixteen years older than I and the hero of my childhood, my brother 6 reigns as our family's political black sheep. His conservative accountant mind embraces enthusiastically every plank of the Republican platform. He believes individual states run best with little or no interference from the federal government, an odd stand for the great-great-grandson of a Quaker abolitionist active in the Underground Railroad and the grandson of a depression farmer whose lands were saved by FDR's moratorium on loan interest. Still, my brother praises corporate tax breaks because they stimulate the economy and denounces military cutbacks because they endanger our country.

**2. Writer**

So, to maintain peaceful coexistence, I rarely discuss politics with him, 7 partially because some vestige of hero worship remains, but mostly because I envision a world more closely aligned with the liberal ideals of the Democratic party—a vision shared by most of my other relatives. I believe the federal government should legislate equality in all states and place people before economics. Thus, I condemn our present tax structure that forces the middle class to pay a higher percentage of their income than the rich do, and I support balancing the federal budget by halting military buildups rather than cutting free lunch programs for needy school children.

**B. Religion**
**1. Brother**

My brother's conservatism also permeates his religion. The fundamen- 8 talist faith he adopted provides clear, if not easy, standards to uphold such as forbidding divorce and perpetuating male dominance in the church. His literal interpretation of the Bible, including baptism by immersion and weekly communion, establishes an absolute line between black and white, between the damned and the saved, leaving little room for gray spaces. He is not fanatical about any of this.

He simply lives his faith, preferring to convert others by example rather than by pushy sermons. 9

2. Writer

Although I once attended the same church as my brother, my religion 10 has grown away from his simple faith. I have no argument with the teachings of Jesus, but I cannot accept the narrow, sexist vision of Paul nor the immense burden of guilt embedded in most Christian doctrine. I believe each person should look within her own mind and imagination, searching for a connection between herself and her world—a connection that will create a sense of responsibility, not guilt. Perhaps that search will lead to Christianity. Perhaps not.

Transition: Connect comparison to card game

Obviously, the old adage "Don't discuss politics or religion" applies to 11 my brother and me. But when the euchre game begins, our political and religious differences cease to matter. Our sole goal is winning, and after years of being partners, we both know how the other will play.

C. Card-playing style
1. Brother

He always sorts his hand without expression and then bids precisely 12 what his cards dictate, adhering to his "bid 'em if you got 'em" philosophy. Next he analytically plays his hand, keeping track of what cards have been played and appearing to know what cards each player holds in her hand. His manner is calm. He prefers to surprise his mother and his wife by silently sneaking a trick to make his bid or to set them, which usually results in at least one of them yelling or throwing her cards at him while he laughs.

2. Writer

I, too, sort my cards without expression, but when bidding I often give 13 away a good hand by sitting up straight and scooting to the edge of my chair. My risky "bid 'em if you got 'em" practice causes me to overbid my hand sometimes. I believe my partner's always good for one trick, and I'm usually right. As the hand progresses, I pull in the cards, talking faster and faster, sometimes louder and louder, drawing attention away from my brother as he sneaks in the crucial winning trick.

Conclusion: Supply reasons for making comparison

After each hand is played, we rehash it as the next one is dealt. What 14 *could* we have done? What *should* we have done? Why does it matter? It does. The discussion is cards, a common interest, a sharing not often possible in the different paths our two lives have taken. Over the years, the card game has helped me respect the differences between us while still valuing our brother and sister relationship. When we do discuss politics and religion, my brother and I discover that, as in euchre, our goals are similar but our game plan differs. He's conservative. I hesitate and then take a chance. Our euchre ritual strengthens our bond, a bond we obviously didn't choose to create, but one we choose to continue.

# The Golden Spike

## JOHN STEELE GORDON

*The Internet is most analogous to the railroad
revolution more than a century ago.*

The Internet in the 1990s is just like the railroads in the 1840s. It is still in its [1]
infancy, its growth is exploding, and no one yet knows how to make money
at it. It also performs the same economic function: connecting things. And
there is no more potent force than connecting buyers and sellers. The GDP
of an economy, after all, is nothing more than the sum of all these connections. The more buyers and sellers there are, the greater the wealth generated. That's why the railroad was the seminal invention of the nineteenth
century and the Internet will undoubtedly be of the twenty-first.

It is hard to imagine just how wretched the overland transportation [2]
system was before the railroads, even in well-developed Europe. Indeed,
*system* is hardly the word for a spotty network of roads, many of which were
hardly better than paths. The Great North Road, the major highway through
the north of England in the eighteenth century, had potholes so large that
men and horses are known to have drowned in them. This meant that
goods, except for luxuries, had to be transported by river or sea or they
could not be transported at all.

As an underdeveloped country, and one of continental size at that, the [3]
young United States' overland transportation problems dwarfed those of
Europe. Worse, most East Coast rivers were navigable for only short distances inland. As a result, there really was no "American economy." Instead
there was a myriad of local ones. Most food was consumed locally, and most
goods were locally produced by artisans such as blacksmiths. The railroads
changed all that in less than thirty years.

When Andrew Jackson made his way from Nashville to Washington, [4]
D.C., for his inauguration in 1829, he traveled by coach and required a
month for the journey. Thirty years later it was possible to make the trip in
three days. Because of the speed and ease of railroads, the volume of passen-
ger traffic increased enormously as well. Before the new technology, passen-
ger traffic between Charleston, south Carolina, and Augusta, Georgia, was
handled by a single stagecoach making three round-trips a week. Five years
after rail service opened between the two cities, traffic was averaging more
than 2,600 passengers a month.

John Steele Gordon, "The Golden Spike," *Forbes* 21 Feb. 2000: 118.

But it was the railroads' ability to haul freight, not people, that trans- 5
formed the world. Before its arrival, shipping a ton of goods 400 miles could
easily quadruple the price. But by rail, the same ton of goods could be
shipped in a fraction of the time and at one-twentieth of the cost. No
wonder the multitude of separate economics began to vanish. "Two generations ago," wrote Arthur Hadley, a Yale economics professor, in 1885, "the
expense of cartage was such that wheat had to be consumed within 200
miles of where it was grown. Today, the wheat of Dakota, the wheat of
Russia, and the wheat of India come into direct competition. The supply at
Odessa is an element in determining the price in Chicago."

Sound familiar? With the internet, it is information and data that can be 6
moved much more quickly and cheaply. According to a Morgan Stanley
Dean Witter report, buying airline tickets over the Internet results in an 87
percent reduction in the distribution cost. Banking online is an 89 percent
reduction. While the railroads produced a national market, the Internet is
producing a truly global one. An example: India's software development services now compete with China's, which compete with Silicon Valley's.

## A New Street

At first most railroads were locally financed by the people and businessmen 7
who stood to benefit from the new transportation. But the securities issued
by these new companies often made their way to Wall Street and played a
major part in the growth of the American financial market. In the 1820s and
early 1830s, state and federal bonds and bank shares dominated securities
trading, and business was often less than brisk. On March 16, 1830, a mere
thirty-one shares changed hands on the New York Stock and Exchange
Board (as the NYSE was then known). By the 1850s, however, average
volume had multiplied manyfold, and two-thirds of the issues being sold
there were railroad stocks and bonds. With the American economy not yet
able to generate enough capital internally, many of these issues were sold to
European investors, especially in Britain, despite the ten-day delay in communication across the Atlantic.

Today, the Internet also is remaking Wall Street, and not just with the 8
upstart online companies, twenty-four hour trading, or the new electronic
exchanges. Volumes and prices have reached all-time highs, thanks in large
measure to companies trading on the hope of the Internet. Nor is the crazi-
ness of the stock prices unique to our time. Because the Erie Railroad had
an erratic, often crooked, management, and an odd route (it ran between
Dunkirk on Lake Erie and Piermont on the Hudson River—two towns of no
commercial importance whatsoever), it became known as "the scarlet
woman of Wall Street," the most notorious railroad stock of the nineteenth
century. But many railroad stocks soared and plunged in the early days of
the industry as the potential profits and the practical realities intersected
with the greed and fear of investors.

## Bigger is Better

It wasn't long before the small, local railway lines began to merge into larger 9 and larger entities, at first regional and then national in scope. In 1853, the New York Central was stitched together out of ten local lines running between Buffalo and Albany. When Cornelius (nicknamed "Commodore") Vanderbilt took control in 1867, he quickly merged it with his Hudson River Railroad, running from Manhattan to Albany, and then with the Lake Shore and Michigan Southern Railway, running west to Chicago. Carrying millions of tons of freight between the nation's two largest cities built the fabulous row of Vanderbilt mansions on Fifth Avenue.

With the growth of national and international markets, economies of 10 scale became possible in nearly all industries, and they quickly began to grow to take advantage of them. Instead of each village blacksmith making horseshoes from scratch, one factory could produce horseshoes by the hundreds of thousands at a fraction of the cost per unit. It was precisely to take advantage of such possibilities that many industries began to merge into larger entities and then into the "trusts" that have been a bogeyman of American politics ever since. But despite the supposed threat of "monopoly pricing," the cost of manufactured goods fell relentlessly as the nineteenth century progressed. In 1911, when Standard Oil was broken up, the price of kerosene was only about one-third of what it had been in 1870, when Standard Oil was formed.

Retailing, as well, could become national in scope, thanks to the rail- 11 roads. Sears Roebuck, Montgomery Ward, and Woolworth could not have offered such low prices and grown into such vast enterprises if they had not had the railroads to deliver their goods. Catalog companies, of course, threatened local retailers and forced them to lower their prices in order to compete effectively. This played no small part in making possible the fact that the period between the Civil War and World War I was an era completely without inflation, despite an economy that was—even with recurrent and severe depressions—growing explosively.

Internet retailers such as Amazon.com are doing to the American 12 economy exactly what Sears and Montgomery Ward did more than a century ago. Amazon is forcing local retailers to compete on a national scale. It is reducing prices and changing how businesses interact with their suppliers and consumers.

While the railroads themselves greatly increased the demand for some 13 goods, they also almost single-handedly gave birth to new industries. The need for rails built the iron and then the steel industries in both Europe and America, the measure of economic power by the dawn of the twentieth century. They, in turn, vastly expanded the mining industry. In a classic example of the synergy that is seldom recognized but is so much a part of economic history, the telegraph companies that sprang up after Samuel Morse demonstrated his invention in 1844 soon realized that the rights-of-way of the railroads were the perfect paths along which to string their lines. (Today, companies laying fiber-optic cable have discovered the same thing.) The railroads also saw that the telegraph could be used as a signaling system, allowing trains to move much more quickly and safely (and thus more cheaply) on the often single-track lines of the early days.

The Internet is proving equally synergistic. It has sparked growth in 14 nearly all sectors of high tech and no doubt will propel the wireless, PDA, and multimedia industries forward. It was not until 1946 that half the households in the country had their own telephones. Half a century later, thanks to the Internet, it is not unusual for middle-class households to have two, three, and even four telephone lines.

## Creative Distinction

By the twentieth century the railroads' endless ramifications had produced 15 our modern economic world. And much of our domestic politics have centered on devising rules needed to distribute fairly the vast wealth created by that world. (These regulations haven't always worked, of course. The Interstate Commerce Commission, established to protect the public from price gouging by the railroad companies, quickly evolved into a government-sponsored price-fixing cartel that devastated the American railroad industry in the long term.) In the future, we can expect much of our energy will go to figuring out how to distribute the vast wealth created by the Internet.

Just as the railroads—the application of the steam engine—were the 16 prime agent of the creative destruction of the pre-industrial world, so the Internet—an application of the computer—is becoming the prime agent in shaping the postindustrial world. And it is doing so a lot quicker than the railroads, which were expensive to build. The Erie Railroad, hardly a model of efficient management, to be sure, cost $23.5 million at a time when that sum was roughly what the federal government was spending per year. The Internet, on the other hand, has been dirt cheap to create.

Much of the infrastructure, such as telephone lines and personal com- 17 puters, already existed. Anyone can go into business as an Internet service provider with little more than a server costing a few thousand dollars and some telephone lines. A Web page can be established so easily and at so little cost that millions of teenagers have already done so. Thus it is no surprise that the Progress and Freedom Foundation reports that the Internet has spread to 25 percent of American households in only seven years, whereas the telephone took 35 years, five times as long, to reach that penetration. Nearly 40 percent of the American adult population now uses the Internet at home, work, or the local library.

## Train Wreck

The railroads overbuilt wildly in the decades after the Civil War, often for 18 competitive rather than economic reasons. In the 1880s and 1890s, as depression hit, two-thirds of the railroad tracks in the United States passed through receivership and were reorganized by the great Wall Street banks such as J.P. Morgan and Kuhn Loeb. This, of course, greatly strengthened the power of these banks. (In the first quarter of the twentieth century, J.P. Morgan's was probably the most powerful bank that ever existed.) But it also made it possible for the banks to impose needed reforms. At that time, it was the banks and the stock exchange, not the government, that required publicly traded companies to adopt generally accepted accounting principles and independent accountants to certify their books.

The Internet will not escape a shakeout of its own at some point. Most 19 of the thousand of entrepreneurs who rushed in at the first sign of opportunity will fall by the wayside, their fortunes as evanescent as rainbows.

The pieces, if the history of the railroads is any guide, will be picked up 20 by people who at first stood on the sidelines. Commodore Vanderbilt never built a railroad in his life. Instead he bought badly run ones, restructured them, merged them into efficient operations, and managed them superbly. (No Vanderbilt railroad went through reorganization at the hands of the banks.) He thus created the largest fortune of the railroad era and died the richest self-made man in the world.

Who the Commodore Vanderbilts of the Internet will be is impossible to 21 say at this point. (If I could, I wouldn't be spending my time writing magazine articles!) But whoever they turn out to be, they're going to make the old Commodore look like a welfare case.

## Questions about Strategy

1. How does Gordon use his introductory paragraph to establish the similarities between the railroad and the Internet?

2. How does Gordon use the alternating pattern to make connections between the railroad and the Internet? Why does he describe various features of the railroad first?

3. How does Gordon use the example of Commodore Vanderbilt as a guide to the possible future of the Internet?

## A Sampler of Other Essays

1. Jon Seidel, "Who Controls Information?" (student essay), p. 182.

2. Michael Rock, "Since When Did *USA Today* Become the National Design Ideal?" p. 120.

3. Gretel Ehrlich, excerpt from *The Solace of Open Spaces*, p. 139.

# Strategy Four: *Division and Classification*

## Selecting Your Subject

To find a suitable subject for a division and classification essay, you need to think about the world in terms of categories. Like the producers of the television game show "Jeopardy," you will never run out of categories, but you need to know how to divide and classify them. When you *divide*, you move downward from some concept (television news) to some system of subcategories within that concept (news, sports, and weather). When you *classify*, you move upward from specific examples (individual news commentators) to some feature they have in common (trustworthiness). Although you can select either strategy for a subject, you will find that the subjects you know best encourage you to use the strategies together. For example, you might divide a college sports program into its units (football, basketball, hockey, volleyball, and so on) and then classify these units according to their budgets (most money for football, least money for volleyball).

## Analyzing Your Audience

As with any writing assignment, when you write a classification essay, you need to think about what your readers already know and what they expect (or need). If you're writing on a new subject (social ceremonies in primitive societies) or explaining a specialized system (the botanist's procedure for identifying plants), your readers need precise definitions and many illustrations for each subcategory. If your readers already know how your subject is classified (G, PG, PG-13, R, NC-17, and X ratings for films), then you don't need to provide elaborate definitions, but you may want to use your illustrations to analyze whether the system works. If you're classifying rock musicians, your readers are likely to regard your system as self-enclosed—something to quibble with, but not something they're likely to use in their everyday lives. On the other hand, if you are classifying stereo equipment, your readers may want to use your system when they shop. In that case, you will need to divide your subject into all its possible categories and illustrate each category with concrete examples.

## Determining Your Purpose

Your chief purpose in writing a classification essay is to *explain* how a system is organized. You might want to explain an established system, such as the Library of Congress system for classifying books. At a deeper level, however, your purpose might be to define, analyze, and justify the principle that underlies the system. You can also write classification essays to *entertain* or to *persuade*. If you classify to entertain (classifying fools, for example), you have an opportunity to be clever and witty, pointing out the dramatic features of each category and providing striking examples of each type. If you classify to persuade, however, you need to be thoughtful and reasonable, as, for example, when you try to convince your readers that a new or controversial rezoning plan for land use is superior to the one already in place.

## Using the Strategy

When you write a classification essay, *divide your subject* into major categories that exhibit a common trait, then subdivide those categories into smaller units. Next, arrange *your categories* into a sequence that shows a logical or dramatic progression. Finally, *divide each of your categories.* First, show how a category is different from others; and second, discuss its most vivid examples. To make this strategy succeed, however, you must be sure that your classification system is *consistent, complete, emphatic,* and *significant.*

When you divide your subject into categories, *apply the same principle of selection to each class.* You may find this difficult if you are trying to explain an established but inconsistent system. You have only to visit a record store to realize that music is often sorted into categories that overlap and cross over. For example, a Dixie Chicks album could be classified as *country, pop, rock, standard,* or *female vocal.* To avoid such tangles, you may decide to create your own system, as Sarah did in Chapter 4 when she classified consumers according to how much they use coupons (pages 88–89).

After you have divided your subject into separate and consistent categories, *make sure your division is complete.* The simplest division separates a subject into A and Not-A. Although you can use this system to tell your readers something about one category (musicians), you won't be able to tell them much about the other (nonmusicians). For this reason, you should try to exhaust your subject by finding *at least three* categories and by acknowledging those examples that won't fit into your system.

Once you have divided your subject, *arrange your categories and examples in an emphatic order.* This strategy encourages you and your readers to think of your categories in some sort of ascending order— from first to last, from simple to complex, from least expensive to most expensive. This technique helps you to show how a category changes, to demonstrate variety in similarity, to distinguish good from bad.

Finally, you need to show *the significance of your system of classification.* The strength of the classifying process is that you can use it to analyze a subject by any number of systems. Its weakness is that you are tempted to classify a subject using all kinds of trivial or pointless categories. You can classify people by their educational backgrounds, their work experience, or their significant achievements; you can also classify them by their shoe size, favorite color, or tastes in ice cream. At the least, you need to demonstrate that your system counts because it analyzes a subject according to a significant subdivision.

# Student Essay

# Listmakers

## LARRY BUSH

**Introduction: Divide subject into three categories**

What's the big deal with lists? They are everywhere—on your refrigerator, on your computer screen, and in virtually every section of the newspaper. Somebody's always coming out with a new list of best sellers, worst picks, or top tens. Irving Wallace even wrote a book entitled *The Book of Lists.* Apparently people can't think about any subject without a list. Well, that's not entirely true. Not everybody thinks about lists in the same way. I have a list. The way I figure it, listmakers can be divided into one of three categories depending on their attitude toward lists. [1]

**Thesis: Establish single principle of division**

**Arrangement: Use numbers to establish order of classification**

**Category one:**    Casual listmakers make lists only on rare occasions. They don't make shopping lists unless they have to purchase more than twelve items. They never make Christmas lists for themselves or for others. Even when they make lists, they don't know how to use them. They forget to look at their list as they stroll through the grocery store. They never check things off their lists when they do their Christmas shopping. They often lose their lists without realizing it. And they have great difficulty reading (much less understanding) other people's lists. [2]

Casual listmakers are actually proud of their "list-less-ness." They proclaim that they don't need lists to run their lives. They can make choices and solve problems without constantly consulting some piece of paper. They view those who are obsessed with lists as slaves to a silly system. When asked, they reply that they have never heard of Irving Wallace's *The Book of Lists.* [3]

**Completeness: List information for each category**

**Category two:**    Careful listmakers make lists for most occasions. They always make detailed shopping and Christmas lists, and they usually make daily, or at least weekly, lists of things to do. They are fairly conscientious about using lists to organize their future plans, and checking these lists to see if they have forgotten something they have planned to do. They often make a new list of things they failed to do on their old list. They like to read other people's lists because they see such systems, however trivial, as interesting and entertaining. [4]

Careful listmakers actually need their lists. They explain that if they can control their lists, they can control their lives. They think (or hope) they live organized lives because they make lists. They view those who live without lists as disorganized, deficient—even irresponsible. When asked, careful listmakers admit that they have skimmed Wallace's *The Book of Lists,* but did not buy it because it wasn't on their shopping list. [5]

**Consistency: Cite Wallace's *The Book of Lists* for each category**

Emphasis: Clarify emphatic order by arranging system by the terms *casual, careful, compulsive*

**Category three:**     Compulsive listmakers make lists for absolutely every 6 occasion. They make lists by the day, by the hour, and by the portion of the hour. They make shopping lists for their family and Christmas lists for their friends. Compulsive listmakers are always inventing new ways to use their lists. They love to write things down so they can check them off. They are at their creative best devising elaborate cross-referencing systems to keep lists of their lists. They have to read, analyze, and debate the details on other people's lists.

Compulsive listmakers cannot live without their lists. They believe that 7 lists (and those who make them) rule the world. These "listamaniacs" cannot think or learn about anything without making a list. They view the "list-less" as hopelessly and extremely lost. When asked, they confess that they had a religious experience when they found *The Book of Lists* listed in the database of their public library. They immediately placed it on their shopping list, checked it off when they purchased it, and now hide it from their family and friends as though it were some sacred relic. They occasionally post tantalizing lists from the book on the refrigerator or the office bulletin board. They also compiled a list of all the people to whom they have given copies of the book and a list of their reactions to it—subdivided into two smaller lists of those people who 1. liked it and 2. loved it.

Significance: Point to significance of system by illustrating how exceptions can be included

Not everyone falls into one of these three categories. Although most 8 people like lists because they represent the orderly way they think they think—top to bottom, first to last—there are people who seem to think in other patterns. According to Wallace, these "holistic" thinkers can be listed in the following categories . . .

# Television Did It First:
# Ten Myths about "New" Media

## JESSICA HELFAND

In 1934, the American biologist William Beebe descended into a bathysphere  1
to a depth of 3,028 feet—a record at the time. While his journey was widely
reported on radio, today this historic event remains all but forgotten,
trapped in the technology of its time. And so it goes, as radio's coverage of
the bathysphere is replaced by television's coverage of the biosphere, sup-
planted by the Web's 62-minute global coverage of our most recent total
lunar eclipse. Will television soon become a forgotten relic now that the Web
is here?

Unlikely. Yet in discussions of new media, television is rarely—if ever—  2
cited. If and when it is, it is granted a kind of nostalgic mention: in the
summer of 1996, a *New York Times* reporter commented that, given its
remarkable coverage of the Mars landing, the Web had finally come into its
own as a popular news medium, "just as the broadcast of John F. Kennedy's
assassination became the defining moment for television as the nation's
information conduit of choice." This is but one of many example of the ways
in which television, as a distribution mechanism capable of capturing the
immediacy of global experience, likens itself to the Web.

*But television did it first.*  3

As a mutable, unpredictable, and increasingly complex cultural ideal,  4
"experience" has never been easy to capture, perhaps least of all by designers. (And if I hear one more designer say, "but what I really want to do is to
design experiences," I think I will scream. One is immediately reminded of
the unemployed actor who swears that what he really wants to do is direct.)
Nonetheless, as the screen becomes a stage upon which media of all kinds
must perform, one could argue that our collective cultural experience of
watching television offers innumerable cues for deciphering the alleged
innovations of contemporary media.

It is still easier to watch TV; it is also perhaps more efficient to surf the  5
Web, given the specificity with which search engines allow us to plot
the minutiae of our own course. Conversely, interactivity—as a two-way
medium—provides perhaps a greater feeling of personal reward that the
inert TV viewer might experience. And there is, too, the very basic fact that

Jessica Helfand, "Television Did It First: Ten Myths about 'New' Media," *Screen: Essays on Graphic Design, New Media, and Visual Culture* (New York: Princeton Architectural P, 2001).

the installed base of couches still greatly overshadows the number of personal computers in general circulation. Most puzzling, however, the prevailing sentiment seems to celebrate the new at the expense of the old. And what is so new about new media, anyway? Herewith, a few myths debunked:

MYTH **01:** The Internet makes everyone a star.                6

FACT: Television game shows did it first.                7

Game shows, quiz shows— people will do anything to be on television, to 8 publicize the silly or sordid details of their own lives, and, to the great delight of the viewing public, to degrade themselves wildly in the process. The Web services this very affliction by empowering users with a kind of *carte blanche* for rampant self-expression: everyone has a Webpage, everyone has an opinion, everyone is a star.

MYTH **02:** Virtual reality invites us to escape normal reality.                9

FACT: "Escapist" situation comedies did it first.                10

In the United States, the 1960s saw a preponderance of comedies produced 11 for television dominated by themes related to magic, witchcraft and fantasy. The popularity of shows like *I Dream of Jeannie* (a genie living in a bottle); *Bewitched* (a witch living in suburbia); *Mr. Ed* (a talking horse) or *My Mother the Car* (a talking car) lay in a slapstick formula that was repeated successfully again and again. In a decade of enormous political upheaval and social change, viewers found respite in watching—and indeed, in identifying with—characters who were at once unthreatening (mother's always in the garage) and clever (how did Jeannie manage to get out of that safe?). Now fast-forward some 30-odd years: consider the creation of virtual worlds we can invent—and inhabit—on the Web. No longer limited by the physical restrictions of the terrestrial world, such alternative environments fuel our imagination and encourage escape. But in today's decidedly less turbulent political climate, just what is it we are escaping from? Devotees of new media claim today's interactive technologies offer immersive experiences: yet while empowering, the capacity for immersion is still so dependent upon innumerable variables—connection speed, monitor settings, entering a URL with no typos—that it remains a distant, if intangible ideal. The Web works best as a kind of giant database, helping us manage the information jungle that threatens to overwhelm us. In this view, television still seems an easier escape from reality.

MYTH **03:** Content online should always play to the user's abbreviated attention 12 span.

FACT: TV viewers have always had a short attention span: variety and "vignette" 13 television did it first.

Comic variety shows such as *Laugh In* and *Saturday Night Live* in the U.S., and 14 *Benny Hill* and *Monty Python* in the U.K., have long been popular, crafted with the impatient viewer in mind. Banter characterized by brevity, pithy one-liners and exaggerated double-takes are a few of the devices that serve this genre well: on TV, they become the entry points for the channel-chasing viewer. On the Web, such percussive dialogue is the fabric of email: to channel-chase is to surf, an equally if not more impatient activity.

**MYTH 04:** "New" media must be kinetic in order to hook users. [15]

**FACT:** Broadcast news television did it first. [16]

In an interview in 1997, *Sixty Minutes* Executive Producer Don Hewitt [17] described his secret for engaging an audience. "You must have action in the first twelve seconds," he said. "It doesn't matter what the action is." The show, a legend in network news television, has won sixty-eight Emmy awards since its inception in 1968 and is the longest continuously-running primetime program ever. (Four years later, in an unusual display of moral conscience, Hewitt acknowledged his complicity in spawning this question-able genre. In his memoir *Tell Me a Story: Fifty Years and 60 Minutes in Television*, Hewitt apologizes for having fathered a form that has since gone horribly awry. Referring to the slippery slope of truth and drama referred to above, Hewitt writes: "We ruined television because we made it so profitable to do this kind of thing.") Certainly this blanket concept, whether intended as a definition of good television (or worse, of good journalism) raises criti-cal questions about the credibility of these shows in general. Does such emphasis on action slant the reporting of news? Is our attention span as a viewing public so short that we need to see things constantly moving in order to stay awake? Have we been so indoctrinated by the lure of action films and crime shows that we yearn to see such dramas unfold in the telling of our nightly news? The degree to which design conspires to build impact—whether through special effects or creative editing techniques—lies at the core of this debate: is "action" merely news made visually manifest? If so, what is the creative role for design? What is the ethical role?

**MYTH 05:** Reality TV is a new programming genre: it is all about voyeurism. [18]

**FACT:** Reality TV has been around since the 1950s. Voyeurism has been [19] around even longer.

Nostalgia buffs may recall a television series in both Britain and the U.S. enti- [20] tled *This Is Your Life* which, beginning in the mid-50s, was modeled on the following "reality TV" model: an unsuspecting celebrity was accosted by a TV host (Eammon Edwards in the U.K.; Ralph Edwards in the U.S.;) and made to publicly endure a retelling of his or her life, in front of a live studio audience, through the surprise appearance of various guests who would share their memories of the subject in question. Unrehearsed and impromptu, the show was a mixture of pulpy nostalgia and pure humiliation. (In England, football star Danny Blanchflower reportedly walked off the set in a stormy public display of embarrassment and anger at the invasion of his personal privacy.)

Today's reality TV offerings (*Survivor, Big Brother, The Weakest Link* 21 among others) differ only in their candor: rather than try to conceal the invasion of privacy, they celebrate it. Participants "share" information that results in exposing the flaws of their opponents, rather than applauding their charms. Clearly, the Internet in general (and Webcams in particular) go to great lengths to facilitate a kind of virtual voyeurism that is simply an updated variant of *This Is Your Life* with greater shock value—but without the celebrity status.

MYTH 06: Hyperlinked storytelling allows for interconnected narratives.  22
FACT: Television (and radio) soap operas did it first.  23
The dramatic genre known broadly as the soap opera depends on a  24 formula of serialized storytelling that has its own pace, unfolding steadily over weeks and months, spawning iterative, obstreperous links to other characters, stories, and occasionally to entire other shows. Character-driven rather than plot-based, soaps quickly become hyperlinked mini-orbits of interconnected people and places, threaded narratives and stories with no endings.

These programs (*EastEnders, Guiding Light*) succeed largely for two  25 reasons: first, because they build viewer interest steadily over time and across multiple plot lines (if you don't like one story you're sure to like another) and second, because the cumulative effect of this kind of viewing has a kind of residual emotional value: it succeeds not because it is physically interactive (click that mouse!) but because it is behaviorally interactive (tune in tomorrow!). Unlike the mathematically-plotted hyperlinks in many digital narratives where the emphasis is on action (think *Myst*), soaps succeed precisely because of this underlying emotional pull.

MYTH 07: Real-Time transmissions on the Web allow users to "experience"  26 history in the making.
FACT: Edward R. Murrow did it first.  27
Reporting daily on the radio from London during the Blitz and several  28 years later (with the support of the then "new" coaxial cable) on television, Murrow made history in the early 1950s by transmitting his reports to both American coasts at once. Premiering in 1951, his 30-minute news program, *See It Now*, opened with Murrow seated at a table, the camera pulling back to show parallel live shots of the Statue of Liberty in New York and the Bay in San Francisco. "We are impressed," he declared solemnly, "by a medium through which a man sitting in his living room has been able to look at both oceans at once." Recent Webcasts (24 Hours in Cyberspace, the chess match between Kasparov and Big Blue) are really no different; yet ironically, we remain perpetually amazed by such experiments in broadcast simultaneity.

**MYTH 08:** Online chatrooms offer a new way to promote social interaction and build community.   29

**FACT:** Television talk shows did it first.   30

The television talk-show format lets viewers watch as an informal dialogue 31 unfolds between interviewer and interviewee(s), the studio audience and the occasional telephone caller. Online chats and threaded discussions do the same: in each medium, there is a tendency toward idiosyncratic topics, a frequent and generally unpredictable splintering of themes, and a sort of uneditable and messy, down-home energy. The more formatted they become, the less modulation there is among voices, or visuals, or the "experiences" these dialogues (or "multilogues") generate. Most talk show sets look alike, as do most online discussions. Chatland . . . or flatland?

**MYTH 09:** Web advertising is annoying. Why can't someone make those banners go away?   32

**FACT:** TV advertising is annoying. Why can't someone make those commercials go away?   33

**MYTH 10:** The lure of selection draws people to surf the Web.   34

**FACT:** Television, in all its multi-channel glory, did it first.   35

It is perhaps ironic that the same things we celebrate about new media are 36 the things we once said we hated about TV. Quantity instead of quality. Edutainment instead of education. Media saturation. Privacy invasion. With satellites and syndication, cable and now the Web, the selection (of channels, of sites) expands; the price (of hardware, of software) diminishes while the input device (remote, mouse) continues to permit steady steering and increased navigation. (Incidentally, the remote had been around since 1955.)

And what of our media addiction? In 1996, *Newsweek* reported that by 37 the age of two, American kids spend an average of twenty-seven hours per week in front of the TV. Now add time spent Websurfing, and there is precious little time left to go froggin' down by the creek. Will the alleged "merger" of Web and TV help minimize this frightening statistic?

Ironically, our dreams of a new hybrid medium are likely to reveal just 38 the opposite: the survival of one medium over the other. Which will it be? Unlike TV, the good news about the Web is that it helps us see things in more digestible portions: critical mass, that terrifying notion of yesteryear, has given way to more rational ideas about community and identity; about hierarchy and chronology; and about efficiency, clarity, and accessibility. The bad news is, such fragmentation isolates individuals and creates a kind of lonely and disenfranchised—if empowered—user. And even this idea of the empowered user is (at least conceptually) not a new one. It was, after all, David Ogilvy who—more than twenty-five years ago—wrote: "The consumer is not a moron: she's your wife."

What we know is that today's media audiences expect the speed and per-<sup>39</sup> formance of TV, with the functionality and scope of the Web. They want to be lazy and they want to be engaged. They are users, viewers, and readers; senders and receivers; the judge and the jury. And it is only going to get more complicated as these lines continue to blur: between WWW and TV; between VDT and VCR; between static media, time-based media, and merged media. Call it what you will, but none of it is new.

## Questions about Strategy

1. What categories does Helfand use to divide her subject?
2. What other categories might she have included?
3. What conclusions does she draw from her division and classification?

## A Sampler of Other Essays

1. Ellen Haack, "A Man with All Reasons" (student essay) p. 75
2. Richard Saul Wurman, "The Five Rings," p. 50
3. Desmond Morris, "Territorial Behavior," p. 140

# Strategy Five: *Definition*

## Selecting Your Subject

All writing is defining. When you write about any subject, you select and connect words that have established meanings. Often, as you compose, you pause to define a special term or define the special way you intend to use a term. When you use definition as a strategy for several paragraphs or a whole essay, however, you have usually stumbled on to a word that needs extended definition. Such words may intrigue you because they seem different (*chutzpah*), difficult (*entropy*), or vague (*stress*). The word *definition* comes from *de* (with regard to) and *finite* (limits). When you are selecting a subject for an extended definition, you are looking for a word whose use or misuse has raised questions or created problems for you and your readers. You hope to clarify the situation by establishing limits for what this word can and cannot mean.

## Analyzing Your Audience

Before you use definition as a writing strategy, think about what your readers already know *or* think they know about the word you have selected to define. Most of your readers may already have a working definition for a word such as *class*. You need to consider these common definitions—how they have been used and misused—as you organize your essay. If you assure your readers that you are familiar with the meanings they know, you may entice them to consider your explanation of the problems these definitions have caused. Similarly, you need to be alert to the problems or questions your readers may have with your attempt to define your term. They may expect you to define other terms before they consider your definition of your term. For example, in order for your readers to follow your definition of *white-collar crime*, they may need definitions for a cluster of related words such as *insider trading*, *junk bonds*, and *privilege*.

## Determining Your Purpose

Your primary purpose in writing a definition is to identify the *special nature* of something. On some occasions, you will need to explain the *exact use* of a particular word or concept. If you are trying to write about a new computer software system, your purpose may be to restrict the meanings of a word such as *file* to a specific one. On other occasions, you will want to argue for the *expanded use* of a word. If you are trying to discuss a historical movement, your purpose may be to open up the use of a word such as *culture* to a variety of interpretations. On still other occasions, you will need to interpret the *conflicting uses* of a controversial word. If you are trying to analyze a social problem, your purpose may be to balance the various uses of a word such as *euthanasia* so that you don't alienate the opposing sides before you have an opportunity to present your definition.

## Using the Strategy

You can select one strategy for defining or use several in combination. Perhaps the most straightforward method for defining anything is *giving examples*. This technique is as natural as a child reading *horse* or *giraffe* in a book and then pointing to the picture on the opposite page. The examples you "point" to should be concrete and cogent. If you introduce vague or unusual examples, you are likely to confuse rather than clarify your discussion.

You can also define by *analyzing qualities* or *attributing characteristics*. These methods build on the procedures followed in dictionaries and thesauruses, which define a word with similar words, or synonyms. Such methods suggest the nuances of a word and avoid the problem of circular definition. For example, to avoid definitions such as "a *charming* person is someone who has *charm*," consider how the following list of synonyms for *charming* might help you identify qualities or characteristics: *pleasant, agreeable, sensual, glamorous, poised, eloquent, tasteful*.

Two other methods that can help you define a term are *defining negatively* and *giving functions*. Most dictionaries provide *antonyms* as well as synonyms to clarify the meaning of a word. For example, you could define *charming* by discussing the meanings of *vulgar*. A more complex procedure might involve using synonyms to define negatively. That is, you could say that a *charming* person may be *sensual* but not *sexual*. Sometimes the most significant (defining) fact about a person, object, or institution is what he, she, or it does. When you define a person as *charming*, you might consider what he or she does: For example, "a charming person *anticipates, empathizes with,* and *responds to* the concerns of others."

Finally, because definition is essential to the writing process, you may find yourself combining it with other strategies. In process analysis you need to define special terms. In comparison and contrast, you need to define the differences and similarities between the subjects of your comparison. In division and classification, you need to define the subcategories you explain. And in any causal analysis or argument, you must define your terms.

# Student Essay

# Depression

## SUE KIRBY

**Introduction: Establish misunderstanding of word**

Depression is a disabling illness we are reluctant to see. People of all ages and socioeconomic groups suffer from depression. Many do not seek treatment because they don't recognize the symptoms. Depression is frequently misidentified as "the blues." "You'll get over it" and "Cheer up" are what people often say to a depressed person. "Look on the bright side." The well-wisher's intent is to snap the person out of the symptoms. Attempts are often made to identify the event that caused the depression. This minimizes the depressed person's experience and implies that if he were stronger willed, he would be well. I have been clinically depressed, and I know that if all it took was wanting to get better, no one would ever be truly depressed. Although traumatic or stressful events may make an individual more vulnerable to depression, it is not the events that must be overcome. 1

**Analyze qualities**

Depression is not merely feeling unhappy or sad but a pervasive feeling of hopelessness and sadness that is unrelenting. Day in and day out most of every day the person with depression is bombarded with negative thoughts, self-doubts, and guilt. Sleep and appetite disturbances almost always accompany depression and affect the overall health of the individual with depression. The person usually has difficulty concentrating. Motivation and interest in work or activities a person once found pleasurable disappear. 2

**Attribute characteristics**

Thoughts of suicide are common and make depression a life-threatening illness. Frequently the depressed person obsesses about suicide. Because depression affects the person's ability to think clearly, logical approaches to talk the person out of suicide rarely are helpful. 3

**Give examples**

The best intervention begins with an honest assessment of the depressed person's thoughts and intents about self-harm. Simply asking the person if he has any thoughts of suicide or self-harm creates an open, honest dialogue. It is important to offer acceptance of the person's thoughts and feelings without condoning suicide as an option. Empathy can be affirming and comforting to the person. Assuring that you will assist the person to get help and working to keep your friend safe from acting upon suicidal thoughts are powerful interventions in suicide prevention. 4

**Clarify purpose for definition**

Depression can be treated. Many people suffer needlessly not only due to lack of recognition of the illness but due to stigma associated with mental illness. Although it is a common illness, people are reluctant to acknowledge they have been treated for depression; that is why I am writing this paper today. Until the Americans with Disabilities Act became law, employers 5 readily discriminated against persons treated for a mental illness such as depression. Insurance companies rarely provide the same levels of coverage for treatment of a psychiatric illness as are allowed for other illnesses. Many physicians are reluctant to diagnose their patients with depression because of society's stigma or their own prejudices.

**Conclusion: Explain that misunderstanding can be resolved**

Depression can be identified and treated. By acknowledging the symptoms, we enable persons suffering with depression to get the treatment needed and make depression a visible illness. 6

# Professional Essay

# Attention! Multitaskers

## JAMES GLEICK

The final, fatal flaw in the time-use pie chart is that we are multitasking crea- [1] tures. It is possible, after all, to tie shoes and watch television, to eat and read, to shave and talk with the children. These days it is possible to drive, eat, listen to a book, and talk on the phone, all at once, if you dare. No segment of time—not a day, not a second—can really be a zero-sum game.

"Attention! Multitaskers," says an advertisement for an AT&T wireless [2] telephone service. "Demo all these exciting features"—namely E-mail, voice telephone, and pocket organizer. Pay attention if you can. We have always multitasked—inability to walk and chew gum is a time-honored cause for derision—but never so intensely or so self-consciously as now. If haste is the gas pedal, multitasking is overdrive. We are multitasking connoisseurs— experts in crowding, pressing, packing, and overlapping distinct activities in our all-too-finite moments. Some reports from the front lines:

David Feldman, in New York, schedules his tooth-flossing to coincide [3] with his regular browsing of on-line discussion groups (the latest in food, the latest in Brian Wilson). He has learned to hit Page Down with his pinky. Mark Maxham of California admits to even more embarrassing arrange- ments of tasks. "I find myself doing strange little optimizations," he says, "like life is a set of computer code and I'm a compiler." Similarly, by the time Michael Hartl heads for the bathroom in his California Institute of Technol- ogy digs each morning, he has already got his computer starting its progress through the Windows boot sequence, and then, as he runs to breakfast, he hits Control-Shift-D to dial into the campus computer network, and then he gets his Web browser started, downloading graphics, so he can check the news while he eats. "I figure I save at least two or three minutes a day this way," he says. "Don't laugh." Then there's the subroutine he thinks of as "the mouthwash gambit," where he swigs a mouthful on one pass by the sink, swishes it around in his mouth as he gets his bicycle, and spits out as he heads back in the other direction, toward a class in general relativity.

The word *multitasking* came from computer scientists of the 1960s. They [4] arranged to let a single computer serve multiple users on a network. When a computer multitasks, it usually just alternates tasks, but on the finest of time scales. It slices time and interleaves its tasks. Unless, that is, it has more than one processor running, in which case multitasking can be truly parallel processing.

James Gleick, "Attention! Multitaskers," *Faster: The Acceleration of Just About Everything* (New York: Pantheon, 1999), 167–72.

Either way, society grabbed the term as fast as it did *Type A*. We apply it to our own flesh-and-blood CPUs. Not only do we multitask, but, with computers as our guides, we multitask self-consciously.

Multitasking begins in the service of efficiency. Working at a computer 5 terminal in the London newsroom of Bloomberg News, Douglas McGill carried on a long telephone conversation with a colleague in New York. His moment of realization came when, still talking on the phone, he sent off an E-mail message to another colleague in Connecticut and immediately received her reply. "It squeezes more information than was previously squeezable into a given amount of time," he says. "I wonder if this contributes to that speeding-up sensation we all feel?" Clearly it does.

Is there any limit? A few people claim to be able to listen to two different 6 pieces of music at once. Many more learn to take advantage of the brain's apparent ability to process spoken and written text in separate channels. Mike Holderness, in London, watches television with closed captioning so that he can keep the sound off and listen to the unrelated music of his choice. Or he writes several letters at once—"in the sense that I have processes open and waiting." None of this is enough for a cerebral cortex conditioned to the pace of life on-line, he realizes:

> Ten years ago, I was delighted and enthralled that I could get a telegram-like E-mail from Philadelphia to London in only fifteen minutes. Three years ago, I was delighted and enthralled that I could fetch an entire thesis from Texas to London in only five minutes. Now, I drum my fingers on the desk when a hundred-kilobyte file takes more than twenty seconds to arrive . . . damn, it's coming from New Zealand . . .

It seems natural to recoil from this simultaneous fragmentation and 7 overloading of human attention. How well can people really accomplish their multitasks? "It's hard to get around the forebrain bottleneck," said Earl Hunt, a professor of psychology and computer science at the University of Washington. "Our brains function the same way the Cro-Magnon brains did, so technology isn't going to change that." But for many—humans, not computers—a sense of satisfaction and well-being comes with this saturation of parallel pathways in the brain. We divide ourselves into parts, perhaps, each receiving sensations, sending messages, or manipulating the environment in some way. We train ourselves as Samuel Renshaw would have trained us. Or, then again, we slice time just as a computer does, feeding each task a bit of our attention in turn. Perhaps the young have an advantage because of the cultural conditioning they received from early exposure to computers and fast entertainment media. Corporate managers think so. Marc Prensky, a Bankers Trust vice president, had to learn to overcome instinctive annoyance when a young subordinate began reading E-mail during a face-to-face conversation; the subordinate explained: "I'm still listening; I'm parallel processing." This whole generation of workers, Prensky decided, weaned on video games, operates at *twitch speed*—"your thumbs going a million miles a minute," and a good thing, if managers can take advantage of it.

At least one computer manufacturer, Gateway, applies multitasking to 8 technical support. Customers call in for help, wait on hold, and then hear voices. "Hello," they are told. "You are on a conference call." William Slaughter, a lawyer calling from Philadelphia, slowly realizes that he has joined a tech-support group therapy session. He listens to Brian helping Vince. Next, Vince listens to Brian helping William. It's like a chess master playing a simultaneous exhibition, William thinks, though Brian seems a bit frazzled. Somehow the callers cope with their resentment at not being deemed worthy of Brian's undivided attention. Why should he sit daydreaming while they scurry to reboot? "Hello, Vicky," they hear him say. "You are on a conference call."

There is ample evidence that many of us choose this style of living. We're 9 willing to pay for the privilege. An entire class of technologies is dedicated to the furthering of multitasking. Waterproof shower radios and, now, telephones. Car phones, of course. Objects as innocent-seeming as trays for magazines on exercise machines are tools for multitasking (and surely television sets are playing in the foreground, too). Picture-in-picture display on your television set. (Gregory Stevens, in Massachusetts: "PIP allows me to watch PBS/C-Span or the like, and keep the ball game on or an old movie. Of course, it is impossible for anyone else to enjoy this, with me changing the pictures and audio feed every few seconds. When the computer and the phone are available in a multiwindow form on the television, things are going to be very different.") Even without picture-in-picture, the remote control enables a time-slicing variation on the same theme. Marc Weidenbaum, in San Francisco, has a shorthand for describing an evening's activities to his girlfriend: "Got home. Ate some soup. Watched twenty or thirty shows." He means this more or less literally:

> I'll watch two sitcoms and a *Star Trek: Voyager* episode and routinely check MTV (didn't they used to run music videos?) and CNN (didn't they used to run news?) in a single hour.
> And really not feel like I'm missing out on anything.

Nothing could be more revealing of the transformation of human sensi- 10 bility over the past century than this widespread unwillingness to settle for soaking up, in single-task fashion, the dynamic flow of sound and picture coming from a television screen. Is any one channel, in itself, monotonous? Marshall McLuhan failed to predict this: the medium of television seemed *cool* and all-absorbing to him, so different from the experience available to us a generation later. For the McLuhan who announced that the medium was the message, television was a black-and-white, unitary stream. McLuhan did not surf with remote control. Sets were tiny and the resolution poor—"visually low in data," he wrote in 1964, "a ceaselessly forming contour of things limned by the scanning finger." People were seen mostly in close-up, perforce. Thus he asserted: "TV will not work as background. It engages you. You have to be *with* it."

No longer. Paradoxically, perhaps, as television has gained in vividness 11 and clarity, it has lost its command of our foreground. For some people television has been bumped off its pedestal by the cool, fast, fluid, indigenously multitasking activity of browsing the Internet. Thus anyone—say, Steven Leibel of California—can counter McLuhan definitively (typing in one window while reading a World Wide Web page in another): "The Web and TV complement each other perfectly. TV doesn't require much attention from the viewer. It fits perfectly into the spaces created by downloading Web pages." If he really needs to concentrate, he turns down the sound momentarily. Not everyone bothers concentrating. Eight million American households report television sets and personal computers running, together in the same room, "often" or "always."

Not long ago, listening to the simpler audio stream of broadcast radio 12 was a single-task activity for most people. The radio reached into homes and grabbed listeners by the lapel. It could dominate their time and attention—for a few decades. "A child might sit," Robinson and Godbey recall sentimentally, "staring through the window at the darkening trees, hearing only the Lone Ranger's voice and the hooves of horses in the canyon." Now it is rare for a person to listen to the radio *and do nothing else*. Programmers structure radio's content with the knowledge that they can count on only a portion of the listener's attention, and only for intermittent intervals. And rarely with full attention. Much of the radio audience at any given moment has its senses locked up in a more demanding activity—probably driving. Or showering, or cooking, or jogging. Radio has become a secondary task in a multitasking world.

## Questions about Strategy

1. How does James Gleick explain the origin of the word *multitasking?*

2. How does Gleick use the routines of people such as David Feldman, Mark Maxham, and Michael Hartl to illustrate multitasking?

3. In what ways does Marshall McLuhan's failure to explain *multitasking* reveal how this new behavior has changed our lives?

## A Sampler of Other Essays

# Strategy Six: *Causal Analysis*

## Selecting Your Subject

When you look for a subject for causal analysis, you are simply being curious. You want to find out why something happened (cause) and what results it produced (effects). Any subject you choose—from why your car won't start to what you can see through a satellite telescope—will have multiple causes and effects. The interrelationship between causes and effects is what makes a particular subject interesting. But to manage your subject effectively, you will need to sort out minor or remote causes so that you can focus on the major causes and effects you want to analyze. You will also need to decide which part of the process seems most significant—the causes or the effects. Do you want to explain why your car wouldn't start, or analyze what happened when you couldn't use your car?

## Analyzing Your Audience

You can assume that your readers, like you, are always curious about why something happens and what results it produces. But you cannot assume that your readers will remain curious for very long if you simply list causes or point to effects. They expect you to show them the connection—they want to know how the causal relationship works. For that reason you must consider some of the following questions: How ready are your readers to follow your analysis? What sort of context do you need to give them to help them see the significance of your subject? How much and what kind of evidence will they need to accept your assertion about the connection between the causes and effects you describe?

## Determining Your Purpose

When you write a causal analysis, you're likely to have one of three purposes. Frequently, you are writing to *explain* how and why things happen. If you are trying to explain how to establish the price of a product or why you exceeded your budget, your purpose is to *isolate* specific causes and effects. At other times, you are writing to *speculate* about the possible causes or potential effects of a certain chain of events. If you are trying to speculate about a new style in fashion, your purpose is to theorize, to *expand* the range of possible causes and consequences. And of course, you can use causal analysis to *argue* that a certain relationship exists between one set of events and another. If you are trying to argue that the consumption of alcohol causes heart disease, your purpose is to acknowledge the possibility of other causal relationships before presenting your best evidence for the relationship you consider the most probable.

## Using the Strategy

You can organize your causal analysis in two ways: (1) you can start with some event or idea and work backward, identifying, analyzing, and speculating about its causes; or (2) you can begin with some event or idea and move forward, theorizing, considering, or forecasting effects. Whether you decide to emphasize causes or effects, you will discover that the motion of life makes your starting point somewhat arbitrary. All causes have effects, which in turn become causes. The more efficient way to bring this process under control in your writing is to (1) state your claim early, (2) explain the connection you are attempting to demonstrate, and (3) present the evidence for connections you intend to analyze.

   To write an effective causal analysis, you should also avoid the following problems:

1. *Exaggerated claim.* Don't overstate your case, particularly when you are writing about complex situations that involve people. Many plausible cause-and-effect relationships are difficult to prove conclusively, so present your analysis as a possible explanation rather than the only explanation.

2. *Hasty generalization.* Don't oversimplify the cause-and-effect relationship. Important events are seldom the result of one simple cause and rarely produce one simple effect. For that reason, qualify your assertions with phrases such as "a major cause," "one result," or "an immediate effect."

3. *Circular cause.* Don't chase your own tail by analyzing effects that are already imbedded in the cause. Circular readings can produce sentences such as "There weren't enough tickets for the concert because there were too many people in line."

   As these problems suggest, causal analysis can be tricky. But that doesn't mean you should avoid using this strategy until you are absolutely sure of your information. You can't always wait to make an analysis or forecast. The best you can do is observe carefully, speculate intelligently, and, when appropriate, qualify your analysis.

# Student Essay

# Only Child Policy

## YILI SHI

Introduction: Establish context and cause of the policy

The biggest problem facing the People's Republic of China in its attempt to build a modern socialist state is its own population. One out of every four people in the world lives in China. This enormous population of over one billion people causes incredibly complex difficulties in virtually every aspect of daily life. In 1979, the Chinese government made a dramatic step to control the growth of this population by declaring that each family could produce only one child. Given the size of the population, the speed at which it was growing, and the strains it was placing on any attempt to chart China's future, the "only child policy" seemed logical and necessary. But implementing it has caused a wide range of social and psychological problems for China's families and their children.

Thesis: Assert that policy has social and psychological effects

Analysis: Consider the immediate effect of policy on traditional family

The immediate problem was that the policy contradicted the long established values of the Chinese family. According to tradition, a family's prosperity is judged by the number of children it produces. In particular, sons are valued because they carry on the family name, cultivate and harvest the family farm, and create additional workers for the family when they marry. By contrast, daughters give up their family name when they marry, move to another place, and work for the prosperity of another family. Given such values, traditional families, especially those in rural areas, resisted the only child policy or sabotaged it by killing baby girls in the hopes that the next "only" child would be a boy.

Analysis: Consider how policy affects aging in city families

The only child policy created another set of problems for families in the city. They looked at the inevitable imbalance between old and young (4:2:1—four grandparents, two parents, and one child) and began to wonder who would take care of them in their old age. On the farm, the eldest son inherits the land and the responsibility for taking care of his parents and aging relatives. In the city, the eldest son has no land and sees his parents and grandparents as an expensive obligation. He prefers to live in his own place, or live off his parents if he can't find a place. In either case, he searches for some form of independence and submits to the wishes of his wife rather than his parents. By contrast, city girls, even after they marry, stay in close contact with their family. They ask their husbands to work for the family, donate money for clothes and food, and look after aging parents and grandparents.

Analysis: Discuss unplanned social effects of policy

Once families accepted the only child policy, they faced the problem of exceptions. What would a family do if it did not plan effectively? Rich families could pay the fine for violating the policy, but poor families would have to find some other, no doubt unpleasant, solution. And what about divorce? If a couple has one child and then decides to separate, who gets the child, who gets to produce another child, and who decides who gets what?

Analysis: Speculate about psychological effects of policy

The biggest problem caused by the implementation of the only child 5 policy was the fear that only children will develop undesirable personalities. If a newly married couple realizes even before their child is born that this child is going to be their only child, how will this knowledge affect the way they raise the child? Will they be over-protective, over-indulgent, catering to their child's every wish and whim? If an only child grows up without siblings, without having to compete for attention and affection, how will he relate to the world outside the family?

The only child policy will be a disaster if it creates a country of self- 6 centered, spoiled brats who do not care about their families, and who do not know how to work and play with others, much less lead their nation into the next century.

Conclusion: Suggest possible long-term effects caused by policy

Apparently, the result of China's only child policy will be the creation of 7 other policies—a policy to establish classes to teach Chinese families how to interpret their new tradition; a policy to establish nursing homes to care for elderly citizens in case their children abandon them; and a policy to establish counseling centers to help parents and only children work out their psychological problems.

# Changing History

## ERIC FONER

All history, the saying goes, is contemporary history. People instinctively 1
turn to the past to help understand the present. Events draw our attention
to previously neglected historical subjects. The second wave of feminism
gave birth to a flourishing subfield of women's history. The Reagan Revolution spawned a cottage industry in the history of U.S. conservatism.

Many years will pass before we can fully assess how our thinking about 2
history has changed as a result of September 11. While historians ponder
this question, conservative ideologues have produced a spate of polemical
statements on how we should teach American history in light of recent
events. In a speech less than a month after the tragedy, Lynne Cheney
insisted that calls for more intensive study of the rest of the world amounted
to blaming America's "failure to understand Islam" for the attack. A letter
distributed by the American Council of Trustees and Alumni, which she
once chaired, chastised professors who fail to teach the "truth" that civilization itself "is best exemplified in the West and indeed in America."

In *What's So Great About America*, Dinesh D'Souza contends that 3
freedom and religious toleration are uniquely "Western" beliefs. The publisher's ad for the book identifies those who hold alternative views as "people
who provide a rationale for terrorism." With funding from conservative
foundations and powerful political connections, such commentators hope
to reshape the teaching of American history.

Historians cannot predict the future, but the past they portray must be one 4
out of which the present can plausibly have grown. The self-absorbed, super-
celebratory history now being promoted will not enable students to make
sense of either their own society or our increasingly interconnected world.

Historians cannot choose the ways history becomes part of our own 5
experience. September 11 has rudely placed certain issues at the forefront of
our consciousness. Let me mention three and their implications for how
we think about the American past: the upsurge of patriotism, significant
infringements on civil liberties and a sudden awareness of considerable dis-
trust abroad of American actions and motives.

The generation of historians that came of age during the Vietnam War 6
witnessed firsthand how patriotic language and symbols, especially the American flag, can be invoked in the service of manifestly unjust causes. Partly as a
result, they have tended to neglect the power of these symbols as genuine

Eric Foner, "Changing History," *The Nation* 5 Sept. 2002. 5 Feb. 2003 <http://www.thenation.com>.

expressions of a sense of common national community. Patriotism, if studied at all, has been understood as an "invention," rather than a habit of the heart.

Historians have had greater success lately at dividing up the American past into discrete experiences delineated along lines of race, ethnicity, gender and class than at exploring the common threads of American nationality. But the immediate response to September 11 cut across these boundaries. No one knows if the renewed sense of common purpose and shared national identity that surfaced so vividly after September 11 will prove temporary. But they require historians to devote new attention to the roots of the symbols, values and experiences Americans share as well as those that divide them.

All patriotic upsurges run the risk of degenerating into a coercive drawing of boundaries between "loyal" Americans and those stigmatized as aliens and traitors. This magazine has chronicled the numerous and disturbing infringements on civil liberties that have followed September 11. Such legal protections as habeas corpus, trial by impartial jury, the right to legal representation and equality before the law regardless of race or national origin have been seriously curtailed.

Civil liberties have been severely abridged during previous moments of crisis, from the Alien and Sedition Acts of 1798 to Japanese-American internment in World War II. Historians generally view these past episodes as shameful anomalies. But we are now living through another such episode, and there is a remarkable absence of public outcry.

We need an American history that sees protections for civil liberties not as a timeless feature of our "civilization" but as a recent and fragile achievement resulting from many decades of historical struggle. We should take a new look at obscure Supreme Court cases—*Fong Yue Ting* (1893), the Insular Cases of the early twentieth century, *Korematsu* during world War II—in which the Justices allowed the government virtual carte blanche in dealing with aliens and in suspending the rights of specific groups of citizens on grounds of military necessity. Dissenting in *Fong Yue Ting*, which authorized the deportation of Chinese immigrants without due process, Justice David Brewer observed that, like today, the power was directed against a people many Americans found "obnoxious." But, he warned, "who shall say it will not be exercised tomorrow against other classes and other people?"

September 11 will also undoubtedly lead historians to examine more closely the history of the country's relationship with the larger world. Public opinion polls revealed that few Americans have any knowledge of other people's grievances against the United States. A study of our history in its international context might help to explain why there is widespread fear outside our borders that the war on terrorism is motivated in part by the desire to impose a Pax Americana in a grossly unequal world.

Back in the 1930s, historian Herbert Bolton warned that by treating the American past in isolation, historians were helping to raise up a "nation of chauvinists"—a danger worth remembering when considering the drumbeat of calls for a celebratory and insular history divorced from its global context. Of course, international paradigms can be every bit as obfuscating as histories that are purely national. We must be careful not to reproduce traditional American exceptionalism on a global scale.

September 11, for example, has inspired a spate of commentary influ- 13 enced by Samuel Huntington's mid-1990s book *The Clash of Civilizations*. Huntington's paradigm reduces politics and culture to a single characteristic—race, religion or geography—that remains forever static, divorced from historical development or change through interaction with other societies. It makes it impossible to discuss divisions within these purported civilizations. The idea that the West is the sole home of reason, liberty and tolerance ignores how recently such values triumphed in the United States and also ignores the debates over creationism, abortion rights and other issues that suggest that commitment to them is hardly unanimous. The definition of "Western civilization" is highly selective—it includes the Enlightenment but not the Inquisition, liberalism but not the Holocaust, Charles Darwin but not the Salem witch trials.

Nor can September 11 be explained by reference to timeless character- 14 istics or innate pathologies of "Islamic civilization." From the Ku Klux Klan during Reconstruction to Oklahoma City in our own time, our society has produced its own home-grown terrorists. Terrorism springs from specific historical causes, not the innate qualities of one or another civilization.

The study of history should transcend boundaries rather than reinforce 15 or reproduce them. In the wake of September 11, it is all the more imperative that the history we teach be a candid appraisal of our own society's strengths and weaknesses, not simply an exercise in self-celebration— a conversation with the entire world, not a complacent dialogue with ourselves.

## Questions about Strategy

1. How does Foner characterize the possible effects of teaching "celebratory history"?

2. What three consequences does Foner see emerging from September 11?

3. How does Foner explain the causes of terrorism?

## A Sampler of Other Essays

1. Andrew Gaub, "The Telephone Paradox" (student essay), p. 122

2. Calvin Trillin, "Comforting Thoughts," p. 73

3. Alan Devoe, excerpt from *Lives Around Us*, p. 144

## Strategy Seven: *Argument*

### Selecting Your Subject

As you think about possible subjects for an argument, think of yourself as an attorney in a courtroom. You have collected your evidence and formed an opinion about your subject, but the other attorney has also collected evidence and formed an opinion that challenges yours. In other words, when you look for a subject, look for the opposition. When you do, you will discover that some subjects are not worth an argument. You can argue about *facts*—who scored the most touchdowns. You can argue about *opinions*—what's the best movie. The first argument can be settled quickly by checking a reference book; the second argument can never be settled because such opinions are based on preference or prejudice. The best subject for an argument is one that can be debated by sensible people presenting evidence, appealing to authorities, and rendering judgments that follow from careful reasoning. See, for example, the various arguments about the military and the media in Chapter 7.

### Analyzing Your Audience

You can never write an argument in a vacuum. If you are an attorney, for example, you are making your argument to a small audience (the jury) and several larger audiences (the people standing outside the courtroom or reading about the trial in a newspaper). The first group is impartial and willing to listen to both sides. The second group contains people who have already made up their minds or who are only vaguely aware of the issues in the trial. Good writers, like good attorneys, must identify readers (friendly and hostile), speculate about potential readers (detached and disinterested), and present all groups with evidence that they will see as appropriate, significant, and reliable. See "Analyzing the Audience" in Chapter 7 (pages 164–166).

### Determining Your Purpose

The most obvious purpose for conducting an argument is to settle a dispute about some controversy or conflict. You make your best case and let the jury, your readers, decide. But you may write arguments for other purposes. Sometimes you may argue to *support a cause*, composing an editorial in favor of subsidized child care on your campus. You may also argue to *promote change*, drafting a petition to reduce student fees. Sometimes you may argue to *refute a theory*, composing a history paper on why you think the antislavery movement was not the chief cause of the Civil War. You can also write arguments to *arouse sympathy*, circulating an essay to support better laws against child abuse. Or sometimes you may argue to *find agreement,* helping apartment residents reach a consensus about a policy on pets. Each of these purposes suggests a slightly different strategy for organizing and presenting your argument.

## Using the Strategy

Two related strategies for conducting an argument are *induction* and *deduction.* In induction, you present a series of individual examples until a particular pattern emerges. Then you make an inductive leap and claim that these examples provide sufficient evidence for your general conclusion. In deduction, you present a general assertion and then attempt to prove its validity by examining individual examples. The two processes are interrelated because to organize your evidence by *induction,* you have to begin with *deduction.* That is, your introduction presents your thesis statement, the generalization you hope to prove by analyzing your individual examples.

Another strategy for organizing an argument borrows from comparison and contrast. In this strategy, you (1) present your opponent's side and then your side (divided pattern), or (2) present one point of your opponent's argument, refute it, assert your point, and move on to the next point (alternating pattern). Another version of this strategy compares each set of points to demonstrate areas of agreement rather than disagreement. In all three methods, you should present the other side first—in a fair and balanced way—and then present your side as the conclusion or accommodation that makes more sense.

As you arrange your argument, avoid oversimplifying or distorting your evidence. An error due to faulty reasoning is called a *fallacy* (see Chapter 7, pages 174–176). When you purposely make such errors to deceive people, you are guilty of *fraud.*

Finally, you need to use the *three appeals* of any argument: *logical, emotional,* and *ethical.* In the logical appeal, use rational methods, such as making claims and citing evidence to support your case. Because such methods appeal to your readers' intelligence, they are probably the best strategies for making your argument convincing. But emotional and ethical appeals have their value too. *Connotative language* and *dramatic examples* appeal to your readers' emotions and persuade them to accept your argument. *Expert testimony* and a *reasonable tone* appeal to your readers' desire for trustworthiness and convince them that they should believe in your competence. Although emotional and ethical appeals must be used with caution (see Chapter 7, pages 170–172), they can enrich and enlighten an otherwise dry and uninspiring argument.

# The Recycling Controversy

## JILL TARASKIEWICZ

Introduction: Identify contending sides

Thesis: Assert new position

Arrangement: Present critics of recycling

Evidence: Cite expert

Evidence: Cite expert's study

Evidence: Cite argument 1. Excessive cost

Recycling has become routine in our culture. We automatically sort plastic containers for curbside pickup, deliver weekly piles of newspapers to community collection bins, and purchase products marked by the symbol ♻ of our collective effort. But recent studies of these common practices have reopened the recycling controversy. Critics contend that recycling has become expensive and inefficient. Advocates assert that it remains essential to our economic and technological development. By considering both sides in this controversy, we can understand how recycling fits into our environmental policy.

The major criticism against recycling is cost. The simple process of sorting plastic containers for curbside pickup does not anticipate the expense of collecting, separating, and reprocessing the seven basic types of plastic at the recycling plant (Van Voorst 53). Indeed, those procedures do not approach cost effectiveness until plants can collect enough raw material to keep the recycling machines running continuously. John Bell reports in the *New Scientist* that "Germany gave up the idea of trying to run a recycling plant at Coburg because it could not find 5 tons of waste plastic a day within 100 kilometers" (44). Even consumer advocate Lynn Scarlett acknowledges that putting one set of trucks on the road "to pick up recyclables, [and] another for remaining waste" not only strains community budgets but also creates more fuel consumption and air pollution.

The cost of recycling is dramatically evident in the elaborate "de-inking" technology required to convert old newspapers into reusable paper. In his study, Dan Charles describes some of the complicated steps in this expensive procedure:

> The process relies on turning old paper into pulp with water and chemicals, before spinning it in tubes to remove any heavy contaminants like staples or sand. . . . Ink particles attach themselves to air bubbles and rise to the surface, where they are scraped off. . . . [T]he paper fibers are bleached with hydrogen peroxide. . . . None of these processes do very well at removing or hiding laser print, glue or paper coatings. (13)

Because of the cost of such procedures—$50 million to build one plant—many newsprint producers are reluctant to invest in de-inking technology. Marcia Berss points out that recycling newspapers does not really save trees: "U.S. virgin newsprint is largely made from trees grown as a crop" (41). This agro-business has created such an "overcapacity of virgin newsprint" that newsprint producers see "no way to recoup the cost of capital outlays" for recycling plants (Berss 41).

Evidence: Cite argument
2. Excessive inefficiency

Although recent studies of recycling discuss cost, they are more concerned about efficiency. The real issues, they contend, are the inequities in supply and demand. Old newspapers are in great supply. "New Jersey towns that just nine months ago pulled in $20 a ton for newsprint must now pay up to $10 a ton to ship it away" (Cahan 116). Indeed, Bruce Van Voorst reveals that over 100 million tons of newspaper collected in the United States never get recycled (52). Moreover, the demand for recycled paper is so depressed that some states have had to pass legislation forcing newspapers to print part of each new edition on recycled paper (Yang 100H). By contrast, plastic is in short supply. Bell reports that although the world produces around 100 million tons of plastic a year, "not enough is reclaimed to enable the manufacturing industry to develop and market products made of recycled material" (44). Wellman, Inc., America's largest plastic recycler, "gobbled up most of the 1.5 billion two liter bottles handed in for recycling" but could supply only half of the demand for its product (Cahan 116–17).

Evidence: Cite expert
testimony

These studies have prompted some critics to conclude that we should abandon recycling. Landfills cost less. Berss points out that this year the citizens of San Jose, California, "will spend $160 a ton to recycle their waste, versus $93 a ton to dump it" (41). Incinerators seem more efficient. Bell explains why plastics are useful for the incineration of municipal waste: "If plastics are removed from waste along with other flammable solids such as paper, what is left is too wet to burn. But if the waste is burned with the plastics still there, potentially useful energy is generated" (44).

Resolution: Cite two
alternatives
A. Landfills
B. Incinerators

These same studies have prompted recycling advocates to generate alternative explanations for the problems of cost and efficiency. Much of what appears as excessive cost, they argue, is really the result of long-established and unexamined business practices. Van Voorst reports that the oil depletion allowance provides a significant subsidy for the producers of oil-based plastics (53). In an interview, environmentalist Pamela Popovich points out that American railroads charge more by the ton to haul recycled paper than they charge to ship virgin paper. "If these costs are taken into consideration," contends Allen Hershkowitz, senior scientist at the Natural Resources Defense Council, "recycling looks economically a lot more competitive" (Van Voorst 53).

Arrangement: Present
advocate of recycling

Evidence: Contest
excessive cost

The inefficiencies in recycling, say advocates, are the result of bad press, poor planning, and underdeveloped technology. "Contrary to popular belief, recycled paper is as high-quality as the conventional stuff and competitively priced" (McAllister). Cahan indicates that when "state officials from Rhode Island, New York, and other Northeastern states met with the region's newspaper publishers and paper industry groups to push for the

Evidence: Contest
excessive inefficiency

increased use of recycled paper," they seemed to get good results (117). Recyclers would get even better results with more effective technology. As Van Voorst suggests, "new processes . . . are needed to remove contaminants. Sorted solid wastes often include contaminants that gum up recycling systems, such as clear plastic tape on envelopes or sticky yellow Post-its on office paper" (54).

**Resolution: Support legislation**

The most direct method for cutting costs and increasing efficiency is legislation. Charles reports that "every one of the 50 states in the U.S. has now passed a law that either encourages or requires local governments to set up some kind of recycling program" (12). Some laws require citizens to sort "each kind of rubbish in its own distinctive container" (Charles 12). Others mandate the minimum use of recycled materials in new products (Berss 41). Still others use tax incentives to encourage companies to develop new technologies (Van Voorst 52). 9

**Evidence: Contest opponents' resolutions
A. Antilandfill**

Recycling advocates are willing to support such extensive legislation because they are adamantly opposed to the alternatives—landfills and incinerators. Landfills may be inexpensive and convenient, but space is limited and continues to decline (Glenn and Riggle 35). Where space is still available—in poor and sparsely populated areas—citizens are concerned about whether the deposit income justifies the dumping of garbage from rich communities out of state. Nobody wants to live next to a landfill, particularly when it can contaminate air, soil, and water (Gialanella and Luedtke SW/RR 18). 10

**B. Anti-incinerator**

Incinerators may cost less than recycling, but they are hardly efficient. Nancy Shute reports that "even if all [of New York's] five incinerators are up and running at full tilt, they could only burn 12,000 tons of garbage a day, less than half the amount the city now creates" (48). More important, incinerators create serious air pollution. In a letter to the *New York Times,* Elizabeth Holtzman indicates that "lead and mercury are emitted from garbage incinerators in large quantities, and can cause brain damage in children." And according to William L. Rathje and Cullen Murphy, authors of *Rubbish! The Archaeology of Garbage,* even "well run incinerators can release into the atmosphere small amounts of more than twenty-five metals . . . which have been implicated in birth defects and several kinds of cancer" (180). 11

**Arrangement: Balance claims of both sides**

Recycling is controversial because both sides present legitimate arguments. The critics are concerned that the public will see recycling as *the* solution to the complex problem of resource management. There is simply too much garbage and too little technology to justify this solution. Even in those instances where economies and technology may justify recycling, the critics are concerned that the procedures may create unacknowledged environmental problems such as high volumes of water waste and energy consumption (Scarlett). 12

The advocates are concerned that the public will give up on recycling before improvements in education, technology, and public policy explore its 13 potential as a solution to resource management. As Rathje and Murphy point out, "recycling is a fragile and complicated piece of economic and social machinery—a space shuttle rather than a tractor; it may frequently break down" (239). But advocates are willing to invest in the eventual success of recycling, particularly when they consider alternatives such as landfills and incinerators.

Arrangement: Introduce new position 1. All types of recycling not equal

Although critics and advocates make legitimate claims, we need a larger perspective to understand the place of recycling in our environmental policy. First, we must realize that all types of recycling are not equal. John E. Young explains how to sort out the different types:

> The most valuable is the manufacture of new products from similar, used items; the least valuable is the conversion of waste materials into entirely different products. The key criterion is whether the recovered material is substituted for the virgin one in production, thus closing the loop. (27)

Some materials—such as glass, steel, and aluminum—rank high in this scheme because they save virgin material from being used. Some—such as plastic—rank low because virtually none is "now being recycled back into original containers" (Young 27). Still others—such as paper—fall somewhere in between because "each time paper is recycled, the fibers it contains are shortened by the process, making the new paper weaker" (Young 27).

2. Recycling can be deceptive

Second, we must become what Rathje and Murphy call "garbage literate" because the label ♻ that identifies products as recycled can be deceptive (242). In most cases, manufacturers use the recycling symbol to indicate that their products are environmentally friendly and responsible. But these products are rarely made from materials that have been turned in for recycling. Instead, they are made from "pre-consumer" waste—that is, material left over from the manufacturing process. Rathje and Murphy point out that the "label one needs to look for is 'post-consumer recycled,' and ideally the label will include a percentage, as in '30 percent post-consumer recycled.' Anything over 10 percent is worthwhile" (243).

Third, we must acknowledge that our garbage problem is so complex that no one process—such as recycling—will ever provide a single solution. Larry Schaper argues that the nation will continue to need landfills, and "as the industry gains more control over the types of materials going into municipal landfills and landfill designs become more reliable, the public may become more accepting of landfills" (65). Similarly, Gialanella and Luedtke argue that recent technological advances in the design of incinerators have improved "their ability to safeguard the environment and public health" (SW/RR 32). Rathje and Murphy contend that the goal is not to "bow" before one single approach but "to discern the varying roles each of these approaches should play locally in America's widely disparate communities and regions" (239).

Finally, we need to develop other environmental policies such as waste  18
reduction. Anne Magnuson reports that some communities encourage their
citizens to precycle—that is, to buy products in bulk rather than in many
small containers that require recycling. Other communities discourage the
accumulation of waste by charging a flat fee for every trash bag. And some
encourage citizens to use preprinted postcards to remove their names from
junk mailing lists (30–37). Such policies discourage the introduction of
more waste into the system. Unless we develop such waste reduction policies, all the recycling, landfills, and incinerators in the world will not save us
from our own garbage.

## Works Cited

Bell, John. "Plastics: Waste Not, Want Not." *New Scientist* 1 Dec. 1990: 44–47.

Berss, Marcia. "Nobody Wants to Shoot Snow White." *Forbes* 14 Oct. 1991:
40–42.

Cahan, Vicky. "Waste Not, Want Not? Not Necessarily." *Business Week* 17 July
1989: 116–17.

Charles, Dan. "Too Many Bottles Break the Bank." *New Scientist* Apr. 1992:
12–13.

Gialanella, Mario, and Louis Luedtke. "Air Pollution Control and Waste
Management." *American City and County* Jan. 1991: SW/RR 17–32.

Glenn, Jim, and David Riggle. "The State of Garbage in America." *Bio Cycle*
(Apr. 1991): 34–38.

Holtzman, Elizabeth. Letter. *New York Times* 24 Jan. 1992: A28.

Magnuson, Anne. "What Has Happened to Waste Reduction?" *American
City and County* Apr. 1991: 30–37.

McAllister, Celia. "Save the Trees—And You May Save a Bundle." *Business
Week* 4 Sept. 1989: 118.

Popovich, Pamela. Personal interview. 12 Oct. 1992.

Rathje, William L., and Cullen Murphy. *Rubbish! The Archaeology of
Garbage.* New York: Harper, 1992.

Scarlett, Lynn. "Will Recycling Help the Environment?" *Consumer Research*
Mar. 1991: 17.

Schaper, Larry. "Trends in Landfill Planning and Design." *Public Works* Apr.
1991: 64–65.

Shute, Nancy. "The Mound Builder." *Amicus Journal* 12 (Summer 1990):
44–49.

Van Voorst, Bruce. "The Recycling Bottleneck." *Time* 14 Sept. 1992: 52–54.

Yang, Dori Jones, William C. Symonds, and Lisa Driscoll. "Recycling Is
Rewriting the Rules of Papermaking." *Business Week* 22 Apr. 1991:
100H–100L.

Young, John E. *Discarding the Throwaway Society.* Washington: Worldwatch,
1991.

# The End of Nature

## BILL MCKIBBEN

Almost every day, I hike up the hill out my back door. Within a hundred yards the woods swallows me up, and there is nothing to remind me of human society—no trash, no stumps, no fence, not even a real path. Looking out from the high places, you can't see road or house; it is a world apart from man. But once in a while someone will be cutting wood farther down the valley, and the snarl of a chain saw will fill the woods. It is harder on those days to get caught up in the timeless meaning of the forest, for man is nearby. The sound of the chain saw doesn't blot out all the noises of the forest or drive animals away, but it does drive away the feeling that you are in another, separate, timeless, wild sphere.

Now that we have changed the most basic forces around us, the noise of that chain saw will always be in the woods. We have changed the atmosphere, and that will change the weather. The temperature and rainfall are no longer to be entirely the work of some separate, uncivilizable force, but instead in part a product of our habits, our economies, our ways of life. Even in the most remote wilderness, where the strictest laws forbid the felling of a single tree, the sound of that saw will be clear, and a walk in the woods will be changed—tainted—by its whine. The world outdoors will mean much the same thing as the world indoors, the hill the same thing as the house.

An idea, a relationship, can go extinct, just like an animal or a plant. The idea in this case is "nature," the separate and wild province, the world apart from man to which he adapted, under whose rules he was born and died. In the past, we spoiled and polluted parts of that nature, inflicted environmental "damage." But that was like stabbing a man with toothpicks: though it hurt, annoyed, degraded, it did not touch vital organs, block the path of the lymph or blood. We never thought that we had wrecked nature. Deep down, we never really thought we could: it was too big and too old; its forces—the wind, the rain, the sun—were too strong, too elemental.

But, quite by accident, it turned out that the carbon dioxide and other gases we were producing in our pursuit of a better life—in pursuit of warm houses and eternal economic growth and of agriculture so productive it would free most of us from farming—*could* alter the power of the sun, could increase its heat. And that increase *could* change the patterns of moisture

Bill McKibben, "The End of Nature," *The End of Nature* (New York: Random, 1989), 47–48, 56–60, 62–64, 66–69, 70.

and dryness, breed storms in new places, breed deserts. Those things may or may not have yet begun to happen, but it is too late to altogether prevent them from happening. We have produced the carbon dioxide—we are ending nature.

We have not ended rainfall or sunlight; in fact, rainfall and sunlight may ₅ become more important forces in our lives. It is too early to tell exactly how much harder the wind will blow, how much hotter the sun will shine. That is for the future. But the *meaning* of the wind, the sun, the rain—of nature— has already changed. Yes, the wind still blows—but no longer from some other sphere, some inhuman place. . . .

. . . Most of the day, the sky above my mountain is simply sky, not "air- ₆ space." Standing in the middle of a grimy English mill town, George Orwell records this "encouraging" thought: "In spite of hard trying, man has yet succeeded in doing his dirt everywhere. The earth is so vast and still so empty that even in the filthy heart of civilization you find fields where the grass is green instead of grey; perhaps if you looked for them you might even find streams with live fish in them instead of salmon tins." When Rachel Carson wrote *Silent Spring* [1962], she was able to find some parts of the Arctic still untouched—no DDT in the fish, the beaver, the beluga, the caribou, the moose, the polar bear, the walrus. The cranberries, the straw- berries, and the wild rhubarb all tested clean, though two snowy owls, prob- ably as a result of their migrations, carried small amounts of the pesticide, as did the livers of two Eskimos who had been away to the hospital in Anchorage.

In other words, as pervasive a problem as DDT was and is, one could, ₇ and can, always imagine that *somewhere* a place existed free of its taint. (And largely as a result of Carson's book there are more and more such places.) As pervasive and growing as the problem of acid rain surely is, at the moment places still exist with a rainfall of an acceptable, "normal" pH. And if we wished to stop acid rain we could; experimenters have placed tents over groves of trees to demonstrate that if the acid bath ceases, a forest will return to normal. Even the radiation from an event as nearly universal as the explo- sion at the Chernobyl plant has begun to fade, and Scandinavians can once more eat their vegetables.

We can, in other words, still plausibly imagine wild nature—or, at least, ₈ the possibility of wild nature in the future—in all sorts of places.

This idea of nature is hardy. Our ability to shut the destroyed areas from ₉ our minds, to see beauty around man's degradation, is considerable. A few years ago I spent some days driving around Arizona in a van with a man named Lyn Jacobs, one of a small number of environmentalists fighting a difficult battle to restrict the grazing of cattle on public lands in the West. The cows, which range over 70 percent of the federal land in the American West under a leasing program that does not pay for itself and each year requires tax subsidies, produce about 3 percent of America's beef. And by their constant grazing, the cattle convert the rangelands into barren pastures. Where there are streams they cave in the banks; where there are wildfowl they trample their nests. In their wake they leave stands of cheatgrass and thistle in place of the natural long-stemmed grasses. But the West has been a pasture so long that practically no one notices. People just assume that grass there can't grow more than a foot high. One morning, Jacobs and I drove along a ranch road that ran just parallel to the Grand Canyon about fifteen miles from the south rim. It was a glorious day, the sky a polarized blue, and though you couldn't see the canyon you knew with heart-stopping precision where it was, for the clouds dropped over its edge, their bottoms obscured like icebergs. "That's the problem," Jacobs said, stopping the van. "When you look at Western panoramas, you don't look down—your eye is trained to think this desert is normal. You tend to look at the mountains and the blue sky above them, and the clouds."

The idea of wildness, in other words, can survive most of the "normal" 10 destruction of nature. Wildness can survive in our minds once the land has been discovered and mapped and even chewed up. It can survive all sorts of pollution, even the ceaseless munching of a million cows. If the ground is dusty and trodden, we look at the sky; if the sky is smoggy, we travel someplace where it's clear; if we can't travel to someplace where it's clear, we *imagine* ourselves in Alaska or Australia or some place where it is, and that works nearly as well. Nature, while often fragile in reality, is durable in our imaginations. Wildness, the idea of wildness, has outlasted the exploration of the entire globe. It has endured the pesticides and the pollution. When the nature around us is degraded, we picture it fresh and untainted elsewhere. When elsewhere, too, it rains acid or DDT, we can still imagine that someday soon it will be better, that we will stop polluting and despoiling and instead "restore" nature. (And, indeed, people have begun to do just this sort of work; here in the Adirondacks, helicopters drop huge quantities of lime into lakes in order to reduce their acidity.) In our midst, nature suffers from a terrible case of acne, or even skin cancer—but our faith in its essential strength remains, for the damage always seems local.

But now the basis of that faith is lost. The idea of nature will not survive 11 the new global pollution—the carbon dioxide and the CFCs and the like. This new rupture with nature is different not only in scope but also in kind from salmon tins in an English stream. We have changed the atmosphere, and thus we are changing the weather. By changing the weather, we make every spot on earth man-made and artificial. We have deprived nature of its independence, and that is fatal to its meaning. Nature's independence *is* its meaning; without it there is nothing but us.

If you travel by plane and dog team and snowshoe to the farthest corner 12 of the Arctic and it is a mild summer day, you will not know whether the temperature is what it is "supposed" to be, or whether, thanks to the extra carbon dioxide, you are standing in the equivalent of a heated room. If it is twenty below and the wind is howling—perhaps absent man it would be forty below. Since most of us get to the North Pole only in our minds, the real situation is more like this: if in July there's a heat wave in London, it won't be a natural phenomenon. It will be a man-made phenomenon—an amplification of what nature intended or a total invention. Or, at the very least, it *might* be a man-made phenomenon, which amounts to the same thing. The storm that might have snapped the hot spell may never form, or may veer off in some other direction, not by the laws of nature but by the laws of nature as they have been rewritten, blindly, crudely, but effectively, by man. If the sun is beating down on you, you will not have the comfort of saying, "Well, that's nature." Or if the sun feels sweet on the back of your neck, that's fine, but it isn't nature. A child born now will never know a natural summer, a natural autumn, winter, or spring. Summer is going extinct, replaced by something else that will be called "summer." This new summer will retain some of its relative characteristics—it will be hotter than the rest of the year, for instance, and the time of year when crops grow—but it will not be summer, just as even the best prosthesis is not a leg.

And, of course, climate determines an enormous amount of the rest of 13 nature—where the forests stop and the prairies or the tundra begins, where the rain falls and where the arid deserts squat, where the wind blows strong and steady, where the glaciers form, how fast the lakes evaporate, where the seas rise. As John Hoffman, of the Environmental Protection Agency, noted in the *Journal of Forestry,* "trees planted today will be entering their period of greatest growth when the climate has already changed." A child born today might swim in a stream free of toxic waste, but he won't ever see a natural stream. If the waves crash up against the beach, eroding dunes and destroying homes, it is not the awesome power of Mother Nature. It is the awesome power of Mother Nature as altered by the awesome power of man, who has overpowered in a century the processes that have been slowly evolving and changing of their own accord since the earth was born.

Those "record highs" and "record lows" that the weathermen are always 14 talking about—they're meaningless now. It's like comparing pole vaults between athletes using bamboo and those using fiberglass poles, or dash times between athletes who've been chewing steroids and those who've stuck to Wheaties. They imply a connection between the past and the present which doesn't exist. The comparison is like hanging Rembrandts next to Warhols; we live in a postnatural world. Thoreau once said he could walk for half an hour and come to "some portion of the earth's surface where man does not stand from one year's end to another, and there, consequently, politics are not, for they are but the cigar-smoke of a man." Now you could walk half a year and not reach such a spot. Politics—our particular way of life, our ideas about how we should live—now blows its smoke over every inch of the globe. . . .

And even as it dawns on us what we have done, there will be plenty of 15 opportunity to forget, at least for a while, that anything has changed. For it isn't natural *beauty* that is ended; in fact, in the same way that the smog breeds spectacular sunsets, there may appear new, unimagined beauties. What will change is the meaning that beauty carries, for when we look at a sunset, we see, or we think we see, many things beyond a particular arrangement of orange and purple and rose.

It is also true that this is not the first huge rupture in the globe's history. 16 Perhaps thirty times since the earth formed, planetesimals up to ten miles in diameter and traveling at sixty times the speed of sound have crashed into the earth, releasing, according to [British scientist] James Lovelock, perhaps a thousand times as much energy as would be liberated by the explosion of all present stocks of nuclear weapons. Such events, some scientists say, may have destroyed 90 percent of all living organisms. On an even larger scale, the sun has steadily increased its brightness; it has grown nearly 30 percent more luminous since life on earth began, forcing that life to keep forever scrambling to stay ahead—a race it will eventually lose, though perhaps not for some billions of years. Or consider an example more closely resembling the sharp divide we have now crossed. About two billion years ago, the microbiologist Lynn Margulis writes, the spread of certain sorts of bacteria caused, in short order, an increase in atmospheric oxygen from one part in a million to one part in just five—from 0.0001 percent to 21 percent. Compared to that, the increase in carbon dioxide from 280 to 560 parts per million is as the hill behind my house to Annapurna. "This was by far the greatest pollution crisis the earth has ever endured," Margulis writes. Oxygen poisoned most microbial life, which "had no defense against this cataclysm except the standard way of DNA replication and duplication, gene transfer and mutation." And, indeed, these produced the successful oxygen-synthesizing life forms that now dominate the earth.

But each of these examples is different from what we now experience, for 17 they were "natural," as opposed to man-made. A pint-sized planet cracks into the earth; the ice advances; the sun, by the immutable laws of stars, burns brighter till its inevitable explosion; genetic mutation sets certain bacteria to spewing out oxygen and soon they dominate the planet, a "strictly natural" pollution.

One can, of course, argue that the current crisis, too, is "natural," because 18 man is part of nature. This echoes the views of the earliest Greek philosophers, who saw no difference between matter and consciousness—nature included everything. James Lovelock wrote some years ago that "our species with its technology is simply an inevitable part of the natural scene," nothing more than mechanically advanced beavers. In this view, to say that we "ended" nature, or even damaged nature, makes no sense, since we *are* nature, and nothing we can do is "unnatural." This view can be, and is, carried to even greater lengths; Lynn Margulis, for instance, ponders the question of whether robots can be said to be living creatures, since any "invention of human beings is ultimately based on a variety of processes including that of DNA replication, no matter the separation in space or time of that replication from the invention."

But one can argue this forever and still not really feel it. It is a debator's point, a semantic argument. When I say that we have ended nature, I don't mean, obviously, that natural processes have ceased—there is still sunshine and still wind, still growth, still decay. Photosynthesis continues, as does respiration. *But we have ended the thing that has, at least in modern times, defined nature for us—its separation from human society.* 19

That separation is quite real. It is fine to argue, as certain poets and biologists have, that we must learn to fit in with nature, to recognize that we are but one species among many, and so on. But none of us, on the inside, quite believe it. . . . 20

The invention of nuclear weapons may actually have marked the beginning of the end of nature: we possessed, finally, the capacity to overmaster nature, to leave an indelible imprint everywhere all at once. "The nuclear peril is usually seen in isolation from the threats to other forms of life and their ecosystems, but in fact it should be seen at the very center of the ecological crisis, as the cloud-covered Everest of which the more immediate, visible kinds of harm to the environment are the mere foothills," wrote Jonathan Schell in *The Fate of the Earth*. And he was correct, for at the time he was writing (less than a decade ago!) it was hard to conceive of any threats of the same magnitude. Global warming was one obscure theory among many. Nuclear weapons were unique (and they remain so, if only for the speed with which they work). But the nuclear dilemma is at least open to human reason—we can decide not to drop the weapons, and indeed to reduce and perhaps eliminate them. And the horrible power of these weapons, which has been amply demonstrated in Japan and on Bikini and under Nevada and many times in our imaginations, has led us fitfully in that hopeful direction. 21

By contrast, the various processes that lead to the end of nature have been essentially beyond human thought. Only a few people knew that carbon dioxide would warm up the world, for instance, and they were for a long time unsuccessful in their efforts to alert the rest of us. Now it is too late—not too late, as I shall come to explain, to ameliorate some of the changes and so perhaps to avoid the most gruesome of their consequences. But the scientists agree that we have already pumped enough gas into the air so that a significant rise in temperature and a subsequent shift in weather are inevitable. 22

Just how inevitable we can see from the remedies that some scientists have proposed to save us—not the remedies, like cutting fossil fuel use and saving the rain forests, that will keep things from being any worse than they need to be, but the solutions that might bring things back to "normal." The most natural method anyone has suggested involves growing enormous numbers of 23 trees to take the carbon dioxide out of the air. Take, for argument's sake, a new coal-fired electric generating station that produces a thousand megawatts and operates at 38 percent thermal efficiency and 70 percent availability. To counteract just the carbon dioxide generated by that plant, the surrounding area to a radius of 24.7 kilometers would need to be covered with American sycamore trees (a fast-growing species) planted at four-foot intervals and "harvested" every four years. It might be possible to achieve that sort of growth rate—a government forestries expert told the Senate that with genetic screening, spacing, thinning, pruning, weed control, fire and pest control, fertilization, and irrigation, net annual growth could be "very much higher than at present." Even if it worked, though, would this tree plantation be nature? A walk through an endless glade of evenly spaced sycamores, with the weed-control chopper hovering overhead, and the irrigation pipes gurgling quietly below, represents a fundamental break with my idea of the wild world.

Other proposals get even odder. One "futuristic idea" described in the [24] *New York Times* springs from the brain of Dr. Thomas Stix at Princeton: he proposes the possibility of using a laser to "scrub" chlorofluorocarbons from the earth's atmosphere before they have a chance to reach the ozone layer. Dr. Stix calculates that an array of infrared lasers spaced around the world could "blast apart" a million tons of chlorofluorocarbons a year—a procedure he refers to as "atmospheric processing." Down at the University of Alabama, Leon Y. Sadler, a chemical engineer, has suggested employing dozens of airplanes to carry ozone into the stratosphere (others have suggested firing a continuous barrage of "bullets" of frozen ozone, which would melt in the stratosphere). To deal with the warming problem, Columbia geochemist Wallace Broecker has considered a "fleet of several hundred jumbo jets" to ferry 35 million tons of sulfur dioxide into the stratosphere annually to reflect sunlight away from the earth. Other scientists recommend launching "giant orbiting satellites made of thin films" that could cast shadows on the earth, counteracting the greenhouse effect with a sort of venetian-blind effect. Certain practical problems may hamper these various solutions; Dr. Broeker, for instance, admits that injecting large quantities of sulfur dioxide into the atmosphere would increase acid rain "and give the blue sky a whitish cast." Still, they just might work. And perhaps, as Dr. Broecker contends, a "rational society needs some sort of insurance policy on how to maintain a habitable planet." But even if they do work—even if the planet remains habitable—it will not be the same. The whitish afternoon sky blessed by the geometric edge of the satellite cloud will fade into a dusk crisscrossed by lasers. There is no way to reassemble nature—certainly not by following the suggestion of one researcher that, in order to increase the earth's reflectivity and thus cool its temperature, we should cover most of the oceans with a floating layer of white Styrofoam chips.

There are some people, perhaps many, to whom this rupture will mean [25] little. A couple of years ago a group of executives went rafting down a river in British Columbia; after an accident killed five of them, one of the survivors told reporters that the party had regarded the river as "a sort of ersatz rollercoaster." Nature has become a hobby with us. One person enjoys the outdoors, another likes cooking, a third favors breaking into military computers over his phone line. The nature hobby boomed during the 1970s; now it is perhaps in slight decline (the number of people requesting permits to hike and camp in the rugged backcountry of the national parks has dropped by half since 1983, even as the number of drive-through visitors has continued to increase). We have become in rapid order a people whose conscious need for nature is superficial. . . .

Still, the passing of nature as we have known it, like the passing of any 26 large idea, will have its recognizable effects, both immediately and over time. In 1893, when Frederick Jackson Turner announced to the American Historical Association that the frontier was closed, no one was aware that the frontier had been the defining force in American life. But in its absence it was understood. One reason we pay so little close attention to the separate natural world around us is that it has always been there and we presumed it always would. As it disappears, its primal importance will be clearer—in the same way that some people think they have put their parents out of their lives and learn differently only when the day comes to bury them.

## Questions about Strategy

1. At the beginning of the essay, how does Bill McKibben use his own experience to establish the ethical appeal of his argument?

2. How does McKibben compare older, untainted ideas of wildness to current, degraded ideas of nature?

3. What kind of solutions does McKibben present for the problem of global warming? To what extent is McKibben convinced that these solutions will work? Explain your answer.

## A Sampler of Other Essays

1. Jon Seidel, "Who Controls Information?," (student essay), p. 182

2. Anna Quindlen, "Execution," p. 180

3. Bill Barich, "La Frontera," p. 217

# Writing Assignments

### 1. NARRATE

Make a list of the special objects you have inherited from members of your family—photographs, tools, clothing. Select one that has become legendary in your family. Then narrate the story of that object, using descriptive details, to make some point about a lesson you inherited with the object.

### 2. OBSERVE

Select someone who does an unusual job—a mechanic, a stockbroker, an actor, a psychic—and ask him or her to analyze a process he or she follows to complete one aspect of his or her job successfully. Use this explanation to prove that a complex job can be made simple or that a job that appears simple can be more difficult than it seems.

### 3. INVESTIGATE

Interview members of two groups of students (for example, male and female, black and white, young and old) about what kinds of jokes make them laugh. Then report your findings in an essay that compares the two groups according to their senses of humor.

### 4. COLLABORATE

Collect information from the members of your writing group on the types of writing teachers they have encountered in their years of schooling. Establish at least three categories of teachers. Then classify them, explaining the strengths and weaknesses of the members of each category.

### 5. READ

Select a word that has always bothered you or that has had significant meaning in your life. Search your library's database for books that might define this word. Then use this information, together with your own experience, to compose an extended definition of the word.

### 6. RESPOND

Respond to one of the essays in this section by writing a letter to its author about the features in his or her essay that you found particularly enjoyable. You may also want to identify those sections of his or her essay that you found difficult to understand. In the latter case, you may want to list the kind of information you need to clarify your misunderstanding.

### 7. ANALYZE

Identify and analyze the unforeseen consequences of some policy enacted in your school or community. Consider what prompted the creation of the policy. Finally, speculate about the policy's future.

### 8. EVALUATE

Read the two essays (student and professional) that illustrate one of the seven strategies in this section and the three essays listed in "A Sampler of Other Essays." Then evaluate which essay makes the most effective use of the strategy. Explain the reasons for your choice.

### 9. ARGUE

Argue that new technology has made incinerators more effective than recycling. You may want to read Mario Gialanella and Louis Luedtke's "Air Pollution and Waste Management," *American City and Country* Jan. 1991: SW/RR 17–32. Then decide whether your source will allow you to argue that burning garbage can be an effective method for converting waste into energy.

### 10. ARGUE

Challenge McKibben's assertion that as a result of humans' continuous presence in nature, "the world outdoors will mean much the same thing as the world indoors." Browse the Web for conservation/environment/technology chat groups. Then ask the members of the group to supply evidence that McKibben's argument is extreme. Compile evidence that we are using new forms of technology to reverse the damage done by older forms of technology.

# PART V

# *Handbook* of Grammar and Usage

**The Evolution of English**

**Understanding Sentence Elements**

**Writing Logical and Effective Sentences**

**Writing Grammatical Sentences**

**Choosing Effective Diction**

**Observing the Rules of Punctuation**

**Observing the Rules of Mechanics**

**A Glossary of Contemporary Usage**

# The Evolution of English

The language that Americans speak and write is descended from the language spoken by the English, Scottish, and Irish immigrants who founded the British colonies in America. Their language, in turn, was descended from the languages of Germanic tribes who, during the fifth and sixth centuries, invaded Britain and settled there. One of these tribes, the Angles, later became known as the Englisc (English) and gave their name to a country and a language, both of which they shared with other peoples—the Saxons, the Jutes, and later, the Danes and the Normans.

The language that has come down to us from that Anglo-Saxon beginning has undergone great changes. Modern college students find Chaucer's fourteenth-century English something of a puzzle. And before Chaucer—well, judge for yourself. Here is the opening of the Lord's Prayer as it was written in the ninth, fourteenth, and seventeenth centuries, respectively:

| *Old English* | *Middle English* | *Modern English* |
|---|---|---|
| Fæder ūre þū þe eart on heofonum, sī þīn nama gehālgod. Tōbecume þīn rīce, Gewurpe ðīn willa on eorðan swā swā on heofonum. | Oure fadir that art in heuenes, halwid be thi name; thi kyngdom cumme to; be thi wille don as in heuen and in erthe. | Our Father which art in heaven, Hallowed be thy name. Thy kingdom come. Thy will be done on earth as it is in heaven. |

A contrast of these three versions offers a brief but revealing impression of the changes that occurred in the language during eight hundred years, and these differences would seem even greater if we could reproduce also the changes in sound that took place. For example, Old English $\bar{u}$ and $\bar{\imath}$ were pronounced like the *oo* in *boot* and the *e* in *me*, respectively, so that $\bar{u}re$ was pronounced "oo'ruh" and $s\bar{\imath}$, "see."

In grammar, the major change has been the simplification of grammatical forms. Old English (700–1100) was a highly *inflected* language, one that made grammatical distinctions by changes in the form of a word. For example, nouns were declined in five cases (nominative, genitive, dative, accusative, and instrumental) as well as in singular and plural numbers. Adjectives and the definite article were declined to agree with the nouns they modified. Here is the declension, in the singular only, of "the good man," with the approximate pronunciation enclosed in quotation marks to the right:

| Case | Declension | Pronunciation |
|---|---|---|
| N. (*man* as subject) | sē gōda mann | "say goada man" |
| G. ("of the good man" or "the good man's") | ðaes gōdan mannes | "thas goadan mannes" |
| D. ("to the good man") | ðǣm gōdan menn | "tham goadan men" |
| A. (*man* as object) | ðone gōdan mann | "thonna goadan man" |
| I. ("by the good man") | ðȳ gōdan menn | "thee goadan men" |

In Modern English the article and the adjective are not declined at all. The noun retains the genitive case and has singular and plural forms. We distinguish between subject and object by word order, and we have replaced the dative and instrumental endings by the prepositions *to* and *by*. As a result, the whole declensional system has been greatly simplified. Verbs still show considerable inflection, though much less than in Old English.

Along with this simplification of grammatical forms went a great increase in vocabulary as new words were introduced through association with foreign cultures. During the eighth and ninth centuries, Scandinavian raiders settled along the coast of England and brought into the language some fourteen hundred place names and about one thousand common words. In 1066 the Normans conquered England, and for three hundred years their French language dominated the court and the affairs in which the nobility was most involved—government, army, law, church, art, architecture, fashions, and recreation. Between 1100 and 1500, over ten thousand French words were absorbed into the language. During the fourteenth, fifteenth, and sixteenth centuries, English writers borrowed heavily from Latin. Language historians estimate that more than half of the present English vocabulary came from Latin, either directly or through one of the Romance languages, especially French. And as the English-speaking countries grew in political, economic, and cultural importance, their language borrowed from all over the world the words it needed to name the things and ideas that Anglo-Americans were acquiring. Today the vocabulary of the English language is international in origin, as the following list illustrates:

| | | |
|---|---|---|
| algebra (Arabic) | dollar (German) | polo (Tibetan) |
| amen (Hebrew) | flannel (Welsh) | silk (Chinese) |
| bantam (Javanese) | garage (French) | shampoo (Hindi) |
| boor (Dutch) | garbage (Italian) | ski (Norwegian) |
| caravan (Persian) | inertia (Latin) | tag (Swedish) |
| cashew (Portuguese) | kimono (Japanese) | toboggan (Micmac) |
| chorus (Greek) | leprechaun (Old Irish) | vodka (Russian) |
| coffee (Turkish) | polka (Polish) | whiskey (Gaelic) |

# Understanding Sentence Elements

The ability to *compose* effective sentences does not depend on an ability to describe sentences grammatically or linguistically. Rather, most proficient writers use intuitive language skills, developed over a number of years, when they compose sentences. Yet when writers understand sentence elements and structure, they are better able to *revise* sentences to achieve a clear form and purpose. To help you in effective sentence revision, the following sections offer a brief overview of basic sentence elements.

## 1 Recognize the Basic Elements of Sentences

Although many sentences are complicated word structures, all sentences, even the most complicated, are built from a few basic elements: **subjects** (S), **verbs** (V), **objects** (O), and **complements** (C). These elements work together to express a central idea that may be further developed or refined by other elements: **modifiers** (M) and **conjunctions** (Conj).

The verb with its objects, complements, and modifiers is known as the **predicate** of the sentence. The predicate describes the action performed by the subject or the state of being of the subject. Subject and predicate are the two main parts of a simple sentence.

>     S    V
> The lawyer wrote. [Subject + Verb.]
>     S    V     O
> The lawyer wrote the brief. [Subject + Verb + Object.]
>       S        V         O CONJ
> The trial lawyer hurriedly wrote the Hernandez brief but then carefully
>     V  O
> revised it.

[Subject + Verb + Object + Conjunction + Verb + Object. Modifiers used throughout.]

These examples show that a sentence composed of the basic elements can be made more specific and informative through expansion.

## 1a *Subjects* identify the people, places, things, ideas, qualities, or conditions that act, are acted upon, or are described in a sentence.

Nouns and pronouns are the most common subjects, but phrases (groups of words without verbs) or clauses (groups of words with subjects and verbs) may also be subjects.

S  V      C
To win is her objective. [Subject *(phrase)* + Verb + Complement.]

S             V   C
What President Aquino wants most is political stability.
[Subject *(clause)* + Verb + Complement.]

**1b**    *Verbs* express action *(select, walk)* or a state of being *(seem, is).* Verbs consist of single words *(develop)* or groups of words *(might have developed).*

A verb that requires an object to complete its meaning is a ***transitive verb.*** A verb that does not require an object to complete its meaning is an ***intransitive verb.*** Notice that some verbs can be either transitive or intransitive.

S      TRANS V    O
President Roosevelt **ordered** the evacuation.

INTRANS V
After two years, Senator Harris **resigned.**

TRANS V     O
The building inspector **examined** the wiring.

INTRANS V
Pandas **eat** voraciously.

A verb connecting a complement to a subject is a ***linking verb.***

The child **seemed** frightened.

After years of study, Fred **became** an aerospace engineer.

**1c**    *Objects* are nouns or pronouns that complete the ideas expressed by subjects and transitive verbs.

***Direct objects*** answer the questions *what?* or *whom?* ***Indirect objects*** answer the questions *to whom or what?* or *for whom or what?*

S    V     D.O.
With great care, Dr. Rodriguez completed the **report.**
[*Report* is *what* Dr. Rodriguez completed.]

S   V   I.O.    D.O.
Dr. Rodriguez sent the **immunologist** the **report.**
[*Report* is *what* Dr. Rodriguez sent; *immunologist* is *to whom* he sent it.]

**1d**    *Complements* are adjectives or nouns that complete the ideas in a sentence by modifying the subject *(predicate adjective)* or by renaming the subject *(predicate noun).*

Complements are joined to the subjects of sentences by linking verbs, such as *am, are, is, was, were, become, get, feel, look,* and *seem.*

S       V        C

Throughout the competition, Warren remained **optimistic.**

[Predicate adjective modifies the subject *Warren.*]

S     V       C

In the end, Warren was first **runner-up.**

[Predicate noun renames the subject *Warren.*]

## 1e    *Modifiers* (typically adjectives, adverbs, and prepositional phrases used as adjectives or adverbs) describe or limit subjects, verbs, objects, complements, or other modifiers.

Modifiers alter the meanings of other words by answering one of these questions: *what kind? which one? how many? whose? how? when? where? how often?* or *to what extent?*

**Long** speeches are unacceptable. [What kind of speeches?]

**Those** four-wheelers are dangerous. [Which four-wheelers?]

We received **sixty-seven** applications. [How many applications?]

The subcommittee shared **its** findings. [Whose findings?]

The immigrant **slowly** completed the form. [How did he complete it?]

**After the tennis match,** we celebrated. [When did we celebrate?]

Leave the carton **in the mailroom.** [Where should it be left?]

Michael called his doctor **frequently.** [How often did he call?]

The glassblower **very** skillfully formed the stem. [What degree of skill did the glassblower use?]

## 1f    *Conjunctions* join and relate two or more words, phrases, or clauses in a sentence.

*Coordinating conjunctions* (*and, but, for, nor, or, so,* and *yet*) link equivalent sentence elements.

John Kander **and** Fred Ebb collaborated on several major musicals. [Conjunction links two subjects.]

The burglars gained access to the vault **yet** left its contents intact. [Conjunction links two verbs.]

He fought unenthusiastically **but** skillfully. [Conjunction links two modifiers.]

I will not do it, **nor** will I recommend anyone else who might. [Conjunction links two clauses.]

*Correlative conjunctions,* such as *both . . . and, either . . . or, neither . . . nor,* and *not only . . . but also,* work in pairs and also link equivalent sentence elements.

**Both** Senator Robins **and** Representative Hershell received contributions from the tobacco industry. [Conjunction links two subjects.]

Marion will go **either** to Butler University to study pharmacology **or** to Indiana University to study dentistry. [Conjunction links two modifiers.]

*Subordinating conjunctions,* such as *after, although, because, even if, so that, until,* and *when,* join clauses, but they subordinate one clause to another. The subordinate clause, introduced by the subordinating conjunction, can be positioned at the beginning, in the middle, or at the end of a sentence.

**Because she was outspoken on the subject of women writers,** Virginia Woolf has become a central figure in feminist criticism. [Subordinate clause first.]

Virginia Woolf has become a central figure in feminist criticism **because she was outspoken on the subject of women writers.** [Subordinate clause last.]

Virginia Woolf, **because she was outspoken on the subject of women writers,** has become a central figure in feminist criticism. [Subordinate clause embedded.]

## EXERCISE

Identify each of the underlined words or phrases as a subject (S), verb (V), object (O), complement (C), modifier (M), or conjunction (Conj). (Consider proper names as single elements, but consider all other words separately.)

1. Although the 1981 baseball strike lasted seven weeks, the 1985 baseball strike lasted only three days.

2. Cadets at West Point are considered members of the regular Army.

3. Jason sent me an application for Duke University, in hopes that I too would apply for admission.

4. In 1967, a <u>fire aboard Apollo 1</u> killed <u>Virgil Grissom , Edward White, and Roger Chaffee</u>.

5. <u>General Washington commissioned seven ships</u> to fight against the <u>British</u> Navy.

6. Universal Studios <u>and</u> 20th Century Fox <u>produced</u> the <u>five</u> motion pictures with the highest revenues in one summer.

7. <u>The Iliad and the Odyssey</u> , composed by the <u>Greek</u> poet Homer, are <u>mainstays</u> of <u>most humanities</u> curricula.

8. <u>Thomas à Becket</u> was the <u>archbishop of Canterbury</u> during the reign of Henry II.

9. <u>In spite</u> of recent declines in sales, <u>General Motors, Ford, and Chrysler</u> are still among the fifteen largest corporations in the United States.

10. <u>U. S. Grant</u> was an effective <u>general</u> but an <u>ineffectual president</u>.

## 2  Recognize Basic Sentence Patterns

There are four basic sentence patterns: simple, compound, complex, and compound-complex.

**2a**    **A *simple sentence* contains one independent clause, that is, a subject and verb that can stand alone as a grammatically complete sentence.**

The subject and verb of a simple sentence may appear in compound form. A simple sentence need not be simplistic, but it does present a single idea. In fact, simple sentences, because they present ideas clearly, are useful for creating emphasis.

       S     V     C
Hurricanes are frightening.

       S                       S   V       C             C
Hurricanes and other tropical storms are both frightening and dangerous.

[Though more complicated than the preceding example, this is a simple sentence because it has one (compound) subject and one predicate; the sentence also includes one compound complement.]

**2b**   A *compound sentence* contains two or more independent clauses joined by a comma and a coordinating conjunction *(and, but, for, nor, or, so,* and *yet)* or by a semicolon alone.

A compound sentence presents a balanced relationship between the clauses that are joined, thus emphasizing that the ideas in the sentence are of equal importance.

> We moved to the Gulf coast to escape the cold Ohio winters, but then we were terrified by tropical storms. [Two independent clauses joined by a conjunction.]

> We moved to Florida in 1978; we stayed only five years, however, and then returned to Ohio. [Two independent clauses joined by a semicolon.]

**2c**   A *complex sentence* contains at least two clauses: one independent and one or more subordinate clauses.

Subordinating conjunctions, such as *although, because, since, when,* and *while,* and relative pronouns, such as *that, what, which,* and *who,* join the clauses in a complex sentence. One clause, and thus the interrelationship of the ideas in the sentence, is emphasized over the others.

> Although it rains in the midmornings, the afternoons are generally sunny. [Subordinate clause, then independent clause.]

> We enjoyed our stay in Florida, even though we knew that we could not remain. [Independent clause, then subordinate clauses.]

**2d**   A *compound-complex* sentence contains three or more clauses—at least two independent clauses and one subordinate clause.

A compound-complex sentence establishes a complicated relationship among a series of ideas.

> While we lived in Florida, we survived four minor hurricanes without injuries or property damage, but we never developed the nonchalance of native Floridians. [Subordinate clause, then independent clause, then another independent clause.]

---

EXERCISE

**Identify the following sentences as simple, compound, complex, or compound-complex.**

1. Lightning is a discharge of electricity between two clouds or between a cloud and the earth.

2. Because of deaths during the war with the Soviet Union and because of massive emigration to Iran and Pakistan, Afghanistan's population has shrunk by one-third in the last decade.

3. According to some statistics, Northern Ireland has the highest unemployment rate in Europe.

4. The original purpose of the Crusades was to take Christianity to the non-Christian "infidels," but the holy wars also served to enrich trade and the arts in Europe.

5. Although the proposed tax cut is supposed to help the average taxpayer, it provides too many loopholes for selected businesses.

6. Mongolia is located in eastern Asia, between Siberia and China, and is slighter larger than Alaska.

7. After his notorious raid on Harpers Ferry in 1859, John Brown was captured and hanged; in the years that followed, his name became a symbol of ineffectual militant protest.

8. Although *bona fide* means "in good faith" in Latin, it is commonly used today to mean "genuine."

9. Because the costs of American materials and labor are high, sales of American-made shoes have plummeted, and sales of imports from Brazil and South Korea have risen.

10. Most Americans assume that the U.S. Navy is our oldest maritime service, yet the U.S. Coast Guard was established in 1790, eight years before the Navy.

## 3   Expand and Vary Sentence Patterns

As writers move from drafting sentences to revising them, they make decisions about diction, about the placement of phrases and clauses, and about the structural patterns of sentences. The larger issue—sentence patterns—is important because sentence construction (and reconstruction) often determines how effectively writing communicates with readers.

## 3a  Use Coordination

When isolated, successive sentences present ideas that together establish an important, parallel relationship; those sentences can be effectively combined by coordination. *Coordination* is the joining of simple sentences to form compound sentences, and it is also the meshing or combining of related sentence elements through pairing or seriation.

> President Reagan initially denied that the United States had traded arms for
> hostages. ~~T~~he Tower commission subsequently revealed otherwise. *but t*
> [Two sentences effectively joined by a coordinating conjunction.]
> Oliver North's *and John Poindexter's* activities were largely unsupervised. ~~John Poindexter's activities were also unsupervised.~~
> [Combining the sentences—by using a compound subject—improves the emphasis.]

## 3b  Use Subordination

When isolated, successive sentences present related ideas; the sentences can be combined through subordination. *Subordination* is the joining of simple sentences to form complex or compound-complex sentences, but it is also the embedding of words, phrases, or clauses in the structure of the most important sentence.

> Marc Chagall ~~was~~ a native of Russia. ~~He~~ emigrated to France. ~~While in~~ ~~France,~~ *where* he produced vibrant and dreamlike paintings.
> [Three independent clauses compressed into one complex sentence.]
> *Because* Chagall's images are often childlike, ~~U~~ndiscerning observers sometimes find his work simplistic. ~~O~~bservant critics see an ingenious use of childhood perception in his work. *but o*
> [Three independent clauses reworked into a compound-complex sentence that reveals a cause-and-effect relationship among the ideas.]

Subordination is a useful means of indicating emphasis and bringing variety to sentences. Consider subordination the groundwork of a mature and effective sentence style and work to use it to achieve your purpose.

## EXERCISE

**Use coordination and subordination to combine the following pairs of sentences.**

1. Four men from the United States have won the Olympic figure-skating title. Only one, Dick Button, won the title twice.

2. *Amadeus* popularized the works of Mozart. The plot of the play and film is historically inaccurate.

3. Ten percent of home-study lawyers pass the California Bar Exam. Sixty percent of law school–trained lawyers pass.

4. Alfred Smith was the first Catholic to run for president. He lost by a wide margin to Herbert Hoover in 1928.

5. Trademarks are usually specialized symbols, products, or company names. They can also be individual words and letters.

## EXERCISE

**The following paragraph contains simple sentences only. Use coordination and subordination to combine sentences and produce an effective and varied paragraph.**

The Beatles were the most successful pop group of all time. They began playing in Liverpool, England. The group had four members. They were John Lennon, Paul McCartney, George Harrison, and Ringo Starr. Their early music was characterized by a simple rhythm-and-blues style. It also had simple harmonies and lyrics. The Beatles' early hits included "She Loves You," "Please Please Me," and "I Want to Hold Your Hand." These simple songs attracted worldwide interest. John Lennon and Paul McCartney later wrote complicated songs. The lyrics became imaginative and philosophical. The music itself became varied. It was also complex. They experimented with new instruments and recording equipment. Their later work included the albums *Rubber Soul, The White Album,* and *Abbey Road.* The Beatles' most sophisticated work was the album *Sergeant Pepper's Lonely Hearts Club Band.* It contained some of the group's most memorable songs. Each member of the band developed separate interests. The group disbanded in 1970.

## UNDERSTANDING SENTENCE ELEMENTS: REVIEW EXERCISES

In the following paragraph, label each of the underlined elements as a subject (S), verb (V), object (O), complement (C), modifier (M), or conjunction (Conj.).

Our Sun is a sphere of superheated gas. Hydrogen atoms at its core fuse, creating the atomic reactions that produce both light and energy. Scientists estimate that the temperature of the Sun's core is twenty million degrees centigrade, while the surface temperature is approximately six thousand degrees centigrade. The diameter of the Sun is roughly 850,000 miles. These figures suggest that our Sun is neither a hot nor a large star when compared with others in our solar system.

The following paragraph contains simple sentences only. Use coordination and subordination to combine sentences to make this paragraph effective. Then label sentences by type: simple (S), compound (C), complex (CX), and compound-complex (CCX).

The Black Death devastated Europe between 1348 and 1666. The disease was brought to Europe through Italy. Traders carried it from the Black Sea area. The epidemic of 1348 killed one-fourth of the population of Europe. The disease was carried by fleas. This was unknown in the fourteenth and seventeenth centuries. The fleas lived on rats. The disease raged, subsided, and reemerged for three hundred years. The worst epidemic in England occurred in 1665. Entire towns and villages were wiped out. London's population decreased by one-tenth. The population was approximately 450,000. People were terrified. They tried all kinds of cures. They didn't understand the nature of the disease. The cures failed. Samuel Pepys wrote about the Black Death in his *Diary.* Daniel Defoe wrote a fictional account titled *Journal of the Plague Year.*

# Writing Logical and Effective Sentences

## 4 Sentence Sense

Creating a uniform impression in your writing is important, especially at the sentence level, because readers need consistency to understand fully your ideas. Unnecessary shifts in point of view, tense, mood, and voice are distracting and may be confusing.

## 4a Use a consistent point of view.

*Point of view* is the standpoint from which you present information. If you select the ***first-person*** point of view, then your subject *(I, we)* is the speaker. If you select the ***second person,*** then your subject *(you)* is being spoken to. If you select the ***third person,*** then your subject *(he, she, it, they)* is being spoken about. Selecting the appropriate point of view and maintaining it are important for clarity.

Swimming instructors must be patient if they work with children. ~~You~~ *They* must acknowledge that some children have never swum before, and ~~you~~ *they* must acclimate children to the water. Instructors must be willing to work slowly and teach skills gradually.
[Elimination of shift from third person *(swimming instructors)* to second person *(you).*]

## 4b Use verb tenses consistently.

Verb tenses signal chronological relationships among ideas. Unnecessary shifts in tense will confuse your readers.

After filling out a tentative class schedule, the student goes to see his or her advisor for approval. The advisor examine*s* the schedule to see that requirements ~~were~~ *are* met, and the student submits the signed computer form.
[The shifts from present tense *(goes)* to the past tense *(examined)* to the present tense *(submits)* make these sentences confusing. It is unclear whether they describe a typically repeated sequence, for which present

tense would be appropriate, or a completed sequence, for which past tense would be suitable.]

## 4c    Use a consistent mood.

Three moods indicate how you view the actions or conditions you are describing in your sentences. The *indicative mood* is used to make statements of fact or opinion and ask questions. The *imperative mood* is used to express commands. The *subjunctive mood* is used to indicate doubt, conditional situations, statements contrary to fact, and wishes. In most writing, mood should remain consistent.

Betting on a horse race, Mr. McMillan explained, can be risky. ~~Bet~~ only *He suggested that people* money that ~~you~~ *they* can afford to lose.

[Elimination of confusing shift from the indicative to the imperative. The first sentence *described;* the second *advised.*]

## 4d    Use a consistent voice.

Active voice and passive voice create different kinds of emphasis in sentences. They should not be mixed in successive sentences that describe the same subject. (See Section 5, "Active and Passive Sentences.")

The research assistants carefully compile the results of the questionnaire. First, they record the sex, age, race, and religion of each respondent. Then, *they record* profession, income, and education ~~were recorded.~~ Next, the assistants note responses to individual interpretive questions. [Elimination of shift into the passive voice.]

---

### EXERCISE

Revise each set of sentences so that it constitutes a paragraph that is consistent in mood, point of view, voice, and tense.

1. Department of Energy spokespersons have suggested that Americans save energy in small but important ways. They suggest walking rather than driving, coordinating short trips, and driving at slower speeds. Turn off lights when you are not in a room. Wash only full loads. Lower your thermostats.

2. The U.S. Fish and Wildlife Service now restricts waterfowl hunting in most areas. Hunters can no longer use lead shot since it poisons birds that are wounded but not killed. You must also restrict hunting to specified seasons, and hunters must limit the number of birds they kill. Penalties are also severe if you are caught violating these protective laws.

3. The National Forest Service has made timberlands available to private logging companies. New logging roads are built, destroying the forest floor. Trees are removed, and fish and wildlife are threatened. Irreparable damage is being done.

4. In the last few years, industrial pollution of water has declined. The Clean Water Act has given government agencies the right to assign stiff fines to plants and foundries in violation of existing pollution standards. These companies then had to correct the problem or risk further fines. Most industries adapted to these procedures.

5. Spokespeople for these agencies and services address important issues at arranged press conferences. Facts are given, and violators are identified. The American people are given information by these spokespeople to help them understand these national concerns.

## 5  Active and Passive Sentences

*Active* sentences emphasize the people or things responsible for actions and conditions. *Passive* sentences focus on people or things that are acted upon. What would be the object in an active sentence is used as the subject in a passive sentence, and a form of the verb *to be* is used with the main verb. As a result, passive sentences are always slightly longer than active sentences. Although most readers and writers prefer active sentences, you should select the sentence pattern that most effectively conveys your purpose.

> *Active:* Congress approved a multibillion-dollar highway improvement bill. [Congress is emphasized.]

> *Passive:* The multibillion-dollar highway improvement bill was approved by Congress. [The highway improvement bill is emphasized.]

## 5a Use Active Sentences Most of the Time

Use active sentences to indicate who takes responsibility for actions and events.

Dr. Taylor misdiagnosed and mistreated Jeremy's respiratory problem.

Use active sentences to create emphasis.

A tornado in Texas destroyed property worth over $50 million.

Use active sentences for economy of expression.

*Active:* Lionel Richie sang the national anthem at the opening game of the season. [13 words]

*Passive:* The national anthem was sung by Lionel Richie at the opening game of the season. [15 words.]

## 5b Use Passive Sentences Selectively

Use passive sentences when the people who are responsible for actions are not known.

The superintendent's window was broken sometime over the weekend.

Use passive sentences to emphasize the receiver of the action instead of those responsible.

Van Gogh's *Sunflowers* was sold for $39.9 million.

Use passive sentences to emphasize actions that are more important than specific people who might be responsible.

Lasers are currently being used to treat medical problems as diverse as cancer, cataracts, and varicose veins.

---

EXERCISE

The following sentences are written in the passive voice. Rewrite those that would be more effective in the active voice.

1. Twenty people were killed when a car bomb exploded in Teheran.

2. Over $800 million had been deposited in personal Swiss bank accounts by Ferdinand Marcos, the ousted president of the Philippines.

3. Favorable trade conditions with China were supported by President Bush, despite controversy over the action.

4. Details of the nuclear accident at Chernobyl were withheld by Soviet officials for several days.

5. Franklin D. Roosevelt was elected to four terms as president.

## **6** Maintain Parallelism among Sentence Elements

*Parallelism* in a sentence requires that similar ideas be presented in similar form and that elements that are similar in function appear in similar grammatical form. Parallelism is an important principle of both grammar and style.

Grammatically, sentence elements linked by coordinating or correlative conjunctions should be similar in form: A clause should be followed by a clause, a phrase by a phrase, a noun by a noun, a verb by a verb of the same tense (see Section 4b), and so on.

Stylistically, parallelism creates balance and emphasis. It can, therefore, be used to create desired effects.

### **6a** Maintain parallelism with coordinating conjunctions.

*with a call for*

The evangelist ended the service with a hymn and ~~calling on~~ sinners to repent.
[Two prepositional phrases separated by a coordinating conjunction.]

### **6b** Maintain parallelism with correlative conjunctions.

The owners of VCRs can either tape films from network broadcasts or ~~can~~ rent films from video clubs.
[Correlative conjunctions followed by two verbs without auxiliaries.]

**6c**   **Repeat key words to clarify a parallel construction.**

The commission has the power to investigate, conciliate, hold hearings, subpoena witnesses, issue cease-and-desist commands, order reinstatements, and direct hiring. [Parallelism emphasized by repeating *to*.]

---

EXERCISE

Revise the following sentences to eliminate faulty parallelism.

1. The narrator of *Invisible Man* was idealistic, intelligent, and tried to advance the cause of black people.

2. Holden Caufield, the main character of *Catcher in the Rye*, rejected hypocrisy in other people but was ignoring his own hypocrisy.

3. Thornton Wilder won Pulitzer Prizes not only for his plays *Our Town* and *The Skin of Our Teeth* but also he won for his novel *The Bridge of San Luis Rey.*

4. The stories of Flannery O'Connor allow readers to examine unusual characters, to explore psychological motivations, and consider macabre situations.

5. Willy Loman could neither understand his own problems nor could he accept the help of friends.

# Word Order

## 7a   Inversions

The common order of words in sentences can be briefly summarized as follows:
- Subjects precede verbs.
- Verbs precede objects or complements.
- Indirect objects precede direct objects.

- Adjectives precede the words they modify.

- Adverbs usually follow verbs they modify, but they precede adjectives or other adverbs.

- Prepositional phrases follow the words they modify.

- Independent clauses often precede subordinate clauses, although three variations are common: (1) clauses used as adjectives follow the words they modify, (2) clauses used as adverbs often precede the independent clause, and (3) clauses used as nouns occupy the subject or object positions.

- Closely related material is best kept as close together as possible.

Although these principles usually govern word order in sentences, any element of a sentence may be moved to create emphasis or interest. Variations of common word order, however, should produce neither awkward nor unidiomatic writing.

| *Common Order* | *Inverted Order* |
|---|---|
| The chancellor **quickly and superficially** responded to the interviewer's questions. | **Quickly and superficially,** the chancellor responded to the interviewer's questions. |
| The team doesn't stand a chance **without Terry.** | **Without Terry,** the team doesn't stand a chance. |
| The computer terminals were installed **at last.** | **At last,** the computer terminals were installed. |
| The company will pay relocation expenses **if employees are transferred.** | **If employees are transferred,** the company will pay relocation expenses. |
| **Jessica said,** "I can attend the Art Institute only if I receive a scholarship." | "I can attend the Art Institute," **Jessica said,** "only if I receive a scholarship." |

## 7b     Emphatic Order

To achieve a desired effect in a sentence, writers can vary the location of key information. In a typical sentence, information placed near the beginning or end will be emphasized. Placing important information in an independent clause, instead of in a subordinate clause or phrase, strengthens emphasis.

Place important information first or last; do not bury it in the middle.
*Unemphatic:* On April 14, 1865, **Abraham Lincoln was shot** at Ford's Theatre.
*Emphatic:* **Abraham Lincoln was shot** at Ford's Theatre on April 14, 1865.
*Emphatic:* At Ford's Theatre on April 14, 1865, **Abraham Lincoln was shot.**
*Unemphatic:* That novel, **as far as I know,** was my biggest commercial failure.
*Emphatic:* **As far as I know,** that novel was my biggest commercial failure.
*Unemphatic:* She is innocent, **in my opinion.**
*Emphatic:* **In my opinion,** she is innocent.

Place key information in independent clauses, not in subordinate clauses or phrases.
*Unemphatic:* He fell from the roof, **thus breaking his neck.**
*Emphatic:* He fell from the roof and **broke his neck.**

## EXERCISE

**Revise the following sentences to improve awkward or unemphatic word order.**

1. The Supreme Court refused to consider the appeal, according to the late news last night.

2. The major evidence had been acquired during a search without a proper warrant, thus resulting in a dismissal of the case.

3. The evidence shows, the prosecuting attorney suggested, that Marshall Tireman is guilty of stealing industrial secrets.

4. The judge agreed to admit the videotape as evidence after the defense attorney made a special appeal.

5. The lawyers, even, had not expected such a large settlement in the case.

## 8   Position Modifiers Carefully

A *modifier* must clearly relate to a word in a sentence and explain, describe, define, or limit the word to which it relates. When a modifier is not positioned properly, the modification can be both awkward and confusing.

## 8a    Long modifiers should not separate a subject and verb or a verb and its complement.

Although modifiers may be placed between a subject and verb or between a verb and its complement, such positioning often makes a sentence difficult to read and interpret. Reposition the modifiers so that they do not break the flow of the sentence.

The renovation, because of fund-raising activities and because of competitive bidding by major contracting firms, was delayed.

The final bid was, even though it was thousands lower than the initial bids, still too high.

## 8b    Avoid dangling modifiers.

Opening modifiers that do not modify the subject of a sentence are said to dangle—hence, the name *dangling modifier.* To correct such an error, either revise the independent clause so that the introductory phrase can logically modify the subject, or revise the introductory phrase to make it a subordinate clause.

To qualify for the award, ~~the committee requires that~~ candidates *must* have sixty class hours and a 3.50 GPA.

While *I was* waiting for my date in the lobby, two men in tuxedos got into a violent argument.

## 8c    Avoid squinting modifiers.

A *squinting modifier* seems to modify the word before it *and* the word after it. Reposition the modifier to clarify the meaning, or use *that* to eliminate confusion.

The reporter said *that* before noon she would finish the article.

The reporter said before noon she would finish the article.

## 8d    Avoid split infinitives.

A *split infinitive* occurs when a modifier falls between *to* and the primary verb. Writers and readers disagree about whether split infinitives are grammatically or stylistically acceptable. To be on the safe side, reposition the modifier.

Darren began to *furiously* pack his luggage to try to make the nine o'clock flight.

---

### EXERCISE

**Eliminate ambiguities in the following sentences by changing the position of misleading modifiers.**

1. At one time his parents said he had been an engineering student.

2. The stage set, based on original paintings and engravings from the eighteenth century, was breathtaking.

3. The car was in the garage that he wrecked.

4. Marc promised on his way home to pick me up.

5. They talked about going on a second honeymoon but never did.

6. My brother hung the painting in the hallway that I gave him for his birthday.

7. The short story was, because of its convoluted sentences and obscure imagery, almost incomprehensible.

8. There is a panel discussion tonight about drug addiction in the student lounge.

9. I thought of writing often but never did.

10. Reading the personal letters of famous people is a way to usefully and completely understand their reactions to public situations.

## 9   Comparisons

When you include *comparisons* in your sentences, consider your diction carefully to ensure that the ideas are clear and complete.

### 9a   Include all the words needed to make a comparison clear and complete.

Flying to Chicago is more convenient than a taking train.

Levi's are more popular than any other jeans.

## 9b   Do not write an implied comparison.

An implied comparison presents only part of the necessary context. The words *better, less, more,* and *worse* and words formed with the suffix *-er* signal the need for fully stated comparisons; use *than* and explain the comparison completely.

The house on Elm Street is better suited to our needs. ^*than the others we've seen*

The orchestra's performance of Beethoven's Ninth Symphony was much worse. ^*than expected*

---

### EXERCISE

**Revise the following sentences to make their comparisons logical and complete.**

1. Once Carla began taking her medication regularly, she felt much better.

2. Having had a two-hour practice session, the students were no longer as confused.

3. Taking a taxi or riding the subway is certainly more convenient than a car.

4. Reeboks are more popular than any tennis shoe.

5. Revising a paper is much easier using a word processor.

## 10   Conciseness

Writing that is concise expresses ideas in as few words as possible; it is free of needless repetition and useless words. To make your writing concise, eliminate words, phrases, and clauses that do not further your purpose.

## 10a   Do not repeat words needlessly.

~~The car~~ We were looking for ~~was~~ a car for highway travel.
[12 words reduced to 9.]

## 10b Do not repeat ideas that are already understood.

~~The~~ frown ~~on Todd's face~~ suggested that he was ~~depressingly~~ saddened by his interview. [14 words reduced to 10.]

## 10c Eliminate expletive constructions whenever possible.

Expletives, such as *it is, there is, there are, here is, here are,* and so on, add words to sentences without clarifying meaning.

~~There were~~ Three cars *were* involved in the accident. [8 words reduced to 7.]

## 10d Write active sentences whenever possible. (See "Active and Passive Sentences," Section 5.)

*My aunt Ruth made* The prize-winning quilt ~~was made by my Aunt Ruth~~.
[9 words reduced to 7.]

## 10e Replace wordy phrases with brief expressions.

I *think* ~~am of the opinion~~ that we should resubmit the insurance claim.
[12 words reduced to 9.]

## 10f Replace forms of the verb *to be* with stronger verbs.

Counselors *must* ~~are responsible for~~ complet*e* the transcript portion of the applications.
[11 words reduced to 9.]

## 10g When possible, replace nonrestrictive clauses with appositives.

Nonrestrictive clauses, clauses that provide useful or interesting but inessential information, can often be replaced with *appositives,* simple words or phrases that provide definitions for other words or phrases in a sentence. (See also Section 20h.) To save words and tighten and clarify your writing, consider using appositives in place of nonrestrictive clauses.

Sandra Day O'Connor, ~~who was~~ the first woman appointed to the Supreme Court, assumed her duties in August 1981.
[19 words reduced to 17 through substitution of an appositive for a nonrestrictive clause.]

## EXERCISE

**Make the following wordy sentences concise. Note the number of words saved through revision.**

1. There should be two waiters to serve every ten people at the banquet, or there will be unnecessary delays occurring. [20 words reduced to _____.]

2. After the violent eruption of Nevada de Ruiz, relief agencies joined together in their efforts to help the unfortunate victims. [20 words reduced to _____.]

3. Wynton Marsalis, who plays both classical and jazz trumpet, scorns pop music. [12 words reduced to _____.]

4. At this point in time, we should prepare for spring floods, in the event that the Wabash River will crest as it did last year. [25 words reduced to _____.]

5. Finalists in the oratory competition will be evaluated by seven judges. [11 words reduced to _____.]

6. The original prototype for the Ford Mustang is on display at the Ford Museum in Detroit, Michigan. [17 words reduced to _____.]

7. A house made of brick is more costly but more maintenance free than a house made of wood. [18 words reduced to _____.]

8. Secret Service agents are responsible for protecting the current president, past presidents, and their families. [16 words reduced to _____.]

9. In the humble opinion of this writer, Academy Awards present indications of popularity rather than quality. [16 words reduced to _____.]

10. The real truth is that there is no money available to support and maintain the scholarship. [16 words reduced to _____.]

—— EXERCISE ——

**Revise the following paragraph to make it concise. Try a number of strategies and notice how much the paragraph improves when you eliminate unnecessary words and bloated phrases.**

Prior to beginning the search for gainful employment, gather together necessary and essential information and materials. Assemble a list of your experiences in educational institutions and in the workplace and be sure to include the months or years involved in each situation. Prepare a résumé that includes facts and information about yourself, personally, and about yourself, academically and professionally. Make sure that there are clear sections in the résumé to cover each of these important and crucial topics. Proofread the final copy of the résumé in order to be aware of and correct any errors or mistakes. Then photocopy the résumé so that you still have at your disposal a copy of the résumé for future reference.

## WRITING LOGICAL AND EFFECTIVE SENTENCES: REVIEW EXERCISES

**Revise the following sets of sentences to create logical and effective sentences. Identify the kinds of problems that require correction.**

1. Human figures were elongated and were rendered in sallow yellows and greens by the Spanish artist El Greco.

2. Cubism is, with its emphasis on presenting the surfaces of all objects—both living and inanimate—in abstract geometric forms, alien to many people's artistic sensibilities.

3. Although his work was not popular during his lifetime, van Gogh paints with bold colors and exaggerated forms. Modern collectors have valued his work since his death.

4. It is clear that there are only a few major pop art paintings of lasting aesthetic value. There are many others that are simply cultural curiosities.

5. When one sees the work of Rembrandt in a well-lighted gallery, you will be impressed by the rich texture of his work and the subtle variations in his gold and brown tones.

6. Neoclassical artists of the eighteenth century objected to the visual excesses of Baroque and Rococo art and imitate the symmetry and simple forms of Greek and Roman art.

7. Picasso's versatility as a sculptor is evident in his ability to skillfully and ingeniously use "junk" in his welded works.

8. Da Vinci, Raphael, David, Rembrandt, van Gogh, Monet, and Picasso would surely be included if one was to make a list of major European painters.

9. New York's Chrysler Building—with its use of zigzag forms, angular metal ornamentation, and strong vertical lines—is an exemplary model of Art Deco architecture.

10. Up until the middle of the twentieth century, most prominent and important painters and sculptors from the United States of America trained and went to school in the countries of Europe.

11. Once, painters worked almost exclusively on wood panels or plaster walls. Then stretched canvas was used. Today, wood is being used again by many artists.

12. The Louvre in Paris houses more major works of art than any museum.

13. Prior to viewing a major exhibition, I would offer encouragement to inexperienced and untrained viewers to peruse or skim the catalogue prepared to accompany the exhibition.

14. To create what he described as an unconscious interpretation of reality, paint was splattered on canvas by Jackson Pollock.

15. Stressing the dreamlike, the unusual, and the bizarre, we found Surrealistic art unsettling.

# Writing Grammatical Sentences

## 11  Eliminate Sentence Fragments

A *sentence fragment* is a group of words presented as if it were a complete sentence—with a capital letter at the beginning and a period at the end. A sentence fragment, however, lacks a subject or a verb or both and does not express a complete thought. Eliminate sentence fragments in one of four ways, depending on the type of fragment.

### 11a  Add a subject when necessary, or join the fragment to another sentence.

Charlie Chaplin was a multitalented man. ^He ~w~Wrote, directed, and starred in his own films.

Charlie Chaplin ~was a~ multitalented man, ~w~Wrote, directed, and starred in his own films.

### 11b  Add a verb when necessary, or join the fragment to another sentence.

Grigori Rasputin, a Russian monk in Czar Nicholas's court. He was assassinated in 1916.

### 11c  Omit the subordinating conjunction, or connect the fragment to an independent clause.

*Mother Teresa*
~Because she~ tirelessly helped the poor in Calcutta. *She* ~Mother Teresa~ was awarded the Nobel Peace Prize in 1979.

### 11d  Attach a phrase to a related sentence.

Leonard Bernstein received wide acclaim on Broadway. *n*Notably for the score of *West Side Story*.

---

### EXERCISE

Eliminate each fragment by making it into a sentence or by combining it with a sentence.

1. The *Robert E. Lee,* a renovated riverboat that now operates as a restaurant. It is an excellent place to eat.

2. We made our way up the mountain trail with much difficulty. Slipping on rocks and snagging our clothes in the underbrush.

3. Chad has only one ambition. To play the violin in a major symphony.

4. Many people dread one part of medical exams more than any other. Having a blood sample taken.

5. In a political speech, candidates should appeal to the entire audience. Not just to those who believe as they do.

6. Even though the cost of automobile insurance is high. Repairs on damaged cars are even more exorbitant.

7. Having come this far. We must see the matter through.

8. Whatever challenge the office presents. I believe our new member of Congress will meet it successfully.

9. When the chairperson stated, "I will not compromise on any issue on which I have taken a stand." I began to question her judgment.

10. Rita Moreno has won all major performance awards. An Oscar, an Emmy, a Grammy, and a Tony.

 ## Eliminate Fused Sentences and Comma Splices

A *fused sentence* (also called a ***run-on sentence***) results when no punctuation or coordinating conjunction separates two or more independent clauses. A *comma splice* results when two or more independent clauses are joined with only a comma. Eliminate these sentence errors in one of four ways.

**12a**   **Use a period to separate independent clauses, forming two sentences.**

> Lorraine Hansberry was the first black female playwright of importance,
> ~~s~~he wrote *A Raisin in the Sun*.

**12b**   **Use a semicolon to separate independent clauses and form a compound sentence.**

> Through flying, Charles Lindbergh gained his notoriety; Amelia Earhart lost her life.

**12c**   **Insert a coordinating conjunction between independent clauses to form a compound sentence.**

> *but*
> Helen Keller was both blind and deaf, she was a skillful author and lecturer.

**12d**   **Use a subordinating conjunction to put the less important idea in a subordinate clause and form a complex sentence.**

> *Although*
> Paul Revere is known to most people as a Revolutionary War patriot, he is known to collectors as a silversmith and engraver.

Be especially sensitive to the use of conjunctive adverbs, such as *consequently, however, moreover, nevertheless,* and *therefore.* They do not link clauses grammatically. Misinterpreting their function in sentences is a common cause of comma splices.

> Oscar Wilde fancied himself a poet and critic; however, he is most remembered as a playwright and wit.

---

#### EXERCISE

Correct the following fused sentences and comma splices.

1. The comma splice can confuse readers, it is usually less troublesome, however, than the fused sentence.

2. Members of the Drama Guild have rehearsed carefully for tonight's show, the director feels certain it will be a success.

3. The war is over the fighting is not.

4. The air traffic controller made the best decision he could at the time, looking back, he saw what he should have done differently.

5. It is too late to sign up for the proficiency exam this term, however, students can sign up for next term's exam.

6. Pay attention to the instructions you must follow them exactly.

7. Much has been done the American Civil Liberties Union believes that much more needs to be done.

8. Stockholders don't have to liquidate their assets this week, all they need to do is sign papers of intent.

9. Clean-up is scheduled for Monday, Tuesday, and Wednesday the plant closes on Friday.

10. No conclusive evidence has been uncovered, the commissioners will meet again tomorrow.

## 13  Agreement

*Agreement* in grammar refers to the correspondence of key sentence elements in number, person, and gender. Two kinds of agreement are grammatically important in most sentences: subject-verb agreement and pronoun-antecedent agreement.

### 13a  Subject-Verb Agreement

In simplest terms, a singular subject requires a singular verb, and a plural subject requires a plural verb. A number of troublesome constructions can cause confusion, however, and require consideration.

**When subjects are joined by *and*, use a plural verb.**

Although each of the subjects may be singular, the compounding makes a plural verb necessary.

O'Connor and Rehnquist **speak** articulately for the dissenters. [Plural verb with compound subject.]

A fool and his money **are** soon parted.

**When subjects are joined by *or, nor, but, either . . . or, neither . . . nor*, or *not only . . . but also*, use a verb that agrees with the subject that is nearer to the verb.**

Either Weixlmann or Stein **is** my choice for president. [Singular verb with two singular subjects.]

The coach or the cocaptains **supervise** the practices each day. [Plural verb agrees with *cocaptains*, the nearer subject.]

Neither Lewis, his two partners, nor their lawyers **were** at the press conference. [Plural verb agrees with *lawyers*, the nearer subject.]

Either Jean or you **are** to accept the award for the entire cast. [Plural verb agrees with *you*, the nearer subject.]

When this rule produces an awkward though correct sentence, consider revising the sentence.

You ~~or he is~~ *two are* the leading contender*s*.

**When a subject is followed by a phrase containing a noun that differs in number or person from the subject, use a verb that agrees with the subject, not with the noun in the phrase.**

The attitude of these men **is** decidedly hostile. [Singular verb agrees with *attitude*, the singular subject.]

The ballots with her name **have** been recalled. [Plural verb agrees with *ballots*, the plural subject.]

**When an indefinite pronoun, such as *anybody, anyone, each, either, everybody, neither, nobody*, and *someone*, is used as a subject, use a singular verb.**

Ultimately, someone **has** to accept responsibility.

Anybody who wants to **has** the right to attend the hearing.

Everyone **has** the same chance.

When a collective noun is used as a subject, use a singular verb *or* a plural verb to clarify the meaning.

When a collective noun emphasizes the unity of a group, use a singular verb. When a collective noun emphasizes group members as individuals, use a plural verb.

The clergy **is** grossly underpaid.
[Singular verb because whole group is meant.]

The clergy **are** using their pulpits to speak out against oppression.
[Plural verb because individual members are meant.]

When an expletive construction, such as *here is, here are, there is,* and *there are,* is used as both subject and verb, match the verb to the noun that follows.

Here **is** your receipt. [Singular verb with singular noun *receipt.*]

Here **are** the copies you requested. [Plural verb with plural noun *copies.*]

There **is** no excuse for such behavior. [Singular verb with singular noun *excuse.*]

There **are** several solutions to the city's problems.
[Plural verb with plural noun *solutions.*]

The verb in a relative clause introduced by *who, which,* or *that* agrees in number with the pronoun's antecedent.

Jessica is one performer who **acts** with restraint.
[Singular verb with singular antecedent *performer.*]

Philip Roth writes books that **illustrate** the absurdities of modern life.
[Plural verb with plural antecedent *books.*]

When a compound subject is preceded by *each* or *every,* use a singular verb.

*Each* and *every* indicate that persons or things are being considered individually.

Each boy and girl **takes** shop and home economics.

Every basket of peaches and flat of strawberries **was** sold.

When a subject is followed by a predicate noun that differs in number from the subject, the verb agrees with the subject, not with the complement.

Although predicate nouns restate the subject of the sentence, their word forms do not always agree in number; that is, the predicate noun and the subject may not be both singular or both plural. Use the subject, not the predicate noun, to determine the appropriate subject-verb agreement.

> Her chief source of enjoyment **is** books.
> [Singular verb with singular subject *source.*]

> Books **are** her chief source of enjoyment.
> [Plural verb with plural subject *books.*]

### When a plural noun has a singular meaning, use a singular verb.

Some subjects may initially appear to be plural, but they are singular. *Electronics, mathematics, semantics,* and *geriatrics* appear to be in plural form but are names of individual fields of study. Expressions such as *gin and tonic* and *ham and eggs* are also singular because they name a single drink and a single dish.

> No news **is** good news.

> Scotch and soda **is** not as popular as it once was.

### When fractions, measurements, money, time, weight, and volume are considered as single units, use singular verbs.

> Three days **is** too long to wait.
> Jerrid feels that 165 pounds **is** his ideal weight.
> Eighteen percent **is** the accepted rate for credit-card financing.

### With titles of individual works, even those containing plural words, use a singular verb.

> *All the King's Men* **is** an enlightening political novel.
> Dorothy Parker's "Good Souls" **is** about congenial, often exploited people.

### Words used as words take a singular verb.

> *Amateur athletes* is used to describe participants as varied as Little League pitchers and endorsement-rich track-and-field stars.

## 13b  Pronoun-Antecedent Agreement

Pronouns must agree with their antecedents (the nouns or pronouns to which they refer) in number and person. A singular pronoun must be used with a singular antecedent; a plural pronoun must be used with a plural antecedent. (See also "Case," Section 14.)

The workers received **their** wages.
[Plural third-person pronoun with plural third-person antecedent *workers.*]

The DC 10 changed **its** course and landed at Cincinnati.
[Singular third-person pronoun with singular third-person antecedent *DC 10.*]

Singular pronouns must also agree in gender with their antecedents. A masculine pronoun must be used with a masculine antecedent; a feminine pronoun must be used with a feminine antecedent; and a neuter pronoun must be used with a neuter antecedent. (See also "Case," Section 14.)

| **Masculine:** | he | him | his | himself |
|---|---|---|---|---|
| **Feminine:** | she | her | hers | herself |
| **Neuter:** | it | it | its | itself |

The generic use of masculine pronouns is no longer universally acceptable. Use both masculine and feminine pronouns when an antecedent could be either male of female *(he or she, his or hers).* Alternatively, use plural, genderless antecedents and pronouns whenever possible.

Each teacher must submit **his** or **her** annual report by March 15.
[Singular masculine and feminine pronouns with male or female antecedent *teacher.*]

Teachers must submit **their** annual reports by March 15.
[Plural pronoun with plural antecedent *teachers.*]

These principles of pronoun-antecedent agreement apply consistently to all situations, but a number of troublesome constructions require special consideration.

When the antecedents *each, either, neither,* and *none* are followed by a phrase that contains a plural noun, use a singular pronoun.

Although the noun in the phrase may be plural, *each, either, neither* and *none* refer to elements individually. Consequently, the pronoun must be singular.

Neither of the boys would accept the responsibility for **his** actions.
[Singular pronoun with *neither* as antecedent.]

Either of these women may lose **her** position.
[Singular pronoun with *either* as antecedent.]

When *everybody, each, either, everyone, neither, nobody,* and *a person* are antecedents, use a singular pronoun.

Although in context these words may imply plurality, the word forms are singular and therefore singular pronouns are required. Do not use masculine pronouns generically to refer to these genderless singular antecedents. Use both masculine and feminine forms, or alternatively, substitute plural antecedents and pronouns for the singular forms.

> Nobody had **his** or **her** work completed on time.
> [Singular pronouns with singular antecedent *nobody.*]

> The committee members had not completed **their** work on time.
> [A plural pronoun with plural antecedent *members.*]

Collective nouns used as antecedents take singular or plural pronouns depending on the meaning of the sentence.

A collective noun that identifies the group as a single unit takes a singular pronoun. A collective noun that identifies the individual members of a group takes a plural pronoun.

> The judge reprimanded the jury for **its** disregard of the evidence.
> [Singular pronoun because reference is to the group as a whole.]

> At the request of the defense attorney, the jury were polled and **their** individual verdicts recorded.
> [Plural pronoun because reference is to group members individually.]

When an antecedent is a person, use *who, whom,* or *that* to introduce qualifying phrases or clauses.

> This is the architect **who** planned the civic center.
> The interior designer **whom** we selected was unavailable.
> The landscaper **that** worked on our property has moved.

When an antecedent is an object or concept, use *which* or *that* to introduce qualifying phrases or clauses.

> Here is the package **that** she left behind.
> The package, **which** she left behind, could not later be found.

When an antecedent is an animal, use *that* to introduce qualifying phrases or clauses.

> Secretariat is the horse **that** you're speaking of.

---

## EXERCISE

**Circle the correct form in parentheses.**

1. Neither she nor her sons (was, were) present at the reading of the will.

2. The jury (is, are) expected to reach a verdict before midnight.

3. Each of the children is expected to bring (his, her, his or her, their) own art supplies.

4. The horse (that, who) won the Kentucky Derby went on to win the Preakness and the Belmont.

5. The team lost (its, their) first game of the season, but (it, they) won the next five games.

6. Every one of the actors who auditioned (was, were) exceptionally talented.

7. There (is, are) both food and firewood in the cabin.

8. Students (which, who) maintain grade-point averages of 3.50 or better are eligible for alumni scholarships.

9. None of the applicants presented (himself, herself, himself or herself, themselves) well in the interview.

10. Thirty hours a week (is, are) a heavy work schedule, especially if you are taking two classes.

## Case

Case is the form or position of a noun or pronoun that indicates its relation to other words in a sentence. English has three cases: *subjective, objective,* and *possessive.* In general, a noun or pronoun is in the subjective case when it acts as a subject, in the objective case when it acts as an object, and in the possessive case when it modifies a noun, as in "*his* bicycle," "the *boy's* dog," "*their* future."

English nouns, pronouns, and adjectives once all showed case by changing their forms. In modern English, word order and idiomatic constructions have largely replaced case endings. Only pronouns—and chiefly the personal pronouns—still make any considerable use of case forms.

Personal pronouns change form dramatically to indicate case.

|  |  | *Subjective* | *Objective* | *Possessive* |
|---|---|---|---|---|
| **Singular** | *1st person* | I | me | my, mine |
|  | *2nd person* | you | you | your, yours |
|  | *3rd person* | he, she, it | him, her, it | his, her, hers, its |
| **Plural** | *1st person* | we | us | our, ours |
|  | *2nd person* | you | you | your, yours |
|  | *3rd person* | they | them | their, theirs |

The indefinite or relative pronoun *who* also changes form to indicate case.

| *Subjective* | *Objective* | *Possessive* |
|---|---|---|
| who | whom | whose |
| whoever | whomever |  |

The case of a pronoun is determined by the pronoun's function in its own clause. Pronouns used as subjects or predicate nouns, that is, nouns that follow linking verbs and restate the subject, are in the subjective case. Pronouns used as direct objects, as indirect objects, or as objects of prepositions are in the objective case. Pronouns that modify a noun or pronoun or that precede and modify a gerund are in the objective case. Use the following guidelines to select the appropriate case.

## 14a Uses of the Subjective Case of Personal Pronouns

▷ As the subject of a verb:

**I** think that **we** missed the flight.

▷ As the complement of the verb *to be:*

I'm sure it was **she.**

▷ As the appositive (restatement) of a subject or predicate noun:

The surveyors, Mr. James and **he,** plotted the acreage.

## 14b Uses of the Objective Case of Personal Pronouns

▷ As the direct object or indirect object of a verb:

Mother likes **her** best.

Todd gave **us** the concert tickets.

▶ As the object of a preposition:

Sara directed the salesman to **him** and **me.**

▶ As the appositive (restatement) of a direct or indirect object:

My sister and I gave them, Mrs. Lester and **her,** nothing but trouble.

▶ As the subject of an infinitive:

I want **them** to take my place.

▶ As the object of an infinitive:

Don't expect to see **her** or **me** at a classical music concert.

## 14c     Uses of the Possessive Case of Personal Pronouns

▶ As a modifier of a noun or pronoun:

These are **my** four children, and those are **his** three.

▶ As a modifier of a gerund:

**Her** skiing improved rapidly.

What's wrong with **my** buying new equipment?

## 14d     Distinguishing Between "We" and "Us" Used with a Noun in Apposition

The subjective case form is *we;* the objective case form is *us.* Select the pronoun that would be correct if the noun were omitted.

**We** tenants must file formal complaints against the management firm.
[Subjective case for subject of the sentence.]

Their inattentiveness has given **us** tenants little recourse.
[Objective case for indirect object.]

## 14e     Personal Pronouns with "Than" or "As"

The case of a pronoun following *than* or *as* in a comparison often causes difficulty. In an elliptical (incompletely expressed) construction, use the case that would be appropriate if all the words were expressed.

He is at least as capable as **she.**
[Subjective case because *she* is the subject of the unexpressed verb *is.*]

The crowd liked Navratilova better than **them.**
[Objective case because *them* would be the object of the verb if the comparison were expressed completely: *better than it liked them.*]

## 14f    Uses of the Subjective Case of the Relative Pronoun "Who"

▷ As the subject of a clause:

Ralph Nader is a consumer advocate **who** gets media attention easily.

▷ As the subject of a clause stated as a question:

**Who** donated the carpets?

## 14g    Uses of "Whom"—The Objective Case of the Relative Pronoun "Who"

▷ As the object of a verb:

Professor Frayne is a man **whom** we admire.

▷ As the object of a verb in a question:

**Whom** should we notify?

## 14h    Distinguishing Between "Whoever" and "Whomever"

The subjective case form is *whoever;* the objective case form is *whomever.* Be aware that even when a subordinate clause functions as an *object,* a pronoun that functions as the *subject* of the clause belongs in the subjective case.

Invite **whoever** will come.
[Subjective case because *whoever* is the subject of *will come.*]

The committee will approve the appointment of **whomever** we select.
[Objective case because *whomever* is the object of the preposition *of.*]

---

EXERCISE

Revise the following sentences to correct any errors in the use of case. Some of the sentences need no correction.

1. The police suspected Boris Kraykov's associates, but he is more likely to be responsible than them.

2. Jim, not me, must make the recommendation.

3. Us gun collectors must be aware of people's objecting to firearms.

4. Reverend Wehrenberg is the person to whom we will go for advice.

5. They gave the finalists, Sandi and he, an enthusiastic round of applause.

6. Whoever we appoint to the council must be willing to present our case with conviction.

7. There is really no excuse for him refusing to comment.

8. The comments were directed to we two, you and I.

9. Carol is at least three years older than him.

10. Sonia will have to train whoever accepts the job.

## 15   Verb Tenses

*Verb tenses* indicate the time of the action or state of being expressed. Most verbs in English have four principal parts and change in a predictable way to form the six basic tenses and the six progressive tenses.

*Present-tense form:* walk
*Present participle:* walking
*Past-tense form:* walked
*Past participle:* walked
*Present tense:* walk, walks
*Past tense:* walked
*Future tense:* will walk, shall walk
*Present perfect tense:* have walked, has walked
*Past perfect tense:* had walked
*Future perfect tense:* will have walked, shall have walked
*Present progressive tense:* am walking, are walking, is walking
*Past progressive tense:* was walking, were walking
*Future progressive tense:* will be walking, shall be walking
*Present perfect progressive tense:* have been walking, has been walking
*Past perfect progressive tense:* had been walking

*Future perfect progressive tense:* will have been walking, shall have been walking

**Irregular verbs** form their past tenses and their past participles through changes in spelling or word form that must be memorized. The following is a list of the principal parts of the most common or troublesome verbs.

| *Present tense* | *Present participle* | *Past tense* | *Past participle* |
|---|---|---|---|
| am, is, are | being | was, were | been |
| bear | bearing | bore | borne |
| beat | beating | beat | beaten |
| begin | beginning | began | begun |
| bite | biting | bit | bitten |
| blow | blowing | blew | blown |
| break | breaking | broke | broken |
| bring | bringing | brought | brought |
| burst | bursting | burst | burst |
| cast | casting | cast | cast |
| choose | choosing | chose | chosen |
| come | coming | came | come |
| deal | dealing | dealt | dealt |
| do | doing | did | done |
| draw | drawing | drew | drawn |
| drink | drinking | drank | drunk |
| eat | eating | ate | eaten |
| fall | falling | fell | fallen |
| fly | flying | flew | flown |
| forbid | forbidding | forbade | forbidden |
| forsake | forsaking | forsook | forsaken |
| freeze | freezing | froze | frozen |
| give | giving | gave | given |
| go | going | went | gone |
| grow | growing | grew | grown |
| hang* | hanging | hung | hung |
| have | having | had | had |
| know | knowing | knew | known |
| lay | laying | laid | laid |
| lie** | lying | lay | lain |

*The verb *to hang,* used in the sense of "to execute," is regular: *hang, hanged, hanged.*
**The verb *to lie,* used in the sense of "to tell an untruth," is nearly regular: *lie, lying, lied, lied.*

| ride | riding | rode | ridden |
| ring | ringing | rang | rung |
| rise | rising | rose | risen |
| run | running | ran | run |
| see | seeing | saw | seen |
| shake | shaking | shook | shaken |
| shoe | shoeing | shod | shod |
| shrink | shrinking | shrank (shrunk) | shrunk |
| sing | singing | sang | sung |
| sink | sinking | sank (sunk) | sunk |
| sit | sitting | sat | sat |
| slay | slaying | slew | slain |
| slink | slinking | slunk | slunk |
| speak | speaking | spoke | spoken |
| spin | spinning | spun | spun |
| spring | springing | sprang (sprung) | sprung |
| steal | stealing | stole | stolen |
| strive | striving | strove | striven |
| swear | swearing | swore | sworn |
| swim | swimming | swam | swum |
| take | taking | took | taken |
| teach | teaching | taught | taught |
| tear | tearing | tore | torn |
| throw | throwing | threw | thrown |
| wear | wearing | wore | worn |
| weave | weaving | wove | woven |
| win | winning | won | won |
| write | writing | wrote | written |

**15a**  **Use the present tense to describe habitual action or actions that occur or conditions that exist in the present.**

Pamela **listens** to classical music when she writes papers.
They **are** exhausted.

**15b**  **Use the present tense to express general truths and scientific principles.**

The earth **tilts** slightly on its axis.

**15c** Use the present tense to describe or discuss artistic works, paintings, sculpture, etc., and literary works, novels, plays, poems, etc.

Polonius **offers** Laertes platitudes, not advice.

The stark black and white in Picasso's large painting *Guernica* **is** the visual equivalent of the starkness of his message.

**15d** Use the past tense to describe completed actions or conditions that existed in the past.

Abolitionists openly **opposed** slavery, often at personal risk.

They **were** exhausted.

**15e** Use the future tense to describe actions that will occur or conditions that will exist in the future.

The Congress **will reconvene** after a brief recess.

**15f** Use the present perfect tense to describe actions that started or conditions that existed at an unspecified time in the past and continue in the present.

For years, Mary Tyler Moore **has been** a spokesperson for the American Diabetes Association.

**15g** Use the past perfect tense to describe actions that started or conditions that existed before a specific time in the past.

In large part, Czar Nicholas **had ignored** the turmoil that preceded the Russian Revolution.

**15h** Use the future perfect tense to describe actions that will be completed or conditions that will exist before a specific time in the future.

Natalie **will have submitted** her dissertation before the school year ends.

**15i**    Use the progressive tenses to express ongoing actions that occur in the present, past, or future.

> I **am learning** to ski.
>
> Sasha **had been planning** to attend the theater opening.
>
> Rebecca **will be working** as a receptionist this summer.

**15j**    Use present participles to express action that coincides with the action described by the main verb.

> **Sensing** that media coverage of the takeover would be negative, Albertson decided to cancel the press conference.

**15k**    Use past participles and perfect participles to express actions that occurred, or to describe conditions that existed, before the action or condition described by the main verb.

> **Shocked** by the disparaging comments, Senator Robertson left the hearing.
>
> **Having completed** her work, Sybil sat down to read.

**15l**    Generally, use the past tense or past perfect tense in a subordinate clause when the verb in the independent clause is in the past or past perfect tense.

This combination of past tenses is used to place one past action in a temporal or other relation with another past action.

> Virginia Woolf **worked** in isolation because she **needed** quiet to concentrate well.
>
> After he **had purchased** tickets for the World Series, Karl **was** unable to use them.

**15m**    When the verb in the independent clause is in the present, future, present perfect, or future perfect tense, use any tense in the subordinate clause that will make the meaning of the sentence clear.

> In *Camelot,* Lancelot **thinks** that he **will succeed** at every venture.
>
> Because twenty-four-carat gold **is** soft, detailed design work **will wear** away over time.

## EXERCISE

**Select the appropriate verb tenses in the following sentences. Be ready to explain your choices.**

1. Rain (is, was) water that (condenses, condensed) around dust particles and (falls, fell) to earth.

2. Normally the incidence of heartworm disease (increases, increased) each year, but last year it (decreases, decreased).

3. On a bimonthly basis, the Citizens' Action Coalition (sends, sent) a newsletter to its supporters.

4. Next fall, tuition at American universities (rises, will rise) to keep pace with inflation.

5. Becky Sharp (is, was) the main character of William Thackeray's *Vanity Fair,* an episodic novel published in 1847.

6. Isaac Bashevis Singer (has written, had written) all of his stories in Yiddish, but they (are, were) immediately translated into English.

7. By the end of this season, we (will play, will have played) in thirty games and two tournaments.

8. (Serving, Having served) on the magazine's board of economic advisors, the woman (is, was) a likely figure to head the Federal Reserve Board.

9. Because Da Vinci (experiments, experimented) with a variety of interesting pigments, many of his works (are, were) deteriorating.

10. (Opening, Having opened) the bomb casing with great care, the explosives expert (disconnects, disconnected) the timing mechanism.

 **16**

## Adjectives and Adverbs

*Adjectives* and *adverbs* are both modifiers, but they serve separate purposes in sentences. Adjectives modify nouns and pronouns. Adverbs modify verbs, adjectives, and other adverbs; they may also modify phrases and clauses.

The -*ly* ending identifies many words as adverbs. It is not foolproof, however. Some adjectives end in -*ly (heavenly, lovely, leisurely),* and many common adverbs *(very, then, always, here, now)* do not end in -*ly.* To avoid faulty modification, be certain to use adjectives only with nouns and pronouns and adverbs with verbs, adjectives, other adverbs, or whole phrases and clauses.

## 16a     Use adjectives to modify nouns and pronouns.

His **thoughtful** assessments are always **welcome.**

They are **dependable.**

## 16b     Use adverbs to modify verbs, adjectives, and other adverbs.

She **carefully** selected the flowers.

She was **especially** careful when she chose the roses.

She **very** carefully examined the buds and leaves on each stem.

## 16c     Recognize the distinct uses of troublesome adjective and adverb pairs.

The following two adjective/adverb pairs, and others you may have had trouble with in your writing, should be used carefully.

*Bad/Badly:* Use *bad,* the adjective form, to modify nouns and pronouns, even with sensory verbs such as *appear, look, taste,* and so on. Use *badly,* the adverb form, only to modify a verb.

Agassi made a series of **bad** volleys during the third match.

His prospects may seem **bad,** but they really aren't.

Although Jimmy Stewart sang several great Cole Porter songs in films, he acknowledged that he sang them **badly.**

*Good/Well:* The word *good,* an adjective, always modifies a noun or a pronoun. The word *well* can function as either an adverb or an adjective. As an adverb meaning "satisfactorily," *well* could modify a verb, an adjective, or another adverb. As an adjective meaning "healthy," *well* could modify only a noun or pronoun.

N
The lasagna smells *good*. [Adjective]

V
Your point is *well* taken. [Adverb]

PRON
Mrs. Biagi says that she feels *well* today. [Adjective]

## EXERCISE

**Revise the following sentences to correct faulty modification.**

1. If you move quiet and slow, you can sometimes see small wildlife in this area.

2. Miss Haversham, eccentric and oppressive, treated Pip bad.

3. Competitive cyclists must react calm and quick when they need to make repairs during tournaments.

4. Make sure that the knots are tied tight and secure, or the rocking of the waves may break the boat loose from the wharf.

5. When receiving chemotherapy treatments, most patients don't feel good.

## WRITING GRAMMATICAL SENTENCES: REVIEW EXERCISE

**Revise the following sentences to make them grammatical. Identify the problem in each sentence that made revision necessary.**

1. Beginning in 1901, Nobel Prizes have been awarded to people who have made major contributions in the areas of peace, literature, physics, chemistry, and physiology or medicine, contributions in economics have been recognized since 1969.

2. A committee representing Yale University and the Bollingen Foundation presents their $50,000 award for poetry every two years.

3. The Harry Chapin Media Award was given to Eric Schlosser who most people recognize as the author of *Fast Food Nation*.

4. *Master of the Senate*, Robert A. Caro's Pulitzer Prize–winning biography, established the links between the personal, political, and historical events in the life of Lyndon B. Johnson.

5. Kennedy Center Honors have recognized the innovative work of a number of choreographers. George Balanchine, Martha Graham, Agnes de Mille, and Jerome Robbins, among others.

6. Although *Thoroughly Modern Millie* won several Tony Awards, it has fared bad with some reviewers.

7. George W. Beadie and Edward L. Tatum, both of the United States, received Nobel Prizes in Physiology for their discovery that genes transmitted hereditary characteristics.

8. Each year, the Randolph Caldecott Medal, awarded by the American Library Association, recognizes whomever has produced the best illustrated book for children.

9. "Don't Know Why," the first cut from Norah Jones's album *Come Away with Me*. Won Grammy Awards in 2002 for best record, best song, and best pop vocal.

10. Henry Kissinger was Secretary of State from 1973 to 1977, under Nixon and Ford, he has received the Nobel Peace Prize (1973), the Presidential Medal of Freedom (1977), and the Medal of Liberty (n.d.).

11. Emory Holloway, Walter Jackson Bate, Justin Kaplan, Lawrence Thompson, Louis Sheaffer, and Richard W. B. Lewis have all won Pulitzer Prizes for biographies of major writers. In spite of the awards, however, their books are more recognized by name than them.

12. MacArthur Foundation Fellowships boast awards of $500,000, spread over five years, these fellowships free recipients to pursue their interests.

13. The Enrico Fermi Award is given to scientists who demonstrated an "exceptional and altogether outstanding" body of work in the field of atomic energy.

14. Milos Forman has won Academy Awards for directing two highly distinct films, *One Flew Over the Cuckoo's Nest*, a black comedy about a psychiatric ward, and *Amadeus*, a selectively retold biography of Mozart, also won Oscars as best film of the year.

15. WGBH, Boston's PBS station, won three George Foster Peabody Awards for Broadcasting in 2002. Their program, *Endgame in Ireland*, were particularly acknowledged.

# Choosing Effective Diction

Effective diction is the choice of words that best communicate your purpose to your audience. Your diction must be tailored to fit the specific context of your sentences and paragraphs and of your paper as a whole. Your choices of effective diction depend on your *subject, audience,* and *purpose.*

## 17  Use a Dictionary

No writer should work without a dictionary. Unabridged dictionaries, like the *Oxford English Dictionary,* usually found in the reference rooms of libraries, contain vast numbers of words and lengthy, thorough definitions. They are useful when you need to find highly detailed information like full word histories or to find the definition of an arcane word. Most of your needs, however, will be met by a standard desk-sized, collegiate dictionary such as

> *American Heritage Dictionary of the English Language*
> *Random House Dictionary of the English Language: College Edition*
> *Webster's New Collegiate Dictionary*
> *Webster's New World Dictionary of the American Language: College Edition*

Those dictionaries, and most other standard-sized collegiate dictionaries, provide a wide variety of general and useful information including

> A brief history of lexicography (the preparation and study of dictionaries)
> A brief history of the language
> An explanatory diagram of a sample word entry, with a key to the abbreviations that are used in the definitions
> Explanations and definitions of and guidance on matters of grammar and usage
> The dictionary of words (the main portion of the reference book)
> Lists of standard abbreviations
> Biographical entries (brief notes on important people)
> Geographical entries (brief notes on important places)
> Lists of foreign words and phrases
> Comparative tables of alphabets, calendars, and currencies
> Tables of measurements (both American and metric)

▶ Lists of signs and symbols in common use

▶ Maps and illustrations

▶ Pronunciation guides

▶ General guides to writing (business-letter forms, forms of address, manuscript preparation guidelines, and so on)

Dictionaries provide much more than definitions; they offer useful information about many subjects related to writing. Most often, however, you will turn to a dictionary to find information about specific words. To make your use of a dictionary efficient and productive, familiarize yourself with its general pattern of presenting information about words.

**Spelling and Syllabication**   Entries begin with the word spelled out and divided into syllables, usually marked with dots: **con•tract.** When a word has several acceptable spellings, each of them will be listed, but the most common spelling will be listed first. If alternative spellings are listed as *Am* (American) and *Brit* (British), use the American spelling in your writing.

**Pronunciations**   The pronunciation (usually enclosed in parentheses) follows, presented in a simplified phonetic transcription. The markings are

**con•tract** (kŏn′trăkt′) *n. Abbr.* **contr., cont.   1.** An agreement between two or more parties, especially one that is written and enforceable by law.  **2.** The writing or document containing such an agreement.  **3.** The branch of law dealing with contracts.  **4.** Marriage as a formal agreement; betrothal.  **5.** In the game of bridge: **a.** The last and highest bid of one hand. **b.** The number of tricks thus bid. **c. Contract bridge** *(see).* —*v.* (kən-trăkt′, kŏn′trăkt′) **contracted, -tracting, -tracts.** —*tr.*  **1.** To enter into by contract; establish or settle by formal agreement.  **2.** To acquire or incur.  **3.** To reduce in size by drawing together; shrink.  **4.** To pull together; wrinkle.  **5.** To shorten (a word or words) by omitting or combining some of the letters or sounds; for example, *I'm* for *I am.* —*intr.*  **1.** To enter into or make a contract.  **2.** To become reduced in size by or as if by being drawn together.  [Middle English, from Old French, from Latin *contractus,* from the past participle of *contrahere,* to draw together, bring about, enter into an agreement : *com-,* together + *trahere,* to draw (see *tragh-* in Appendix*).] —**con•tract′i•bil′i•ty, con•tract′i•ble•ness** *n.* —**con•tract′i•ble** *adj.*
  **Synonyms:** *contract, condense, compress, constrict, shrink.* These verbs refer to decrease in size or content of a thing and sometimes to a resultant change in its form. *Contract* applies to internal drawing together that reduces the volume of a thing. *Condense* refers to an increase in compactness produced by the removal or reduction of parts or by a change in physical form of the thing involved, such as a change from gas to liquid or from liquid to solid. *Compress* applies to increased compactness brought about by external force; the term implies reduction of volume and change of form or shape. *Constrict* refers to decreasing the extent of a thing, usually by external pressure. *Shrink* refers to contraction that produces reduction in physical extent.

matched to a pronunciation guide, which is usually printed at the bottom of each page. When words have more than one syllable, accent marks ( ´ ´ ) indicate which syllables receive primary or secondary stress.

**Parts of Speech**    Abbreviations such as *n., v.,* and *adj.* indicate how a word can be used in a sentence. When a word can be used in various ways, the definitions are divided by parts of speech with, for instance, all meanings of the noun grouped together, followed by all meanings of the verb.

**Abbreviations**    If a word is commonly abbreviated, some dictionaries include the abbreviation in the entry; other dictionaries list abbreviations in a special section.

**Grammatical Features**    Distinctive grammatical features are noted in the entry. The principal parts of a verb are included, information that is especially helpful with irregular verbs—for example, *go, went, gone, going, goes.* Plural forms are provided for nouns that form plurals irregularly—for example, *mouse, mice.* When comparative and superlative degrees of adjectives and adverbs are formed in ways other than by adding *-er* or *-est*—for example, *good, better, best* or *many, more, most*—dictionaries generally list them.

**Meanings**    Within part-of-speech groups, meanings are most commonly presented in order of their frequency of use. Some dictionaries, however, present definitions in historical order (from oldest to newest) or hierarchical order (from primary to secondary). Read the front matter of the dictionary you are using to see which pattern it follows.

**Etymology**    When word origins are known, they are provided, sometimes in abbreviated form (*Gk.* for Greek, *ME* for Middle English, and so on). Thus *contract* is one of a large class of words that came into English from Latin by way of Old French. It is made up of the prefix *con-* (from the Latin *com-,* meaning "together") and the root word *tract* (from the Latin *trahere,* meaning "to draw").

**Labels**    Labels are used to identify words according to a number of specific criteria: general level of usage (*Nonstandard, Informal, Slang, Dia.,* and so on), regional usage (*Brit., Southern*), and usage within an area of specialization (*Law, Med., Computer Sci.*).

**Synonyms and Antonyms**    Many dictionaries include brief lists of synonyms for defined words (often introduced by the abbreviation *syns.*), to illustrate comparable word choices. Some dictionaries include antonyms as well (often introduced by the abbreviation *ant.*). Check the front matter of your dictionary to see whether these aids are used and where they are placed in the entries.

## EXERCISE

Use the following questions to familiarize yourself with your own collegiate dictionary. You will have to use all parts of the dictionary to find your answers—the front matter, entries, and appended materials. Keep in mind that your responses may vary slightly from those of people using other dictionaries.

1. If you have to hyphenate *maleficence* at the end of a line, where could you appropriately place a hyphen before finishing the word on the next line?

2. How are the following words pronounced: *acclimate, banal, data, impotent, Wagnerian?*

3. Which is the preferred spelling, *aesthetics* or *esthetics?* Is the word listed under both spellings or under only one?

4. What synonyms does your dictionary list for *ghastly, lure, puzzle, single,* and *yield?*

5. What is the British meaning of the word *torch?* When *torch* is used as slang, what does it mean? What idiomatic expression uses the word *torch?*

6. What is a *schlemiel?* What is the origin of the word?

7. How many meanings are recorded for the word *vulgar?* By what pattern are the definitions arranged?

8. As what parts of speech can the word *square* be used? In what order do the parts of speech appear in the entry?

9. What are the plural forms of *alumna, fungus, graffito, hippopotamus,* and *medium?*

10. For what do the abbreviations AAUW, EST, FNMA, MCAT, and VISTA stand?

11. In what years were *Marian Anderson, D. W. Griffith, Marie Antoinette, Alfred Nobel, George H. Ruth,* and *Mary Cassatt* born?

12. In what countries are *Addis Ababa, Caracas, Kuala Lumpur, Mecca,* and *Sarajevo* located?

## 18 Consider Issues of Diction

Standard English is the language of educated speakers and writers of English. American schools, government, businesses, and media have long used Standard English as the criterion by which speech and expository writing are judged; yet judgments about acceptable usage are sometimes hard to make because of the fluid nature of language and the effect of different writing situations. In a larger sense, word choices must be made in the context of a given piece of writing, depending on your subject, audience, and purpose. As a result, a word choice that is appropriate in one context may be inappropriate in another.

## 18a Changes and Variations in Language

Language is constantly evolving, and as a result standards of usage are also constantly changing. New words are introduced, old words assume new meanings, and some words are discarded. As a writer, you must be aware of such changes and keep your diction current. A newly coined word such as *houseperson* may at the present time be questionable usage, but another fairly recent word such as *chair* is generally acceptable. You need to remain sensitive to such subtleties and make your word choices on the basis of what currently seems to be acceptable. A dictionary and your instructor can provide useful guidance.

Be aware as well that language varies from one region of the country to another. *Tag* may easily be understood in some areas, but in other regions the term *license plate* may be necessary to make your meaning clear. It is therefore important to familiarize yourself with regional word choices and to use or avoid using them, depending on your writing context.

## 18b The Writing Situation—Formal or Informal

Writers vary their diction and sentence structure to suit the writing context. A letter to the editor of the local newspaper in support of its position on a local issue, for example, AIDS education in the schools, would differ in many ways from a letter to a friend on the same subject. The difference is one of level of formality within Standard English. Formal usage—which typically uses an extensive vocabulary including learned words, no slang, few contractions, and long, often complex sentences—may be appropriate for some topics and in some circumstances. Informal usage—generally characterized by the use of popular and colloquial words and some slang and contractions and short, simple sentences, often including fragments—may be appropriate for other topics and other circumstances. Whether a writer chooses a formal or informal style, or something in between, depends not on "correctness," for a broad

527

range of styles is acceptable; rather, it depends on what is *appropriate* to the specific writing situation.

The following discussions address some key issues of diction, both formal and informal, and will help you choose your words selectively. (See Chapter 10, "Diction: The Choice of Words," for a fuller discussion.)

## 18c    Considering Denotation and Connotation

When you choose words, consider their **denotations** (the meaning in the dictionary) and their **connotations** (the meaning derived from context). Look at these two sentences:

> Nell Gwynn, a **famous** actress during the English Restoration, became the mistress of King Charles II.

> Nell Gwynn, a **notorious** actress during the English Restoration, became the mistress of King Charles II.

Both of the words in bold type indicate that Nell Gwynn was well known; the denotations are similar. *Famous* and *notorious* have different connotations, however. *Famous* implies "celebrated," "renowned"; *notorious* implies "infamous," "widely but unfavorably known."

## 18d    Distinguishing Between Often-Confused Words

Some words are easily mistaken for each other because of similarities in spelling or pronunciation. When such confusion occurs, ideas become jumbled or unclear. Look at these two sentences:

> In her closing remarks, the district attorney stated that the defendant had been **persecuted** because the evidence proved him guilty.

> Darren received a summons for **wreckless** driving.

In the first, the verb *persecute* has been mistaken for *prosecute;* in the second, *wreckless* for *reckless.*

Commonly confused words include *advice* and *advise; cite, sight,* and *site; council* and *counsel; farther* and *further; loose* and *lose;* and *principal* and *principle.* Others are listed in "A Glossary of Contemporary Usage" (page 576).

## 18e    Avoiding Trite Language

Trite language is diction that is commonplace and unimaginative and consequently ineffective. Once-original expressions like *white as snow, in the final analysis,* and *rough and ready* have been used so often, in so many contexts, that they no longer offer new insight. Avoid using clichés and instead strive to communicate your meaning in your own language.

*Ideally, aging*

~~In an ideal world~~ boxers ~~who are over the hill~~ would retire before they ~~were~~ *lost their*

*strength and agility.*

~~past their prime.~~

## 18f    Avoiding Jargon

*Jargon,* the specialized or technical language of a particular group, is sometimes appropriate when you are writing only to members of the group, but it is inappropriate when you are writing for a general audience. Keep your audience clearly in mind, and use specific but common words instead.

*interdepartmental memos,*

By improving the quality and clarity of ~~horizontal transmittal correspon-~~

*save money.*

~~dence,~~ companies can ~~become more cost efficient~~.

## 18g    Using Figurative Language

Figurative language imaginatively compares dissimilar things to present a significant insight. Figurative language can add interest to your writing, but you should be aware of some potential problems in its use.

▸ *Mixed metaphors* bring together images that clash because they establish incompatible impressions.

Shannon dove into her studies to reach the top of the class standings. [*Dove,* denoting downward movement, clashes with *reach the top,* connoting upward movement.]

▸ *Exaggerated personifications* result when inanimate objects or abstractions are given human or animal characteristics, thus creating images that are so far-fetched that readers find them strained—even laughable—rather than effective.

The craggy peak, covered with a few scraggly pines, brooded over the valley like a disapproving parent.

▸ *Unrecognizable allusions* are references to obscure historical or literary events or people. An allusion should illuminate a discussion, so use references that are likely to be recognized by a general audience.

Jeremy's letter to the editor, a condensed *Areopagitica,* railed against censorship. [The allusion to John Milton's tract on freedom of the press might be lost on many readers.]

---

### EXERCISE

**Revise the following sentences to eliminate problems with diction. Consult your dictionary, if necessary.**

1. The sight for the new city counsel building has already been chosen.

2. We racked our brains for solutions to our financial problems, but solutions seemed few and far between.

3. The berserk parents shouted at the school's principle and refused to believe that Danny, their pride and joy, could have done anything wrong.

4. Purchasing a residence in a noncity environment was the Smiths' fondest wish.

5. Like a ship without a sail, Scott wandered threw the office building, looking for the lawyer's office.

6. The intelligence operative arranged for telephone surveillance of Dr. Russell's office.

7. For reasons too numerous to mention, Bradley Jennerman resigned.

8. One should always masticate one's food completely.

9. Like a scared monkey, the small child clung to his mother.

10. Researchers suggest that excessive involvement in the television-viewing process can effect the way a young person preforms in an educational institution.

### EXERCISE

**Revise the following paragraphs to eliminate problems with diction.**

    In these troubled financial times, one is likely to find adults returning to their family domiciles to cohabitant with their parents. After attaining degrees from institutions of higher learning, many offspring return to their home areas to find gainful employment and save money by sharing the family dwelling. The money they save they often invest in automobiles, stereos, and haberdashery. Some save money to allow them to invest later in living quarters of their own or save money for a rainy day.

The psychological affects of adults returning to live with parents can be unfortunate. Offspring sometimes feel that they are not establishing their independence from Mom and Pop. Parents sometimes feel that their children, now grown, are imposing on their independence, and returning children create storm and strife when they return to the nest. But at this point in time, adults living with their parents is becoming more commonplace, and many people will have to learn to live with the situation.

## Choosing Effective Diction: Review Exercise

**Revise the following sentences to improve their diction.**

1. An effective piece of transcribed discourse must be easily decipherable.

2. Like a sponge absorbs water, the dancer listened to and analyzed the comments of her choreographer.

3. In the final analysis, the institution of higher learning's operation was not cost-effective.

4. The NSC's clandestine operations in Central America and the Middle East were less than effective.

5. The aggressive salesperson amassed a sizable commission.

6. It goes without saying that in this day and age oral communication is crucial for getting ahead in this dog-eat-dog world.

7. Sometime or other everyone will have difficulties with interpersonal relations.

8. The principal's principal objection was not to the principal the students presented but to their method of implementing it.

9. The Herculean task of planning the reunion fell on the shoulders of the two organizers.

10. The microscopic listening devices implanted in the concrete structural members of the U.S. Embassy in Moscow would make surreptitious monitoring of conversations possible.

# Observing the Rules of Punctuation

Marks of punctuation serve specific purposes in sentences. They show where thoughts end, where ideas are separated, and where pauses occur. Punctuate sentences according to the principles noted here. Remember that using punctuation unnecessarily is as confusing as omitting it when it is required.

## 19 Periods, Question Marks, and Exclamation Points (./?/!)

Three marks of punctuation end sentences: the **period,** the **question mark,** and the **exclamation point.** They indicate that a thought is complete, and they perform—especially the period—other functions as well.

### 19a Accurate Use of Periods

#### Use a period to end a sentence that makes a statement.

Solar power is not yet a widely used energy source.

#### Use a period at the end of a question that is a courteously stated request or a command.

Will you please hand in your papers now.

Give your forms to the secretary when you've finished.

#### Use a period to end a sentence that contains an indirect question.

The landlord asked if we understood the terms of the lease.
[The sentence states that a question was asked; it does not directly pose the question.]

#### Use a period with most abbreviations.

Although a period in an abbreviation indicates that letters have been omitted, some standard abbreviations do not require periods. Consult a dictionary for guidance. (See also Section 35, "Abbreviations.")

| *With periods* | *Without periods* |
|---|---|
| Mr. | FCC (government agency) |
| M.D. | IL (state) |
| Trans. | PBS (television network) |

**Use a period before a decimal point and with dollars and cents.**

Production standards vary by only .14 millimeter.

Pi equals 3.14159.

The price was reduced to $39.95.

## 19b    Accurate Use of Question Marks

**Use a question mark after a direct question.**

The need for a question mark is usually indicated by inverted word order: Part or all of the verb in the independent clause precedes the subject of the clause. In some instances, however, intent transforms a statement into a question.

Can we assume that the order has been shipped?

[*Can,* part of the verb, precedes the subject *we.*]

You mean he's ill?

[Intent, not word order, indicates that the sentence is a question; the question mark, though optional, confirms the writer's intent.]

**Use a question mark in parentheses to indicate uncertainty about the accuracy of dates or numbers or other facts.**

Modern scholars question whether Homer, a Greek poet of the ninth century (?) B.C., was the sole author of the famous epics attributed to him, the *Iliad* and the *Odyssey.*

It is not good usage to indicate possibly inaccurate words or to indicate irony by using a question mark in parentheses; changes in diction or sentence structure are more effective means of achieving these ends.

## 19c    Accurate Use of Exclamation Points

**Use an exclamation point only to express strong emotion or to indicate unusual emphasis.**

Be quiet!

Don't just stand there. Do something!

In most writing, exclamation points are not necessary or appropriate. Use them selectively.

## 20    Commas (,)

The *comma* is used to make the internal structure of a sentence clear. It does so in three general ways: (1) by separating elements that might otherwise be confused, (2) by setting off interrupting constructions, and (3) by marking words that are out of normal order.

### 20a    Use commas to separate three or more coordinate items in a series.

Using a comma before the conjunction (the word that joins the items in the series) is always correct and will avoid possible confusion.

> Her favorite novelists were Melville, Lawrence, and Faulkner.
> [Commas separating nouns.]

> We considered displaying the statue in three places: in the lobby, in the president's office, and in the reception room. [Commas separating phrases.]

> Jack designed the set, Ira did the flat painting, and Margo did the detailed painting.
> [Commas separating independent clauses.]

### 20b    Use commas between coordinate adjectives or adverbs that are not joined by a conjunction but that modify the same word individually.

When each of several adjectives modifies a noun individually or when each of several adverbs modifies a verb, adjective, or adverb individually, commas should separate the modifiers. No comma separates the last modifier from the word it modifies. (See also Section 21d.)

> It was a dark, drizzly, depressing day. [Each adjective individually modifies *day.*]

> Rick slowly, methodically rechecked his documentation.
> [Each adverb individually modifies *rechecked.*]

### 20c    In a compound sentence, use a comma before the coordinating conjunction that links the independent clauses.

This usage prevents the subject of the second clause from being misread as an additional object in the first clause. When there is no danger of a confused reading, the comma may be omitted.

Because of financial difficulties, the farmer sold his tractor and his plows, and his land remained uncultivated in the spring.

[Without the comma, *land* could be misread as another direct object in a series with *tractor* and *plows*.]

T. S. Eliot's poetry is highly regarded but his drama is not.

[No comma necessary because no confusion is likely.]

## 20d  Use one comma or a pair of commas to set off a conjunctive adverb.

Conjunctive adverbs, such as *however, moreover, therefore, consequently,* and *nevertheless,* establish logical connections between sentences. Usually they provide a transition between two statements, and they often come near or at the beginning of the second statement. If no confusion will result, the comma or commas may be omitted, but using commas in these cases will always be correct.

The warehouse was severely damaged by fire. Subsequently, the property was sold at a loss.

Recent advances in medical research have brought hope to victims of AIDS. Some medical experts, however, feel the optimism is premature.

Streamlining corporate management helps companies operate more smoothly; moreover, it can save on operating costs.

## 20e  Use a comma after an introductory subordinate clause in a complex or compound-complex sentence.

Because oil prices were high, American drivers began to conserve gasoline, showing that for once they were responsive to environmental issues.

Although Middle English is somewhat difficult to read, the rewards of reading Chaucer make learning his language worth the effort.

### Use a comma after an introductory infinitive or participial phrase.

To prepare for her language proficiency exam, Pam skimmed five study guides.

Moving cautiously through the rubble, the insurance agent made notes for the damage report.

## 20f  Use a comma after introductory elements that function as adjectives or adverbs unless the phrase is short and the meaning of the sentence is clear without the comma.

A prepositional phrase at the beginning of a sentence that answers the questions *when, where,* or *under what conditions* is functioning like an adverb.

Since such phrases modify the entire sentences of which they are a part, they should be followed by commas.

> After four weeks of intensive work, Jason finished the first draft of his master's thesis.

> After classes the five of us met to play basketball.
> [Short phrase does not require a comma.]

**Use a comma to set off an introductory adverb that modifies an entire sentence.**

> Finally, attending conferences and workshops is an important way to meet other professionals.

## 20g    Use one comma or a pair of commas to set off a nonrestrictive clause or phrase.

A *nonrestrictive clause* or *phrase* does not limit a class to a particular group or individual but modifies the whole class. It supplies additional information but can be omitted from a sentence without substantially altering the sentence's meaning.

A *restrictive clause* or *phrase* specifies a particular member or members of a group. It supplies information that is necessary to the meaning of the sentence. Restrictive clauses or phrases are not set off by commas.

> The audio designer, **who creates sound effects for a play,** is an important member of a theater staff.
> [*Nonrestrictive clause* could be omitted without altering sentence meaning.]

> New recruits, **who may join after finishing high school,** must make numerous adjustments before they are acclimated to military life.
> [*Nonrestrictive clause* could be omitted without altering sentence meaning.]

> The audio designer **who worked on *Equus*** should be fired.
> [*Restrictive clause* identifies a specific audio designer.]

> All soldiers **who complete basic training** will be assigned to duty within three weeks. [*Restrictive clause* identifies a specific group of soldiers.]

## 20h    Use one comma or a pair of commas to set off nonrestrictive appositives.

An *appositive*—a word, phrase, or clause that renames a word or group of words in a sentence—can be nonrestrictive or restrictive. Nonrestrictive appositives provide inessential information and are set off by commas. Restrictive appositives provide essential information and are not set off by commas. Appositives are grammatically equivalent to the noun or pronoun they rename.

> PBS, **a nonprofit broadcasting network,** relies on corporate donations to cover most of its operating expenses.
> [*Nonrestrictive appositive* could be omitted without altering sentence meaning.]

> The superstation **TBS** broadcast the first colorized versions of many American film classics.
> [*Restrictive appositive* identifies a specific station.]

## 20i   Use one or a pair of commas to set off contrasted elements.

> Young children react best to positive comments, not negative ones.
> South Korea, not Japan, has the highest literacy rate in Asia.

## 20j   Use commas to set off the words *yes* and *no*, mild interjections (*well, okay,* and so on) that begin sentences, and words in direct address.

> Yes, James Joyce's *Ulysses* is a difficult novel to read.
> I suspect, my fellow Americans, that we are the victims of a hoax.
> Sarah, would you please share your interpretation of the poem?

## 20k   Use commas to separate directly quoted material from explanatory expressions.

Expressions that signal direct quotations, such as "he said," "she replied," and so on, vary widely in form and position (they may be positioned at the beginning, in the middle, or at the end of a quotation). Wherever such expressions occur, they must be separated from the quotation, most often with commas.

> **Reverend Tobias said,** "State lotteries are nothing but state-sanctioned gambling."

> "Lotteries, however, provide revenues that can be used to support education," **Representative Fulwiller noted.**

> "If we ignore the lottery as a way of increasing revenues," **he added,** "our state's finances will continue to suffer."

**201**    **Use commas with numbers containing four or more digits, dates, addresses, place names, and titles and academic degrees, according to the conventions shown below.**

▷ *Numbers:* Place a comma after every three digits, moving from right to left.

1,399 2,776,100

▷ *Dates:* In month-day-year order, a comma separates the day and year. If a date including month, day, and year appears in the middle of a sentence, a comma also follows the year.

No commas are required in the day-month-year order or when only the month and year are used.

George Washington was born on February 22, 1732.

On October 30, 1905, Tsar Nicholas issued the October Manifesto, guaranteeing individual liberties.

Sixty percent of Hiroshima was destroyed by the atomic bomb dropped on 6 August 1945.

Hitler annexed Austria in March 1938.

▷ *Addresses:* When an address is written in a sentence, separate each element with a comma. If the address appears in the middle of a sentence, a comma must follow the last element.

She moved to **719 Maple Avenue, Cleveland, Ohio,** shortly after the Thanksgiving holidays.

The Convention Center in **Landover, Maryland,** was the site of the "Welcome Home" concert honoring Vietnam veterans.

The Olympics in **Munich, West Germany,** were plagued by terrorism.

▷ *Titles and academic degrees:* Use commas to set off these nonrestrictive elements.

At Honors Convocation, Rebecca Kingsley, **professor emerita,** presented the scholarship that bears her name.

William Leeds, **M.D.,** serves on the Marion County Health Board.

---

ᴇxᴇʀᴄɪsᴇ

Supply periods, question marks, exclamation points, and commas in the following sentences. Make sure that a rule guides your placement of each punctuation mark.

1. CBS NBC and ABC America's largest networks are now advertising programs regularly on

 small independent cable networks

2. The novel originally priced at $2595 did not sell well but sales increased when the price was reduced to $1795

3. Address women as Ms unless you are certain that they prefer Miss or Mrs

4. Should we send our order to the Chicago Illinois distribution center or to the Atlanta Georgia center

5. Angered that her glares did not quiet the jabbering child the old woman finally shouted "Shut up"

6. The tour guide concerned that he adapt himself to the visitors' preferences asked if they wanted to spend more time in the chapel

7. The San Francisco earthquake of April 18 1906 measured 8.3 on the Richter scale but the March 2 1933 earthquake in Japan measured 8.9

8. Much to my surprise the word *calf* is used to describe young cattle elephants antelopes rhinoceroses hippopotamuses and whales

9. Even though he was reporting on the war he repeated what the generals told him.

10. Did you know that the West Indian island Jamaica is smaller (4244 square miles) than Connecticut

11. Because she was aware of prejudice against women Amadine Aurore Dupin published her novels under the name George Sand

12. After four months of work the restorers gave up their attempts to salvage the Venetian fresco

13. Peonies irises roses and day lilies are among Americans' favorite perennial not annual flowers

14. To be competitive in a declining market American auto manufacturers slashed interest rates and offered special rebates

15. The Tyrannosaurus Rex with teeth that measured six inches long was the fiercest of the meat-eating dinosaurs

16. Passengers who need special assistance are always asked to board airplanes before other travelers

17. Ironically taking out a mortgage is considered more stressful than having a foreclosure on a mortgage

18. Many taxpayers choose to use the "short form"; however taxpayers who wish to itemize deductions must use the "long form"

19. The mineral calcium is needed to develop and maintain bones and teeth but it is lacking in many diets

20. The film *Gandhi* begins with the leader's assassination on January 30 1948 and then recounts his life in a long flashback

## 21 Unnecessary Commas

Too many commas in sentences can be as confusing as too few. To avoid excessive use of commas, observe the following rules.

### 21a Do not use a comma before a coordinating conjunction that joins only two words, phrases, or dependent clauses.

> Isak Dinesen married a Danish baron and subsequently moved to Africa.
> [No comma with compound verb *married and moved*.]

> I asked for advice first from my classmates and then from Professor Bakerman.
> [No comma between two prepositional phrases joined by *and*.]

### 21b Do not use a comma between subjects, verbs, and complements unless specific rules require that commas be used.

In the simplest sentences, no commas should break the subject-verb-complement pattern. When other information is added—appositives, nonrestrictive clauses, coordinate modifiers—commas may be necessary, but only as required by specific comma rules.

> The angry soprano walked out of the rehearsal.
> [No comma with subject-verb pattern.]

The angry soprano, **unhappy with the conductor,** walked out of the rehearsal.
[Nonrestrictive appositive set off by commas.]

Our university's pole vaulter was, a strong contender for the title.
[No comma with verb-complement pattern.]

Our university's pole vaulter was, **by general agreement,** a strong contender for the title.
[Parenthetical comments, in this case a nonrestrictive prepositional phrase, require commas; see Section 20g.]

## 21c Do not use a comma before the first or after the last item in a series.

Carla began attending exercise classes, to build her stamina, to lose weight, and to tone her muscles. [Comma would interrupt verb-complement pattern.]

*Time, U.S. News & World Report,* and *Newsweek,* are the most popular weekly magazines in America. [Comma would interrupt subject-verb pattern.]

## 21d Do not use commas to separate adjectives or adverbs that cumulatively modify the same word.

When adjectives or adverbs work together to create meaning, they should *not* be separated by commas.

Four, small, red candles burned on the mantelpiece.
[No commas because *red* modifies *candles, small* modifies *red candles,* and *four* modifies *small red candles.*]

## 21e Do not use a comma between an adjective or an adverb and the word it modifies.

An especially, talented, pianist opened the recital. [No commas because the adverb *especially* modifies the adjective *talented,* which modifies the noun *pianist.*]

## 21f Do not use commas to set off restrictive elements in sentences.

Roman Polanski's film, *The Pianist,* won an Oscar in 2003.
[No commas because film title is necessary for sentence clarity. (Polanski has made other films.)]

## 21g    Do not use a comma before an expression in parentheses.

When a comma is necessary with a parenthetical expression, it should follow the closing parenthesis.

> In hopes of graduating early, Brian took six English classes, (English 307, 320, 337, 339, 412, and 445), but he could not manage the reading.

## 21h    Do not use a comma before either an indirect or a direct quotation introduced by *that*.

> President Bush said, that the war on terror is only begun.
>
> *But:* President Bush said, "The war on terror is well begun, but it is only begun."
>
> Wasn't it Winston Churchill who said that "an iron curtain has descended across the Continent"?

## 21i    Do not place a comma after either a question mark or an exclamation point in a direct quotation.

Question marks and exclamation points replace the commas that are frequently required with direct quotations.

> "Will we never recover from the wounds created by the Vietnam War?," asked Representative Martin.

---

### EXERCISE

Remove unnecessary commas from the following sentences. Be ready to explain why each comma you delete is not needed.

1. Sandy Koufax was named Most Valuable Player of the World Series in 1963, and in 1965.

2. Two American cities, (Chicago, and New York City) each employ more than ten thousand police officers.

3. Four, very, small cars can park in the spaces normally allotted to three full-sized cars.

4. The geriatrician said, the symptoms suggest that Uncle Rupert probably has Alzheimer's disease.

5. Chicago's O'Hare International Airport, is the busiest airport in the United States.

6. The aging movie theater, which was once the small city's pride, needed extensive, expensive, renovation.

7. The playwright, Sophocles, is known for perfecting the form, of classical Greek tragedy.

8. Since early 1982, the copper penny has been gradually replaced, by a copper-plated zinc coin.

9. "How can we expect students, who have never taken calculus, to perform well on this portion of the exam?," Professor Carino asked.

10. California, Pennsylvania, Illinois, Michigan, and Ohio, each distributes over $1.5 million annually in unemployment benefits.

 **Semicolons (;)**

The *semicolon* most often functions like a period, separating independent clauses. Though it can in some specialized instances replace a comma, the semicolon should not be used routinely as a substitute for a comma.

**22a    Use a semicolon to join closely related independent clauses that are not connected by a coordinating conjunction.**

In this usage, the semicolon most clearly functions like a period. As a result, make certain that each clause is, in fact, independent.

Take care of the children; let the adults take care of themselves.

**22b    Use a semicolon to join independent clauses that are linked by a conjunctive adverb, or separate the clauses with a period.**

The defense attorney's closing statements were brilliantly presented; however, the facts of the case favored the prosecution.

**22c    Use a semicolon to separate three or more items in a series when one or more of the items contain internal commas.**

In their essays, students commented on *The Fire Next Time,* an essay-novel by James Baldwin; *Soul on Ice,* a polemic by Eldridge Cleaver; and *Anger and Beyond,* a collection of critical essays edited by Herbert Hill.

**22d    Do not use a semicolon in place of a comma with a subordinate clause.**

Although revisions of the tax code will eliminate many deductions, most Americans will benefit from a reduction in their overall tax rate.

**22e    Do not introduce a list or a clarifying phrase with a semicolon.**

The colon (:) and the dash (—) are traditionally used to introduce a list or a clarification. The semicolon is not interchangeable with these marks of punctuation.

A number of long-distance services vied for consumers' business, AT&T, MCI, and Sprint.

# 23    Colons (:)

Using a *colon* is a formal way to introduce a list or a clarification. The colon means "Note what follows." Use colons selectively to add clarity to your writing.

**23a    Use a colon to introduce a list.**

The items in the series should never be direct objects, predicate nouns, predicate adjectives, or objects of prepositions. An independent clause must precede the colon. As suggested in Section 22e, a dash may be used in place of the colon.

American theater and film have produced a number of notable acting families: Barrymore, Bridges, Fairbanks, Fonda, and Sheen.

**23b    Selectively use a colon between two independent clauses when the second explains the first.**

The second clause may start with either a lowercase letter (as shown here) or with a capital letter.

Except for differences in the subject matter, the rules of grammar are like the laws of chemistry: they are generalizations describing accepted principles of operation.

**23c    Use a colon to emphasize an appositive that comes at the end of a sentence.**

Marlowe and Shakespeare introduced the dramatic use of blank verse: unrhymed iambic pentameter.

**23d**　Use a colon in place of a comma to introduce or emphasize a long quotation.

> Churchill concluded an eloquent speech with this visionary statement: "Out of the depths of sorrow and sacrifice will be born again the glory of mankind."

**23e**　Use a colon between numerals designating hours and minutes, after formal salutations in formal or official correspondence, between titles and subtitles, between chapter and verse in biblical citations, and between city and publisher in works-cited entries.

> The speaker was scheduled to arrive on a 9:40 A.M. flight from Los Angeles.
> Dear Mr. Harper:　　　　Dear Professor Smithson:
> *Some Sort of Epic Grandeur: The Life of F. Scott Fitzgerald*
> Isaiah 12:2–4
> Cambridge: Harvard UP
> Boston: Houghton Mifflin

**23f**　Do not use a colon between a verb and its complement or between a preposition and its object.

> Jerrid's favorite restaurants are: Richard's Townhouse, The Broken Blossom, and Fernucchi's.

---

### EXERCISE

Revise these sentences, using semicolons or colons.

1. Two lizards found in the southwestern United States and northern Mexico are venomous. They are the Gila monster and the Mexican bearded lizard.

2. The Democratic party considered five cities for its national convention. Those cities were Dallas, Texas, Chicago, Illinois, Atlanta, Georgia, Washington, D.C., and Los Angeles, California.

3. Phil Jackman was only an adequate basketball player. However, he is an excellent basketball coach.

4. Infertility counselor Roselle Shubin made this epigrammatic comment on parenthood, "There is more to being a mother than giving birth, and more to being a father than impregnating a woman."

5. Morocco, Algeria, Libya, Tunisia, and Egypt border the Mediterranean Sea. These are the only African countries that do.

## Dashes (—)

A **dash** (made in typing with two hyphens with no space between or before or after them) serves a number of purposes in punctuating sentences. But it should be used with restraint because if overused, the dash can become distracting and will lose its impact.

**24a**    **Use dashes to set off appositives that contain commas in midsentence.**

> Five states—Indiana, Iowa, Kentucky, Missouri, and Wisconsin—share borders with Illinois.

**24b**    **Use a dash to set off a series that introduces or ends a sentence.**

> Beaumont, Fletcher, Jonson, Kyd, Marlowe, and Webster—these dramatists were respected contemporaries of Shakespeare.

**24c**    **Use dashes, singly or in pairs, to set off interpretations, evaluations, or interruptions.**

> This answer—if we can call it an answer—is completely meaningless.
> This answer is completely meaningless—if we can call it an answer.

## Parentheses (( ))

**Parentheses,** used in pairs to set off secondary information in sentences, can foster clarity. Use them selectively, however, because they break the flow of sentences and if overused make your writing seem choppy and fragmented.

**25a** Use parentheses to enclose an explanation, qualification, or example that is not essential to the meaning of the sentence.

Phnom Penh is the capital of Kampuchea (known to most Americans as Cambodia).

**25b** Use parentheses around numbers or letters that identify a sequence within a sentence.

Withdrawing money from an automatic teller machine requires following seven simple steps: (1) insert your validated bank card, (2) type in your personal access code, (3) identify the account you want to take the money from, (4) indicate the amount of money you desire, (5) open the drawer and remove the money, (6) indicate that the transaction is complete, and (7) remove your bank card and the withdrawal slip.

## EXERCISE

Using dashes and parentheses, revise these sentences.

1. In 1755, roughly 4,000 Acadians settlers in Nova Scotia, Canada, were forcibly relocated to Louisiana.

2. Sagamore Hill, Theodore Roosevelt's home at Oyster Bay, New York, became a national memorial in 1962.

3. Mali, Niger, and Nigeria these are the countries through which the river Niger flows.

4. Changing a tire requires following five relatively simple steps: 1. turn off the car's engine and engage the emergency brake, 2. jack up the car on the appropriate side, 3. remove the damaged tire, 4. put on the spare, and 5. lower the car and remove the jack.

5. Margaret Higgins Sanger 1883–1966 led the birth-control movement in America during the early years of the twentieth century.

## 26 Quotation Marks ("/")

*Quotation marks* are most commonly used to enclose direct quotations (see also "Quoting Sources" in Chapter 14). The most important issues with quotation marks are accuracy in recording other people's comments and accuracy in the placement of other punctuation marks.

## 26a   Place commas and periods *before* quotation marks.

My favorite story, "The Fall of the House of Usher," is by Poe.

## 26b   Place colons and semicolons *after* quotation marks.

Shelley creates a vivid image of a decayed civilization in his poem "Ozymandias": "Round the decay / Of that colossal wreck, boundless and bare / The lone and level sands stretch far away."

For the university newspaper, Rachel wrote "The Dilemma of Drug Testing"; the article won the school's journalism award in the spring.

## 26c   If a quotation is a question or an exclamation, place the question mark or exclamation point *before* the quotation marks.

If the whole sentence in which a quotation (or an exclamation) appears is a question (or an exclamation) but the quotation is not, place the question mark (or exclamation point) after the quotation marks.

I can't remember who wrote the ballad "What'll I Do?"

Were we supposed to read "What It Takes to Be a Leader"?

## 26d   Use single quotation marks ('and') around material that would be enclosed by full quotation marks if it were not already within a quotation.

Jeremy said, "Although 'Dover Beach' is one of Matthew Arnold's greatest poems, it is not one of my favorites."

# Brackets ([/])

*Brackets* are used to enclose an editorial or a clarifying explanation or comment inserted into a direct quotation.

Richardson commented, "Using both systems [the U.S. Customary System and the International Metric System] has caused considerable confusion for American consumers and has put U.S. industries at a trade disadvantage."

# 28 Ellipses (. . .)

*Ellipses,* three spaced periods, are used to indicate the omission of one or more words from a quotation. The three periods, or points, that form the ellipsis are considered a unit. When the omission comes at the end of a sentence, a fourth point must be added as end punctuation. When a comma is required, it follows the ellipsis.

**28a** **Use ellipsis points to show where words have been omitted from a direct quotation.**

Omit extraneous material—like parenthetical expressions or unnecessary clarifications—but do not leave out material if the omission changes the meaning of the original text.

| *Original Quotation* | *Elliptical Quotation* |
|---|---|
| Lincoln's antislavery views, clarified in the Republican party platform of 1860, served to alienate not only the residents of southern states but also southern sympathizers in the North. | According to Walter Holtmire, "Lincoln's antislavery views . . . served to alienate not only the residents of southern states but also southern sympathizers in the North." |

**Use ellipsis points very selectively to indicate hesitation, a trailing off of thought, or an incomplete statement.**

The deathbed scene in James Brooks's *Terms of Endearment* is . . . manipulative.

## OBSERVING THE RULES OF PUNCTUATION: REVIEW EXERCISE

Correct the punctuation errors in the following sentences. Be ready to identify the rules that guided your thinking.

1. The Internal Revenue Service IRS is responsible for administering the tax laws passed by Congress

2. From 1791 to 1862 the US government relied on tariffs to generate income in 1862 however Congress enacted the first income tax law to pay for the debts of the Civil War

3. Did you know that income taxes were not universally instituted until 1913

4. Following the current tax law only a few major deductions will be allowed mortgage payments state and local taxes medical expenses and charitable contributions

5. Nevada South Dakota Texas Washington and Wyoming these states do not impose a corporate tax based on net income

6. The IRS operates from its various headquarters one national office in Washington seven regional offices sixty-three district offices and tax service centers and processes roughly 200 million returns annually

7. Beginning in 1943 taxes were withheld from wages a plan that increased the number of people who equitably paid taxes

8. According to new tax laws corporate rates will drop from 46 percent to 34 percent however a minimum tax will also be imposed to prevent major companies from paying no taxes

9. The nation's first sales taxes enacted in 1812 affected consumers of only four kinds of commodities gold silver jewelry and watches

10. Did you know that it was Benjamin Franklin who said But in this world nothing can be said to be certain except death and taxes

11. James Otis spoke the sentence that became a catch phrase of the American Revolution Taxation without representation is tyranny

12. In 2000 our public debt was $5,674,178,886.86 a figure so large it is hard to imagine

13. Most Americans do not object to paying taxes many however object to how the tax money is spent

14. Various tables Schedule X Y or Z are used to compute the taxes of people with incomes of more than $50000

15. Taxpayers who wish to appeal a tax charge must follow four steps 1 discuss the charge with a local appeal's office 2 submit a written protest 3 wait for a judgment 4 pay the charge or file yet another appeal with the District Claims Court

# Observing the Rules of Mechanics

Mechanical errors in the use of capitalization, italics, quotation marks, apostrophes, hyphenation, number style, abbreviations, and spelling distract readers from the content of your writing. Heeding certain rules as you prepare the final copy of a paper will help ensure that your reader's attention is focused not on preventable mechanical errors but on what you have to say.

## 29 Capitalization

### 29a Capitalize the first word of every sentence and of every line in conventional poetry.

> Using a word processor saves time during revision.

> Standardized tests present a major problem for minorities; they do not allow for cultural differences.

> Whenas in silks my Julia goes
> Then, then, methinks, how sweetly flows
> That liquefaction of her clothes. . . .
>     —Robert Herrick,
>       "Upon Julia's Clothes"

### 29b Distinguish between *proper names,* which require capitalization, and *common names,* which do not.

> I left the assignment in my professor's mailbox.
> *But:* I left the assignment in Professor Sheldon's mailbox.
> I worked in summer stock to gain experience.
> *But:* I worked at the Summer Festival Theater to gain experience.

### 29c In titles, capitalize the first and last words and all important words.

As a general rule, capitalize all nouns, pronouns, verbs, adjectives, and adverbs in titles. In addition, capitalize all prepositions and conjunctions of five or more letters. In words with two-part titles, the first word of the subtitle is also capitalized, regardless of the word's length.

Zora Neale Hurston's *Their Eyes Were Watching God*

Derrick Ashford's "Eighteenth-Century Comedy on the Modern Stage"

Marya Mannes's "TV Advertising: The Splitting Image"

**29d**   **Capitalize the names of people, races, nationalities, languages, and places, whether used as nouns or as adjectives.**

In American usage, the terms *black* and *white* are not capitalized. Native American, Hispanic, and Asian are capitalized.

| | |
|---|---|
| Thomas Paine | Caucasian |
| Malaysia | Danish customs |
| Nairobi | Greek festival |

**29e**   **Capitalize the names of historical and cultural periods; historical, political, and cultural events; and documents.**

| | |
|---|---|
| the Age of Reason | the Emancipation Proclamation |
| the Romantic Movement | Elizabethan drama |
| the Battle of Hastings | Prohibition |

**29f**   **Capitalize the names of days, months, and secular and religious holidays.**

| | |
|---|---|
| Thursday | the Fourth of July |
| September | Hanukkah |

**29g**   **Capitalize the names of businesses and other organizations and government agencies and offices.**

| | |
|---|---|
| General Electric Company | National Rifle Association |
| Phi Delta Kappa | United States Senate |

**29h**   **Capitalize the names of schools, colleges, and universities; academic departments; specific sources; and degrees—but not general references.**

Amherst College [But *college classes*]

Thomas Jefferson High School [But *high school teachers*]

Department of Education [But *department meeting*]

Sociology 245 [But *sociology course*]

Bachelor of Arts [But *baccalaureate degree*]

**29i**  **Capitalize the names of religions and their followers and religious terms for sacred persons, books, and events.**

| | |
|---|---|
| God | Islamic law |
| Buddha | Christian traditions |
| the Koran | the Immaculate Conception |

**29j**  **Capitalize titles that precede proper names.**

| | |
|---|---|
| Doctor Erica Weinburg | Prime Minister Tony Blair |
| Secretary of State Colin Powell | President Abraham Lincoln |
| Professor Leon Edel | |

A title used alone or following a proper name is not capitalized.

A college professor is the catalyst in a classroom.

Jimmy Carter, the former president, has contributed even in retirement to the benefit of the country.

**29k**  **Capitalize nouns designating family relationships only when they are used as proper names or when they precede proper names.**

After arthroscopic surgery, Mother's chances of leading a normal life improved.

I arrived at the apartment before Uncle Will got home from work.

Do not capitalize common nouns that name family relationships, even when the noun is preceded by a personal pronoun in the possessive case.

After arthroscopic surgery, my mother's life improved.

I arrived at the apartment before my uncle got home from work.

Never underestimate the influence of brothers and sisters.

**29l**  **Capitalize *A.M.* and *P.M.* and *A.D.* and *B.C.*; capitalize the call letters of radio and television stations; capitalize abbreviated forms of business, organization, and document names. (Periods may or may not be required, according to convention; consult a dictionary.)**

| | |
|---|---|
| 705 B.C. | ERA |
| A.D. 1066 | WPFR radio |

| | |
|---|---|
| 4:30 A.M. | KTVI television |
| 4:30 P.M. | IBM |

## 29m   Capitalize the first word of a direct quotation if the quotation is a complete sentence or an interjection that can stand alone.

Mr. Bennett remarked, "Though ornate by present standards, Baroque sculpture remains aesthetically pleasing."

Carla, surprised by the harsh criticism, responded, "Oh."

---

### EXERCISE

**Supply capitalization in the following sentences, noting the rule that guides each correction.**

1. the elizabethan period, a cultural and aesthetic awakening in england, began roughly a century after the italian renaissance.

2. yom kippur, the holiest jewish holiday, was observed on thursday, september 15, this year.

3. although my mother and aunt beatrice are both normally critical television viewers, they both love *the young and the restless.*

4. an mba from harvard is an excellent passport to a lucrative job on wall street or with a fortune 500 firm.

5. students in french secondary schools are expected to learn english as well as one other foreign language.

6. Colin Powell, the secretary of state, travels extensively in europe and the middle east for the department of state.

7. the reverend thomas r. fitzgerald serves as president of st. louis university, a catholic university enrolling over eleven thousand students.

8. who was it who said, "i cried all the way to the bank"?

9. the abbreviation ira could refer to the irish republican army, the international reading association, or an individual retirement account.

10. dorothy parker once described katharine hepburn's performance in a play with this caustic sentence: "she ran the whole gamut of emotions from a to b."

 ## Italics

In print, *italics,* slanted type, is used to give words distinction or emphasis. In handwritten or typed manuscript, the same effects are achieved using underlining.

### 30a    Italicize the titles of books, periodicals, newspapers, pamphlets, plays, films, television series (but not individual programs), radio programs, long poems, long musical compositions, record albums, paintings, and sculpture.

Marcel Proust's *Swann's Way* (book)
The *Washington Post* (newspaper)
NCTE's *Essentials of English* (pamphlet)
Oscar Wilde's *The Importance of Being Ernest* (play)
Rob Marshall's *Chicago* (film)
HBO's *The Sopranos* (television program)
Casey Kasem's *Top-Twenty Count Down* (radio program)
Walt Whitman's *Leaves of Grass* (long poem)
Tchaikovsky's *The Nutcracker Suite* (long musical composition)
Dixie Chicks' *Wide Open Spaces* (album)
Pablo Picasso's *Three Musicians* (painting)
George Segal's *Girl in Doorway* (sculpture)

### 30b    Italicize the names of individual ships, trains, airplanes, and spacecraft.

Jacques Cousteau's *Calypso* (ship)
the *Orient Express* (train)

*Air Force One* (airplane)

*Voyager 1* (spacecraft)

## 30c   Italicize foreign words and phrases.

Confined to a hospital bed, Rachel had to vote ***in absentia.***

Many foreign terms have been assimilated into standard usage and, as a result, do not require italics. Consult a dictionary for guidance.

## 30d   Italicize words used as words, letters used as letters, numbers used as numbers, and symbols used as symbols.

French contains two variations of *you,* one formal and one informal.

The letters *a* and *e* used to be printed *æ.*

Make sure that you distinguish your *1s* from your *7s.*

The ampersand, *&,* is unacceptable in formal prose.

## 30e   Italicize words selectively for emphasis.

In formal prose, this is not considered good usage.

Jason played the song *twenty-three* times in a row!

# 31   Quotation Marks (""/"")

*Quotation marks* are most commonly used to set off direct quotations, but they have a mechanical use as well.

## 31a   Use quotation marks with the titles of brief works or parts of complete works.

"Winning Hearts Through Minds" in *Time* (article)

Ernest Hemingway's "Old Man at the Bridge" (short story)

Gerard Manley Hopkins's "God's Grandeur" (poem)

Stephen Jay Gould's "Darwinism Defined: The Difference Between Fact and Theory" (essay)

Norah Jones's "Don't Know Why" (song)

"The Spirit of Scholarship" in Richard Altick's *The Art of Literary Research* (chapter in a book)

"The Long Goodbye" from *The West Wing* (episode from television program)

## EXERCISE

**Insert italics (underlining) and quotation marks in the following sentences. Remember to place them accurately in relation to other punctuation.**

1. Paul Conrad won Pulitzer Prizes for editorial cartooning when he worked for two different publications: the Denver Post and the Los Angeles Times.

2. Grammies for best song and best album went to Tina Turner for What's Love Got to Do With It? and Private Dancer, respectively.

3. To demonstrate aerodynamic possibilities, engineers developed the Gossamer Albatross, an airplane propelled by peddling.

4. Blattela germanica is an eloquent sounding term to use when you mean cockroach!

5. Stuart called here sixteen times while you were gone this weekend.

6. On your final charts, please write female and male rather than ♀ and ♂.

7. A View to a Death, a pivotal chapter in Golding's novel Lord of the Flies, offers a vision of primitive, ritualistic execution.

8. Richard Brookhiser wrote an article entitled The Mind of George Bush in The Atlantic Monthly.

9. Many American musicals have plays as their source, among them Hello, Dolly (The Matchmaker), My Fair Lady (Pygmalion), and Cabaret (I Am a Camera).

10. Kurtz, a character in Conrad's novel The Heart of Darkness, has reemerged in T. S. Eliot's Hollow Men, a brief poem, and Apocalypse Now, a long film.

## Apostrophes (')

The ***apostrophe*** has three general uses: to indicate the possessive case of nouns and some pronouns, to indicate the omission of letters and numbers, and to indicate the plural of letters, numbers, and words used as words.

**32a**    Use an apostrophe and an *s* to form the possessive of a singular noun, a plural noun not ending in *s*, or an indefinite pronoun.

> Oprah Winfrey's guests
> somebody's car
> the men's dressing room
> a month's rental fee
> Harry Jones's first flight

**32b**    Use only an apostrophe, without an *s*, to form the possessive of a plural noun ending in *s*.

> scientists' projections
> the Joneses' first flight

**32c**    To show joint possession, add an apostrophe and an *s* to the last name in the group. To show individual possession, add an apostrophe and an *s* to each name in the group.

> Lerner and Loewe's musical reputation [Joint possession]
> Shakespeare's and Marlowe's dramatic innovations [Individual possession]

**32d**    Use an apostrophe to show the omission of letters and numbers.

> | couldn't | could not | there's | there is |
> |----------|-----------|---------|----------|
> | I'll | I will (*or* I shall) | the '04 Olympics | the 2004 Olympics |

**32e**    Use only an *s* to form the plurals of numbers, letters, and words used as words.

> Kirsten received four *10s* during the final round of competition.
> Her *s*'s look like *8s*.
> His writing was cluttered with *verys*, *reallys*, and *especiallys*.

# Hyphenation (-)

*Hyphens* are used for two purposes: to divide a multisyllable word at the end of a line and to join two or more words of a compound.

**33a**   **Hyphenate a word that must continue on a new line**

Place hyphens between the syllables of words that must be divided (if necessary, consult a dictionary to see where a break may be made). Do not break one-syllable words or leave fewer than three letters at the end or beginning of any line. Do not hyphenate proper names.

The hurricane battered the coastline, damaging property in four cities.

**33b**   **Hyphenate compound words according to convention; consult a dictionary.**

Some compound words are hyphenated; others are "closed up," written as one word; still others are written as two words.

| *Hyphenated* | *Closed Up* | *Two Words* |
|---|---|---|
| sister-in-law | applesauce | wedding ring |
| razzle-dazzle | blackboard | living room |
| master-at-arms | landowner | free fall |

**33c**   **Hyphenate words that precede a noun and combine to modify it.**

heart-to-heart talk

off-the-cuff comments

never-ending problems

When the modifiers follow the noun, no hyphens are necessary.

The comments were off the cuff.

His problems were never ending.

**33d**   **Hyphenate compound numbers ranging from twenty-one to ninety-nine; hyphenate fractions.**

a test score of sixty-seven

two-thirds of the voters

**33e**   **Hyphenate words using the prefixes *all-*, *ex-*, and *self-*; hyphenate words using the suffix *-elect*.**

all-consuming pride                          ex-wife

self-motivated student                       secretary-elect of the city council

**33f**   **Hyphenate a compound consisting of a prefix and a proper noun.**

anti-Iranian                    un-American
pre-Enlightenment               post-Kantian

**33g**   **Hyphenate words formed with a prefix if the unhyphenated form would be a homonym, a word with the same spelling and pronunciation but a different meaning.**

re-cover (to cover again)       recover (to regain)
re-lease (to lease again)       release (to let go)

# 34   Numbers

**34a**   **Spell out numbers that can be expressed in one or two words.**

thirty-two source cards         twenty-six thousand dollars
five million voters             fourteen hundred miles

**34b**   **Use digits for numbers that would require three or more words if spelled out.**

319 graduates (*not* three hundred and nineteen)
101 pages (*not* one hundred and one)

**34c**   **Spell out a number that begins a sentence, or revise the sentence so that it does not open with a number.**

*Not:* 412 art dealers attended the convention.
*But:* Four hundred and twelve art dealers attended the convention.
*Or:* There were 412 art dealers at the convention.

**34d**   **Use digits for addresses, dates, divisions of books and plays, dollars and cents, identification numbers, percentages, scores, and times.**

2300 North 12th Street (address)
11 January 1912 or January 11, 1912 (dates)
700 B.C., A.D. 700 (dates)
Chapter 17, Volume 2, Act 1, Scene 2 (divisions of books and plays)
$7.95, $1,230,000, $4.9 million (dollar amounts)

314-77-2248, UTC 41 69490 (identification numbers)
81 percent, 3 percent (percentages)
117 to 93 (scores)
6:10 A.M., 2:35 P.M. (times)

# 35 Abbreviations

*Abbreviations,* shortened forms of words, should be used sparingly. Any abbreviations you use should be familiar to your readers, and they must be appropriate to the writing context. To double-check conventional abbreviations, consult a dictionary.

## 35a Abbreviate titles that precede or follow people's names.

| | |
|---|---|
| Wiliam D. Grenville, Jr. | Judith Haverford, Ph.D. |
| Ms. Abigail Hample | Rebecca Blair, M.D. |
| Dr. Terence McDonald | the Rev. Stephen Pierson |

## 35b Use standard abbreviations and acronyms for names of organizations, corporations, and countries. Many of these abbreviations do not require periods.

*Organizations:* AFL-CIO, YMCA, FBI
*Corporations:* GTE, NBC, GM
*Countries:* USA, (*or* U.S.A.), UK (*or* U.K.)

## 35c Before using an abbreviation that might be unfamiliar to some readers, spell out the complete name or term at its first appearance.

Idaho State University—located in Pocatello, Idaho—is a state-supported university serving over three thousand students. ISU offers especially strong programs in health-related professions.

## 35d Use standard abbreviations with times, dates, and specific numbers. Use the dollar sign with specific amounts.

Note the placement of the abbreviations A.M., P.M., *B.C.,* and *A.D.*

| | |
|---|---|
| $1,245.78 | 500 B.C. |
| 11:20 A.M. | A.D. 496 |
| 4:15 P.M. | part no. 339 (*or* No.) |

## 35e    Use standard abbreviations in works-cited entries.

(See "Documenting Sources" in Chapter 14.)

| *Abbreviation* | *Meaning* |
|---|---|
| ed. | editor, edition |
| et al. | and others |
| rev. | revised |
| rpt. | reprint |
| trans. | translator, translated by |
| vol. | volume |

## 35f    Use Latin abbreviations sparingly in prose.

| *Latin Abbreviation* | *English Equivalent* |
|---|---|
| cf. *(confer)* | compare |
| e.g. *(exempli gratia)* | for example |
| et al. *(et alii)* | and others |
| etc. *(et cetera)* | and others, and so on |
| i.e. *(id est)* | that is |
| n.b. *(nota bene)* | note well |

## 35g    In most writing, do not abbreviate business designations (unless the company does), units of measurement, days of the week, months, courses of instruction, divisions of books and plays, geographical names (except in addresses), or personal names.

| *Not* | *But* |
|---|---|
| Co., Inc. | Company, Incorporated |
| lb, tbs. | pound, tablespoon |
| Fri., Oct. | Friday, October |
| psych., Eng. | psychology, English |
| chap., vol. | chapter, volume |
| L.A., VA | Los Angeles, Virginia |
| Wm., Robt. | William, Robert |

## EXERCISE

Insert necessary apostrophes and hyphens in the following sentences. In addition, correct the number style and forms of abbreviations.

1. 6 members of the committee returned the questionnaire, refusing to comment on MSUs drug testing program.

2. The suicide that ends Act four of *Hedda Gabler* shocked many narrow minded critics.

3. Doctor Connelly, a graduate of U. of TX at Austin, spoke to our faculty on Oct. 15, 2003.

4. To attract first rate teachers to our public schools, we will have to increase teachers salaries.

5. Stephen Sondheims *Sunday in the Park with George* presents a neo Impressionist view of human relations and art.

6. Karin was delighted to receive 2 *8s* and 2 *9s* on her performance until she realized that *15s* were possible.

7. The post Civil War period was a time of exploitation and manipulation in the South.

8. The Rams won the game thirty-six to seven, having passed for one hundred and fifty four yards and having made seventy four percent of the games interceptions.

9. My father in laws Social Security check ($24967) covers slightly over two thirds of his monthly expenses.

10. The president elect of the N.C.T.E. felt that her work would require working with a state of the art computer and printer, so she bought the pair.

---

### EXERCISE

Revise the following paragraph so that it is mechanically correct and consistent with conventional usage. Errors in capitalization, italics, quotation marks, apostrophes, hyphenation, number style, and abbreviations are present in the paragraph.

> 1600 Pennsylvania Ave., Washington, District of Columbia, is perhaps the *most famous* address in the U.S. At that site is the "White House," the residence of the President and his family. The design for the Original house was selected by Pres. Washington and Pierre L'Enfant, the french born designer of the city, and the cornerstone was set on Oct. 13, 1792. In 1814, the building was razed during a Battle of the war of 1812, and in subsequent years the interior of the structure had to be rebuilt. But the original design was heavily modified. As Mrs. John N. Pearce notes in The White House: A Historic Guide Ever changing personalities and styles of living and building have inspired the continuing metamorphosis that has marked the history of the White House. Over the years, the "White House" has served as both the official and the private residence of the first family. The 1st floor's rooms are used for public functions like Receptions and State Dinners, and its expansive, public rooms are decorated with such famous artwork as Gilbert Stuarts portrait George Washington. The limited access rooms on the second and third floors are used by the presidents family and friends. In all, the "White House" has one hundred and thirty-two rooms.

## 36 Spelling

Errors in spelling, like other mechanical errors, interfere with communication because readers notice and are distracted by them. To avoid such distractions in your writing, develop good spelling habits. If you are a naturally good speller, then you have only to refresh your memory of common spelling rules. If you are a weak speller, then you need to hone your spelling skills.

Do not worry about spelling while you are planning and working on early drafts of your papers. If you interrupt your writing to check the spelling of a word, you might lose a thought that you cannot recapture. Instead make a mark near the word in question—a check mark in the margin, the abbreviation *sp.* above the word, or a circle around the word—and continue your writing. Then, when your final draft is complete, look up the spelling of the words you have marked. This approach—checking spelling during revision—will allow you to write with a sense of continuity and attend to potential problems before typing your final copy.

## 36a   Review Spelling Rules

**Form plurals according to the pattern of the singular word.**

▶ When words end in a consonant plus *o,* add *-es.*

| | |
|---|---|
| fresco | frescoes |
| motto | mottoes |
| tomato | tomatoes |

*Exceptions*

| | |
|---|---|
| auto | autos |
| dynamo | dynamos |
| piano | pianos |

and other "music" terms, e.g., cello

▶ When words end in a vowel plus *o,* add *-s.*

| | |
|---|---|
| cameo | cameos |
| radio | radios |
| studio | studios |

▶ When words end in a consonant plus *y,* change the *y* to *i* and add *-es.*

| | |
|---|---|
| daisy | daisies |
| remedy | remedies |
| victory | victories |

▶ When words end in a vowel plus *y,* add *-s.*

| | |
|---|---|
| attorney | attorneys |
| key | keys |
| survey | surveys |

▶ When words end in *s, ss, sh, ch, x,* or *z,* add *-es.*

| | | | |
|---|---|---|---|
| bonus | bonuses | match | matches |
| overpass | overpasses | tax | taxes |
| wish | wishes | buzz | buzzes |

▶ When words that are proper names end in *y*, add *-s*.

the Bellamys

the three Marys

two Germanys

**Add prefixes, such as *dis-*, *mis-*, *non-*, *pre-*, *re-*, and *un-*, without altering the spelling of the root word.**

| | |
|---|---|
| similar | dissimilar |
| spell | misspell |
| restrictive | nonrestrictive |
| historic | prehistoric |
| capture | recapture |
| natural | unnatural |

**Add suffixes according to the spelling of both the root word and the suffix.**

▶ When words end with a silent *e* and the suffix begins with a consonant, retain the *e*.

| | |
|---|---|
| achieve | achievement |
| definite | definitely |
| refine | refinement |

*Exceptions*

| | |
|---|---|
| argue | argument |
| awe | awful |
| true | truly |

▶ When words end with a silent *e* and the suffix begins with a vowel, drop the *e*.

| | |
|---|---|
| accommodate | accommodating |
| grieve | grievance |
| size | sizable |
| tolerate | tolerating |

▶ When words end with a silent *e* that is preceded by a "soft" *c* or *g* and the suffix begins with a vowel, retain the *e*.

| | | | |
|---|---|---|---|
| notice | noticeable | singe | singeing |
| trace | traceable | outrage | outrageous |
| change | changeable | | |

▶ When a one-syllable word ends with a single consonant and contains only one vowel and the suffix begins with a vowel, double the final consonant.

| | |
|---|---|
| blot | blotted |
| clip | clipping |
| fit | fitting |
| skip | skipper |
| stop | stopping |
| trip | tripped |

**Distinguish between words spelled with *ie* and *ei*.**

The order of the vowels *ie* and *ei* is explained in this familiar poem:

Write *i* before *e*

Except after *c*

Or when sounded like *ay*

As in *neighbor* and *weigh*.

These are some exceptions to this rule:

| | |
|---|---|
| counterfeit | leisure |
| either | neither |
| foreign | seizure |
| forfeit | sovereign |
| height | weird |

## 36b Improving Your Spelling Skills

**Use a full-sized dictionary to check meanings and spellings of words that are often mistaken for each other.**

A standard dictionary provides definitions that will help you distinguish between *affect* and *effect, elicit* and *illicit,* and other confusing word pairs.

**Use a spelling dictionary for easy reference when you know a word's meaning but are unsure of its spelling.**

Spelling dictionaries contain lists of commonly used words with markings to indicate syllable breaks. These special dictionaries are helpful as quick references.

**Concentrate on the most troublesome parts of easily misspelled words.**

Give particular attention to the parts of words that lead to spelling errors—usually a single syllable or small cluster of letters.

accident**all**y                    des**per**ate

se**pa**rate                        se**cre**tary

main**ten**ance

### Keep a record of words you have misspelled in your writing.

Most people have individual sets of words that they regularly use and regularly misspell. Use a note card, a sheet of paper, or a small notebook to record your personal list of troublesome words.

### Carefully check the spelling of technical terms.

When your writing requires specialized language, verify the spelling of technical terms because their spelling is often tricky.

### Use a spellchecker if you are using a word-processing program.

If you use a word processor to prepare your papers, take advantage of software that can check spelling. Although spelling programs are not without problems, they can be quite helpful.

### Consult the following list of frequently misspelled words.

| | | |
|---|---|---|
| abbreviate | aggravate | analysis |
| absence | aggression | analyze |
| absurd | airplane | annual |
| accelerate | alleviate | antecedent |
| accidentally | alley | anxiety |
| accommodate | allotted | apartment |
| accomplish | allowed | apparatus |
| according | ally | apparent |
| accumulate | although | appearance |
| accustom | always | appropriate |
| achievement | amateur | arctic |
| acoustics | ambiguous | argument |
| acquaintance | ammunition | arising |
| acquitted | among | arithmetic |
| across | amount | arouse |
| address | analogous | arranging |

article
artillery
ascend
association
athlete
athletics
attempt
attractive
audible
audience
authorities
automobile
auxiliary
awkward
bachelor
balance
balloon
barbarous
barring
battalion
bearing
becoming
beggar
beginning
believe
beneficial
benefited
biscuit
boundaries
breathe
brilliant

Britain
Britannica
bulletin
buoyant
bureau
buried
burying
business
busy
cafeteria
calendar
candidate
carburetor
carrying
casualties
causal
ceiling
celebrity
cemetery
certain
changeable
changing
characteristic
chauffeur
chief
choosing
chosen
clause
climbed
clothes
colloquial

colonel
column
coming
commission
commitment
committed
committee
companies
comparatively
compel
compelled
competent
competition
complaint
completely
compulsory
concede
conceivable
conceive
condemn
condescend
connoisseur
conqueror
conscience
conscientious
considered
consistent
contemptible
control
controlled
convenient

*Continued on next page*

copies

corner

coroner

corps

corpse

costume

countries

courteous

courtesy

cries

criticism

criticize

cruelty

cruise

curiosity

curriculum

custom

cylinder

dealt

debater

deceitful

deceive

decide

decision

defendant

deferred

deficient

definite

definition

democracy

dependent

descendant

description

desirable

despair

desperate

destruction

developed

development

diaphragm

diary

dictionary

dietitian

difference

digging

diphtheria

disappearance

disappoint

disastrous

discipline

discussion

disease

dissatisfied

dissipate

distribute

doesn't

dominant

don't

dormitories

dropped

drunkenness

echoes

ecstasy

efficiency

eighth

eligible

eliminate

embarrass

emphasize

employee

encouraging

encyclopedia

enthusiastic

environment

equipment

equipped

equivalent

erroneous

especially

eventually

exaggerate

exceed

excel

excellent

exceptional

excitement

exercise

exhaust

exhilaration

existence

experience

explanation

extensive

extracurricular

extremely

exuberance

fallacious

fallacy

familiar

| | | |
|---|---|---|
| fascinate | heinous | intellectual |
| February | heroes | intelligence |
| fiery | hesitancy | intentionally |
| financial | hindrance | intercede |
| financier | hoarse | interested |
| forehead | hoping | interpret |
| foreign | horde | interrupt |
| foremost | humorous | irreligious |
| forfeit | hurries | irresistible |
| forty | hygiene | irresponsible |
| frantically | hypocrisy | itself |
| fraternities | hysterical | judicial |
| friend | illiterate | khaki |
| fulfill, fulfil | illogical | knowledge |
| gaiety | imaginary | laboratory |
| generally | imagination | legitimate |
| genius | imitative | leisure |
| genuine | immediately | library |
| glorious | implement | lightning |
| government | impromptu | literature |
| grammar | inadequate | loneliness |
| grandeur | incidentally | losing |
| grievous | incredible | magazine |
| guarantee | indefinitely | magnificent |
| guardian | independent | maintain |
| guidance | indicted | maintenance |
| handicapped | indispensable | maneuver |
| handkerchief | inevitable | manual |
| harass | influential | manufacture |
| hearse | innocent | mathematics |
| height | inoculate | mattress |

*Continued on next page*

| | | |
|---|---|---|
| meant | occasionally | playwright |
| medicine | occur | pleasant |
| medieval | occurred | possess |
| messenger | occurrence | possessive |
| millionaire | official | possible |
| miniature | omission | potatoes |
| minute | omit | practice |
| mischievous | omitted | prairie |
| misspelled | opinion | preceding |
| modifies | opportunity | predominant |
| modifying | optimistic | preference |
| momentous | organization | preferred |
| mosquitoes | original | prejudice |
| mottoes | orthodox | preparation |
| mountainous | outrageous | prevalent |
| murmur | overrun | primitive |
| muscle | pamphlet | privilege |
| mysterious | parallel | probably |
| necessary | parliament | professor |
| necessity | participle | prominent |
| neither | particularly | pronounce |
| nervous | pastime | pronunciation |
| nevertheless | peaceable | propeller |
| nickel | perceive | protein |
| niece | perform | psychology |
| ninety | permissible | pursue |
| ninth | perseverance | pursuing |
| noticeable | persuade | putting |
| notorious | phrase | quantity |
| nowadays | physical | quarantine |
| obedience | physician | questionnaire |
| obliged | picnicked | quizzes |
| obstacle | piece | realize |

recede

receipt

receive

receiving

recognize

recommend

reference

referred

relevant

religion

religious

remembrance

reminiscence

rendezvous

repetition

replies

representative

reservoir

resistance

restaurant

rhetoric

rheumatism

rhythmical

ridiculous

sacrifice

sacrilegious

safety

salary

sanctuary

sandwich

scarcely

scene

scenic

schedule

secretarial

secretary

seized

sensible

sentence

sentinel

separate

sergeant

severely

shining

shriek

siege

sieve

similar

sincerely

sincerity

skeptical

slight

soliloquy

sophomore

source

specifically

specimen

spontaneous

statement

statue

stomach

stopped

strength

strenuously

stretched

struggle

studying

subordinate

subtle

succeed

success

successful

suffrage

superintendent

supersede

suppress

surprise

swimming

syllable

synonym

synonymous

tangible

tariff

tasting

technical

technique

temperament

tenant

tendency

thorough

thought

tournament

traffic

*Continued on next page*

| | | |
|---|---|---|
| tragedy | usually | whole |
| transferred | vacancy | wholly |
| tremendous | vacuum | wiry |
| tries | valuable | woman |
| truly | vengeance | women |
| twelfth | victorious | won't |
| typical | view | worried |
| tyranny | vigilant | worrying |
| unanimous | vigorous | writing |
| undoubtedly | village | written |
| unnecessary | villain | yacht |
| until | warrant | your |
| usage | warring | you're (you are) |
| useful | weird | zoology |
| using | welfare | |

---

## EXERCISE

Use the following activities to help you eliminate any spelling problems that you happen to have. Keep in mind that your work will vary from that of other writers because individuals have individual difficulties with spelling.

1. Scan the list of frequently misspelled words (pages 568–574) and underline the words you know you have trouble spelling. Then write them on a 4" × 6" card for handy reference when you proofread your papers.

2. Review your graded papers from classes this term (or other recent samples of your writing), and make a list of the words you have misspelled. Include in this list any specialized terms that you frequently use.

3. Prepare a 4" × 6" card with a list of important names and terms used in your major and minor courses, especially those that present spelling problems. Include the names of writers, theorists, organizations, cities, titles, scientific terms, commonly used foreign phrases, and so on.

## OBSERVING THE RULES OF MECHANICS: REVIEW EXERCISE

**Correct the mechanical errors in the following paragraph.**

The civil war period in american history has had a tremendous impact on modern Culture, Science, Politics, and Economics—in fact, on almost all aspects of american life. Yet the real influences of the civil war are typically ignored because of the myths which americans prefer to perpetrate. Who has not created a fictionalized view of antebellum culture based on Historical Novels like Margaret Mitchells Gone With The Wind, Harriet Beecher Stowes Uncle Toms Cabin, or Margaret Walkers Jubilee? Who has not been influenced by the Ken Burns's documentary The Civil War. Modern Americans have seen president Lincoln portrayed by dozens of actors, have seen reenactments of the battle of Gettysburg, and have witnessed the sea battles of the Iron ships: The Monitor and others. Who has not seen dramatized versions of soldiers—both from the north and the south—heading to their homes, with The Battle Hymm of the Republic or Dixie as background music. We have stored images of generals Lee and Grant, as often as not based on the idealized statuary of the Franklin Mints Civil War Chess Set. Yet few of us have seen the civil war through the disturbing Psychological perspective of Stephen Cranes The Red Badge of Courage. Few have acknowledged in any real way that the reconstruction depressed the southern economy, gave rise to the ku klux klan, and failed to solve the ideological problems that continued to divide the country long after the deaths of six-hundred and fifty thousand soldiers.

# A Glossary of Contemporary Usage

This glossary identifies words and constructions that sometimes require attention in composition classes. Some of the entries are pairs of words that are quite different in meaning yet similar enough in spelling to be confused (see **principal, principle**). Some, such as the use of *without* as a synonym for *unless,* are nonstandard usages that are not acceptable in college writing (see **without** = **unless**). Some are informal constructions that may be appropriate in some situations but not in others (see **guess**).

The judgments recorded here about usage are based on the Usage Notes contained in the *American Heritage Dictionary,* supplemented by other sources. Because these authorities do not always agree, it has sometimes been necessary for the author of this textbook to decide which judgments to accept. In coming to decisions, I have attempted to represent a consensus, but readers should be aware that on disputed items the judgments recorded in this glossary are finally mine.

Because dictionaries do not always distinguish among formal, informal, and colloquial usages, it has seemed useful to indicate whether a particular usage would be appropriate in college writing. The usefulness of this advice, however, depends on an understanding of its limitations. In any choice of usage, the decision depends less on what dictionaries or textbooks say than on what is consistent with the purpose and style of the writing. The student and instructor, who alone have the context of the paper before them, are in the best position to answer that question. All that the glossary can do is provide a background on which particular decisions can be based. The general assumption in the glossary is that the predominant style in college writing is moderate rather than formal or colloquial, so calling a usage informal in no way suggests that it is less desirable than a formal usage.

**ad** *Ad* is the clipped form of *advertisement.* The full form is preferable in a formal style, especially in letters of application. The appropriateness of *ad* in college writing depends on the style of the paper.

**adapt, adopt** *Adapt* means "to adjust to meet requirements": "The human body can adapt itself to all sorts of environments"; "It will take a skillful writer to adapt this novel for the movies." *Adopt* means "to take as one's own" ("He immediately adopted the idea") or—in parliamentary procedure— "to accept as law" ("The motion was adopted").

**advice, advise**   The first form is a noun, the second a verb: "I was advised to ignore his advice."

**affect, effect**   Both words may be used as nouns, but *effect,* meaning "result," is usually the word wanted: "His speech had an unfortunate effect"; "The treatments had no effect on me." The noun *affect* is a technical term in psychology. Although both words may be used as verbs, *affect* is the more common. As a verb, *affect* means "impress" or "influence": "His advice affected my decision"; "Does music affect you that way?" As a verb, *effect* is rarely required in college writing but may be used to mean "carry out" or "accomplish": "The pilot effected his mission"; "The lawyer effected a settlement."

**affective, effective**   See **affect, effect.** The common adjective is *effective* ("an effective argument"), meaning "having an effect." The use of *affective* is largely confined to technical discussions of psychology and semantics, in which it is roughly equivalent to "emotional." In this textbook, *affective* is used to describe a tone that is chiefly concerned with creating attitudes in the reader.

**aggravate**   *Aggravate* may mean either "to make worse" ("His remarks aggravated the dispute") or "to annoy or exasperate" ("Her manners aggravate me"). Both are standard English, but there is still some objection to the second usage. If you mean *annoy, exasperate,* or *provoke,* it would be safer to use whichever of those words best expresses your meaning.

**ain't**   Except to record nonstandard speech, the use of *ain't* is not acceptable in college writing.

**all together, altogether**   Distinguish between the phrase ("They were all together at last") and the adverb ("He is altogether to blame"). *All together* means "all in one place"; *altogether* means "entirely" or "wholly."

**allow**   When used to mean "permit" ("No smoking is allowed on the premises"), *allow* is acceptable. Its use for "think" ("He allowed it could be done") is nonstandard and is not acceptable in college writing.

**allusion, illusion**   An *allusion* is a reference: "The poem contains several allusions to Greek mythology." An *illusion* is an erroneous mental image: "Rouge on pallid skin gives an illusion of health."

**alright**   A common variant spelling of *all right,* but there is still considerable objection to it. *All right* is the preferred spelling.

**among, between**   See **between, among.**

**amount, number**   *Amount* suggests bulk or weight: "We collected a considerable amount of scrap iron." *Number* is used for items that can be counted: "He has a large number of friends"; "There are a number of letters to be answered."

**an**   Variant of the indefinite article *a*. Used instead of *a* when the word that follows begins with a vowel sound: "an apple," "an easy victory," "an honest opinion," "an hour," "an unknown person." When the word that follows begins with a consonant, or with a *y* sound or a pronounced *h*, the article used should be *a*: "a yell," "a unit," "a history," "a house." Such constructions as "a apple," "a hour" are nonstandard. The use of *an* before *historical* is an older usage that is now dying out.

**and/or**   Many people object to *and/or* in college writing because the expression is associated with legal and commercial writing. Generally avoid it.

**angle**   The use of *angle* to mean "point of view" ("Let's look at it from a new angle") is acceptable. In the sense of personal interest ("What's your angle?"), it is slang.

**anxious = eager**   *Anxious* should not be used in college writing to mean "eager," as in "Gretel is anxious to see her gift." *Eager* is the preferred word in this context.

**any = all**   The use of *any* to mean "all," as in "He is the best qualified of any applicant," is not acceptable. Say, "He is the best qualified of all the applicants," or simply "He is the best-qualified applicant."

**any = any other**   The use of *any* to mean "any other" ("The knife she bought cost more than any in the store") should be avoided in college writing. In this context, use *any other*.

**anyone = all**   The singular *anyone* should not be used in writing to mean "all." In "She is the most talented musician of anyone I have met here," omit "of anyone."

**anywheres**   A nonstandard variant of *anywhere*. It is not acceptable in college writing.

**apt = likely**   *Apt* is always appropriate when it means "quick to learn" ("He is an apt student") or "suited to its purpose" ("an apt comment"). It is also appropriate when a predictable characteristic is being spoken of ("When he becomes excited, he is apt to tremble"). In other situations the use of *apt* to mean "likely" ("She is apt to leave you"; "He is apt to resent it") may be too colloquial for college writing.

**as = because**   *As* is less effective than *because* in showing causal relation between main and subordinate clauses. Since *as* has other meanings, it may in certain contexts be confusing. For example, in "As I was going home, I decided to telephone," *as* may mean "while" or "because." If there is any possibility of confusion, use either *because* or *while*—whichever is appropriate.

**as = that**   The use of *as* to introduce a noun clause ("I don't know as I would agree to that") is colloquial. In college writing, use *that* or *whether*.

**as to, with respect to** = **about**    Although *as to* and *with respect to* are standard usage, many writers avoid these phrases because they sound stilted: "I am not concerned as to your cousin's reaction." Here *about* would be more appropriate than either *as to* or *with respect to*: "I am not concerned about your cousin's reaction."

**at**    Avoid the redundant *at* in such sentences as "Where were you at?" and "Where do you live at?"

**author**    *Author* is not fully accepted as a verb. "To write a play" is preferable to "to author a play."

**awful, awfully**    The real objection to *awful* is that it is worked to death. Instead of being reserved for situations in which it means "awe inspiring," it is used excessively as a utility word. Use both *awful* and *awfully* sparingly.

**bad** = **badly**    The ordinary uses of *bad* as an adjective cause no difficulty. As a predicate adjective ("An hour after dinner, I began to feel bad"), it is sometimes confused with the adverb *badly*. After the verbs *look, feel,* and *seem,* the adjective is preferred. Say: "It looks bad for our side," "I feel bad about the quarrel," "Our predicament seemed bad this morning." But do not use *bad* when an adverb is required, as in "He played badly," "a badly torn suit."

**bank on** = **rely on**    In college writing *rely on* is generally preferred.

**being as** = **because**    The use of *being as* for "because" or "since" in such sentences as "Being as I am an American, I believe in democracy" is nonstandard. Say "Because I am an American, I believe in democracy."

**between, among**    In general, use *between* in constructions involving two people or objects and *among* in constructions involving more than two: "We had less than a dollar between the two of us"; "We had only a dollar among the three of us." The general distinction, however, should be modified when insistence on it would be unidiomatic. For example, *between* is the accepted form in the following examples:

> He is in the enviable position of having to choose between three equally attractive young women.
>
> A settlement was arranged between the four partners.
>
> Just between us girls . . . (when any number of "girls" is involved)

**between you and I**    Both pronouns are objects of the preposition *between* and so should be in the objective case: "between you and me."

**bi-, semi-**    *Bi-* means "two": "The budget for the biennium was adopted." *Semi-* means "half of": "semicircle." *Bi-* is sometimes used to mean "twice in." A bimonthly paper, for example, may be published twice a month, not once every two months, but this usage is ambiguous; *semimonthly* is preferred.

**but that, but what**    In such a statement as "I don't doubt but that you are correct," *but* is unnecessary. Omit it. "I don't doubt but what . . ." is also unacceptable. Delete *but what* and write *that.*

**can = may**    The distinction that *can* is used to indicate ability and *may* to indicate permission ("If I can do the work, may I have the job?") is not generally observed in informal usage. Either form is acceptable in college writing.

**cannot help but**    In college writing, the form without *but* is preferred: "I cannot help being angry." (Not: "I cannot help but be angry.")

**can't hardly**    A confusion between *cannot* and *can hardly.* The construction is unacceptable in college writing. Use *cannot, can't,* or *can hardly.*

**capital, capitol**    Unless you are referring to a government building, use *capital.* The building in which the U.S. Congress meets is always capitalized ("the Capitol"). For the various meanings of *capital,* consult your dictionary.

**censor, censure**    Both words come from a Latin verb meaning "to set a value on" or "judge." *Censor* is used to mean "appraise" in the sense of evaluating a book or a letter to see if it may be released ("All outgoing mail had to be censored") and is often used as a synonym for *delete* or *cut out* ("That part of the message was censored").

    *Censure* as a verb means "to evaluate adversely" or "to find fault with"; as a noun, it means "disapproval," "rebuke": "The editorial writers censured the speech"; "Such an attitude will invoke public censure."

**center around**    Center on" is the preferred form.

**cite, sight, site**    *Cite* means "to refer to": "He cited chapter and verse." *Sight* means "spectacle" or "view": "The garden was a beautiful sight." *Site* means "location": "This is the site of the new plant."

**compare, contrast**    *Compare* can imply either differences or similarities; *contrast* always implies differences. *Compare* can be followed by either *to* or *with.* The verb *contrast* is usually followed by *with.*

    Compared to her mother, she's a beauty.

    I hope my accomplishments can be compared with those of my predecessor.

    His grades this term contrast conspicuously with the ones he received last term.

**complement, compliment**    Both words can be used as nouns and verbs. *Complement* speaks of completion: "the complement of a verb"; "a full complement of soldiers to serve as an honor guard"; "Susan's hat complements the rest of her outfit tastefully." *Compliment* is associated with praise: "The instructor complimented us for writing good papers."

***complement of* to be**    The choice between "It is I" and "It's me" is a choice not between standard and nonstandard usage but between formal and colloquial styles. This choice seldom has to be made in college writing since the expression, in whatever form it is used, is essentially a spoken rather than a written sentence. Its use in writing occurs chiefly in dialogue, and then the form chosen should be appropriate to the speaker.

The use of the objective case with the third person ("That was her") is less common and should be avoided in college writing except when dialogue requires it.

**continual, continuous**    Both words refer to a continued action, but *continual* implies repeated action ("continual interruptions," "continual disagreements"), whereas *continuous* implies that the action never ceases ("continuous pain," "a continuous buzzing in the ears").

**could of = could have**    Although *could of* and *could have* often sound alike in speech, *of* is not acceptable for *have* in college writing. In writing, *could of, should of, would of, might of,* and *must of* are nonstandard.

**council, counsel**    *Council* is a noun meaning "a deliberative body": "a town council," "a student council." *Counsel* can be either a noun meaning "advice" or a verb meaning "to advise": "to seek a lawyer's counsel," "to counsel a person in trouble." A person who offers counsel is a *counselor*: "Because of his low grades, Quint made an appointment with his academic counselor."

**credible, creditable, credulous**    All three words come from a Latin verb meaning "to believe," but they are not synonyms. *Credible* means "believable" ("His story is credible"); *creditable* means "commendable" ("John did a creditable job on the committee") or "acceptable for credit" ("The project is creditable toward the course requirements"); *credulous* means "gullible" ("Only a most credulous person could believe such an incredible story").

**cute**    A word used colloquially to indicate the general notion of "attractive" or "pleasing." Its overuse shows lack of discrimination. A more specific term is often preferable.

His daughter is cute. [lovely? petite? pleasant? charming?]

That is a cute trick. [clever? surprising?]

He has a cute accent. [pleasant? refreshingly unusual?]

She is a little too cute for me. [affected? juvenile? clever?]

**data is**    Because *data* is the Latin plural of *datum,* it logically requires a plural verb and always takes a plural verb in scientific writing: "These data have been double-checked." In popular usage and in computer-related contexts, *datum* is almost never used and *data* is treated as a singular noun and given a singular subject: "The data has been double-checked." Either *data are* or *data is* may be used in popular writing, but only *data are* is acceptable in scientific writing.

**debut**    *Debut* is a noun meaning "first public appearance." It is not acceptable as a transitive verb ("The Little Theater will debut its new play tonight") or as an intransitive verb ("Cory Martin will debut in the new play").

**decent, descent**    A decent person is one who behaves well, without crudeness and perhaps with kindness and generosity. *Decent* can mean "satisfactory" ("a decent grade," "a decent living standard"). *Descent* means "a passage downward"; a descent may be either literal ("their descent into the canyon") or figurative ("hereditary descent of children from their parents," "descent of English from a hypothetical language called Indo-European").

**desert, dessert**    The noun *desert* means "an uncultivated and uninhabited area"; it may be dry and sandy. *Desert* can be an adjective: "a desert island." The verb *desert* means "to abandon." A *dessert* is a sweet food served as the last course at the noon or evening meal.

**different from, different than**    Although both *different from* and *different than* are common American usages, the preferred idiom is *different from*.

**disinterested, uninterested**    The distinction between these words is that *disinterested* means "unbiased" and *uninterested* means "apathetic" or "not interested." A disinterested critic is one who comes to a book with no prejudices or prior judgments of its worth; an uninterested critic is one who cannot get interested in the book. Dictionaries disagree about whether this distinction is still valid in contemporary usage and sometimes treat the words as synonyms. But in college writing the distinction is generally observed.

**don't**    *Don't* is a contraction of "do not," as *doesn't* is a contraction of "does not." It can be used in any college writing in which contractions are appropriate. But it cannot be used with a singular subject. "He don't" and "it don't" are nonstandard usages.

**double negative**    The use of two negative words within the same construction. In certain forms ("I am not unwilling to go") the double negative is educated usage for an affirmative statement; in other forms ("He hasn't got no money") the double negative is nonstandard usage. The observation that "two negatives make an affirmative" in English usage is a half-truth based on a false analogy with mathematics. "He hasn't got no money" is unacceptable in college writing, not because two negatives make an affirmative, but because it is nonstandard usage.

**economic, economical**    *Economic* refers to the science of economics or to business in general: "This is an economic law"; "Economic conditions are improving." *Economical* means "inexpensive" or "thrifty": "That is an economical purchase"; "He is economical to the point of miserliness."

**effect, affect**   See **affect, effect.**

**effective, affective**   See **affective, effective.**

**either**   Used to designate one of two things: "Both hats are becoming; I would be perfectly satisfied with either." The use of *either* when more than two things are involved ("There are three ways of working the problem; either way will give the right answer") is a disputed usage. When more than two things are involved, it is better to use *any* or *any one* instead of *either:* "There are three ways of working the problem; any one of them will give the right answer."

**elicit, illicit**   The first word means "to draw out" ("We could elicit no response from them"); the second means "not permitted" or "unlawful" ("an illicit sale of drugs").

**emigrant, immigrant**   An emigrant is a person who moves *out* of a country; an immigrant is one who moves *into* a country. Thus refugees from Central America and elsewhere who settle in the United States are emigrants from their native countries and immigrants here. A similar distinction holds for the verbs *emigrate* and *immigrate.*

**eminent, imminent**   *Eminent* means "prominent, outstanding": "an eminent scientist." *Imminent* means "ready to happen" or "near in time": "War seems imminent."

**enormity, enormous, enormousness**   *Enormous* refers to unusual size or measure; synonyms are *huge, vast, immense:* "an enormous fish," "an enormous effort." *Enormousness* is a noun with the same connotations of size and can be applied to either good or bad effects: "The enormousness of their contribution is only beginning to be recognized"; "The enormousness of the lie almost made it believable." But *enormity* is used only for evil acts of great dimension: "The enormity of Hitler's crimes against the Jews shows what can happen when power, passion, and prejudice are all united in one human being."

**enthused**   *Enthused* is colloquial for *enthusiastic:* "The probability of winning has caused them to be very enthused about the campaign." In college writing use *enthusiastic.*

**equally as**   In such sentences as "He was equally as good as his brother," the *equally* is unnecessary. Simply write, "He was as good as his brother."

**etc.**   An abbreviation for the Latin *et cetera,* which means "and others," "and so forth." It should be used only when the style justifies abbreviations and then only after several items in a series have been identified: "The data sheet required the usual personal information: age, height, weight, marital status, etc." An announcement of a painting contest that states, "Entries will be judged on the basis of use of color, etc." does not tell contestants very much about the standards by which their work is to be judged. Avoid the redundant *and* before *etc.*

**expect = suppose or suspect**    The use of *expect* for *suppose* or *suspect* is colloquial. In college writing use *suppose* or *suspect:* "I suppose you have written to him"; "I suspect that we have made a mistake."

**fact**    Distinguish between facts and statements of fact. A fact is something that exists or existed. A fact is neither true nor false, it just *is.* A statement of fact, or a factual statement, may be true or false, depending on whether it does or does not report the facts accurately.

Avoid padding a sentence with "a fact that," as in "It is a fact that all the public opinion polls predicted Truman's defeat in the 1948 election." The first five words of that sentence add no meaning. Similarly, "His guilt is admitted" says all, in fewer words, that is said by "The fact of his guilt is admitted."

**famous, notorious**    *Famous* is a complimentary and *notorious* an uncomplimentary adjective. Well-known people of good repute are famous; those of bad repute are notorious, or infamous.

**farther, further**    The distinction that *farther* indicates distance and *further* degree is not unanimously supported by usage studies. But to mean "in addition," only *further* is used: "Further assistance will be required."

**feature = imagine**    The use of *feature* to mean "give prominence to," as in "This issue of the magazine features an article on juvenile delinquency," is established standard usage and is appropriate in college writing. But this acceptance does not justify the slang use of *feature,* meaning "imagine," in such expressions as "Can you feature that?" "Feature me in a dress suit," "I can't feature him as a nurse."

**fewer = less**    *Fewer* refers to quantities that can be counted individually: "fewer male than female employees." *Less* is used for collective quantities that are not counted individually ("less corn this year than last") and for abstract characteristics ("less determination than enthusiasm").

**field**    *Field,* in the sense of "an area of study or endeavor," is an overused word that often creates redundance: "He is majoring in the field of physics"; "Her new job is in the field of public relations." Delete "the field of" in each of these sentences.

**fine = very well**    The colloquial use of *fine* to mean "very well" ("He is doing fine in his new position") is probably too informal for most college writing.

**flaunt = flout**    Using *flaunt* as a synonym for *flout* confuses two different words. *Flaunt* means "to show off": "She has a habit of flaunting her knowledge to intimidate her friends." *Flout* means "to scorn or show contempt for": "He is better at flouting opposing arguments than at understanding them." In the right context either word can be effective, but the two words are not synonyms and cannot be used interchangeably.

**fortuitous, fortunate**   *Fortuitous* means "by chance," "not planned": "Our meeting was fortuitous; we had never heard of each other before." Do not confuse *fortuitous* with *fortunate,* as the writer of this sentence has done: "My introduction to Professor Kraus was fortuitous for me; today she hired me as her student assistant." *Fortunate* would be the appropriate word here.

**funny**   Often used in conversation as a utility word that has no precise meaning but may be clear enough in its context. It is generally too vague for college writing. Decide in what sense the subject is "funny" and use a more precise term to convey that sense.

**get**   A utility word. The *American Heritage Dictionary* lists thirty-six meanings for the individual word and more than sixty uses in idiomatic expressions. Most of these uses are acceptable in college writing. But unless the style is deliberately colloquial, avoid slang uses in which *get* means "to cause harm to" ("She'll get me for that"), "to cause a negative reaction to" ("His bad manners really get me"), "to gain the favor of" ("He tried to get in with his boss"), and "to become up to date" ("Get in the swing of things").

**good**   The use of *good* as an adverb ("He talks good"; "She played pretty good") is not acceptable. The accepted adverbial form is *well.* The use of *good* as a predicate adjective after verbs of hearing, feeling, seeing, smelling, tasting, and the like is standard. See **bad.**

**good and**   Used colloquially as an intensive in such expressions as "good and late," "good and ready," "good and tired." The more formal the style, the less appropriate these intensives are. In college writing use them sparingly, if at all.

**guess**   The use of *guess* to mean "believe," "suppose," or "think" ("I guess I can be there on time") is accepted by all studies on which this glossary is based. There is objection to its use in formal college writing, but it should be acceptable in an informal style.

**had (hadn't) ought**   Nonstandard for *ought* and *ought not.* Not acceptable in college writing.

**hanged, hung**   Alternative past participles of *hang.* For referring to an execution, *hanged* is preferred; in other senses, *hung* is preferred.

**he or she, she or he**   The masculine form (*he, his, him*) of the personal pronoun used to refer to an individual who could be either male or female: "The writer should revise his draft until he achieves his purpose." Substituting pronouns that refer to both males and females in the group, such as *he or she,* or *she or he,* corrects the implicit sexism in the traditional usage but sometimes sounds awkward. An alternative is to use plural forms: "Writers should revise their drafts until they achieve their purpose."

**hopefully**   Opinion is divided about the acceptability of attaching this adverb loosely to a sentence and using it to mean "I hope": "Hopefully, the plane will arrive on schedule." This usage is gaining acceptance, but there is still strong objection to it. In college writing the safe decision is to avoid it.

**idea**   In addition to its formal meaning of "conception," *idea* has acquired so many supplementary meanings that it must be recognized as a utility word. Some of its meanings are illustrated in the following sentences:

The idea (thesis) of the book is simple.

The idea (proposal) she suggested is a radical one.

I got the idea (impression) that he is unhappy.

It is my idea (belief, opinion) that they are both wrong.

My idea (intention) is to leave early.

The overuse of *idea,* like the overuse of any utility word, makes for vagueness. Whenever possible, use a more precise synonym.

**illicit, elicit**   See **elicit, illicit.**

**illusion, allusion**   See **allusion, illusion.**

**immigrant, emigrant**   See **emigrant, immigrant.**

**imminent, eminent**   See **eminent, imminent.**

**imply, infer**   The traditional difference between these two words is that *imply* refers to what a statement means, usually to a meaning not specifically stated but suggested in the original statement, whereas *infer* is used for a listener's or reader's judgment or inference based on the statement. For example: "I thought that the weather report implied that the day would be quite pretty and sunny, but Marlene inferred that it meant we'd better take umbrellas." The dictionaries are not unanimous in supporting this distinction, but in your writing it will be better not to use *imply* as a synonym for *infer.*

**individual**   Although the use of *individual* to mean "person" ("He is an energetic individual") is accepted by the dictionaries, college instructors frequently disapprove of this use, probably because it is overdone in college writing. There is no objection to the adjective *individual,* meaning "single," "separate" ("The instructor tries to give us individual attention").

**inferior than**   Possibly a confusion between "inferior to" and "worse than." Use *inferior to:* "Today's workmanship is inferior to that of a few years ago."

**ingenious, ingenuous**   *Ingenious* means "clever" in the sense of "original": "an ingenious solution." *Ingenuous* means "without sophistication," "innocent": "Her ingenuous confession disarmed those who had been suspicious of her motives."

**inside of, outside of** *Inside of* and *outside of* generally should not be used as compound prepositions. In place of the compound prepositions in "The display is inside of the auditorium" and "The pickets were waiting outside of the gate," write "inside the auditorium" and "outside the gate."

*Inside of* is acceptable in most college writing when it means "in less than": "I'll be there inside of an hour." The more formal term is *within*.

Both *inside of* and *outside of* are appropriate when *inside* or *outside* is a noun followed by an *of* phrase: "The inside of the house is quite attractive"; "He painted the outside of his boat dark green."

**in terms of** An imprecise and greatly overused expression. Instead of "In terms of philosophy, we are opposed to his position" and "In terms of our previous experience with the company, we refuse to purchase its products," write "Philosophically, we are opposed to his position" and "Because of our previous experience with the company, we refuse to purchase its products."

**irregardless** A nonstandard variant of *regardless*. Do not use it.

**irrelevant, irreverent** *Irrelevant* means "having no relation to" or "lacking pertinence": "That may be true, but it is quite irrelevant." *Irreverent* means "without reverence": "Such conduct in church is irreverent."

**it's me** This construction is essentially a spoken one. Except in dialogue, it rarely occurs in writing. Its use in educated speech is thoroughly established. The formal expression is "It is I."

**-ize** The suffix *-ize* is used to change nouns and adjectives into verbs: *civilize, criticize, sterilize*. This practice is often overused, particularly in government and business. Avoid such pretentious and unnecessary jargon as *finalize, prioritize,* and *theorize*.

**judicial, judicious** Judicial decisions are related to the administering of justice, often by judges or juries. A judicious person is one who demonstrates good judgment: "A judicious person would not have allowed the young boys to shoot the rapids alone."

**kind of, sort of** Use a singular noun and a singular verb with these phrases: "That kind of person is always troublesome"; "This sort of attitude is deplorable." If the sense of the sentence calls for the plural *kinds* or *sorts,* use a plural noun and a plural verb: "These kinds of services are essential." In questions introduced by *what* or *which,* the singular *kind* or *sort* can be followed by a plural noun and verb: "What kind of shells are these?"

The use of *a* or *an* after *kind of* ("That kind of a person is always troublesome") is usually not appropriate in college writing.

**kind (sort) of = somewhat**    This usage ("I feel kind of tired"; "He looked sort of foolish") is colloquial. The style of the writing will determine its appropriateness in a paper.

**latter**    *Latter* refers to the second of two. It should not be used to refer to the last of three or more nouns. Instead of *latter* in "Michigan, Alabama, and Notre Dame have had strong football teams for years, and yet the latter has only recently begun to accept invitations to play in bowl games," write *last* or *last-named* or simply repeat *Notre Dame.*

**lay, lie**    *Lay* is a transitive verb (principal parts: *lay, laid, laid*) that means "put" or "place"; it is nearly always followed by a direct object: "She lay the magazine on the table, hiding the mail I laid there this morning." *Lie* is an intransitive verb (principal parts: *lie, lay, lain*) that means "recline" or "be situated" and does not take an object: "I lay awake all night until I decided I had lain there long enough."

**leave = let**    The use of *leave* for the imperative verb *let* ("Leave us face it") is not acceptable in college writing. Write "Let us face it."

**less**    See **fewer.**

**liable = likely**    Instructors sometimes object to the use of *liable* to mean "likely," as in "it is liable to rain," "He is liable to hit you." *Liable* is used more precisely to mean "subject to" or "exposed to" or "answerable for": "He is liable to arrest"; "You will be liable for damages."

**like = as, as though**    The use of *like* as a conjunction ("He talks like you do"; "It looks like it will be my turn next") is colloquial. It is not appropriate in a formal style, and many people object to it in an informal style. The safest policy is to avoid using *like* as a conjunction in college writing.

**literally, figuratively**    *Literally* means "word for word," "following the letter," or "in the strict sense." *Figuratively* is its opposite and means "metaphorically." In informal speech, this distinction is often blurred when *literally* is used to mean *nearly*: "She literally blew her top." Avoid this usage by maintaining the word's true meaning: "To give employees a work vacation means literally to fire them."

**loath, loathe**    *Loath* is an adjective meaning "reluctant," "unwilling" ("I am loath to do that"; "He is loath to risk so great an investment") and is pronounced to rhyme with *both*. *Loathe* is a verb meaning "dislike strongly" ("I loathe teas"; "She loathes an unkempt man") and is pronounced to rhyme with *clothe*.

**loose, lose**    The confusion of these words frequently causes misspelling. *Loose* is most common as an adjective: "a loose button," "The dog is loose." *Lose* is always used as a verb: "You are going to lose your money."

**luxuriant, luxurious**  These words come from the same root but have quite different meanings. *Luxuriant* means "abundant" and is used principally to describe growing things: "luxuriant vegetation," "a luxuriant head of hair." *Luxurious* means "luxury-loving" or "characterized by luxury": "He finds it difficult to maintain so luxurious a lifestyle on so modest an income"; "The furnishings of the clubhouse were luxurious."

**mad = angry or annoyed**  Using *mad* to mean "angry" is colloquial: "My girl-friend is mad at me"; "His insinuations make me mad." More precise terms—*angry, annoyed, irritated, provoked, vexed*—are generally more appropriate in college writing. *Mad* is, of course, appropriately used to mean "insane."

**majority, plurality**  Candidates are elected by a *majority* when they get more than half of the votes cast. A *plurality* is the margin of victory that the winning candidate has over the leading opponent, whether the winner has a majority or not.

**mean = unkind, disagreeable, vicious**  Using *mean* to convey the sense "unkind," "disagreeable," "vicious" ("It was mean of me to do that"; "He was in a mean mood"; "That dog looks mean") is a colloquial use. It is appropriate in most college writing, but since using *mean* loosely sometimes results in vagueness, consider using one of the suggested alternatives to provide a sharper statement.

**medium, media, medias**  *Medium*, not *media*, is the singular form: "The daily newspaper is still an important medium of communication." *Media* is plural: "Figuratively, the electronic media have created a smaller world." *Medias* is not an acceptable form for the plural of *medium*.

**might of**  See **could of**

**mighty = very**  *Mighty* is not appropriate in most college writing as a substitute for *very*. Avoid such constructions as "He gave a mighty good speech."

**moral, morale**  Roughly, *moral* refers to conduct and *morale* refers to state of mind. A moral man is one who conducts himself according to standards for goodness. People are said to have good morale when they are cheerful, cooperative, and not too much concerned with their own worries.

**most = almost**  The use of *most* as a synonym for *almost* ("I am most always hungry an hour before mealtime") is colloquial. In college writing *almost* would be preferred in such a sentence.

**must (adj. and n.)**  The use of *must* as an adjective ("This book is must reading for anyone who wants to understand Russia") and as a noun ("It is reported that the President will classify this proposal as a must") is accepted as established usage by the dictionaries.

**must of**  See **could of.**

**myself** = **I, me**  *Myself* should not be used for *I* or *me*. Avoid such constructions as "John and myself will go." *Myself* is acceptably used as an intensifier ("I saw it myself"; "I myself will go with you") and as a reflexive object ("I hate myself"; "I can't convince myself that he is right.")

**nauseous** = **nauseated**  *Nauseous* does not mean "experiencing nausea"; *nauseated* has that meaning: "The thought of making a speech caused her to feel nauseated." *Nauseous* means "causing nausea" or "repulsive": "nauseous odor," "nauseous television program."

**nice**  A utility word much overused in college writing. Avoid excessive use of *nice* and, whenever possible, choose a more precise synonym.

That's a nice dress. [*attractive? becoming? fashionable? well-made?*]

She a nice person. [*agreeable? charming? friendly? well-mannered?*]

**not all that**  The use of *not all that interested* to mean "not much interested" is generally not acceptable in college writing.

**off, off of** = **from**  Neither *off* nor *off of* should be used to mean "from." Write "Jack bought the old car from a stranger," not "off a stranger" or "off of a stranger."

**OK, O.K.**  Its use in business to mean "endorse" is generally accepted: "The manager OK'd the request." In college writing *OK* is a utility word and is subject to the general precaution concerning all such words: Do not overuse it, especially in contexts in which a more specific term would give more efficient communication. For example, contrast the vagueness of *OK* in the first sentence with the discriminated meanings in the second and third sentences:

The mechanic said the tires were OK.

The mechanic said the tread on the tires was still good.

The mechanic said the pressure in the tires was satisfactory.

**one**  See **you.**

**only**  The position of *only* in such sentences as "I only need three dollars" and "If only Mother would write!" is sometimes condemned on the grounds of possible ambiguity. In practice, the context usually rules out any but the intended interpretation, but a change in the word order would result in more appropriate emphasis: "I need only three dollars"; "If Mother would only write!"

**on the part of**  The phrase *on the part of* ("There will be some objection on the part of the students"; "On the part of business people, there will be some concern about taxes") often contributes to wordiness. Simply say "The students will object," "Business people will be concerned about taxes."

**party = person**   The use of *party* to mean "person" is appropriate in legal documents and the responses of telephone operators, but these are special uses. Generally avoid this use in college writing.

**per, a**   "You will be remunerated at the rate of forty dollars per diem" and "The troops advanced three miles per day through the heavy snow" show established use of *per* for *a*. But usually "forty dollars a day" and "three miles a day" would be more natural expressions in college writing.

**percent, percentage**   *Percent* is used when a specific portion is named: "five percent of the expenses." *Percentage* is used when no number is given: "a small percentage of the expenses." When *percent* or *percentage* is part of a subject, the noun or pronoun of the *of* phrase that follows determines the number of the verb: "Forty percent of the wheat is his"; "A large percentage of her customers pay promptly."

**personal, personnel**   *Personal* means "of a person": "a personal opinion," "a personal matter." *Personnel* refers to the people in an organization, especially employees: "Administrative personnel will not be affected."

**phenomenon, phenomena**   *Phenomenon* is singular; *phenomena* is plural: "This is a striking phenomenon." "Many new phenomena have been discovered with the radio telescope."

**plenty**   The use of *plenty* as a noun ("There is plenty of room") is always acceptable. Its use as an adverb ("It was plenty good") is not appropriate in college writing.

**practical, practicable**   Avoid interchanging the two words. *Practical* means "useful, not theoretical," and *practicable* means "feasible, but not necessarily proved successful": "The designers are usually practical, but these new blueprints do not seem practicable."

**première**   *Première* is acceptable as a noun ("The première for the play was held in a small off-Broadway theater"), but do not use it as a verb. Instead of "The play premièred in a small off-Broadway theater," write "The play opened . . ."

**preposition (ending sentence with)**   A preposition should not appear at the end of a sentence if its presence there draws undue attention to it or creates an awkward construction, as in "They are the people whom we made the inquiries yesterday about." But there is nothing wrong with writing a preposition at the end of a sentence to achieve an idiomatic construction: "Isn't that the man you are looking for?"

**principal, principle**   The basic meaning of *principal* is "chief" or "most important." It is used in this sense both as a noun and as an adjective: "the principal of a school," "the principal point." It is also used to refer to a capital sum of money, as contrasted with interest on the money: "He can live on the interest without touching the principal." *Principle* is used only as a noun and means "rule," "law," or "controlling idea": "the principle of 'one man, one vote'"; "Cheating is against my principles."

**proceed, precede**   To *proceed* is to "go forward"; to *precede* means "to go ahead of": "The blockers preceded the runner as the football team proceeded toward the goal line."

**prophecy, prophesy**   *Prophecy* is always used as a noun ("The prophecy came true"); *prophesy* is always a verb ("He prophesied another war").

**proved, proven**   When used as past participles, both forms are standard English, but the preferred form is *proved:* "Having proved the first point, we moved to the second." *Proven* is preferred when the word is used primarily as an adjective: "She is a proven contender for the championship."

**quote**   The clipped form for *quotation* ("a quote from *Walden*") is not acceptable in most college writing. The verb *quote* ("to quote Thoreau") is acceptable in all styles.

**raise, rise**   *Raise* is a transitive verb, taking an object, meaning to cause something to move up; *rise* is an intransitive verb meaning to go up (on its own): "I raised the window in the kitchen while I waited for the bread dough to rise."

**rarely ever, seldom ever**   The *ever* is redundant. Instead of saying, "He is rarely ever late" and "She is seldom ever angry," write, "He is rarely late" and "She is seldom angry."

**real = really (very)**   The use of *real* to mean "really" or "very" ("It is a real difficult assignment") is a colloquial usage. It is acceptable only in a paper whose style is deliberately colloquial.

**reason . . . because**   The construction is redundant: "The reason he couldn't complete his essay is because he lost his note cards." Substitute *that* for *because:* "The reason he couldn't complete his essay is that he lost his note cards." Better yet, simply eliminate *the reason* and *is:* "He couldn't complete his essay because he lost his note cards."

**refer back**   A confusion between *look back* and *refer*. This usage is objected to in college writing on the ground that since the *re-* of *refer* means "back," *refer back* is redundant. *Refer back* is acceptable when it means "refer again" ("The bill was referred back to the committee"); otherwise, use *refer* ("Let me refer you to page 17").

**regarding, in regard to, with regard to**   These are overused and stuffy substitutes for the following simple terms: *on, about,* or *concerning:* "The attorney spoke to you about the testimony."

**respectfully, respectively**   *Respectfully* means "with respect": "respectfully submitted." *Respectively* means "each in turn": "These three papers were graded respectively A, C, and B."

**right (adv.)**   The use of *right* as an adverb is established in such sentences as "He went right home" and "It served her right." Its use to mean *very* ("I was right glad to meet him") is colloquial and should be used in college writing only when the style is colloquial.

**right, rite**   A *rite* is a ceremony or ritual. This word should not be confused with the various uses of *right*.

**said (adj.)**   The use of *said* as an adjective ("said documents," "said offense") is restricted to legal phraseology. Do not use it in college writing.

**same as = just as**   The preferred idiom is "just as": "He acted just as I thought he would."

**same, such**   Avoid using *same* or *such* as a substitute for *it, this, that, them*. Instead of "I am returning the book because I do not care for same" and "Most people are fond of athletics of all sorts, but I have no use for such," say "I am returning the book because I do not care for it" and "Unlike most people, I am not fond of athletics."

**scarcely**   In such sentences as "There wasn't scarcely enough" and "We haven't scarcely time," the use of *scarcely* with a negative creates an unacceptable double negative. Say, "There was scarcely enough" and "We scarcely have time."

**scarcely . . . than**   The use of *scarcely . . . than* ("I had scarcely met her than she began to denounce her husband") is a confusion between "no sooner . . . than" and "scarcely . . . when." Say, "I had no sooner met her than she began to denounce her husband" or "I had scarcely met her when she began to denounce her husband."

**seasonable, seasonal**   *Seasonable* and its adverb form *seasonably* mean "appropriate(ly) to the season": "She was seasonably dressed for a late-fall football game"; "A seasonable frost convinced us that the persimmons were just right for eating." *Seasonal* means "caused by a season": "increased absenteeism because of seasonal influenza," "flooding caused by seasonal thaws."

**-selfs**   The plural of *self* is *selves*. Such a usage as "They hurt themselfs" is nonstandard and is not acceptable in college writing.

**semi-**   See **bi-, semi-**.

**sensual, sensuous**   *Sensual* has unfavorable connotations and means "catering to the gratification of physical desires": "Always concerned with satisfying his sexual lust and his craving for drink and rich food, the old baron led a totally sensual existence." *Sensuous* has generally favorable connotations and refers to pleasures experienced through the senses: "The sensuous comfort of a warm bath," "the sensuous imagery of the poem."

**set, sit**   These two verbs are commonly confused. *Set* meaning "to put or place" is a transitive verb and takes an object. *Sit* meaning "to be seated" is an intransitive verb. "You can set your books on the desk and then sit in that chair."

**shall, will**   In American usage the dominant practice is to use *will* in the second and third persons to express either futurity or determination and to use either *will* or *shall* in the first person.

In addition, *shall* is used in statements of law ("Congress shall have the power to . . ."), in military commands ("The regiment shall proceed as directed"), and in formal directives ("All branch offices shall report weekly to the home office").

**should, would**   These words are used as the past forms of *shall* and *will* respectively and follow the same pattern (see **shall, will**): "I would [should] be glad to see him tomorrow"; "He would welcome your ideas on the subject"; "We would [should] never consent to such an arrangement." They are also used to convert *shall* or *will* in direct discourse into indirect discourse:

| *Direct Discourse* | *Indirect Discourse* |
|---|---|
| "Shall I try to arrange it?" he asked. | He asked if he should try to arrange it. |
| I said, "They will need money." | I said that they would need money. |

**should of**   See **could of.**

**sight, site, cite**   See **cite, sight, site.**

**so (conj.)**   The use of *so* as a connective ("The salesperson refused to exchange the merchandise, so we went to the manager") is thoroughly respectable, but its overuse in college writing is objectionable. There are other good transitional connectives—*accordingly, for that reason, on that account, therefore*—that could be used to relieve the monotony of a series of *so*'s. Occasional use of subordination ("When the salesperson refused to exchange the merchandise, we went to the manager") also brings variety to the style.

**some**   The use of *some* as an adjective of indeterminate number ("Some friends of yours were here") is acceptable at all levels of writing. Its use as an intensive ("That was some meal!") or as an adverb ("She cried some after you left"; "This draft is some better than the first one") should be avoided in college writing.

**sort of**   See **kind of.**

**stationary, stationery**   *Stationary* means "fixed" or "unchanging": "The battle front is now stationary." *Stationery* means "writing paper": "a box of stationery." To remember the distinction, associate the *e* in *stationery* with the *e*'s in *letter*.

**suit, suite**   The common word is *suit:* "A suit of clothes"; "Follow suit, play a diamond"; "Suit yourself." *Suite,* pronounced "sweet," means "retinue" ("The President and his suite have arrived") or "set" or "collection" ("a suite of rooms," "a suite of furniture"). When *suite* refers to furniture, an alternative pronunciation is "suit."

**sure = certainly**   Using *sure* in the sense of "certainly" ("I am sure annoyed"; "Sure, I will go with you") is colloquial. Unless the style justifies colloquial usage, use *certainly* or *surely.*

**terrific**   Used at a formal level to mean "terrifying" ("a terrific epidemic") and at a colloquial level as an intensive ("a terrific party," "a terrific pain"). Overuse of the word at the colloquial level has made it almost meaningless.

**than, then**   *Than* is a conjunction used in comparison; *then* is an adverb indicating time. Do not confuse the two: "I would rather write in the morning than in the afternoon. My thinking seems to be clearer then."

**that, which, who**   *That* refers to persons or things, *which* refers to things, and *who* refers to persons. *That* introduces a restrictive clause, and *which* usually introduces a nonrestrictive clause: "John argued that he was not prepared to take the exam, but the exam, which had been scheduled for some time, could not be changed"; "Anyone who was not ready would have to take the test anyway."

**there, their, they're**   Although these words are pronounced alike, they have different meanings. *There* indicates place: "Look at that dog over there." *Their* indicates possession: "I am sure it is their dog." *They're* is a contraction of "they are": "They're probably not home."

**thusly**   Not an acceptable variant of *thus.*

**tough**   The use of *tough* to mean "difficult" ("a tough assignment," "a tough decision") and "hard fought" ("a tough game") is accepted without qualification by reputable dictionaries. But its use to mean "unfortunate," "bad" ("The fifteen-yard penalty was a tough break for the team"; "That's tough") is colloquial and should be used only in a paper written in a colloquial style.

**troop, troupe**   Both words come from the same root and share the original meaning, "herd." In modern usage *troop* can refer to soldiers and *troupe* to actors: "a troop of cavalry," "a troop of scouts," "a troupe of circus performers," "a troupe of entertainers."

**try and**   *Try to* is the preferred idiom. Use "I will try to do it" instead of "I will try and do it."

**type = type of**   *Type* is not acceptable as a variant form of *type of.* In "That type engine isn't being manufactured anymore," add *of* after *type.*

**uninterested, disinterested**   See **disinterested.**

**unique**   The formal meaning of *unique* is "sole" or "only" or "being the only one of its kind": "Adam was unique in being the only man who never had a mother." The use of *unique* to mean "rare" or "unusual" ("Americans watched their television sets anxiously as astronauts in the early moon landings had the unique experience of walking on the moon") has long been popular, but some people still object to this usage. The use of *unique* to mean merely "uncommon" ("a unique sweater") is generally frowned upon. *Unique* should not be modified by adverbs that express degree: *very, more, most, rather.*

**up**   The adverb *up* is idiomatically used in many verb-adverb combinations that act as verbs—*break up, clean up, fill up, get up, tear up.* Avoid the unnecessary or awkward separation of *up* from the verb with which it is combined, since such a separation makes *up* look at first like an adverb modifying the verb rather than an adverb combining with the verb in an idiomatic expression. For example, "They held the cashier up" and "She made her face up" are awkward. Say "They held up the cashier," "She made up her face."

**use to**   The *d* in *used to* is often not pronounced; it is elided before the *t* in *to.* The resulting pronunciation leads to the written expression *use to.* But the acceptable written phrase is *used to*: "I am used to the noise"; "He used to do all the grocery shopping."

**very**   A common intensive, but avoid its overuse.

**wait on**   *Wait on* means "serve": "A clerk will be here in a moment to wait on you." The use of *wait on* to mean "wait for" ("I'll wait on you if you won't be long") is a colloquialism to which there is some objection. Use *wait for*: "I'll wait for you if you won't be long."

**want in, out, off**   The use of *want* followed by *in, out,* or *off* ("The dog wants in"; "I want out of here"; "I want off now") is colloquial. In college writing supply an infinitive after the verb: "The dog wants to come in."

**want to = ought to, should**   Using *want to* as a synonym for *should* ("They want to be careful or they will be in trouble") is colloquial. *Ought to* or *should* is preferred in college writing.

**where . . . at, to**   The use of *at* or *to* after *where* ("Where was he at?" "Where are you going to?") is redundant. Simply write, "Where was he?" and "Where are you going?"

**whose, who's**   *Whose* is the possessive of *who; who's* is a contraction of *who is* or *who has*: "In the play, John is the character whose son leaves town. Who's going to try out for that part?"

**will, shall**   See **shall, will.**

**-wise**   Avoid adding the suffix *-wise,* meaning "concerning," to nouns to form such combinations as *budgetwise, jobwise, tastewise.* Some combined forms with *-wise* are thoroughly established (*clockwise, otherwise, sidewise, weatherwise*), but the fad of coining new compounds with this suffix is generally best avoided.

**without = unless**   *Without* is not accepted as a conjunction meaning "unless." In "There will be no homecoming festivities without student government sponsors them," substitute *unless* for *without.*

**with respect to**   See **as to.**

**worst way**   When *in the worst way* means "very much" ("They wanted to go in the worst way"), it is too informal for college writing.

**would, should**   See **should, would.**

**would of**   See **could of.**

**would have = had**   *Would* is the past-tense form of *will,* but its overuse in student writing often results in awkwardness, especially, but not only, when it is used as a substitute for *had.* Contrast the following sentences:

| *Awkward* | *Revised* |
|---|---|
| If they *would have done* that earlier, there *would have been* no trouble. | If they *had done* that earlier, there *would have been* no trouble. |
| | *or:* |
| | *Had* they *done* that earlier, there *would have been* no trouble. |
| We *would want* some assurance that they *would accept* before we *would make* such a proposal. | We *would want* some assurance of their acceptance before we *made* such a proposal. |

In general, avoid the repetition of *would have* in the same sentence.

**you = one**   The use of *you* as an indefinite pronoun instead of the formal *one* is characteristic of an informal style. If you adopt *you* in an informal paper, be sure that this impersonal use will be recognized by your readers; otherwise, they are likely to interpret a general statement as a personal remark addressed specifically to them. Generally avoid shifting from *one* to *you* within a sentence.

**yourself**   *Yourself* is appropriately used as an intensifier ("You yourself told me that") and as a reflexive object ("You are blaming yourself too much"). But usages such as the following are not acceptable: "Marian and yourself must shoulder the responsibility" and "The instructions were intended for Kate and yourself." In these two sentences, replace *yourself* with *you.* The plural form is *yourselves,* not *yourselfs.*

# Acknowledgments

**CHAPTER 1**

*Page 6:* Photo © Phil Schermeister/CORBIS.

*Page 14:* Photo © Susan Holtz.

*Page 23:* Gail Godwin, "Becoming a Writer," from "A Writing Woman," *Atlantic* October 1979: 84. Copyright © 1979 by Gail Godwin. Reprinted by permission of John Hawkins & Associates, Inc.

**CHAPTER 2**

*Page 37:* Photo © Ed Bock/CORBIS.

*Page 46:* Photo © Langevin Jacques/CORBIS SYGMA.

*Page 49:* Excerpt from "Los Angeles Notebook" from *Slouching towards Bethlehem* by Joan Didion. Copyright © 1966, 1968, renewed 1996 by Joan Didion. Reprinted by permission of Farrar, Straus and Giroux, LLC.

*Page 50:* "The Five Rings" from *Information Anxiety* by Richard Saul Wurman, copyright © 1989 by Richard Saul Wurman. Used by permission of Doubleday, a division of Random House, Inc.

**CHAPTER 3**

*Page 62:* Photo © 2003 Susan Holtz.

*Page 72 (top):* Photo Pierpont Morgan Library, New York.

*Page 72 (bottom):* Photo © Bettmann/CORBIS.

*Page 73:* "Comforting Thoughts" by Calvin Trillin. From *Enough's Enough.* Published by Ticknor & Fields. Copyright © 1988, 1990 by Calvin Trillin. Reprinted by permission of Lescher & Lescher, Ltd. All rights reserved.

*Page 74:* Photo © Jose Luis Pelaez, Inc./CORBIS.

**CHAPTER 4**

*Page 87:* Photo © Mark Richards/PhotoEdit. All rights reserved.

*Page 94:* Photo © Dave G. Houser/CORBIS.

*Page 95 (top):* Photo TBWA/Chiat/Day for V&S Vin & Spirit AB, Stockholm.

*Part 95 (bottom):* Photo, an Adbusters ad parody, 604-736-9401.

*Page 96:* "New Products" by Andy Rooney. Reprinted with the permission of Scribner, an imprint of Simon & Schuster Adult Publishing Group, from *And More by Andy Rooney* by Andrew A. Rooney. Copyright © 1982, 1986 by Essay Productions, Inc.

*Page 98:* Photo © Susan Holtz.

**CHAPTER 5**

*Page 108 (Table 5.1 and Figure 5.1):* "Cell Phone Bill of Rights," <http://www.Let'sTalk.com/company/bill_study.htm >.

*Page 109 (Figure 5.2):* "Cell Phone Bill of Rights," <http://www.Let'sTalk.com/company/bill_study.htm>.

*Page 109 (Figure 5.3):* <http://www.verniernetworks.com/products.html>.

*Page 110 (Figure 5.4):* <http://www.attws.com/general/coverage_maps/coveragemaps.jsp>.

*Page 111 (Figure 5.5):* <http://www.Qualcomm.com/globalstar/about/satellites.html>.

*Page 113:* Robert Qually, "White Space," from *WHITEGRAPHICS: The Power of White in Graphic Design* by Gail Deibler Finke, Rockport Publishers. Reprinted by permission of Gail D. Finke.

*Page 118:* David Carson, "Don't Mistake Legibility for Communication," from *The End of Print: The Grafik Design of David Carson,* San Francisco: Chronicle Books, 2000. Reprinted by permission of the author.

*Page 119 (top):* Photo courtesy Susan Holtz, newspaper public domain.

*Page 119 (bottom):* Photo © Susan Holtz.

*Page 120:* Michael Rock, "Since When Did *USA Today* Become the National Design Ideal?," *I.D. Magazine* (New York) March/April 1992. Reprinted by permission of the author.

**CHAPTER 6**

*Page 131:* Reprinted with permission of Simon & Schuster Adult Publishing Group, from *Adam and Eve and the City* by Francine duPlessix Gray. Copyright © 1987 by Francine duPlessix Gray.

*Page 133:* Photo © Paul Souders/Image Bank/Getty.

*Page 138 (top):* Photo © Orlando Nelson Grillo.

*Page 138 (bottom):* Photo public domain.

*Page 140:* Extract from *Manwatching* by Desmond Morris published by Jonathan Cape. Used by permission of The Random House Group Limited.

*Page 147 (top and bottom):* Photo © Susan Holtz.

*Page 148:* Excerpt from "The Encircled River" from *Coming into the Country* by John McPhee. Copyright © 1977 by John McPhee. Reprinted by permission of Farrar, Straus and Giroux, LLC.

## CHAPTER 7

*Page 160:* Photo © Greg GibsonAP/Wide World.

*Page 178:* Photo © Gross National Products, 1986 (Wayzata, MN).

*Page 179:* Photo © 2002 TM and E. C. Publications, Inc. All rights reserved.

*Page 180:* "Execution" from *Living Out Loud* by Anna Quindlen, copyright © 1987 by Anna Quindlen. Used by permission of Random House, Inc.

*Page 183 (top):* Photo © Al Jazeera/AP/Wide World.

*Page 183 (bottom):* Photo © NBC News/AP/Wide World.

## CHAPTER 8

*Page 199:* Photo © Bettmann/CORBIS.

*Pages 204, 205, 208:* Bill Barich, "The Crazy Life," November 3, 1986. Reprinted by permission. Copyright © 1986 Bill Barich. Originally appeared in *The New Yorker*.

*Page 214 (top):* Photo © Tom Nebbia/CORBIS.

*Page 214 (bottom):* Photo © Evanian Phillippe/CORBIS SYGMA.

*Page 215 (bottom):* Photo © Earl and Nazima Kowall/CORBIS.

*Page 215 (bottom):* Photo © The Norman Rockwell Family Trust.

*Page 216:* Reprinted with permission of Simon & Schuster Adult Publishing Group, from *Close to Home* by Ellen Goodman. Copyright © 1979 by The Washington Post Company.

*Page 217:* Bill Barich, "La Frontera," December 17, 1990. Reprinted by permission. Copyright © 1990 by Bill Barich. Originally appeared in *The New Yorker*.

## CHAPTER 9

*Page 239:* Photo © Jefferson Medical College, Thomas Jefferson University, Philadelphia.

*Page 241:* Photo © 2003 Museum of Fine Arts, Boston. All rights reserved.

*Page 248 (top):* Photo © Albright-Knox Art Gallery/CORBIS.

*Page 248 (middle):* Photo © Lester Lefkowitz/CORBIS.

*Page 248 (bottom):* Photo © Ric Ergenbright/CORBIS.

*Page 249 (top):* Photo © royalty-free/CORBIS.

*Page 249 (bottom):* Photo © Paul A. Souders/CORBIS.

*Page 250:* Pam Smith, "Powerful Red Dogs: Excerpts from a Painter's Studio Notes," originally appeared in *The Georgia Review*, Volume 44, Nos. 1 & 2 (Spring/Summer 1990). Copyright © 1990 by the University of Georgia. Copyright © 1990 by Pam Smith. Reprinted by permission of Random House, Inc.

*Page 252:* "The Knife" from *Mortal Lessons: Notes on the Art of Surgery* by Richard Selzer. Copyright © 1974, 1975, 1976, 1987 by Richard Selzer. Reprinted by permission of Georges Borchardt, Inc., Literary Agency.

## CHAPTER 10

*Page 260:* "Colloquial" definition, copyright © 1981 by Houghton Mifflin Company. Reproduced by permission from *The American Heritage Dictionary of the English Language*.

*Page 261:* "Slang" from *The Oxford English Dictionary*, 2/e. Copyright © Oxford University Press 1989. Reprinted by permission of Oxford University Press.

*Page 261:* Excerpt from *Pygmalion* reprinted by permission of The Society of Authors on behalf of the Bernard Shaw Estate.

*Page 265:* Photo © Danny Lehman/CORBIS.

*Page 268:* Photo © Brenda Tharp/CORBIS.

*Page 271:* Excerpt from "Los Angeles Notebook" from *Slouching towards Bethlehem* by Joan Didion. Copyright © 1966, 1968, renewed 1996 by Joan Didion. Reprinted by permission of Farrar, Straus and Giroux, LLC.

*Page 280 (left):* Photo © Alan Goldsmith/CORBIS.

*Page 280 (right):* Photo © Chris Vincent/CORBIS.

*Page 281 (left):* Photo © Adam Woolfitt/CORBIS.

*Page 281 (right top):* Photo © Stocktrek/CORBIS.

*Page 281 (right bottom):* Photo courtesy of NASA/JPL/Caltech.

*Page 282:* "The Microscope" from *My Life and Hard Times* by James Thurber, published by Harper & Row. Copyright © 1933, 1961 by James Thurber.

*Page 283:* "Total Eclipse" from *Teaching a Stone to Talk: Expeditions and Encounters* by Annie Dillard. Copyright © 1982 by Annie Dillard. Reprinted by permission of HarperCollins Publishers, Inc.

## CHAPTER 11

*Page 295:* Photo © The Mariner's Museum/CORBIS.

*Page 295:* "Style" definition, copyright © 1981 by Houghton Mifflin Company. Reproduced by permission from *The American Heritage Dictionary of the English Language*.

*Page 302:* Excerpted from "Hong Kong Dream" © 1983 by Calvin Trillin. Appears in a book entitled *Third Helpings* by Calvin Trillin. Published by Ticknor & Fields. Reprinted by permission of Lescher & Lescher, Ltd. All rights reserved.

*Page 306 (left and right):* Photo © Swim Ink/CORBIS.

*Page 307 (top):* Photo © The Image Bank/Getty.

*Page 307 (bottom):* Photo © AFP/CORBIS.

*Page 308:* P. J. O'Rourke, "Third World Driving Hints and Tips," *Holidays in Hell.* Copyright © 1988 by P. J. O'Rourke. Used by permission of Grove/Atlantic, Inc.

*Page 310:* Patricia Hampl, "Prague," *A Romantic Education* (Boston: Houghton, 1981), 145–148, 149–152.

**CHAPTER 12**

*Page 334 (top and bottom):* Lexis/Nexis Academic. Copyright 2002.

*Page 336:* Google™ Search is a trademark of Google Inc.

**CHAPTER 14**

*Page 404:* "Digging" from *Meditations from a Moveable Chair* by Andre Dubus, copyright © 1998 by Andre Dubus. Used by permission of Alfred A. Knopf, a division of Random House, Inc.

*Page 418:* "Selling in Minnesota" from *Nickel and Dimed: On (Not) Getting by in America* by Barbara Ehrenreich. Copyright © 2001 by Barbara Ehrenreich. Reprinted by permission of Henry Holt and Company, LLC.

*Page 426:* John Steele Gordon, "The Golden Spike," *Forbes* 21 Feb. 2000: 118. Reprinted by permission of Forbes Magazine, copyright © 2003 Forbes Inc.

*Page 435:* Jessica Helfand, "Television Did It First: Ten Myths about 'New' Media," *Screen: Essays on Graphic Design, New Media, and Visual Culture* (New York: Princeton Architectural Press, 2001). Reprinted by permission.

*Page 445:* "Attention! Multitaskers" from *Faster: The Acceleration of Just About Everything* by James Gleick. Copyright © 1999 by James Gleick. Reprinted by permission of Pantheon Books, a division of Random House, Inc.

*Page 453:* "Changing History" by Eric Foner. Reprinted with permission from the September 5, 2002 issue of *The Nation.*

*Page 463:* "The End of Nature," from *The End of Nature* by William McKibben. Copyright © 1989 by William McKibben. Used by permission of Random House, Inc.

**PART 5**

*Page 524:* "Contract" definition, copyright © 1981 by Houghton Mifflin Company. Reproduced by permission from T*he American Heritage Dictionary of the English Language.*

# Index of Authors and Names

# Subject Index

Raisz, Erwin, 294
Rand, Paul, 8–9
*Reader's Guide to Periodical Literature*, 332
Reading
  evaluation of, 47
  from Web, 47
  journal use in, 43
"The Recycling Controversy" (Taras-kiewicz), 458–462
Red herring, 176
Reidenbach, Susan, (student writer) 40–42
Reinhardt, Joanne (student writer), 32–34
Repetition
  coherence through use of, 202
  as design element, 116
  emphatic, 240
Representational graphics, 107–110
Research paper planning
  evaluating sources and, 338–341
  finding sources and, 324–338. (See also Sources)
  making a schedule for, 320–321
  overview of, 318–319
  subject selection and, 321–323
  taking notes and, 341–346
  using computer for, 347
Research papers, 319–320
Research paper writing
  creating the introduction for, 354–357
  developing a thesis for, 353
  drafts for, 354, 377
  overview, 350–351
  preliminary outline for, 351–352
  quoting sources for, 357–362
  sample of, 379–393
  using your computer for, 378
Resolution, 209
Restatement, 208
Restrictive clauses, 536
Revision
  agenda for, 84–85
  of arguments, 174–176
  for audience, 82–83, 90–92
  authors on, 80
  case study of, 85–93
  on computer, 93
  diction in, 271–278
  explanation of, 6–7, 79–80, 130
  global, 6, 79, 174, 304
  local, 6, 79, 174, 304
  looking objectively at, 80–81
  process of, 79–80

of paragraphs, 209–212
for purpose, 83–84, 92–93
for subject, 82, 88–90
for style, 304, 305
of sentences, 236–246
*Rio* (Gibson), 302
Rock, Michael, 120–122
Rodriguez, Richard, 191–192
*A Romantic Education* (Hampl), 196
Rooney, Andy, 96–97, 208, 291
Rozin, Skip, 270
Run-on sentence, 501–502

Salinger, J. D., 267
"Same Goal, Different Plan" (Modlin), 424–425
Sarton, May, 54–55
Schedules, 320–321
Scheffel, Robert (student writer), 30–32
Schlissel, Lillian, 201
Scratch outlines, 55–58. *See also* Pre-liminary outline
Search engines, 326–327, 335
Search strategy, 324, 325, 327
Second–person point of view, 486
Seidel, Jon, 160, 161, 162–163, 170, 182–184, 397
"Selling in Minnesota" (Ehrenreich), 418–420
Selzer, Richard, 223, 234, 252–253
Semicolons,
  independent clauses and, 503, 543
  quotation marks and, 548
  use of, 543–544
Sentence fragments, 501
Sentence modifier, 224
Sentence revision,
  for clarity, 236–237
  for economy, 242–243
  elements of, 236
  for emphasis, 238–242
  for variety, 244–246
Sentences
  active, 488, 489
  agreement in, 504–510
  balanced, 234
  basic elements of, 476–480
  basic patterns of, 480–481
  case in, 510–513
  combined by coordination, 117
  combined by subordination, 230–231
  combined for purpose, 231–233
  comma splices in, 501
  comparisons in, 495–496

complex, 481
compound, 481
compound–complex, 481
conciseness in, 496–497
consistency in, 486–487
cumulative, 235–236
elements of, 223
expanded by modification, 225–226
expanding and varying patterns of, 482–484
function of, 223–224
fused, 501–502
parallel structure in, 227–230, 490–491
passive, 488, 489
periodic and cumulative, 235
sense of, 486–487
simple, 480
topic, 190–193
types of, 234–236
using computer to compose, 247
variety in, 246–247
verb tenses in, 514–518
word order in, 491–493
Sentence structure
  and style, 297–301
  and tone, 295
Shakespeare, William, 234
Shaw, George Bernard, 261–262
Shea, Rachel Hartigan, 343–344, 345, 353, 360
Sheppard, R. Z., 230
Shi, Yili (student writer), 205–206, 451–452
"Sight Into Insight" (Dillard), 264
Simile, 267
Simple sentences, 480
"Since When Did *USA Today* Become the National Design Ideal?" (Rock), 120–122
"The Size of Things" (Jastrow), 269
Slang, 261–262
Slanting of facts, 161
Slater, Philip, 195–196
"Smart Degrees Take Center Stage" (Shea), 360
Smith, H. Allen, 135
Smith, Pam, 250–251
*The Solace of Open Spaces* (Ehrlich), 139
*Something to Declare* (Alvarez), 30
Sources. *See also* Citations; *specific sources*
  documenting, 362–364
  evaluating, 338–341
  finding library and Internet,

324–328. (*See also* Library
resources; Internet)
overview of, 324
quoting, 357–362. (*See also*
Quotations)
taking notes on, 343–345
Special paragraphs
concluding paragraphs as, 207–208
explanation of, 187, 204
introductory paragraphs as, 204–207
revision of, 211–212
transitional paragraphs as, 207
Specificity, 263–266
*Specimen Days*, (Whitman), 298
Speculation
approaches to, 35
on computer, 38
evaluating, 37
explanation, 34
Spelling
computer spellchecks and, 305, 568
frequently misspelled words,
568–574
improving skills in, 567–568
rules for, 565–567
use of dictionary for, 524, 567
Split infinitive, 494–495
Squinting modifiers, 494
Stafford, William, 29
Sturma, Rob (student writer), 414–417
Style
advice about, 303–304
example of, 296
explanation of, 295–296
inconsistent, 303
range of, 297–301
revising for, 304, 305
using computer to check, 305
Subject archive, 326–327, 335
Subject headings, 328–329
Subjective case, 510–511, 513
Subjects
agreement between verbs and,
504–507
for arguments, 156
bibliographic use for sources on,
326, 329–330
finding subject headings related to,
328–329
for research papers, 321–323
revision for, 82, 88–90
selection of, 9–11
of sentences, 476–477
Subjunctive mood, 487
Subordinating conjunctions, 479, 502
Subordination, 230–231, 483–484

Suffixes, 559
Summarizing sources, 344, 261
"Summer Pond" (Hoagland), 267
Survey, as type of research paper, 319
Synonyms, 525

Taraskiewicz, Jill (student writer), 209,
458–462
"The Telephone Paradox" (Gaub),
122–123
"Television Did It First: Ten Myths
about 'New' Media" (Helfand),
435–440
"Territorial Behavior" (Morris),
140–141
Testimony, as type of evidence, 158
Textual graphics, 106–107
"Their Side" (Seidel), 162–163
Theroux, Paul, 294–295
Thesis
composing effective, 65–66
development in research papers,
353
explanation of, 18
purpose and, 18–19
"They Know How to Get Us" (Penning), 90–92
Third–person point of view, 131, 292,
486
"Third World Driving Hints and Tips"
(O'Rourke), 308–310
Thomas, Lewis, 225, 268
Thoreau, Henry David, 49, 268
Thurber, James, 7–8, 282–283
*Time* (Sheppard), 230
Titles
abbreviations of, 562
capitalization of, 553
italicizing, 555
quotation marks and, 556
verb use and, 507
Tone
deciding on, 292
distance as element of, 294–295
importance of appropriate, 289
range of, 291–292
style and, 297–301
using computer to check, 305
Topical paragraphs
coherence in, 198–203
completeness in, 193–195
explanation of, 187, 189
order in, 195–198
revising, 209–211
topic sentence in, 190–193
unity in, 189–190

Topics. *See* Subjects
Topic sentences, 190–193
"Total Eclipse" (Dillard), 283–285
Transitional markers, 202
Transitional paragraphs, 207
Transitive verbs, 477
Trillin, Alice, 235
Trillin, Calvin, 8, 73–75, 302
Triteness, 276–277, 528–529
Tuan, Yi-Fan, 142–143
Tuchman, Barbara, 318, 350
Twain, Mark, 296
Typeface, as element of design, 104–106

*Uncommon Grounds: The History of
Coffee and How It Transformed the
World* (Pendergrast), 361–362
Unity, 189–190
Unrecognizable allusion, 529

Vagueness, 271–272
Variety, revising sentences for, 244–246
Verbs
active and passive, 240–242
agreement between subject and,
504–507
consistency in tenses, 486
explanation of, 477
irregular, 515–516
tenses, 514–518
Viorst, Judith, 196–197
Visual culture, 20–21
Vocabulary, 475
Voice
active and passive, 240–242, 487
consistency in, 487
emphatic, 240–242

Walden (Thoreau), 268
Walker, Lou Ann, 193–194
Warrants, 168–169
"Watching Whales" (Graham),
150–152, 206–207, 208
"A Way of Writing" (Stafford), 29
Weissman, Gerald, 225
Weltfish, Gene, 190–191
Welty, Eudora, 79–80
*West with the Night* (Markham), 302
*Where Do We Go from Here: Chaos or
Community?* (King), 202
"Where's the Beef?" (Shea), 343–344
White, E. B., 192, 229
White space, as design element,
112–113
"White 'Space'" (Qually), 113
Whitman, Walt, 298–299